EVILLE: PASEO DE COLÓN ▲ 184 | SEVILLE: PARQUE MARÍA LUISA ▲ 200 | CÓRDOBA ▲ 236

AS ALPUJARRAS ▲ 343 | BAEZA AND ÚBEDA ▲ 347-348 | CABO DE GATA ▲ 352

CÓRDOBA
The magic of a visit to La Mezquita, one of Spain's most imposing monuments, continues as you explore the streets of the ancient Judería.

DOÑANA NATIONAL PARK
Almost 6,000 square miles of lagoons, marshes and dunes. A stopover for numerous species of migrating bird.

THE ALHAMBRA
The world's best-preserved medieval Arab palace is a highlight of Hispanic-Moorish art.

LAS ALPUJARRAS
High valleys that provide sanctuary for both wildlife and popular traditions inherited from the Moors.

BAEZA AND ÚBEDA
An exceptionally rich heritage of Renaissance architecture.

CABO DE GATA
A promontory facing the African coast, with Andalusia's loveliest beaches.

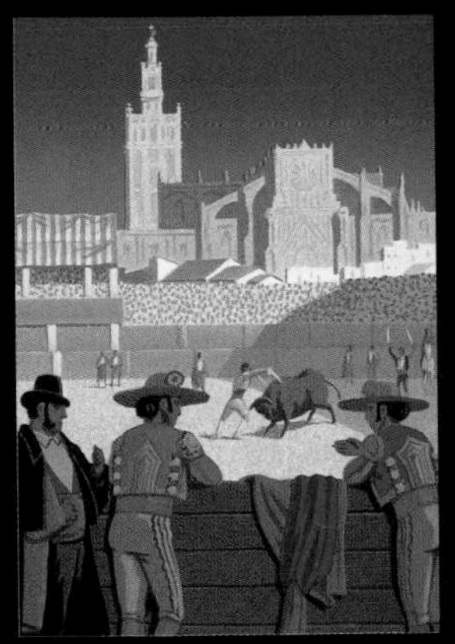

SEVILLE AND ANDALUSIA

KNOPF GUIDES

● Encyclopedia section

■ **NATURE** The natural heritage: species and habitats characteristic of the area covered by the guide, annotated and illustrated by naturalist authors and artists.
HISTORY The impact of international events on Andalusian history, from the arrival of the first inhabitants to modern days, with key dates appearing in a timeline alongside the text.
ARTS, CRAFTS AND TRADITIONS Traditions (costumes, crafts, festivals and gastronomy) and their continuing role in contemporary Andalusian life.
ARCHITECTURE The architectural heritage from ancient times to today; a look at the great monuments, both civil and religious, focusing on style and topology.
AS SEEN BY PAINTERS How the image of the city has evolved in the hands of the great Sevillian artists.
AS SEEN BY WRITERS An anthology of texts taken from works of writers from several periods and nationalities, arranged thematically.

Itineraries

Each itinerary begins with a map of the area to be explored.
✪ **NOT TO BE MISSED** The top sites, highlighted in gray in the margins. The emphasis is on the practical aspects of visiting these sites.
★ **EDITOR'S CHOICE** Sites singled out by the editor for special attention.
INSETS On richly illustrated double pages, these insets turn the spotlight on subjects deserving more in-depth treatment.

Practical information

All the travel information you will need before you go and when you get there.
PLACES TO VISIT A handy table of addresses and opening times.
USEFUL ADDRESSES A selection of hotels, restaurants, cafés, tapas bars and hotspots of Andalusian nightlife.
APPENDICES Bibliography, list of illustrations and index.
MAP SECTION Maps of the Andalusian region, plus street maps of Seville, Córdoba, Granada and Cádiz, preceded by a street index.

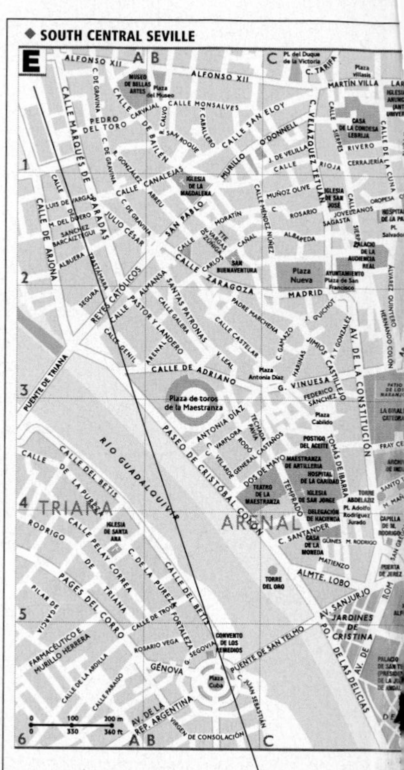

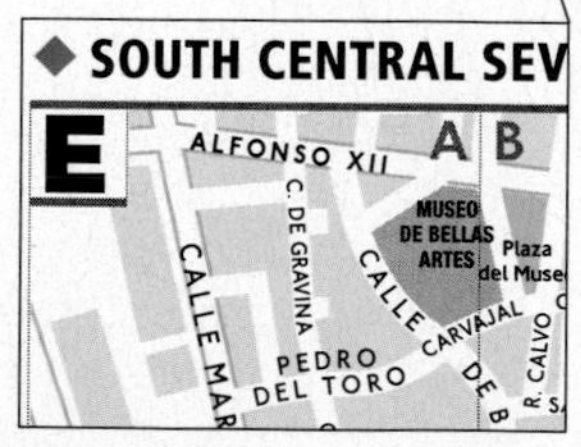

Each map in the map section is designated by a letter. In the itineraries, all the sites of interest are given a grid reference (for example: ◆ E A1).

✪ This symbol indicates a place not to be missed.

★ The star symbol signifies sites singled out by the editors for special attention.

The itinerary map shows the main sites.

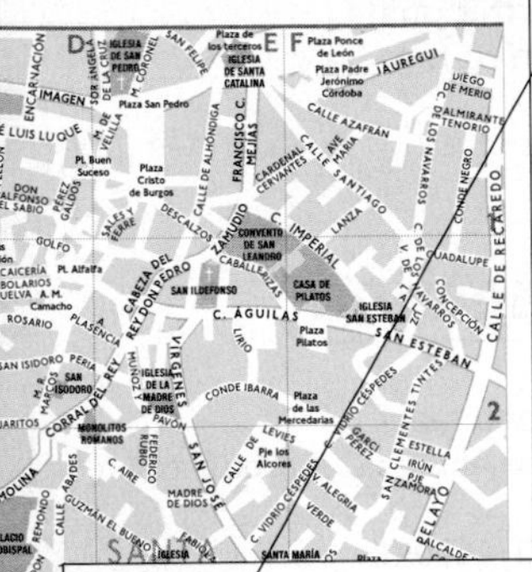

▲ THE OLD PORT DISTRICT

This astrolabe can be seen on the exterior of the chapel of the Palacio de San Telmo.

1. Río Guadalquivir 2. Torre del Oro 3. Puente de San Telmo 4. Jardines de Cristina 5. Hotel Alfonso XIII 6. Palacio de San Telmo 7. Fábrica de Tabacos 8. Puerta de Jerez

9. Avenida de la Constitución 10. Casa de la Moneda 11. Teatro de la Maestranza 12. Hospital de la Caridad 13. Postigo del Aceite 14. Plaza de Toros de la Maestranza 15. Paseo de Cristóbal Colón 16. Puente de Triana 17. Mercado del Barranco 18. Calle Reyes Católicos 19. Iglesia de la Magdalena 20. Plaza de Armas 21. Puente de Chapina

PASEO DE COLÓN, A WINDOW ONTO HISTORY ✪
Past and present collide on the bank of the Guadalquivir: opposite the Torre del Oro ("golden tower"), a Moorish construction dating from the 13th century, rises an emblem of contemporary Seville, the headquarters of the contingency fund, completed by Rafael Moneo in 1986. In a similar fashion, the Plaza de Toros de la Maestranza (1761), a temple to bullfighting, is juxtaposed by the Teatro de la Maestranza, a theater and opera house inaugurated in 1991.

"The Casa de la Moneda mints 700 gold and silver marks per day and employs 180 men. Loads of gold and silver coins leave the building as if they were ordinary merchandise." (Extract from a chronicle, 1548)

TORRE DEL ORO
The tower, originally a bastion overlooking the river and port, formed part of the fortifications of the Alcázar. Seville was captured after the breaking of a chain stretched between the tower and its replica on the Triana bank in 1243.

THE OLD PORT

The historic port of Seville extended along the strip of land running parallel to the river, now the *paseos* de Colón and del Marqués de Contadero, and occupied the districts of La Carretería, El Postigo, El Arenal, El Baratillo and La Cestería. When its center of activity was displaced, this former port became a popular area for taking a leisurely stroll.
TORRE DEL ORO ★. The tower was built by the Almohads in 1221–2 to reinforce the Alcázar's defenses and control access to the port. Indeed, when Admiral Ramón de Bonifaz took control of it in 1243, in doing so cutting supply lines to Seville from Triana, the city fell. The upper section was added in 1760. Its name has three possible origins: its proximity to the Casa de la Moneda; its use to store treasure brought back from the Indies; or its former cladding of gold *azulejos* ● 56, 73. Today the tower belongs to the Navy and houses the MUSEO MARITIMO. Two circular, vaulted rooms contain documents, paintings, models, weapons and other reminders of the city's maritime history.
CASA DE LA MONEDA. The Calle Santander leads from the Torre del Oro to the Casa de la Moneda, the part of the Alcázar that received gold and silver from America, as indicated by the names of the streets and gardens in the district. For example, the Torre de la Plata ("silver"), a Muslim and Christian edifice surrounded by buildings, was the counterpart of the Torre del Oro ("gold") and defended the 12th-century Casa de la Moneda. The complex was built in 1587, in response to the huge influx of precious metals. It can still be seen today, albeit much restored. Its monumental entrance (1761) opens onto the Calle Habana.

The FUNDICIÓN REAL (royal foundry) and the crucible furnaces, now exhibition rooms, attest to its former activity. In the 19th century production ceased and the building was converted into apartments, though you can still visit the old blast furnaces.

PUERTA DE JEREZ

The Avenida de la Constitución runs past the Casa de la Moneda and the Jardines de Cristina to the Puerta de Jerez, an extremely busy intersection and the point of exit for Cádiz. The HOTEL ALFONSO XIII to the south is a fine example of Sevillian regionalism. It was the birthplace of Vicente Aleixandre (1898–1989), a poet of the "Generación del 1927" ▲ 304 and winner of the Nobel Prize for Literature.

◆ C A3-A4-B4-B5-C5
◆ E A2-A3-B4-B5-C5-C6

ARQUILLO DE LA PLATA
Gate (14th-century) on the avenue from the port to the Casa de la Contratación (also still known as the Casa del Océano) where metals from America ● 36 were stored.

Galleons on the Arenal, in front of La Giralda, in the summer of 1617.

184 185

●■▲◆ The above symbols within the text provide cross-references to a place or theme discussed elsewhere in the guide.

The mini-map pinpoints the itinerary within the wider area covered by the guide.

Beneath the mini-maps are cross-references to the map section.

● Encyclopedia section

▲ Itineraries in Andalusia

◆ Practical information

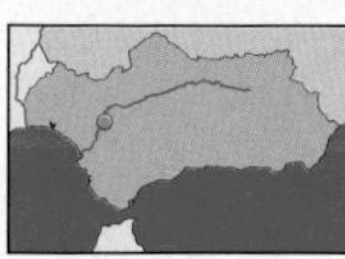

SEVILLE ▲ 121
Visit the cathedral and La Giralda, the symbol of the Andalusian capital, followed by the Alcázar, the masterpiece of Mudéjar art. Afterwards, wander the old districts, with their palaces and churches, as far the Museo de Bellas Artes and the old port. Cross the Guadalquivir to explore Triana, the old gipsy *barrio*, and the island of La Cartuja, returning via Parque María Luisa.

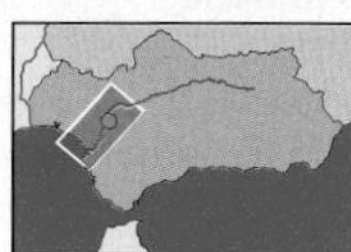

AROUND SEVILLE ▲ 206
Four itineraries that allow you to discover, respectively, the ancient site of Itálica, north of Seville; the imposing Moorish fortress of Alcalá de Guadaira and the Roman remains at Carmona, to the east; then the megalithic monuments of Valencina, before following the Guadalquivir down to its estuary.

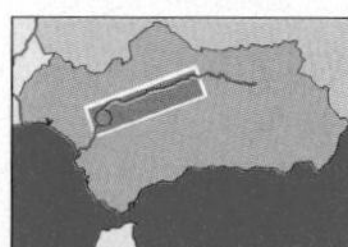

SEVILLE TO CÓRDOBA ▲ 229
Coming back up the Guadalquivir valley, stop off at the medieval castle of Almodóvar del Río and the ruins of Medina Azahara, the Ommiad caliphs' palatial city. Then savor Córdoba: the "forest of columns" of La Mezquita and the labyrinth of the ancient medina, where you will find the major monuments of the "city of three cultures".

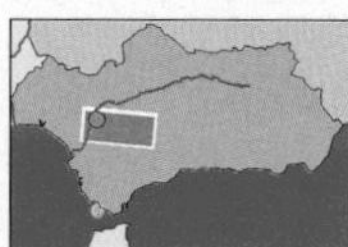

LA CAMPIÑA ▲ 245
Roam the vast plains of this farming region to the east of Seville, visiting the classical palaces and Mudéjar-Gothic churches of Écija, "the town of sun" with its recordbreaking summer temperatures; the "castle-hacienda" of Monclova; Marchena; Utrera; and the archeological museum and Baroque palaces of Osuna. Make sure to taste Estepa's *mantecados* (sweet biscuits).

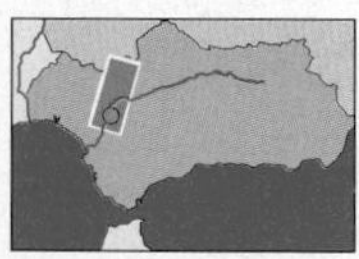

SIERRA MORENA ▲ 261
Follow ancient roads through this stunning chain of mountains separating Andalusia from the rest of Spain. After Aracena, the region's "capital", and the "cave of marvels", visit the nature reserves and the little Roman or Moorish villages, finishing at Riotinto, where mining has been carried out for almost five thousand years.

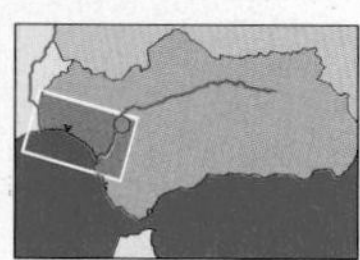

THE PROVINCE OF HUELVA ▲ 275
From Seville, cross the Niebla plain, studded with Baroque bell towers, to get to Huelva, the provincial capital, the Monasterio de la Rábida, then the ports of Palos de la Frontera and Moguer, infused with memories of Colombus and the "discovery" of America. Venture into Doñana National Park, on the Guadalquivir estuary, and end with El Rocío hermitage.

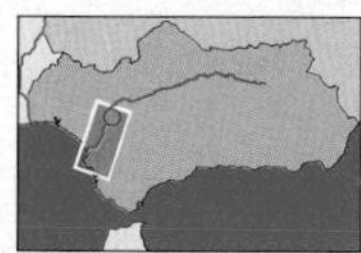

SEVILLE TO CÁDIZ ▲ 291
Make your way to Jerez de la Frontera, the aristocratic home of sherry and of Spanish riding. Follow the "wine route" toward Sanlúcar de Barrameda, with its castle and *bodegas*, then the Costa de la Luz as far as walled Cádiz, one of Europe's oldest cities, situated at the end of a narrow peninsula.

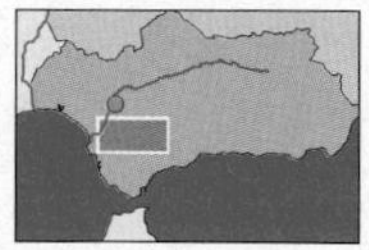

THE WHITE TOWNS ROUTE ▲ 317
From Cádiz, cross the Sierra de Cádiz and the Serrenía de Ronda, mountains long fought over by Christians and Muslims and a former haunt of *bandoleros*. Appreciate the wild landscapes of the nature reserves of Grazalema and the Sierra de las Nieves, as well as the rustic architecture of the *Pueblos Blancos*, then discover Ronda, a romantic eagle's nest and cradle of modern bullfighting.

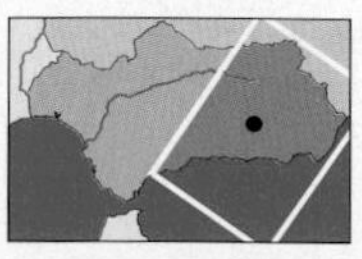

EASTERN ANDALUSIA ▲ 329
After Málaga, where Picasso discovered his artistic vocation, visit Granada, the capital of eastern Andalusia, which is dominated by the unforgettable Alhambra; ascend the Sierra Nevada; and experience the unique charms of the white villages of Las Alpujarras. Witness the Renaissance architectural heritage of Jaén, Baeza and Úbeda, as well as the barren landscapes of Almería.

NUMEROUS SPECIALISTS AND ANDALUSIA ENTHUSIASTS HAVE CONTRIBUTED TO THIS GUIDE, BUT WE PARTICULARLY THANK MIGUEL AZAOLA.

● Encyclopedia section

■ **NATURE**
Angel Martín
■ **HISTORY**
Diego Carrasco, Fernando Olmedo
■ **ARTS AND TRADITIONS**
Pedro Barbadillo, Diego Carrasco, Nicolás Ramírez
■ **ARCHITECTURE**
Nicolás Ramírez
■ **SEVILLE AS SEEN BY PAINTERS**
Diego Carrasco
■ **SEVILLE AS SEEN BY WRITERS**
Lucinda Gane

▲ Itineraries in Andalusia

José M. Astilleros (Cádiz, Serranías de Cádiz, Ronda), Pedro Barbadillo (Córdoba), Diego Carrasco (Seville, Río Abajo), Francisco Gallardo, Juan F. Lacomba (Los Alcores, La Campiña), Fernando Olmedo (Seville, Itálica, El Aljarafe, eastern Andalusia), Nicolás Ramírez (Sierra Morena, Huelva), Nieva Capote, Amalia Góngora, Santiago Arce (eastern Andalusia)

◆ Practical information

Carmen Bruña, Nieva Capote, Amalia Góngora, José Márquez, Carmen de la Calle, María Larreta, Isabel Lovillo, Cristina Peralta, Carlos Jesús Sagrario García, and Robert Graham of the *Financial Times* for the hotels and restaurants

This is a Borzoi Book
published by Alfred A. Knopf

Completely revised and updated in 2003

Published in the United States by Alfred A. Knopf, a division of Random House, Inc., New York, and simultaneously in Canada by Random House of Canada Limited, Toronto. Distributed by Random House, Inc., New York.

Knopf, Borzoi Books, and the colophon are registered trademarks of Random House, Inc

www.aaknopf.com

Library of Congress
Cataloging-in-Publication Data

Seville and Andalusia
ISBN 0-679-75568-3
LC–97–80537

Originally published in France by Nouveaux-Loisirs, a subsidiary of Editions Gallimard, Paris, 1995. Copyright © 1995 by Editions Nouveaux-Loisirs

Translated by
Wendy Allatson

Edited and typeset by
Book Creation Services, London

Printed and bound in Italy by
Editoriale Lloyd

SEVILLE AND ANDALUSIA

SPANISH EDITORS
Equipo 28
FRENCH EDITORS
Patrick Jézéquel, Catherine Bray
PICTURE RESEARCH
Equipo 28
UPDATING
Anne-Valérie Cadoret, Nicolas Christich, Jean-Gérald de Baecker, Sybille d'Oiron, Odile Simon, Marie Tychyj
LAYOUT
Carole Gaborit, Michele Bisgambiglia (nature)
MAPS
Atelier de Bayonne: Dominique Duplantier, Frédéric Liéval, Rémy Etcheberry, Martine Gros, Lydiem Rousset
MAP SECTION
Édigraphie

ILLUSTRATIONS
Nature: Frédéric Bony, Jacqueline Candiard, Jean Chevalier, Denis Claveul, Gismonde Curiace, François Desbordes, Claire Felloni, Bruno Lenormand, Dominique Mansion, François Place, Pascal Robin, Franck Stefan, John Wilkinson
Architecture: Philippe Candé, Jean-Marie Guillou, Jean-Michel Kacédan, Maurice Pommier, Claude Quiec, Amato Sorro, François Pichon, Jean-Claude Sené, Jean-Sylvain Roveri, Gabor Zitia
Itineraries: Jean-Marc Lanusse, Maurice Pommier
Computer graphics: Paul Coulbois, Kristof Chemineau, Patrick Mérienne

PHOTOGRAPHY
AGESA, Javier Andrada, Archivo J. Granados, Arenas, Atín Aya, Juan C. Galán, F.O. Granados, Bibliothèque Nationale, Bibliothèque de l'Opéra de Paris, E. Briones, J.C. Cazalla, El Viso publication, DC. Fernández, FOAT., Grupo Espiral, Iñaki Iturriaga, P. Juliá, L.L. Roger-Viollet, British Museum, Oronoz, J.M. Pérez Cabo, M. Regidor, Gloria Rodríguez, Equipo 28 (Seville), Tecnifoto, José Morón, José A. Sierra, Anselmo Valdés, M. Zapke

SPECIAL THANKS TO
Miguel Azaola, Colette Olive, Javier Baselga (Turismo Andaluz S.A.), Provincial Tourism Institute of Seville, Tourist Board head office, the Archives of Cartuja manufacture, the Archives of the Indes of Seville, Tablada Base Aéra, port of Seville, Loïc Menanteau and all museums and places of interest mentioned in this guide

Encyclopedia section

A tug (above) sailing past the Convento de los Remedios ▲ *194*.

The polacca *Cortés* (left) in the port of the Torre del Oro ● *69* ▲ *184*.

Seville's Feria de Abril was established in 1847. The fair was originally a cattle market and gradually became a festival ● *50*. It takes place after the Semana Santa (Holy Week) ● *44*.

Group with a water carrier in the Plaza de San Francisco ▲ *132*

Nature

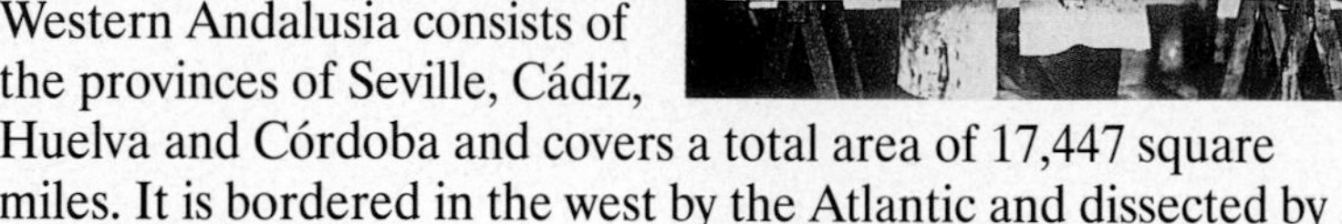

STURGEON
The sturgeon, once fished for caviar, has today disappeared from the Guadalquivir.

Western Andalusia consists of the provinces of Seville, Cádiz, Huelva and Córdoba and covers a total area of 17,447 square miles. It is bordered in the west by the Atlantic and dissected by the Río Guadalquivir, whose deep, broad valley runs between the Sierra Morena (the southern edge of the Castilian plateau) in the north, and the karstic ranges of the Baetic Cordillera in the south. Between Seville and its estuary, the river flows through marshland. Within a radius of barely 62 miles, the region offers a range of very different landscapes.

RÍO GUADALQUIVIR
The basin of the Guadalquivir (22,138 square miles) covers 11 percent of peninsular Spain.

SIERRA MORENA ▲ *262*
The Sierra Morena forms the southern edge of the Iberian range and rises to a height of 3,280 feet above the level of the valley floor.

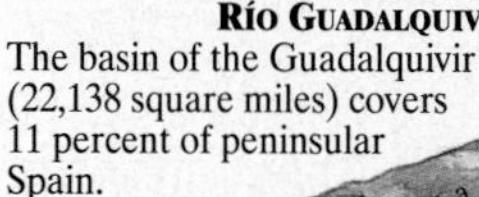

ODIEL MARSHES
These tidal marshes border the Río Odiel near Huelva ▲ *279*.

GUADALQUIVIR MARSHES
This vast expanse of marshland, which today occupies the site of the ancient Lake Ligustinus, stretches from Seville to the coast. The marshes on the northern right bank have been partially reclaimed and given over to market gardening, while those on the southern left bank have been left untouched. The flora and fauna are protected as part of the Coto Doñana National Park ▲ *286*.

La Campiña
La Campiña is an important cereal- and olive-producing area that lies between the mountains and the river.

El Aljarafe ▲ *218*
Olive and orange trees are grown on these densely populated slopes.

Baetic Cordillera
High rainfall and fertile soil produces a wide variety of plant life.

Sierra Morena
A stock-farming and forested region, mainly planted with cork-oak.

El Tajo ▲ *328*
Ronda's famous gorge provides evidence of the erosion of the Baetic Cordillera.

High-altitude meadows
These meadows, planted with holm-oaks, are typical of the mountain regions.

Córdoba
Seville
Río Guadalquivir
Guadalquivir marshes
Coto Doñana National Park
de
la
Luz
Jerez de la Frontera
Cádiz
Gibraltar

Vineyards of Jerez
Since ancient times vines have been grown in the low, sandy regions of the valley.

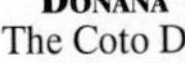

Doñana
The Coto Doñana National Park covers an area of some 192,050 acres around the Guadalquivir estuary. Its flora and fauna are extremely well preserved.

Bay of Cádiz
The bay's coastline, where dunes alternate with all types of marshland, is a fine example of coastal geomorphology.

■ THE DOÑANA DUNES

UMBRELLA PINE
Reintroduced in 1856, this pine has adapted well to the environment.

The 192,050 acres of the Coto Doñana National Park combine three different ecosystems: active dunes, static dunes and marshland. The 18½-mile line of active dunes moves northward at a rate of 16½ feet per year. The static dunes or *cotos* are covered with vegetation adapted to the dry, higher zones or to the damp, lower zones liable to flooding.

Valleys supporting pines and scrub and surrounded by active dunes are known as *corrales*.

COARSE-FRUITED JUNIPER
Today this juniper, once a common sight in the *corrales*, is only found in coastal enclaves.

SPINY-LEAVED THRIFT
Its bright pink flowers add a touch of color to sandy areas.

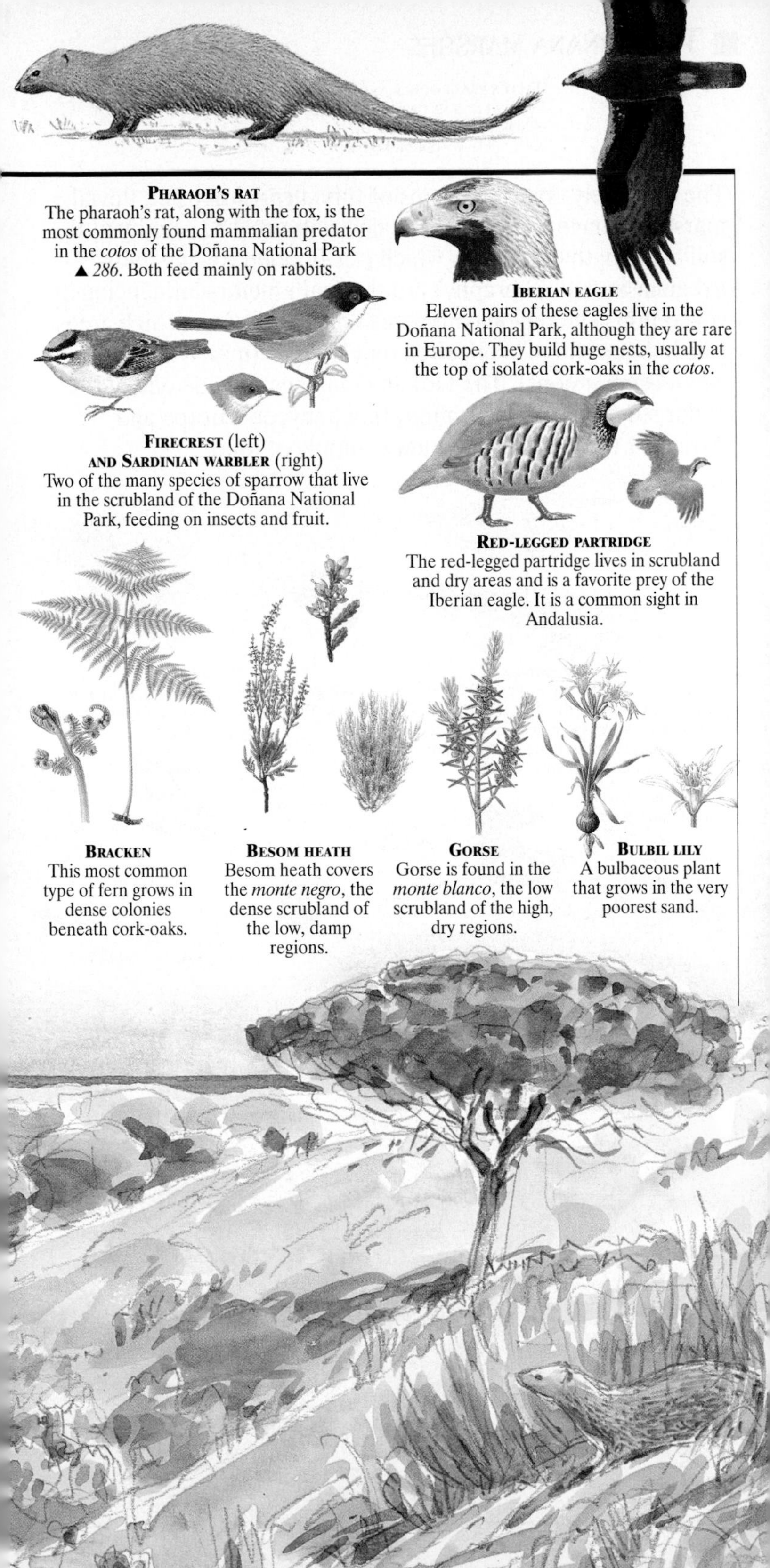

Pharaoh's rat
The pharaoh's rat, along with the fox, is the most commonly found mammalian predator in the *cotos* of the Doñana National Park ▲ *286*. Both feed mainly on rabbits.

Iberian eagle
Eleven pairs of these eagles live in the Doñana National Park, although they are rare in Europe. They build huge nests, usually at the top of isolated cork-oaks in the *cotos*.

Firecrest (left) **and Sardinian warbler** (right)
Two of the many species of sparrow that live in the scrubland of the Doñana National Park, feeding on insects and fruit.

Red-legged partridge
The red-legged partridge lives in scrubland and dry areas and is a favorite prey of the Iberian eagle. It is a common sight in Andalusia.

Bracken
This most common type of fern grows in dense colonies beneath cork-oaks.

Besom heath
Besom heath covers the *monte negro*, the dense scrubland of the low, damp regions.

Gorse
Gorse is found in the *monte blanco*, the low scrubland of the high, dry regions.

Bulbil lily
A bulbaceous plant that grows in the very poorest sand.

WALTL'S PLEURODELE NEWT
This newt lays its eggs in the least saline waters of the marsh lakes.

The extremely rich ecosystems of this surprisingly flat, fluvial marshland have marked seasonal variations. The salinity of the soil and length of time for which it is flooded (owing to its irregular microtopography) are the main factors influencing its vegetation. The region comprises *vetas* and *vetones* (high areas which do not flood), *caños* (channels), *ojos* (marsh lakes) and *lucios* (depressions). The Doñana marshes provide one of the major stopovers for birds migrating between Europe and Africa, as they offer an abundant supply of food.

GRAYLAG GOOSE
Every winter between 60,000 and 70,000 geese arrive from northern Europe. They use their beaks to forage in the sand for their main source of food: the hard roots of Andalusian cypress grass.

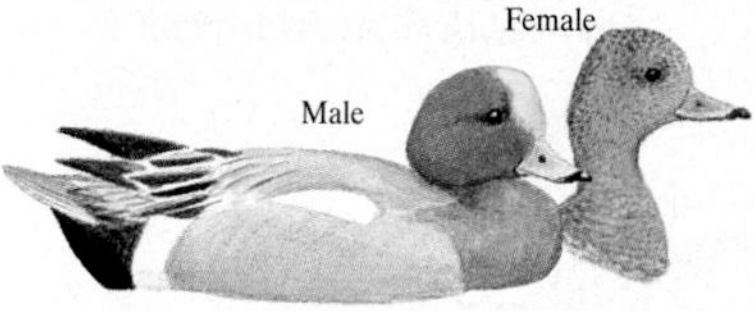

Female

Male

WIDGEON
Widgeon account for more than half the ducks that overwinter in the Guadalquivir marshes ▲ *286*.

WINTER. Arrival of migrating geese.

BULRUSH OR TYPHA
Found at the edge of rivers, lakes and marshes.

LAKE ACEBRON
This small lake situated near La Rocina, a stream that runs across the marshes, is one of the few whose shores are still covered with deciduous forest.

GULL-BILLED TERN
Gull-billed and other terns frequent the marshes along the coast of Huelva ▲ *279*.

WHITE WAGTAIL
The white wagtail, with its distinctive black-and-white plumage, is found on river banks in the Doñana marshes.

PURPLE GALLINULE.
Extremely rare in Europe, it lives in the reed beds of the Doñana marshes. It uses its feet to carry food to its beak.

MARSHLAND VEGETATION
Bulrushes border the *caños* and *lucios* (freshwater channels and depressions) where white celandines grow.

Areas with saline soil that do not flood are smothered with saltwort or marsh samphire.

CORK-OAK
Large colonies of birds nest in the coastal cork-oaks, known locally as *pajareras* (aviaries).

SUMMER
The marshes dry up and are replaced by steppe covered with dry pasture.

SPRING
As the days lengthen, aquatic plants begin to grow and the waders arrive.

■ Wildlife of the Doñana marshes

Eel
The young eels swim along the *caños* of the marshes and spawn in the Sargasso Sea.

As Europe's protected areas decrease and its wetlands dry out, the Coto Doñana National Park plays a vital role in preserving many species that have become rare elsewhere. Its marshes, in particular, provide refuge for water birds, while its sand dunes are the home of birds of prey, large predators like the lynx, and herbivores such as the wild boar, red deer and fallow deer.

Gambusia
The gambusia was introduced from North America to control mosquitos, as it feeds on the aquatic larvae.

Black-headed and white-eyed gull
These gulls form noisy flocks on the beaches and further inland where they scavenge for food in the garbage dumps. The white-eyed gull is a common sight along the coast.

Spotless starling
In winter, large flocks of these birds roost in the reed beds.

Lesser short-toed lark
Nests in the clumps of short grass where it looks for food.

Warbler
Found in the thick bramble bushes on the edge of Doñana's *monte negro* ▲ *286.*

Collared pratincole
Noisy flocks of these birds inhabit the areas of low vegetation at the water's edge.

Flamingo. Flamingos are found in lagoons and the clear, shallow waters of large marshes. Some twelve thousand individuals make seasonal stopovers in Doñana as they move between Doñana, Fuente de Piedra (where they nest), Odiel and the Camargue.

Spoonbill
Large colonies gather, with other species, in the trees of the coastal areas and marshland.

Green woodpecker
This bird makes holes in the trunks of pines to build its nest and search for insects.

Lapwing or green plover
The lapwing is the harbinger of winter.

Black-winged stilt
This bird acts as an early warning system in the lagoons it inhabits.

Redshank
The redshank winters in Doñana where it feeds on shellfish and larvae.

Red-knobbed coot
This extremely rare species is resident in Doñana.

Coot
This commonly found aquatic species dives for its food.

Marsh-harrier
The marsh-harrier has a wing span of up to 4 feet. It perches in the rush and reed beds at the edge of lagoons and rivers, and hunts small rodents, frogs and toads by flying just above the ground.

Black kite
In summer it disputes its hunting ground with the sedentary kite.

Common acanthodactyl
In summer it moves into the scrub of the *monte blanco* to escape the heat of the sand.

Montpellier snake
This snake can measure over 6½ feet. It is very aggressive and attacks all kinds of prey.

Pardelle lynx
The lynx is the only big cat in southern Europe. It is the emblem of the Doñana National Park.

Wild boar

Doe

Red deer

The large herbivores of the Coto Doñana. As well as cattle, these include the (usually small) red deer that browse on the new shoots of low branches, the fallow deer (introduced in the 17th century) that graze on the marshland and the wild boar that inhabit the marshes and lagoons.

LITTLE OWL
This nocturnal bird of prey nests in hollows in olive trees and holm-oaks.

The flora of the pastures and olive groves which, as well as trees, includes up to fifty herbaceous species per square yard, meets the needs of an extremely diverse fauna. These areas of agricultural exploitation provide shelter for many different kinds of wild animals and are the winter stopover for large numbers of Europe's insect-eating birds. Pastures and oak trees, providing acorns, constitute an extensive stock-farming area for different breeds of cattle adapted to the harsh conditions of summer drought.

BULL
The bull is the symbol of this region ▲ *227*, *276*, which breeds and selects bulls: *bravo* (brave) or *lidia* (fighting).

ANDALUSIAN HORSE
The crossing of Spanish horses with the Berber and Arab has produced this extremely beautiful breed, which has itself been crossed with American and European blood. Its excellent temperament makes it ideal for herding cattle.

BANDED HOOPOE

From olive to oil
The olives are crushed using a granite millstone. The resulting pulp is spread on oil-bags (circular trays) which are stacked in the oil press. The liquid produced is decanted to separate the oil from the water.

Olive tree
The cultivated variety of the wild olive tree is the most widely grown tree in Andalusia.

Civet
This small carnivore has distinctive spotted fur and weighs between 2½ and 4½ lbs. It is a timid and solitary nocturnal hunter that climbs trees and large shrubs with great agility.

Blackbird
Like the starling and thrush, the blackbird hunts for food in the olive groves.

BEE-EATER
The bee-eater arrives in spring and builds its nest in crevices in banks. It feeds mainly on bees and wasps.

The mountain regions, or sierra, that have not been converted into pasture or reforested, are covered in a woody, Mediterranean vegetation that can be divided into two types. The forest of the *monte alto* (high mountain) harbors the oldest species of trees (cork-oak, holm-oak and arbutus) and large shrubs (mastic tree, caper bush and buckthorn). The scrub of the *monte bajo* (low mountain) has poorer, drier vegetation consisting of smaller, aromatic and flowering plants and bushes: cistus, heathers, rosemary and thyme.

The rivers and streams of the sierra have an irregular rate of flow and a vegetation adapted to these variations.

GOLDEN EAGLE
This large, diurnal bird of prey flies above the oak groves and scrub. Its young have pale markings on their wings and tail.

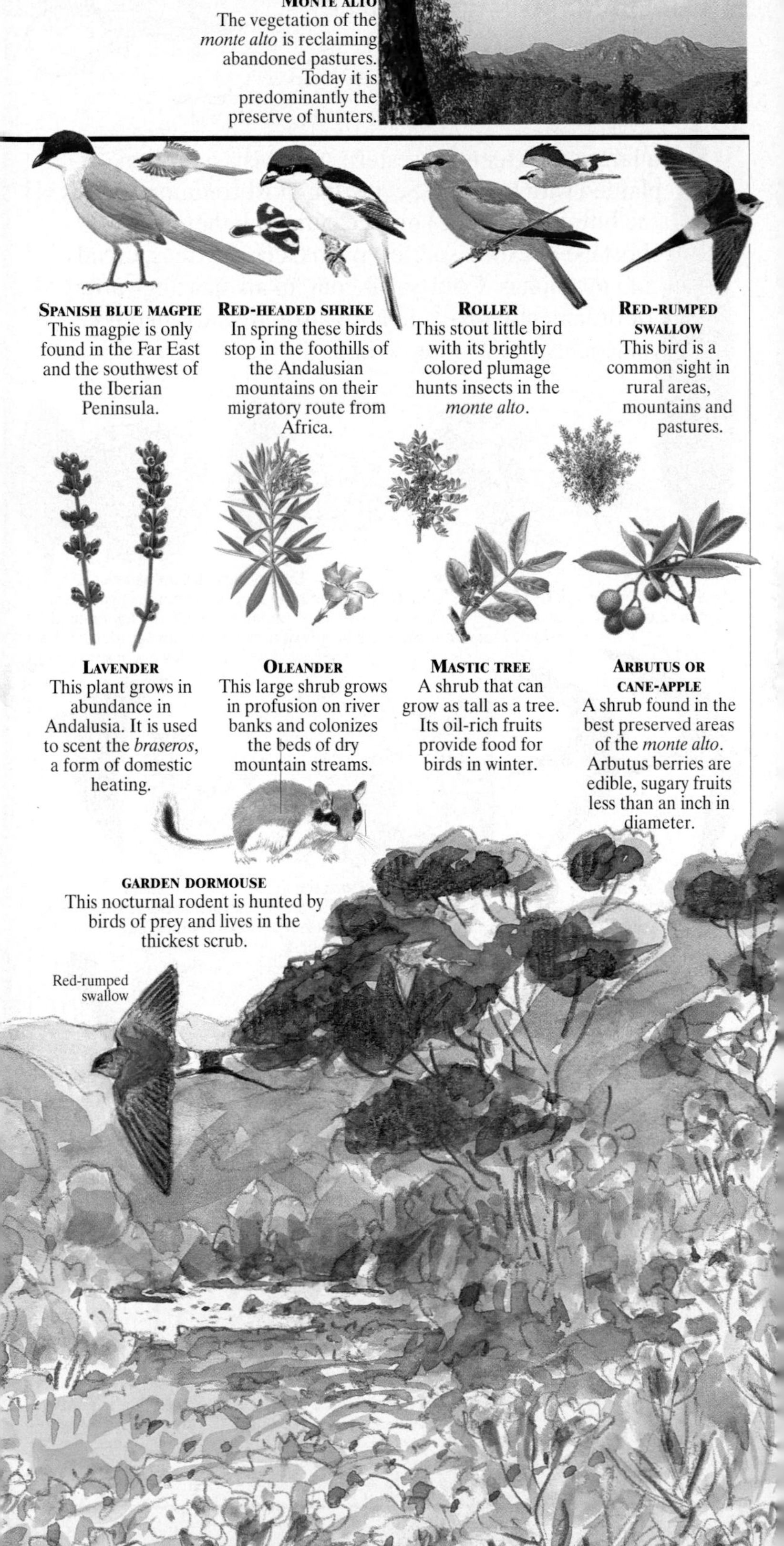

Monte alto
The vegetation of the *monte alto* is reclaiming abandoned pastures. Today it is predominantly the preserve of hunters.

Spanish blue magpie
This magpie is only found in the Far East and the southwest of the Iberian Peninsula.

Red-headed shrike
In spring these birds stop in the foothills of the Andalusian mountains on their migratory route from Africa.

Roller
This stout little bird with its brightly colored plumage hunts insects in the *monte alto*.

Red-rumped swallow
This bird is a common sight in rural areas, mountains and pastures.

Lavender
This plant grows in abundance in Andalusia. It is used to scent the *braseros*, a form of domestic heating.

Oleander
This large shrub grows in profusion on river banks and colonizes the beds of dry mountain streams.

Mastic tree
A shrub that can grow as tall as a tree. Its oil-rich fruits provide food for birds in winter.

Arbutus or cane-apple
A shrub found in the best preserved areas of the *monte alto*. Arbutus berries are edible, sugary fruits less than an inch in diameter.

Garden dormouse
This nocturnal rodent is hunted by birds of prey and lives in the thickest scrub.

Red-rumped swallow

SPANISH LIZARD
This lizard spends most of its time hidden in cracks and crevices, coming out on fine days to bask in the sun, high up on a wall.

Squares and streets in western Andalusia are often planted with trees. In Seville the most common species is the bitter (or Seville) orange, although there is no shortage of exotic species: palm trees, fig trees, cycads and magnolias. Courtyards contain an amazing variety of ornamental plants in pots, also often arranged on balconies and window ledges.

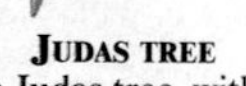

CYPRESS
A tree traditionally seen in cemeteries.

JUDAS TREE
The Judas tree, with its heart-shaped leaves, is widely found in parks.

LEMON AND ORANGE TREES
The bitter orange is a common sight in the streets of Andalusia, while the lemon tends to be grown in courtyards and gardens. Both have sweetly scented flowers in spring.

HOUSE MARTIN
The house martin nests under eaves and balconies.

BARN OWL OR SCREECH OWL
Its silent, white shadow often surprises human night-birds near the cathedral where it nests.

SWIFT
Seville has large colonies of swifts which, like swallows, hunt insects in flight.

LESSER KESTREL
Three families of this small bird of prey nest in Seville: in the church of El Salvador, the cathedral and the Hospital de las Cinco Llagas. The cathedral family can be seen hunting bats and nocturnal insects in the floodlights.

STORK
Like other migratory birds, storks fly over Seville and the Guadalquivir marshes.

History

HISTORY OF ANDALUSIA

Arrow heads from the 4th or 3rd millennium BC, discovered beneath the dolmens of Valencia.

2500 BC
Bronze Age.

900 BC
Phoenician colonies (Iberian peninsula).

FROM TARTESSOS TO THE CARTHAGINIANS

600 BC
Greek colonies on the Andalusian coast.

550 BC
Decline of Tartessos.

Melkart (right, on Seville town hall), the mythical founder of Hispalis.

500 BC
Punic influence in Hispania.

264 BC
Punic wars.

206 BC
Roman domination of Hispania.

The kingdom of Tartessos (11th–6th century BC), whose capital lay at the mouth of the Baetis (now the Guadalquivir), was the first known monarchy in the western Mediterranean basin. It was the result of Phoenician influence on local Iberian culture and was at its height during the reign of Arganthonius (6th century BC). A staging post on the western pewter route inhabited by crop and livestock farmers, the state exploited the mines, worked the gold and maintained maritime relations with the North and Asia Minor.

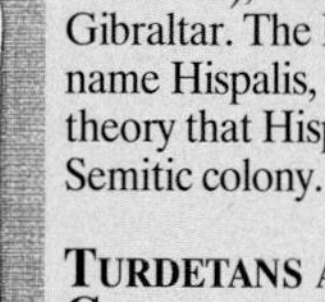

8TH CENTURY BC: THE FOUNDATION OF HISPALIS. Mythology attributes the foundation of ancient Seville to Melkart, a Semitic deity associated with the Greek god Heracles and the Roman god Hercules. The myth describes attempts by the Mediterranean peoples to colonize the region around the Pillars of Hercules (*Herculis columnae*), now the Straits of Gibraltar. The Phoenician root of the name Hispalis, "Spal", supports the theory that Hispalis was originally a Semitic colony.

Roman tombs discovered in Seville.

27 BC
Principate of Augustus.

TURDETANS AND CARTHAGINIANS. Evidence of Turdetan (a local Iberian culture) and Punic (6th–3rd century BC) influences was discovered on the site of Hispalis, above the Tartessian layer. During this period, local uprisings and the Roman conquest put an end to Carthaginian supremacy. Hispalis was burnt in c. 216 BC. In 206 BC Scipio's legions defeated the last of the Punic armies in the neighboring town of Ilipa.

ROMAN BAETICA

19 BC
Foundation of the Roman province of Baetica.

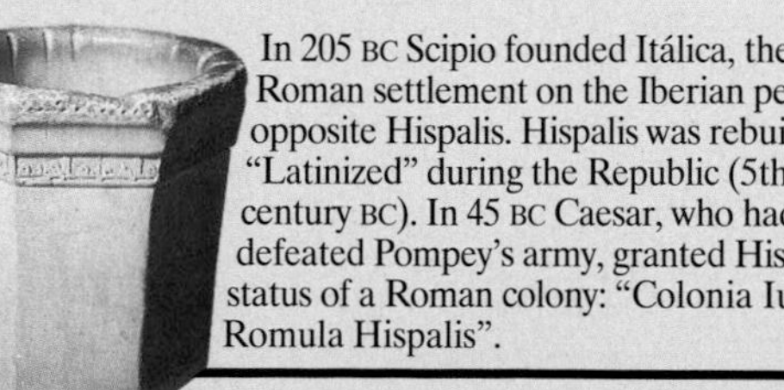

White marble well (Seville, Muslim period).

In 205 BC Scipio founded Itálica, the first Roman settlement on the Iberian peninsula, opposite Hispalis. Hispalis was rebuilt and "Latinized" during the Republic (5th–1st century BC). In 45 BC Caesar, who had defeated Pompey's army, granted Hispalis the status of a Roman colony: "Colonia Iulia Romula Hispalis".

"The change which most deeply affected cultural (and linguistic) history was the conversion of the Goths to Catholicism, consecrated by the Council of Toledo in 589."

Michel Banniard

HISPALIS, AN IMPERIAL CITY. The Romanization of Hispalis was part of a project to colonize Baetica, named after the river Baetis that flowed through it. Towns were built and Latin became the official language. For seven hundred years this rich Roman province supplied the Roman world with metals, oil, wheat and wine. It also produced philosophers and the first two Roman emperors born outside Italy: Trajan (53–117) and Hadrian (76–138), both from Itálica. During the Empire (1st century BC–5th century AD), and especially under Hadrian, Hispalis experienced a period of remarkable urban development. In 287, the martyrdom of Justa and Rufina, the city's patron saints, was the first indication of Christianity in the region. The city was at its height toward the end of the Empire. Ausonius (310–95), a Roman poet and a Christian, referred to it as the leading Hispano-Roman city and the eleventh largest city in the world.

Viking ship: the Normans sailed up the Baetis and sacked Seville in 844.

AD 98–117
Trajan reigns as emperor.

AD 117–138
Hadrian reigns as emperor.

AD 410
Rome is sacked by the Visigoths, led by Alaric. End of the western Roman Empire.

AD 552
Byzantium occupies part of Baetica.

AD 732
The Arab offensive in the West is halted at Poitiers.

VANDALS AND VISIGOTHS. The Vandals occupied Baetica from 409 until 429, and gave it the name of Vandalusia. They sacked Hispalis in 426. In 476 the Visigoths founded a kingdom which lasted for two hundred years. Hispalis became Spali and remained the political and cultural center. The bishop, Leander (d. c. 600), and the archbishop, Isidore (560–636), made it a rich center of Latin culture whose influence spread throughout the Western World.

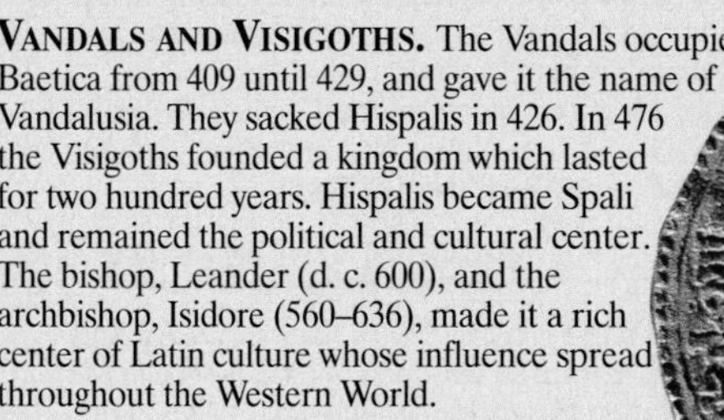

EL-ANDALUS

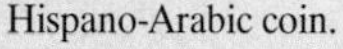

Hispano-Arabic coin.

CALIPHATE OF CÓRDOBA. In 711 Arab forces landed on Gibraltar and defeated the Goths. This opened the way into Europe for Islam and soon most of the Iberian peninsula was under Islamic control. Spali prospered and became the Islamic capital of El-Andalus, corresponding to ancient Vandalusia. A society of Muslims, Christians and Jews was formed and Arabs and North Africans joined the indigenous population. In 756 Abd el-Rahman I, the last survivor of the Arabian Ommiad dynasty, founded the independent emirate of Córdoba. In 929 it was established as a rival caliphate to Baghdad. In the

AD 756
Ommiad emirate in Andalusia.

AD 800
Charlemagne reigns as emperor of the Western World.

1085
Toledo is captured by Alfonso VI.

1099
The Crusaders conquer Jerusalem.

Muslim Seville, by the Romantic artist Genaro Pérez Villaamil (1848).

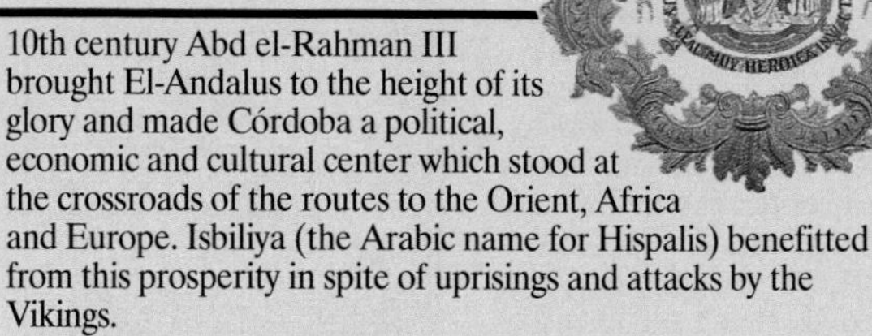

ARMS OF SEVILLE
Alfonso X (the Wise) is flanked by the bishops Isidore and Leander. The monogram "No Do", which was a contraction of "No madeja do" ("It did not abandon me") expresses the sovereign's gratitude to the city for remaining faithful to him during the civil war fought against his son, Don Sancho.

1212
Battle of Las Navas de Tolosa. The Guadalquivir valley is opened up to the Christians.

10th century Abd el-Rahman III brought El-Andalus to the height of its glory and made Córdoba a political, economic and cultural center which stood at the crossroads of the routes to the Orient, Africa and Europe. Isbiliya (the Arabic name for Hispalis) benefitted from this prosperity in spite of uprisings and attacks by the Vikings.

THE GOLDEN AGE OF ISBILIYA. Following the collapse of the Caliphate of Córdoba in 1031, El-Andalus was divided into a patchwork of small kingdoms, or *taifas*, which came under pressure from the Christian armies. As the capital of the most important Andalusian kingdom, Isbiliya enjoyed a brief period of glory under the Abbadids, who established a sophisticated and cultured court in the city. At the end of the 11th century the scale of the Christian advance led the North African Muslims to intervene. Following the removal from power of the caliph El-Mu'tamid in 1091, a succession of Almoravid and Almohad caliphs ruled El-Andalus. Isbiliya became the peninsular capital of the Almohad Caliphate of Marrakesh and, with eighty thousand inhabitants, the largest city in Spain. In 1198 a huge mosque was built, flanked by a superb minaret, now La Giralda. The fortifications were extended to include some 740 acres and some suburbs, such as Triana and La Macarena, were also fortified.

Seville captured by Ferdinand III (the Saint).

MEDIEVAL CHRISTIANITY

Ferdinand III (the Saint), King of Castile and Léon, captured Córdoba (1236), Seville (1248) and then the entire Guadalquivir valley. The Muslims of El-Andalus withdrew to Granada, which was the last Hispano-Arabic stronghold on the peninsula.

1250
The Christians occupy lower Andalusia.

1264
Uprising of the Andalusian Mudéjars.

1275
Intervention of the Moroccan Benimerin dynasty in Andalusia.

SEVILLE: FORTRESS AND TRADING CENTER. In spite of frontier wars with the Muslims, wars of succession, disputes among the aristocracy and the ravages of plague, Seville was revitalized during the 14th and 15th centuries. It was the capital of a kingdom that covered the whole of western Andalusia and the favorite residence of Alfonso X (the Wise), Alfonso XI and Pedro I (the Cruel). Its essentially agricultural and commercial economy, with some regional and traditional crafts, made it a trading center for agricultural, woolen and manufactured products at regional, national and international level. Once incorporated into the Christian world, it became the staging post between the Mediterranean and northern Europe, and the spearhead of expansion into Africa and the New World. It was a melting pot for a wide range of different cultures and welcomed cosmopolitan merchant communities: Mudéjars (Muslims allowed to remain in Spain after the Christian

Map of the kingdom of Seville (1597), according to the work of the cartographer Jerónimo de Chaves (1523–74).

> "In the space of twenty or thirty years, the few hundred small vessels that set sail from Cádiz, Palos and Lisbon discovered more continents than the entire human race during the course of the previous centuries."
> Stefan Zweig

Reconquest) and an extremely active Jewish minority which lived in the Jewish quarter or *juderia*. However, the situation of the religious minorities deteriorated. In 1483 the Jews were expelled from Seville, the seat of the first tribunal of the Inquisition. On January 2, 1492 Boabdil, King of Granada, relinquished the keys of the city, the last Muslim stronghold in Spain, to Isabella I of Castile and her husband, Ferdinand II of Aragon. After uniting the Christian kingdoms of Spain, the Catholic Monarchs, or Reyes Católicos (the title given to Isabella and Ferdinand by Pope Alexander VI) proceeded to build an empire that their successors extended across Europe and the New World. The expulsion of the Spanish Jews (1492) and Muslims (1502) deprived Andalusia of its intellectual elite.

THE GOLDEN AGE

Trade with the Indies, established by the voyages of Christopher Columbus, flourished via the Atlantic ports of Andalusia. The city benefitted greatly from the establishment of the Spanish colonial empire. Its strong position on the European and African markets was extended to include its role of "port and gateway to the Indies" which controlled all expeditions and fleets.

PROSPERITY FROM THE AMERICAS. In 1503 the Casa de la Contratación, which functioned not only as a chamber of commerce but also as a commercial tribunal, granted Seville the monopoly on trade between Europe and America. During the 16th and early 17th centuries, it overtook Venice and Genoa as one of the world's leading cities. Its only weakness was that, in an economy dominated by agriculture and traditional crafts, Seville tended to act as an intermediary rather than a center of production. Between the 15th and 16th centuries the number of people living in the city tripled to 120,000, a total population that was rivalled only by Paris, London and Naples. Suburbs such as Triana spread, and as well as the Spanish inhabitants, there was a mixed assortment of foreigners attracted by Seville's opulence that included large numbers of Genoese and Flemings. In 1526 Charles V married Isabel of Portugal in Seville. In 1570 the Parliament of Castile met there in the presence of Philip II. As the seat of an archdiocese and the tribunal of the Inquisition, the city was at the head of Catholic orthodoxy and the Counter-Reformation, as well as being the religious center that gave birth to a number of mystic sects and engendered various movements that pressed for reform.

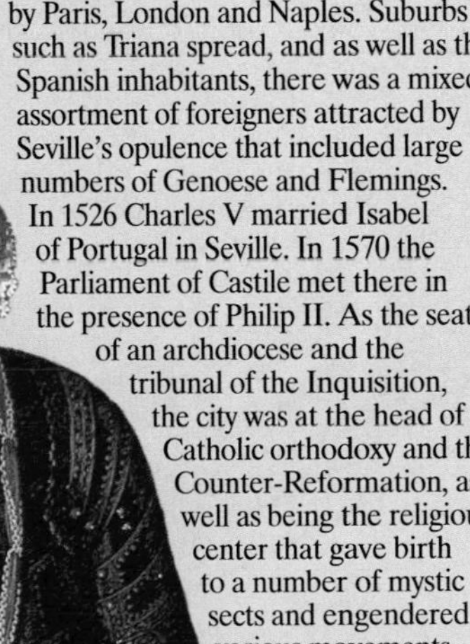

1348
Europe is devastated by the Black Death.

1369
Civil war and death of Pedro I (the Cruel).

Globe, detail of *El Geógrafo* (c. 1640), by Vélazquez.

1403–84
Conquest of the Canaries from Andalusia.

1453
Constantinople is conquered by the Ottomans.

1479
Unification of the Kingdom of Spain.

1492
Discovery of America, capture of Granada and end of the Reconquest.

1519–56
Charles V reigns as emperor.

1519–22
Juan Sebastián Elcano, Magellan's lieutenant, is the first man to sail around the world.

Philip II of Spain (1527–98) from a painting by Alonso Sánchez Coello.

By the late 15th century Seville was one of the most prosperous cities on the Iberian peninsula. In the 16th century its port and chamber of commerce, established in 1503, controlled all maritime passenger and cargo traffic between Europe and America. As a major European trading center, Seville played a leading role in the world's economy.

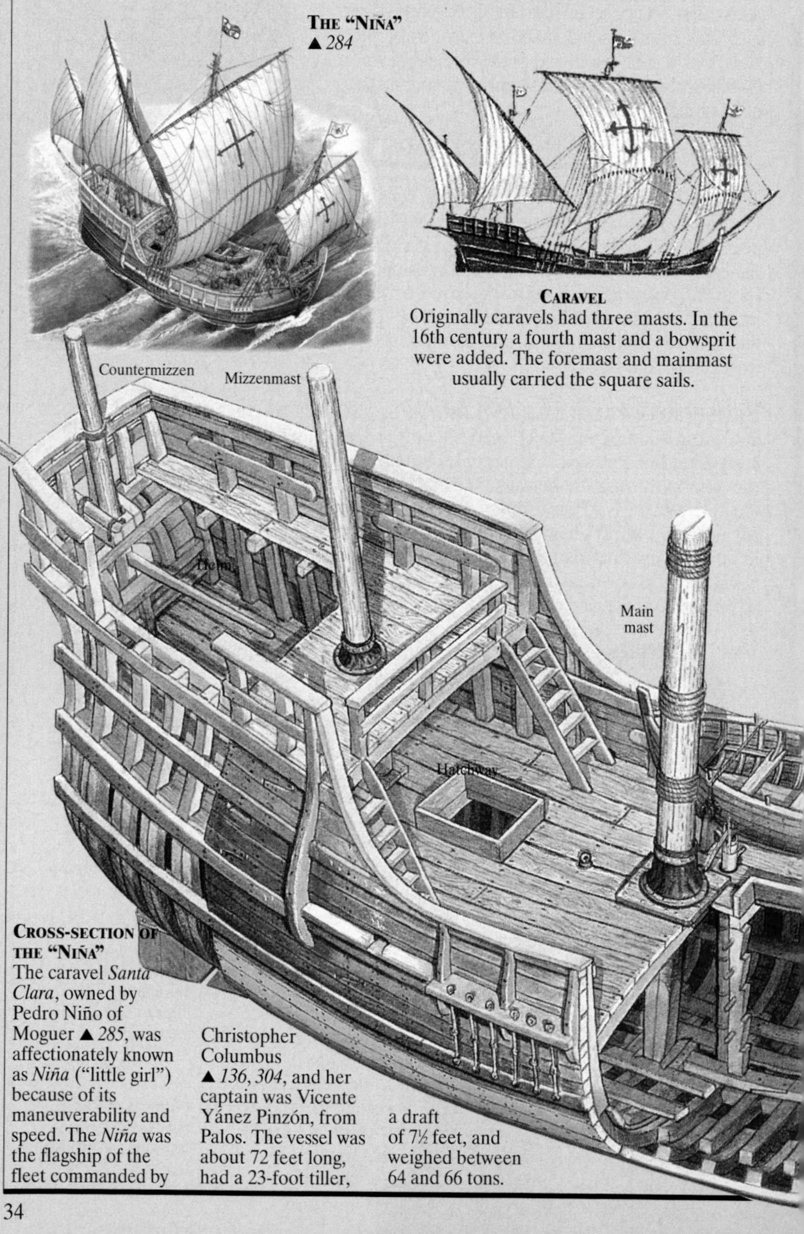

THE "NIÑA"
▲ *284*

CARAVEL
Originally caravels had three masts. In the 16th century a fourth mast and a bowsprit were added. The foremast and mainmast usually carried the square sails.

CROSS-SECTION OF THE "NIÑA"
The caravel *Santa Clara*, owned by Pedro Niño of Moguer ▲ *285*, was affectionately known as *Niña* ("little girl") because of its maneuverability and speed. The *Niña* was the flagship of the fleet commanded by Christopher Columbus ▲ *136*, *304*, and her captain was Vicente Yánez Pinzón, from Palos. The vessel was about 72 feet long, had a 23-foot tiller, a draft of 7½ feet, and weighed between 64 and 66 tons.

"February 14, 1493. The *Niña* is in grave difficulty. Her sails are torn and she is constantly assailed by mountainous waves... outraged that this ridiculously small vessel should presume to sail the waters of the ocean."

Cees Nooteboom

VOYAGE TO THE INDIES
Map preserved in the *Archivo de Indias* (Archives of the Indies) ▲ *150*, showing the port of Cartagena de Indias in Venezuela. In spring and summer, when the winds were favorable, two fleets set sail: the *Tierra Firme* fleet for Cartagena de Indias and Portobello, and the *Nueva España* fleet for San Juan de Ulúa and Veracruz.

THE INDIES FLEET
Caravels were gradually replaced by fighting galleons, while merchantmen and other vessels, such as carracks, cutters and frigates, were improved. A 16th-century treatise on navigation (left) by Pedro de Medina of Seville.

PILOTS AND SAILORS
The pilot (center) was responsible for directing the ship's course, a task which required experience and technical expertise. He had to understand swells and currents, be able to read navigational charts, keep a steady course using a compass and calculate latitude with an astrolabe. A sailor (left) from the Indies fleet in 1529.

THE "SANTA MARÍA"
The flagship commanded by Christopher Columbus on his first voyage was not a caravel but probably a carrack, a larger vessel which was much more difficult to maneuver.

FROM CARAVEL TO GALLEON
The typical vessel used for the Indies fleets was heavily armed and weighed about 330 tons. Although originally Spanish, the galleon was soon adopted throughout Europe. Its name was derived from "galley".

Seville and, later, Cádiz experienced unprecedented expansion from their privileged position regarding Spain's relations with America. For three hundred years their ports channeled precious metals, products and knowledge that affected every aspect of contemporary life and ended the old medieval order. With the collapse of the Spanish empire, however, they were discreetly forgotten.

A GEOGRAPHICAL REVOLUTION
Mid-16th century *Mappa mundi* by Pedro de Medina (1493–1567), cosmographer for the Casa de la Contratación. The expeditions that left the ports of Andalusia brought back conclusive evidence that the earth was round.

GOLD AND SILVER
During the course of the 16th century alone, 330,693 lbs of gold and 16,535 lbs of silver passed through the port of Seville, with the same amount smuggled in illegally. Doubloon worth 8 *escudos* (right) made from Peruvian gold (1748).

THE OLD AND THE NEW
Allegorical engraving of the meeting between the Old World (the cultured man or "civilization") and the New World (the naked woman or "barbarism"). In 1506 a gathering of humanists in Saint-Dié, in the French province of Lorraine, called the New Continent "America" in honor (although not necessarily justly so) of the Italian Amerigo Vespucci (1451–1512). In 1501–2 Vespucci, who worked for an Italian company in Seville, took part in a Portuguese expedition along the coast of Brazil which resulted in the discovery of the New Continent and its attribution to the Italian. He entered the service of Spain and replaced the disgraced Columbus ▲ *136, 283* as *piloto mayor*.

"The face of the world is changing… What was thought to be an island was in fact a peninsula, and what was thought to be the Indies was an undiscovered continent."

Stefan Zweig

THE MONOPOLY OF SEVILLE AND CÁDIZ
In 1503, shortly after the discovery of the New World, the Casa de la Contratación (or del Océano) was founded by the Crown to manage relations between Spain and the Indies. It organized expeditions, decided their routes, granted permits to pilots, assessed business and regulated the movement of passengers and merchandise. Ships had to put into the port of Seville. In the 17th century Seville began to decline as a result of the increasing prosperity of Cádiz, which had become the new metropolis of the Indies. In 1778 a decree authorizing free trade abolished the monopoly and opened up the field to other Spanish ports.

PORT OF SEVILLE: LATE 16TH CENTURY
Although Seville had all the disadvantages of a river port, it was chosen because its position eliminated the danger of foreign invasion and made it easier to control maritime traffic. Above: Oil painting attributed to Alonso Sánchez Coello.

BAY OF CÁDIZ: 18TH CENTURY
In 1680 Cádiz was granted the monopoly on relations with the New World. The Casa de la Contratación was transferred there in 1717.

EXOTIC AND INDIGENOUS PLANTS
The importing of plants from the Old and New Worlds changed the world's eating patterns, customs and landscapes. American plants such as potatoes and corn became basic foods in Europe, while manioc became a staple in Africa. Tomatoes, sweet peppers, cocoa (below) and tobacco soon became popular.

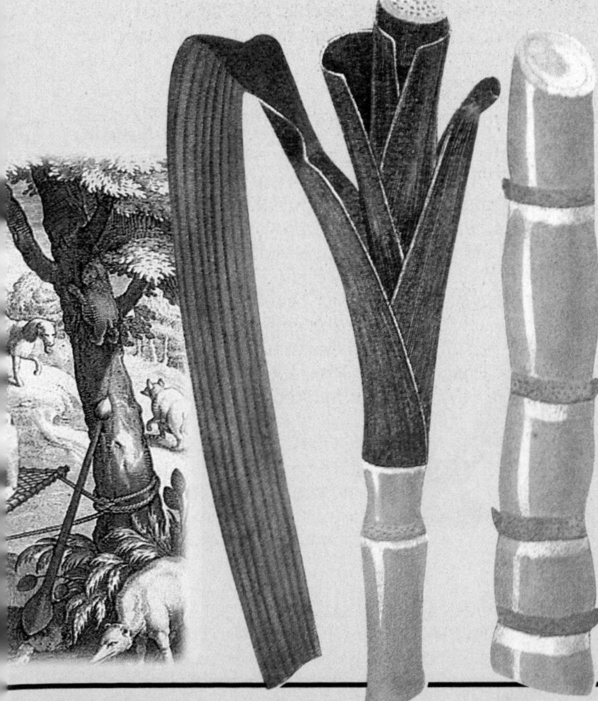

Nicolás Monardes (1507–84) of Seville played a major role in acclimatizing and propagating these plants. Conversely, sugar cane (left), cotton, wheat, vines and olives grew well in the soil of the New World.

El Arenal and Triana (1710).

SEVILLE: CULTURAL AND ARTISTIC CENTER. Seville became a cultural center for writers (Arias Montano, Mateo Alemán and Miguel de Cervantes) and artists (Francisco de Zurbarán, Velázquez and Bartolomé Estebán Murillo) and took on the appearance of a Renaissance city: squares were built, public buildings constructed and the gates in the city wall transformed into monumental arches.

DECLINE OF SEVILLE. During the first half of the 17th century there was widespread evidence that the Spanish empire was in a state of crisis. Disastrous military campaigns in Europe, rebellions in Portugal and Catalonia (1640) and the loss of maritime supremacy, combined with other factors such as the displacement of maritime trade to Cádiz, political instability (the Andalusian succession plot in 1640), economic chaos, food shortages, epidemics (almost half the population died of plague in 1649) and floods, to bring about the decline of Seville.

1521
In Seville, the Pendón Verde rebellion against the high cost of living. Cortés conquers Mexico.

1532
Pizarro conquers Peru.

1556–98
Reign of Philip II.

1566
The Dutch rebellion against Spain.

THE MONARCHY IN CRISIS

Following the loss of its trade monopoly with the Indies in 1717, Seville was nothing more than the agricultural market for lower Andalusia and the seat of several institutions. From 1729 to 1733 it was somewhat revitalized by the presence of the court of Philip V, the first of the Spanish Bourbons. During the second half of the 18th century the city benefitted from the reforms of the Enlightenment: Jovellanos (1744–1811) introduced liberal policies and revived education; Pablo de Olavide (1725–1803), administrator of Andalusia, undertook the modernization of the urban infrastructure and the colonization of the depopulated areas of the Sierra Morena.

Sevilla
SE PUBLICA DIARIAM
El Liberal en Sevilla
HUELVA

WARS AND SOCIAL UNREST IN THE 19TH CENTURY. The instability provoked by the American and French revolutions was exacerbated in the early

1580
Spain annexes Portugal.

1588
The Spanish Armada is defeated.

1596
Cádiz is sacked by the Earl of Essex.

1610
The Moors are expelled from Spain.

1701–15
The Spanish War of Succession.

1759–88
Reign of Charles III.

Ferdinand VII (Anon., 1820's).

“Qien no ha visto Sevilla, no ha visto maravilla!”
(“Those who have not seen Seville have missed a wondrous sight!”)
Popular saying

19th century by military confrontations. In 1805 the British fleet defeated the French and Spanish at Trafalgar, south of Cádiz. In 1807 the French invasion of Spain gave rise to the War of Independence. The first defeat of Napoleon’s army at the Battle of Bailén (1808) postponed the invasion of Andalusia and, for two years, Seville was the capital of Spain. However, in 1810 Joseph Bonaparte captured Seville and laid siege to Cádiz, where Parliament had taken refuge. In 1812 the latter elected the country’s first liberal constitution. The crisis in Spain led to rebellion in the American colonies which gained independence in 1824, to the detriment of the ports of Andalusia.

Political and social unrest. During the reigns of Ferdinand VII and his successors, there was increasing political conflict and social unrest. The 1820 military rebellion, led by General Rafael de Riego from the Seville region, opened the way for liberalism. This was followed three years later by a violent absolutist reaction. Although not without major incident (the bombing of Seville by the supporters of Isabel II, who was invested as regent in 1840), the constitutional regime became more firmly established during the 1830’s. Measures designed to liberalize the economy dismantled the old order, enriched the emergent bourgeoisie and relegated craftsmen and peasants to the status of journeymen. There was further political and social unrest when Isabella II was deposed in 1868. The first anarchist congress was held in Córdoba in 1872, when uprisings in Seville and Jerez were strengthening the Andalusian peasants’ revolt. A two-year period of republican government beginning in 1873 was followed by a return to monarchy which gave the country relative stability until the end of the century.

Liberal
Sevilla
MADRID · BARCELONA · BILBAO · MURCIA Y SEVILLA
DE LA MAÑANA
BODAS

Seville: a regional capital. The secularization of Church wealth had far-reaching consequences for Seville. Its beneficiaries formed a wealthy upper-middle class who tried to re-launch the economy. In 1847 the Feria de Abril, an important cattle market, was established. In 1848 the dukes of Montpensier took up residence in Seville and established a liberal court that favored progress and the arts. The predominantly agricultural economy strengthened, the population increased and the city’s railroad and port, which received ever greater volumes of maritime traffic, made it an important trading center. Seville, the capital of western Andalusia, exported agricultural (oil, cork and oranges) and mining products, while industry was expanding (particularly tobacco, foundries and ceramics).

1808–14
War of Independence fought against Napoleon.

1808–24
The Spanish colonial empire is in crisis.

1820–23
Liberal government.

The Battle of Seville, W. Heath (1815).

1860
War with Morocco.

1868
“La Gloriosa”: liberal revolution.

1873
First Spanish Republic.

1875
Restoration of the monarchy.

1926 edition of *El Liberal*, a progressive newspaper (left).

1892
Peasant unrest in Andalusia. Jerez uprising.

Poster for the joint Hispanic-American Exhibition of 1929.

Postage stamp issued for Expo '92.
Plan (below) of the 1929 exhibition.

1898
War with the United States and the loss of Cuba, Puerto Rico and the Philippines.

1917
Social unrest in Andalusia. The Rif war.

1923
Dictatorship of General Primo de Rivera.

1931
Second Republic.

20TH-CENTURY SEVILLE

1936–9
Spanish Civil War.

1939–75
Dictatorship of General Franco.

1975
Death of Franco. Coronation of Juan Carlos I and the institution of democracy.

Sevilla la Roja, drawing by Martínez de León.

1977
First free elections.

1981
Attempted coup d'état.

1992
Expo '92 is held in Seville.

The economy was weakened by the war with the United States and the loss of the last overseas colonies in 1898. Between the launch of the joint Hispanic-American Exhibition project in 1909 and its opening in 1929, Seville experienced a period of renewed activity, in particular centered around the port. The city, which was the subject of an extensive building program, spread both southward and eastward, and impressive, broad avenues were opened up in the historic center.

REPUBLIC, CIVIL WAR AND DICTATORSHIP. The general crisis of 1929 and the failure of the joint Hispanic-American Exhibition led to increased tensions, and Seville became a center of conflict during the Second Republic (1931–6). It was also an important political battleground for the confrontation between the ruling conservative classes and the powerful anarchist-union and communist movements. During the Civil War, the city fell into the hands of the rebels, in July 1936. The economic and political isolation of Franco's dictatorship led to a period of post-war stagnation. However, the 1960's marked the development of steady economic growth.

MODERNIZATION AND DEMOCRACY. During the 1970's economic growth and the institution of democracy transformed Seville into a modern city whose population increased to 700,000 during the next decade. The creation of the *comunidad autónoma* of Andalusia in 1982 made it the capital of the province, and the seat of the Andalusian parliament and government. Expo '92 bequeathed the city the futuristic site on the Isla de la Cartuja, and also resulted in a strengthening of its resources in the service industries.

The Andalusian parliament.

Arts and traditions

The *traje de flamenca* (the *traje de faralaes* is the best known), the *traje de amazona* and the men's *traje de corto* are traditional costumes, now only worn for festivals. Their exact history is unknown. The flamenco dress, the *bata* (probably from the Arabic *batt* meaning "cloak"), is thought to have its most distant origins in Crete and to have been embellished by Roman, Arab and gipsy fashions.

19TH-CENTURY ROMANTIC SCENE
The costumes worn for festivals and *romerías*, popular festivities held to celebrate a pilgrimage, have not changed over the years.

"TRAJE DE CORTO" AND "TRAJE DE FLAMENCA"
The men's costume comprises a pair of black or gray waisted trousers, a short jacket, false-fronted shirt, belt, boots and a *sombrero cordobés* (Cordovan hat). The women's costume consists of a brightly colored, frilled or flounced dress, necklaces, bracelets, high-heeled shoes and a flower worn in the hair.

"TRAJE DE AMAZONA"
The extremely elegant *traje de amazona* is less common than the *traje de corto*. It consists of a short velvet jacket, with gold embroidery, and a matching *sombrero calañes*. This brimless hat, originally from the mountain regions, is sometimes worn with a hairnet.

FANS
Fans are in everyday use in summer as well as being an accessory carried at festivals. They can be expensive, very simple or decorated with regional designs.

"SOMBRERO DE ALA ANCHA"
This broad-brimmed hat, also known as the *sombrero cordobés* (Cordovan hat), is typically Andalusian and a must for festivals. In the past it was the standard headgear in rural areas, but is now usually only worn by people of the older generation.

"Her pink skirt made it easy to guess that she was from Andalusia. Catalan women prefer dark colors, French black or German brown."
Pierre Louÿs

Mantilla
The word "mantilla" originates from the Arabic *mantil*, which is derived from the *mantum* of Gothic times. There are two types of mantilla. The white lace or silk mantilla is worn for festivals and grand occasions, especially bullfights. The black lace mantilla is worn on formal occasions, at funerals, and on the Thursday and Friday of the Semana Santa in Seville. The mantilla is held in place by a high, finely worked tortoiseshell comb.

"Mantón de Manila"
The shawl, an elegant accessory worn with the *traje de flamenca* at fairs and festivals, was introduced to Spain via the Spice Route. Its name is a reminder that, in the 17th century, embroidered silks were imported from Japan and Manila. It is also worn in the evening.

Origins
The *traje de flamenca* originated from the *bata de faena*, an overall worn by Andalusian women in the mid-19th century, especially those working in tobacco factories ▲ *186*. It was made of percale and had a single or double flounced hem. The gradual addition of braid and lace, and then the shawl, flowers and combs, turned it into a costume worn at festivals.

The Semana Santa commemorates the Passion and, because it is derived from the penitence ritual of the medieval brotherhoods, has retained the Baroque inspiration of the Counter-Reformation. From Palm Sunday to Easter Sunday, fifty-eight brotherhoods leave their respective churches and make their way to the cathedral (one every half-hour) from where they return to their church. For six days, the heart of Seville beats to the rhythm of *pasos* and *saetas* as the penitents and general public take part in this ardent and sumptuous celebration.

PROCESSIONS
The processions date from 1520, when the first Marquis of Tarifa organized a Via Dolorosa which ran from his residence (today known as the Casa de Pilatos ● *80* ▲ *158*, *160*) to the Cruz del Campo on the road from Seville to Carmona ▲ *214*. The processions of brotherhoods (*cofradías*) leave their churches carrying an image or statue of their patron saint.

BLUE SUITS AND MANTILLAS
According to tradition, men who are not participating in the processions wear blue suits and the women mantillas. Balconies provide an ideal vantage point for watching the processions. In this way the Sevillians are able to take part in a festival during which religious treasures usually housed in the churches are carried through the streets.

THE ROLE OF THE BROTHERHOODS
The processions are only one aspect of a brotherhood's activities. Each brotherhood has a council whose members are elected from among the brothers and led by a senior brother. The council is responsible for administering the congregation, preparing the processions, restoring statues and, if necessary, improving the organization of worship.

OFFICIAL ROUTE AND STRICT TIMETABLE
The official route, known as the Carrera Oficial, is shared by all the brotherhoods. It runs from the Plaza de la Campana ▲ *130* to the Puerta de San Miguel of the cathedral ▲ *133*, via the Calle Sierpes, the Plaza de San Francisco and the Avenida de la Constitución, and is lined with VIP seats and "boxes". The general council of the brotherhoods imposes a very strict timetable.

"The statues of the Virgin arouse more interest than the statues of Christ… They bring up the rear… the most famous, those most dear to the Sevillians, are careful to maintain this sense of longing."
Dominique Fernandez

"La Macarena" ▲ *167*. The *Virgen de la Esperanza*, sculpted in the 17th century by an unknown artist, is the best known of Seville's statues of the Virgin. It is carried beneath a silver canopy and on its breast shine the *mariquillas*, flower-shaped jewels presented by the bullfighter Joselito ▲ *211*. La Macarena, Seville's most powerful brotherhood, was founded in the 16th century by the gardeners' corporation.

"La Trianera" ▲ *195*. The procession of the patron saint of Triana, the *Esperanza de Triana*, takes place at dawn on Good Friday. The brotherhood was founded in the 17th century by ceramists and sailors.

"La Saeta". Since 1918–20 the *saeta* ("arrow"), the only one of the great *cantes* ● *54* that is purely religious, has been closely related to the flamenco. The *saeta* is sung *a cappella* by one person. Antonio Machado described it in a poem as the "Song of the Andalusian people/sung every spring/to pray for the stairway/ that leads to the Cross."

The processions are slow and the route complicated. The brotherhoods nearest the cathedral take at least four hours to complete their penitence, while those furthest away may take up to twelve hours. Six, seven or eight brotherhoods set out on each day of the week. Each brotherhood consists of between three hundred and two thousand penitents, called *nazarenos*.

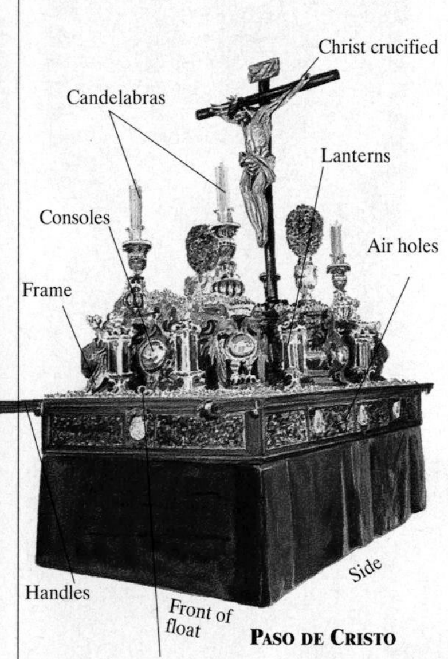

PASO DE CRISTO

PASO DE LA VIRGEN DE PALIO

LES "PASOS"
Each brotherhood usually prepares two *pasos* (floats) which are carried in procession through the streets. The first is dedicated to Christ and presents Christ on the Cross or a scene from the Passion. The second, dedicated to the Virgin, always consists of a *mater dolorosa* beneath a canopy. The richness and lavish decoration of the floats that bear the statues is legendary.

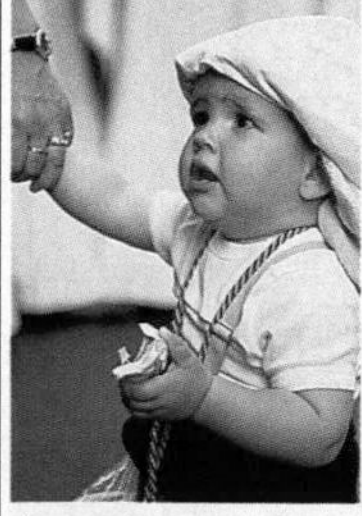

AGE-OLD TRADITIONS
Traditions are passed on in early childhood and future penitents are registered with a brotherhood at birth. Children taking part in the processions do not wear masks.

BEARERS
The *paso* is carried by 36 to 48 *costaleros*, named after their cotton headgear or *costal*, which forms protective folds at the back of their neck. Since they cannot see where they are going, their slow progress is directed by a *capataz*, dressed in black, who walks ahead of the *paso* and strikes a hammer to indicate when to stop and move off again.

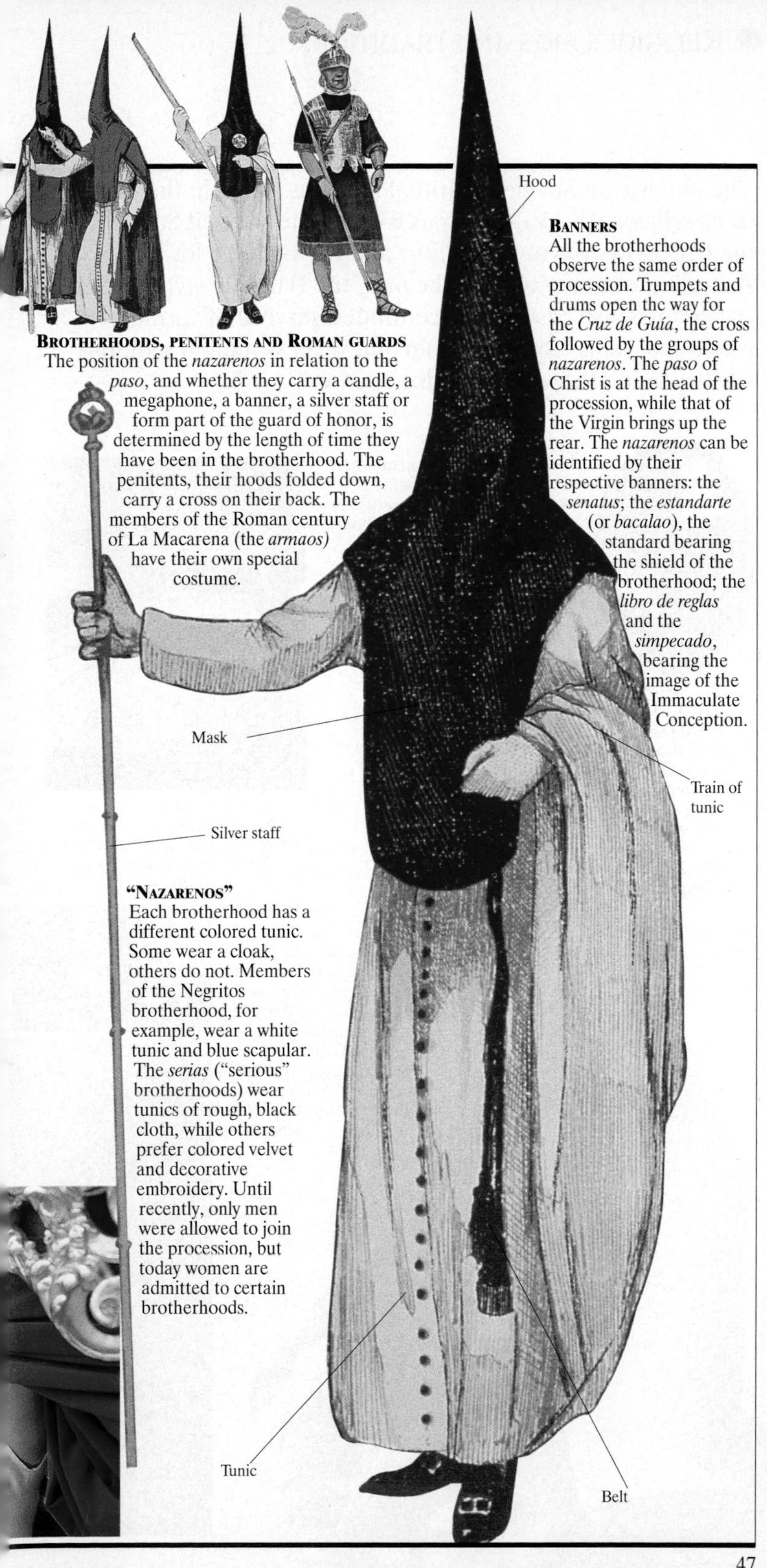

Brotherhoods, penitents and Roman guards
The position of the *nazarenos* in relation to the *paso*, and whether they carry a candle, a megaphone, a banner, a silver staff or form part of the guard of honor, is determined by the length of time they have been in the brotherhood. The penitents, their hoods folded down, carry a cross on their back. The members of the Roman century of La Macarena (the *armaos)* have their own special costume.

Banners
All the brotherhoods observe the same order of procession. Trumpets and drums open the way for the *Cruz de Guía*, the cross followed by the groups of *nazarenos*. The *paso* of Christ is at the head of the procession, while that of the Virgin brings up the rear. The *nazarenos* can be identified by their respective banners: the *senatus*; the *estandarte* (or *bacalao*), the standard bearing the shield of the brotherhood; the *libro de reglas* and the *simpecado*, bearing the image of the Immaculate Conception.

"Nazarenos"
Each brotherhood has a different colored tunic. Some wear a cloak, others do not. Members of the Negritos brotherhood, for example, wear a white tunic and blue scapular. The *serias* ("serious" brotherhoods) wear tunics of rough, black cloth, while others prefer colored velvet and decorative embroidery. Until recently, only men were allowed to join the procession, but today women are admitted to certain brotherhoods.

The intensity of Seville's spiritual life is reflected in the number of its religious festivals: Corpus Christi, the Blessed Sacrament, the Cruces de Mayo, Santa Cruz and the Baile de los Seises. As well as commemorating the past, the Baroque style of these ceremonies also ensures the continued survival of various traditional skills, especially gold and silver work and sculpture, which would otherwise have disappeared.

Juan Martinez Montañés (1568–1649)
Some of the *pasos* in the Semana Santa processions include examples of the work of one of the most renowned religious sculptors. Portrait by Velázquez ● *91*.

Sculpture: in the tradition of the masters
Local sculptors are still inspired by the example of the great schools: the *montañesina* (Martínez Montañés) and the *roldanesca* (Pedro Roldán). Alvarez Duarte rolls up his sleeves before what will be a Christ of the Passion (below).

Wax
One of Seville's wax factories where religious tapers and candles are made from virgin and paraffin wax.

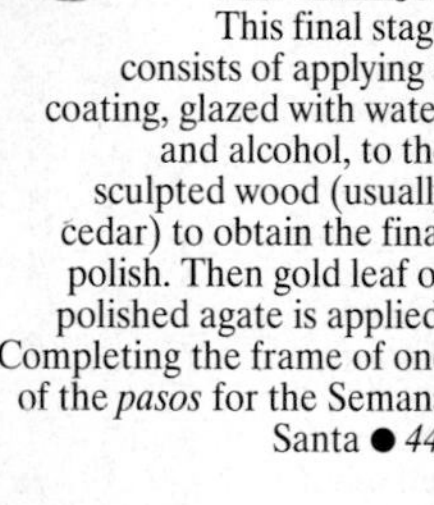

The "aparejo"
This final stage consists of applying a coating, glazed with water and alcohol, to the sculpted wood (usually cedar) to obtain the final polish. Then gold leaf or polished agate is applied. Completing the frame of one of the *pasos* for the Semana Santa ● *44*.

COSTUME OF THE "SEISES"
The costume (red for the festival of the Corpus Christi, blue for the Immaculate Conception) is similar to those worn by page boys. It consists of a hat with a feather, a doublet (*vaquero*) and white breeches embellished with gilt braid and a taffeta sash.

"EL BAILE DE LOS SEISES"
One of Seville's most elegant traditions, *el baile de los seises*, dates back to the reign of Ferdinand III (the Saint). In the 15th century the *seises* (*seis* means "six") were the six boys who sang in the cathedral. Today ten boys sing on three occasions: the festivals of the Blessed Sacrament ("El Corpus") and the Immaculate Conception ("La Purísima") and during the three days of the carnival. As they sing, they perform a simple dance and play the castanets.

GOLDSMITHS AND SILVERSMITHS
A flourishing art sustained by the creation of silver staffs, lamps, banners and *pasos*.

"CRUCES DE MAYO"
On May 3 the discovery of the Holy Cross on hallowed ground is celebrated in public squares and private courtyards.

CORPUS CHRISTI. The city's social, religious and civil bodies are all represented in the Corpus Christi procession held each Thursday throughout June to commemorate the institution of the sacraments and Eucharist. The streets are strewn with aromatic herbs. *Procesión del Corpus*, by Manuel Cabral Bejarano, showing the procession leaving the cathedral ▲ *133*.

A number of festivals and processions are held in spring and summer in western Andalusia: *ferias*, originally cattle markets, and *romerías*, pilgrimages to places of worship where pilgrims sing and pray.

"CASETAS"
Casetas are the wood and canvas stands, decorated with flowers, large earthenware jars and embroidered shawls, erected at *ferias* by organizations, companies and institutions. They are divided in two with a dance platform at the front and, at the back, a counter serving vintage wines, soups and cooked meats from the sierra. Prizes are awarded for the best decorated stands.

"REAL"
The *real* is the fairground enclosure bounded by the line of the *casetas* and the whitewashed streets. Individual horses and teams are displayed there, as in this 1930's photograph.

"FERIAS"
Ferias were first held in the 13th century. Over the ages they have become veritable institutions. The Feria de Abril, established in 1847 on the initiative of a Catalan and a Basque who suggested the idea to the town council of Seville, has remained faithful to the tradition of the *feria*. It marks the beginning of a three-month cycle of festivals, from April to June, during which towns and villages in the region celebrate their own festivals according to a pre-arranged calendar.

ENJOYMENT AND COURTESY
La Feria de Sevilla, by Joaquín Domínguez Bécquer (1817–79) ● *93* captures the atmosphere of the Feria de Abril: obvious enjoyment, hospitality and courtesy.

Virgen del Rocio ▲ *290*
The *Virgen del Rocío* is the focus of Spain's most famous pilgrimage. The statue of the Virgin is housed in a hermitage in the village of El Rocío, near Almonte, in the province of Huelva. Pilgrims belonging to brotherhoods from Seville, Cádiz, and the villages of Huelva arrive on foot, on horseback and by car. They set out on the Wednesday before Whitsun, at the end of May or beginning of June. Almost one million people and more than a hundred brotherhoods gather to pay homage to the Virgin and to follow the young people from Almonte who carry her through the streets for more than twelve hours.

Young gipsy pilgrims
Young pilgrims, in traditional gipsy costume, taking part in the pilgrimage of El Rocío in the early 20th century.

Pilgrimage of Santa Maria de las Rocinas
In the 13th century the hermitage of Santa María de las Rocinas was already a center of pilgrimage for the mountain dwellers of Mures (Villamanrique), the shepherds of Almonte ▲ *290* and the colliers of Sanlúcar de Barrameda ▲ *298*. The pilgrimage was the forerunner of a ceremony which, over the centuries, would attract increasing numbers of people.

Pilgrims in the Almonte region
The pilgrimage can take three or four days as the procession makes its way across the Doñana marshes ■ *18*, ▲ *286* to the sound of pipes and tambourines. At night pilgrims sleep in the pine forests, in the shelter of their ox carts decorated with garlands.

Seville's great *toreros*, its well-informed enthusiasts (*aficionados*) and the grandeur and beauty of La Maestranza, its bullring, make it one of Spain's leading bullfighting cities. The season begins on Easter Sunday with a *corrida* (bullfight) that opens the Feria de Abril, and is one of the world's major bullfighting events. It continues throughout the summer with the *novilladas* (using young bulls) and ends in September with the Feria de San Miguel.

SAND, SWEAT AND BLOOD
The *peones* assist the matador by using their capes to tire the bull at the beginning of the fight. Every bullfight takes place under the watchful gaze of the *aficionados*. Ernest Hemingway was a true *aficionado* ● 107.

RITUAL PRELUDE
The *corrida* begins with a procession of bullfighters (*paseillo*). Before the fight (*lidia*), they perform *verónicas*, downward passes of the cape executed with the hands together.

DEADLY TRINITY
In the course of an afternoon bullfight, three matadors confront six bulls. The fight takes place in three stages. During the first stage (*tercio de varas*), the matador uses a cape while mounted picadors stick three spears in the bull. These are followed by three pairs of *banderillas* (barbed darts) during the *tercio de banderillas*. Finally there is the *tercio de espadas*: the matador executes several passes (*faena de muleta*) before dealing the death blow.

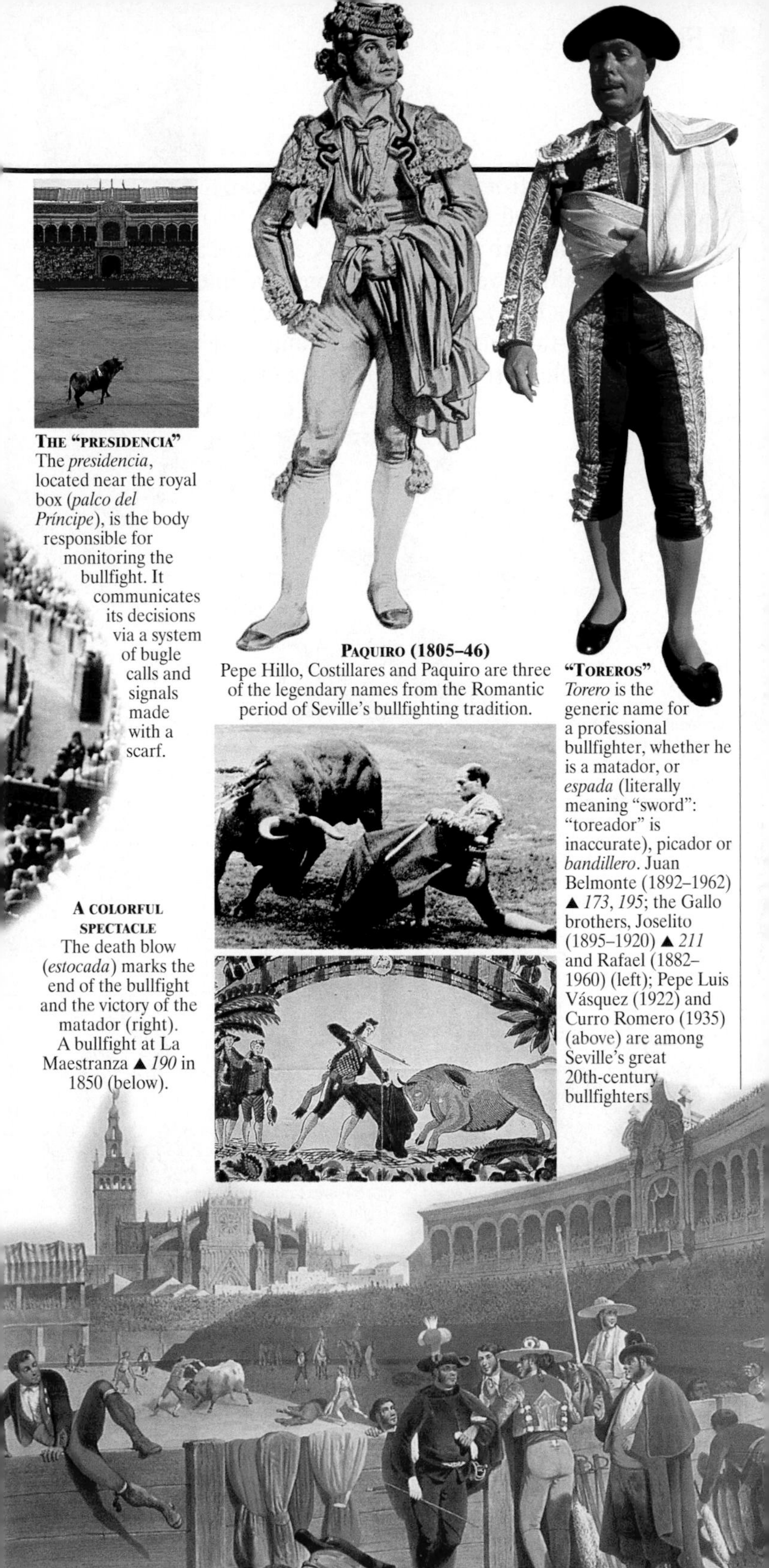

THE "PRESIDENCIA"
The *presidencia*, located near the royal box (*palco del Príncipe*), is the body responsible for monitoring the bullfight. It communicates its decisions via a system of bugle calls and signals made with a scarf.

PAQUIRO (1805–46)
Pepe Hillo, Costillares and Paquiro are three of the legendary names from the Romantic period of Seville's bullfighting tradition.

"TOREROS"
Torero is the generic name for a professional bullfighter, whether he is a matador, or *espada* (literally meaning "sword": "toreador" is inaccurate), picador or *bandillero*. Juan Belmonte (1892–1962) ▲ *173*, *195*; the Gallo brothers, Joselito (1895–1920) ▲ *211* and Rafael (1882–1960) (left); Pepe Luis Vásquez (1922) and Curro Romero (1935) (above) are among Seville's great 20th-century bullfighters.

A COLORFUL SPECTACLE
The death blow (*estocada*) marks the end of the bullfight and the victory of the matador (right). A bullfight at La Maestranza ▲ *190* in 1850 (below).

Flamenco, derived from traditional Andalusian singing (*cante andaluz* or *cante jondo*), first appeared with the arrival of gipsies in Cádiz and Seville in the 15th century. Initially relegated to an entertainment performed in brothels, flamenco became generally accepted during the 19th century. In the 1920's Manuel de Falla, Federico García Lorca and Angeles Ortiz established flamenco's wide popularity.

GUITAR: "EL TOQUE"
Although classical guitar has been the national instrument since the 17th century, it was not used for flamenco until the second half of the 19th century.

DANCE: "EL BAILE"
Sevillanas, movements performed by four individual couples, are derived from *seguidillas* (which appeared in La Mancha in the 16th century) and the *bolero*. They originated in Seville and spread to the rest of Spain during the 18th century.

SONG: "EL CANTE"
Flamenco was reserved for family gatherings and private celebrations until the second half of the 19th century when it became a popular entertainment in "music" cafés. The first and most famous of these was opened by Silverio Franconetti (right, ▲ *175*) in Seville in 1885. They proved extremely popular in Andalusia and Madrid until the 1920's. In theory the *cante* (singing) is either *jondo* (deep) or *chico* (high). But *jondo* also means performing the oldest and technically most difficult repertoire and singing in a particular way. Famous *cantaor* Antonio Chacón (1869–1929) (right).

Camarón de la Isla (1952–92)
José Monge, Camarón de la Isla, was a great singer in the gipsy tradition. Performing both new and traditional flamenco songs, he brought this style to the height of its international popularity.

Traditional duo
The *cantaor*, wearing a black suit and white shirt, sits on one of two chairs. His hands are placed flat against his thighs or hold a willow cane between his knees. The guitarist sits on the other chair, leaning toward the *cantaor* and following every inflection of the song. The guitar is always subsidiary to the dominant *cante*.

Manolo Caracol (1910–76)
At the age of twelve, this gipsy *cantaor* from Seville entered the Granada song contest organized by Federico García Lorca ● 99, *106* in 1922. He gave a brilliant performance of all the most difficult forms of flamenco.

Paco de Lucía
His collaboration with Camarón de la Isla produced a collection of recordings which summarizes the world of the *cante* in an unprecedented virtuoso performance. Flamenco owes its international reputation to his talent and musical research. He has played with guitarists from other countries, such as Al di Meola and John McLaughlin.

Aurora Vargas

There are any number of ceramic votive tablets and name plaques in the streets of Seville. It was the gold reflections of the *azulejos* which once covered the Torre del Oro ● *68* ▲ *184* that gave the tower its name.

Ceramics and pottery are the most important traditional crafts in the lower Guadalquivir valley. Although pottery was first produced there in the Neolithic age, it acquired its uniquely decorative character during the Islamic period (8th–13th centuries), later to be further embellished by classic 16th-century techniques.

TRIANA CERAMICS
Most of Seville's artistic ceramics are produced in the Triana district ▲ *194* which has given its name to a particular style. It combines various techniques, with a preference for hand-painted, popular motifs. Its most remarkable items are *azulejos* ● *77*, architectural features, dishes and earthenware jars.

GUADALQUIVIR POTTERY
The Guadalquivir valley has rich clay soil and produces coarse (*en basto*) domestic and rustic pottery: white (*en blanco*) ceramics for earthenware pitchers and water jugs, and glazed ceramics (*vidriada*) for terrines. The pitchers from Lebrija ▲ *293* and earthenware oil jars from Coria are particularly renowned.

DECORATIVE CERAMICS
Decorative ceramics were first produced in Seville during the Islamic period. Spanish Muslim artists were responsible for the dissemination of glazing techniques and their systematic use in architecture for façades, floors, arcaded upper galleries and roofs. Mudéjar art was, in turn, enriched by imported oriental techniques and regional production developed accordingly. *Alicatado*, a mosaic of carved fragments (left), began to be used for wall coverings and *azulejos*, usually blue (*azul* actually means "blue") decorative tiles, for wall panels. *Azulejos* were also used for floors, in small *olambrillas,* for covering the spaces between roof beams and to decorate stair risers.

Decorative motifs
The geometric motifs of the Islamic period (center) were embellished by the classical Italianate designs of the 16th and the popular Baroque motifs of the 18th centuries.

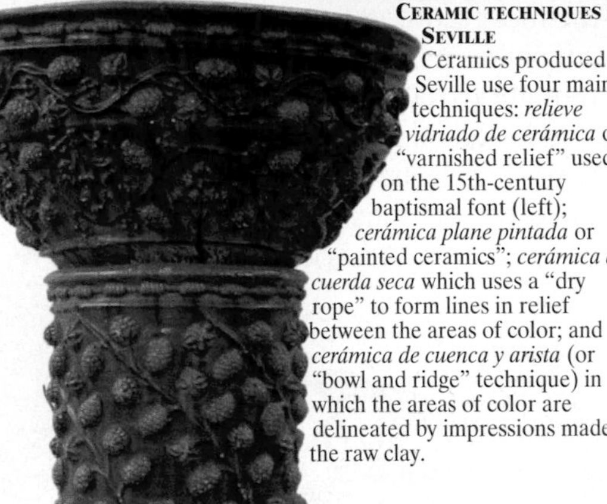

Ceramic techniques in Seville
Ceramics produced in Seville use four main techniques: *relieve vidriado de cerámica* or "varnished relief" used on the 15th-century baptismal font (left); *cerámica plane pintada* or "painted ceramics"; *cerámica de cuerda seca* which uses a "dry rope" to form lines in relief between the areas of color; and *cerámica de cuenca y arista* (or "bowl and ridge" technique) in which the areas of color are delineated by impressions made in the raw clay.

Street plaques
Ceramic plaques were already being used in the 18th century to indicate street names and house numbers (*azulejos de proprios*). *Azulejo de proprios* of the Alcázar (above).

Cartuja ceramics
The Cartuja factory ▲ *198*, founded in 1839 by the Englishman Charles Pickman ▲ *199*, heralded the industrialization of ceramics. It produced pieces whose motifs, taken from various European and regional styles, were either painted on or obtained by chromolithography (color reproduction by lithography).

Gazpacho is one of the most representative dishes of Andalusian cuisine, which has its roots in the rural tradition. It is an ancient dish thought to date from the time of the Iberians or Romans and based on a simple mixture of bread, water, oil and salt. The garlic and vinegar were added later, while other ingredients, such as tomatoes and sweet peppers from America, were added in the 17th century.

INGREDIENTS FOR GAZPACHO
Serves 4–6:
2¼ lbs ripe tomatoes;
2 green peppers;
1 medium cucumber;
1–2 cloves of garlic;
1 cup dried white breadcrumbs;
6–7 tablespoons olive oil; 1–2 tablespoons wine vinegar;
1½ pints water; salt.
Proportions can be varied to taste.

1. Soak the breadcrumbs in water. Remove the pith and seeds from the peppers and cut them into small pieces. Taste the cucumber to make sure it is not bitter and then peel (leaving a little of the skin to give it more taste) and shred it.

MORTAR OR MIXER
Traditionally gazpacho is prepared using a mortar (*almirez*) in which the various ingredients are mixed by hand. Today mixers tend to be used. In fact, although the method is the same, mixers produce a thicker soup.

4. When you have obtained a smooth mixture, gradually add the oil (as for mayonnaise). As you mix in the oil, add the vinegar and thin down with a little of the water.

5. Strain through a conical strainer. Flush the residue through the strainer with the rest of the water until only the cucumber seeds and tomato skins are left. Season to taste.

"Gazpacho is supposed to be very refreshing, an opinion which seems to me somewhat rash. And yet, however strange it may appear when you first taste it, in the end you get used to it and may even like it."

Théophile Gautier

Simple and refreshing
The word "gazpacho", which first appeared in a document in 1611, is thought to be derived from the pre-Roman term *caspa*, meaning "residue" or "fragment". This simple dish, once the staple diet of peasants and journeymen, still appears on the tables of western Andalusia at the first sign of warm weather.

2. Crush the garlic in the mortar or mixer (make sure you salt it so that it doesn't spurt out) and then add the less tender vegetables such as the chopped peppers and shredded cucumber.

3. Mix to a fine paste. Add the chopped tomatoes and then the breadcrumbs, which have been squeezed to remove any excess water. Beat vigorously to bind the mixture.

Variations
Apart from regional differences, there are as many variations as there are individual tastes. *Gazpachos rojos* are typical of Seville and its environs. *Salmorejo* and *porra* are thicker versions (made with less water), served with a more substantial accompaniment. In *ajo blanco* the tomatoes, cucumber and peppers are replaced by almonds. Finally, some are heated up before being served.

6. Gazpacho can be chilled in the refrigerator or by adding a few ice cubes. Serve in a tureen with a selection of garnishes: peppers, cucumber, tomatoes, onion, bread and hard-boiled eggs.

At the end of spring, when temperatures rise to around 35 °C, it is much more pleasant to sit in a bar (often open onto the street) than in the enclosed atmosphere of a restaurant. The oldest bars are well worth a visit, if only for their evocative, Baroque décor. But, above all, bars are very lively places and almost all of them serve *tapas* (snacks) in the afternoon and evening.

BEER
Spanish beer is pale, served cold and has become more popular than wine. *Cruzcampo* is Seville's most famous beer.

WINE ▲ *306*
The wine cellars, *tabernas* and bars of Seville are well stocked with wines, particularly from Jerez (*finos*, *soleras* and *manzanilla* from Sanlúcar ▲ *298*), but also from El Condado de Huelva, Córdoba ▲ *236* and Valdepeñas.

BARS IN SEVILLE
The great majority and the oldest (wooden casks and counters, and *azulejos*) of Seville's many bars are found in the old city center ▲ *155* and in Triana ▲ *194*. Bars in Seville are an important part of everyday life: as well as breakfast, they serve *tapas* and *raciones*, a range of snacks and hors d'oeuvres.

OLIVE AND OTHER TAPAS

In Seville bars serve olive-based snacks such as *banderillas picantes* (olives, gherkins and sweet or chilli peppers seasoned with vinegar, brine and garlic), *aceitunas gordales* (large olives heavily seasoned with garlic, peppers, spices and salt) and *aceitunas manzanilla* (fairly small olives grown in the Seville region, and the best), as well as *altramuces* (lupin seeds left to swell in brine).

Pescaito frito (small, fried fish) is a favorite with the Sevillians. They are eaten at *veladores*, communal tables installed on bar terraces.

"CHURRERÍAS" AND "FREIDURÍAS"

Churrerías and *freidurías* sell mainly fried, take-away food. *Churrerías* (donut stalls) sell *churros*, the long donuts eaten for breakfast, and potato donuts eaten in the evening. In the late afternoon *freidurías de pescaitos* sell squid, hake (*pescada*), small sole (*acedías*), firm-fleshed fish marinaded in a sweet pepper sauce (*adobo*) before they are cooked, and other types of fish from the coast of Cádiz and Huelva. They also sell croquettes, olives, capers, radishes, and thick, crunchy donuts (*regañas y picos*). This fried food is eaten in bars, on terraces and in open-air movie theaters.

TAPAS

Tapas refers to all cold and hot snacks (cooked meats, cheeses, cooked dishes, fried food) served with drinks. Seville has many *bares tienda*, combined bars and grocery stores. The term *tapas* probably referred to the rounds of sausage that used to be placed on a glass of wine (*tapar* means "to cover") in *bares tienda* and served as an aperitif.

JEREZ-SOLERA 1670
CHATO 40 CÉNTIMOS

TYPICAL ANDALUSIAN PRODUCTS

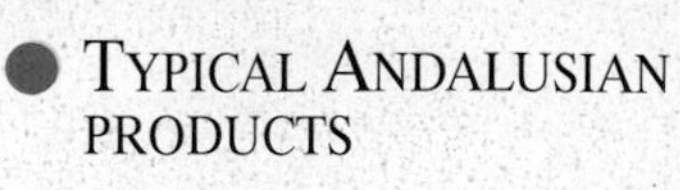

ANDALUSIAN FAN ● *42*
Fans were imported from the Far East in the 16th century and became extremely popular in Spain during the 18th century. Paper or fabric is stretched across wood or ivory ribs and painted or embroidered with geometric motifs, popular scenes or *goyescas*.

LIQUEURS
Although less well-known than the wines ▲ *306*, brandies from the sierra are just as popular.

CÓRDOBA LEATHER ▲ *236*
The repoussé (or embossed) leather is painted with bright colors and partly covered with silver leaf. It is decorated with scenes in relief, plant forms or geometric motifs.

COMBS. Combs were originally designed to secure the mantilla, the ornate veil worn during Catholic ceremonies. The most beautiful Andalusian combs are made of tortoiseshell.

GOLD AND SILVER WORK
Cordovan filigree consists of interlaced gold or silver.

EMBROIDERED SHAWL
Hand-embroidered silk shawls have been worn by Andalusian women since the 19th century. Today they are made by the few remaining craft workshops or are imported from China.

CERAMICS ● *56*
The ceramics workshops of Triana continue the local tradition of floral and naive designs.

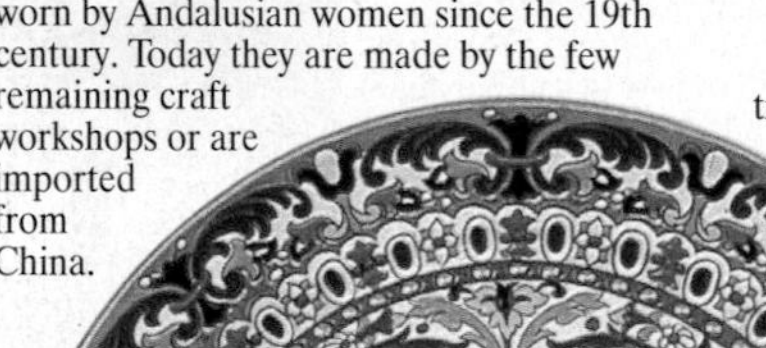

JAMS
The Convento de Santa Paula ▲ *168* is renowned for its *mermeladas*.

Architecture

The dolmens and hut settlements of lower Andalusia belong to the megalithic culture that developed along the Atlantic coast of Europe in the 6th century BC. The inhabitants lived by agriculture and stock-farming and by exploiting the region's mineral resources. The first cities were founded by Phoenician and Greek settlers, but the Romans were the major urban developers: they rebuilt Hispalis (Seville) and founded nearby Itálica.

THE GODDESS FORTUNA. The Greek marble (above), found on the site of Itálica ▲ *208*, most probably represents the Roman goddess Fortuna, the city's protectress. The head is crowned with a crenelated tower of bonded freestone pierced by a door.

DOLMEN OF MATARRUBILLA ▲ *219*
This tomb from the 3rd millennium BC was sealed with flat stones and covered by a barrow. An interior passageway leads to the circular chamber where a block of black marble was probably used as an offering table.

NEOLITHIC RURAL DWELLING
The structure of the *chozas* (reed huts) found in lower Andalusia is similar to that of Neolithic huts. Their wooden framework is covered with reeds.

ROMAN HOUSE
The rectangular layout of the single-story Roman *domus* was organized around the axis formed by the entrance and covered entrance hall. The bedrooms (*cubicula*) opened onto a central colonnaded courtyard (*peristylum*) with a gallery and cistern (*impluvium*). At the far end of the courtyard was the dining room and main living room (*tablinum* or *triclinium*). The houses discovered at Itálica were of this type.

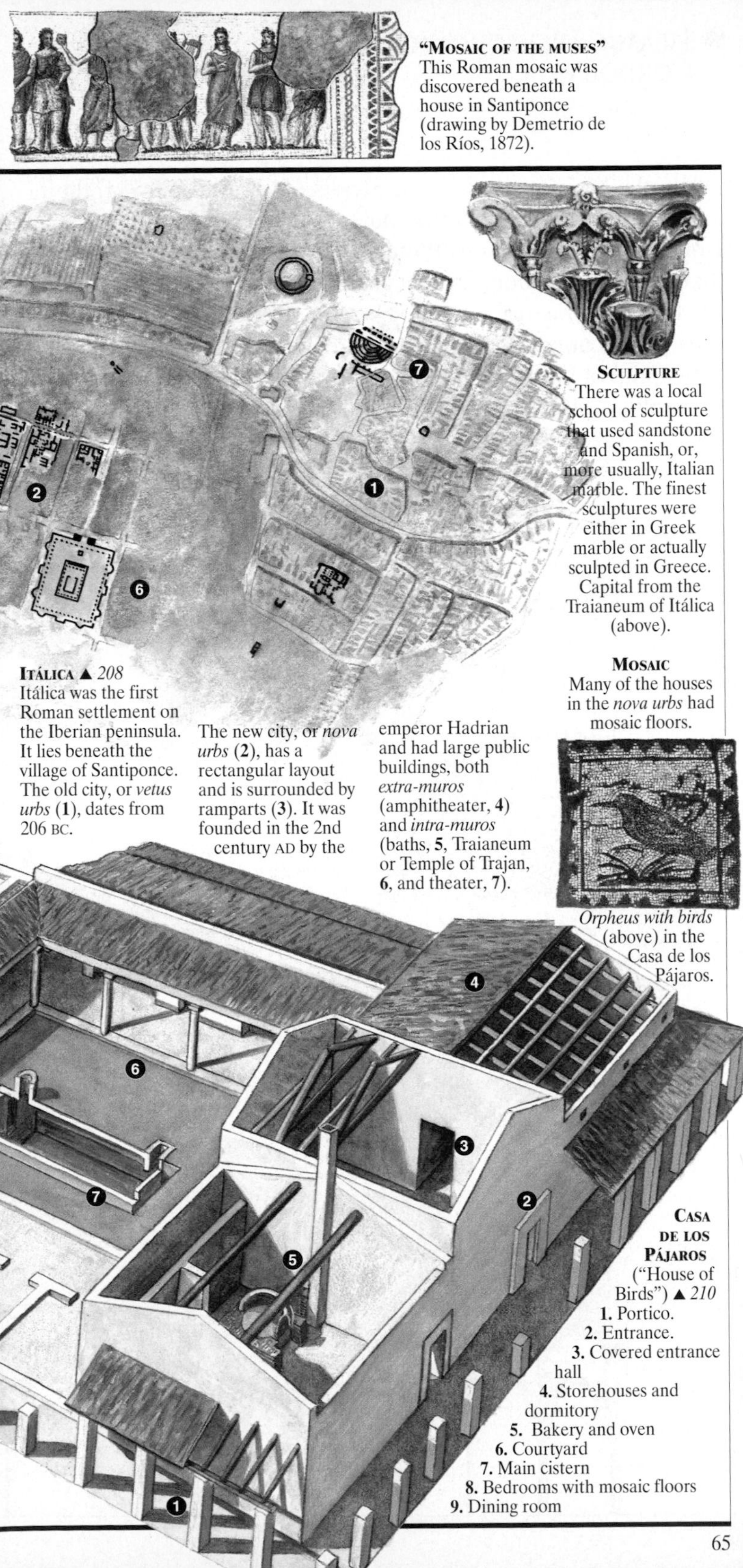

"Mosaic of the muses"
This Roman mosaic was discovered beneath a house in Santiponce (drawing by Demetrio de los Ríos, 1872).

Sculpture
There was a local school of sculpture that used sandstone and Spanish, or, more usually, Italian marble. The finest sculptures were either in Greek marble or actually sculpted in Greece. Capital from the Traianeum of Itálica (above).

Itálica ▲ *208*
Itálica was the first Roman settlement on the Iberian peninsula. It lies beneath the village of Santiponce. The old city, or *vetus urbs* (**1**), dates from 206 BC. The new city, or *nova urbs* (**2**), has a rectangular layout and is surrounded by ramparts (**3**). It was founded in the 2nd century AD by the emperor Hadrian and had large public buildings, both *extra-muros* (amphitheater, **4**) and *intra-muros* (baths, **5**, Traianeum or Temple of Trajan, **6**, and theater, **7**).

Mosaic
Many of the houses in the *nova urbs* had mosaic floors.

Orpheus with birds (above) in the Casa de los Pájaros.

Casa de los Pájaros
("House of Birds") ▲ *210*
1. Portico.
2. Entrance.
3. Covered entrance hall
4. Storehouses and dormitory
5. Bakery and oven
6. Courtyard
7. Main cistern
8. Bedrooms with mosaic floors
9. Dining room

When the Muslims crossed the Straits of Gibraltar in 711, their architects began to apply their talents to the legacy left by the Romans and Visigoths. Although they concentrated on three main areas (irrigation, and religious and defensive architecture) the Muslim influence can also be seen in the characteristically intricate urban architecture. Abd el-Rahman I made Córdoba the capital of his caliphate and honored it by building a mosque. In Seville, Abd el-Rahman II built arsenals and ramparts to protect the city from the Norman invasions.

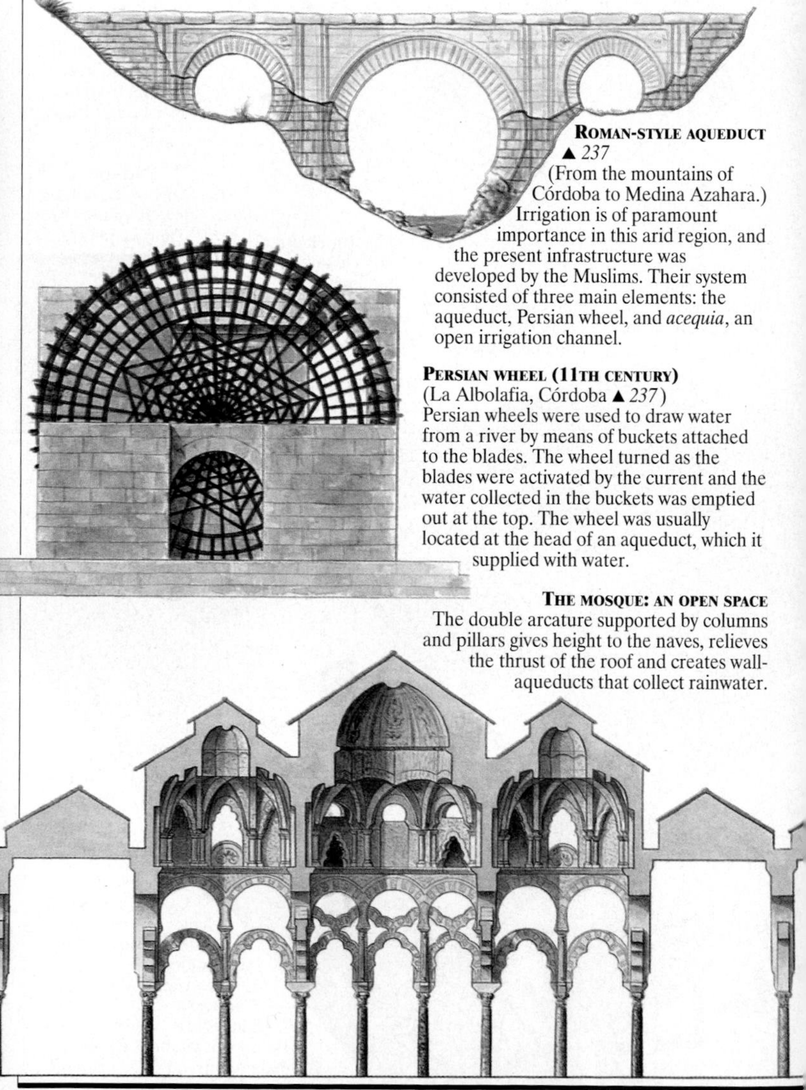

ROMAN-STYLE AQUEDUCT ▲ *237*
(From the mountains of Córdoba to Medina Azahara.) Irrigation is of paramount importance in this arid region, and the present infrastructure was developed by the Muslims. Their system consisted of three main elements: the aqueduct, Persian wheel, and *acequia*, an open irrigation channel.

PERSIAN WHEEL (11TH CENTURY)
(La Albolafia, Córdoba ▲ *237*)
Persian wheels were used to draw water from a river by means of buckets attached to the blades. The wheel turned as the blades were activated by the current and the water collected in the buckets was emptied out at the top. The wheel was usually located at the head of an aqueduct, which it supplied with water.

THE MOSQUE: AN OPEN SPACE
The double arcature supported by columns and pillars gives height to the naves, relieves the thrust of the roof and creates wall-aqueducts that collect rainwater.

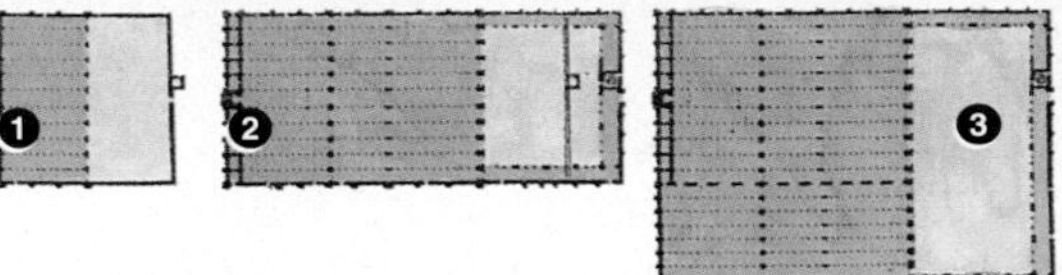

1. *Qibli* wall, indicating the direction of Mecca (*qibla*).
2. The *qibli* wall contains the *mihrab* (niche).
3. Patio de los Naranjos ("courtyard of orange trees").

The great mosque of Córdoba ▲ *238*
The early plan for the construction of La Mezquita, begun in 785, was drawn up during the reign of Abd el-Rahman I. El-Hakam II extended its length (961–76) and Hisham II doubled its width (976–1009).

Ribbed domes
Three high domes above the central aisle precede and announce the *mihrab*. The ribbed arches forming the framework of the domes divide their vaulted space into smaller areas.

Arches of the Caliphate
Two types of arch were used in the construction of the mosque: the mainly decorative, multifoil arch (left) and the horseshoe arch (right). The latter, a legacy of Visigoth architecture, was widely used by the caliphate.

Ornate decoration
The decoration is particularly ornate on the *qibli* wall, around the *mihrab*. It comprises a mosaic of marble, sculpted with Koranic verses, and *pâte de verre*, imported from Byzantium and decorated with Byzantine motifs.

RECONSTRUCTION OF THE MINARET OF THE GREAT MOSQUE
▲ *109, 134*
The tower, known as La Giralda since the 18th century, was originally the minaret of the Great Mosque of Seville built by the Almohads (1184–98). The upper story, which has since been replaced, was once surmounted by a dome crowned with four golden balls. The brick tower is built on a freestone base (nearly 45 feet square).

"SEBKA"
The windows on the sides of the tower have a central mullion and decorative facing known as *sebka*, a brick motif whose arches and lobules interlace to form a network of lozenges characteristic of Almohad art.

MATERIALS
The Almohad dynasty (12th–13th centuries) used stone (above) for more detailed structures and, more generally, *pisé* (layers of dried clay, as seen on the detail above) which was less costly and easier to use.

RAMPARTS ▲ *166*. Seville's enclosure wall (6½ feet thick) was built of *pisé* in the 12th century by the Muslims. It includes a barbican (**1**), a rampart walk (**2**) and towers, such as the two-story, hexagonal Torre Blanca (**3**), decorated with bands of brick and surmounted by prism-shaped merlons (**4**).

Puerta de Córdoba
The Puerta de Córdoba is set in a projecting tower on the enclosure wall. It has freestone foundations but is mainly built of *pisé*. Above the gate is a brick relieving arch.

Decoration
The only decorative element in this military structure is a horseshoe arcature surmounted by ceramics. The Torre del Oro is thought to have been named after the gold reflections of its original covering of glazed faience tiles.

Restoration of the Torre del Oro
▲ *184*
The Torre del Oro was built in c. 1220 by the Almohads as an angle tower on the city's enclosure wall. It must have been the counterpart of a similar structure on the opposite bank of the river and there was probably a chain stretching between the two bastions to control access to the port. The tower is a twelve-sided polygon built on freestone foundations. The main body (three stories) and the upper section of the tower are of *pisé*.

Ceramic detail.

Central rosette of the façade of the Iglesia de Omnium Sanctorum ▲ *173*.

The Islamic artistic tradition flourished in western Andalusia from the 13th to the 15th century, at the same time as the Gothic and Renaissance styles. This gave rise to a unique art form of Mudéjar, which derived its name from the Muslims who remained in Andalusia and worked for Christians (*mudayyan* means "vassal"). Mudéjar architecture in Seville used local materials (brick, plaster, ceramics and wood) and combined Almohad and Granadan influences with Gothic and Renaissance features.

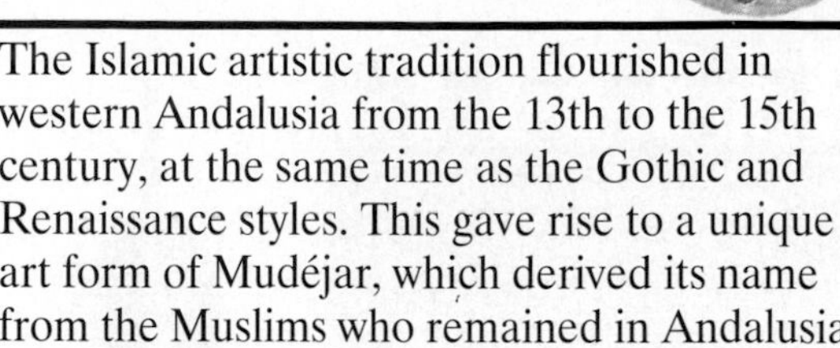

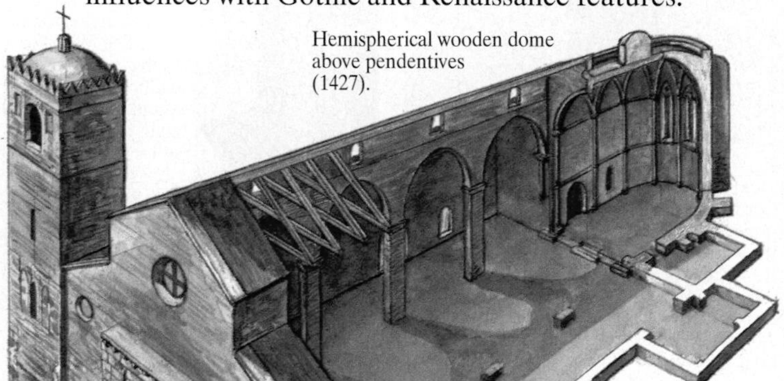

Hemispherical wooden dome above pendentives (1427).

IGLESIA DE SANTA MARINA ▲ *167*
(14TH CENTURY)
The church's three naves, rampant pointed door arch, oculus and polygonal apse with its Gothic, freestone vault and intersecting ribs are reminiscent of the Mudéjar style combined with Islamic art, which favors brick, slender pillars, wooden roof structures, and cubic chapels built against minaret-style towers.

WINDOWS AND FLOORS
Lobate window inscribed in a blind arch decorated with *azulejos* (Iglesia de Omnium Sanctorum). Brick floor with polychrome *azulejos* (2½ inches square). Mudéjar uses bricks or flags, tiles, or a combination of the two.

Floral and interlaced motifs
A 15th-century panel decorated with the most commonly found Mudéjar decorative motifs.

Polychrome plaster reliefs
The balls, stylized plant motifs, interlacing (rows of stalactites) and Kufic inscriptions (**3**) are in the Islamic artistic tradition. These various elements are combined with scenes depicting typically Gothic figures (**1** and **2**). (Alcázar, Seville ▲ *142*, 14th century)

Interior decoration
Mudéjar art excelled in the field of interior decoration. For example, the Salón de Embajadores has plinths covered with *azulejos*, plaster decorations with plant motifs, small blind arches, plaster interlacing, wrought-iron balconies and 16th-century paintings.

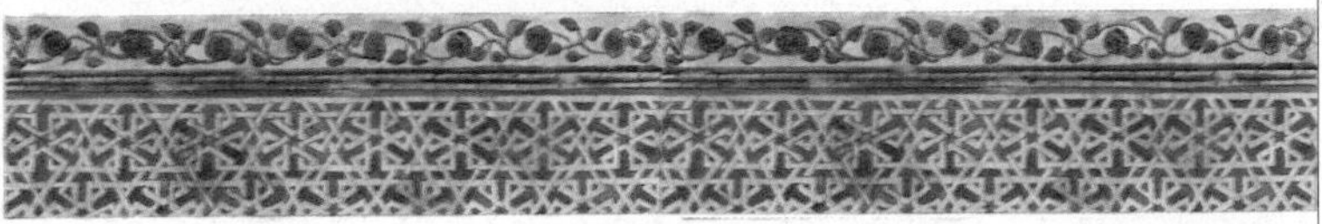

Salón de Embajadores ▲ *146.* The decoration of the Salón de Embajadores (Salon of the Ambassadors) is Mudéjar art at its very best. It forms part of the palace of King Don Pedro, built by Pedro I in the Alcázar from 1364 onward. The square *salón* is surmounted by a wooden dome and flanked by alcoves with double geminate windows.

The Plateresque (or Charles V) style originated in Lombardy and was introduced into Spain via the marble architectural elements imported by sea from Genoa during the 15th century, and the arrival of Italian, Florentine and Lombard artists during the 16th century. This decorative style, consisting of arabesques, garlands and scrolls, gradually replaced Gothic and Moorish elements. Later, the incorporation of these Italianate motifs into the architectural structure produced the Renaissance style.

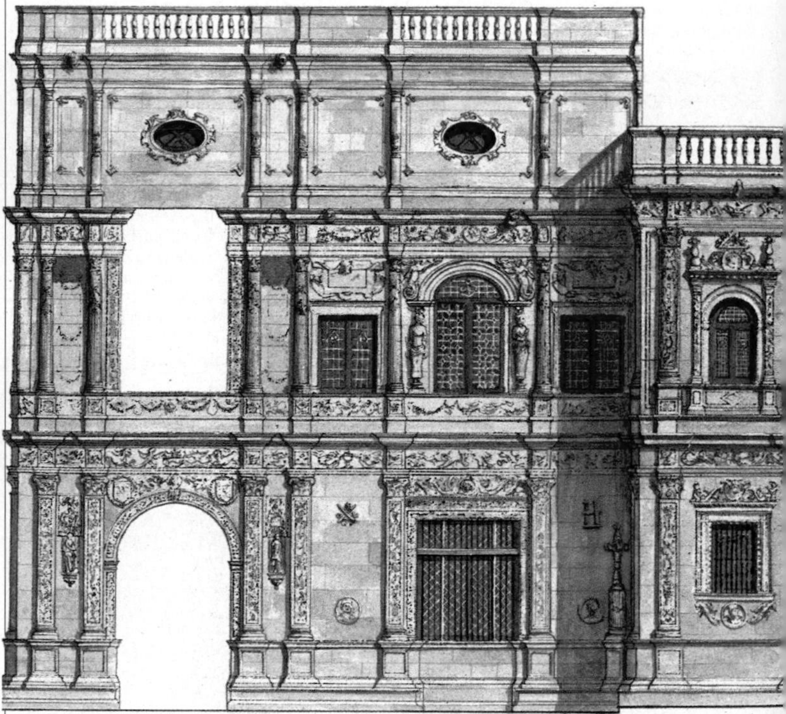

AYUNTAMIENTO ▲ *132*
The façade of the town hall is a masterpiece of Renaissance architecture and a fine illustration of Plateresque building. The finely carved stonework of this style influenced all types of art, including silver work, from which it took its name (*platero* means "silversmith"). This Renaissance section (1526–70) was designed by Diego de Riaño and built in stone in traditional Lombard style.

HOSPITAL DE LAS CINCO LLAGAS ▲ *166*
Martín de Gaínza began the construction of the hospital in 1545. Its two intersecting naves, based on an almost square layout (186 yards square), echo the structure of the Great Hospital of Milan by Filarete. The main façade and entrance (1617), by Asensio de Maeda.

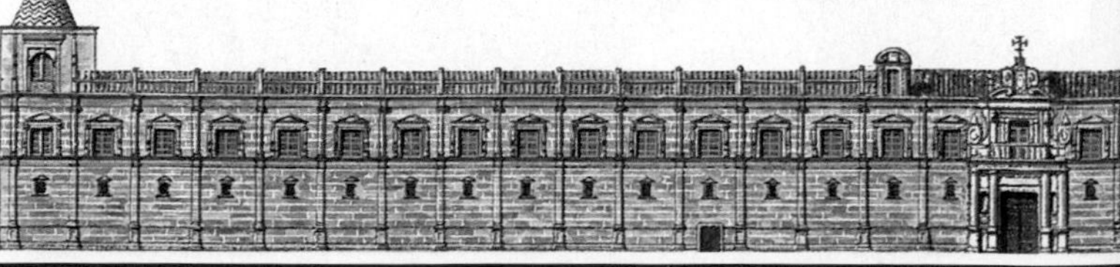

Pavilion of Charles V (Alcázar ▲ *142*)
The Cenador de la Alcoba is a Renaissance adaptation (1543–6) by Juan Fernandez, of an Islamic oratory. The porticoed galleries of this square pavilion have semicircular arches supported by columns, while its hemispherical dome has a coffered ceiling and is decorated with Triana ceramics from the Polido ● *56* factory. The *azulejos* used in the *cenador* are decorated with geometric Moorish motifs.

"Azulejo" from the Gothic palace of the Alcazar
The Renaissance-style *azulejo*, decorated with classical motifs, was introduced to Seville by Italian artists in the early 1500's. (Niculoso Pisano, 1503.)

The town hall seen from the Plaza de San Francisco ▲ *132*, showing the Renaissance section (left), and the neo-Renaissance section built in the 19th century (right).

La Giralda ● *68* ▲ *134.* The Renaissance bell tower (1558–68) was added to the Almohad minaret. Its four stories of stone, brick and ceramics culminate in a 25-foot, bronze weather vane: *la giralda* or *giraldilla*. Architect Hernán Ruiz the Younger (1508–69) ▲ *166*, son of Hernán Ruiz the Elder and father of Hernán Ruiz III, left two major works: the cathedral Chapterhouse (Sala Capitular) and the church of the Hospital de las Cinco Llagas.

1. Present entrance
2. Monastery parvis
3. Visiting rooms
4. Main courtyard
5. Former dormitories
6. Abbatial hall
7. Passage of San Cristóbal
8. Chapterhouse
9. Mudéjar cloister
10. Main cloister
11. Choir
12. Church
13. Church parvis and porch
14. Sacristy
15. Former garden
16. Kitchen
17. Refectory
18. Cells

The monastic system was established in Seville in the 13th century as a result of the Christian conquest. A succession of religious foundations then converted it into a convent-city and, by the 17th century, there were some one hundred convents. Today, Seville has one of the highest concentrations of convents in Spain with seventeen monastic establishments representing a major part of its architectural and artistic heritage.
The organization of these convents is based on a distorted Benedictine system, but makes a distinction between the areas open to the public (parvis and church) and the enclosed areas around the cloisters.

San Clemente ▲ *176*

The present layout of the monastery (which covers an area of 9,568 square yards) was designed in the 15th and completed in the 16th and 17th centuries. Although it is based on the Benedictine system, certain aspects have been adapted to suit the urban environment: for example, the church (**12**) lies on a north–south axis.

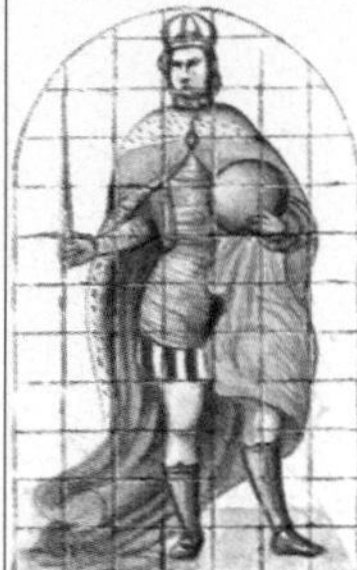

San Fernando and San Clemente
San Fernando (above) is usually associated with the foundation of the Monastery of San Clemente, inhabited by Cistercian nuns, in the 13th century.

Seville was conquered on the festival of San Clemente (below), who became its patron saint. In the 18th century, these two *azulejos* were placed on the 17th-century doors of the church parvis (**13**).

Patio de la Abadesa. The Patio de la Abadesa (Court of the Abbess or main courtyard, **4**), comprises the monastery's oldest section of outbuildings. The infirmary, work and study rooms, the abbess's apartment and the former dormitories (two L-shaped naves supported by cylindrical wood columns which were coated during the 16th century to protect them against the climate, **5**) open onto Genoese Renaissance colonnaded galleries.

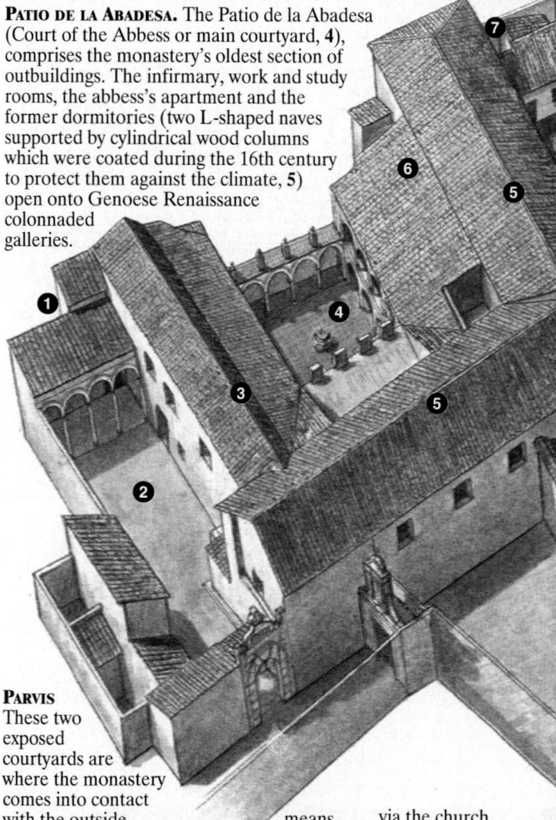

Parvis
These two exposed courtyards are where the monastery comes into contact with the outside world. The parvis of Santa Clara (**2**), overlooked by the visiting rooms (**3**), was the traditional means of access to the monastery and services. Those coming to worship in the church entered via the church parvis (**13**), built in the 17th century, and the porch with its two Mannerist-style doors.

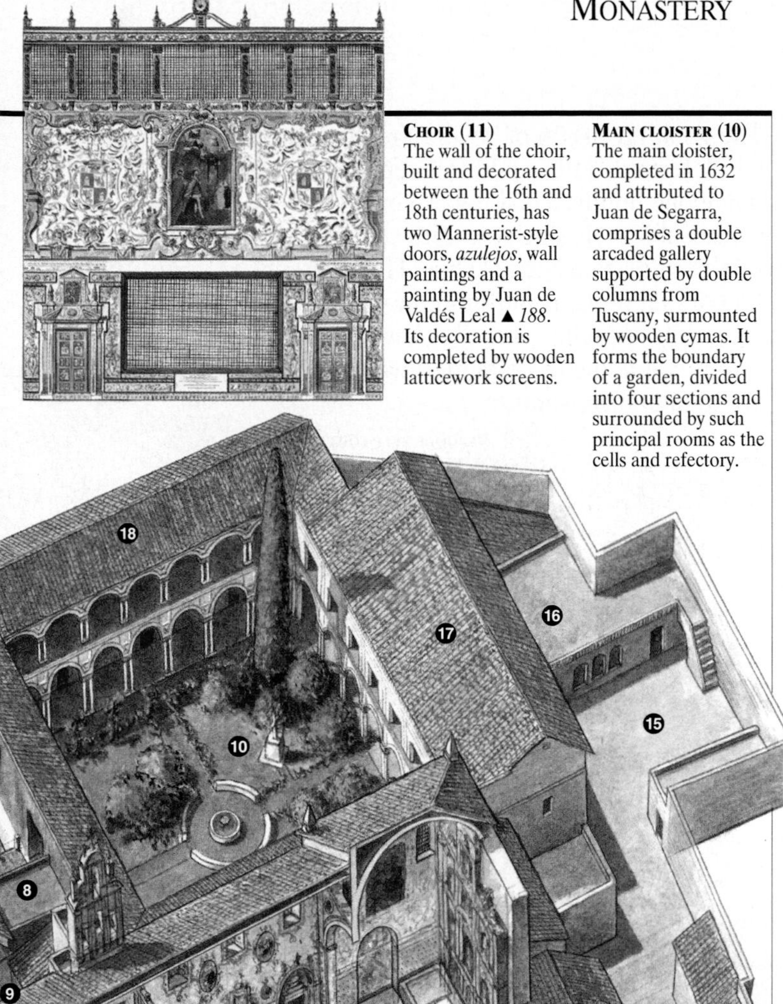

CHOIR (11)
The wall of the choir, built and decorated between the 16th and 18th centuries, has two Mannerist-style doors, *azulejos*, wall paintings and a painting by Juan de Valdés Leal ▲ *188*. Its decoration is completed by wooden latticework screens.

MAIN CLOISTER (10)
The main cloister, completed in 1632 and attributed to Juan de Segarra, comprises a double arcaded gallery supported by double columns from Tuscany, surmounted by wooden cymas. It forms the boundary of a garden, divided into four sections and surrounded by such principal rooms as the cells and refectory.

CHURCH WITH WALL-BELFRY (12)
(1588)
The church's single nave, spanned by a Mudéjar coffered ceiling, is extended to the south by a chapel surmounted by a hemispherical, coffered vault and, to the north, by a choir with a gallery for the nuns.

The great profusion of Seville's religious buildings has determined the city's architectural profile. Some one hundred bell towers, built in every conceivable style since the 13th century, are silhouetted against the skyline. However, La Giralda remains the supreme example. Generally speaking, churches have bell towers, while the more modest wall belfries are found on convents.

BAROQUE BELL TOWER
The body of the tower is pierced by semicircular arches and surmounted by a cornice and spire. Piers and arches are built in mortar and brick, and are rough-rendered, painted, embossed or decorated with ceramics (*azulejos* are plain-colored or decorated with motifs). The towers are covered with glazed roof and ridge tiles.

MUDÉJAR BELL TOWER
The 14th-century Mudéjar church of Santa Catalina ▲ *170* has a brick bell tower. The horseshoe arch of the window is in the Moorish tradition and is emphasized by an *alfiz*, a frame rising from the imposts.

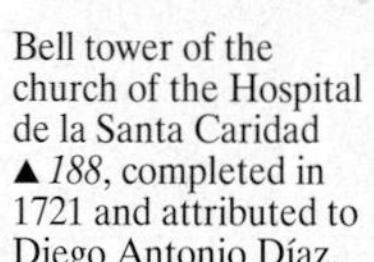

Bell tower of the church of the Hospital de la Santa Caridad ▲ *188*, completed in 1721 and attributed to Diego Antonio Díaz.

THE BELLS OF SEVILLE
The bells of La Giralda ring out every morning at 9.30am. They are fitted with a balance-weight placed counter to the central axis or shaft on which they are mounted. The shaft rests on two roller bearings and is activated by ropes. On other bell towers the ropes are mounted on pulleys, or the wrought-iron tongue is pierced with a hole through which a rope is passed and pulled from the ground below. Some bell towers are protected by characteristic small iron balconies.

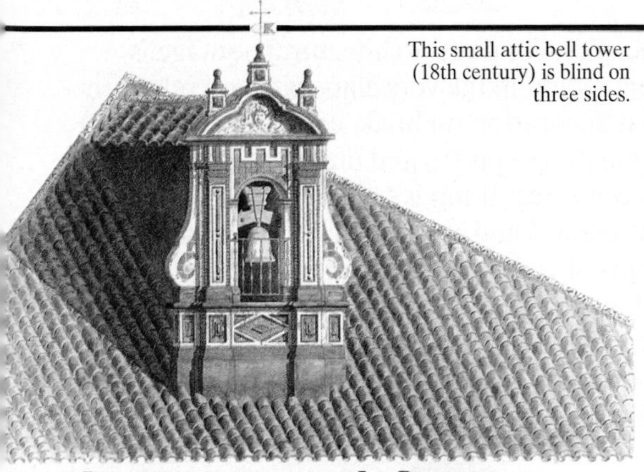

This small attic bell tower (18th century) is blind on three sides.

BELL TOWER OF THE CHAPEL OF LOS PANADEROS
The open side is decorated with a semicircular arch resting on a base, flanked by pilasters and surmounted by a frieze, cornice and pediment. The roof is decorated with three inset dies and the tympanum with an enameled, ceramic cherub.

“ESPADAÑA”
Espadaña is the Castilian term for a wall belfry or open bell tower. It comes from the word *espada* meaning “sword”.

“ESPADAÑA” DE SANTA PAULA ▲ *168*
The *espadaña*, built between 1600 and 1640, was renovated in 1751 and 1950. It comprises four compartments, three with depressed arches and one with a semicircular arch. The openings are flanked by pilasters edged with scrolls. The entablature and cornice of the lower section support a straight pediment surmounted by two pyramidal pinnacles. The curved pediment of the upper section is decorated with a weather vane and two bulbous pinnacles.

Santa Paula occupies the tympanum of the upper pediment.

“AZULEJOS”
● *56*, ▲ *128*
The base, pilasters and consoles of the *espadaña* of the Iglesia de Santa Paula are decorated with ceramics painted in cobalt blue, black and orange.

Coat of arms of the Order of San Jerónimo.

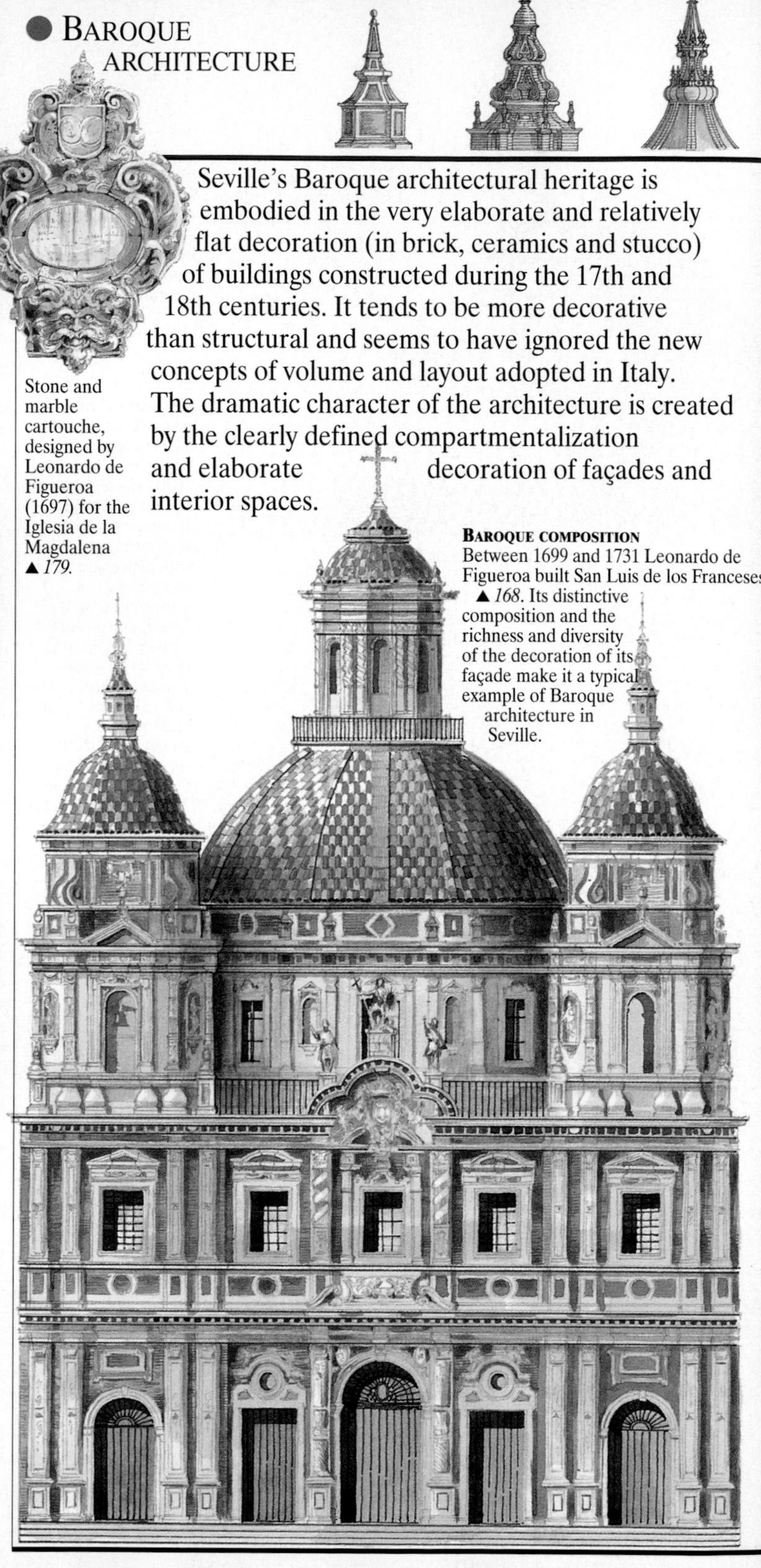

Seville's Baroque architectural heritage is embodied in the very elaborate and relatively flat decoration (in brick, ceramics and stucco) of buildings constructed during the 17th and 18th centuries. It tends to be more decorative than structural and seems to have ignored the new concepts of volume and layout adopted in Italy. The dramatic character of the architecture is created by the clearly defined compartmentalization and elaborate decoration of façades and interior spaces.

Stone and marble cartouche, designed by Leonardo de Figueroa (1697) for the Iglesia de la Magdalena ▲ *179*.

BAROQUE COMPOSITION
Between 1699 and 1731 Leonardo de Figueroa built San Luis de los Franceses ▲ *168*. Its distinctive composition and the richness and diversity of the decoration of its façade make it a typical example of Baroque architecture in Seville.

Spires
Spires and pinnacles (17th and 18th centuries).

Stucco
The dome of the Iglesia Santa María la Blanca ▲ *157* is a fine example of the densely ornate motifs in high relief used in its decoration.

Other characteristic (but less ornate) examples of stuccoed *intaglio* motifs.

Eclecticism. The spire, designed by Leonardo de Figueroa to surmount the dome and light the transept of the church of the former Convent of San Pablo, is made of brick and polychrome ceramics. It is crowned with wrought iron and decorated with Indian figures, a reminder of Spain's links with the New World ● *36*.

Formal variety
The terracotta entrance of the church (1690–1713) of the Convento de los Terceros ▲ *169*. Its composition is an example of the formal variety that can be achieved with pilasters and Baroque capitals.

Centralized plan
(San Luis)
Preceded by a portico, the church is organized around the central dome.

Proportions and outline
The façade of San Luis is built of contrasting stone and red brick. The two distinct bodies of five bays are separated by an entablature on which two Solomonic (twisted) columns support a curvilinear pediment. The roofs of the central dome, its lantern and flanking towers are covered with glazed tiles.

The Casa de Pilatos ("Pilate's House"), the most luxurious nobiliary residence in Seville, is a fine example of the urban mansions built in western Andalusia from the 15th century onward. The main part of the mansion was constructed between 1519 and 1570. The lines of the inward-facing layout are broken by four large, open areas. The mansion perpetuates the Roman heritage of the interior courtyard, the *casa-patio*, center of domestic life, and also incorporates an Islamic influence in its proliferation of styles and irregularity of its layout.

Coat of arms on a panel of *azulejos* on the outside of the staircase.

CERAMICS, PLASTER, STONE AND MARBLE
The plinths and floors are decorated with

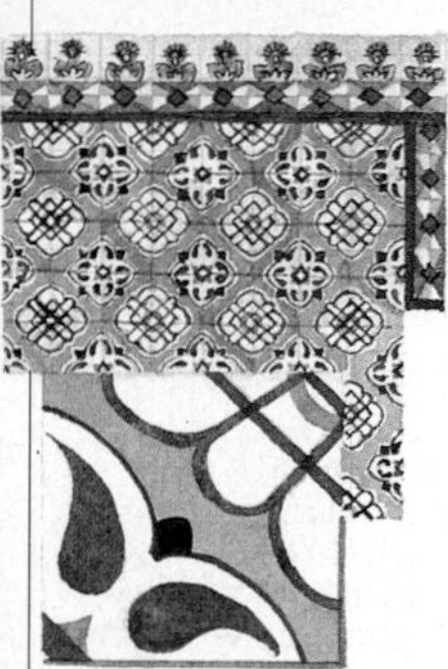

Mudéjar *azulejos* (above) and the arches with plaster. The balustrades are in Gothic-style carved stone and the Renaissance columns and capitals are in Genoese marble (below).

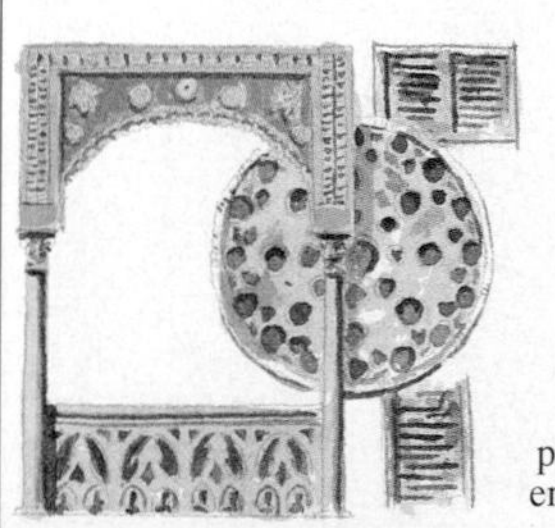

FAÇADE AND ENTRANCE HALL
The exterior of the Casa de Pilatos consists of a blank wall pierced by a classical entrance (1529). This leads into an open entrance hall which in turn gives access to the stables opposite.

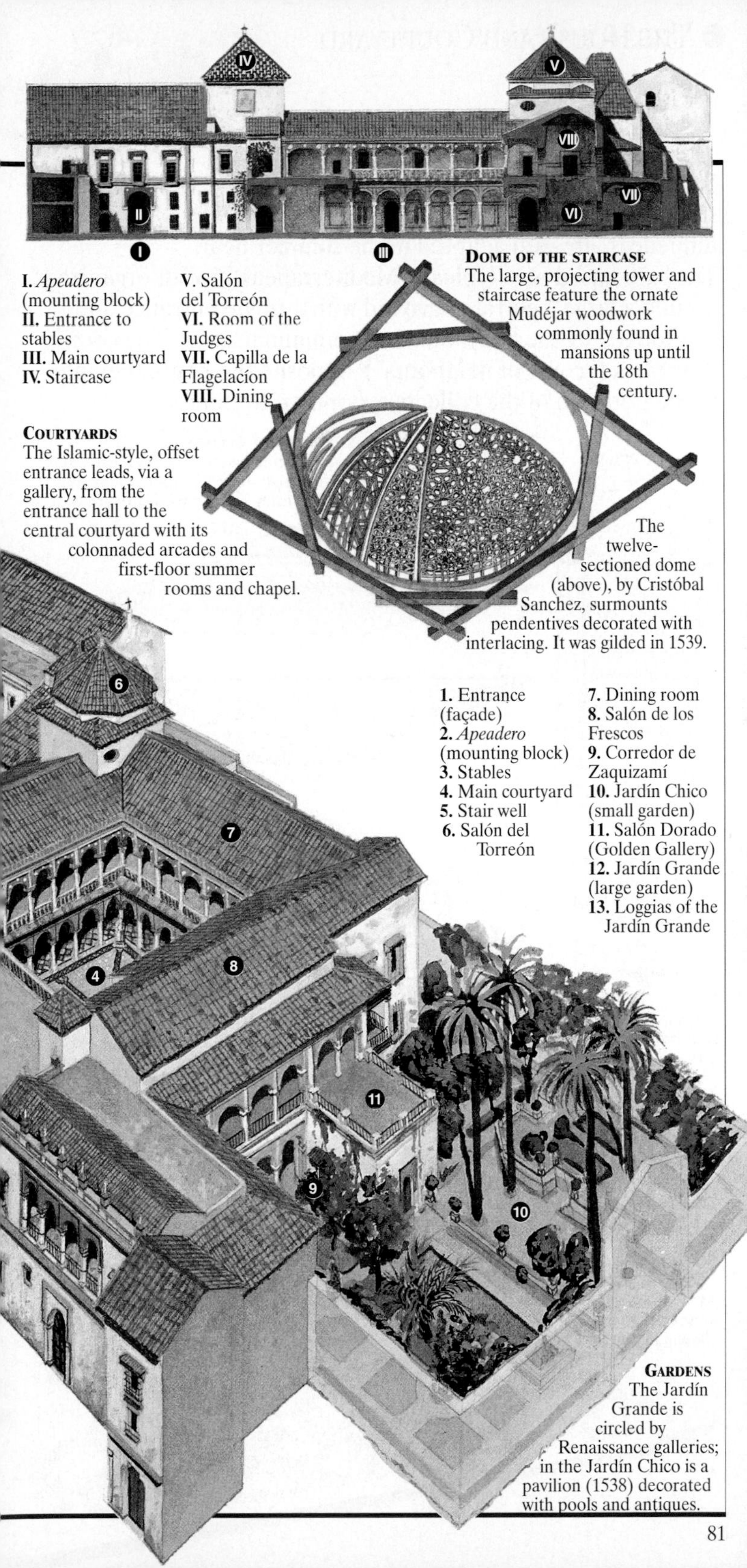

I. *Apeadero* (mounting block)
II. Entrance to stables
III. Main courtyard
IV. Staircase
V. Salón del Torreón
VI. Room of the Judges
VII. Capilla de la Flagelacíon
VIII. Dining room

DOME OF THE STAIRCASE
The large, projecting tower and staircase feature the ornate Mudéjar woodwork commonly found in mansions up until the 18th century.

COURTYARDS
The Islamic-style, offset entrance leads, via a gallery, from the entrance hall to the central courtyard with its colonnaded arcades and first-floor summer rooms and chapel.

The twelve-sectioned dome (above), by Cristóbal Sanchez, surmounts pendentives decorated with interlacing. It was gilded in 1539.

1. Entrance (façade)
2. *Apeadero* (mounting block)
3. Stables
4. Main courtyard
5. Stair well
6. Salón del Torreón
7. Dining room
8. Salón de los Frescos
9. Corredor de Zaquizamí
10. Jardín Chico (small garden)
11. Salón Dorado (Golden Gallery)
12. Jardín Grande (large garden)
13. Loggias of the Jardín Grande

GARDENS
The Jardín Grande is circled by Renaissance galleries; in the Jardín Chico is a pavilion (1538) decorated with pools and antiques.

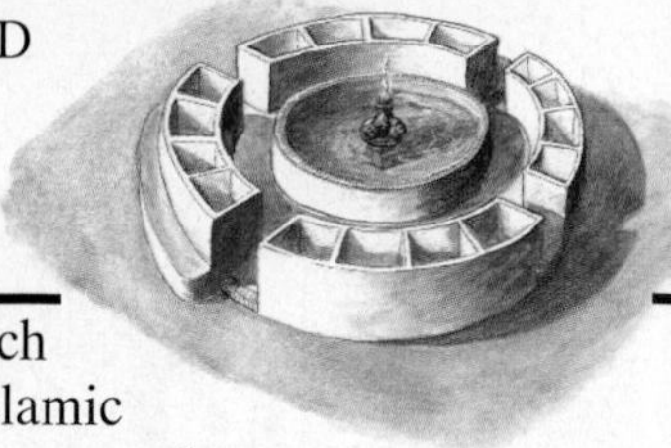

The *corral del conde*'s fountain-laundry.

Seville's traditional *casas-patio*, which still bear the mark of Roman and Islamic influences, are well adapted to the summer heat. They are based on a typically Mediterranean layout, organized around a large, central courtyard with a single entrance and overlooked by the bedrooms and communal areas. The *corral de vecinos* ("court of neighbors"), opposite the house, belongs to the tradition of the collective, popular dwelling.

GLASS ROOFS AND AWNINGS

Some courtyards are protected from bad weather by a glass roof (*montera*) installed above wire mesh. In summer an awning (*vela*), made of canvas or netting, is erected to keep the courtyard cool.

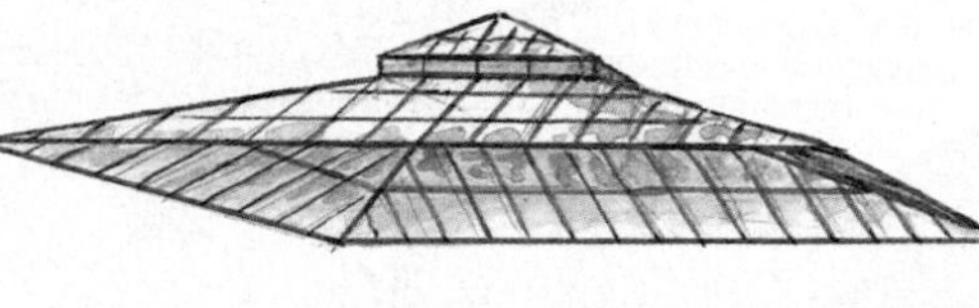

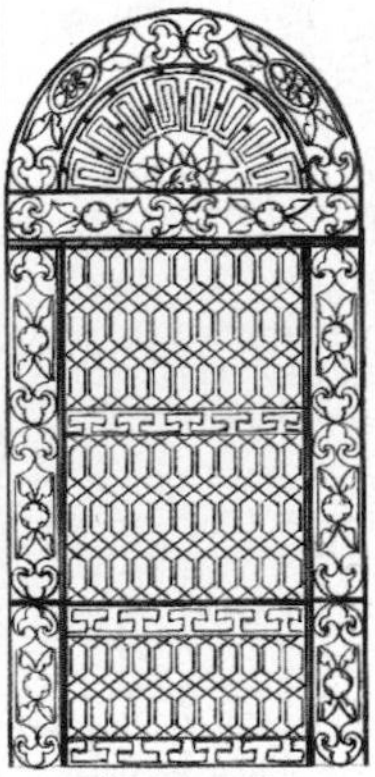

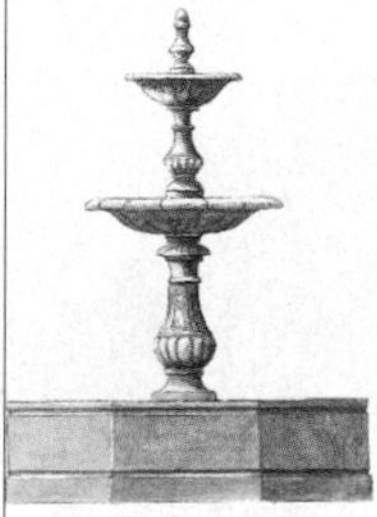

"CANCELA"

The *cancela* is a wrought-iron grille separating the entrance hall from the courtyard.

FOUNTAIN

The fountain occupies the same position, in the center of the courtyard, as the Roman cistern or Moorish *aljibe*. Many fountains are made of Italian marble.

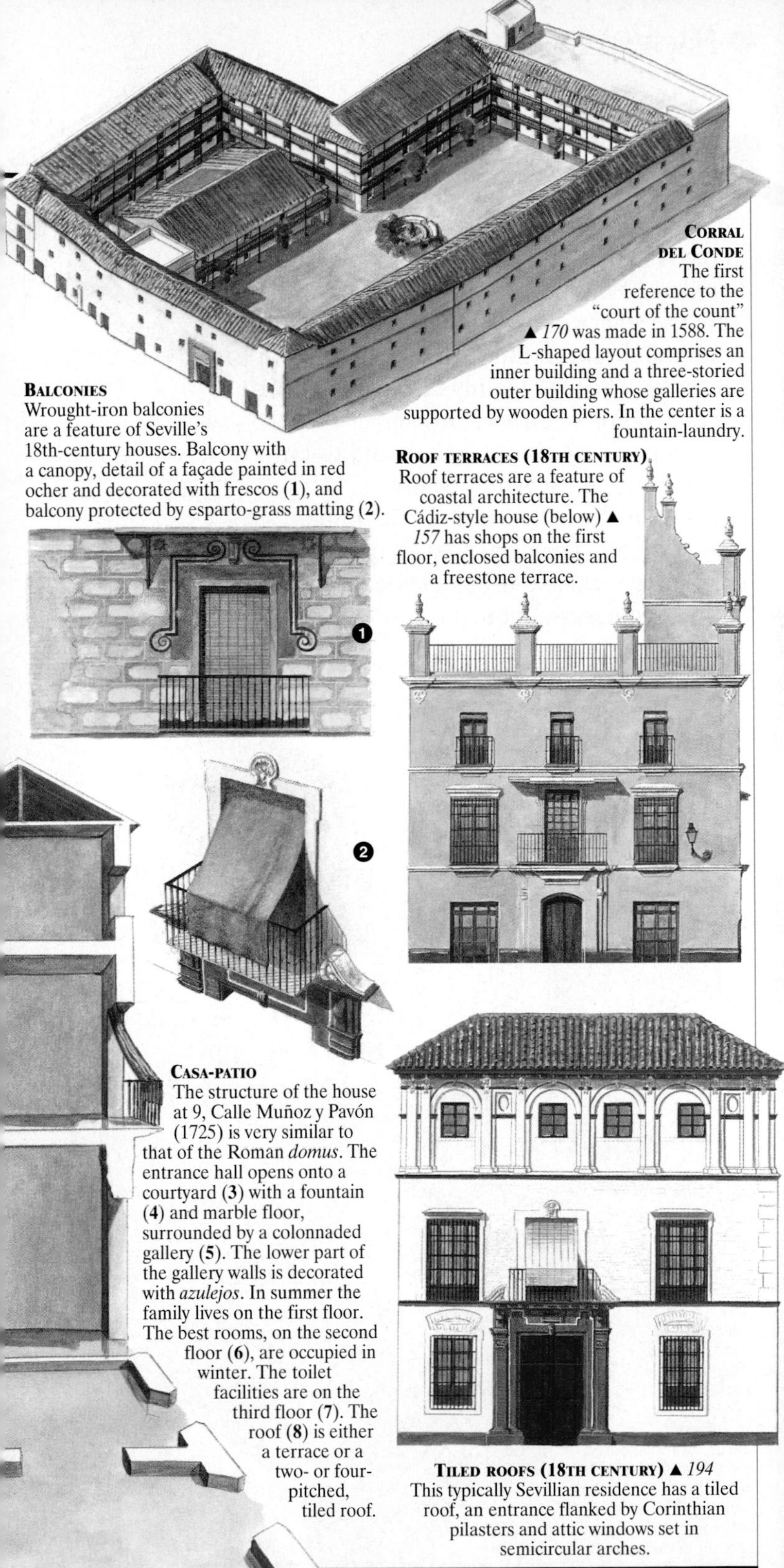

CORRAL DEL CONDE The first reference to the "court of the count" ▲ *170* was made in 1588. The L-shaped layout comprises an inner building and a three-storied outer building whose galleries are supported by wooden piers. In the center is a fountain-laundry.

BALCONIES
Wrought-iron balconies are a feature of Seville's 18th-century houses. Balcony with a canopy, detail of a façade painted in red ocher and decorated with frescos (**1**), and balcony protected by esparto-grass matting (**2**).

ROOF TERRACES (18TH CENTURY)
Roof terraces are a feature of coastal architecture. The Cádiz-style house (below) ▲ *157* has shops on the first floor, enclosed balconies and a freestone terrace.

CASA-PATIO
The structure of the house at 9, Calle Muñoz y Pavón (1725) is very similar to that of the Roman *domus*. The entrance hall opens onto a courtyard (**3**) with a fountain (**4**) and marble floor, surrounded by a colonnaded gallery (**5**). The lower part of the gallery walls is decorated with *azulejos*. In summer the family lives on the first floor. The best rooms, on the second floor (**6**), are occupied in winter. The toilet facilities are on the third floor (**7**). The roof (**8**) is either a terrace or a two- or four-pitched, tiled roof.

TILED ROOFS (18TH CENTURY) ▲ *194*
This typically Sevillian residence has a tiled roof, an entrance flanked by Corinthian pilasters and attic windows set in semicircular arches.

The hacienda is the most impressive building in the Andalusian countryside. Large numbers of these vast farms, which were the legacy of the Roman villa, were built between the 17th and the 19th centuries. They are mainly devoted to the cultivation of olives (often in conjunction with vines), cereals and stock-farming. The most widely found Andalusian farm, the rural *cortijo*, only grows cereals. The hacienda is a complex architectural structure combining rural and urban elements and marked by a strong popular tradition.

The gate of San Ignacio de Torrequemada (1708) at Gelves ▲ 2 has a plaster decoration.

Gates are sometimes decorated with *azulejos* ● *56* bearing the coat of arms of the owner of the property (left) or religious figures.

THE PRESSING YARD
The pressing yard (**5**) with its rows of earthenware jars used to collect olive oil. The tower houses the balance-weight of the press. In the adjoining patio, the oil is stored in jars set in the ground.

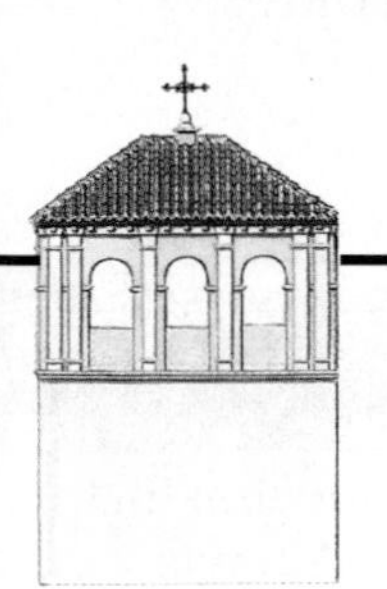
Mirador with semicircular openings and pilasters.

Mirador surmounted by a lobate roof culminating in a pinnacle.

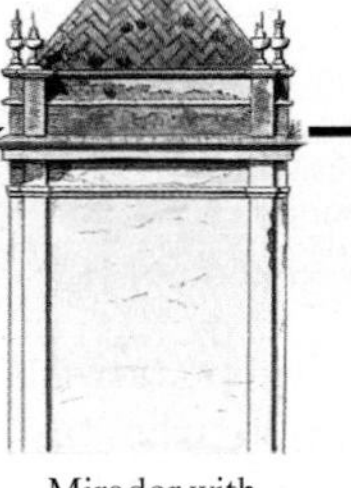
Mirador with a pyramidal, tiled roof.

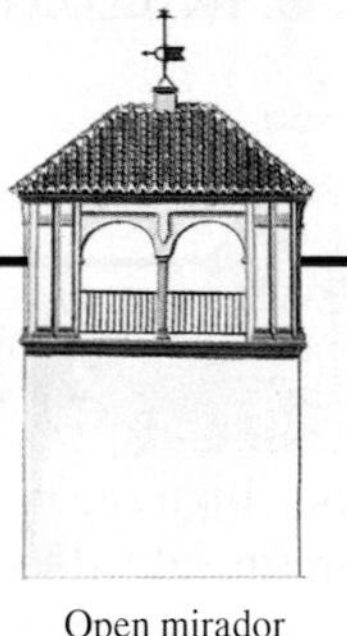
Open mirador with a central column.

Mirador tower for the press

Mirador towers are a characteristic feature of haciendas. They are built, using a technique widely employed from antiquity to the 19th century, to house the balance-weight of the lever presses. The solidly built, massive tower was surmounted by a mirador which made it possible to oversee the work being done on the farm and survey the surrounding area.

Mill press

The first stage in olive pressing: the olives are placed on the circular stone "tray" of the press and crushed by the mule-operated, granite millstone.

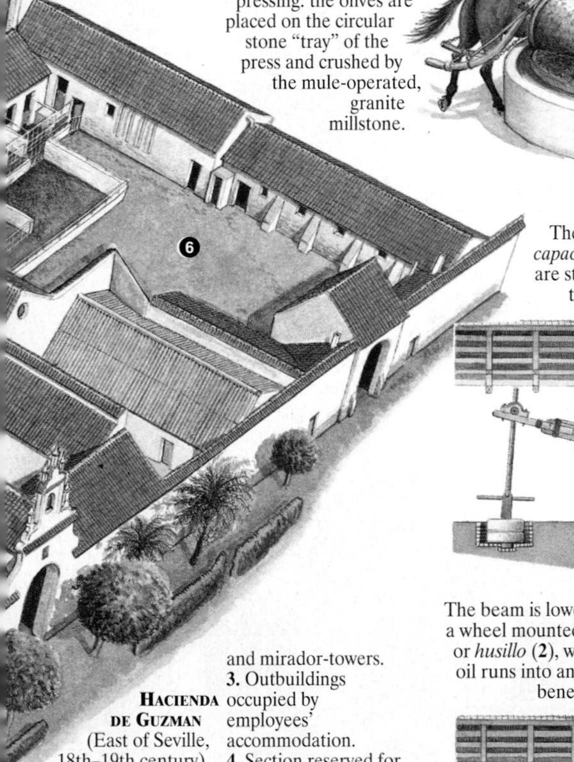

"Viga" press

The olive pulp is placed on *capachos,* circular trays, which are stacked and pressed using the *viga* or beam (**1**).

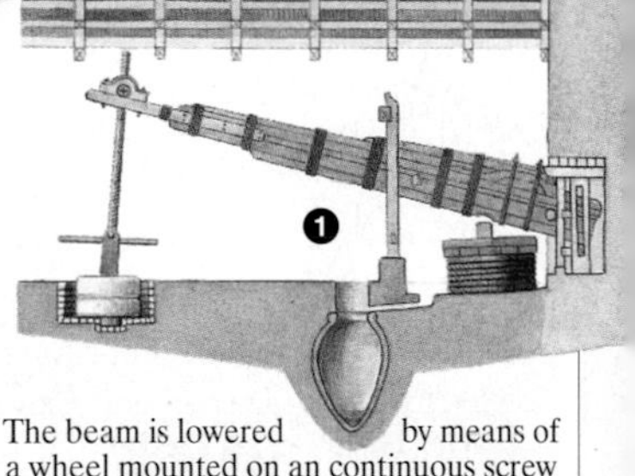

The beam is lowered by means of a wheel mounted on an continuous screw or *husillo* (**2**), weighted at one end. The oil runs into an earthenware jar placed beneath the press.

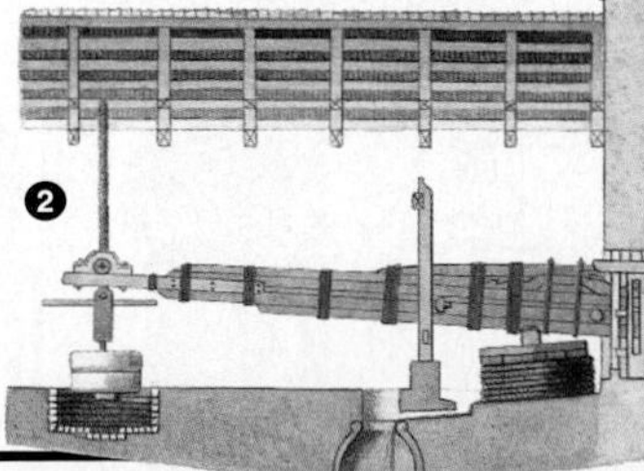

Hacienda de Guzman

(East of Seville, 18th–19th century)

Each section has its own courtyard.
1. Master courtyard-garden.
2. The owners live in the elegant, two-story wing with its colonnaded galleries and mirador-towers.
3. Outbuildings occupied by employees' accommodation.
4. Section reserved for oil production, with its mill, presses (**5**) and storehouses.
6. The *patio de labor* (work yard) includes the stables and cattle sheds and has its own separate entrance.

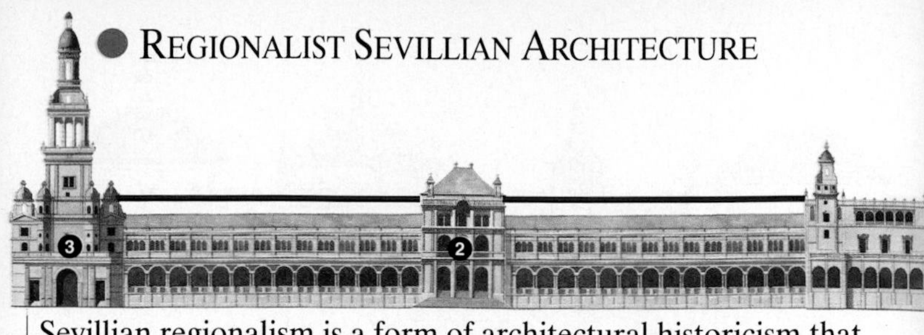

Sevillian regionalism is a form of architectural historicism that, in the late 19th and early 20th century, incorporated motifs from past styles into modern buildings. It favored the forms and decorative elements most typical of Andalusia. For example, the highly prized neo-Mudéjar style is an inspired recreation of medieval Islamic-Andalusian architecture. The modern age was also marked, to a lesser extent, by the development of the neo-Renaissance and neo-Baroque styles. Regionalist esthetics were applied to both public buildings and private residences.

PABELLÓN MUDÉJAR
The pavilion was built between 1911 and 1914 on the Plaza de América for the 1929 Exhibition ▲ *203*. The architect, Aníbal González, drew his inspiration for the façade from the Alcázar. The central body of the building (below) and the wings are faced with brick and decorated with ceramics.

COSTURERO DE LA REINA ▲ *202*
The "Queen's Arbor", built in 1890 by Juan Talavera de la Vega for the gardens of the Palacio de San Telmo ▲ *187*, was one of the first neo-Mudéjar structures.

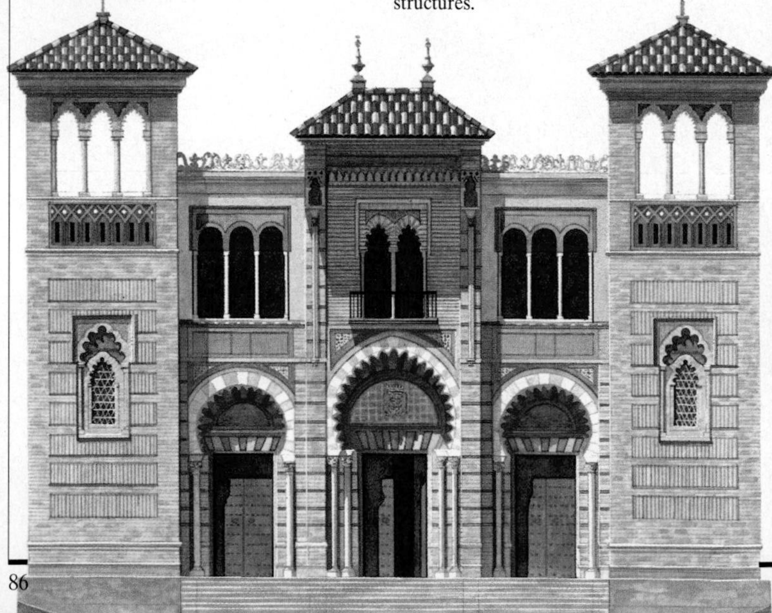

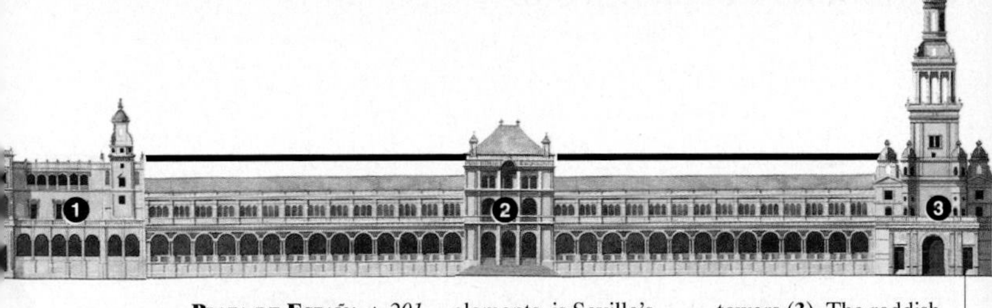

Plaza de España ▲ *201*
The main square of the 1929 Exhibition was built between 1914 and 1928. Its vast edifice, inspired by 16th-century classicist and Plateresque styles but also incorporating certain local 17th-century Baroque elements, is Seville's finest example of neo-Renaissance building. It forms a semicircle of 558 x 320 feet with a central pavilion (the Capitanía General, **1**) and two intermediary pavilions (**2**) midway along each arc. At either end of the structure are two bell towers (**3**). The reddish brick façade is emphasized by balustrades and decorated with ceramics. The semicircular arches of the raised gallery are supported by marble columns.

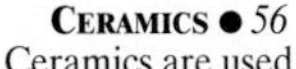

Ceramics ● *56*
Ceramics are used to decorate the base of walls, balustrades, roofs and all kinds of decorative elements, for example, this pinnacle in Triana ceramics (Plaza de España).

Decorative arts
Traditional decorative arts such as ceramics were an important part of regionalist architecture. Brick *en limpio* (carved and worked in relief) was also widely used in the decoration of façades.

Casino de la Exposición ▲ *202*
The neo-Baroque *casino* was built between 1925 and 1928 for the 1929 Exhibition. The vast central circular room is spanned by a dome covered with *azulejos* that is in turn surmounted by a lantern. Its façade is decorated with plaster pilasters, moldings and *intrados*.

The bell tower on Plaza de España, reminiscent of La Giralda, stands at over 260 feet and is six stories high.

Hispanic-American Exhibition (1929)
A number of symbolically regionalist edifices were built for this international event, preparations for which lasted from 1909 until 1929.

Estación de plaza de Armas (Córdoba) ▲ *191*
The façade of Córdoba station, completed in 1901, combines the brick and ceramics of neo-Mudéjar with the glass and iron of industrial architecture, a combination frequently used for stations.

The creation of the Sevillian School of Architecture (1960) and the city's election as capital of the *comunidad autónoma* of Andalusia (1982) and venue for Expo '92 had a beneficial effect on architecture and urban development. Recent projects to develop Seville's infrastructure have included the construction of new buildings (airport, Santa Justa station, La Maestranza theater) and the rehabilitation of part of its historic district. The Isla de la Cartuja, center of Expo '92, offers a selection of contemporary architectural styles.

PUENTE DEL ALAMILLO ▲ *198*

This impressive viaduct, designed by Santiago Calatrava, links the old town with the Isla de la Cartuja. It is supported at one end by a 453-foot pylon inclined at an angle of 58° and attached by thirteen pairs of cables.

SANTIAGO CALATRAVA

The work of the engineer and architect Santiago Calatrava evokes the articulated, organic forms of animal and vegetable fossils.

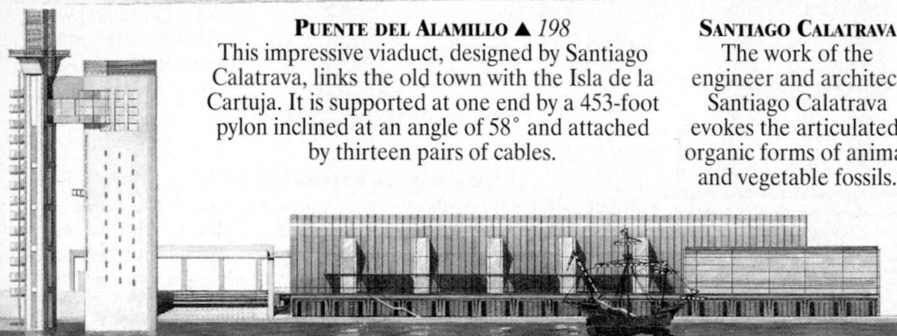

PABELLÓN DE LA NAVEGACIÓN

The main façade of this project by Guillermo Vazquez Consuegra overlooks the Guadalquivir. It is extended by a curved metal roof and five huge stained-glass windows, while a mirador-tower juts out above the river. Inside, huge curved wooden beams span a width of 131 feet. The metal roof, wooden beams and convex lines are reminiscent of naval architecture and the vast spaces of old dockside warehouses.

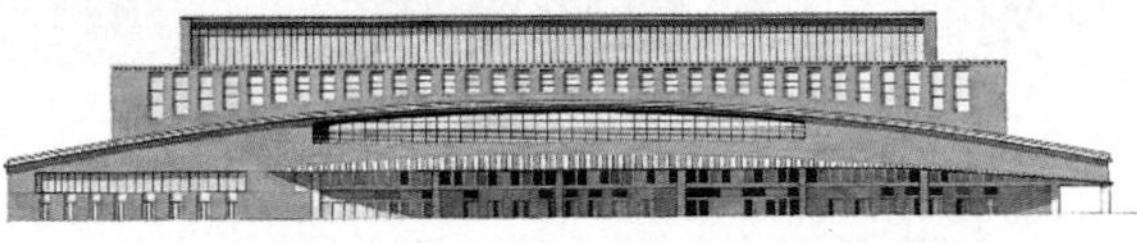

ESTACIÓN DE SANTA JUSTA

The lines of the station, designed by Antonio Cruz and Antonio Ortiz, are a metaphor for movement. The architects have made extensive use of brick, with a curved concrete canopy marking the main entrance. The platforms are surmounted by a vaulted metal structure which is oval in cross-section. The building received the leading national architectural award for its restrained use of materials, its transparent and well-organized interior, its masterly proportions and levels of light. Façade (above) and cross-section of main hall (below).

Seville as seen by painters

“Strength, clarity, excellent groupings, a desire for realism and the greatest power of imagination.”

Francisco Pacheco, on *Velázquez*

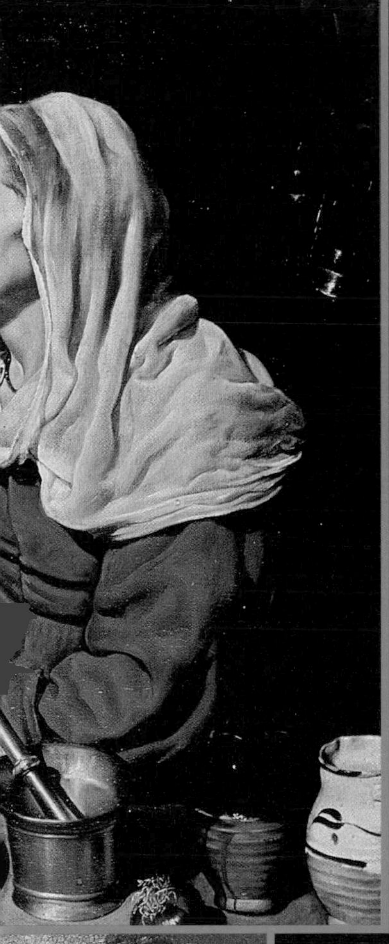

Diego Velázquez (1599–1660) (**5**) was born in Seville and studied under Francisco Pacheco, the master of the Sevillian school who later became his father-in-law. He soon made a name for himself and, in 1617, established his own school as a master in his own right. In 1623 he left for Madrid and became the official artist at the court of Philip IV, his great protector. His Sevillian period is characterized by two main themes: the religious subjects that formed the greater part of the commissioned work of 17th-century artists, and scenes from the life of the lower classes, such as the *Old Woman Frying Eggs* (**1**) and *Water-seller in Seville* (**2**).

Bartolomé Estebán Murillo (1617–82) (**6**) was born and died in Seville. He lived the impecunious and devout existence befitting a renowned local master and was overburdened with commissions, especially after his marriage in 1645. He lent a more human touch to Baroque art by giving his saints expressions observed among poorer people, worn down by their harsh living conditions. Part of his work was devoted to the street urchins who lived by begging and petty theft in a time of shortage (**4**).

La Alameda de Hércules (**3**) is attributed to Martínez del Mazo (1612–67), son-in-law of Velázquez and influenced by him. This widely emulated genre painting depicts one of the favorite walks of contemporary Sevillians.

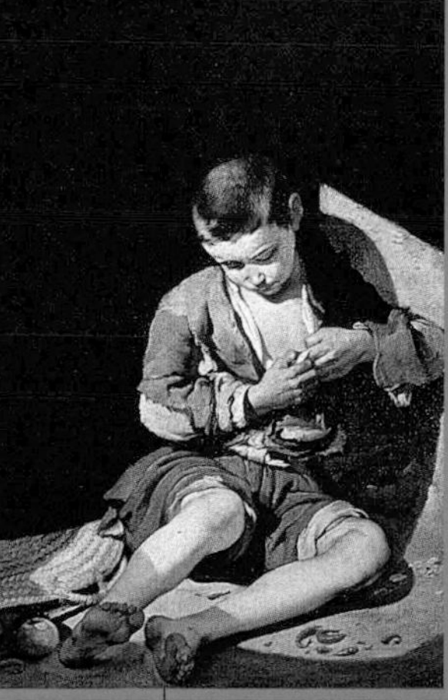

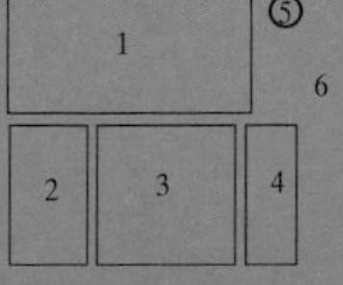

The Romantic period in Spanish painting, which benefitted from the contribution of, and was strongly influenced by, foreign artists, was one of the most productive for Sevillian art. During the reign of Isabella II (1833–68) the Church ceased to be the main source of commission for artists, who turned toward genre painting and landscapes.

Self-portrait (**4**), above, the work of the Sevillian artist Joaquín Domínguez Bécquer (1817–79), illustrates this trend. *El Patio de las Doncellas* (*Court of the Damsels*) (**1**) demonstrates his artistic precision and mastery of color. His compatriot Manuel Cabral Bejarano (1814–84) depicted such picturesque landscapes as the *Paseo de las Delicias* (**3**). He was visibly influenced by the English artist David Roberts (1796–1864) who was among his friends. Roberts produced some very interesting works in which he imposed his view of the city, notably *La Giralda seen from La Borceguinería* (**2**).

Gonzalo Bilbao (1860–1938) (**2**) was one of the Sevillian artists who marked the transition from Romanticism to a more open and subtle Realism. His characteristic use of brush strokes and portrayal of light were reminiscent of the Impressionists, whom he admired. *Las cigarreras cruzando el puente de Triana*, depicting women workers from the tobacco factories crossing the Triana bridge (**1**), is a treatment of one of the subjects for which he became famous. Other paintings representing local scenes and customs include his *Noche de verano en Sevilla* (**3**).

Like many of his contemporaries, the prolific artist José García Ramos (1852–1912) traveled widely in Europe. His technical virtuosity was renowned throughout Spain where his work was considered the finest expression of the Andalusian character. He was inspired by (sometimes anecdotal) scenes from everyday life which featured dandies, bullfighters, the guitarists who played in inns and taverns, gipsies, and dancers, as in the famous *Baile por bulerías* (**5**). José Arpa (1860–1952), a native of Carmona, was one of the first open-air artists whose landscapes (for example, *Seville seen from Triana*, **4**) reveal a very personal touch.

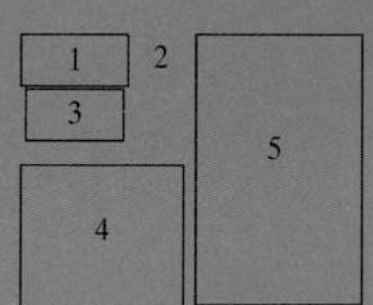

"This languid sensuality gave way to leaps and bounds worthy of a young jaguar, thus proving that these soft, silky bodies contain muscles of steel."

Théophile Gautier

El Vanity panameño en el desguace, showing the demolition of the Panamanian ship *Vanity*, is by Joaquín Saenz (b. Seville, 1931), one of the great modern Realists.

Seville
as seen by writers

LANDSCAPE

FERTILE SOIL

Between 1830 and 1834, Richard Ford (1796–1858) traveled through Spain, often on horseback. He acquired a knowledge of the country that was unrivaled in his day.

❝The soil of [this] province is most fertile, and the climate delicious; the land overflows with oil and wine. The vines of Xerez, the olives of Seville, and the fruits of Malaga, are unequalled. The yellow plains, girdled by the green sea, bask in the sunshine, like a topaz set around with emeralds. Strabo could find no better panegyric for the Elysian fields of Andalucia, than by quoting the charming description of the father of poetry: and here the classics following his example, placed the Gardens of the Blessed, and these afterwards became the real paradise, the new and favoured world of the Oriental. Here the children of Damascus rioted in a European Arabia Felix. On the fame of the conquest reaching the East, many tribes abandoned Syria to settle in Andalucia, just as the Spaniards afterwards emigrated to the golden S. America. The new comers kept chiefly apart, isolated in clans, each tribe hating each other; hence a seed of weakness was sown in the very cradle of the Moorish dominion. Thus the Yemenite Arabs of the stock of Kháttan lived in the plains, while the Syrians of the stock of Adhán lived in the cities, and thence were called "*Beladium*," to both of which the Berbers from the Atlas were opposed.

When these heterogeneous ingredients became more amalgamated, it was here, in a congenial soil, that the Oriental took the deepest root. Here he has left the noblest traces of power, taste, and intelligence – here he made his last desperate struggle. Six centuries after the chilly north had been abandoned to the Gotho-Spaniard, Granada still was held; and from this gradual recovery of Andalucia, the Oriental divisions into separate principalities are still retained, and it is still called *Los Cuatro Reinos*, the "Four Kingdoms," viz. Seville, Cordóva, Jaen, and Granada. . . .

However fertile the soil, and favourable the climate, no province in Spain, except Estremadura, has been turned to less account by the natives, who with strange apathy have allowed the two richest districts and those the best cultivated under the Roman and Moor, to relapse into weed and underwood; everywhere the luxuriance of wild vegetation shows what crops might be raised with even common cultivation. Hence from the recesses of the barrier Sierra Morena down to the plains which fringe the Straits of Gibraltar, there is a wide and unexplored field for the botanist and sportsman. Nothing is more striking than the brilliant

"They have hotter daies in *Spain* than we have here, but our daies are longer; and yet we are hotter in our business here, and they are longer about it."

John Donne

Flora of May and June: it is that of a hothouse growing wild; flowers of every colour, like perfumed cups of rubies, amethysts, and topazes filled with sunshine, tempt the stranger at every step. They bloom and blush unnoticed by the native. The nomenclature of the commonest plants is chiefly taken from the Arabic, which sufficiently denotes whence the Spaniard derived his limited knowledge.❞

RICHARD FORD, *A HANDBOOK FOR TRAVELLERS IN SPAIN – VOL. I*,
PUB. CENTAUR PRESS, LONDON, 1966

TRAVELING BY RAIL

Matilda Betham Edwards (1836–1919) evokes the changing colors and atmosphere of Andalusia as seen from a train.

❝There is a cant phrase about railways having done away with the poetry of travelling. Was ever such an absurdity uttered and believed in? I think if ever the poetry of travel was realised, it is now, especially at night and in Spain. You are whirled from region to region apparently by elemental fire alone. You pass through new, sweet, starry atmospheres, like a bird; you go to sleep, and never know under what strange or happy auspices you will awake. This beautiful moonlight landscape of tiny homesteads lying on the banks of a silvery river, of green meadows skirting snow-tipped mountains, and long lines of fir-trees pricking against a blue-black sky, – is it real or a picture only? These dreary table-lands that seem to stretch into infinity, these sloping olive-grounds, these sharp sierras, these alternating scenes of loveliness, and grandeur, and desolation, seem more like the phantasmagoria of dreams than anything else.

And then the aspects of human life, though fleeting, are yet so full of charm. You see faces that tell their own story, and in a moment they have vanished. You are let into little domestic scenes touching, or comic, or painful, or passionate, as the case may be. You cannot stop five minutes at a village station, or linger five minutes in a village waiting-room, without being moved to smiles or tears.

For my part I have never taken a railway journey, however short, that has not had some incident worth remembering; but in Spain, which is a collection of kingdoms, each rich in different sorts of interest, one is troubled, like the silk-merchant at Toledo, with the *embarras de richesses.* You see a hundred landscapes in a day you would fain remember. You see a hundred faces and hear a hundred things, that seem too characteristic to forget. But, like the changing colours of the sunset, these impressions melt one into the other, and, unless seized at the moment, are utterly lost.❞

MATILDA BETHAM EDWARDS, *THROUGH SPAIN TO THE SAHARA*,
PUB. HURST AND BLACKETT, LONDON, 1868

SEVILLE IN SPRING

Most famous for his pioneering work in the field of sexology, Henry Havelock Ellis (1859–1939) published works on a number of other subjects. Here he writes lovingly of his favorite season in southern Spain.

❝'Thanks be to God,' exclaimed the great admiral, Christopher Columbus, as he approached the new Indies on the 8th of October 1492, 'the air is very soft, as of April in Seville, and it is a pleasure to be there!' There can, indeed, be no place where it is a greater pleasure to be than in Seville in April, as every Spaniard well knows. 'What would you do if you came in for a fortune? a Spaniard was asked.

'Give half to the poor, and with the other half buy a house in Seville and spend the spring there,' this true Spaniard replied. In summer Seville is too hot, the narrow serpentining Sierpes – the main artery of life in the city and reserved for foot passengers – becomes a furnace, although covered by awnings, and no breath of air is felt save in the great Plaza Nueva. In winter, indeed, it is often pleasant, but even in Seville it is sometimes cold, and then the Spaniard has no resource but his great cloak, which he folds more closely across his breast and mouth. But at the beginning of April spring comes to Seville in a flash with the heat of a northern summer. The acacias and other deciduous trees seem to burst into radiant verdure in a day; the orange trees throughout the city leap into blossom and scatter their deep perfume everywhere; and everywhere, too, in the street and in the hair and bosoms of the women, there are roses and carnations, the two preferred flowers of Spain, so tenderly and lovingly treated that they scarcely seem the mere flowers we know them elsewhere.”

HENRY HAVELOCK ELLIS, *THE SOUL OF SPAIN*,
PUB. CONSTABLE & CO., LONDON, 1929

THE ARCHITECTURE OF SEVILLE

VARIETY

Children's story-teller Hans Christian Andersen (1805–75) had a life-long love of travel. Here he explains why he prefers Seville to Paris.

“In Paris one tires oneself out looking at shops which can be amusing enough: one goes as in a treadmill, looking and looking and time passes and one gets home weary – and has profited nothing. It is quite otherwise in Seville. The streets are narrow and one is not dazzled by shops. The houses and courtyards look very ordinary, rather tediously over-whitewashed – but it is very much the same

with them as it is with human beings: outside one looks very like another, but inside, there lies the difference and it is this that one comes to love more than the outward appearance. Walk through the streets of Seville and look inside; the doors and gates are open. *El patio*, as the little courtyard is called, is both the heart and the face which reveals to us the taste of the inhabitants. In one court there is a lovely statue, in another a big, carved, stone wall; the next house has perhaps a Moorish hall with stucco-work and artistic decoration. Let us cross the street where there lies a palatial building: its court is a whole rose-garden with fountains and statuettes. The little house close by has only a low small door into a tiny courtyard, but it is filled with lovely flowers around a single, tall palm. Now we are standing before a larger building with a colonnaded courtyard, three storeys high, decorated with oil paintings. Such is the variety of Seville. In late November there was not the outside life that goes on at other times. One should come to Seville in the spring when the flowers are at their best, or in the summer when one can see how the southerner lives. Then each little *patio* presents a conversation piece. The inhabitants spend their whole day down there, a big sun-awning is spread high over the courtyard or a vine forms a thick roof with its broad, shade-giving leaves. The family and servants sit there in the shade, working, gossiping or just dreaming lazily. During the long, warm days they stay out in the open air and go inside only at night to sleep.❞

HANS CHRISTIAN ANDERSEN, *A VISIT TO SPAIN AND NORTH AFRICA 1862*, TRANS. GRACE THORNTON, PUB. PETER OWEN, LONDON, 1985

MOORISH INFLUENCE

Biographer and travel writer Augustus Hare (1792–1834) remarks on the Moorish style of the architecture.

❝The people of Seville all seem proud now of its Moorish history, and aware of the advantages which that period has bequeathed to them. All the best Moorish houses are preserved, and the hot season of the 'oven of Spain' is rendered endurable by the forethought which made the streets so narrow that it is generally impossible for two carriages to pass one another, while the houses which line them have large gardens, or are built round open courts, which, in summer, are covered with an awning or *velo*; while the windows are defended by the thick matted blinds called *esteras*. The names which are written up at the entrance of the streets in Seville are in themselves always picturesque and interesting, and have reference to events which occurred in them, or persons who have lived there. . . . All are whitewashed, as at Córdova, and the clear shadows of the passers-by fall blue upon the dazzling walls. In the streets where most business is carried on, barriers are placed at each end of the broad flagged pavement to prevent a carriage from

attempting to enter, so that only mules and donkeys jostle the foot-passengers with their heavy burdens. Here the chief shops have no doors or windows, but are open porticos, supported on pillars, like oriental bazaars. Conspicuous among these are the shops of the gaily-coloured Mants, generally kept by solemn-looking old Moors, who insist upon their customers being seated, and regale them with dates and sweetmeats, while they exhibit their wares and those of the common earthenware, with their picturesque forms and bright green and red enamel. In the engravers' windows strangers will notice that some of the visiting-cards are black, with the name in white – these are the cards of the doctors, and, rather ominously, signify their calling.❞

Augustus Hare, *Wandering in Spain*,
pub. Smith, Elder & Co., London, 1885

The streets of Seville

Virginia Woolf (1882–1941) was on the whole complementary about Seville in her diary entries in April 1905, despite commenting on its "elephantine beauty".

❝We began to explore Seville this morning. First to the Cathedral, which looms everywhere. It is vast. That is the first impression. I dont very much care for such elephantine beauty – but it is fine. Service was going on – & so we could not see much. In the afternoon we took a carriage & drove for an hour in the gardens which are lovely, though somewhat faded & out of repair, like everything else. The streets are very narrow, cobbled, with no pavement to walk on. Trams bad & not easy to get. It is a difficult town to find ones way about in – We went to the great hospital & saw the yellow city walls, which enclose the city. . . .

Woke this morning under my mosquito curtains – which the beasts merely laugh at – to find, firstly the maid carrying on a long & emphatic speech in Spanish – & 2ndly a rain of pure English blood pouring outside. (That sentence by the way may be read 2 ways – but we do not live in the time of the Inquisition.) Out in a clear space to the Giralda, which is the Cathedral Tower, from which we gazed over Seville; a small town it looks from that height, soon dwindling off into the fields. White houses with brown roofs for the most part. The rain was such that we sat a long time in the Cathedral – which is not really beautiful, though certainly impressive – in the same way that a steep cliff or a bottomless well is. In the afternoon we 'did' Alcázar, a splendid gilt & mosaic Moorish building – a sight again which does not charm me. . . .

A showery morning again, but not so bad, it turned out, as yesterday. We went out & bought photographs – our solitary extravagance, & then saw the Church of the Caridad, which was not very interesting. The most interesting part of Seville is its streets. After lunch we took a cab & drove to the Casa Pilatos, as it was raining. There are court yards leading to court yards, all of white marble – simpler & more stately than the Alcázar. Also a great many dark long rooms, round the court yards, lined with beautiful tiles, cool & hushed. Then we bought a spirit lamp with great skill, & various necessaries for our 2 meals in the train tomorrow. I shant be sorry to move on, though I have enjoyed this.❞

VIRGINIA WOOLF, *A PASSIONATE APPRENTICE – THE EARLY JOURNALS 1897–1909*, ED. *MITCHELL A. LEASKA*, PUB. THE HOGARTH PRESS, LONDON, 1990

SMILING SEVILLE

Czech novelist and dramatist Karel ¢apek (1890–1938) wrote various travel books, replete with atmospheric description.

❝I wager a bottle of aljarafe, or anything you like, that every guide, every journalist, and even every young lady tourist, will refer to 'smiling' Seville. Certain stock phrases and epithets possess the ghastly and irritating quality of being right. You can knock me down or call me a purveyor of tushery or an arrant babbler for saying so, but 'smiling' Seville really is smiling Seville. Nothing can be done about it; in fact, there is no other way of describing the place. It is just 'smiling' Seville; in every corner of its eyes and mouth there is a flutter of merriment and tenderness.

And perhaps it is only that a street, however narrow, glistens as if it were freshly whitewashed every Saturday. And that from every window, from every lattice in it are thrust garlands, pelargonia and fuchsias, small palms and all kinds of greenery, blossoming and leafy. Here the awnings have still remained from the summer, stretched from roof to roof, and intersected by the sky, as by a blue knife; and when you stroll along, you seem to be, not in the street, but in the flower-laden passage of a house where you are paying a visit; at this corner somebody may perhaps shake you by the hand and say: 'We *are* pleased to see you' or '¿Qué tal?' or something cheerful of that sort. And everything here is as clean as a new pin; there is a smell of garlands and frying oil; every door with its lattice leads to a trim heavenly garden which is called a patio, and here again is a church with a majolica dome and a portal as ornate as if a great festival were on, and above all this the gleaming minaret of the Giralda is uplifted. And this narrow, crooked lane is called Sierpes because it twists like a snake; here the life of Seville flows along densely and slowly: casinos and taverns, shops full of lace and flowered silk, caballeros in light Andalusian sombreros, tiny streets where vehicles cannot be driven, because of the crowds of people drinking wine, chatting, haggling, laughing and generally idling there in various ways. Then there is an old cathedral embedded in the old quarter among the houses and patios, so that you can only see bits of it wherever you are, as if it were too big to be viewed as a whole by mortal eye. And then another small faience church, miniature palaces with bright and graceful frontages, arcades and balconies and embossed lattices, a notched wall, from behind which palms and broad-leaved musas lean over; always something attractive, a snug corner where you feel at ease and which you never want to forget. Just recall that wooden cross on the little square, as white and restful as a nun's cell; those delightful, quiet quarters of the city which contain the narrowest streets and the most charming nooks in the world.❞

KAREL ¢APEK, *LETTERS FROM SPAIN*,
TRANS. PAUL SELVER,
PUB. GEOFFREY BLES, LONDON, 1931

A CURIOSITY SHOP

The Moorish aspects of the city impressed H.V. Morton (1892–1979).

❝The streets of the old city are among the most picturesque in Spain, and in true eastern fashion the outside of a house is no indication of its interior. Beautiful wrought-iron doors give glimpses into charming courtyards where you can see a fountain, some geraniums in pots, a palm tree, and a dado of Moorish tiles.

I wandered through a labyrinth of narrow streets, coming to unexpected little plazas, then on through more white tunnels which might have been in Africa. Sometimes I heard a voice singing a high-pitched wail in a minor key that ended suddenly, as if bitten off in mid-air. It is extraordinary that though Ferdinand and Isabel expelled the Moors, the voice of Andalusia is still Moorish.

It was in one of these old streets that I came across the perfect curiosity shop. There were baroque saints, old pictures, bits of jewellery, mirrors, swords and daggers, coins, strips of beautifully carved and gilded wood, chairs, tables, glass cabinets bursting with knick-knacks; and the whole place was covered with a sheet of dust. Imprisoned behind this wreckage of another world I saw a pair of sad old Spanish eyes under an aged felt hat. When I spoke the old eyes gleamed for a second believing me to be an Americano, then filled again with their habitual gloom. In a galvanized tin bath I found a beautiful seventeenth century box lock, complete with its key. The bolt was jammed with rust and for a moment I thought I should buy it for the pleasure of cleaning it and getting the key to work again as once it did – to admit who knows and to whom? Another enchanting and ridiculous object was a musical box that actually worked. Upon the lid sat a mouse in a cage and facing it was an old woman dressed like a witch, with a stick in her hand.❞

H.V. MORTON, *A STRANGER IN SPAIN*,
PUB. METHUEN & CO LTD., LONDON, 1955

A VIEW OF THE CATHEDRAL

Rainer Maria Rilke (1875–1926) was not a fan.

❝As for Seville, up to the very last there was no understanding between us, none at all, although the inhabitants take the Festival of the Virgin very personally and a whole series of ceremonies was impending, whose beginning I shared. But I found the cathedral thoroughly repulsive, indeed hostile, – it is never serious, there is something hazy and imponderable about this high-blown overweening dome, an *out-trumping* spirit that seeks to out-trump God himself and seize him as it were from above. And the infamous organ makes the interior so sweet with its treacly tone that the colossal pillars grow quite faint; it leaves you unmoved, this deliquescent architecture, a tour de force – it can go and do what it likes with itself.❞

RAINER MARIA RILKE, *SELECTED LETTERS OF RAINER MARIA RILKE*, TRANS. R.F.C. HULL,
PUB. MACMILLAN & CO., LONDON, 1946

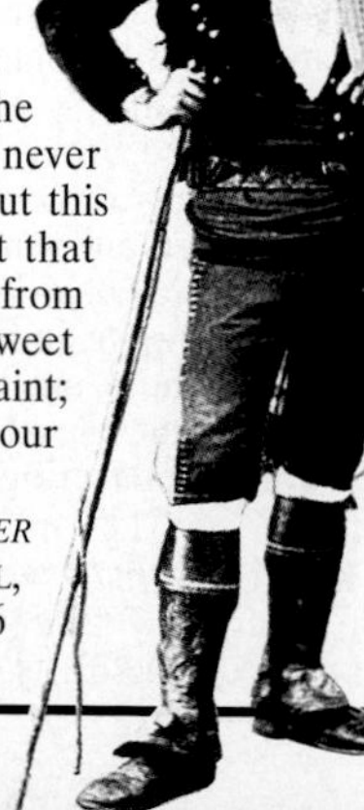

Another view

Although generally known for his cynicism and satirical criticisms, Evelyn Waugh (1903–66) was a great admirer of the city of Seville.

❝I did not begin to master the geography of the town, and remember it now in a series of isolated magic lantern slides. The cathedral is magnificent; one of the finest in Europe; a great, spacious, Gothic church full of superb sculpture hidden in dark corners and behind metal gates. The dome was never a great success technically, as it has twice fallen in since it was originally built; the last restoration was by Casanova, in the late eighties, and it is hoped that he has succeeded in making it relatively permanent; just outside the cathedral is a large *patio*, once the courtyard of a mosque, in which hangs a stuffed crocodile sent by the Sultan of Egypt to Alfonso the Learned, with a suit for the hand of his daughter.❞

Evelyn Waugh, *Labels – A Mediterranean Journey*, pub. Duckworth, London, 1930

Andalusians

Great Boasters

Richard Ford analyses the character of the men of southern Spain.

❝Of all Spaniards the Andalucian is the greatest boaster; he brags chiefly of his courage and wealth. He ends in believing his own lie, and hence is always pleased with himself, with whom he is on the best of terms. His redeeming qualities are his kind and good manners, his lively, social turn, his ready wit and sparkle: he is ostentatious, and, as far as his limited means will allow, eager to show hospitality to the stranger, after the Spanish acceptation of that term, which has no English reference to the kitchen. As in the days of Strabo, he rather affects the foreigner than dislikes him, for the intercourse of his rich maritime cities has broken down somewhat of inland prejudices.

The Oriental imagination of the Andalucians colours men and things up to the bright hues of their glorious sun; their exaggeration, *Ponderacion*, is only exceeded by their credulity, its twin sister. Everything is in the superlative or diminutive, especially as regards talk in the former, and deeds in the latter. They have a yearning after the unattainable, and a disregard for the practical; never, in fact, either much knowing or caring about the object in pursuit. They are incapable of sustained sobriety of conduct, which alone can succeed in the long run. Nowhere will the stranger hear more frequently those talismanic words which mark national character – *No se sabe, no se puede, conforme*, the 'I don't know,' 'I can't do it;' the *Mañana, pasado mañana*, the 'tomorrow and day after tomorrow;' the *Boukra, balboukra*, of the procrastinating Oriental. Here remain the Bakalum or *Veremos* 'we will see about it;' the Pek-éyi or *muy bien*, 'very well;' and the Inshallah, *si Dios quiere*, the 'if the Lord will' of St. James (iv. 15); the *Ojala*, or wishing that God would effect what he wants, the Moslems *Enxo-Allah*. In a word, the besetting sins of the Oriental, his ignorance, indifference, procrastination, tempered by a religious resignation to Providence. ❞

RICHARD FORD, *A HAND-BOOK FOR TRAVELLERS IN SPAIN – VOL. I*, PUB. CENTAUR PRESS, LONDON, 1966

THE PARISIANS OF SPAIN

According to Havelock Ellis, Sevillians have a sense of grace and aristocracy.

❝The Sevillians may be said to be the Parisians of Spain. They possess a certain well-poised gaiety, – *alegria*, as they themselves call it, – a fine sense of temperance and harmony. They have that wit which is the sign of an alert intelligence; they are sufficient to themselves, and they are a people of artists. In most of these respects they differ from their fellow-countrymen in temperament. Spaniards generally are a grave and silent people, tending to run to extremes, by no means artists, with fine moral qualities indeed, but, while very honest, also, it must be said sometimes lacking in quick intelligence. The Sevillians, and especially the women of Seville, possess a quality which, like the ancient Romans, the Spaniards call 'salt,' a sapid and antiseptic quality of bright intelligence which permeates all that they are and all that they do. They do nothing quite in the same way as other people, and are thus placed, perhaps a little consciously, apart from other people. The meanest girl of the people in Seville has an easy consciousness and pride in this superority, and in every movement shows a gracious dignity which we mostly seek in vain elsewhere, even in the cities that lie nearest. If we go to Córdova we feel that we are among a people from whom the tide of life has retired, and who have proudly shut themselves up within their palatial and beautifully various *patios*. If we go to Granada we find ourselves among a busy bourgeois set of small tradesmen. The distinction of Seville is at once aristocratic and democratic. We feel here the presence of an ancient civilisation that has been matured through many generations and has penetrated the whole people. Everything at Seville bears the touch of a finely tempered race, and the imprint is always gracious, noble, harmonious. We see this indicated even in the varied colouring of the houses. Sevillian houses, while very charming inside, are very simple outside, and it is usual to give them a coloured wash according to the taste of the owner. At Granada, where the same custom prevails, the colouring is often harsh, with a preference for an unpleasant brown, but at Seville an instinctive feeling for harmony seems everywhere to have presided over its arrangement. Again, Spain is a land where wrought iron has always been largely used. The iron *rejas* or gratings outside the windows, the iron gates of the *patios* or courtyards, the great iron screens enclosing the chapels in the churches, have everywhere offered scope for the development of skill in such work, but nowhere in Spain is the ironwork so bold and yet so felicitous as in Seville. And the same qualities we find in the highest degree in the people themselves, more especially in the women.❞

HENRY HAVELOCK ELLIS, *THE SOUL OF SPAIN*, PUB. CONSTABLE & CO., LONDON, 1929

SPANISH BELLES

Lord Byron (1788–1824) found Spanish women pleasingly attentive.

❝Seville is a beautiful town, though the streets are narrow they are clean, we lodged in the house of two Spanish unmarried ladies, who possesed *six* houses in Seville, and gave me a curious specimen of Spanish manners. – They are women of character, and the eldest a fine woman, the youngest pretty but not so good a figure as Donna Josepha, the freedom of women which is general here astonished me not a little, and in the course of further observation I find that reserve is not the characteristic of the Spanish belles, who are in general very handsome, with large

"Three Spaniards, four opinions."

Spanish proverb

black eyes, and very fine forms. – The eldest honoured your *unworthy* son with very particular attention, embracing him with great tenderness at parting (I was there but 3 days) after cutting off a lock of his hair, & presenting him with one of her own about three feet in length, which I send, and beg you will retain till my return. – Her last words were 'Adio tu hermoso! me gusto mucho' 'Adieu, you pretty fellow you please me much.' – She offered a share of her apartment which my *virtue* induced me to decline, she laughed and said I had some English 'Amante,' (lover) and added that she was going to be married to an officer in the Spanish army.❞

GEORGE GORDON BYRON, *IN MY HOT YOUTH – BRYON'S LETTERS AND JOURNALS, VOL. 1,* ED. *LESLIE A. MARCHAND,* PUB. JOHN MURRAY, LONDON, 1973

"LA SAL"

Theophile Gautier (1811–72) takes a romantic view of the charms of Sevillian women.

❝On the Alameda del Duque, where people take a breath of air between the acts outside the theatre, which is quite near by, and, above all, on La Cristina, it is charming to see the pretty Sevillanas parading with little airs and graces between seven and eight o'clock, in groups of three or four, accompanied by their present or future lovers. Their movements are alert, vivacious and mettlesome, and they seem to paw the ground like a horse rather than to walk. The rapidity with which their fans open and close beneath their fingers, the flash of their eye, the assurance of their movements, the willowy lissomness of their figures, add a characteristic touch to their appearance. There may be women in England, France and Italy whose beauty is of a more perfect and regular type, but there are certainly none prettier and more piquant. They possess in a high degree what Spaniards call *la sal*. This is a thing of which it is difficult to give an idea in France: a mixture of nonchalance and vivacity, of daring retorts and childish wiles, of a grace, a piquancy, and a *ragoût*, as the painters say, which may be found quite apart from beauty, and is often preferred to it. And so in Spain they say to a woman: 'How *salada* (full of salt) you are!' There is no greater compliment.❞

THEOPHILE GAUTIER, *A ROMANTIC IN SPAIN,* TRANS. CATHERINE ALSION PHILLIPS, PUB. ALFRED A. KNOPF, NEW YORK AND LONDON, 1926

A FALSE PICTURE

The generally accepted, picturesque view of Andalusians was the invention of French writers like Theophile Gautier, according to V.S. Pritchett (b. 1900).

❝Andalusia is what for a century or more the foreigner has understood to be Spain. It is the Spain of the romantic legend, as Castile is the Spain of the 'black legend', *la leyenda negra*. We see in our mind's eye the Córdoba hat of the Feria, the women with the high combs, the proud carriage, and the rose or carnation in their hair; we see the dangerous gypsy dancer, the long-toothed, narrow-hipped bullfighter, the figure of Don Juan. We see the cool tiled patios of Córdoba, Seville, and Granada, hear the lazy talking of the guitar, the electric crackle of castanets, as the twisting arms swing down. We are in the heart of the Moorish Kingdom and have one foot in the East. Flowers, singing, sunlight, black shade, and the rustle of water.

Is it like this? Shall we be deceived? No – as always in Spain, if we look at one face it is like this; the face turns and we see the opposite. Romantic Andulasia was an invention of the French, especially of Théophile Gautier, Mérimée, and, later, of Maurice Barrès; the country of *'Le sang, la volupté, et al mort,'* and in the enchantment of Holy Week in Seville these ideas easily catch the northern imagination. Nor must we underrate them: the French are more intelligent and imaginative than the Spaniards, and have simply prolonged certain Andalusian characteristics into a higher key and turned them into general ideas.❞

V.S. PRITCHETT, *THE SPANISH TEMPER*, PUB. CHATTO & WINDUS, LONDON, 1954

ENCOUNTERS

Hugo Williams (b. 1942) describes some characters he met on his travels.

❝Borgos seemed to specialize in pharmacies – ancient chapels to Chemistry, with panelling and painted ceilings, cupids and no shampoo. Salamanca was pastry shops and frantic displacement activity. Seville is a Martini ad with scooters and balconies and royal palms, high heels and steep shadows up alleyways, tales of scooter crimes. I wrote the first line of a short story: 'He went upstairs and entered her room without knocking.' A German woman in the hotel is interested in dancing Flamenco Sevillana, but there is no room to give me a demonstration. Tapas: a bowl of tiny snails, which I extract with my teeth, Harry Lime in the background, the first two bars only.

I find Seville extremely difficult. The Museo de Bellas Artes is closed for reconstruction. The Great Tower closes while I am up it. A man lets me out and I spill blinking into the dazzling, deserted street. I take a nap on one of the mosaic benches in the Murillo Gardens and wake to find a beggar making cigarette noises in my ear. I don't have any, so I get up and walk away, cross to have been woken. He follows, muttering. 'Lend me money, lend me money.' He has drawn a knife. I head towards a busy road, only to find it is a cul-de-sac of wire netting. By now he is poking my bottom with the knife. I can feel its point through my money folded in my back pocket, just enough to get me to Portugal tomorrow. I walk faster, edging out of the trap. When I look round, he has fallen back. I feel the flimsy gooseflesh between my ribs that might so easily have provided his revenge on society. Beautiful Seville oranges lie where they have fallen under the trees.❞

HUGO WILLIAMS, *FREELANCING*,
PUB. FABER AND FABER, LONDON AND BOSTON, 1995

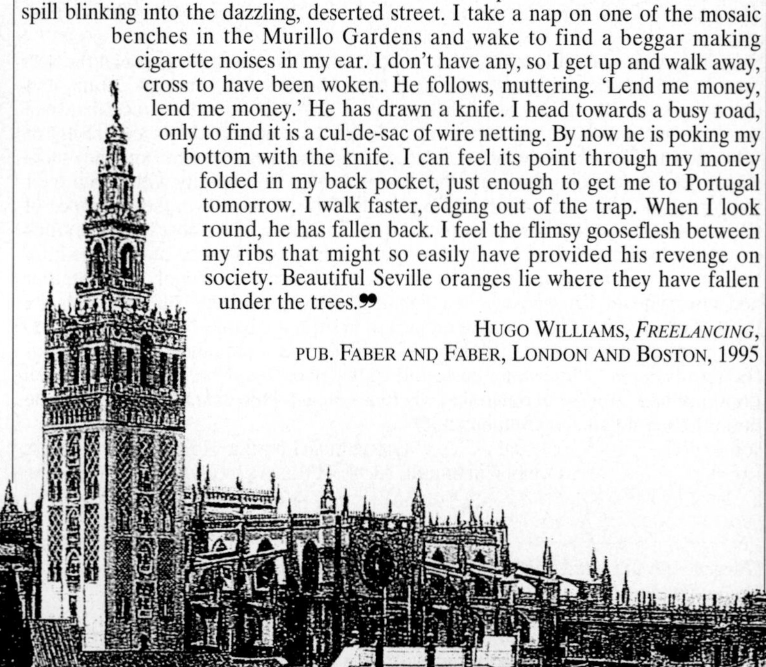

"Seville lights up for a feast-day as a face lights up with a smile."
Arthur Symons

LIFESTYLE

SHERRY

One of the region's best-known exports is described by John Lomas (1846–1927).

❝If a man wishes to disabuse his mind of the notion that he is being robbed when he is asked a high figure for a good sherry, if he would harbour only pleasant feelings when his neighbour assures him that he has bought the 'same thing at half the price,' or appreciate the dense ignorance of after-dinner talkers upon the subject of wine in general, let him pay a week's visit to Jerez, and follow up with some degree of real care the birth, nursing and development of a really fine Manzanilla or Amontillado. He will tread vineyards which were in cultivation six hundred years ago, when the land was in the occupation of the Moors. He will probably bewail the little advance that has been made all these centuries in the paths of scientific process and appliance; but that will in some sort only increase his interest in all that he sees, while he cannot fail to be duly impressed by the honest care and vigilance bestowed upon his beloved liquor. He will not only attain at last – after many years of more or less dictatorial holding forth upon the subject – to some real knowledge of the differences between natural, vintage, and *solera* wines, or the blended types which alone he is likely to come across in England, but he may even store up useful *data* concerning the more intricate ways of *vino dulce*, *vino de color*, *finos palmas*, and *olorosos*. He will no longer marvel at the loud and deep disputing at which he has been accustomed to assist, when he sees what an amusing variety of tastes in the directions of colour, flavour, age, and price are provided for in the vast bodegas in which he will be treated as an honoured guest. He will not be sceptical again about such prices as even £300 per butt, after he has been once made to put together the annual cost of tending an acre of vines, the loss by blight, 'scud,' and other similar causes, the amount of evaporation, and the percentage of failures and sourings during the four or five years of probation which a wine should undergo, and all the expenses of blending, nursing, casking and storing.❞

JOHN LOMAS, *SKETCHES IN SPAIN FROM NATURE, ART AND LIFE*,
PUB. LONGMANS GREEN & CO., LONDON, 1884

A FEAST

Two middle-aged ladies devoured an unusual feast, as described by Penelope Chetwode (1909–86).

❝When we got back to the *posada* in the late afternoon everyone was busy in the kitchen making pork sausages and white puddings. Three enormous bowls of mince stood ready on the table, the one destined for the puddings containing, among other delicacies, the colossal lights of the pig, boiled and put through the mincing-machine and the tripe treated in the same way.

That night we had a royal feast to celebrate the *matanza* (pig killing): ten grown-ups sat round the two tables while the four children sat on low chairs by the fire. We had not plates or glasses or forks, just a spoon and a *navaja* apiece.

First course: Pig's broth with bits of bread floating it it.

Second course: Extra good *cocido* (chickpea and potato soup with cloves of garlic).

Third course: Two large earthenware bowls containing slices of fried black pudding and assorted chitterlings eaten of the points of our *navajas* with pickled pimientos.

Fourth course: A delicious port and chicken stew served in the *olla* in which it was cooked, swimming in yellowish brown gravy and accompanied by a mountain of olives. This was great fun: you jabbed your *navaja* into a bit of meat and took potluck; you gnawed all the meat off the bone held in your fingers and tossed it over your shoulder onto the floor. At one point Felicidad fished out a hen's claw which she sucked clean with great relish. *Fifth course:* Pomegranates.

White wine was passed round and round in a *porrón*, and after the excellent meal was over the women washed the spoons and the serving dishes, scrubbed the tables and swept up all the bones off the floor, leaving the kitchen cleaner than many a one I have visited in the British Isles, and what a way to solve the washing-up problem!❞

PENELOPE CHETWODE,
TWO MIDDLE-AGED LADIES IN ANDALUSIA,
PUB. JOHN MURRAY, LONDON, 1963

THE PASOS

Gertrude Bone (1883–1962) describes the atmosphere of this supposedly religious occasion.

❝As I was returning home in a little mountain town I was unexpectedly caught in a crowd which was waiting for the procession. Those in the rear of the advancing pasos saw an opportunity to intercept them by running behind the street buildings and emerging farther on. But the returning stream made progress impossible in the old Moorish street. The pasos were wedged in the crowd. The balconies were filled with spectators, and barely lifted above the heads of the people stood the figure of Christ mocked, hands tied, head drooping and wounded, torn garments, a roughly carved figure of some tragic intensity. Excited by the jostling crowd, a drunken gipsy began to sing a ribald song. The people, from rebukes, passed to jeering. Jests and protests were shouted from one to another. Suddenly an old woman whose fierce profile was cut, as it were, from her black shawl, began to sing a *saeta* of devotion in a piercing voice. The gipsy refused to stop and sang louder, taking it as a challenge. The people laughed aloud at both, and in the middle of the swaying, noisy crowd stood the tragic and abandoned figure, taking on in circumstance something of the fickleness and triviality which had brought about its Passion.

But this is the emotion broken about the pasos by accidental human lighting. There are, too, moments of dramatic intention. One day in a southern town I was in the plaza at the hour of the Crucifixion. Windless sunshine and the bright air of the mountains caught the crimson and purple of the guild dresses and gave them solidity and sumptuousness as the procession circled the plaza. The black mantillas and dresses of the women made darker the shadows of the heavy cornices and balconies. Suddenly a silence which was not of decorum fell on the crowd, and I noticed for the first time that the high blank wall to the side of the square held the great iron portal of the prison. As the suffering Christ drew near, the iron gates were flung open, the outstretched arms were lowered to pass under them, and He who gathered the souls whom men cast out passed into the prison. 'He was numbered among the malefactors.' It was a great gesture and the only religious one of the day. The crowd dispersed in silence.❞

GERTRUDE BONE,
DAYS IN OLD SPAIN,
PUB. MACMILLAN AND CO. LTD,
LONDON, 1938

SPANISH CATS

Most Spaniards dislike cats, according to Nina Epton.

❝The trunk of one of the larger trees in the garden had been fenced in, leaving a small aperture on one side, and filled with wood shavings for the caretaker's cat and her three kittens. 'He must be fond of cats,' I remarked in surprise. Spaniards usually dislike cats and never speak to them except to shoo them off. Most Spanish cats are thin, wary and wild.

Even the lady director of the Sevillan Society for the Protection of Animals and Plants (they are lumped together in Spain, so little is thought to differentiate them. They are all classed as 'irrational'), was not a cat lover. 'They do such strange things,' she observed. 'They hide themselves in such odd places, they get squeezed into such tight corners. They even hurl themselves from balconies . . . you never know what they will be up to next.' (After looking at several typical English cats a Spanish socialist friend observed: 'Your cats look so *bourgeois*!'.)

Spanish cats rarely appear in works of art, but this is partly due to the fact that Spanish artists have been contemptuous of conversation pieces. Their only opportunity to present pets was in their pictures of the Holy Family. El Greco painted a cat, but as one would expect from him, it is a fierce Siamese with malevolent eyes and a hieratic air, not a cosy kind of cat to live with. Valdés Leal (who should not be judged by his 'death' pictures alone) painted a sociable, contented cat in *his* picture of the Holy Family which hangs in the Museum of Fine Arts in Seville. This is an ordinary black and white cat, plump by Spanish feline standards, sitting relaxedly with its forepaws tucked inwards, head raised, eyes glancing sideways with an alert friendly expression, obviously a well cared for family pet. Picasso, too, understands and likes cats as is evident from the three acutely observed bronze sculptures of cats which were shown in the 1967 Paris and London exhibitions, so expressive of feline delicacy, timidity and inquisitiveness. His cats vibrate, especially the one making water in a characteristic half abashed pose.❞

NINA EPTON, *ANDALUSIA*,
PUB. WEIDENFELD & NICOLSON, LONDON, 1968

BULLFIGHTING

Ernest Hemingway (1899–1961) was an aficionado of the bullfight.

❝The days on which there will be fights in other towns in Spain than Madrid vary, but, in general . . . the dates coincide with the national religious festivals and the times of the local fairs or ferias, which usually commence on the Saint's day of the town. . .

Aside from the novilladas and the two subscription seasons at Madrid the best place to see a series of bullfights in the early spring is at the feria in Sevilla where there are at least four fights on successive days. This feria starts after Easter. If you are in Sevilla for Easter ask anyone when the feria starts or you can find the dates from the big posters advertising the fights. If you are in Madrid before Easter go to any of the cafés around the Puerta del Sol, or the first café on your right on the Plaza de Canalejas going down the Calle de San Jeronimo from the Puerta del Sol toward the Prado and you will find a poster on the wall advertising the feria of Sevilla. In this same café you will always find in the summer the posters or cartels advertising the ferias of Pamplona, Valencia, Bilbao, Salamanca, Valladolid, Cuenca, Malaga, Murcia and many others.

On Easter Sunday there are always bullfights in Madrid, Sevilla, Barcelona, Murcia, Zaragoza, and novilladas in Granada, Bilbao, Valladolid and many other places. There is also a bullfight in Madrid on the Monday after Easter. On the 29th of April of each year there is a bullfight and fair at Jerez de la Fontera. This is an excellent place to visit with or without bulls, and is the home of sherry and everything distilled from it. They will take you through the cellars of Jerez and you may taste many different grades of wines and brandies, but it is best to do this on another day than the one you plan to go to the corrida.”

ERNEST HEMINGWAY, *DEATH IN THE AFTERNOON*,
PUB. PENGUIN BOOKS IN ASSOCATION WITH JONATHAN CAPE,
NEW YORK/LONDON, 1966

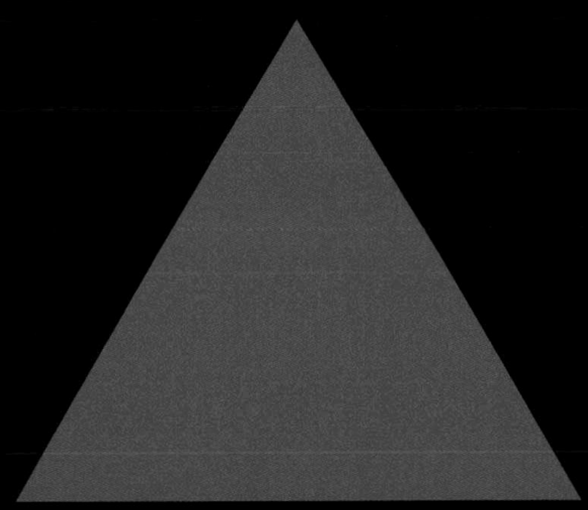

Itineraries in Andalusia

▲ Flock of sheep in the Carmona region.

▲ Olive grove, La Campiña.

▼ Holm-oaks at the foot of the Sierra Morena.

▲ Riotinto cattle on open pastureland.

▲ Pine forest, Alcalá.

▼ Orange grove, El Aljarafe.

▲ Río Guadalquivir and the Vega valley. ▼ Río Guadalquivir in the Marisma (marsh regi

▼ Hacienda de la Florida, Carmona.

▲ The cathedral, Seville.

▼ La Giralda and the Iglesia del Divino Salvador.

▼ Seville from the Puente del V Centenario.

▼ Plaza de Toros de la Maestranza.

▲ Río Guadalquivir, Seville.

The city center from Triana. ▼

Seville and around

▲ THE CITY CENTER: SOUTH

See also the map section at the end of the guide.
◆ C, D, E

1. Convento de Santa Paula
2. Convento de Santa Isabel
3. Iglesia de San Marcos
4. Iglesia de Santa Marina
5. Iglesia de San Luis
6. Iglesia Omnium Sanctorum
7. Alameda de Hércules
8. Convento de Santa Clara
9. Iglesia de San Lorenzo et Jesús del Gran Poder
10. Iglesia de Santa Catalina
11. Iglesia de San Pedro
12. Iglesia de la Anunciación
13. Palacio de Lebrija
14. La Campana
15. Iglesia de San Esteban
16. Casa de Pilatos
17. Iglesia de San Ildefonso
18. Iglesia de Salvador
19. Calle Sierpes
20. Museo de Bellas Artes
21. Iglesia de la Magdalena
22. Ayuntamiento

15
16
17
10
11
Plaza
de la
Encarnación
12
18
13
22
19
14
21
20

32
24
23
28
36
25
29
37
38
27
26
30
31
22
42
41
44
43
47

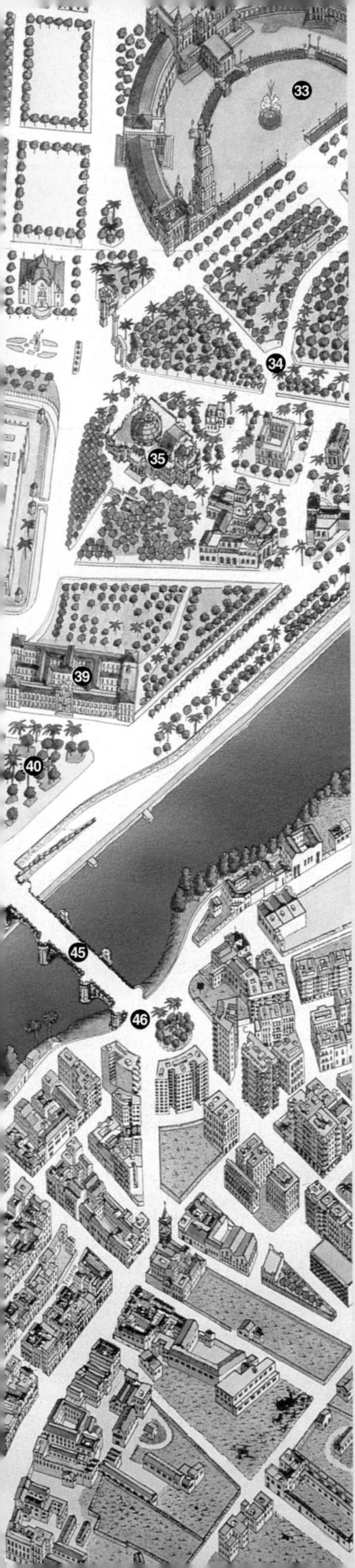

See also the map section at the end of the guide.

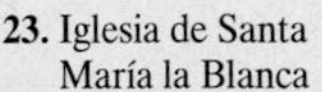

◆ **C, D, E**

23. Iglesia de Santa María la Blanca
24. Jardines de Murillo
25. Iglesia de Santa Cruz
26. Palacio Arzobispal
27. Catedral and La Giralda
28. Jardines de Alcazar
29. Reales Alcazáres
30. Archivo de Indias
31. Avenida de la Constitución
32. Prado de San Sebastián
33. Plaza de España
34. Parque María Luisa
35. Casinó de la Exposición
36. Fábrica de Tabacos (Universidad)
37. Hotel Alfonso XIII
38. Puerta de Jerez
39. Palacio de San Telmo
40. Jardines de Cristina
41. Torre del Oro
42. Hospital de la Caridad
43. La Maestranza, Plaza dc Toros
44. La Maestranza theater
45. Puente de San Telmo
46. Plaza de Cuba
47. Calle Betis

SEVILLE BY ANY OTHER NAME
In the 1st millennium BC the city was called "Spalis". The etymology of the name (probably derived from the Phoenician root "Spal") is uncertain, although one school of thought translates it as "founded on marshland". It was known to the Romans as "Hispalis", and the Visigoths called it "Spali". Between the 8th and 13th centuries the Muslims Arabized the name to "Isbiliya" ● *32*. It was finally incorporated in the Romance language of Catalan as "Sevilla". 
Panel of *azulejos* ● *56, 77* (right) representing Seville, seen from Triana, in 1738.

PATRON SAINTS OF SEVILLE
Seville's patron saints are the Christian martyrs, Justa and Rufina ▲ *138, 139*, and the Gothic scholar-bishops, Leander and Isidore, shown in the sketch (below) by Murillo ● *91*, ▲ *157, 315*. The festivals of San Fernando (May 30) and the Virgen de los Reyes (August 15) are the most important.

BIRTH AND GROWTH OF A CITY

The history of Seville is that of a city occupying a privileged geographical position on a major river, at a junction of natural communication routes linking the heart of Andalusia with the coastal plains and maritime routes. At the beginning of the 1st millennium BC, the total area of the port established on a promontory by the Phoenicians was no greater than 490 x 220 yards. By the 1st century BC the city was already surrounded by walls. Under the Romans it covered an area of almost 100 acres and its center was established at the highest point, between the modern districts of El Salvador and Alfalfa ▲ *162*. Although it changed very little until the Muslim period, during the 8th and 9th centuries it was extended still further (to more than 222 acres) and the suburb of Triana ▲ *194* was mentioned for the first time as a permanent settlement on the far side of the river. The city's greatest period of expansion was during the 12th and 13th centuries when it spread over an area of almost 740 acres and acquired the structure that it retained for several centuries.

THE MODERN CITY. In 1252 Alfonso X divided the city into twenty-four parishes (*collaciones*) and several suburbs. The golden age led to renewed expansion as the city extended

A CONVENT-CITY
View of Seville from the monastery of La Cartuja, in 1665. In spite of the disasters and crises of the 17th century, the Church retained its power. As many as seventy-three convents stood within the city walls and some one hundred religious edifices were constructed.

"Seville is surrounded by crenelated enclosure walls, flanked at intervals by huge towers (several of which have fallen into ruins), and ditches that are now almost completely filled in. These walls would offer no form of defense against modern artillery but their serrated, Moorish crenelations are extremely picturesque. Their foundation, like so many other walls and encampments, is attributed to Julius Caesar."

Théophile Gautier, *Journey to Spain*, 1851

beyond the ramparts and streets were widened. The oriental character of the houses was gradually modified and transformed until they became more European in style. At the end of the 19th century the population had grown to such an extent that, in 1861, parts of the city walls and gates had to be demolished. Between 1900 and 1940 the city's population increased tenfold, to 300,000, within an area of 2,347 acres. The Hispanic-American Exhibition of 1929 ● *87* ▲ *201* accentuated this phenomenon. Today Seville's 8,895 acres is home to over 700,000 inhabitants (one million, if the suburbs are included). Although the oldest part only occupies 9 percent of the city's total surface area, it is still the largest in Europe.

SEVILLE: FACTS AND FIGURES. Seville stands on the Río Guadalquivir, 50 miles from the Atlantic Ocean, at a latitude of 37°N and 5°W in the lower Guadalquivir valley. At its highest point, it is 56 feet above sea level. It has a Mediterranean climate with an oceanic influence, moderate temperatures (annual average 19°C), infrequent and irregular rainfall (annual average 20 inches) and high levels of sunshine (2,796 hours per year).

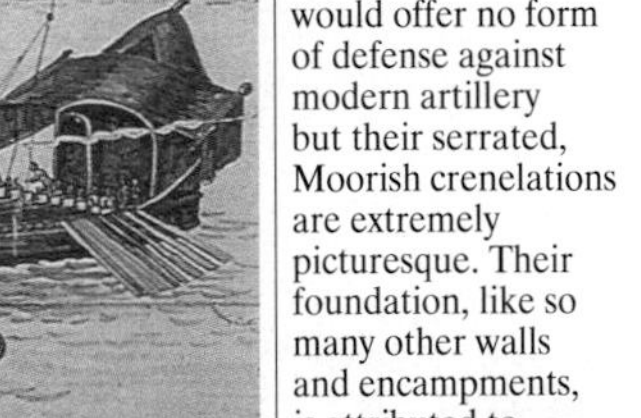

SEVILLE SEEN FROM TRIANA (1840)
From the end of the 18th century, the provincial capital was a source of great

fascination for travelers. Its Muslim past, artistic wealth, literary tradition, the hospitality of its inhabitants and its festivals attracted increasing numbers of tourists.

1. La Campana 2. Calle Sierpes 3. Iglesia de la Anunciación 4. Calle Cuna 5. Calle Tetuán 6. Iglesia del Salvador 7. Ayuntamiento 8. Avenida de la Constitución 9. Plaza Nueva 10. Calle H. Colón 11. Cathedral

◆ C B3-4, C3-5
◆ E C1-2, D2-5

THE HEART OF THE CITY

THE HEART OF THE CITY. For Sevillians, La Campana is the real heart of the city. Although not a plaza in the strict sense, it is the hub of the residential, commercial and business districts located to the south of the historic part of Seville. The city center lies on either side of a line running from La Campana, via the Calle Sierpes and the Avenida de la Constitución, to the cathedral and the Alcázar, through a maze of narrow streets that jealously guards the city's major sites and historic monuments.

LA CAMPANA AND THE PLAZA DEL DUQUE. These two adjacent areas form the "entrance" to the city center. La Campana was once the confectioners' district and still has a great many patisseries. It takes its name (meaning "bell") from its proximity to the fire station.

CALLE SIERPES ★. In the Middle Ages the Calle Sierpes was known as the Calle de los Armeros. It was renamed "Sierpes" in the 16th century after an inn sign depicting the jaws of a snake or, quite possibly, just because it was a winding street (*serpiente* means "snake"). It was famous for the legendary liveliness of its many cafés (for example, *Los Corales*, a favorite rendezvous for such celebrities as Juan Belmonte and El Gallo ▲ *173, 195*) and *casinos* (the Andalusian version of private clubs), some of which, such as the *Labradores* and *El Mercantil,* still exist. Today the Calle Sierpes is a narrow, winding pedestrian precinct, almost half a mile long. During shopping hours and in the late afternoon, its rather old-fashioned, typically Sevillian animation makes it an ideal place to feel the pulse of life in the Andalusian capital. This narrow, busy street, with its wider intersections, is bordered by

PLAZA DEL DUQUE
In the Middle Ages, the mansions built by the powerful Duke of Medina Sidonia made the plaza one of the focal points of the city. They have been replaced by buildings occupied by department stores. A statue of Velázquez ● *91* by Antonio Susillo stands in the center of the plaza.

Velas (awnings) above the Calle Sierpes.

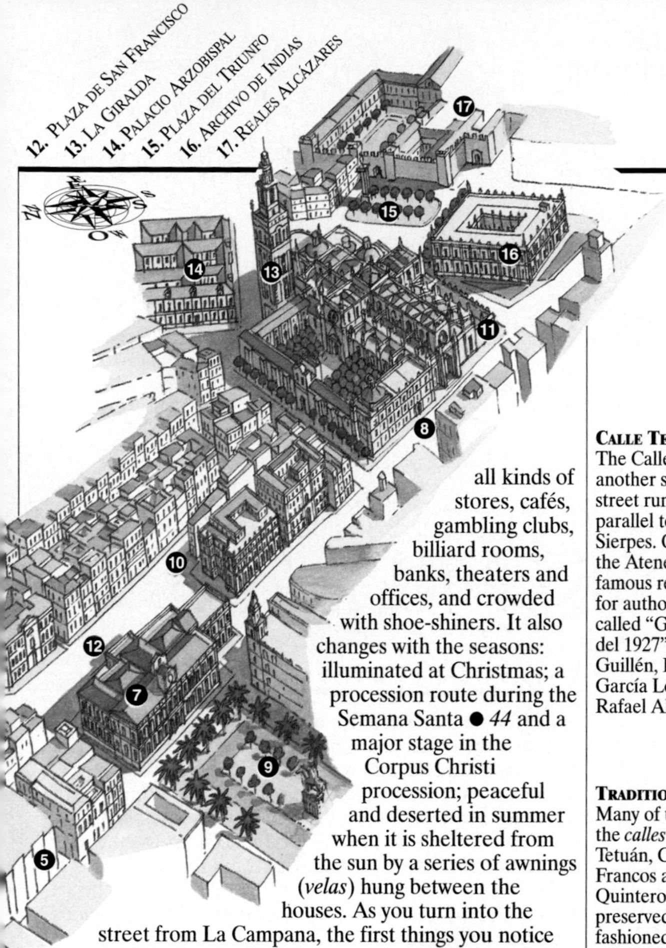

12. Plaza de San Francisco
13. La Giralda
14. Palacio Arzobispal
15. Plaza del Triunfo
16. Archivo de Indias
17. Reales Alcázares

all kinds of stores, cafés, gambling clubs, billiard rooms, banks, theaters and offices, and crowded with shoe-shiners. It also changes with the seasons: illuminated at Christmas; a procession route during the Semana Santa ● *44* and a major stage in the Corpus Christi procession; peaceful and deserted in summer when it is sheltered from the sun by a series of awnings (*velas*) hung between the houses. As you turn into the street from La Campana, the first things you notice are the Cronómetro (housing an amazing collection of clocks), and the huge verandahs of the *casinos* where members can sit and watch what is going on in the street. After the *calles* Cerrajería and Rioja, you come to the San José intersection and the Chapel of San José, a tiny jewel of Baroque architecture begun in 1699. Its double entrance is decorated with terracotta sculptures and *azulejos*, while its richly decorated interior includes a *retablo* signed by two Sevillian masters, Cayetano de Acosta and Pedro Duque Cornejo. The street opens onto the Plaza de San Francisco where, on the wall of the Hispanic-American bank, a faience plaque marks the site of the royal prison which was so often evoked in picaresque literature. Its inmates included Mateo Alemán and, in 1597, Miguel de Cervantes. Cervantes is said to have been inspired to write *Don Quixote* while incarcerated in this place, and indeed, in his preface to the reader, the author describes his work as "engendered in some dismal prison, where wretchedness keeps its residence, and every dismal sound its habitation".

Calle Tetuán
The Calle Tetuán is another shopping street running parallel to the Calle Sierpes. On it stands the Ateneo, once a famous rendezvous for authors of the so-called "Generación del 1927": Jorge Guillén, Federico García Lorca and Rafael Alberti ▲ *304*.

Traditional stores
Many of the stores on the *calles* Sierpes, Tetuán, Cuna, Francos and Alvarez Quintero have preserved the old-fashioned charm of the stores of yesteryear. The flower-sellers at the San José intersection on the Calle Sierpes set the tone.

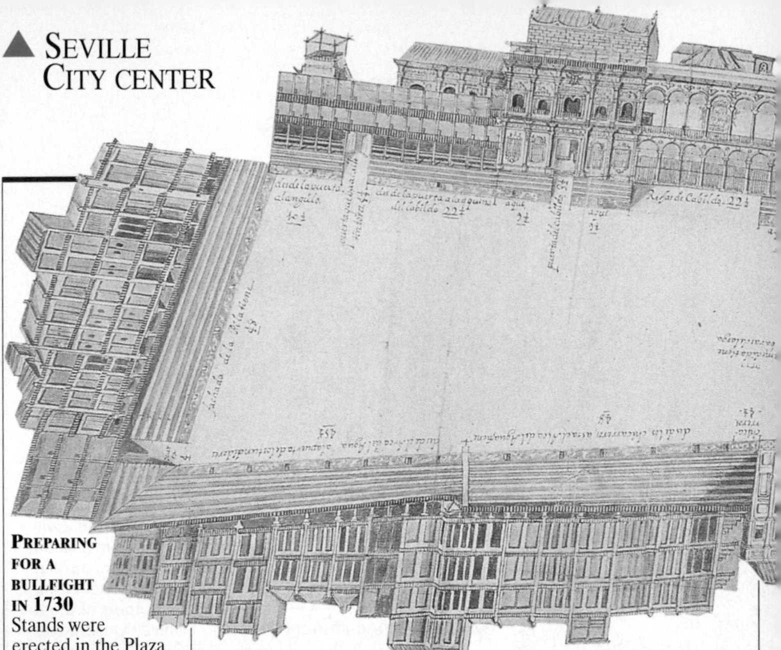

PREPARING FOR A BULLFIGHT IN 1730
Stands were erected in the Plaza de San Francisco and balconies and platforms were decorated with hangings. The main stands, including the official stands, were installed along the arcades of the town hall (top). The law courts can be seen (bottom right) opposite the tribunal. Philip II, Philip V and Isabel II entered Seville via the plaza. In 1560, fifty-one executions were held here, by order of the Inquisition. In 1634 Juan de Benavides, commander-in-chief of the new Spanish fleet, was executed in the plaza, as was the bandit Veneno in 1832. Today it is decorated for the annual Semana Santa and Corpus Christi ● *44* processions.

PLAZA DE SAN FRANCISCO ★

The Plaza de San Francisco, otherwise known as the Plaza Mayor, is the oldest plaza in Seville. Its architecture, general atmosphere and the different views that it offers of the city also make it one of the most attractive. It took its name from the monastery built on one side of it in the second half of the 13th century. Described in the 16th century as "the most public plaza in Seville", it was already the site of the town hall and several tribunals, and the venue for all kinds of official ceremonies: processions, receptions, tournaments, religious trials and executions.

AUDIENCIA. This former tribunal building became a royal court in 1250. It was replaced in 1597 by a new edifice which underwent a series of modifications and today houses a bank. Its courtyard, surrounded by an arcature whose severity is reminiscent of the Castilian Renaissance style, often provides the setting for exhibitions.

AYUNTAMIENTO ★. The building that stands between the Plaza de San Francisco and the Plaza Nueva has been the seat of the municipal authorities since the 16th century ● *72*. After the Reconquest a council of "twenty-four knights", all honorable "Sevillians of rank and property", sat in premises near the cathedral. With the marriage of the Emperor Charles V in 1526, they decided to build council chambers worthy of their function in the vicinity

PLAZA MAYOR AND LA GIRALDA
Photograph of the Plaza Mayor in the 19th century, when it was still bordered by houses with long balconies, and arcades with goldsmiths' and silversmiths' stores.

of the monastery of San Francisco. Diego de Riaño designed the houses and began their construction, which continued until 1572, with the help of a number of brilliant craftsmen and artists. Although completed much later, the façade overlooking the plaza and the Renaissance-style south wing of the edifice date from this period. During the second half of the 19th century, the main neoclassical façade of the Plaza Nueva was added to the building. The oldest rooms, the SALA DEL APEADERO ("halt") and the SALA DEL ARQUILLO ("little bow"), are decorated with allegories of the city and the monarchy. The remarkable cut stonework in the Sala del Apeadero is a harmonious blend of late Gothic and early Renaissance styles. The room opens onto the SALA CAPITULAR BAJA (lower chapterhouse) surmounted by a coffered vault carved with effigies of the kings of Spain. \A staircase with a finely carved dome leads to the SALA CAPITULAR ALTA (upper chapterhouse) where historic exhibits, including the city's banner, the chapter's silver maces and paintings, are on display.

MERCURIO
Bronze statue (1576) on the fountain in Plaza de San Francisco.

According to the Romans, Mercury protected trade, thieves and travelers.

PLAZA NUEVA, OR PLAZA DE SAN FERNANDO. This vast plaza was opened in 1852 on the site of the former building of the Franciscan Casa Grande, which was demolished after the confiscation of clerical wealth by the State. The MONUMENT TO SAN FERNANDO shows King Ferdinand accompanied by other heroes of the Conquest of Seville.

AVENIDA DE LA CONSTITUCION. The city center's main thoroughfare runs between the town hall and the cathedral, through what was formerly a residential district for Genoese immigrants. It still has some fine architectural examples of Sevillian regionalism ● *86*.

CATHEDRAL AND LA GIRALDA ★

FROM MOSQUE TO CATHEDRAL. In the 12th century Seville became the Almohad capital of El-Andalus ● *31*. Abu Yacub Yusuf, the second caliph of the Moroccan dynasty established in the city, ordered a huge mosque to be built next to what is today known as the Alcázar (from *al-qasr*, meaning "fortress") ▲ *142*. Work began in 1172 under the direction of Ahmed Ibn Baso, an architect from Toledo, and the first prayers were offered ten years later. The minaret was not completed until 1198. The mosque, known as Dhema Mukyarrim, was in every way superior to the principal mosque of the Almohad capital of Marrakesh. In 1248, following the Conquest of Seville by Ferdinand III ● *32*, the Islamic edifice became a place of Catholic worship and was renamed the Iglesia de Santa María la Mayor. It was used as a cathedral until the 15th century.

THE CATHEDRAL AND LA GIRALDA, SYMBOLS OF A DUAL CITY ✪
Europe's largest Gothic cathedral is more impressive for the extraordinary works of art it contains than for its size. After lingering in front of the world's biggest reredos, make sure to climb La Giralda for its exquisite views over the city. The best place to admire this former minaret of the Almohad Great Mosque, Seville's emblematic colossus, is from the Patio de Banderas in the Alcázar.

PATIO DE LOS NARANJOS. The visit starts in the Patio de los Naranjos ("courtyard of orange trees"), where the ritual ablutions were performed. The courtyard forms the main body of the largest surviving Moorish building and is surrounded by a crenelated wall in which the PUERTA DEL PERDÓN ("pardon"), with its bronze door-knockers and door panels, is a masterpiece of Almohad art. It is decorated with 880 hand-carved Koranic inscriptions, as well as sculpted Renaissance elements which were added in c. 1520. A Roman fountain and basin stand in the center of the courtyard, which is still planted with orange trees. The side galleries, decorated with wrought-iron arcatures, house a library (BIBLIOTECA CAPITULAR Y COLOMBINA) and chapel (CAPILLA DE LA VIRGEN DE LA GRANADA), the only surviving section of the cathedral-mosque. The PUERTA DEL LAGARTO ("lizard"), surmounted by a vault bearing a replica of a crocodile (which was a gift from the Sultan of Egypt to Alfonso X ● *32*), leads to the cathedral and La Giralda.

LA GIRALDA ● *68*, *72***.** The characteristic outline of La Giralda has become the very emblem of Seville, and was acclaimed as such by Alexandre Dumas in *De Paris à Cadix*. The tower was in fact the minaret of the Great Mosque, built between 1184 and 1198 by Ibn Baso and the North-African architect, Ali de Gomara. Along with the Kutubiyya tower in Marrakesh and the Hassan tower in Rabat, La Giralda belongs to a group of towers known as the "Three Sisters", built during the same period and in the same architectural style. The 250-foot minaret was surmounted by four large golden spheres, sculpted by Abu Layz (the Sicilian) and visible for a distance of 25 miles. They were destroyed by an earthquake in 1356. A second major modification, between 1558 and 1568, added a bell tower above the turret, which brought the overall height of the tower to almost 312 feet. The master of works was the Cordovan architect Hernán Ruiz the Younger (1500–69), who

FROM MINARET TO BELL TOWER
La Giralda in its original form (bottom, far right) and surmounted by the Renaissance bell tower (above), built in 1558. A staircase was added to the famous thirty-five ramps, intersected by landings, that gave access (even on horseback) to the top of the tower, from where there is an unparalleled view of the city.

Seal of the Church of Seville.

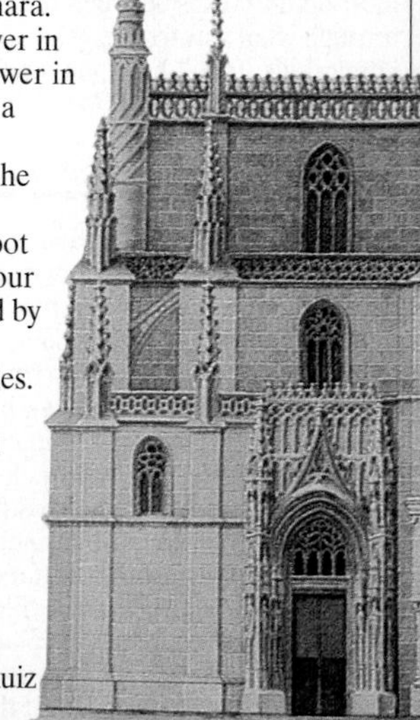

"Florence has its ancient palaces, Pisa its Campo Santo, Naples has Herculanum and Pompeii, Granada the Alhambra, Córdoba its Mosque and Seville La Giralda."
Alexandre Dumas

gave the tower its present appearance and called it "La Giralda" after the (1.3-ton) bronze weather vane in the form of a figure of Faith ("Giraldillo") on its summit.

Cathedral. At the beginning of the 15th century the church of Santa María la Mayor was in such a poor state of repair that in 1401 the Chapter decided to build a new, and truly exceptional, cathedral. The construction of the largest Gothic church in Christendom lasted from 1402 to 1509. Because of the vastness of the site and the use of freestone (commonly found in Gothic architecture but an unfamiliar material in a region which favored brick), it was decided to use Castilian, French, Flemish and German craftsmen and to bring the stone from Cádiz and Portugal. Certain sections were left unfinished and the entire structure was not completed until the 20th century.

At ground level, the cathedral proper covers an area of 127 x 83 yards. Its five naves lie along an east–west axis, while its chapels, which are built against the exterior wall of the cathedral, give it the characteristic horizontality of late Gothic architecture. Sixty pillars support the elevation of the central nave, which reaches a maximum height of 130 feet below the vault of the transept.

Stained-glass windows. The first glazed panels were set in the central nave in 1428, under the direction of the Alsatian Henri Allemand. The stained-glass windows depicting scenes from the Old and New Testaments were installed a hundred years later, and are one of Europe's richest collections.

A tripartite complex
The sanctuary covers an area of 175 x 155 yards and consists of three buildings: the cathedral, La Giralda and the Patio de los Naranjos.

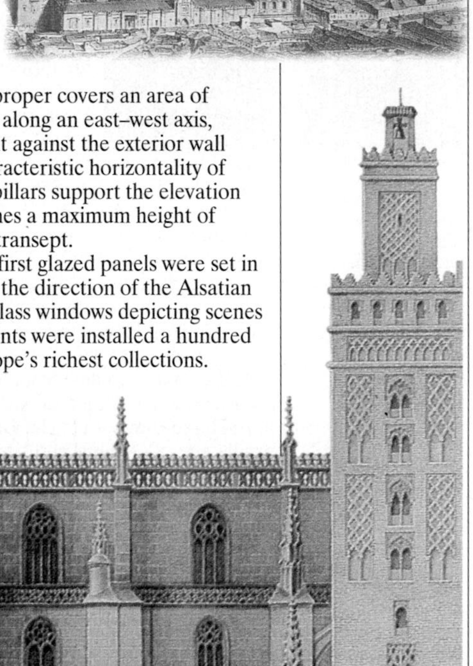

Merchants cast out from the temple
Bas-relief (1519–20), by Miguel Florentín, on the Puerta del Perdón, in the Patio de los Naranjos, where trade used to take place.

Capilla Mayor
Opposite the choir stalls of the cathedral, the chapel houses a reredos 65 feet high and 59 feet wide. This masterpiece of flamboyant Gothic art, begun by the Fleming Pieter Dancart in 1482, was completed in 1564. Dedicated to the Christ of the Million and the Virgin of the See, it consists of 44 raised gilt panels.

Tomb of Columbus
The kings of Castile, Aragon, Leon and Navarra carry the explorer's coffin ● *36* ▲ *283*, brought back from Cuba in 1899 (above, right) and placed in front of the cathedral's south door.

Above the grilles of the Capilla Real (1773), the Moor Axataf surrenders the keys of the city to Ferdinand III ● *32*.

The chapels. Beyond the Puerta del Lagarto ("lizard") is a series of chapels rich in the heritage of the religious art of the 15th, 16th and 17th centuries. Near the apse the Capilla de San Pedro (Saint Peter) houses works by Zurbarán ▲ *158*, whose famous *retablo* (1625) relates the life of Saint Peter, and paintings by Juan de Valdés Leal: *Saint Mary Magdalene* and *Saint Martha*. The lighter and more richly decorated Capilla Real ★ (royal chapel) to the south is markedly Renaissance in style. Martín de Gaínza drew up the plans in 1551 and worked on it from 1553, though was soon taken over by Hernán Ruiz the Younger ▲ *239*, then by Juan de Maeda, who finished it in 1575. It contains the tombs of Ferdinand III, his wife Beatrix and his son Alfonso X. On its altar is a 13th-century *Virgen de los Reyes*, showing a seated Virgin granting her patronage to the kings. The adjoining Sala de Juntas (council chamber) contains the relics of Ferdinand III (the Saint). Three chapels

in the left island deserve close attention. The Capilla de Santiago (Saint James) in the north wing, the first of three remarkable chapels, contains the early 15th-century alabaster tomb of the archbishop Gonzalo de Mena. The second, the Capilla de Scalas, has an Italian marble altarpiece (1539) and a glazed terracotta Virgin from the studio of the Florentine sculptor, Andrea della Robia. The third chapel, the Capilla de San Antonio (Saint Anthony), houses Murillo's ● *91*, ▲ *138*, *182* masterpiece, *La Visión de San Antonio* (1656). The choir has 117 stalls in costly woods in the Gothic-Mudéjar style, completed in 1478 by the sculptor Nufro Sánchez, as well as jasper porticos, four sculpted alabaster shrines and two elaborately decorated Baroque organs (1725). Finally there are two chapels in the right aisle that are well worth a visit. The Capilla de la Virgen de la Antigua takes its name from the 14th-century painting that hangs there. The Virgin of Antigua, one of the patron saints of El Descubrimiento ("The Discovery"), was worshiped in Seville after Columbus had landed on the island of Antigua, in the Antilles. The chapel also houses the marble tomb of Archbishop Hurtado de Mendoza (1509) by Doménico Fancelli, and the high altar by Pedro Duque Cornejo (1740). The Capilla de San Hermenegildo contains the terracotta tomb (1485) of Archbishop Juan de Cervantes.

Gothic portals
The cathedral's carved portals, which are decorated with terracotta statues (1464–7) by Lorenzo Mercadente de Bretaña, date from the 15th and 16th centuries. The east portals are known as the Puerta de las Campanillas ("small bells") and the Puerta des los Bastones ("staffs"), and the west portals as the Puerta del Nacimiento (Nativity), or de San Miguel (Saint Michael), and the Puerta del Baptisterio (Baptism).

Sacristies and chapterhouse. The Renaissance-style rooms built along the south wall today house important art collections. Constructed between 1529 and 1543 by the architects Diego de Riaño and Martín de Gaínza, the Sacristía Mayor (main sacristy) contains the treasury of the cathedral, including a reliquary, the so-called Tablas Alfonsíes, presented by Alfonso X (1824), an imposing silver monstrance created by Juan de Arfe (1580-87), and works by Pedro Campaña, Zurbarán and Murillo. The Sacristía de los Cálices (chalice sacristy), built between 1509 and 1537, also contains valuable religious objects. The Sala Capitular (chapterhouse) was completed in 1591 by Juan de Minjares with the aid of various sculptors, according to plans by Hernán Ruiz the Younger. Beneath the dome hangs an *Immaculate Conception* by Murillo. Its antechamber (Anticabildo) is lined with hymn books and miniature manuscripts.

Iglesia del Sagrario. The Iglesia del Sagrario ("Church of the Tabernacle"), which was designed by Miguel de Zumárraga, Alonso de Vandelvira and Cristóbal de Rojas, lies on the west side of the Patio de los Naranjos. Work on the building began in 1618 and continued for the next forty-four years. As its name suggests, the Iglesia de Sagramento (now a parish church) was once the shrine of the cathedral, to which it is still connected. The edifice is characteristic of early Baroque architecture, and each element within its vast interior exudes grandeur, from the statues of the Evangelists and the Fathers of the Church (by José de Arce) above the galleries to the *retablo mayor*, a beautiful *Descent from the Cross* by Pedro Roldán (1624–99) ● *48*, ▲ *189*.

Sala Capitular
The Sala Capitular is elliptical in design. It was based on Michelangelo's plans for the Capitole in Rome.

Seville's cathedral houses a unique collection of paintings and sculptures, as well as some fine examples of decorative and applied arts. To this treasury is added that of the cathedral archives and the Biblioteca Capitular y Colombina, which contain a priceless collection of manuscripts and printed books.

ARCHBISHOP'S CHALICE
by Damián de Castro (c. 1777) for Delgado y Venegas.

"SAN ISIDORO" ● *31* ▲ *128*
The cathedral contains a remarkable collection of works by the Sevillian artist Bartolomé Estebán Murillo (1618–82) ● *91*.

"SAN LEANDRO"
"San Leandro" and "San Isidoro" form a diptych of the patron saints of Hispalis, the learned Visigoth bishops. Oil on canvas (1655).

EARLY 19TH-CENTURY SILK AND GOLD CHASUBLE
The cathedral's extensive collection of sumptuous embroidery and lace comprises over three thousand items that date from the 14th to the 19th centuries.

"SANTA JUSTA Y SANTA RUFINA"
This painting (1553–5) by Hernando de Esturmio (c. 1515–56), a Flemish artist living in Seville, not only reveals the influence of Raphaël, but is also a fine example of Renaissance esthetic principles. The two patron saints ▲ *128* were martyred at the foot of La Giralda.

“Santa Teresa de Jesús”
This painting (c. 1650) by Francisco de Zurbarán is in the Sacristía Mayor. Zurbarán, a native of Fuente de Cantos, went to Seville as a young man where he studied and made a career of painting for churches and convents.

Biblioteca Capitular y Colombina ▲ *134*
Hernando Colón (1488–1539), the library’s founder, was the son of Christopher Columbus. He traveled with his father to the Indies and, later, with Charles V to Italy, Flanders and Germany. He also visited Africa and Asia. From these voyages he brought back over twenty thousand books to Seville, where he had chosen to live, and subsequently bequeathed them to the city.

“Privilegio rodado”
A privilege or “freedom” granted by Henry III in 1317. It is part of the large collection of illuminated manuscripts preserved in the cathedral archives, the Archivo de la Catedral de Sevilla.

“Santa Justa y Santa Rufina»
Oil on canvas by Francisco de Goya (1817) ▲ *159*.

“Cristo de la Clemencia”
The *Cristo de la Clemencia* (also known as the *Cristo de los Cálices* because it hangs in the Chalice Sacristy) was created in 1603 by Juan Martínez Montañéz (1568–1649), who was nicknamed “El Dios de la Madera” (“the god of wood sculpture”) ● *48*. The design, expressiveness, relief and exquisite polychromy of this masterly figure, over 6 feet high, have earned it the reputation of being the best sculpture of Christ Crucified in Spanish Baroque art.

La Custodia Grande
The 13-foot custodial, used during the Corpus Christi festival, was engraved in 1587 by Juan de Arfe (1535–1602). It took 990 lbs of American silver. Its decoration represents the exultant triumphialism of the Catholic Church.

AROUND THE CATHEDRAL

APPROACHES TO THE CATHEDRAL. Streets lead from all directions to the area of monuments and stores formed around the cathedral by the Calle Alemanes, the Avenida de la Constitución, the Plaza de la Virgen de los Reyes and the Plaza del Triunfo. This constitutes Seville's major tourist district and is also one of the best places to see the Semana Santa, Corpus Christi and Virgen de los Reyes ● *44, 49* processions. In the late 12th century the district enjoyed a period of intense commercial activity when the Almohads constructed a covered market selling valuable merchandise near the newly built Great Mosque. This *alcaicería* ("silk merchants' district") extended between the cathedral and the Plaza de San Francisco along the line of what is now the Calle Hernando Colón. This commercial activity has been continued by the businesses in these same, and the adjoining, streets (mainly Argote de Molina, Francos and Alvarez Quintero), where the most characterful and traditional stores are found.

VASE OF LILIES
View from La Giralda toward the Plaza de San Francisco. The vase of lilies symbolizes the Church of Seville.

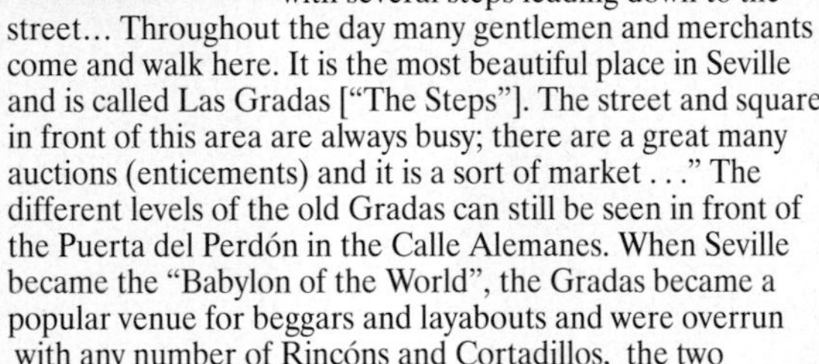

Scenes of everyday life in the galleries of the Calle Alemanes.

LAS GRADAS AND THE CALLE ALEMANES. Open-air trading was also conducted near the cathedral, on makeshift stalls or on the steps, as described by the Venetian ambassador, Andrea Navagero, in 1526: "All around the edifice, around the church and cloister and in front of the façades, is a fairly wide area of marble paving, closed off by chains, with several steps leading down to the street… Throughout the day many gentlemen and merchants come and walk here. It is the most beautiful place in Seville and is called Las Gradas ["The Steps"]. The street and square in front of this area are always busy; there are a great many auctions (enticements) and it is a sort of market . . ." The different levels of the old Gradas can still be seen in front of the Puerta del Perdón in the Calle Alemanes. When Seville became the "Babylon of the World", the Gradas became a popular venue for beggars and layabouts and were overrun with any number of Rincóns and Cortadillos, the two heros of Cervantes ● *103*.

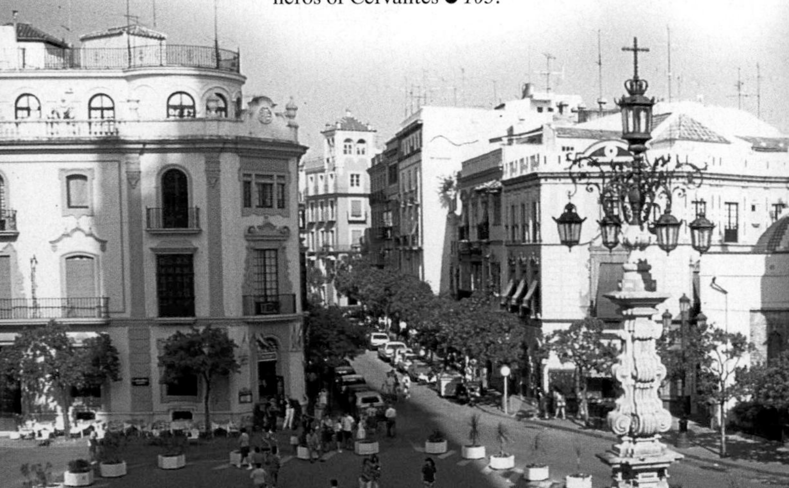

"Behind the cathedral, the red Baroque façade of the Archbishop's Palace would appear to be the perfect setting for the final act of *Don Juan*."

Arturo Uslar Pietri

Façade of the Palacio Arzobispal
In 1251 Ferdinand III gave the first Bishop of Seville, Don Remondo, the land on which the Archbishop's Palace was built. It was constructed in several stages, acquiring its present form in the early 17th century. The monumental staircase was erected between 1663 and 1669, and the Baroque façade was completed in 1705.

Business (auctions, slave trading) was conducted on the steps, in the Patio de los Naranjos and even in the cathedral, if it was raining. This caused an outcry and was subsequently banned by the Church, which led to the construction of the Lonja de Mercaderes (Merchants' Exchange).

Plaza de la Virgen de los Reyes. The former Corral de los Olmos, which belonged to the Mosque and then the cathedral, became the venue for meetings of the ecclesiastical chapter and the municipal council. In 1790 the buildings occupying the courtyard were demolished and the plaza was opened up to create more space around La Giralda and the Palacio Arzobispal.

Palacio Arzobispal. The Archbishop's Palace houses Seville's third largest art gallery. Its collection of some three hundred paintings consists mainly of works from the 17th- and 18th-century Spanish, Italian and Dutch schools.

Plaza del Triunfo. The plaza services some of Seville's principal buildings, since "the essence of its history is concentrated between the cathedral, the Alcázar and the Casa Lonja, which contains the Archivo de Indias". *La Inmaculada*, a monument to the Immaculate Conception, stands in the center of the plaza and, on one side, a chapel commemorating the 1755 earthquake that devastated Andalusia.

The plaza de la Virgen de los Reyes in the 19th century.

The whitewashed façade and bell tower of the Convento de la Encarnación, on the southeastern edge of the Plaza de la Virgen de los Reyes.

The Alcázar is one of the highlights of Seville's civil architecture. Founded by the first caliphs, extended by their successors and transformed by the first Christian monarchs, it provides a perfect illustration of the synthetic art known as Mudéjar. The gardens that adorn the palace provide more proof of Andalusian genius.

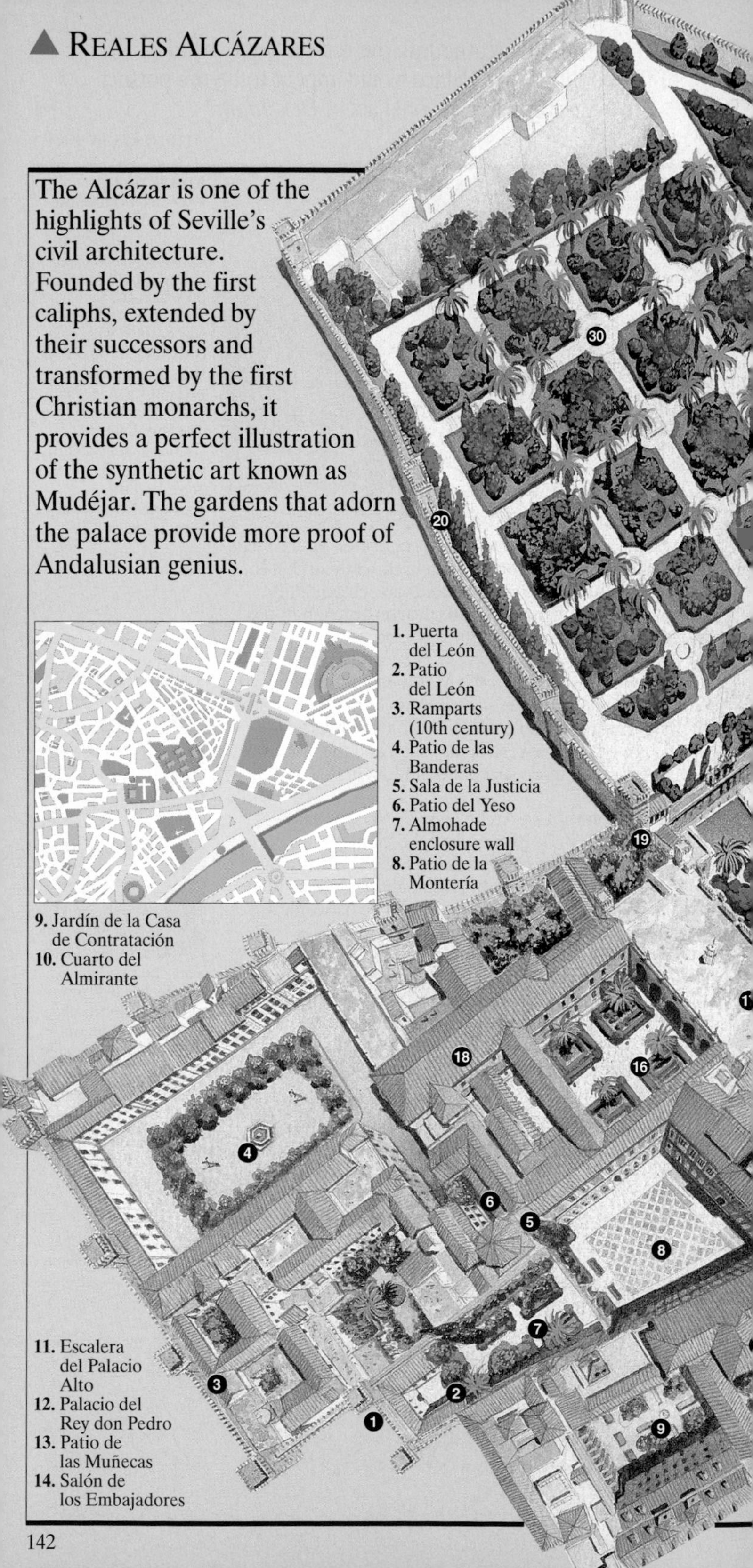

1. Puerta del León
2. Patio del León
3. Ramparts (10th century)
4. Patio de las Banderas
5. Sala de la Justicia
6. Patio del Yeso
7. Almohade enclosure wall
8. Patio de la Montería
9. Jardín de la Casa de Contratación
10. Cuarto del Almirante
11. Escalera del Palacio Alto
12. Palacio del Rey don Pedro
13. Patio de las Muñecas
14. Salón de los Embajadores

15. Patio de las Doncellas
16. Patio del Crucero
17. Palacio Gótico and Salas de las Bóvedas
18. Apeadero
19. Torre del Agua and Puerta de Marchena
20. Muralla del Callejón del Agua
21. Fuente de los Grutescos
22. Jardín de la Danza
23. Jardín de las Damas
24. Cenador de Carlos V
25. Cenador del León
26. Jardín Nuevo
27. Huerta de la Alcoba
28. Laberinto
29. Jardín de los Poetas
30. Huerta del Retiro

THE ALCAZAR, WHERE MOORISH HISTORY LIVES ON ✪
The jewel of Mudéjar art, the palace of Pedro the Cruel (Palacio del Rey don Pedro) is the most spectacular part of the Alcázar. The palace gardens, which are embellished with terraces, false grottos and elegant fountains, are an ideal place to spend a peaceful few hours far from the bustle of the city.

REALES ALCÁZARES ★

PUERTA DEL LEÓN
The main entrance of the Alcázar takes its name from the emblem of a lion on the panel of *azulejos* above the doorway.

The Alcázar, with its many palaces, gardens and outbuildings, occupies a vast fortified area at the southern end of Seville's historic center. For over one thousand years it has received governments and royalty and has distinguished itself from other royal palaces belonging to the Spanish Crown by the originality of its architecture. Moorish influences combine with Gothic, Renaissance and Baroque elements to make it a composite complex with a very particular charm, as is borne out by many literary and anecdotal accounts.

ALCÁZAR DE LA BÉNÉDICIÓN. The walls and towers that overlook the Plaza del Triunfo and the Alcázar's main entrance are its oldest surviving section. In 913 the Emir of Córdoba, Abd el-Rahman III, ordered a fortress to be built for the governor with a view to strengthening a power threatened by sporadic rebellions. The fortress occupied the site of what is now the Patio de Banderas, in the northeast corner of the current complex. The main entrance section around the Puerta del León was built under the Abbadids when, in the 11th century, they made Seville the capital of one of the most powerful *taifas* of El-Andalus ● *31*. The fortress became a palace protected by walls (*al-qasr*), around which adjacent areas intended to receive other structures were marked out. The poet-king El-Mu'tamid (1040–95) built the Palace of El-Mubarak (Alcázar de la Benedición, or "Palace of Benediction"), a theater of political intrigues and a literary salon. In the 12th century the Almohad caliphs built the Sala del Yeso near the entrance and began to extend the outer walls. The Alcázar became an elaborate complex of fortifications that extended as far as the banks of the river at the Torre del Oro ▲ *184* and overlooked the most vulnerable part of the city.

PATIO DEL YESO
Laid out in the late 12th century, this is a rare vestige of the Almohad palace. It has a splendid portico with openwork galleries and a fountain.

ROYAL PALACE. The victory of the Christian armies in 1243 did not alter the original functions of the palace in any way. Before he died there in 1252, Ferdinand III made it the residence of his royal court, as did his successors. The Seville residence of the kings of Spain for seven centuries, it underwent regular additions and restoration work, though the majority of the current buildings, such as the 14th-century Sala de la Justicia, a fine example of the purest Mudéjar style, date from the reign of Pedro the Cruel (1350–9).

ART COLLECTIONS
The rich collections of objets d'art and paintings housed in the Alcázar include this canvas of the Saint Ildefonso by Velázquez ● *48, 91*, from the municipal collection.

"As soon as you enter a place as a tourist, it ceases to exist as a place in its own right. It becomes a place to be visited."
François Weyergans

Patio de la Montería. The three arches set in the Almohad wall open onto the Patio de la Montería ("hunt"), overlooked by the impressive façade of the Palacio del Rey Don Pedro (Palace of King Pedro). The Casa de Contratacíon ● *36*, the office of the Crown which, from 1503 to 1717, managed relations with the New World, occupied the Cuarto del Almirante (Admiral's Room) on the right. All that remains of the outbuildings of this *casa del Océano* are a large hall hung with tapestries by Goya ▲ *139, 159* and paintings, the small Museo Romántico and the Sala de Audiencia and its chapel. In these two rooms Columbus, Vespucci and Magellan ● *101* ▲ *194* met the Catholic kings to develop plans for the voyage to the Indies ● *35*.

Palacio del Rey Don Pedro. This superb example of Mudéjar architecture is the principal building of the Alcázar. Built between 1364 and 1366 by craftsmen from Toledo, Granada and Seville, on the site and in the stead of the old Abbadid *alcázar* and surrounding palaces, the Palacio del Rey Don Pedro gave the Alcázar its present appearance. The inscriptions on the façade of the palace attest to the various cultural influences brought to bear over the years. Next to the motto of the Nasrid dynasty ("God alone is Conqueror"), inscribed on *azulejos* in Kufic script, is an epigraph in Gothic lettering dedicated to Pedro I, King of Castile and León, who commissioned the work.

Pedro, the Cruel or the Just ▲ *162*. The figure of Pedro I (1334–69) is closely linked to the history of Seville, where he established his court. Throughout a reign undermined by uprisings opposing royal authority, dynastic factions and the nobility, the Alcázar became the setting for his cruel sentences and amorous adventures. Pedro, who was finally assassinated by his half-brother, Henry II (the Magnificent), was known by his opponents as "the Cruel", but as "the Just" by his followers. One of the actions that earned him his notoriety was the assassination, on his order, of his brother Fadrique in the Sala de la Justicia of the Alcázar.

Private apartments. The richly decorated vestibule with columns with Visigoth capitals, its domes and its coffered ceilings bends round to open out onto the Patio de las Doncellas ("maidens"), the splendid central court of the palace's official quarters ▲ *146*. Crossing the Dormitorio de los Reyes Morors (the Moorish kings' bedroom) brings you to the small Patio de las Muñecas ("dolls"), subtly decorated with sculptured plasterwork. Around it are the royal apartments, of which the largest, to the north, has a beautiful coffered ceiling created in 1543. It is in this Cuarto del Príncipe (prince's room) that Isabelle the Catholic gave birth to her only son, Prince Juan, who died aged eighteen.

Public areas. Crossing the Dormitorio de Felipe II brings you to the Salón de Embajadores (ambassadors' room),

Cuarto del Almirante
Its chapel has a *Virgin of the Seafarers* painted by Alejo Fernández in 1536. It depicts the Virgin unfurling her protective cape over a flotilla and over a group of people including Charles V, Christopher Columbus ▲ *283* and some American Indians.

Patio de Banderas
Once troops were inspected in the Patio de Banderas ("flags"), the former parade ground of the Alcázar. It dates from the time of the original Muslim *alcázar* (9th and 10th centuries), when the rectangular fortress with its freestone walls and towers was built near the river, on the site of a former Roman forum and Visigoth basilica.

Façade of the Palacio del Rey Don Pedro
The façade overlooks the Patio de la Montería.

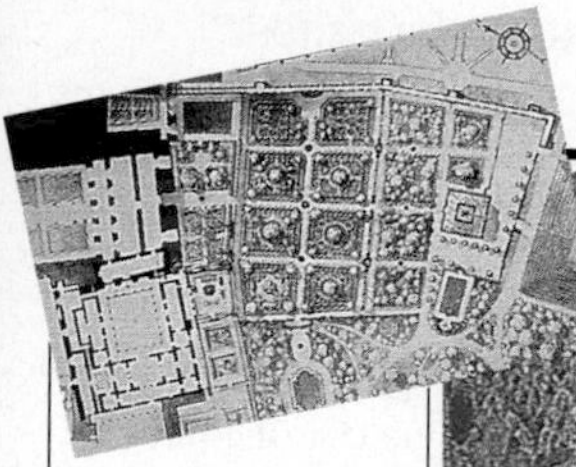

Plan of the gardens of the Alcázar.

PATIO DE LAS MUÑECAS
The arches, decorated with delicate stucco openwork, are supported by colored marble columns surmounted by Moorish capitals that were probably brought back from from Medina Azahara by El-Mu'tamid or his Almohad successors.

PATIO DE LAS DONCELLAS
The 14th-century Mudéjar Patio de las Doncellas includes Renaissance elements added in the 16th century: the upper gallery, columns and stucco motifs.

reception room of Pedro I's palace. The sumptuous salon stands on the site of the legendary throne room of the *Qasr-al-Mubarak*, a pavilion with a décor of heavenly constellations known as the Sala de las Pléyades, *El-Turayya*, and greatly extolled by the poets. Pedro I preserved the original structure and conserved the 10th-century galleries brought back from the Medina Azahara ▲ *234* by El-Mu'tamid. The Salón de los Embajadores was restored and reworked many times, most notably for the marriage of Charles V and Isabel of Portugal, which was celebrated in Seville in 1526. It owes its other name, Media-Naranja ("half-orange"), to its extraordinary wooden dome (1427), which has a frieze of royal portraits set in Gothic niches around its base. The walls of the room are covered with magnificent panels of *azulejos* and stucco decorations. The Patio de las Doncellas is one of the masterpieces of Mudéjar art, with its galleries with magnificent multifoil arcatures, its walls covered with *azulejos* and its stucco panels. The Genoese columns and the upper gallery with semicircular arches, Plateresque stuccowork and a tiled floor, date from a major renovation project carried out between 1540 and 1572. On the western side of the courtyard, the majestic ARCO DE LOS PAVONES ("arch of the

Salones de Carlos V
(seen from the Patio del Crucero) The apartments of Charles V are part of the Palacio Gótico (Gothic palace), built in the 13th century. They have been altered several times, most notably after the 1755 earthquake.

peacocks"), a triple Cordovan-style arcature decorated with gold stucco birds, leads to the Salón del Techo de Felipe II ("ceiling of Philip II") with its Renaissance coffered ceiling (1589–91).

Palacio Alto. The monumental staircase situated in one corner of the Patio de la Montería leads to the second story of the Palacio del Rey Don Pedro. This upper palace, where the Spanish royal family resides when in Seville, was renovated for the main part in the late 15th century and early 16th century. The Oratorio de los Reyes Católicos (oratory of the Catholic monarchs), the Cuarto de Don Pedro (bedroom of Pedro I) and the other royal apartments are fine examples of integrated architectural styles.

Patio del Crucero and Palacio Gótico

An 18th-century Baroque gallery links the Patio de la Montéria to the Patio del Crucero or Patio de Maria de Padilla, named after Pedro I's mistress. Dating back to the Almohad era, it has raised alleys in the shape of a cross evoking the four rivers of life that flow in the gardens of Islamic Paradise. It is part of the Palacio Gótico built by Alfonso X (1221–84, known as Alfonso the Wise). It was here that, under the direction of this enlightened monarch, a group of Christian, Muslim and Jewish scholars developed such major works as *Songs to the Virgin* and the *Book of Chess, Dice and Backgammon*. The palace, into which Pedro the Cruel's mistress moved in the 14th century, owes its current name (Salones de Carlos V) to the modifications carried out under Charles V. It has some admirable *azulejos* painted by Cristóbal de Augusta between 1577 and 1583 and some fine tapestries depicting the conquest of Tunisia by the emperor in 1535 ▲ *148*.

The gardens. The Palacio Gótico opens onto the Jardín del Estanque y de los Grutescos ("pool and grotesques") with its Mannerist-style gallery created in 1612 by the Milanese artist Vermondo Resta. Alongside the palace the orderly flower beds of the Moorish gardens (de la Danza, de Troya, de la Galera and de las Flores) create a peaceful oasis. A vaulted gallery links the Jardín de la Danza to the Baños de Doña Maria de Padilla, beneath the Patio del Crucero. Further on are the 16th- and 17th-century tunnels of Charles V and Léon, a maze, the Jardín Nuevo ("new garden"), and, beyond the "gallery of the grotesques", the Huerta del Retiro, an ancient kitchen garden restructured by Alfonso XIII. Coming out of the gardens, you cross the Apeadero, a vast 17th-century room, then the Patio de Banderas to get to the exit.

Royal apartments
The rooms constituting the so-called Dormitorio de los Reyes Moros (bedroom of the Moorish Kings) open onto the Patio de las Doncellas. They used to include the royal bedchamber and summer apartments. They are decorated with superb *azulejos*, flooring, stuccowork and coffered ceilings.

Cenador de Carlos V
The Cenador de Carlos V is a pavilion (1543) combining classical and Mudéjar architectural styles.

Huerta del Retiro
The Huerta (market garden) del Retiro, the back of the Fuente de los Grutescos and the Torre del Enlace.

The first of the Salones de Carlos V in the Alcázar contains a series of twelve Flemish tapestries recording the Emperor's Tunis Expedition of 1535. Their quality of manufacture and narrative realism, combined with an innovative style introduced at the height of the Renaissance, make them a masterpiece in the art of court tapestry.

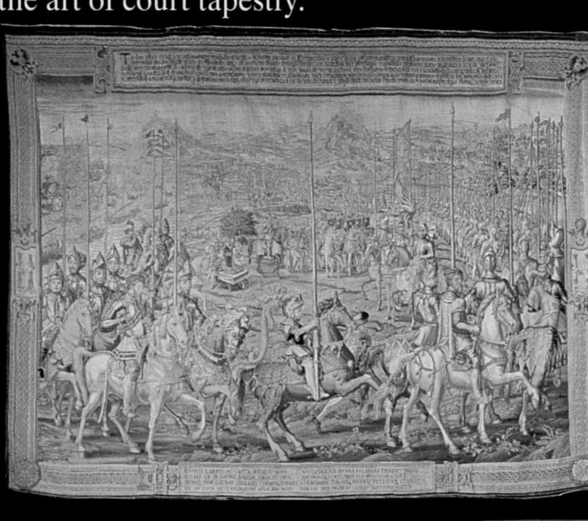

The tapestries were commissioned in 1546 by Maria of Hungary, governor of the Netherlands, to commemorate her brother's victorious expedition. They were drawn by Jan Vermeyen, in collaboration with Pieter Van Aelst, and woven by Willem Pannemaker.

PREPARING FOR WAR Tapestry (left) showing the Emperor inspecting his troops in Barcelona, before setting sail for Africa.

"The city's main sights, the ones that everyone visits, are the Alcázar, the cathedral and Pilate's House."

Alexandre Dumas

Charles V is depicted as an heroic warrior, surrounded by gentlemen and knights, inspecting the regular regiments of Spanish infantry and the German and Italian detachments that took part in the Tunis Expedition.

Military map
Tapestry (below) depicting the map of the Mediterranean coast of Europe, from where the military and naval forces of Charles V set sail, and the part of Africa where they pitched camp.
The inverse of current cartographic convention, the orientation of the map shows south at the top. The armies sailed round the Iberian peninsula toward Barbary. Next to the small poster is the portrait of the Flemish artist Jan Vermeyen (known as Barbalunga), who drew the cartoons for the tapestries.

By land and sea
Tapestry (above) showing the attack upon the fortress of Goletta after the imperial armies had landed near the ancient city of Carthage. Galleys, galleons, carracks and caravels supported the land attack that opened the way to Tunis, the last position of the Barbary chieftain, Barbarossa. The use of the new technique of perspective in the tapestries in this collection marked the definitive adoption of the canons of the Renaissance in this field. The series is completed by various views of the capture and sack of Tunis, which was placed in the hands of Moulay Hassan, the Emperor's vassal.

Self-portrait
Another tapestry shows Vermeyen making sketches from real life (above), accompanied by his assistant Van Aelst. This collection of tapestries was first exhibited in London in 1554, on the occasion of the marriage of Prince Philip, heir to the Spanish crown, and Queen Mary Tudor. The first of the many reproductions made was in Granadan silk and Milanese gold thread. The original tapestries became worn and in 1740 were replaced by the silk and wool copies on display today.

SPECIAL JURISDICTION Chains, like those of the nearby cathedral, outline the area which came under the special jurisdiction of the consulate of the merchants of Seville. The area adjoining the building was known at the time as the Plaza de la Lonja.

GREAT STAIRWAY The magnificent stairway of the Archivo de Indias was built (1614–27) by Miguel de Zumárraga. During the renovations of 1785, under the direction of Lucas Cintora, it was covered with pink- and gray-veined marble (jasper) quarried at Morón de la Frontera, a district of Seville.

In the upper-story rooms is a library with mahogany and cedarwood shelves made in 1788 by Blas Mölner. A number of plans and drawings are on display in the reading rooms.

LA CASA LONJA (ARCHIVO DE INDIAS)

The cathedral ▲ *133*, Alcázar ▲ *142* and Casa Lonja, housing the Archivo de Indias, form the monumental core of Seville.

A LATE-RENAISSANCE MASTERPIECE. The sober and severe design of the Casa Lonja was the work of Juan de Herrera (1530–97), a humanist intellectual who oversaw, in collaboration with Juan Bautista, the building of the Monastery of Escorial near Madrid, and who was the most important representative of Spanish Renaissance architecture. Herrera, assisted by Francisco de Mora and Asensio de Maeda, merely drew up the plans (for which he received 1,000 ducats), entrusting the actual construction of the Lonja to a group of craftsmen, including Juan de Minjares, Alonso de Vandelvira, Miguel

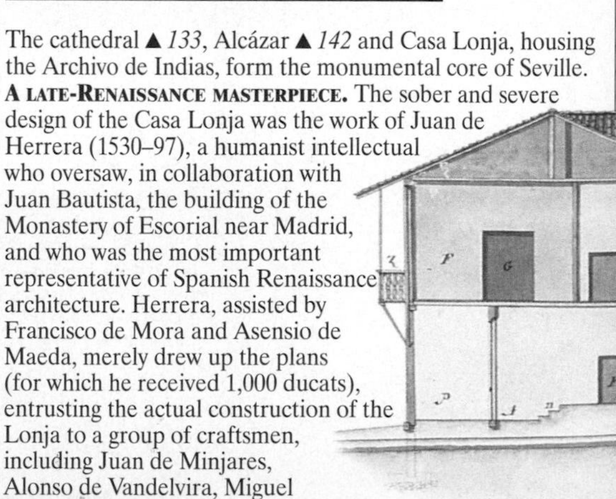

"Scholars from all over the world come here to research, sift through documents and secretly play the detective, for everything is classified in these files, according to colony and historical period."
Cees Nooteboom

de Zumárraga, Marcos Soto, Juan Bernal and Pedro Sánchez Falconete. Work began in 1583 and lasted until 1646. In 1785 Félix Carazas and Lucas Cintora (a man of the Enlightenment and a member of the Seville Academy) undertook renovation work in order to preserve documents.

A COMMERCIAL CENTER. During the 16th century Seville became a successful commercial center and attracted large numbers of merchants who established specialist guilds. The largest of these was the guild of merchants and shipping agents involved in trade with the West Indies. Its members formed the "Universidad de Mercaderes" which, from 1543, had its own *consulado* (consulate) responsible for protecting the group's interests. In the absence of suitable premises in which to conduct their business and hold meetings, it established itself in the Lonja, which became the symbol of Sevillian trade. With the commercial decline of the 17th century, the consulate left the Lonja which, between 1660 and 1674, housed the Academy of Art established by Esteban Murillo ● *91*, ▲ *138, 182*. In the 17th century it was also used as living accommodation for local people.

CREATION OF THE ARCHIVES. In response to the critical attacks leveled against Spain by the Scotsman William Roberts and the Frenchman Abbé Raynal in their respective histories of the Indies (1770 and 1774), the ministers of Charles III decided to publish more favorable texts. But to do this, they had to gather together the countless and widely dispersed documents of the various institutions of the Spanish "overseas Empire". This led to the creation of the Archivo General de Indias, housed in the Casa Lonja. The first cartloads of documents arrived in 1785, as work to refurbish the building was getting underway, and the Archives of the Indies have continued to be extended until very recently. They constitute the most extensive collection of information on America and the Pacific between the 16th and the 19th centuries ● *34, 36*.

A cross of allegiance near the Casa Lonja symbolizes the good faith of its commercial transactions.

EXPLORERS' ACCOUNTS
Account by Juan Sebastián Elcano (1476–1526), who took part in the first voyage around the world (1519–22).

Storm scene during Manuel Pando's expedition to Tierra del Fuego and Patagonia in 1769 (above). Naguinoui Indian from New Zealand (left). Plan for a tobacco factory in Guayaquil, Ecuador (1778) (below).

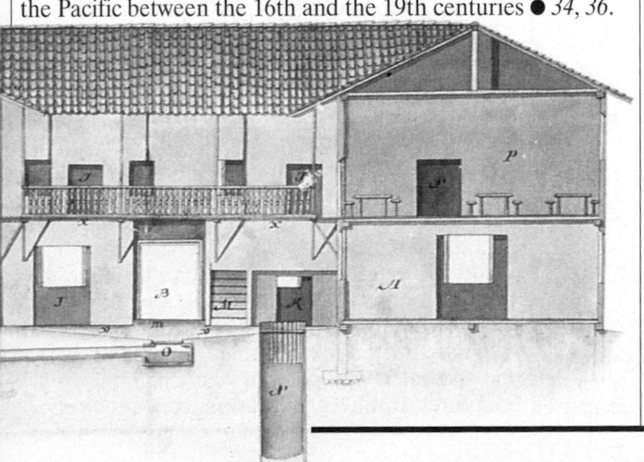

THE MEMORY BANK OF THE WORLD
The stone and brick treasury of the Archivo de Indias contains over seven thousand maps, plans and drawings, and ninety million pages, stored in forty-three thousand files, on more than 5½ miles of shelving.

1. Calle Abades
2. La Giralda
3. Reales Alcázares
4. Hospital de los Venerables
5. Iglesia de Santa Cruz
6. Jardines de Murillo
7. Monumento a Colón
8. Iglesia de Santa María la Blanca
9. Iglesia de San Bartolomé
10. Iglesia de San José

◆ C B3, C3-4
◆ E C1-2, D1-4, E1-4, F1-5

HISTORIC DISTRICTS OF SEVILLE

This itinerary starts at the foot of La Giralda ● *66*, *72*, 109 ▲ *134*, in the PLAZA DE LA VIRGEN DE LOS REYES, and follows the Calle Mateos Gago, lined with orange trees, into the oldest districts and narrow streets of Seville: Abades, La Judería, San Isidoro, La Alfalfa and El Salvador.

CALLE ABADES. The Calle Mateos Gago leads into what was originally the *cardo maximus*, the main thoroughfare of the Roman city of Hispalis ● *30*, and later the Calle Mayor del Rey. Its elevated status is somewhat surprising given that its dimensions date from a very early period of urban planning. The Calle Abades has retained its original proportions and is protected from vehicular traffic by huge millstones and, at the intersections, by marble or bronze bollards. In the 14th century it was known as the Cal de los Abades (from *calle*, "street" and *abad*, "abbot"), since it was inhabited by the canons and other officials of the cathedral.

CASA DE LOS PINELO. The Calle Abades and the Calle Guzmán el Bueno ("the Good") ▲ *206*, *298* offer some fine examples of 16th-, 17th- and 18th-century *casas-patio* (houses centered around a courtyard). The *patios* are protected by wrought-iron grilles and decorated with porticos where paintings, sculptures, furniture and various copper objects

CALLE MATEOS GAGO
The Calle Mateos Gago, widened in 1923, is the busiest tourist thoroughfare in the Santa Cruz district.

11. Iglesia de San Esteban
12. Casa de Pilatos
13. Convento de San Leandro
14. Calle San José
15. Iglesia de San Nicolás
16. Plaza de San Pedro
17. Iglesia de San Ildefonso
18. Iglesia de San Isidoro
19. Plaza de la Alfalfa
20. Plaza de la Encarnación
21. Iglesia de la Anunciación
22. Palacio de Lebrija
23. Iglesia del Salvador

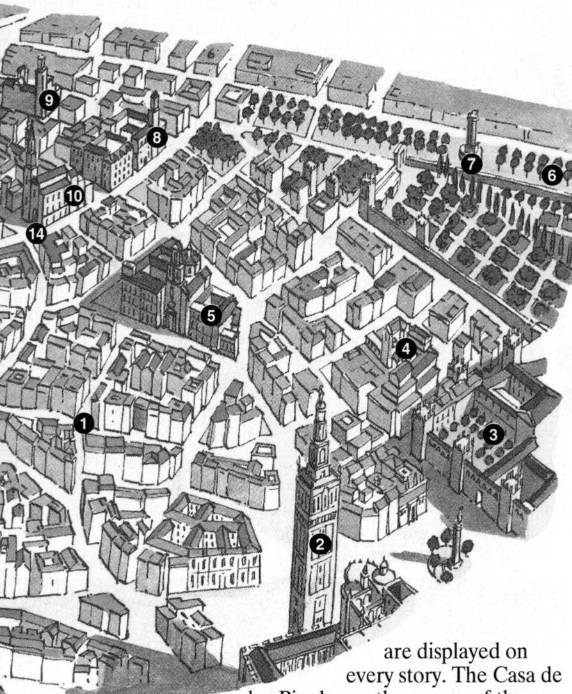

are displayed on every story. The Casa de los Pinelo, on the corner of the Calle Segovias, houses the academies of Fine Art and Literature and is a prominent example of an early Sevillian residence: a discreet façade, belvedere, flight of steps, interior courtyard and, at the back, a garden. The banker Francisco Pinelo, a member of one of the richest Genoese families, lived there from 1496 until his death in 1509. He was the friend and partner of Christopher Columbus ● *36*, ▲ *283* and played an important part in the organization of his expeditions and the Casa de la Contratación.

CALLE MARMOLES AND CALLE AIRE. A few steps from the Calle Abades are the three monumental columns of a TEMPLE OF HERCULES AND MARS, built during the reign of Hadrian ▲ *208*. According to legend the columns or marbles are all that remains of the seven pillars supposedly planted in the ground by Hercules ● *30* when he founded the city. Nearby is the narrow Calle Aire where the poet Luis Cernuda ▲ *163*, *165* lived.

LA JUDERÍA

From the Calle Abades, the *calles* Aire and Guzmán el Bueno lead back into the Calle Mateos Gago near the CASA SALINAS. The steps of the *casa* (which, from the 16th to the 19th century, belonged to the Jaén family) are decorated with a remarkable *azulejo*. Opposite is the IGLESIA DE SANTA CRUZ, the Baroque church (1665–1728) of the parish of La Judería, the old Jewish quarter.

THE UPPER CITY
The district adjacent to Seville's main monuments is the oldest and highest part of the city. Superimposing successive cultural strata has resulted in a dense, irregularly shaped urban complex with few plazas and open areas. Remains of the early city, dating from around the 8th century BC, were discovered in this district, at the highest point of the historic center (about 50 feet above sea level).

POPULAR SONG
"En la calle de los Abades/todos han tíos y ninguno padres." ("In the Calle de los Abades/everyone has [religious] fathers and no one has a father.")

A Renaissance motif on the Casa de los Pinelo; the Roman columns of the Temple of Hercules in the Calle Mármoles; and the façade of the Iglesia de Santa Cruz.

CALLE JUDERÍA
This street joins the Barrio de Santa Cruz at the Alcázar. It leads to the Patio de Banderas via the Callejón de los Suspiros.

HISTORY OF SEVILLE'S JEWISH COMMUNITY. Although the Jewish community (first mentioned in Seville in the 4th century) had flourished under the Visigoths, the persecutions suffered toward the end of this period led the Jews of Spain to welcome the arrival of the Muslims in 711. Initially tolerated by Islam, in the 11th century they were driven into the Christian kingdoms by the Almohads. When, in the 13th century, other Christian kingdoms expelled them, the Jews returned to Seville under Ferdinand III and Alfonso X. They were allocated the area to the north of the Alcázar: 40 acres of buildings surrounded by a wall. Today it is covered by the districts of Santa Cruz, Santa María la Blanca and San Bartolomé. During the reign of Pedro I the Jewish community numbered some two thousand people and was represented by a class of affluent financiers in the service of the Crown. But the effects of the Crusades could soon be felt. In 1391 a riot brought about their downfall: the sermons of Archdeacon Ferrán Martínez incensed the population and precipitated an attack on the Jewish quarter that left many dead and led to enforced conversions and exiles. The most important synagogues were converted into churches and the Jewish community was reduced to some sixty families scattered throughout the city.

"JAMERDANA"
Jamerdana is an Arabic word meaning "street of taverns". The façade of the Casa de los Venerables is painted in red and white, the

colors of Seville, and its church is dedicated to Ferdinand, patron saint of the Spanish.

A shady courtyard at the end of a narrow passageway (*zagüane*) in the old city.

Model for tourism The Barrio de Santa Cruz was rebuilt between 1912 and 1920 by the Ministry for Tourism to create a model for tourism in Andalusia.

Their situation worsened during the 15th century, at a time when converted Jews were experiencing increased economic and social power. In 1483 the Inquisition took its toll and Seville's remaining Sephardic Jews were expelled by decree.

Barrio de Santa Cruz. Since it was restored in the early 20th century, the part of the Judería adjacent to the Alcázar has become a major tourist district. The Barrio ("district") de Santa Cruz is bounded by the Calle Mateos Gago, which follows the line of what was once the old enclosure wall of the Jewish quarter. In the Calle Mesón del Moro (where a local restaurant houses some well-preserved Arab baths), a passageway leads into the heart of the district whose narrow streets can be glimpsed from the intersection of the *calles* Ximénes de Enciso and Santa Teresa. Nearby are the Casa de Murillo (Murillo's house) and a Convent founded in 1575 by Saint Theresa of Avila (1515–82) and established in this district, surrounded by a whitewashed enclosure wall, in 1586. The sacristy of the church contains the manuscript of one of Saint Theresa's mystic works: *Las Moradas* (*The Foundations*, or *The Castle of the Soul*, 1577), and her portrait, painted by Fray Juan de la Miseria (1576).

Hospital de los Venerables Sacerdotes. The small plaza of the Hospital de los Venerables is reached via the Calle Lope de Rueda and a series of picturesque passageways. The elegant Baroque building houses FOCUS (Fondo de Cultura de Sevilla), a cultural foundation responsible for organizing art exhibitions. It was built between 1676 and 1697 as accommodation for elderly priests, at the instigation of Canon Don Justino de Neve, the friend and patron of Murillo. The architects Juan Domínguez and Leonardo de Figueroa ▲ *168*, *178*, *181* built it around a square courtyard, with an arcaded first floor and large doorways and windows on the upper story. Paintings cover the walls of the nave. Juan de Valdés Leal ▲ *188* painted the frescos of the presbytery vault and the remarkable perspective in the sacristy. His son Lucas (1661–1725) completed his father's work and later painted *La Sagrada Cena* (*The Last Supper*) on the reredos of the high altar and *L'Apoteosis de San Fernando* (*The Apotheosis of Saint Ferdinand*), his most successful work. His paintings on marble include *La Inmaculada* (*The Immaculate Conception*), which makes a pair with a *Madonna* by Sassoferrato in the presbytery.

From the plaza de Doña Elvira to the calle Judería. The Plaza de Doña Elvira and Plaza de la Alianza are also adjacent to the Alcázar. A 17th-century statue of the *Cristo de*

Opposite the Hospital de los Venerables is the *Hostería del Laurel*, the scene of Don Juan's amorous adventures.

Casa de Murillo The artist's life is closely linked to the Barrio de Santa Cruz, where he lived and worked on several different occasions. In 1682 he fell from scaffolding while painting frescos in Cádiz. He was taken back to Santa Cruz, where he died and was buried in the parish church. His house (left) in the Calle Santa Teresa has been converted into a museum that perpetuates his memory.

Santa Cruz, the soul of Seville ✪ Little plazas shaded by palms and orange trees, whispering fountains, small markets, tapas bars, and restaurants hidden away in the greenery-filled courtyards of ochre and white residences... The lacework of paved alleys in the ancient Judería is a perfect spot for aimless wandering, though it pays to get there early to savor its charms without the crowds.

PLAZA DE SANTA CRUZ
The wrought-iron cross of the Cerrajería, the Brotherhood of Locksmiths, stands in the center of the district's largest plaza.

DON JUAN
Standing in the Plaza de Refinadores, the scene of some of his amorous adventures and the home of his historic models (Don Pedro, Don Juan Tenorio and Miguel de Mañara) is a statue of Don Juan, the universal myth that originated in Seville. He was immortalized by Juan de la Cueva, Tirso de Molina, Molière, Goldoni, Mozart, Byron, Mérimée, Dumas and Zorrilla.

GARDENS OF MURILLO
The gardens and the Avenida Catalina de Ribera were once part of the vegetable garden of the Alcáza almshouse.

la Misericordia, the patron saint of the Brotherhood of Santa Cruz, stands in the PLAZA DE LA ALIANZA, where the brotherhood makes a particularly moving halt during the processions of the Semana Santa ● *44*. Doña Elvira stands as the symbol of this plaza, which is planted with orange trees and entwined by the Calle Judería as it winds its way between towers, fountains and vaults to the PATIO DE BANDERAS. It is said that those who jump over the chain between the guard-stones will never marry.

CALLEJON DEL AGUA. This narrow street runs alongside a wall bordering the canal that carries water to the Alcázar ▲ *142*. Opening onto it are the Calle de la Pimienta and the Calle Susona, in the very heart of the Judería. The legend of Susona has been handed down from the last days of the Jewish community. In 1480 Susona, a remarkable woman from a rich Jewish family, denounced her father and other relatives implicated in a conspiracy, in order to save the life of her lover, a Christian knight. The accused were sent to the scaffold. Susona, overcome by remorse, wanted her skull displayed, after her death, in the street where she had lived as a warning to others.

GARDENS AND PLAZAS OF SANTA CRUZ. At the end of the Callejón del Agua is the tiny Plaza de Alfaro, the famous setting for the adventures of Rossini's Figaro. Opening onto it are the Jardines de Murillo, the gardens bordering the Santa Cruz district. Beyond is the PLAZA DE SANTA CRUZ, the former site of a succession of religious buildings: a mosque, a synagogue and, in 1391, a parish church. In 1810 the Napoleonic authorities had the church demolished in order to open up the site. Today the plaza forms the sober architectural setting for the CRUZ DE LA CERRAJERÍA, a masterpiece of Sevillian wrought-iron work, created in 1692 by Sebastián Conde. The plaza gives access to the Calle de la Mezquita, the Plaza de Refinadores and the tiny, isolated

"Men are made of fire,
women of fiber,
the Devil fans the flames of disquiet."

Desdenes (*Disdain*), watercolor by Gonzalo Bilbao ● *94*.

Plaza de las Cruces, where Don Juan fought, carried off beautiful women and encountered his own burial.

IGLESIA DE SANTA MARÍA LA BLANCA. The Barrio de Santa Cruz ends at the PUERTA DE LA CARNE ("gate of meat"), so called because it was located near the slaughterhouses, opposite the San Bernardo district (traditionally associated with bullfighters ● *52*, ▲ *107*). The Calle San José, once the main thoroughfare of the Judería, also opens onto the gate. The façade of the Iglesia de Santa María la Blanca is dominated by a bell tower and the pointed archway of the entrance opens onto trompe-l'oeil naves separated by reddish marble columns heavily decorated with stuccowork. The interior, with its paintings and extremely elaborate 17th-century Baroque stuccowork, houses a *Last Supper* by Murillo ● *91*, ▲ *138*, *182*, which is one of the artist's finest works, and the *Pietà* (1546), a painting on wood by Luis de Vargas. The Calle San José is overlooked by such rampart walks as the DOS HERMANAS ("two sisters"), near the Altamira Palace with its 17th-century façade. From here several streets lead to the urban islands of San Bartolomé, Archeros, Céspedes and Levíes, ending at the impressive wall of the IGLESIA DE LA MADRE DE DIOS (completed in 1572) with its finely carved entrance. It houses a worthy collection of 16th- and 17th-century paintings, sculptures and ceramics beneath its superbly constructed, Mudéjar coffered ceilings (1564). There are also two gisants, one of Doña Juana de Zúñiga, the wife of Hernán Cortés, the other of their daughter, Doña Catalina Cortés, sculpted by Juan de Oviedo and Miguel Adán in 1589. At the end of the street is the IGLESIA DE SAN NICOLÁS, built in 1758. Inside, the Genoese marble pillars and painted wall panels are a fine example of extremely ornate Baroque architecture.

BARRIO DE SAN BARTOLOMÉ. The Calle Conde de Ibarra runs through the Barrio de San Bartolomé, one of the unrestored districts of the Judería, and opens onto the district's most pleasant spot, the PLAZA DE LAS MERCEDARIAS. Also opening onto the plaza is the Calle Levíes, the narrow, winding street in which the family of Samuel Leví (treasurer of Pedro I ● *32*, ▲ *145*) once lived and where the parish church and several remarkable palaces can still be seen today. The neoclassical Iglesia de San Bartolomé, designed by José Echamorro in 1779, stands in a small plaza on the corner of the extremely narrow Calle Verde, which winds its way through a labyrinth of narrow streets and enclosed courtyards. This group of houses built one against the other, which

PUERTA DE LA CARNE
The archway and walls were demolished in 1865, and all that remains is the gate-house, with its distinctive, narrow Baroque belvedere in the form of a seat.

SYNAGOGUE AND CHURCH
The parish church of Santa María la Blanca was built on the site of a 13th-century synagogue. It was restored in Gothic style in 1391.

MADRE DE DIOS
In 1496 this Dominican convent in the Calle San José was installed in a synagogue and a complex of buildings requisitioned by the Inquisition.

CALLE LEVÍES
A former coal-merchant's yard has been converted into a bar, with an open-air terrace at the back, in the heart of the district. It evokes the popular tradition of gatherings around the table, and celebrations held in courtyards and gardens. Inside, the bar and cellar are reminiscent of another tradition: the flamenco ● *53*, ▲ *391*.

was the last retreat of the Jews of Seville, is itself a microcosm steeped in the atmosphere of the popular districts.

CASA-PALACIO DE MAÑARA. This *casa-palacio* has the most ostentatious façade in the Calle Levíes. The recent restoration of this (now official) building has highlighted the superposed Almohad, Mudéjar and Renaissance ● *70*, *72* architectural styles. It was built for Señor Juan de Almansa who, in 1532, had the columns and other architectural elements in white marble and black stone sculpted in the Genoese workshops of Antonio María de Aprile. It acquired its present appearance after the restoration commissioned in 1623 by its new owner, Don Tomás de Mañara, Leca y Colona, a Corsican merchant from Calvi who had grown rich through trade with the Americas. This small mansion is also associated with the memory of the son of Don Tomás, Miguel de Mañara (1627–79), who provided the Romantics with an archetype for Don Juan. This proud and haughty young man led a carefree existence until, devastated by the death of his wife, he decided to devote himself to God and spent his time reorganizing the charitable works of the Hospital de la Caridad ▲ *188*. Legend attributes this sudden conversion to the fact that he saw an image of his own funeral procession in the streets of the Judería on his way home from a ball, a scene featured in *Don Juan* ● *101* ▲ *156*.

IGLESIA DE SAN ESTEBAN. The Calle Vidrio leads out of the Judería to the Iglesia de San Esteban, designed by the "Master of 1356", so called because he restored several churches after the earthquake that struck the city in that year. In the 15th century a sculpted portal decorated with friezes of blind Mudéjar arches was added. Inside, beneath the 15th-century Mudéjar coffered vaults, stand an altar covered with 14th-century polychrome *azulejos* and a huge altarpiece with paintings on wood (c. 1635) by Zurbarán. A side chapel houses a highly venerated statue of the *Cristo de la Salud y del Buen Viaje* (17th century).

CASA DE PILATOS ★ ● *80*, ▲ *160*. A statue of the painter Zurbarán stands in the plaza overlooked by the simple enclosure (whitewashed walls, single entrance and belvedere) of the Casa de Pilatos. In 1481 Pedro Enríquez and his wife Catalina de Ribera, a titled and wealthy woman of noble birth (whose line dated from the time of the Reconquest), began to buy up sections of this block of houses in order to build the Palacio de San Andrés, named after the family's patron saint. Their son Don Fadrique, first Marqués de Tarifa (1476-1539), undertook the completion of the edifice on his return from

SAINT PETER
The paintings of Saint Peter and Saint Paul are the most remarkable in the series executed by Francisco de Zurbarán ▲ *139*, *182* for the Iglesia de San Esteban.

CASA-PALACIO DE MAÑARA
The reliefs of the porch and courtyard are truly remarkable.

the Holy Land in 1521. His *via dolorosa*, between the mansion and the tiny Iglesia de la Cruz del Campo, was the forerunner of the processions of the Semana Santa. The popular imagination associated the residence with that of Pontius Pilate. In a niche in the façade are the resplendent polychrome jaspers (1630) of the first station of the *via dolorosa*, which is next to the PORCHWAY that Don Fadrique had brought from the Genoese workshops of Antonio María de Aprile. It was installed in 1533, at the same time as the columns, fountains and marbles that symbolized the influence exerted by that great Italian Renaissance workshop upon Seville. Throughout the 16th century the Enríquez y Ribera family rivaled the Medicis, making the Casa Pilatos the symbol of the Renaissance in Seville. Don Fadrique's successors, Pedro Afán and Fernando, first and third dukes of Alcalá and viceroys of Naples, continued his work until the 17th century as the patrons of other "Roman-style" works imported from Italy. The artistic heritage of this period constitutes one of the finest collections on view in a private house.

PALACIO DE MEDINACELI. In the 17th century the house of the Enríquez y Ribera family formed an alliance with the house of Medinaceli, the present owners of the mansion. Before they regained possession in the mid-19th century, the *palacio* fell into disrepair and has only recently been completely restored. A collection of paintings hangs in the *piano nobile*. The frescoed galleries and *salón*, with its stained-glass windows and painted ceilings, once welcomed the humanist court of the dukes of Alcalá. The most important paintings, in the Salón del Torreón and the adjoining rooms, include a bullfight by Goya, a *Pietà* (1539) by Sebastiano del Piombo and a series of portraits. There is also an exceptional collection of archives. The dining room is of particular interest, with its portraits of the dukes of Lerma de Pantoja de la Cruz, black slate fireplace (17th century) and still life by Giuseppe Recco (1679). In the next apartment visitors can admire a *Prometheus* by the Naples School before they leave.

To set it off to advantage, the masters of the Casa de Pilatos cleared a plaza in front of the mansion.

AN URBAN MANSION
The Casa de Pilatos is undoubtedly the finest urban mansion in Andalusia. Its architecture, Mudéjar decoration, Gothic elements and Italian marbles provide a harmonious blend of the architectural tastes that dominated the early decades of the 16th century. The Regionalists called this combination the "Sevillian style" ● *86*.

TREASURES OF THE CASA DE PILATOS

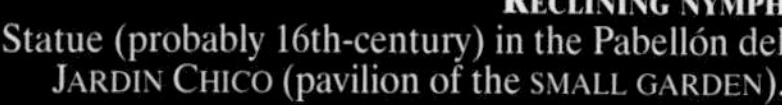

RECLINING NYMPH
Statue (probably 16th-century) in the Pabellón del JARDIN CHICO (pavilion of the SMALL GARDEN).

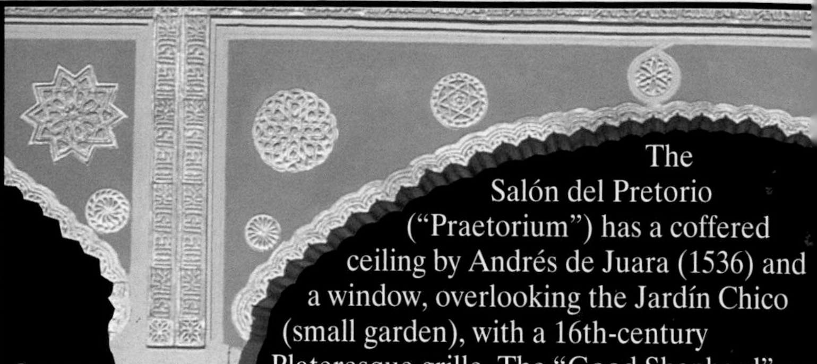

The Salón del Pretorio ("Praetorium") has a coffered ceiling by Andrés de Juara (1536) and a window, overlooking the Jardín Chico (small garden), with a 16th-century Plateresque grille. The "Good Shepherd" on the altar of the 15th-century Gothic Capilla de la Flagelación is a masterpiece of 4th-century Christian art. The base of the walls of the monumental staircase are covered with *azulejos*, and the staircase is surmounted by a wooden Mudéjar dome carved by Cristobal Sanchez and painted in distemper by Antón Perez (1539).

COURTYARD SCULPTURES
The first duke of Alcalá, who was viceroy of Naples from 1559 to 1571, assembled the collection of classical Roman and Renaissance sculptures. The setting for the sculptures was designed by Benvenuto Tortello and G. Menichini along the lines of an ancient Roman garden. The niches of the portico contain a collection of twenty-five busts of patricians brought from Rome, and a bust of Charles V.

THE FALL OF PHAETON
Detail of the *Apoteosis de Hércules* (in the SALÓN DEL TECHO DE HÉRCULES), a mythological exaltation of the dukes of Alcalá, painted in 1603–4 by the humanist and art theoretician Francisco Pacheco (1564–1644) ● *91*.

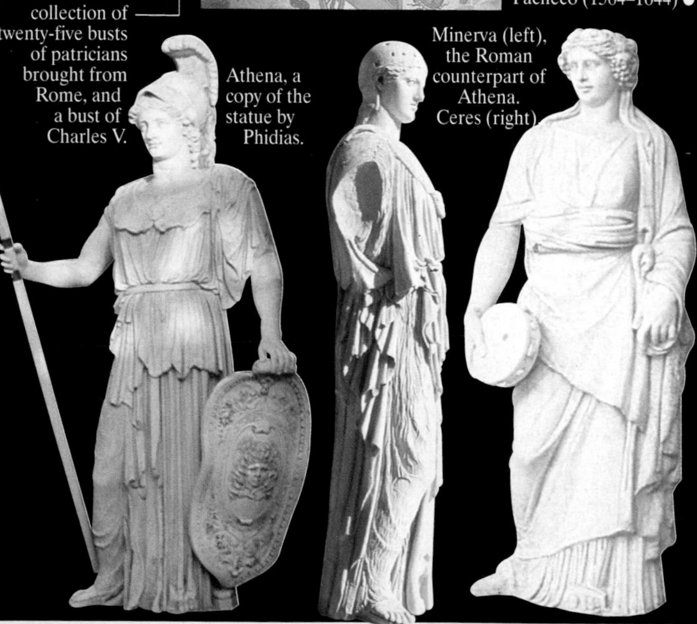

Athena, a copy of the statue by Phidias.

Minerva (left), the Roman counterpart of Athena. Ceres (right).

"Nowhere have I seen such beautiful faïence wall coverings as in the Casa de Pilatos."

Alexandre Dumas

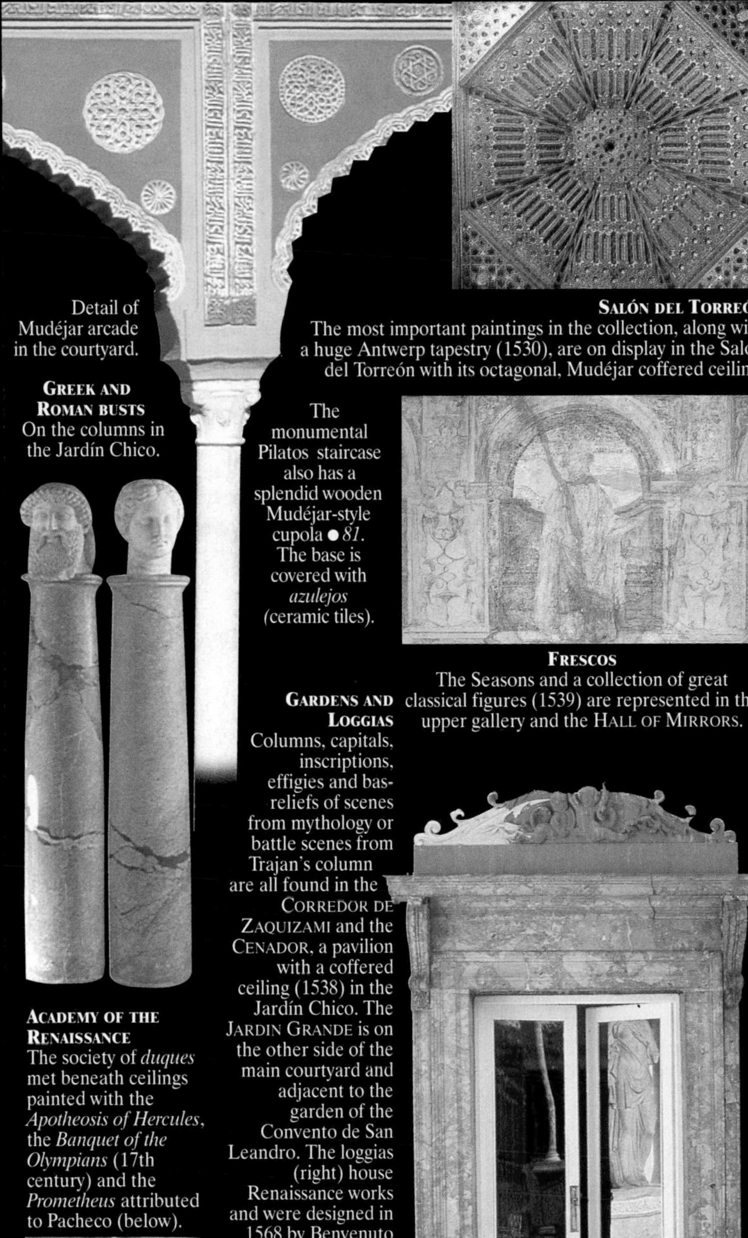

Detail of Mudéjar arcade in the courtyard.

SALÓN DEL TORREÓN
The most important paintings in the collection, along with a huge Antwerp tapestry (1530), are on display in the Salón del Torreón with its octagonal, Mudéjar coffered ceiling.

GREEK AND ROMAN BUSTS
On the columns in the Jardín Chico.

The monumental Pilatos staircase also has a splendid wooden Mudéjar-style cupola ● *81*. The base is covered with *azulejos* (ceramic tiles).

FRESCOS
The Seasons and a collection of great classical figures (1539) are represented in the upper gallery and the HALL OF MIRRORS.

GARDENS AND LOGGIAS
Columns, capitals, inscriptions, effigies and bas-reliefs of scenes from mythology or battle scenes from Trajan's column are all found in the CORREDOR DE ZAQUIZAMI and the CENADOR, a pavilion with a coffered ceiling (1538) in the Jardín Chico. The JARDIN GRANDE is on the other side of the main courtyard and adjacent to the garden of the Convento de San Leandro. The loggias (right) house Renaissance works and were designed in 1568 by Benvenuto Tortello. The outbuildings to the north were built in 1603, under the direction of Juan de Oviedo, on the edge of this orchard in the heart of the city.

ACADEMY OF THE RENAISSANCE
The society of *duques* met beneath ceilings painted with the *Apotheosis of Hercules*, the *Banquet of the Olympians* (17th century) and the *Prometheus* attributed to Pacheco (below).

IGLESIA DE SAN ILDEFONSO
Opposite San Leandro is the colonial-style neoclassical church (1796–1841) of San Ildefonso, with its twin-towered, polychrome façade.

FROM SAN LEANDRO TO EL SALVADOR

From the Casa de Pilatos the Calle Aguilas leads to the Calle Alfalfa, and the Calle de los Caballerizas to the Iglesia de San Ildefonso on the edge of the San Leandro district. A simple vestibule opens onto the convent enclosure, where visitors can buy *yemas*, the famous patisserie specialty of Seville, prepared by the nuns ● *62*.

CONVENTO DE SAN LEANDRO. Since 1369 the monastery (founded in 1295) has stood on the site of the early buildings granted by Pedro I. The complex forms a network of courtyards and passages and shares a building with the Casa de Pilatos. A wall pierced with ornamental openwork divides the entire height of the church's single nave, which is separated from the choir enclosure by grilles and screens. It houses the *retablos* of *San Juan Bautista* and *San Juan Evangelista*, two masterpieces created by Juan Martínez Montañés between 1621 and 1632. The church is open on the 22nd of every month for the worship of Santa Rita de Casia, the patron saint of lost causes and the subject of great popular devotion.

IN THE SHADE OF A BAY TREE. The Plaza de San Leandro and its fountain, the PILA DEL PATO ("duck's basin"), is shaded by the huge leaves of one of Seville's most venerable trees. Don Juan Tenorio, who inspired Tirso de Molina's *El Burlador de Sevilla* (*The Rake of Seville*), may well have lived in this plaza ● *101*.

CALLE MORERÍA. The Calle Morería runs into the PLAZA DEL CRISTO DE BURGOS Y SAN PEDRO from the old district of El Adarvejo, formerly inhabited by the Jews and then the Mudéjars of Seville. In the 15th century these families were scattered throughout the city and subjected to the hostility directed against religious minorities. They moved into and lived in this district until the Sevillian Mudéjars were officially expelled in 1502.

PLAZA DE LA ALFALFA. The streets leading to the Plaza de la Alfalfa are named after such corporations as the Boteros and Odreros (makers and sellers of wineskins) and offer ideal vantage points from which to watch the Semana Santa ● *44* processions. The Roman forum and medieval markets (selling meat and alfalfa) were located near the plaza. On Sunday mornings there is a small cattle market, held here since the early 19th century.

IGLESIA DE SAN ISIDORO. The church is ensconced in the upper part of the city, away from the busy plaza. It was built immediately after the Reconquest on the site of a mosque (which had itself been

The fountain in the Plaza de San Leandro, the so-called Pila del Pato ("duck's basin"), and the house, near the Calle Morería, where the artist Diego Velázquez was born.

BUST OF DON PEDRO
A bust of Don Pedro at the end of the Calle del Candilejo commemorates the "exploits" of King Pedro I ● *32*, ▲ *145*. It was here that Don Pedro, who had just killed a man in a night-time skirmish, was recognized by an old woman. Having promised her the head of the guilty party (his own), he had the bust erected on the scene of the crime.

PICTURESQUE PICARESQUE
According to the inscription on these *azulejos* ● *56, 77*, the Plaza del Pan, Calle de la Pescadería and nearby side streets provided the setting for several of Miguel de Cervantes' *novelas ejemplares* and novels by other authors.

built on the foundations of an early church) and was dedicated to Saint Isidore, the Visigoth Bishop of Seville from 599 until his death in 636. Isidore of Seville (Cartagena c. 560–Seville 636) was the author of the renowned twenty books of the *Etymologías* or *Origenes* ● *31*, ▲ *138*. The pointed archway of the entrance to the tower and the structure of the edifice date from the mid-14th century. The church houses the *Tránsito de San Isidoro* (*Death of Saint Isidore*), by the Sevillian artist Juan de los Roelas (1558–1625), who founded the Sevillian Naturalist School, the *Cristo de las Tres Caídas* (*Christ Thrice Fallen*), and the *Cirineo* (*Simon of Cyrene*), painted by Ruiz Gijón in 1687. The *retablo* (completed in 1740) of the CAPILLA SACRAMENTAL (Chapel of the Holy Sacrament) is a masterpiece of Baroque art ● *78*.

LA ALCAICERÍA, THE OLD SILK MERCHANTS' DISTRICT. On the way down from the Iglesia de San Isidoro and the Plaza de la Alfalfa to the Plaza del Pan and the Plaza del Salvador, the CALLE DE LA PESCADERÍA ("fish market"), the CUESTA DEL ROSARIO ("rosary"), which is the only steep street in Seville, and the *calles* Alcaicería and Lineros ("linen makers") pass through the city's oldest merchants' district, with its half-timbered houses. The district was established in the 9th century around the Great Mosque

"The tiny shops on the Plaza del Pan were built against the Iglesia del Salvador... They were like holes dug out of the walls of the church. Some lay behind small shop windows, while others – like those on the plaza at the back of the church – were open-fronted."
Luis Cernuda, *Ocnos*

PLAZA DEL PAN
Formerly known as the Plaza de Jesús de la Pasión, the plaza's present name was derived from the fact that bread was sold here. For this reason, and because it was small, it was always bustling with all kinds of different people. Today small 17th-century locksmiths', watchmakers' and jewelers' workshops, with their vaulted ceilings supported by massive pillars, exist alongside department stores. These stores were built between 1900 and 1930, at a time when increased commercial activity led to the transformation of many of the city's buildings. One of the stores (left) in the Pedro Roldán group (1930), designed by José Espiau (1884–1938) in a combination of different styles.

THE GREAT MOSQUE
The Iglesia del Salvador (Saint Savior) was built on the site of a mosque whose general layout, base of the minaret and courtyard have been retained. The mosque was itself built in 830, according to plans by Ibn Adabbas, on the foundations of a Visigoth cathedral and Roman basilica. An inscription dating from 1079 mentions the reforms carried out by El-Mu'tamid.

and surrounding *souks* in the Barrio del Salvador. The Calle Alcaicería, with its shops and banner signs, was once the district's main thoroughfare bordered by prestigious shops and businesses. In the 12th century the city's religious and economic center was moved nearer the cathedral.

IGLESIA DEL DIVINO SALVADOR. From a Roman basilica to a Visigoth cathedral, mosque and, finally, a collegiate church, the Iglesia del Divino Salvador (Saint Savior) is Seville's second largest religious building after the cathedral. In the early 17th century the badly damaged medieval and Islamic section of the edifice was demolished. The Roman and Visigoth buildings of the oratory, courtyard and tower were preserved. Work began in 1674 and lasted forty years. Donations from a wealthy parish endowed the church with an unrivaled artistic heritage. The *retablo mayor* and the one in the Capilla Sacramental (Chapel of the Holy Sacrament) are masterpieces by Cayetano de Acosta (1711–80), who gave Rococo art its highest form of expression. On a silver altar in the chapel stands a *Jesús de la Pasión* (1619) by the great Sevillian sculptor Juan Martínez Montañés (1568–1649) ● *48* ▲ *139*, *206*. The serenity of his *Nazareno* (*Christ carrying the Cross*) contrasts with the dramatic *Cristo del Amor* (*Christ of Love*), sculpted in 1620 by Juan de Mesa (1583–1627) ▲ *179*, a pupil of Montañés and a master of the expressive realism of Baroque art. The tiny but richly decorated CAPILLITA DE LOS DESAMPARADOS ("Lost Souls") (above) stands against one of the walls of the Patio de los Naranjos.

PLAZA DEL SALVADOR. The modest Plaza del Salvador, once the main plaza of the old city, is dominated by the impressive stone and pink brick façade of the Iglesia del Salvador. Its small trees and porches make it an ideal place to relax on the café terraces or in the crowded *bodegas* (wine bars) ● *60*. During the festivals of the Semana Santa and Corpus Christi, ● *44*, the plaza is transformed into one of the stations on the procession route and is covered with awnings and temporary altars. In front of the towered gateway of the HOSPITAL DE LA PAZ (or San Juan de Dios) is a MONUMENT TO JUAN MARTINEZ MONTAÑÉS. The interior decoration of the late 16th-century hospital was renovated at the end of the 18th century. Inside are Rococo stuccowork, sculptures and *azulejos* ● *56*, ▲ *128* covering the base of the walls.

Layers accumulated over one thousand years had covered the shafts of the columns in the courtyard.

CALLE CUNA AND PALACIO DE LEBRIJA ★. The Calle Cuna is a commercial street running parallel to the Calle Sierpes, from the Plaza del Salvador toward the *calles* Campana and

"In memoriam Luis Cernuda"
Commemorative plaque in the house in the Calle Acetres where Luis Cernuda (1902–63) was born. Cernuda was one of Spain's greatest modern poets.

Encarnación. On the corner of the Calle Cerrajería is a Mudéjar-style edifice, built in 1912 by José Espiau ▲ *163*. At the end of the street is the severe, classical entrance of the Palacio de Lebrija, with its studded mahogany door. In 1914 Doña Regla Manjón transformed the mansion (built in the 15th and refurbished in the 16th century) and decorated it with mosaic flooring brought from Itálica ● *65*, ▲ *208*, architectural remains and various works of art. The entire first floor is decorated with Roman mosaic flooring. The vestibule (with its 18th-century Triana *azulejos* ▲ *194*) and corridors comprise Spain's finest collection of the remarkable *opus sectile*, a flooring technique using pieces of marble arranged in geometric patterns. The collection, which dates from the 4th century, is dominated by the rare and much sought-after yellow marble, *giallo antico*. The Renaissance courtyard, with its neo-Mudéjar stuccowork, was built around the mosaic of the *Amores de Zeus* (2nd century). Its medallions represent the Cyclops Polyphemus, the Seasons and the loves of the Master of Olympus. The garden room has a first-century mosaic of fish, and other mosaics are to be found in the octagonal Medusa and Ganymede rooms. The Plateresque frieze and Mudéjar coffered ceiling of the staircase came from the mansion of the Ponce de León de Marchena family. The second-floor apartments comprise a series of *salones* and a library, all richly decorated with furniture, carpets and sculptures.

Iglesia de la Anunciación. In a corner of the Plaza de la Encarnación stands the former Jesuit Church of the Annunciation, designed by Hernán Ruiz the Younger ▲ *136, 239, 264* and built from 1565 onward. Its great nave houses 18th-century paintings and *retablos* by Juan Martínez Montañés, including the *San Ignacio*, *San Juan de Borja* and the representation of *San Juan Bautista* on the *retablo mayor*. The *Virgen del Valle*, a frame in the form of a chandelier, with only the head and hands, attributed to Juan de Mesa, is also housed in the church.

La Encarnación
The main commercial streets, such as the Mercado de Puente y Pellón, and the most distinctive bars and cafés are found near the Plaza de la Encarnación.

Palacio de Lebrija
At the foot of the splendid, and typically Sevillian, staircase, with its three flights of stairs, the Roman mosaic floor has retained all its detail and brightness of color. The *azulejos* decorating the walls were painted in the Triana district between 1585 and 1611.

1. PUERTA DE LA MACARENA
2. HOSPITAL DE LAS CINCO LLAGAS
3. MURALLAS (RAMPARTS)
4. BASILICA DE LA MACARENA
5. IGLESIA DE SAN GIL
6. CALLE SAN LUIS

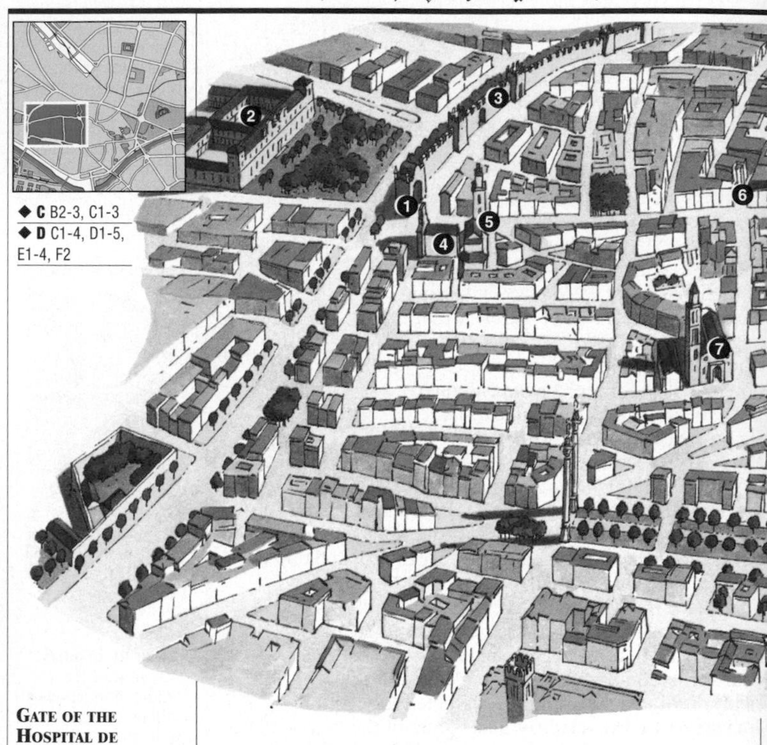

◆ C B2-3, C1-3
◆ D C1-4, D1-5, E1-4, F2

GATE OF THE HOSPITAL DE LA SANGRE
Asensio de Maeda built this huge, white marble gate. The church, designed by Hernán Ruiz the Younger ● *73,* ▲ *136* in 1558, is a triumph of Spanish Mannerism. The reliefs on the portal were sculpted in 1564 by Bautista Vásquez.

View of the ramparts of Seville, 19th-century engraving.

LA MACARENA AND SAN LUIS

The rare vestiges of the fortified enclosure that defended the city are in the heart of the popular Macarena district.
THE RAMPARTS. The *pisé* walls built by the Almoravids in the first half of the 12th century were extended and reinforced by the Almohads and then the Christians. The preserved section, with its SEVEN QUADRANGULAR BASTIONS and POLYGONAL TOWER, runs from what used to be the Puerta de Córdoba, built against the Iglesia de San Hermenegildo, to the ARCO DE LA MACARENA. It can be best seen from a barbican or the renovated rampart walk. In the 16th century the fortifications became redundant and the principal gateways were widened. The kings entered via the Puerta de la Macarena where they received the keys of the city on the occasion of their first visit. At dawn on Good Friday, the

7. Iglesia Omnium Sanctorum
8. Calle Feria
9. Convento de Santa Paula
10. Iglesia de Santa Marina
11. Iglesia de San Marcos
12. Iglesia de San Luis
13. Palacio de las Dueñas
14. Iglesia de Santa Catalina
15. Iglesia de San Pedro
16. Iglesia de San Juan de la Palma
17. Iglesia de San Andrés
18. Alameda de Hércules

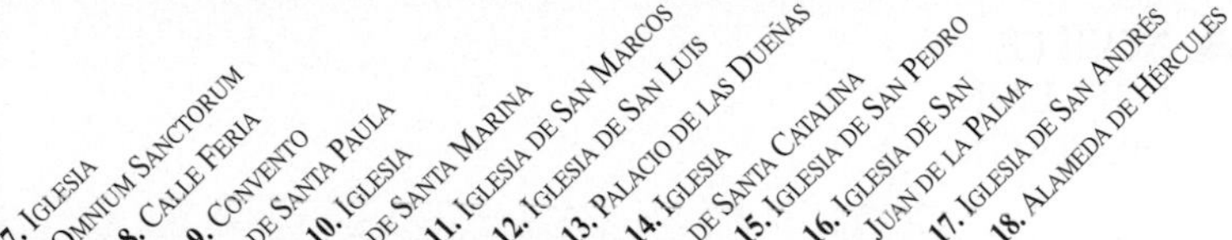

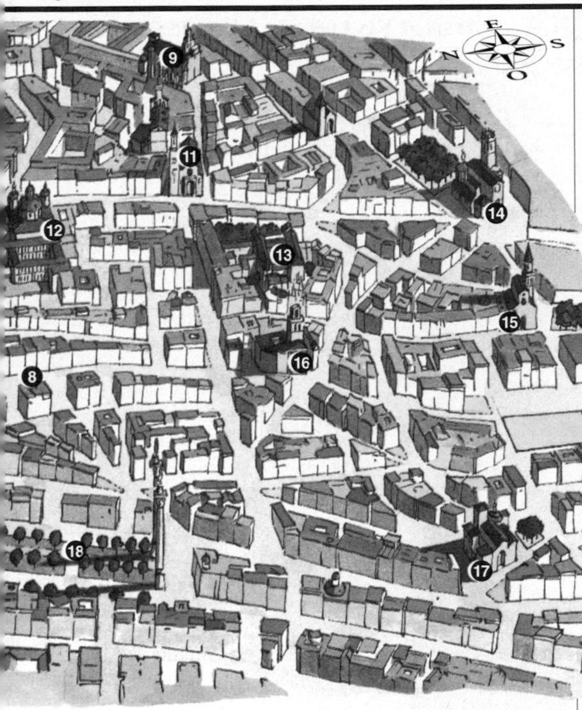

Hospital de las Cinco Llagas
The hospital, founded by Catalina de Ribera, is one of the most majestic Renaissance buildings in Seville, and the seat of the Andalusian parliament. It was begun in 1545 and completed in the 17th century under a succession of architects: Martín de Gaínza, Hernán Ruiz, Benvenuto Tortello and Asensio de Maeda.

Arco (restored in the 19th century) provides a grandiose setting for the procession of the *Virgen de la Esperanza*.

Calle San Luis. The Calle San Luis, formerly the Calle Real (Royal), used to border a district that incorporated the Puerta del Arenal and the old city. The street, whose present name dates from 1845 and pays homage to Saint Louis (Louis IX of France) was the street of kings and churches. It passes through a part of the city which is typical of post-Reconquest urban development. The district's patron saint, the *Virgen de la Esperanza*, is worshiped in the form of a beautiful Baroque sculpture ● *45*, in the Basilica de la Macarena (1949). Behind the basilica stands the much-renovated, 13th-century Iglesia de San Gil, whose Mudéjar tower and bell tower (18th-century) have been preserved. Inside, its walls are covered with late 13th-century *azulejos* ● *56*, *77*, ▲ *128* and paintings by Juan de Espinal (1770). There are several other churches in the street, including the 14th-century Mudéjar Iglesia de Santa Marina, which was renovated by Pedro I in 1356. Unfortunately, it was badly damaged by fire in 1869 and all that remains of the church today are the admirable proportions of its tower, the pointed arch of its sober entrance and walls decorated with *oculi*.

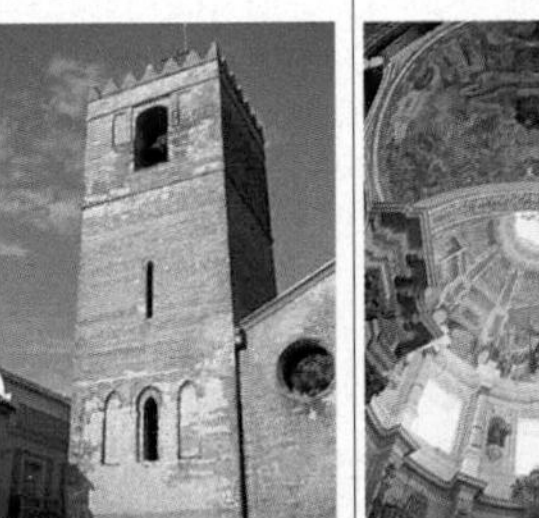

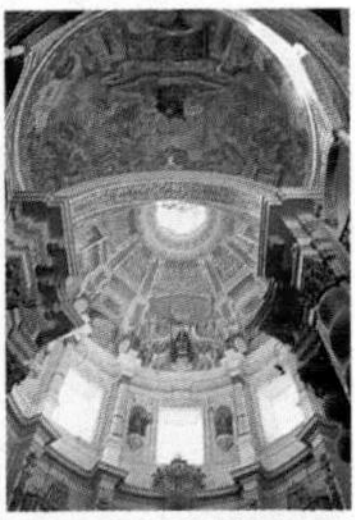

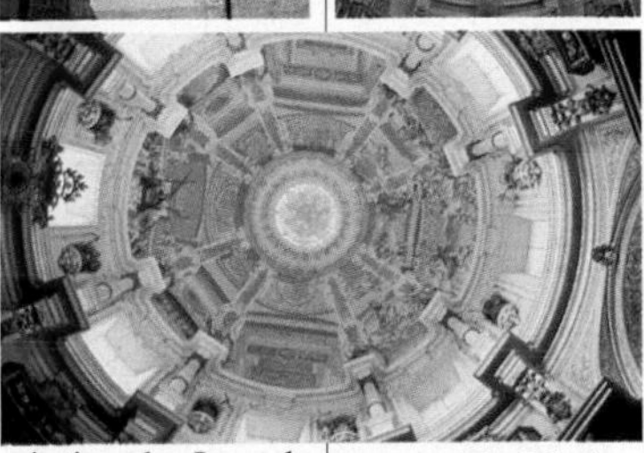

Tower of the Iglesia de Santa Marina (top left). Views (top right, and above) of the dome of the Iglesia de San Luis, one of the finest examples of Baroque architecture in Seville.

SAN MARCOS
This 14th-century Mudéjar church, with its unusually elegant tower, stands in the heart of a dense network of convents and parish churches. Three bare naves are all that remains of an interior badly damaged by fire.

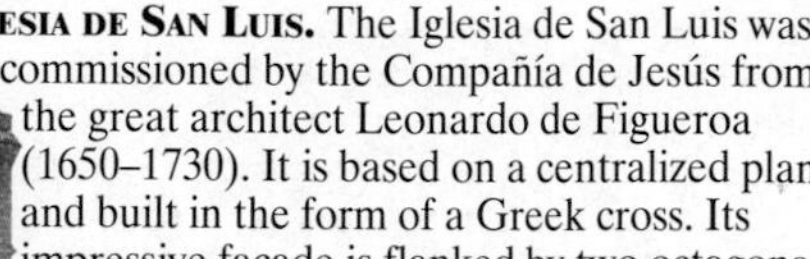

IGLESIA DE SAN LUIS. The Iglesia de San Luis was commissioned by the Compañía de Jesús from the great architect Leonardo de Figueroa (1650–1730). It is based on a centralized plan and built in the form of a Greek cross. Its impressive façade is flanked by two octagonal towers, while the sophisticated decoration of the high dome is enhanced by paintings attributed to Lucas Valdés ▲ *155*, *179*. The side walls are covered by some remarkable paintings, and the masterly *retablos* include that of the high altar (1730), by Pedro Duque Cornejo, which is a bold blend of brightly colored Baroque motifs. The overall effect is dazzling and extremely representative of the tastes of the period. The Centro Andaluz de Teatro (Andalusian Theater Center) occupies the outbuildings of the former Jesuit novitiate.

PLAZA DEL PUMAREJO. The Calle San Luis crosses this vast plaza, named after Don Pablo Pumarejo, a Sevillian gentleman who bought the land and adjacent lots from the friars of San Jerónimo in the late 18th century. He built an elegant villa (today converted into small rented apartments) whose door, coat of arms and Cuban mahogany columns have been preserved. The area used to be covered by a maze of narrow streets known as Los Cuatro Cantillos ("four knucklebones"), where the inhabitants of the islands of San Gil and Santa María conducted their business.

PORTAL OF THE CHURCH OF THE CONVENTO DE SANTA ISABEL
Nothing is known of the life of Alonso de Vandelvira, the architect of this early 17th-century portal (below).

MAIN ENTRANCE OF THE CONVENTO DE SANTA PAULA
The 16th-century brick entrance (above, right) opens onto the cloister garden.

PLAZA DE SANTA ISABEL. The Convento de Santa Isabel, founded in the late 15th century, stands on the plaza of the same name. In 1835 it became a women's prison and was later inhabited by the sisters of a community who ran a Magdalen hospital. It houses works by Juan Martínez Montañés and Juan de Mesa ▲ *139*, *179*.

CONVENTO DE SANTA PAULA. The occupations of the sisters of the Hieronymite Convento de Santa Paula range from prayer to embroidery and crochet work, making religious objects, running a small museum and making confectionery. The order was founded by Ana de Santillán y Guzmán, a Sevillian woman of noble birth who, in 1473, obtained permission from Sextus IV to establish a religious community in one of the buildings on her property. The church was begun in 1483, at the instigation of the Marquesa Isabel Enríquez de Montemayor. Extensions carried out in the 16th and 17th

"I have seen much of the country, La Macarena, but never a face to equal yours"

Romantic quatrain

centuries created a city within the city, with gardens, huge cloisters, courtyards, outbuildings and several large buildings. The CHURCH has a remarkable coffered ceiling (1623), created under the direction of López de Arenas, and houses the tombs of the *marqueses* of Montemayor. The high altar has an 18th-century *retablo*, while the side walls were the work of three great 17th-century sculptors (1635–8): Alonso Cano (*retablo* of *San Juan Evangelista* on the left-hand wall), Felipe de Rivas (*retablo* of *San Juan Bautista*) and Juan Martínez Montañés (the two figures of the two patron saints). In 1810 Marshal Soult ▲ *181* helped himself to the works of Alonso Cano, which were replaced by less valuable paintings.

CONVENT-MUSEUM. Because of the wealth of its artistic heritage, the Convento de Santa Paula has been classified as an historic monument. Its museum, which occupies a vestibule, two large *salones* and the choir, houses a collection of 16th-, 17th- and 18th-century paintings, sculptures, ceremonial caskets and urns, reliquaries and some masterpieces of gold and silver work. The window of the second *salón* offers a view of the convent's most impressive cloister, the delicately arcaded, double CLAUSTRO REAL, or Royal Cloister (17th century). Before leaving, visitors can buy traditionally made confectionery and *mermeledas* ● *62* in the tower.

IGLESIA DE SAN ROMÁN. This much-renovated church (the oldest part is in the Mudéjar-Gothic style), with its 18th-century tower, overlooks the Plaza de San Román. Gipsies gather here during the Semana Santa for the procession of El Manué (the patron saint of their brotherhood) held under the auspices of the dukes of Alba. During the 16th century the increasing number of churches and convents attracted vagabonds and beggars, who saw Christian charity as a means of alleviating their suffering. The Sevillian nobility recruited armies from this population to meet the needs of their fratricidal struggles.

CALLE SOL AND CALLE SANTIAGO One of the façades in the old Calle Sol is that of the CASA DEL REY MORO, once part of a mansion said to have belonged to Abenamafor, Emir of Niebla. The building is considered the oldest *casa-patio* in Seville. Across the plaza, opposite the Iglesia de Santa Catalina, is the venerable Calle Santiago. It leads into the old district of LOS CIPRESES, with its aristocratic residences on the site of the Palacio de Abdelmón, Emir of Baza (like Niebla, a small kingdom of the dislocated Almohad empire

ENTRANCE OF THE CONVENTO DE SANTA PAULA
Designed in 1504 by Pedro Millán and Francisco Niculoso, this combines Gothic, Mudéjar and Renaissance elements.

LOS TERCEROS
Courtyard of the old Franciscan convent of Los Terceros, whose church (17th-18th century) has a curious portal reminiscent of certain examples of Hispanic-American architecture.

CHORROJUMO
The gipsy Chorrojumo, a popular 19th-century figure.

SANTA CATALINA
This 14th-century church still has its Mudéjar apse and tower ● *76*, as well as a magnificent coffered ceiling. On the western side, the Gothic portal, dating from the same era, comes from the Iglesia de Santa Lucía, which was destroyed in 1930.

▲ *277*). The district's main monuments are the CORRAL DEL CONDE, the former residence of the Duke of Olivares (now rented apartments), the 18th-century PALACIO DE VILLAPANÉS, the 17th-century Iglesia de Santiago (with a *retablo* sculpted by Andrés de Ocampo and paintings by Francisco Pacheco ● *91*, ▲ *160*), and the CONVENTO DE SANTA MARIA DE LOS REYES, with its elegant porch and church, where the Dirección General de Arquitectura holds its exhibitions.

SANTA CATALINA INTERSECTION

The delightful PARISH CHURCH OF SANTA CATALINA stands on the site of a former mosque. The church is the starting point for the following itinerary, which runs between small plazas and churches, past the bars that have replaced old hostelries and 18th- and 19th-century inns. In the Calle Almirante Apodaca, the huge, ruined building of the POSADA DE LUCERO is all that remains of the muleteers' inn.

IGLESIA DE SAN PEDRO AND CONVENTO DE SANTA INÉS. The Iglesia de San Pedro, in the Mudéjar-Gothic style common to most of the churches on this itinerary, houses an interesting collection of paintings by Zurbarán, Pedro de Campaña, Lucas Valdés and Francisco de Herrera ▲ *139*, *155*, *158*. The statue of the *Cristo de Burgos* (1573) that stands in one of the chapels is carried on one of the *pasos* during the Semana Santa ● *44*. It has given its name to the *plaza* (PLAZA DE BURGOS), with its four huge magnolia trees, in front of the church entrance. In Calle María Coronel stands the FRANCISCAN CONVENTO DE SANTA INÉS, inhabited by nuns of the Order of Saint Clare ("Clarisses"). It was founded in 1374 by Doña María Coronel, a Sevillian woman of noble birth who disfigured herself to escape the designs of Pedro I. Her embalmed body lies in the Mudéjar-Gothic building of the convent church, situated inside the cloister and restored by Herrera el Viejo in 1630 ▲ *280*. One of the two streets running alongside the outbuildings is named after the

Muleteers, oil painting on a medallion (19th century).

"EL RINCONCILLO"
This *taberna*, thought to be the oldest in Seville, was opened in 1670 and restored in the 19th century. It has some fine *azulejos* ● *56*, ▲ *128* and is well worth a visit for its atmosphere, *tapas* ● *60* (for example, spinach, cod omelette), *coroneles* (glasses of red wine) and its history, associated with the bullfighting fraternity ● *52, 107* and popular gatherings.

Azulejo for a dance school.

Sevillian nun Sor Angela de la Cruz, a cobbler's daughter who founded the community of the Hermanas de la Cruz (Sisters of the Cross), well known in the city for their charitable works. The poet Fernando Villalón (1881–1930) was born in the aristocratic residence (4, Calle Sor Angela de la Cruz) that houses the seat of the community.

PALACIO DE LAS DUEÑAS
"My childhood, it is memories of a courtyard in Seville."
Antonio Machado

PALACIO DE LAS DUEÑAS. This 15th-century mansion is the property and residence of the dukes of Alba and can only be visited with special permission. It is a fine example of Mudéjar-Renaissance architecture. The remarkable main courtyard, with its Gothic balustrade and Plateresque stuccowork, is reached via the gardens where the poets Antonio and Manuel Machado, the sons of one of the ducal administrators, played as children. The residence and street are named after the former monastery of Santa María de las Dueñas, founded by Saint Ferdinand and demolished in the 19th century. The CONVENTO DE LAS TERESAS and several beautiful, late 19th-century houses (including the birthplace of the writer Manuel Chaves Nogales) can still be seen in the street. A little further on, in the street of the same name, are the 17th-century bell tower and church of the Augustinian CONVENTO DEL ESPIRITU SANTO.

Summer evening in a street (early 20th century).

ENTRANCE OF THE IGLESIA DE SAN ANDRÉS (below, left).

PLAZA DEL POZO SANTO. Turn your back on the Iglesia de San Juan de la Palma and make your way along the narrow shopping streets to the Plaza del Pozo Santo ("holy well"). According to a 14th-century legend a child is said to have fallen into the well, whereupon the waters rose and brought him back to the rim. On the plaza is the HOSPITAL DEL SANTÍSIMO CRISTO DE LOS DOLORES, a two-story building housing a church. The Calle Cervantes runs between the churches of San Andrés and San Martín, and leads to the Calle Feria which marks the end of this short detour.

PARISH CHURCH OF SAN JUAN DE PALMA
This Mudéjar-Gothic church from the 14th and 15th centuries stands on the plaza of the same name.

CHURCHES OF SAN ANDRÉS AND SAN MARTIN. The painter Valdés Leal ▲ *155, 188* was baptized in the Iglesia de San Andrés, a triple-naved edifice containing panels painted by his

Stalls at the antiques and bric-à-brac market of El Jueves, held in the Calle Feria. Nowhere else will you see so many paintings by Murillo.

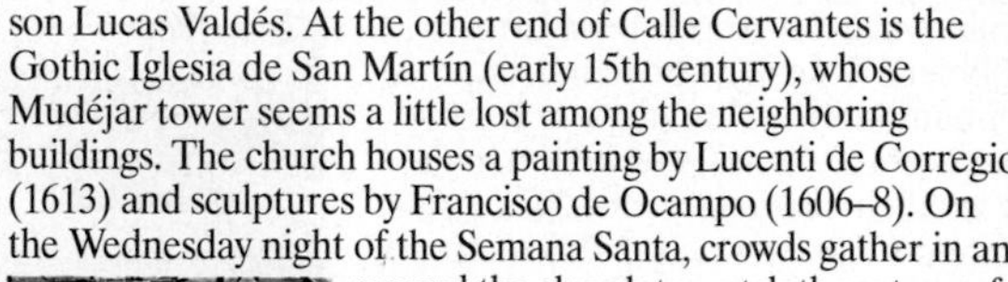

son Lucas Valdés. At the other end of Calle Cervantes is the Gothic Iglesia de San Martín (early 15th century), whose Mudéjar tower seems a little lost among the neighboring buildings. The church houses a painting by Lucenti de Correggio (1613) and sculptures by Francisco de Ocampo (1606–8). On the Wednesday night of the Semana Santa, crowds gather in and around the church to watch the return of the penitents of the Brotherhood of the Sagrada Lanzada (the so-called "Lanza").

IGLESIA DE SAN JUAN DE LA PALMA. The church was renovated in the 17th and 18th centuries, but the entrance and base of the tower betray its Mudéjar origins. In a niche in the *retablo* of the high altar are two works by Hita de Castillo: the *Virgen de la Amargura* and *San Juan* (1760).

BARRIO DE LA FERIA

The Calle Feria, one of the widest streets in Seville, was created in 1868 from various streets that bore the names of traditional trades: Laneros, Caño Quebrado, Pozo de los Hurones and Ancha de Feria. This was the district of wool craftsmen, makers of *banderillas* and capes, carpenters and linen makers. The extent of its economic activity can be gauged by the fact that it was already paved in the 16th century. However, in 1861, after the opening up of a gate in the city walls, a number of old houses had to be demolished. The famous bullfighter

CASA DE LOS ARTISTAS
This 14th-century house, restored and transformed into a luxurious Renaissance residence by Hernán Ponce de León in the 16th century, was bought by the Levanto family in 1634. It was later converted into accommodation leased by artists, sculptors and craftsmen (above and right).

"Juan Belmonte took what he wanted from the inventions of El Gallo, combined them with the Classic style, and developed both methods into his own great, revolutionary style."

Ernest Hemingway

Earthenware crockery sellers at the Thursday market (El Jueves), early 20th-century photograph.

Juan Belmonte ● *53*, ▲ *195* was born in Calle Feria. The district's medieval atmosphere has been best preserved in the area that lies between the *iglesias* de San Juan de la Palma and Omnium Sanctorum, where the two rows of narrow, irregularly shaped houses are mostly occupied by small stores and workshops. On the Plaza Montesíon stands the Capilla de Montesíon, a bookshop and a *taberna* that has preserved its old-fashioned atmosphere and is particularly lively on Thursdays, the day of the market. The former Convento de Monte Sión, with its crumbling entrance and tall bell tower, houses the Archivo de Protocolos (Archives of the Protocol). The intersection has been known successively as the Caño Quebrado, the Plaza de los Trapos, the Plaza de los Carros and, since 1845, Los Maldonados, in honor of a family whose main residence stood there. The building, later occupied by a factory making natural orange-flower water, has today disappeared and there is now an open space adjoining the Plaza de la Capilla de Monte Sión.

THE PENDON VERDE REBELLION. In 1520 Seville was the scene of a political and economic power struggle between two of the city's great families: Guzmán (dukes of Medina Sidonia ▲ *206*, *277*) and Ponce (dukes of Arcos ▲ *252*). The two camps recruited their troops in the popular districts of La Heria and La Feria, among the homeless, vagabonds and miscreants. Lured by the promise of being allowed to plunder the houses of rich Jewish merchants, they were sent to launch an attack on the Alcázar, which ended in a bloodbath. A year later the discontented populace rebelled and insurgents from the districts of La Feria, San Gil and San Román burst into the Iglesia Omnium Sanctorum and seized the Pendón Viejo, an old standard captured from the Moors, before threatening to sack the city. They freed prisoners and took up arms, but the newly reconciled authorities and nobility joined forces to quell the rebellion.

THE RIOT OF 1652. In the 17th century the populace rioted in protest against the bad management of municipal affairs, abuses and corruption. Food prices had soared. On May 22, 1652 a dispute between a baker from Alcalá and a customer over a loaf was the spark that lit the powder keg. The governor and assistant provost marshal (*asistente*) of Seville were forced to leave the city, but there was no pillaging or any form of offence other than the opening of the prisons and a general search to discover the whereabouts of wheat reserves. A month later mercenaries hired by the nobility had re-established law and order.

OMNIUM SANCTORUM

This Mudéjar-Gothic church, whose sculpted entrance belongs to the original 13th-century structure, was renovated in the 14th century. The ornamentation of the tower added in the 15th century is similar to that of La Giralda ● *73*. It was here that the Pendón Verde rebellion began and ended in 1520, and the Pendón Viejo is still preserved in the church. In an attempt to escape, the insurgents sought refuge in the church but were later executed. The church required further restoration after a fire in 1936, during the Spanish Civil War ● *40*. A cattle market is held nearby, and it is still possible to see the remains of the Palacio de los Marqueses de Algaba, built in the 14th century and abandoned since the 19th.

Sevillian couple, 19th-century engraving.

CASA DE LAS SIRENAS
The most distinctive building on the Alameda de Hércules is now little more than a ruin, although it was once a French-style residence of the Romantic period, built in 1864 for the Marquis of Esquivel. Rumor has it that it represented the taste of the Princess Ratazzi, the poetess wife of a Bonaparte. Its name is derived from the two bronze statues that stood at the entrance and evokes a past filled with entertainments, horse-drawn carriages and damask.

HERCULES
Statues of Hercules and Julius Caesar stand on Roman columns at the southern end of the Alameda.

COURTESANS OF THE ALAMEDA
At the end of the 19th century, the respectable society of the Alameda was replaced by those on the fringes of society as it opened its bars and brothels. Today it remains a nightlife hotspot, and hosts a flea market on Sunday mornings.

Right, flamenco dancers around 1930.

EL JUEVES. This small antiques and bric-à-brac market has been held in the Calle Feria every Thursday since the 13th century, perpetuating the ancient privilege granted to the merchants. Its very special atmosphere was immortalized by Miguel de Cervantes and other writers of the Spanish golden age and, in the 19th century, by the travelers Richard Ford and Baron de Davillier, when it attracted enthusiastic amateurs and antique dealers in search of masterpieces and archeological remains.

LA CRUZ VERDE. This is the name of the intersection where the Calle Feria widens and continues in a straight line. In the 16th century, it was known as the Pozo de los Hurones ("ferrets' well") and was a favorite meeting place for privateers.

LA ALAMEDA DE HÉRCULES

The Alameda was once a branch of the Guadalquivir that flooded when the river was in spate. In the 12th century the Almoravids incorporated it within their fortified enclosure wall and drained it. However the area was still flooded in the rainy season since it acted as an overflow for the reservoirs and water conduits in the north of

Baroque ceramics
Azulejos ● *56, 77,* ▲ *128* showing the flood levels of the Guadalquivir and a view of the Alameda ▲ 192.

the city. This earned it the name of the Laguna de Feria, as it was right next to the popular district of La Feria. It was not until 1574 that any form of urban development took place, on the initiative of the then assistant provost marshal, the Conde de Barajas.

Los Hércules. The count decided to remove the two marble columns from a large Roman edifice in the Calle Mármoles ▲ *153* and erect them on the Alameda. The columns were surmounted by sculptures by Diego de Pesquera (1574): one of Hercules, the mythical founder of Seville ● *30*, and the other of Julius Caesar, who built the city walls. The monuments were dedicated to Charles V and his son Philip II. The removal and erection of the columns took a year and was done with the assistance of the artillerist Bartolomé Morel, who was responsible for erecting the Giraldillo ▲ *125, 135*. Draining the area involved installing three marble fountains and planting some 1,700 trees, including alders, white and black poplars (*álamos* in Spanish, a noun that gave rise to *alameda*), cypresses, thujas, and orange trees. In the 17th and 18th centuries the avenue of the Alameda was much frequented by elegant carriages on warm summer nights. However it still suffered from the effects of high water and flooding, with stagnant, fetid pools left behind when the floodwater receded. In 1764 it was drained once again and two columns were erected at the southern end, on which lions hold up the Sevillian and Spanish coats of arms. In the 19th century new blocks of houses were built and reduced the avenue to its present dimensions. All that remains of the gardens that once followed the line of the façades are a few isolated sections protected by railings. The Pila del Pato ("duck's basin"), the fountain erected in the northern section in 1852, was moved to the Plaza de San Leandro in 1942.

La Alameda, once the mecca of the "Cante Andaluz". For a long time the Alameda was the venue *par excellence* of flamenco. In 1878 the *cantaor* Silverio Franconetti opened a music café during the summer months. After 1900 it attracted the very best flamenco artists, as evidenced by the BUST OF AURORA PAVÓN (La Niña de los Peines), at the northern end of the avenue, and the STATUE OF MANOLO CARACOL, at the southern end ● *55*.

Drummer
Photograph (19th century) of one of the traditional late-night celebrations and popular festivals held on summer evenings.

La Alameda Vieja
Until the 1930's park-keepers and water-sellers, in their small glass-fronted kiosks with metal canopies, were a common sight on the Alameda. Although they are no longer there, the Alameda Vieja still looks much the same as it did in 1936.

Sevillians being ferried across the Alameda during a flood in the early 20th century ▲ *192*.

▲ From Santa Clara to the Museo de Bellas Artes

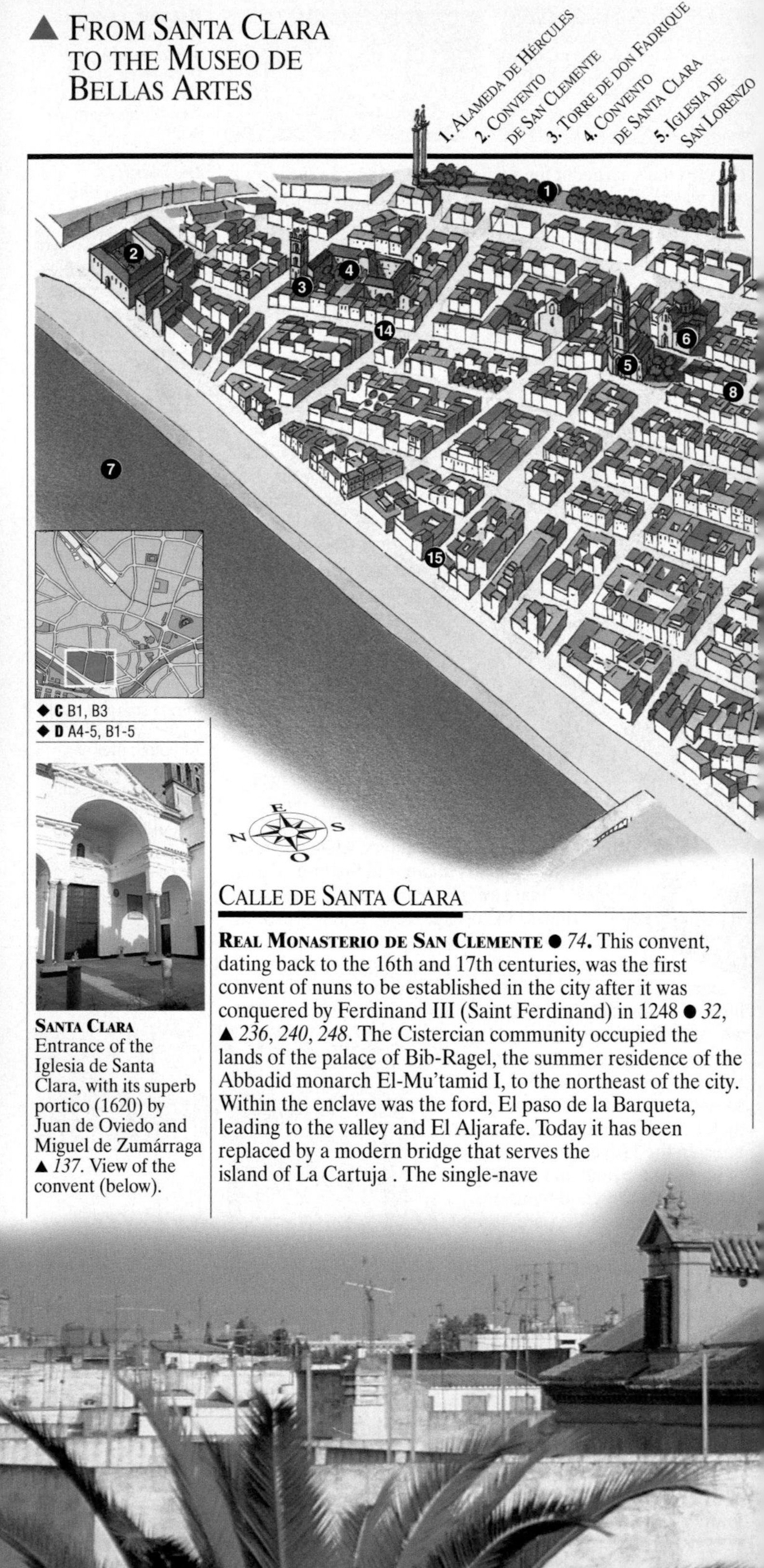

◆ **C** B1, B3
◆ **D** A4-5, B1-5

Santa Clara
Entrance of the Iglesia de Santa Clara, with its superb portico (1620) by Juan de Oviedo and Miguel de Zumárraga ▲ *137*. View of the convent (below).

Calle de Santa Clara

Real Monasterio de San Clemente ● *74***.** This convent, dating back to the 16th and 17th centuries, was the first convent of nuns to be established in the city after it was conquered by Ferdinand III (Saint Ferdinand) in 1248 ● *32*, ▲ *236*, *240*, *248*. The Cistercian community occupied the lands of the palace of Bib-Ragel, the summer residence of the Abbadid monarch El-Mu'tamid I, to the northeast of the city. Within the enclave was the ford, El paso de la Barqueta, leading to the valley and El Aljarafe. Today it has been replaced by a modern bridge that serves the island of La Cartuja . The single-nave

church, transformed in the 18th century, has a 16th-century Mudéjar coffered ceiling and 16th-century *azulejos*. The *retablo mayor* by Felipe de Rivas (1639-47) is decorated with polychrome paintings by Juan de Valdés Leal ▲ *188*.

Real Monasterio de Santa Clara. The second royal monastery in the Calle de Santa Clara was also one of the first convents established in Seville by Ferdinand III after his victory over the Muslims. It was built in 1289 and greatly extended in the 16th and 17th centuries. There is little to be seen from the street, but the narrow 17th-century entrance opens onto the church parvis, a delightful little garden with a marble fountain, orange trees and a date palm. It is surrounded by buildings once occupied by priests, clerics and the nuns' male servants. Today they house craft and study workshops. The 15th-century Mudéjar-Gothic church ● *70* has a beautiful coffered ceiling. Its *retablo mayor* and four lateral altars are the work (1621) of Juan Martínez Montañés ● *48*, ▲ *139*, *206*.

Torre de Don Fadrique
Built in 1252, the tower illustrates the transition from Romanesque to Gothic architecture.

Courtyard and *apeadero* (staging post) of the Santa Colomá mansion, in the Calle de Santa Clara.

PLAZA DE SAN LORENZO
The red and ocher façade of the Iglesia de San Lorenzo and the nearby entrance of the Basilica del Gran Poder stand on the edge of the plaza, whose plane trees were planted during the Napoleonic era.

Baroque bell tower surmounting the tower of the Iglesia de San Lorenzo (15th century).

COURTYARDS
Private house in the Calle de San Vicente,

which runs through one of the city's old aristocratic districts, characterized by elegant, two-story buildings and romantic courtyards.

IGLESIA DE LA MAGDALENA
The already considerable height of the naves was further increased by the octagonal dome, supported by a drum, added by Leonardo de Figueroa ▲ *155, 168, 180*, the founder of a rich "dynasty" of architects.

TORRE DE DON FADRIQUE. The tower is the oldest part of the first convent of nuns of the Order of Saint Clare, built on the site of the palace of the infante, Don Fadrique. Since 1920 it has housed the MUSEO ARQUEOLOGICO.

CONVENTO DE SANTA ANA. The community of Calced Carmelite nuns took up residence here in 1606. The complex, which stands at the intersection of the *calles* Santa Ana and Santa Clara, dates from the 17th and 18th centuries and has been restored several times. Its single-nave church, built between 1625 and 1650, contains a *retablo* decorated with a central sculpture (1627) by Juan Martínez Montañés.

PEACEFUL DISTRICTS

A commemorative plaque and the façade are all that remains of the house in the Calle Conde de Barajas, where the 17th-century Romantic poet Gustavo Adolfo Bécquer was born. The life of the peaceful and romantic district of San Lorenzo is centered around its beautiful plaza. The IGLESIA DE SAN LORENZO was built in the 16th century on the remains of a mosque, and was renovated in the 18th and 19th centuries. The door opening onto the plaza is one of two designed by Diego López Bueno in 1625 and set in the side walls of the church. It is surmounted by a niche containing a sculpture of San Lorenzo. The five naves and numerous chapels offer a blend of different styles. The church houses the statues of the

Although it no longer exists, in the 16th and 17th centuries the Dominican Convento de San Pablo was an extremely influential center for religious study, with a famous library and numerous works of art. In c. 1535 it had more than eighty friars. Bartolomé de las Casas studied there.

brotherhoods of El Dulce Nombre and La Soledad, which are carried in the final procession of the Semana Santa ● *44*, as well as beautiful Baroque *retablos*.

BASÍLICA DE JESUS DEL GRAN PODER. This modern building with its neo-Baroque entrance houses Seville's most venerated statue, *Jesús del Gran Poder*, by Juan de Mesa (1620) ▲ *164*, *252*. It is considered to represent the height of Sevillian Baroque art and is carried through the streets on the morning of Good Friday in an extremely devout and beautiful procession. The statue stands next to the *Virgen del Mayor Dolor y Traspaso* (18th century) and *San Juan Evangelista*, also by Juan de Mesa. As one of Seville's major spiritual centers, the basilica is much visited and is a popular setting for weddings.

CALLE CARDENAL SPÍNOLA. This quiet, narrow street was named after Marcelo, Archbishop of Seville, who founded the newspaper *El Correo de Andalucía* in 1899. Its beautiful buildings include the 18th-century CONVENTO DE SANTA ROSALIA. The parallel *calles* Cardenal Spínola and San Vicente, the Plaza de San Lorenzo and Museo de Bellas Artes enclose a delightful residential district (18th–19th centuries).

IGLESIA DE SAN VICENTE. Standing on the plaza of the same name, this 14th-century Mudéjar-Gothic church is the parish church of an aristocratic district. It was later modified, particularly in the 19th century. Inside, its collection of *retablos*, paintings and sculptures also represent different styles and periods. The original architectural style can still be seen from the stone portal, the bell tower and the CAPILLA DE LA HERMANDAD DE LAS SIETE PALABRAS.

IGLESIA DE LA MAGDALENA. The church is all that remains of the Dominican Convento de San Pablo, founded by Ferdinand III in 1248. The original edifice was destroyed in 1691. Rebuilding by Leonardo de Figueroa, according to the medieval layout of three naves, a transept and five chapels, commenced the same year and lasted until 1709. In 1810 it became the parish church of Santa María Magdalena and is one of Seville's great Baroque churches, with its distinctive openwork bell towers and the ornate lantern of its great dome. The extremely rich interior includes wall paintings, niches, gilt wood moldings, plasterwork, frescos by Lucas Valdés, canvases by Valdés Leal and Zurbarán, remarkable works of Baroque inspiration. There is also the sculpted group of *El Descubrimiento* (17th century). The CAPILLA DE LA HERMANDAD DE LA QUINTA ANGUSTIA contains the only surviving section of the original, late 14th-century church.

BARTOLOMÉ DE LAS CASAS (1474–1566)
This influential figure twice crossed the Atlantic (in 1502 and 1508) and wrote his famous *Historia General de las Indias*, based on personal documents belonging to his close friend Columbus ▲ *136*, *283* and his descendants, at San Pablo. Las Casas was the first to defend the rights of the Indians of South America.

"CABO PERSIANAS"
The popular name for this Rationalist building on the Plaza de la Magdalena.

MUSEO DE BELLAS ARTES
Claustro Grande and openwork bell tower (top, left); main hall, the former church (top, right); main entrance (above).

MUSEO DE BELLAS ARTES

Since 1839 the provincial Museo de Bellas Artes de Sevilla (Museum of Fine Arts) has occupied the former Convento de la Merced. After the Christian conquest of the city, Ferdinand III ● *32*, ▲ *176*, *240*, *248* gave the friars of La Merced land to cultivate and the site on which the convent was built. Its construction, originally in Mudéjar-Gothic style, lasted from the 13th to the 15th century.

A MUSEUM WITHIN A CONVENT. Insufficient information makes it impossible to form a complete picture of the layout and characteristics of the original building. The work that gave the museum its present structure was carried out under Sevillian architect and sculptor Juan de Oviedo; it began with the church (1602–12) with its casket-like design in the form of a Latin cross and its two side chapels, including that of the Cristo de la Expiración (which has a beautiful coffered ceiling). Its magnificent dome, painted by Domingo Martínez, still bears witness to its lively decoration. Work continued with the CLAUSTRO GRANDE (great cloister), the PATIO DE LOS BOJES ("box-trees"), the PATIO DEL ALJIBE ("cistern"), the PATIO DE LAS CONCHAS ("shells"), the sacristy, the noviciate and other outbuildings. The three main cloisters are arranged around a large, imperial-style central staircase that dominates the complex. It is an architectural masterpiece as well as being extremely beautiful. It was the forerunner of the "imperial staircases" inspired by those of the *alcázares* of Madrid and Toledo and served as a model for a great many convents in Latin America. The architect designed the open spaces and access to courtyards and staircases in the manner most appropriate to where they led. In this way, the former entrance of the convent opens onto the official courtyard, which in turn leads to a more private courtyard, and finally to the Patio del Aljibe, the modern entrance at the far end of the building. The edifice underwent various modifications, in particular the work to the Claustro Grande, completed in 1724, by Leonardo de Figueroa ▲ *155*, *168*, *178*, and the neoclassical façade (19th century).

BIRTH AND FORTUNES OF THE MUSEUM
In 1835 the confiscation of Church wealth by the Mendizábal government led to the expropriation of the works of art owned by convents and monasteries. The task of monitoring and preserving this wealth was entrusted to a museum committee, or Junta de los Museos, responsible for collecting and cataloging

Claustro Grande (great cloister).

Detail of the ceiling of the main staircase.

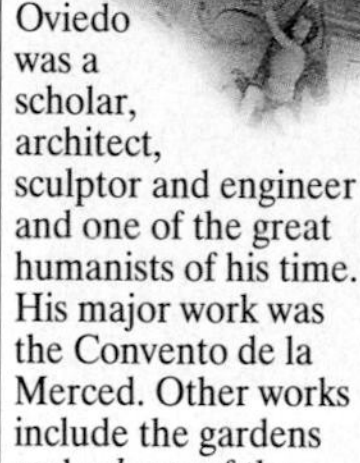

Oviedo was a scholar, architect, sculptor and engineer and one of the great humanists of his time. His major work was the Convento de la Merced. Other works include the gardens and *salones* of the Casa de Pilatos. The former nave and main staircase (below).

"Oviedo… was the representative of a humanist culture which… allowed the imagination the freedom to indulge in techniques that broke with the rigor forming the very essence of Classicism."

A. Bonet Correa

the paintings and works of art taken from churches. The Seville Arts Academy was founded in the same year and in 1839 was given the Convento de la Merced. The convent had been ravaged by fire in 1810 and its dependencies were, for the most part, in an extremely poor state of repair. The committee for the protection of works of art stipulated that the building should be partially renovated and repaired to restore it to a reasonable state. Work continued until 1985, when the restoration was finally completed. For more than one hundred years the roof of the museum had frequently collapsed and, until recently, its rooms were often closed.

Juan de Oviedo y de la Bandera
Bust of the architect of the museum, from the *Book describing the true portraits of great and famous men* (1599), by his friend Francisco Pacheco ● *91*, ▲ *160*.

The collections. The museum's collections fell victim to the artistic plundering of Seville in the 19th century. In 1810 Marshal Soult requisitioned 999 very valuable paintings, many of which were never returned. In 1835 Baron Isidore Taylor paid an extremely low price for five hundred works of art that were displayed at the Louvre for a while. The museum's present collections can be divided into two main groups. The first, devoted to Sevillian Baroque art and including major works signed by Zurbarán and Murillo, is alone enough to justify the museum's existence. The second group comprises 19th- and early 20th-century canvases related to Romanticism and *costumbrismo* (genre painting). The museum also has collections of sculpture, pottery, gold work, furniture, embroidery and decorative arts.

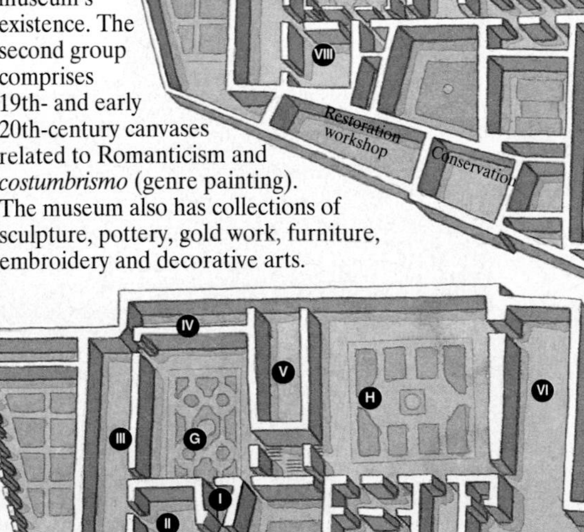

Second floor
VII. 17th-century Sevillian paintings
VIII. Murillo and his school
IX. Valdés Leal
X. European Baroque paintings
XI. Zurbarán
XII. 17th-century Spanish and 18th-century Sevillian paintings
XIII. Goya and Romanticism
XIV. *Costumbrismo* (genre painting)
XV. 20th century

First floor
A. Reception area
B. Store
C. Rest rooms
D. Temporary exhibitions
E. Patio de las Conchas
F. Patio del Aljibe
G. Patio de los Bojes
H. Claustro Grande
I. Spanish medieval art
II. Sevillian medieval art
III. Renaissance
IV. *Retablos*
V. Mannerism
VI. Baroque

Spanish painting is well represented in the Museo de Bellas Artes. Most comes from southern Spain; in fact, Zurbarán, Cano, Pacheco, the Herreras, Valdés Leal, Murillo and Velázquez either came from or worked in Seville. There are also great works from northern Spain and Italy.

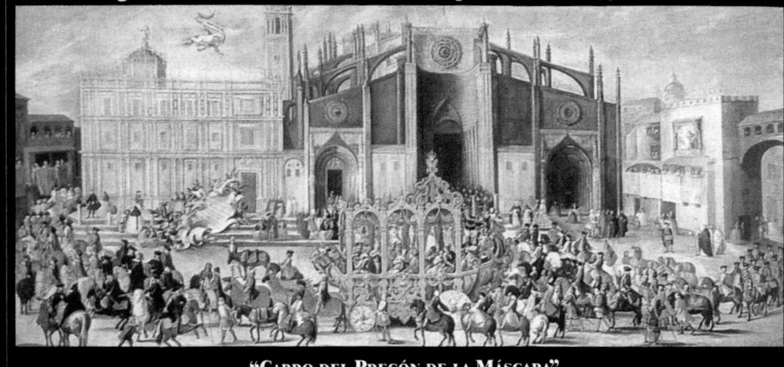

"CARRO DEL PREGÓN DE LA MÁSCARA"
Oil on canvas, painted in 1748 by Domingo Martínez. One of a decorative group of eight canvases depicting the procession of carriages that drove through Seville on the occasion of the coronation of Ferdinand VI.

SAINT JEROME
Polychrome terracotta figure (1525), by Pedro Torrigiano (1472–1528).

"LA VIRGEN DE LA MISERICORDIA"
This painting by de Zurbarán ▲ *139*, was one of a series for the Carthusians.

"LA INMACULADA" (1650) **AND "SAN TOMAS DE VILLANUEVA"** (1678)**.** Two oils on canvas by Bartolomé Estebán Murillo ● *91,* ▲ *138*.

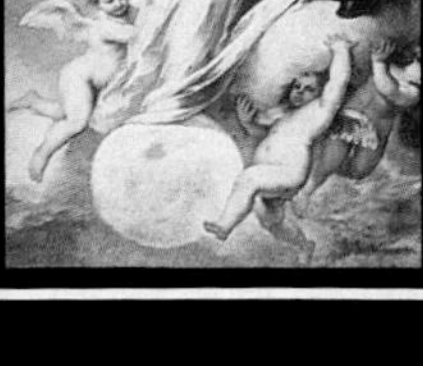

15TH CENTURY
Juan Sánchez de Castro (dates unknown) is the most worthy representative of 15th-century Sevillian painting. Although the museum does not possess any of his works, these paintings of San Antonio Abad and San Cristóbal (c. 1480) were the work of a group of masters influenced by his style. These and six other panels were painted in oils for a church *retablo*.

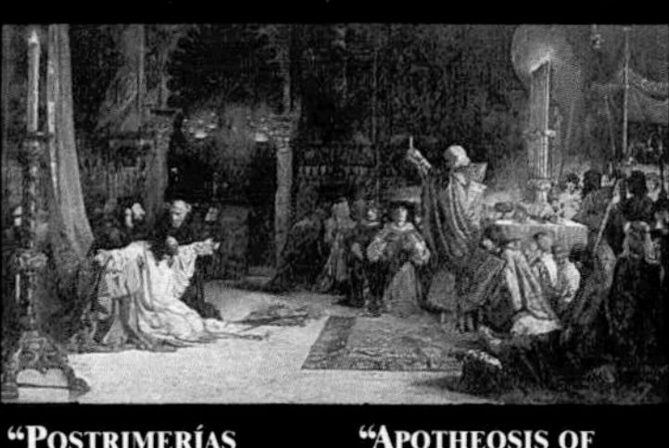

"POSTRIMERÍAS DE SAN FERNANDO"
"The Dying Moments of Saint Ferdinand" is an oil on canvas painted in 1887 by Virgilio Mattoni (1842–1923).

"APOTHEOSIS OF SAINT THOMAS OF AQUINUS"
This oil on canvas (1631) by Francisco de Zurbarán ▲ *139*, *158* is considered his finest work.

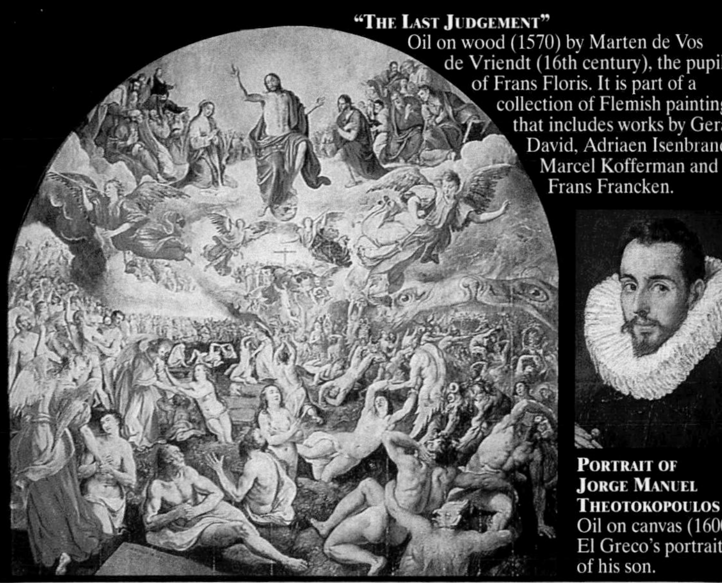

"THE LAST JUDGEMENT"
Oil on wood (1570) by Marten de Vos de Vriendt (16th century), the pupil of Frans Floris. It is part of a collection of Flemish painting that includes works by Gerard David, Adriaen Isenbrandt, Marcel Kofferman and Frans Francken.

PORTRAIT OF JORGE MANUEL THEOTOKOPOULOS
Oil on canvas (1600). El Greco's portrait of his son.

1. Río Guadalquivir
2. Torre del Oro
3. Puente de San Telmo
4. Jardines de Cristina
5. Hotel Alfonso XIII
6. Palacio de San Telmo
7. Fábrica de tabacos
8. Puerta de Jerez

This astrolabe can be seen on the exterior of the chapel of the Palacio de San Telmo.

PASEO DE COLÓN, A WINDOW ONTO HISTORY ✪
Past and present collide on the bank of the Guadalquivir: opposite the Torre del Oro ("golden tower"), a Moorish construction dating from the 13th century, rises an emblem of contemporary Seville, the headquarters of the contingency fund, completed by Rafael Moneo in 1986. In a similar fashion, the Plaza de Toros de la Maestranza (1761), a temple to bullfighting, is juxtaposed by the Teatro de la Maestranza, a theater and opera house inaugurated in 1991.

"The Casa de la Moneda mints 700 gold and silver marks per day and employs 180 men. Loads of gold and silver coins leave the building as if they were ordinary merchandise." (Extract from a chronicle, 1548)

TORRE DEL ORO
The tower, originally a bastion overlooking the river and port, formed part of the fortifications of the Alcázar. Seville was captured after the breaking of a chain stretched between the tower and its replica on the Triana bank in 1243.

THE OLD PORT

The historic port of Seville extended along the strip of land running parallel to the river, now the *paseos* de Colón and del Marqués de Contadero, and occupied the districts of La Carretería, El Postigo, El Arenal, El Baratillo and La Cestería. When its center of activity was displaced, this former port became a popular area for taking a leisurely stroll.

TORRE DEL ORO ★. The tower was built by the Almohads in 1221–2 to reinforce the Alcázar's defenses and control access to the port. Indeed, when Admiral Ramón de Bonifaz took control of it in 1243, in doing so cutting supply lines to Seville from Triana, the city fell. The upper section was added in 1760. Its name has three possible origins: its proximity to the Casa de la Moneda; its use to store treasure brought back from the Indies; or its former cladding of gold *azulejos* ● *56, 73.* Today the tower belongs to the Navy and houses the MUSEO MARITIMO. Two circular, vaulted rooms contain documents, paintings, models, weapons and other reminders of the city's maritime history.

CASA DE LA MONEDA. The Calle Santander leads from the Torre del Oro to the Casa de la Moneda, the part of the Alcázar that received gold and silver from America, as indicated by the names of the streets and gardens in the district. For example, the Torre de la Plata ("silver"), a Muslim and Christian edifice surrounded by buildings, was the counterpart of the Torre del Oro ("gold") and defended the 12th-century Casa de la Moneda. The complex was built in 1587, in response to the huge influx of precious metals. It can still be seen today, albeit much restored. Its monumental entrance (1761) opens onto the Calle Habana.

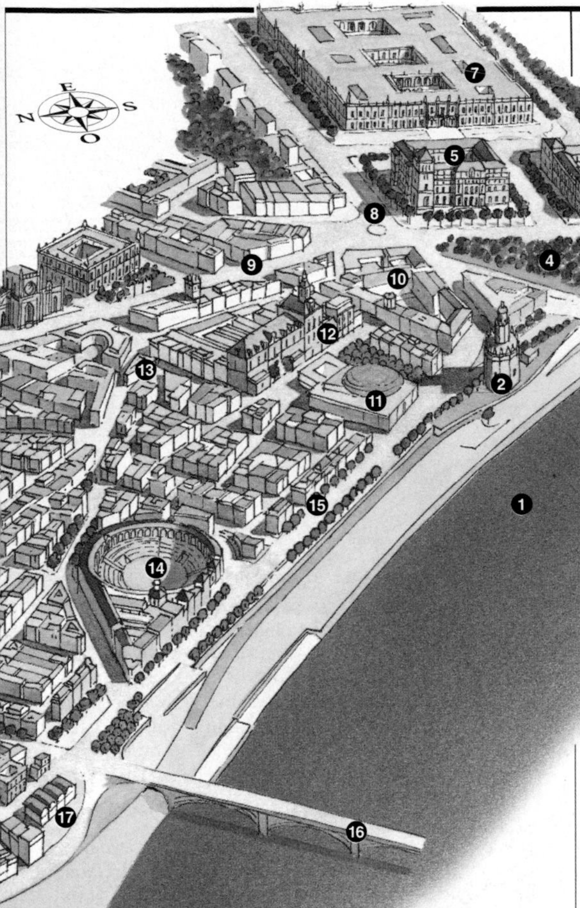

9. Avenida de la Constitución
10. Casa de la Moneda
11. Teatro de la Maestranza
12. Hospital de la Caridad
13. Postigo del Aceite
14. Plaza de toros de la Maestranza
15. Paseo de Cristobal Colón
16. Puente de Triana
17. Mercado del Barranco
18. Calle Reyes Católicos
19. Iglesia de la Magdalena
20. Plaza de Armas
21. Puente de Chapina

◆ C A3-A4-B4-B5-C5

◆ E A2-A3-B4-B5-C5-C6

Arquillo de la Plata
Gate (14th-century) on the avenue from the port to the Casa de la Contratación (also still known as the Casa del Océano) where metals from America ● *36* were stored.

The Fundición Real (royal foundry) and the crucible furnaces, now exhibition rooms, attest to its former activity. In the 19th century production ceased and the building was converted into apartments, though you can still visit the old blast furnaces.

Puerta de Jerez

The Avenida de la Constitución runs past the Casa de la Moneda and the Jardines de Cristina to the Puerta de Jerez, an extremely busy intersection and the point of exit for Cádiz. The Hotel Alfonso XIII to the south is a fine example of Sevillian regionalism. It was the birthplace of Vicente Aleixandre (1898–1989), a poet of the "Generación del 1927" ▲ *304* and winner of the Nobel Prize for Literature.

Galleons on the Arenal, in front of La Giralda, in the summer of 1617.

TOBACCO ● *37*
The Sevillian doctor Nicolás Monardes (1508–88) was the first to introduce the plant into Europe and defend its therapeutic properties.

URBAN OVERSPILL
Industrial and port installations developed outside the walls of the old Muslim city, along with the suburbs. The first buildings to be finished were the Palacio de San Telmo and the Fábrica de Tabacos.

CAPILLA DE PUERTA JEREZ. The chapel is the only part that remains of the College of Santa María, which was the first Hispanic university, founded in 1506 by Maese Rodrigo de Santaella. A *retablo* painting in the chapel shows the Virgen de la Antigua receiving the college building from the hands of its founder.

"CIGARRERAS"
Women workers leaving the tobacco factory were a favorite subject with Romantic artists. In the 19th and 20th centuries the factory employed an essentially female workforce (which provided inspiration for the character of Carmen ▲ *190*), of over three thousand women and only a few hundred men. The *rancho de cigarreras*, headed by a woman, was the basic unit of cigar production.

FÁBRICA DE TABACOS

The Calle San Fernando runs between the Alcázar and the old Fábrica de Tabacos, one of the largest factory buildings of its time, which today houses the rectorate of the University of Seville. The city pioneered the import of tobacco from the Indies, as well as potatoes, tomatoes and corn. In 1492 Christopher Columbus had observed the use of tobacco among the inhabitants of the Caribbean Islands, and the first shipments arrived in the port of Seville soon after. In the 17th century the first tobacco factories to be established on this side of the Atlantic were producing "Sevillian gold", a fine snuff which was the delight of snuff-takers until "smoking" tobacco became fashionable. Seville's vast tobacco factory was built in the 18th century to meet the increasing demand for the plant, whose flourishing trade was controlled by the State. It has an elaborate entrance decorated with inlays representing Christopher

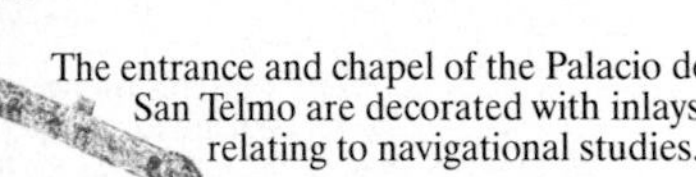
The entrance and chapel of the Palacio de San Telmo are decorated with inlays relating to navigational studies.

ROYAL FACTORY
The vast Fábrica de Tabacos was built in response to the increasing popularity of tobacco. Between 1728 and 1770 such architects and military engineers as Ignacio Sala and the Dutchman Sebastian van der Borcht directed the construction of a vast stone rectangle that looked more like a fortress. It covered an area of 200 x 160 yards and was surrounded by a ditch and turrets to protect the precious merchandise.

Columbus ▲ *136*, *283*, *304* and Hernán Cortés ▲ *221* (one of the first Europeans to smoke), cloistered courtyards, fountains, and two small structures used as a chapel and a prison for smugglers. The corridors echoed with the noise made by the workforce which, although originally male, had become predominantly female by the beginning of the 19th century. Women were paid less and were ideally suited to this light factory work.

PALACIO DE SAN TELMO

The white entrance and façades of San Telmo can be seen between the tobacco factory and the Guadalquivir. The *palacio*, dedicated to the patron saint of seafarers and built to house a school of navigation, was begun in 1682 at the request of the Universidad de los Mareantes, the Brotherhood of Navigators. It was built in the form of a quadrilateral with four towers, a central courtyard, a chapel and gardens. The most remarkable architectural elements are the entrance, the staircase and the Salón de Columnas. In 1695 twelve statues of illustrious Sevillians, sculpted by Antonio Susillo, were placed on the north façade. In the Baroque chapel through the cloister is a statue (1600) of *Nuestra Señora del Buen Aire*, protectress of seafarers, who presided over the foundation of Buenos Aires.

ROMANTIC COURT. Antoine d'Orléans, duke of Montpensier and son of the French king, Louis-Philippe, married a Spanish infanta. In 1849 he acquired the Palacio de San Telmo where he established his small court. It was frequented by politicians

SCHOOL AND PALACE
The Palacio de San Telmo, a fine example of Sevillian Baroque architecture, was completed in 1796. Its construction was directed by several architects, including members of the Figueroa "dynasty" ● *79*, ▲ *155*, *215*. It housed a naval school until the Duke of Montpensier made it his residence in the mid-19th century.

FAÇADE OF THE CAPILLA DE LA CARIDAD
The chapel was built by Bernardo Simón Pineda. Its *azulejo* panels, attributed to Murillo, represent saints George and James, and Faith, Hope and Charity.

and artists and became the center of Seville's social and romantic life. At the end of the 19th century the duchess María Luisa donated the palace for use as a seminary and gave its gardens to the people of Seville. Today the Palacio de San Telmo is the seat of the Presidencia de la Junta de Andalucía (the regional government's executive).

HOSPITAL DE LA SANTA CARIDAD

After the Puente de San Telmo, linking the Puerta de Jerez with Triana, the port itinerary returns to the Torre del Oro. Beyond the Teatro de la Maestranza lie the royal dockyards, among the first in Castile, built in 1252 by Alfonso X. In the 16th century they became the warehouse area of the port and naval artillery and merchants' depots were erected. All that remains of the original structure are the halls occupied by the Hospital de la Caridad and the former Maestranza de Artillería.

THE VANITIES OF THE WORLD TRAMPLED UNDERFOOT
Death arrives in the twinkling of an eye: *In ictu Oculi* . . . by Juan de Valdés Leal (1672).

AN ALMSHOUSE. The Hospital de la Caridad, in the Calle Temprado, was founded by the brotherhood of the same name, created in the 16th century to provide shelter for the poor and burial for the destitute and executed criminals. The hospital was established in the chapel of the dockyards, under the patronage of San Jorge, the patron saint of Genoa, the birthplace of the traders who controlled the finances and major trade of Castile. Between 1645 and 1670 the church was rebuilt according to a design by Pedro Sánchez Falconete and, in 1682, the hospital was

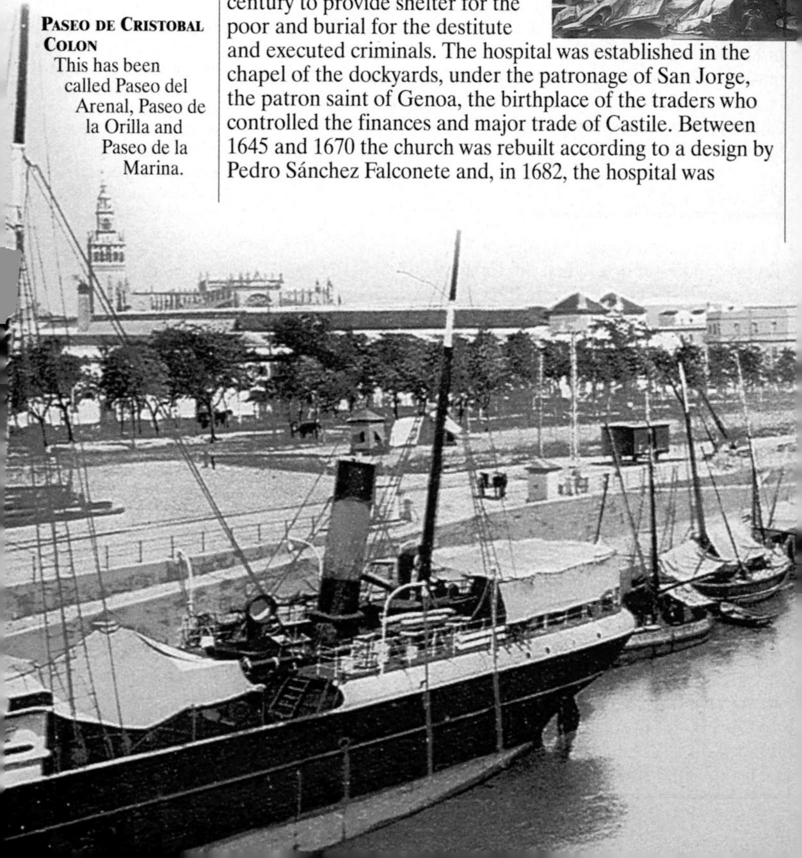

PASEO DE CRISTOBAL COLON
This has been called Paseo del Arenal, Paseo de la Orilla and Paseo de la Marina.

"If we encountered Truth, that, and that alone, would be the shroud that we should wear."

Miguel de Mañara

completed according to plans by Leonardo de Figueroa ▲ *155, 168, 178*.

"The best man that ever lived". This is the inscription on the memorial stone of Miguel de Mañara's tomb, beneath the portal of the entrance of the Capilla de la Santa Caridad. Mañara was certainly humble and pious, but this rich Corsican nobleman is remembered first and foremost as a lover of art and a senior brother in the Cofradía de la Caridad from 1663 until his death. He personally supervised the construction and decoration of one of Europe's major religious centers and was responsible for the chapel's fine blend of Sevillian Baroque architecture based on the spiritual chiaoscuro of his age.

Capilla de la Santa Caridad ★. The visit begins in a beautiful courtyard, with a double gallery by Bernardo Simón Pinela, fountains and panels of 17th-century Dutch *azulejos*. Inside the chapel, on either side of the entrance, are two canvases painted in 1672 by the Sevillian artist Juan de Valdés Leal (1622–90): *In ictu Oculi* and *Finis Gloriae Mundi*. Behind the altar stands a *retablo* sculpted by Pedro Roldán ● *48*, ▲ *137* and painted by Valdés Leal ▲ *136, 155*: ten life-sized figures compose an Entombment against a gilded décor of wreathed columns, atlantes and angels. The art collection is completed by a dozen or so paintings by Murillo ● *91*, ▲ *138, 182*, who was a member of the brotherhood and a close friend of Mañara. The series is missing the four paintings taken by the French field-marshal Soult. On the side walls are depicted Saint John of God carrying a dying man on his shoulders, and Saint Isabella of Hungary nursing a leper; in front of the presbytery there are Moses making the waters of a spring gush forth, and the Feeding of the Five Thousand. It is possible to have the chapterhouse opened to see a portrait of Mañara by Valdés Leal.

Postigo del Aceite
The Postigo del Aceite is one of the few surviving rampart gates near the dockyards. It was also known as the Postigo de los Azacanes ("water carriers"). It was through this gate that oil was brought into the city. Originally Moorish, its present appearance is the result of the transformations carried out in 1573, during the reign of Philip II. The arched entrance was widened and decorated with inscriptions and the city's coat of arms. It houses a small chapel to the Virgen de la Concepción where it is customary to drop a coin through the slot in the glass case that protects her.

Theater and opera house
The Teatro de la Maestranza, with its distinctive ceramic dome, stands on the banks of the river. It

was built in 1991 on the site of an artillery barracks, and is the city's main theater. Productions have included *Don Juan*, *Figaro* and *Carmen*.

Corrida at the Real Maestranza around 1850. The bullring's arcades, unfinished at the time, offered a view of La Giralda and the cathedral in the background.

EL ARENAL
The district behind the bullring is Seville's old tidal dock (*arenal* means "sand bank").

SUBURBS OF THE PORT DISTRICT. The Calle Dos de Mayo opens onto the picturesque plaza of the POSTIGO DEL ACEITE, which offers a unique view of the Semana Santa processions ● *44*. To the east stretches the SUBURB OF LA CARRETERÍA with its old grocers' stores, wine cellars and stores selling all kinds of delicacies. The streets become busier as you approach the intersection of the *calles* Arfe and García de Vinuesa, formerly the Calle de la Mar, that ran from the port to the cathedral. This former lagoonal area became Seville's Mancebiá district, famous for its prostitution and a popular setting in picaresque literature until it was cleaned up by the famous administrator, Pablo de Olavide, in 1778. The CAPILLA DE LA VIRGEN DEL BARATILLO stands in the Calle Adriano, in the heart of El Arenal and adjoining the Plaza de Toros. Bullfighters, in particular, worship in the chapel.

THE EL BARATILLO BULLRING
Built on the small hill of El Baratillo ("bric-à-brac"), the *plaza de toros* owes its oval shape to the fact that it was built over a period of 120 years. When there are no bullfights, the visitors' entrance is near the central gateway on the Paseo de Cristóbal Colón.

PLAZA DE TOROS DE LA MAESTRANZA

REAL MAESTRANZA. The bullring is the private property of La Real Maestranza de Caballería de Sevilla, a "riding society" set up in 1670 to replace a 13th-century order of knights that had become obsolete. Dedicated to training the aristocracy, as future king's officers, in mounted combat, La Maestranza

CARMEN ▲ *186*
There is a statue of Carmen, the operatic and literary heroine, opposite the bullring, scene of her tragedy in Bizet's opera.

organized public displays, including bullfights and tournaments, on Seville's plazas. When the court of Philip V was established in Seville, c. 1730, the King bestowed upon La Maestranza the honor of being presided over by a member of the royal family.

Fisherman on the quayside of the Guadalquivir.

STONE AND BRICK BULLRING. In the 1730's La Real Maestranza had the Baratillo flattened in order to build a wooden bullring there. From 1749, a series of stone buildings to accommodate stables, workshops and other outbuildings were constructed alongside the bullring's fence. In 1761 construction of a permanent bullring began. The royal box (*palco del Príncipe* ● *53*) and the main gate were completed in 1765, but the rest of the works were suspended several times and dragged on until 1881. The bullring is surrounded by two sections of tiered seats, one open (*tendidos*) and the other sheltered beneath the colonnaded gallery (*gradas*). The *presidencia* ● *53* and the *palco del Príncipe* are oppssite the *puerta de cuadrillas*, the gate through which the alguazils, picadors and mounted toreadors enter. The bulls emerge from the bull pens and exit, dead, via the *puerta de arrastre* ("haulage" exit).

ENTRANCES AND COURTYARDS
An iron grille surrounds the only section of the bullring's façade that is not hidden by other buildings. Several

entrances open directly onto buildings, and the courtyard where the horses are saddled and the picadors prepare for the *corrida* is cramped.

THE CATHEDRAL OF BULLFIGHTING
La Maestranza bullring is one of the oldest and loveliest in Spain (seating capacity 12,500). Its sheer beauty, excellent acoustics and long-standing tradition have made it a cathedral of bullfighting. During the fight spectators can hear the very rustling of the capes and the breathing of the bull. In the early decades of the 20th century Joselito and Belmonte ● *107* ▲ *173, 195* fought here. One of the corridors of the bullring houses the MUSEO TAURINO, which exhibits the dazzling costumes and portraits of famous bullfighters.

PUENTE DE TRIANA. Beyond the bullring are the quays of the Puente de Triana, Seville's first fixed bridge which, in the mid-19th century, replaced the pontoon linking Seville and Triana. All that remains of the city's early industrialization are the iron depots of the former Mercado del Barranco, built along the port in 1883 and now an exhibition center, and the ESTACÍON DE PLAZA DE ARMAS, which lies beyond the Calle Arjona. The station is still known as Córdoba station. The building itself incorporates an interesting combination of metal, filigree brickwork and *azulejos*.

The former Córdoba train station on Plaza de Armas.

HIGH-WATER MARK
The plaque (below) on the Torre del Oro marks the level of the flood waters in 1892.

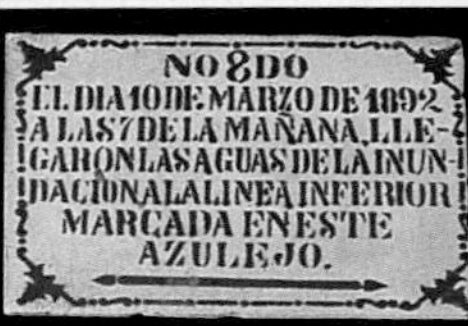

NO 8DO
EL DIA 10 DE MARZO DE 1892
A LAS 7 DE LA MAÑANA LLE-
GARON LAS AGUAS DE LA INUN-
DACION A LA LINEA INFERIOR
MARCADA EN ESTE
AZULEJO.

Although the Río Guadalquivir has always been vital to the prosperity of Seville, until the mid-20th century it was also the cause of the city's greatest disasters. Periodically the river was swollen by torrential rain and the water level rose . . . until it burst its banks and flooded the valley and low-lying areas between El Aljarafe and Los Alcores. Seville became an island in the center of a vast lake. Even the ramparts, which tended to act as a dike, were often submerged.

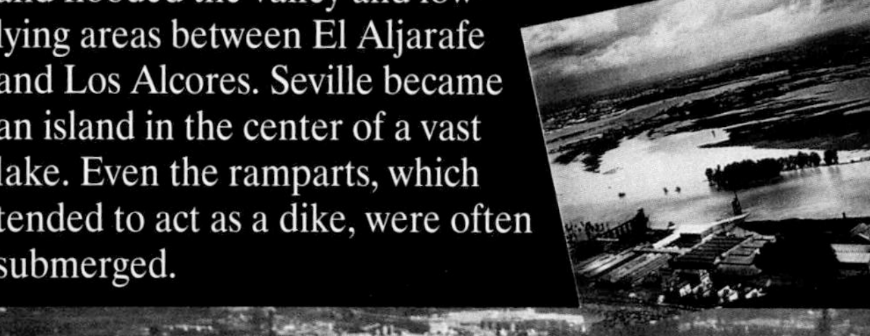

A FORMIDABLE ENEMY
Traditionally the ramparts of Seville were a defense against the floods of the Guadalquivir. The most vulnerable parts of the city were the outlying districts: El Arenal, the port (left, in 1892), and Triana. Although the city gates were closed using huge planks jointed with a mix of earth, the water often flowed in through the sewers and other openings. Engineering work carried out in the 19th century gradually reduced the risk of flooding. Flood defenses were constructed on the outskirts of the city and the river's rate of flow was controlled with artificial canalization and dikes.

"The water rose in the Calle Betis, spread through the tile works, the Calle Castilla, the soap factory, the market... and flooded the houses."
Rafael Laffón, 1947

ENDEMIC DANGER
A low-lying position (almost at sea level), a combination of heavy rain and high tides and the progressive narrowing of the river bed explain why Seville has been constantly exposed to the risk of flooding. Numerous *azulejos* in various parts of the city mark the level of the flood waters and act as a reminder that floods have been a constant feature of Seville's history.

A FORMER RIVER BED
Until the 11th century a branch of the river flowed near what are now the Alameda de Hércules, the Calle Sierpes and the Plaza Nueva. The Alameda remained a marshy area until it was drained in the 16th century. Once the city was flooded, the Guadalquivir went even further and flooded the low-lying plains. Photograph of the Alameda (right) in 1947.

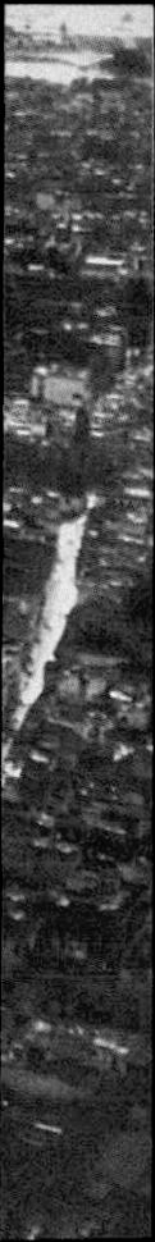

FAMOUS FLOODS. Official records refer to the floods of 1626, described as the "year of the deluge", 1796 and 1892. The last flood caused by the Guadalquivir (opposite page) was in 1947, although flooding caused by other rivers, such as the Tamarguillo, continued until 1961.

FLOOD VICTIMS
People took refuge on the upper floors (Triana in c. 1912, above) and had to travel by boat (Calle Trajano in 1947, below).

WHEN THE FLOOD WATERS SUBSIDED . . . The heavy flooding destroyed houses, docks, port installations and merchandise. When the waters subsided the banks of the river were covered with a thick layer of mud that often reached a depth of over 3 feet. The quays in 1947 (above).

1. PLAZA DE TOROS DE LA MAESTRANZA
2. TORRE DEL ORO
3. PUENTE DE SAN TELMO
4. PLAZA DE CUBA
5. IGLESIA DE SANTA ANA

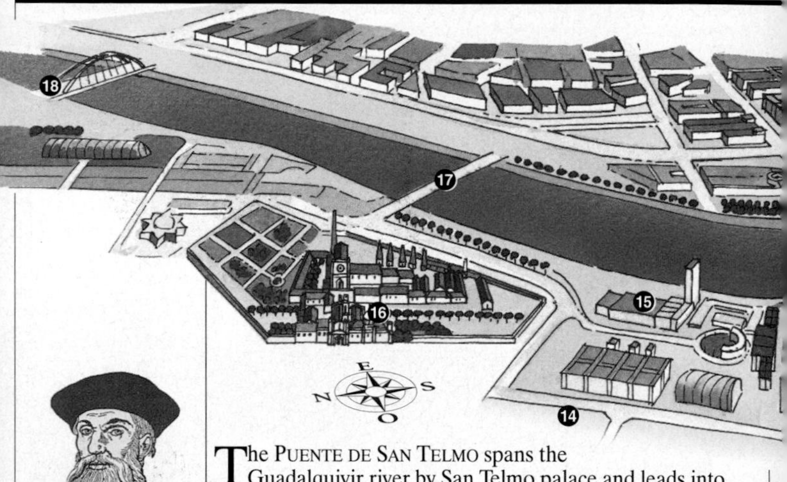

MAGELLAN
After distinguishing himself during the East Indies expedition (1505) and the capture of Malacca (1511), the Portuguese navigator envisaged a route to the Moluccas. He arrived in Seville in 1517 and, with the support of the Spanish Crown, set sail from Triana down the Guadalquivir to Sanlúcar ▲ *298*. From there he completed the first round-the-world voyage. He died in 1521 on the Island of Mactan (Philippines) and only eighteen of his men returned to Triana, in 1522.

Triana, drawing by Anton van Wyngaerde (1567).

The PUENTE DE SAN TELMO spans the Guadalquivir river by San Telmo palace and leads into the streets of Triana, which is almost as old as the district on the opposite bank and which got its name from the emperor Trajan. It is one of Seville's poorer areaz and, on several counts, one of the most interesting. The gipsies, who were ordered to live here by royal decree after the Reconquest, were displaced to the suburbs in the 1960's and 1970's, but the heart of this ancient Gypsy district still beats to the rhythm of the flamenco ● *54*. It also has associations with seafaring, as this was where sailors were recruited for long sea voyages, and remains attached to its maritime traditions, as well as to the tradition of pottery production dating back to ancient times.

CONVENTO DE LOS REMEDIOS. The Puente de San Telmo leads into the Plaza de Cuba, on the left of which is the Convento de los Remedios. The Virgen de los Remedios ("remedies"), worshiped in the church, is particularly dear to seafarers. The convent is adjacent to the former Puerto de la Mulas ("port of mules"), which was once an obligatory "port of call" for those, such as Ferdinand Magellan and his companions, who were about to embark upon a long voyage. The old monastery gave its name to a new district that sprang up south of the Avenida de la República Argentina in the 1950's, which proved to be the forerunner of the much-disparaged urban development that took place in Seville over the following two decades.

CALLE BETIS. The Calle Betis ("Baetis" was the Roman name for the Guadalquivir) lies above the Puente de San Telmo and is reached by following the river bank upstream. It is a true belvedere, offering a magnificent view of the opposite bank and the majestic architecture of the historic districts of Seville ● *83*. Ramps and steps lead down to the shore and the quays of the former shrimp port, now a marina. Although river fishing is almost obsolete, Triana has retained all the appearance of a port and traditional craft district, and certain Sevillian customs and characteristics remain fiercely alive. You only have to take one of the narrow streets leading from the Calle Betis into the heart of Triana to find this out for yourself: you will

6. Calle Betis
7. Plaza del Altozano
8. Puente de Triana
9. Iglesia de San Jacinto
10. Capilla del Patrocinio
11. Calle Castilla
12. Paseo Nuestra Señora de la O
13. Puente de Chapina
14. Parque Tematico de la Cartuja
15. Pabellón de la Navegación
16. La Cartuja
17. Pasarela de la Cartuja
18. Puente de la Barqueta

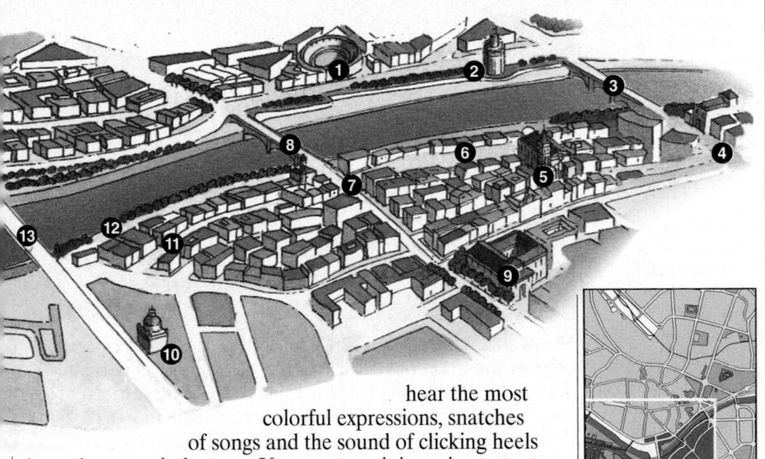

hear the most colorful expressions, snatches of songs and the sound of clicking heels through open windows . . . You can even join an impromptu meeting in one of the district's many *tabernas.* In the Calle Troya an *azulejo* reminds passers by that this was the setting for Cervantes' Court of Monipodio, the vagabonds' meeting place in *Rinconete y Cortadillo*.

Plaza de Santa Ana. To the right of the Calle Troya, the Calle Pureza leads to the tiny Plaza de Santa Ana and one of the oldest Christian churches in the city. It was built in the late 13th century by Alfonso X, who had been miraculously cured of an eye disease, and was used for a long time as a cathedral. Visitors to the church can admire the Renaissance *retablo* of the high altar, a 16th-century tomb inlaid with *azulejos* by Niculoso Pisano, and the silver monstrance by Mateo Ximénez, which is the central feature of Triana's "Corpus Chico" procession.

Capilla de los Marineros. A little further on, in the Calle Pureza, stands the Capilla de los Marineros ("chapel of seafarers") housing the *Esperanza de Triana*. The splendor of her procession, at dawn on Good Friday, competes with that of the *Virgen de la Esperanza* ("La Macarena") ● *45*. The statue, by an unknown sculptor, was restored in the 19th century by Juan de Astorga, although the face, by Castillo Lastrucci, is more recent. On the way back to the Calle Betis is Figaro's barber's shop (its real name is "Los Pajaritos"). The present owner has decorated the building with designs reminiscent of *Marriage of Figaro* by Mozart and *The Barber of Seville* by Rossini.

◆ **C** A1-6, B1, B5-6
◆ **E** A4-6, B5-6

Feria de la Velá
The festival, dedicated to Santa Ana (the patron saint of the district of Triana) and Saint James the Apostle (Santiago), is held on July 24 and 25 on the banks of the river. The Calle Betis is crowded with canvas stalls, flamenco performances, greased poles and vendors selling fresh hazelnuts.

Juan Belmonte
In the Plaza del Altozano a bronze statue of Juan Belmonte ● *53*, ▲ *173* looks across the river at the Maestranza ● *52*, ▲ *190* opposite. In the first three decades of the 20th century, he revolutionized bullfighting. His motto was "Stop, pacify and control".

PUENTE DE TRIANA
(Puente de Isabel II)
Opened in 1852, this was Seville's first fixed bridge. Until then river crossings had been made using an ingenious Moorish floating bridge (12th century), a wooden pontoon placed on a series of boats that rose and fell with the movement of the river.

Retablo of the *Virgen de la Esperanza de Triana*.

CAPILLA DEL CARMEN
Also known as the Capilla del Mechero ("oil lamp").

PLAZA DEL ALTOZANO. The Calle Betis comes to an end on the edge of the Plaza del Altozano. On the right the Puerta de Triana opens onto the bridge of the same name (officially the PUENTE DE ISABEL II), built between 1845 and 1852. The design of the bridge, by Fernando Bernadet and Gustavo Steinacher, was based on that of the (now non-existent) Pont de Carrousel in Paris.

PASEO DE LA O. The Calle San Jorge runs from the northwest of the plaza and the route is extended further on, by the Calle Castilla. To the right the Callejón de la Inquisición leads down to the river where a beautiful avenue, the Paseo de la O, provided the setting for one of the darkest episodes in Spanish history. The Castillo de San Jorge (built by the Muslims) that once stood on this spot became the Castillo de la Inquisición, a prison for those accused of heresy, witchcraft and Judaism. Several famous people died here, including the Italian sculptor Torrigiano who, according to the Inquisitors, committed suicide to escape being burnt at the stake. Seville's first *auto-da-fé* was held here in 1481. Until 1520 many converted Jews were pursued by the ecclesiastic tribunal. With the abolition of the Inquisition in the 19th century, the castle was demolished and a market installed on the site.

CALLE CASTILLA. Some of Seville's most famous ceramics workshops ● *56* are found near the Calle Castilla. Crockery, decorative *azulejos*, plant-pot holders and polychrome ceramic reproductions of religious images are just some of the more typical Triana ceramic items

"[Flamenco] originally described the manners and bearing of Spanish soldiers returning from Flanders. They were found... to have adopted strange, and somewhat bizarre manners."

Dominique Fernandez

being produced. According to a long-standing tradition Triana is also Seville's district of festivity and enjoyment, with hundreds of *tabernas* and bars offering tapas ● *61* and other specialities. Calle Castilla's most popular establishment is the brasserie Ruiz, also known as the *Peña Trianera*, renowned for its picturesque architecture and the quality of its cuisine. Opposite it, near the Callejón de la Inquisición, the Corral de las Flores is one of the few traditional working-class communal housing projects to have survived the rehabilitation campaign carried out in the district in the 1960's.

FLAMENCO DISTRICT. The conviviality and sociable atmosphere of the *corrales*, galleried apartments surrounding a central courtyard, are closely linked to the appearance and dissemination of flamenco singing which, according to some experts, was born in the cellars of Triana. It was in the "music" cafés near the Plaza del Altozano, such as the *Peña Flamenca* (a bar were flamenco enthusiasts meet), the *Casa Anselma* and the *taberna El Berrinche*, that such 19th-century pioneers of the modern *cante jondo* ● *54*, ▲ *391* as Manuel Torres, Tomás "el Nitri" and "el Fillo" made a name for themselves. Several flamenco groups still meet today in the Calle Alfarería near the Calle Castilla, and guitarists, *cantaores* and enthusiasts get together over a glass of wine and a plate of fried fish.

CHRISTIAN WORSHIP AND CEREMONY. In the Calle Castilla are the IGLESIA NUESTRA SEÑORA DE LA O and the CAPILLA DEL CRISTO DE LA EXPIRACION. The statues of the district's patron saint, *Nuestro Padre Jesús Nazareno*, belonging to the church, and the famous *Cristo del Cachorro* (sculpted in 1682 by Ruiz de Gijón), housed in the chapel, are carried in the torchlit procession held on the evening of Good Friday. As the procession crosses the Triana bridge, the light of the torches are reflected in the waters of the river, making it one of the most impressive sights of the Semana Santa ● *44*.

"CORRALES" AND GIPSIES

Atmospheric Triana is largely so thanks to the lay presence of its large Gipsy community and to its *corrales de vecinos* ● *82* (below).

Flamenco festival in the courtyard of the Hotel Triana.

Paseo de la O.

LA CARTUJA

Near the Puente del Cachoro, the Triana district comes to an end and the modern district of La Cartuja begins.
MONASTERIO CARTUJO DE SANTA MARIA DE LAS CUEVAS. The district was named after the Carthusian monastery (*cartuja*) founded in 1400 by Archbishop Gonzalo de Mena. The Carthusian monks chose the site for its remoteness, far from the noise and bustle of the city and completely cut off when the river was in spate. The monastery expanded during the 15th century under the patronage of the powerful Ribera family. The CAPILLA MAGDALENA, the CHAPTERHOUSE and the CHURCH were constructed around a small, elegant cloister in pure Mudéjar-Gothic style. During subsequent centuries the monastery was further extended and its art collections enriched with masterpieces. After it was impoverished by the plundering of the 19th century, some of these works found their way back to their place of origin. Visitors can see the MONUMENTAL MARBLE TOMBS of Pedro Enríquez and Catalina de Ribera, sculpted in c. 1530 in the Genoese workshops of Aprile de Carona and Pace Gazini. On his return from his first voyage, Christopher Columbus ▲ *136*, *283* took up residence in La Cartuja where, with the help of the Carthusian monks who placed their knowledge and their well-stocked library at his disposal, he prepared future expeditions. At the time the orchard of La Cartuja was highly praised and provoked the following comment from a traveler in 1526: ". . . the monks are on the right ladder to climb straight up to Heaven".
The last religious modification took place in c. 1759 when the CAPILLA PÚBLICA (public chapel) was built.

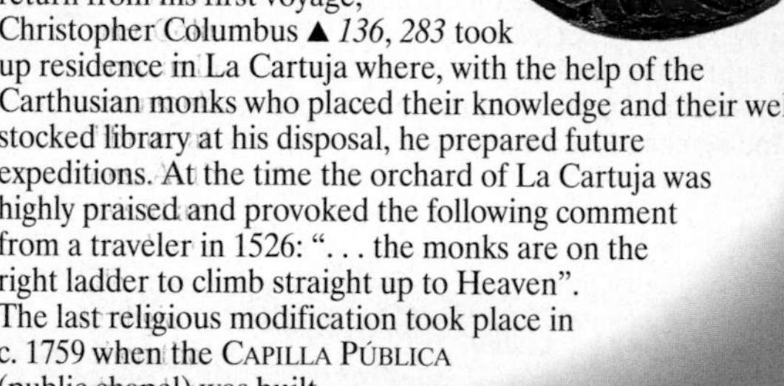

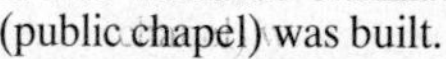

LA CARTUJA TRANSFORMED
In 1992 the Isla de la Cartuja, previously devoted to agriculture and the extraction of clay for the pottery industry, was spectacularly transformed into the site for Expo '92.

View of La Cartuja on an exhibition poster.

CHRISTOPHER COLUMBUS'S HERALDIC SHIELD (right).

NEW BRIDGES
Four bridges were built across the river, between Seville and

La Cartuja, for Expo '92: the *puentes* de la Chapina, de la Cartuja, de la Barqueta and del Alamillo, which is a true feat of engineering.

"The depth of civilization and the impression of being in a capital city when you are in Seville would be inexplicable if you didn't take into account that... [it] was once a leading commercial center."

Dominique Fernandez

Pickman china. In 1841 the Englishman Charles Pickman installed a ceramics factory in the monastery buildings, which had been auctioned off, as part of the process of the secularization of Church property, and extensively transformed it. The new factory of La Cartuja, which manufactured "English china of every type and color", was one of the first few experiments of the Sevillian industrial revolution. Today Pickman's china still graces some of the finest tables in the world.

The "Age of Discovery". La Cartuja's tenuous connection with Christopher Columbus explains its selection as the site for Expo '92, commemorating the fifth centenary of the discovery of America. A carefully renovated Cartuja gave its name to the exhibition center and became the Royal Pavilion. The theme of Expo '92 was the "Age of Discovery". The development of navigation and technology was presented in thematic pavilions, while other areas were presented in national and corporate pavilions. A total of 110 countries and 22 international organizations were represented over an area of 198 acres, and the exhibition welcomed over forty million visitors. The work for Expo '92 affected not just the district of La Cartuja, but had an impact upon the entire city, which was modernized in several areas.

After the exhibition. Although temporary structures were dismantled at the end of the exhibition, the permanent pavilions constituted the nucleus of the "Cartuja '93" project. The former exhibition center is now occupied by a technical center and a discovery park, including the famous pavilions of Navigation, the Future and Andalusia. Finally the landscaping of the banks of the Guadalquivir river has made this a popular place to walk.

Expo '92
The exhibition center (below) and an aerial view of the newly completed urban development of La Cartuja (bottom).

La Cartuja footbridge, with the Puente del Alamillo ● *88* in the background.

1. Parque María Luisa
2. Plaza de España
3. Pabellón de Portugal
4. Avenida del Cid
5. Glorieta San Diego
6. Prado de San Sebastián
7. Avenida de Isabel la Católica
8. Casino de la Exposición and Teatro Lope de Vega

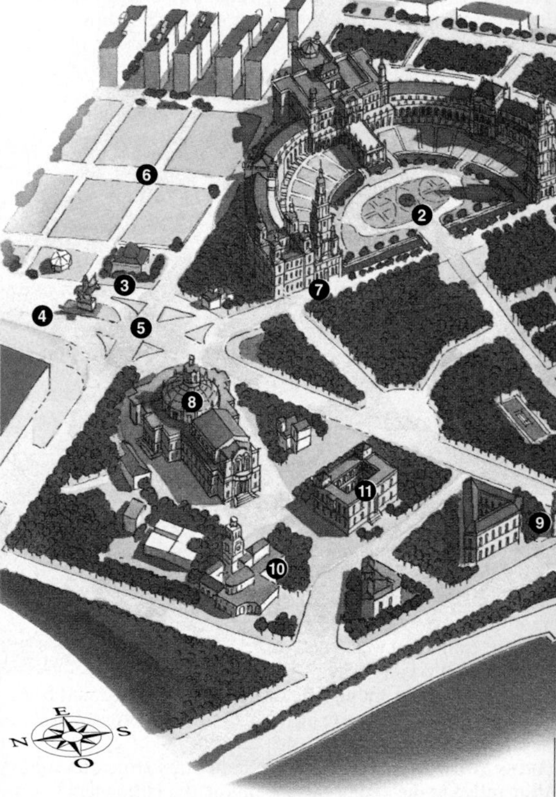

El Cid
This itinerary begins at the monument to El Cid, which stood at the main entrance to the Hispanic-American Exhibition. A replica of the equestrian statue, by the American sculptor Hyatt Huntington, stands opposite the Hispanic Society in New York.

TAKING A BREAK ✪
A favorite spot among Sevillians looking for fresh air, the park juxtaposes wild vegetation with neat flower beds, and European plants with more exotic species. Take a boat trip on the little canal of Plaza de España before visiting the museums of Plaza de América.

The Parque María Luisa, the largest and most pleasant park in Seville, runs along the left bank of the Guadalquivir river from the Palacio de San Telmo to the Avenida de la Palmera ("palm tree"). The park was created in successive stages, a fact that is apparent from its general layout and the blocks of greenery of which it is made up.

The office of architect Aníbal González, right, shortly before the Hispanic-American exhibition of 1929.

9. Costurero de la Reina
10. Pabellón de Chile
11. Pabellón de Peru
12. Glorieta de los Marineros Voluntarios
13. Pabellón Real
14. Pabellón Mudéjar (Museo de Artes y Costumbres Populares)
15. Plaza de América
16. Pabellón Plateresco (Museo Arqueológico)
17. Jardines de las Delicias
18. Paseo de las Delicias
19. Glorieta Buenos Aires

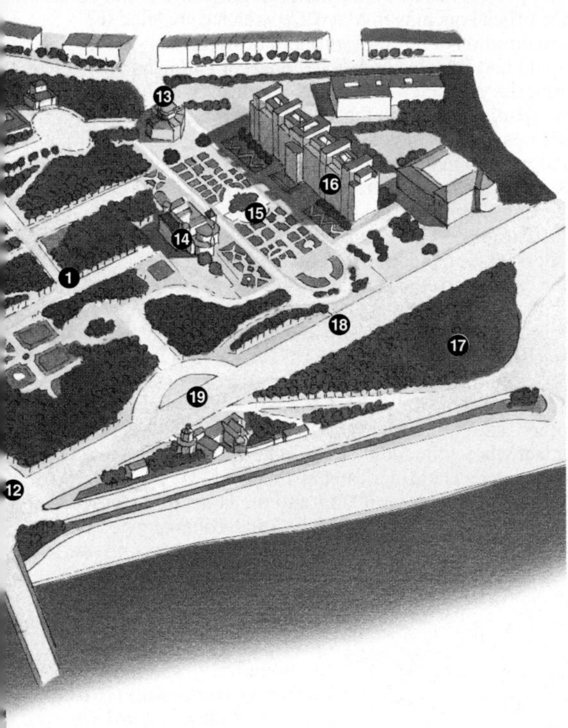

◆ C C6-D6

Plaza de España
The Plaza de España, the emblem of the 1929 Exhibition and the symbol of Spain, is a masterpiece created by the architect Aníbal González, who sadly died a few days before the exhibition opened. Between 1914 and 1928 more than a thousand workmen were employed on the construction of the site. The neo-Renaissance Pabellón de España, which overlooks the plaza and its central fountain, forms a vast semicircle flanked by two 260-foot towers. The ceramic facings decorating its arcaded gallery represent the various Spanish provinces. A half-moon canal, traversed by bridges adorned with *azulejos*, runs around the plaza.

HISTORY OF THE PARK

In 1830 the Jardines de las Delicias ("delights") were opened on the banks of the Guadalquivir. It was the first enclave of ornamental plants in what had, until then, been an area of fertile market gardens. In 1849 the French landscape gardener Lecolant designed the romantic gardens of the Palacio de San Telmo, the residence of the dukes of Montpensier. The gardens, given to the city in 1893 by the dowager duchess María Luisa Fernanda de Bourbon (daughter of Ferdinand VII of Spain), lay within the park named after their donor. In 1929 the park was redesigned according to its present layout and became the centerpiece of the Hispanic-American Exhibition.
Hispanic-American Exhibition. This international event, initiated in 1909, was intended to lift Seville out of a period of economic stagnation through a program of public works, while encouraging tourism. In 1911 the task of redesigning the 346 acres of park and surrounding area to accommodate the exhibition was entrusted to Jean-Claude Nicolas Forestier (1861–1930), a French landscape gardener and warden of the Bois de Boulogne. The architect Aníbal González (1876–1929) ● *87* was responsible for the construction of the buildings.

A wide range of species
The park boasts a particularly rich collection of botanical species. A huge fig tree on one of the park's *glorietas* (below).

ROMANTIC GARDEN
The park's central lake, with its beautiful Mudéjar arbor, is a remnant of the original gardens of the Palacio de San Telmo. It stands in landscaped grounds embellished with exotic trees, shrubs, grottos and fountains.

The project was delayed by endless difficulties, right up until the official opening in May 1929, which completed the urbanisation of Seville's southern districts. The pavilions of Spain and Portugal and the colonies of Latin and Portuguese America competed with those of industrial and commercial companies. Although the actual event was a failure for various reasons (it coincided with the Wall Street Crash), it did succeed in promoting significant urban development.

ARCHITECTURE AND THE ENVIRONMENT. The landscaping and structural work carried out for the 1929 Exhibition has made the Parque de María Luisa doubly interesting for visitors, as it offers an harmonious blend of architecture and vegetation. At the entrance to the park, opposite the statue of El Cid and the Prado de San Sebastián, are the PABELLÓN DE PORTUGAL (the former Portuguese Pavilion and now the Consulate) on one side, and the CASINO DE LA EXPOSICIÓN (formerly the Pabellón de Sevilla) and the TEATRO LOPE DE VEGA (an eminent Seville theater for dramatic art and music) on the other. They are the work of Vicente Traver (1889–1970) under whose direction the exhibition buildings were completed. The American pavilions of PERU (inspired by Incan art), URUGUAY, CHILE and the UNITED STATES (in Californian colonial style) are near the river. The nearby COSTURERO DE LA REINA ("queen's arbor") ● *86* is one of the remaining small decorative structures in the gardens of the palace of the dukes of Montpensier.

AMERICA COMES TO SEVILLE
The 117 buildings of the 1929 Exhibition included the distinctive American pavilions ("Argentina", above). Most still stand in the Paseo de las Delicias and the Avenida de la Palmera.

EUROPEAN PARK, ORIENTAL GARDEN. In the park there is a striking alternation of open spaces and densely planted areas. Forestier in fact decided to "respect the essence of the place" by incorporating the structural elements and planting of the former gardens of San Telmo into his formal design. The old orange trees flourished and multiplied to such an extent that they became the symbol of Seville. The Parque de María Luisa was transformed into an extraordinary blend of bustling European avenues, peaceful oriental courtyards and romantic landscaped gardens, deserving of every kind of praise and, according to the landscape artist Joaquín Sorolla y Bastida (1863–1932),

The park's *glorietas* are islands of vegetation with a central monument commemorating an event or famous person.

"making all the other gardens of Europe pale by comparison".

AVENUES AND "GLORIETAS". Avenues lead from the entrance, through an exuberance of widely varied planting, to *glorietas* bordered by ponds, fountains, pergolas and benches covered with *azulejos*. Not far from the Plaza de España is a SCULPTED GROUP dedicated to the memory of the Romantic poet Gustavo Adolfo Bécquer (1836–70): three female figures representing Love Deceived, Love Fulfilled and Love Lost, embraced by a huge bald cypress planted in 1870. From the center of the Plaza de España, the PASEO DE LOS MAGNOLIOS ("avenue of magnolias") leads to avenues bordered by plane trees and Japanese pagoda trees. Hidden away in the heart of the park are a little lake with the ISLETA DE LOS PATOS ("island of ducks"), the FUENTE DE LAS RANAS ("fountain of frogs") and the FUENTE DE LOS LEONES ("fountain of lions")at the foot of MONTE GURUGÚ, the only hill in this vast green space.

PLAZA DE AMÉRICA. The Plaza de América lies at the southern end of the park. It was created in 1912 by Aníbal González and was the most outstanding plaza of the Ibero-American Exhibition. It is elliptical in shape and bordered by the Pabellón Real, the Museo Arqueológico and the Museo de Artes y Costumbres Populares, built especially for the 1929 Exhibition and offering a synthesis of the three great Sevillian styles: Mudéjar, Gothic and Renaissance. The *glorietas* (including one dedicated to Cervantes) and *plazoletas* (small squares such as Las Palomas) are bordered by flower beds. The PABELLÓN REAL (royal pavilion) (1911–16) was built in flamboyant Gothic style for the royal family. The exterior is

Until recently organ-grinders were a common sight in the parks of Seville, as were people selling cinnamon wafers (small cone-shaped waffles) and the photographers with their *papier-mâché* horses.

MUSEO DE ARTES Y COSTUMBRES POPULARES
The pieces in this museum of folklore and popular art attest to the importance of rural life in Lower Andalusia (harrow, left). The first floor, devoted to traditional trades and occupations, houses reconstructions of a press, a forge, a baker's oven, a potter's wheel and a tanner's workshop.

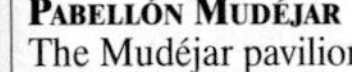

PABELLÓN MUDÉJAR
The Mudéjar pavilion in the Plaza de América was built between 1911 and 1914 as the "Palace of Decorative Arts" for the 1929 Exhibition. It is one of Aníbal González' most celebrated works and gave its name to this picturesque style.

PABELLÓN PLATERESQUE
The Renaissance-inspired Plateresque pavilion (which today houses the Museo Arqueológico) was designed by Aníbal González and built between 1911 and 1919. Its sobriety provides a striking contrast to the Pabellón Mudéjar.

PHOENICIAN ART
Statuette of Astarte, goddess of fertility, which bears one of the oldest Phoenician inscriptions on the Iberian peninsula.

decorated with ceramics in relief and the interior with pictorial *azulejo* panels. The Pabellón Mudéjar (MUDÉJAR PAVILION) ● *86* houses the MUSEO DE ARTES Y COSTUMBRES POPULARES (the Museum of Popular Art and Folklore) which presents various aspects of the region's cultural heritage: costume, jewelry, gold work, religion, festivals, musical instruments, agricultural and pastoral farming, housing, weaving and pottery. The collection of ceramics is probably the most remarkable. It contains pieces made between the 14th and the 20th centuries, which represent the various techniques of this typically Sevillian craft. *Azulejos*, pharmacists' jars and products from the Cartuja factory ▲ *198* form the basis of the collection.

MUSEO ARQUEOLÓGICO

The Pabellón Plateresco, the former "Palace of Fine Arts" of the 1929 Exhibition, stands on one side of the Plaza de América. Today it houses the Museo Arqueológico, one of Spain's most important archeological museums, which was opened to the public in 1946. This antiquities museum was created in 1835. It is comprised of exhibits from the Roman town of Itálica ▲ *208*, the municipal collection and such private collections as the one put together in the latter part of the 18th century by Don Francisco de Bruna, who was governor of the Alcázar.

FROM PREHISTORIC TO COLONIAL TIMES. The visit begins in the basement, with archeological remains from the Stone, Bronze and Iron ages and objects imported by Phoenician, Greek and Carthaginian settlers. Of particular

PREHISTORIC ART
One of the stone idols (right), decorated with eyes and carved in the form of cylinders or plaques, that appear to be linked to funerary monuments dating from the early Bronze Age. They are the region's earliest religious representations.

ROMAN ART
Altars, *cippi*, sarcophagi, coins, mosaics, bronzes, ceramics and jewelry offer, along with the Salón Imperial and the rooms presenting studies of archeological strata, a complete overview of Roman Baetica. Leg of a horseman (right), discovered in the Cerro Macareno.

Carambolo treasure
The treasure contains masterpieces of Tartessian culture ● *30* and some of the museum's key pieces (right). Copper and Bronze Age objects (far right).

interest are the items from dolmens in the region, mysterious funerary steles and examples of Tartessian culture, the result of the Phoenician influence on local Iberian culture. There are also the amazingly rich treasures from the sites of El Carambolo, near Seville, and Evora. Ceramics and other products from the Levant attest to the importance of trade between the eastern Mediterranean countries and southern Spain.

Splendors of Roman art. The first few rooms on the next floor have an impressive collection of sculptures (lions, bulls and warriors) from the local Iberian civilization of the Roman period. These are followed by rooms devoted to Roman art (the most important section of the museum), starting with bronzes and sculptures, including the group of the Niobides (4th century BC, probably Greek), and mosaics. The Greek-inspired Roman statuary from Itálica, sculpted during the reign of Hadrian, are the most valuable pieces, on display in Rooms XIV–XX. The most remarkable of these are Mercury, Venus, Meleager, Diana the Huntress and the huge torso of Diana. The elliptical central room, the so-called Salón Imperial, contains an impressive collection of Roman emperors: a huge statue of Trajan, a bust of Hadrian ● *31*, ▲ *208* and, among others, representations of Augustus, Nero and Marcus Aurelius. The visit ends with the less important collections, featuring art from paleo-Christian, Visigoth and Hispano-Moresque periods.

Fortuna and Mercury
The museum houses Spain's most prestigious collection of Roman sculpture. It consists primarily of divinities and emperors from the Roman town of Itálica ● *65*. Statues (left) of Fortuna (2nd century) and Mercury, god of commerce and travelers.

Alexander the Great
2nd-century copy of a lost Hellenistic original.

Venus of Itálica, with marine attributes.

Paseo de las Delicias

The last section of the gardens on this itinerary lies between the Paseo de las Delicias, adjoining the Plaza de América, and the Guadalquivir river. It is an area characterized by groves and fountains and, as well as an attractive summerhouse, it contains several of the former exhibition pavilions. These are the Pabellón de Guatemala, looking like a small casket of brightly colored *azulejos*, in the shade of a monkey-puzzle tree; the colonial-style Pabellón de Argentina; the Pabellón de Colombia with its strange Indian décor; the Pabellón de Marruecos ("Morocco"), carved by craftsmen from the Maghreb; and the geometric Aztec-style Pabellón de Méjico. The avenue, which extends the magnificent vista of the majestic Avenida de la Palmera in the direction of Cádiz, once marked the boundary of the 1929 Exhibition site ● *87*.

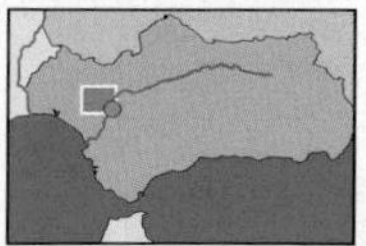

Half a day
6–7 miles

◆ A C2

SCULPTURES OF SAN ISIDORO
Among the sculptors who worked on the Monasterio de San Isidoro was Juan Martínez Montañés ● *48*, ▲ *139*. From 1609 until 1613 Martínez Montañés worked on the great *retablo mayor* of the Iglesia de Guzmán el Bueno, on which the delicate reliefs (below) of the panels represent aspects of Christian beliefs. The *retablo mayor* of the Capilla Sacramental and the *orants* (carved effigies) of the donors, Guzmán and his wife, are also his work.

IGLESIA DE SAN ISIDORO
The church is built predominately in the early Gothic style of the stone masons who appeared after the Reconquest. The far wall and ribbed vault of the refectory are decorated with frescos.

Four short itineraries in the environs of Seville are described in this section (pages 206–27). The first of these takes you north of the city, on the N-630 in the direction of Mérida, to Santiponce and Itálica, returning via La Algaba, San Jerónimo, the C-431 and the cemetery of Seville.

SANTIPONCE. The site of this small town matches almost exactly the site of the Roman town of Itálica. The village of Santiponce that once existed on the banks of the Guadalquivir, on the island of El Hierro, was destroyed by the great floods of 1595 and 1602 ▲ *192*. The local inhabitants sought refuge with the monks of San Isidoro, who gave them the land bordering the monastery where they built a new village.

SAN ISIDORO DEL CAMPO

Although not permanently open to the public, the Monasterio de San Isidoro is well worth a visit.

GUZMAN EL BUENO. Guzmán is the ancestral name of the dukes of Medina Sidonia. Alonso Pérez de Guzmán ("El Bueno", 1256–1309), lord of Santiponce, built San Isidoro in 1301 as a family pantheon. A heroic deed during the siege of Tarifa (on the Straits of Gibraltar)

1. Ruins of Itálica 2. Santiponce 3. Monasterio de San Isidoro del Campo 4. La Algaba 5. Río Guadalquivir 6. Convento de San Jerónimo de Buenvista 7. Cementerio de San Fernando 8. Canal de Alfonso XIII 9. Cathedral 10. Corta de la Cartuja 11. Camas

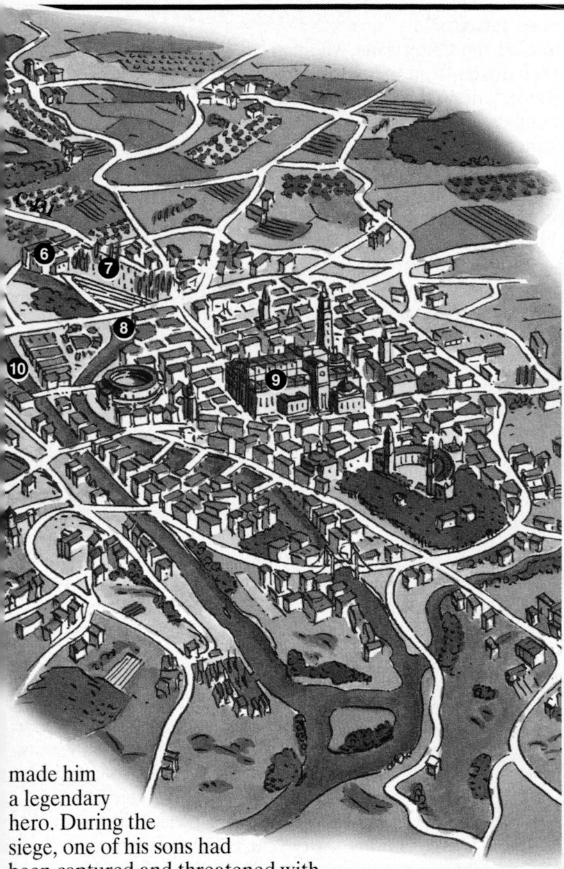

"Itálica, the birthplace of Trajan, Hadrian and Theodosus, is more than three-quarters buried beneath the ground. But its mosaics and statues bear witness to a splendor created by the diligence of local Greek craftsmen, and the luxury imported from Greece and Rome. For the great 17th-century Spanish poet, Rodrigo Caro, Itálica is the symbol of solitude and melancholy, the dried-up river bed that remains after the vast outflow of a life that is no more."
Marguerite Yourcenar
Le Temps, ce grand sculpteur

made him a legendary hero. During the siege, one of his sons had been captured and threatened with execution if Guzmán did not surrender. He replied that "he would rather they killed this son, and five more besides, if they had captured them, than surrender his king's city".

Monasterio del Cister. The monastery took its name from its first community, who were Cistercians. In the 14th century Guzmán el Bueno and his son, Juan, each had Gothic churches built there. In the first church are the tombs of Juan and his wife (with 14th-century gisants) and a niche containing the rim of a well hollowed out by the water that, according to legend, bestowed wisdom on Saint Isidore, the patron of the monastery. The church of Guzmán el Bueno houses sculptures by Juan Martínez Montañés.

Portals and frescos
Mudéjar portal of the Iglesia de San Isidoro (15th century). Frescos painted between 1431 and 1436 combine Italian and French influences with Mudéjar-style motifs.

Horse trader
The *feria* of Santiponce was a faithful reflection of the purism of Andalusian traditions.

In the 1st century AD Trajan and Hadrian, the first emperors from the Roman provinces, were born in Itálica. With Augustus, they formed the great triad of Imperial Rome.

"LOS ISIDROS"
In 1431 the Cistercians, who had become increasingly lax, were driven from the monastery and replaced by the Hieronymites. The construction of the Mudéjar cloisters was completed by giving the Claustro de los Muertos its commemorative plaques and the Claustro de los Evangelistas its paintings. The sacristy, chapterhouse, chapels, a new cloister and the 17th-century tower gave the complex its present appearance. In 1547 Hernán Cortés ▲ *187, 221* was buried at San Isidoro, but was later conveyed to Mexico. During the 16th century the monks of San Isidoro, known as the "Isidros", were renowned for their intense intellectual activity. This was brought to an end by the Inquisition when the community was purged in 1562. A number of its members had already fled, including Fray Casiodoro de Reina (1520–94), who produced the first translation of the Bible into Catalan.

ITÁLICA ★

The entrance to the archeological site lies to the north of the village of Santiponce.

A MILITARY AND AGRICULTURAL TOWN. Itálica was founded in 206 BC by Scipio Africanus ● *30* after his victory over the Carthaginians at nearby Ilipa. For the first time Rome exercised direct control over territory located outside Italy. Appian (AD 95–106), the Greek historian from Alexandria, noted in the section of his *Romaica* (history of Rome) devoted to Iberia: "From then on, the Romans began to send generals, every year, among the peoples of Spain to maintain peace. Scipio gave them the necessary troops for the task and installed the wounded from his army in a town that he called Itálica, after the name of Italy." It was the first *municipium* of Roman citizens established outside the Italian peninsula, populated by soldiers who were born there and had been rewarded with gifts of land. Itálica was an aristocratic, military and agricultural town that monitored movements between the mines of the Sierra Morena and the lower Guadalquivir ▲ *192, 222*. As such, Itálica distinguished itself from the neighboring port of Hispalis, which was a trading center of Semitic origin.

HADRIAN AND TRAJAN
Bust of Hadrian (above) and the huge statue of Trajan (below) found at Itálica.

"NOVA URBS"
Streets and houses cover the part of Itálica built in the 2nd century.

"VETUS URBS". The original town, whose remains can still be seen in the cellars and courtyards of Santiponce, was built during the Roman Republic (mid-5th century BC–beginning of the early Roman Empire, in 27 BC) on the hill later occupied by Santiponce. It had solid enclosure walls and public buildings. Most of what remains is located in the area known as Los Palacios: the site of the forum and the Great Temple of Diana, in what was the town

OCTAVIA
This portrait of Octavia, the wife of Mark Antony, was one of many found at Itálica.

AUGUSTUS
The first Italican coins were struck in 23 BC, during the reign of Augustus.

AMPHITHEATER
The elliptical amphitheater (about 170 x 148 yards) is the most important structure on the site and the third largest amphitheater in the Roman world. It could hold 40,000 spectators, who came to watch the games.

center. The amphitheater is situated on the slopes of the hill of Santiponce. During the Empire, the power of the Italican lines of descent extended as far as Rome in the persons of Hadrian and Trajan, born and brought up in the *municipium* of Baetica until their duties called them elsewhere. With the support of the senators of Hispania and Gaul, Trajan became Emperor in AD 98 and extended the possessions of the Empire. His nephew and successor, Hadrian, who built the famous Hadrian's Wall in the north of Britain, strengthened the boundaries of the Empire, founded towns and cities and fought for peace.

"NOVA URBS". The site of Itálica open to the public is that of the great urban extension undertaken in the 2nd century by Hadrian, who gave it the honorific title of "Colonia Aelia Augusta" ("Venerable Colony of Aelius"). With the protection of the Emperor's sons, the community of Itálica, which barely had more than eight to ten thousand inhabitants, soon became one of the most prosperous towns in Hispania. New Itálica (*nova urbs*) then covered an area of around 100 acres to the north of the old town (*vetus urbs*). The site includes a reconstruction of a ROMAN HOUSE, containing a collection of figurines and inscriptions, and the massive AMPHITHEATER, with its covering of freestone and marble, which was designed to hold the entire population of the town and the surrounding area. The ruins near the coliseum give some idea of the dimensions of the wall surrounding the town and the huge sewer, over three feet deep, that formed the central axis of a complex system of underground conduits.

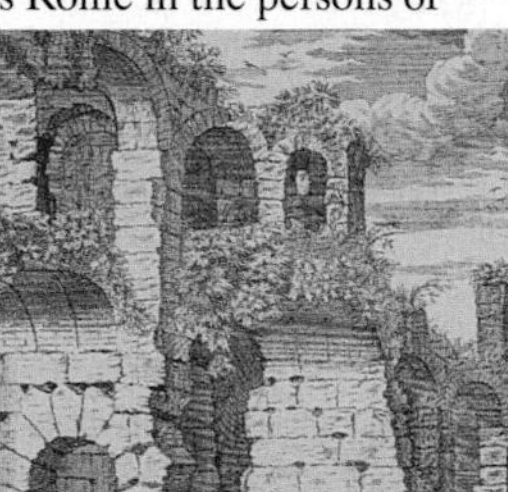

Rodrigo Caro (1573–1647), the Sevillian poet born in Utrera, dedicated his most beautiful lines to the Roman town of Itálica.

THEATER
The theater, built in limestone in the 1st century BC, lies below the town of Santiponce. In the 2nd century AD it was decorated with marbles, statues and carved altars representing bacchantes. These were gifts from Lucius and Gaius Polius, as indicated by an inscription on the *proscenium*.

CASA DE LOS PAJAROS
In the House of Birds, in Itálica, 32 species of bird, in their mosaic pictures, surround Orpheus.

MOSAICS
Some of the remarkable mosaic floors of the luxurious Roman villas ● *65* can still be seen on the site today. They are arranged around the *peristylum* (colonnaded courtyard), as Andalusian houses were later arranged around a central courtyard, each with a different design. The most remarkable are those of the Casa de la Exedra (or Manzana del Gimnasio), with its summer garden; the Casa de Hylas, whose terraced rooms are linked by flights of steps; the Casa de los Pájaros and the Casa del Planetario (both late 2nd century).

CIVIL AND DOMESTIC ARCHITECTURE. The streets, paved with huge polygonal slabs, intersected at right angles. They were laid out using marking lines. Those bordering blocks of houses (*insulae*, or "islands") were porticoed, a feature usually only found in Greek and Roman towns and cities in the eastern Mediterranean (Antioch and Palmyra). At the western end of the town is the huge BATHS complex, with its large pools and rooms (which were originally covered).
RUINS AND QUARRY. The short history of the *nova urbs* of Itálica makes it unique. With buildings cracking because of landslides, and its vast size making it effectively useless, it was abandoned in favor of the old town and the ruins were used as a quarry. Until the Arab conquest Itálica survived as a small fortified town and the Visigoth episcopal see. It was forgotten during the Muslim period and the site, known as Campos de Talca or Sevilla la Vieja, became confused with the old town. It was rediscovered during the Renaissance when it became the symbol of the glories of the classical world. Quarrying continued apace until the 19th century when it was decided to preserve the site, and archeological digs were conducted, as they are still today.
THE ARTISTIC LEGACY OF ITÁLICA. The sculptures, excavated objects and mosaics recovered from Itálica constitute an important part of the legacy bequeathed by Ancient Rome. It has provided Seville's Museo Arqueológico with one of its major collections of sculpture, as well as enriching other museums and several private and corporate collections.

MONASTIC ESTATES
Seville was surrounded by a belt of monasteries that owned vast rural estates. The Gambogaz farm (top), belonged to the Carthusian monastery, and the cloister of San Jerónimo (above).

ITÁLICA TO SEVILLE

Beyond Itálica a track leads from an intersection on the N-630 to the village of La Algaba, a name of Islamic origin meaning "forest",

La Algaba. In the center of La Algaba, it is impossible to miss the 89-foot-high, crenelated bastion of the Torre de los Guzmanes. Throughout its three floors, its rooms have freestone vaults and elegant windows. The tower, built in 1446 by the Guzmán family, is a fine blend of civil and military Andalusian Mudéjar architecture. It is open to the public and houses a modern art gallery.

Convento de San Jerónimo de Buenvista. Now a cultural center, the cloister is reached from San Jerónimo, a district of Seville that grew up around the former monastery (founded in 1414). The church once housed the famous statue of San Jerónimo (Saint Jerome), today in the Museo de Bellas Artes ▲ *180*, by the Italian sculptor Pietro Torrigiano (1472–1528). Torrigiano was master of works for the tomb of Henry VII and Elizabeth of York in Westminster Abbey, and influenced the school of Seville where he carried out several important commissions, the last of which proved fatal. The Duke of Arcos asked him to work on a statue of the Virgin, but the sculptor considered the fee too small. He was tried for heresy and imprisoned in the Castillo de la Inquisición in Triana where he starved himself to death.

Cementerio de San Fernando. Seville's main cemetery lies between the districts of San Jerónimo and La Macarena, and is typically Andalusian, with its niches, whitewashed walls, avenues and cypress trees. The central rotunda is dominated by *El Cristo de las Mieles*, by the Sevillian sculptor Antonio Susillo (1857–92) who was buried at the foot of the statue after his suicide. Shortly after, the statue's mouth began to drip with honey from a swarm of bees that had nested there. The mausolea of the great bullfighters are of particular note. The funerary monument on the tomb of Joselito contrasts with the sober, geometric lines of the monument to Belmonte ▲ *173, 195*. A bronze statue commemorates Francisco Rivera, alias Paquirri. When he died, in 1984, 100,000 people paid their last respects.

Mosaics
A fine collection of Roman *musivium opus* can be admired in situ in the mansions of Seville or the Museo Arqueológico ▲ *204*.

Royal monastery
The monastery of San Jerónimo de Buenvista received the Reyes Católicos (Catholic Monarchs), Charles V, Philip II and Philip IV before they made their triumphant entrances into Seville. Its vast 16th-century Renaissance courtyard (50 yards square), built in freestone on 15th-century Gothic foundations, has sculpted galleries and porches.

Death of a hero
The death of José Gómez Ortega (alias Joselito), fatally wounded by the bull Bailaor in 1920, caused an unprecedented display of public grief. The entire district of La Macarena went into mourning and crowds of people followed his funeral procession. His tomb, by Mariano Benlliure, is the most remarkable monument in the Cementerio de San Fernando.

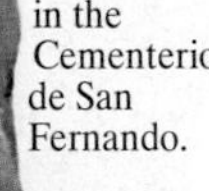

1. Seville
2. Alcalá de Guadaira
3. Mairena del Alcor
4. El Viso del Alcor
5. Carmona

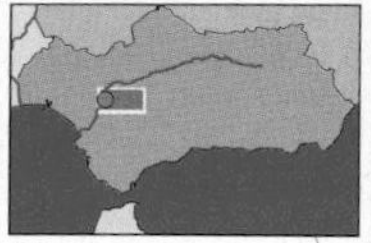

One day
28 miles

◆ A D2-3

Alcalá and the Fortress
The name "Alcalá de Guadaira" is derived from the Arabic, meaning "the fortress of Guadaira". The town's fortified castle is one of the most impressive in Andalusia and consists of a double enclosure wall, with the second wall (the *alcazaba*, or "casbah") higher than the first. It was built by the Almohads in the 12th century and was modified by the Christians in the 14th and 15th centuries.

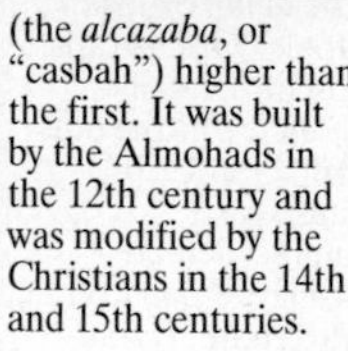

Los Alcores form a series of hills, rising to a height 820 feet, to the east of Seville between the Guadaira and Mairena rivers. The C-432 links the main towns of Alcalá de Guadaira, Mairena del Alcor, El Viso del Alcor and Carmona.

Alcalá de Guadaira

Alcalá is known as the "Ciudad de los Panaderos" ("town of bakers"), as it used to be Seville's main supplier of bread.

Castle and town. Centered around the castle are the town's principal monuments: the Mudéjar churches of Nuestra Señora del Aguila (14th century), Santiago (16th century) and San Sebastián.

"He was a leading light. He was certainly masterly, and was considered (and considered himself) to be the master of masters."

Mario Bois, on Antonio Mairena

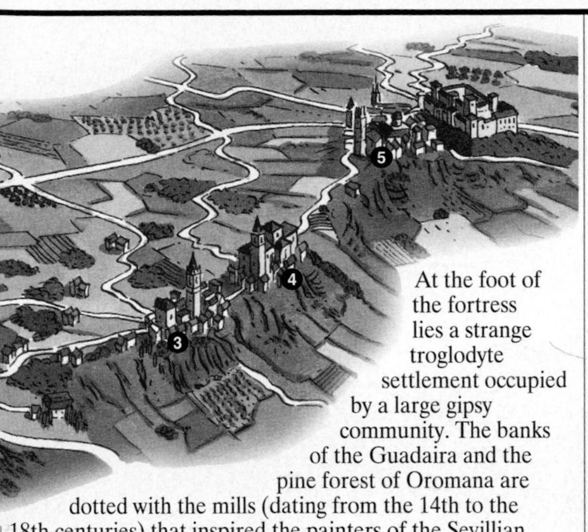

At the foot of the fortress lies a strange troglodyte settlement occupied by a large gipsy community. The banks of the Guadaira and the pine forest of Oromana are dotted with the mills (dating from the 14th to the 18th centuries) that inspired the painters of the Sevillian Romantic school ● *92*.

GANDUL. This hamlet next to Alcala has an interesting architectural and archeological heritage: not far from a 12th-century Almohad tower, a medieval church and a 17th-century palace, the remains of a Roman town and a necropolis, dating from the early Copper Age, have been excavated on the slopes of Bencarrón.

MAIRENA DEL ALCOR

THE MASTER OF EL CANTE

This charming village, home to a settled gipsy community, has given its name to a flamenco dynasty. Every year the famous Festival Flamenco, dedicated to the memory of the *cantaor* Antonio Mairena (1909–83), described as the master of *el cante* ● *54,* is held in the courtyard of the Academia.

FERIA DE MAIRENA
The *feria*, today a famous spectacle, was once one of the largest cattle markets in Andalusia ● *50*. The Feria de Mairena was the first of the season and occupied a

strategic position on one of the routes linking Seville with the agricultural plains.

PALACIO DE GANDUL
This beautiful 17th-century Baroque mansion was the residence of the village *marqués*.

The Via Augusta, linking Cádiz to Rome, crossed this bridge. In the distance, Carmona.

Santa María de Gracia
The church of the priory of Carmona stands in the center of the fortified town. It occupies the site of a great 11th-century mosque, "with marble columns and stone pilasters", of which only the Patio de los Naranjos ("orange trees") remains. The church houses some fine works of art: the sculptures of the *retablo mayor*, the gold work of the treasury, and paintings that include the San José *retablo* (1540), signed by the Flemish artist Pierre de Champaigne.

Castillo de la Luna. This Moorish castle was the residence of the British artist and archeologist George Bonsor, a pioneer in the field of Andalusian archeology. His collections are on display in a neo-Moorish house within the castle walls.
El Viso del Alcor. The town occupies the site of the ancient Roman town of Basilipo. Its Mudéjar church, Santa María, was founded by the hermits living there in the Middle Ages.

Carmona ★

From its vantage point on the summit of Los Alcores, Carmona overlooks the fertile agricultural valley. This ancient city has been inhabited on a permanent basis since 3000 BC and was the seat of the campaniform-vase culture. During the 1st millennium BC, it was occupied successively by the Phoenicians, Carthaginians and Romans. Its present name is derived from "Khar-Hammon" ("Hammon" is the name of the Carthaginian sun god). The Romans referred to it as the "city of cheerfulness" because of the pleasant aspect of the countryside. Julius Caesar described it as the most important fortified town in Baetica. Its fortress was unassailable and its agricultural market has flourished up to the present day.

Roman remains. A truly exceptional archeological site lies on the edge of the town, near the road to Seville. The remains of a vast necropolis and an amphitheater, discovered here in 1868, attest to the prosperity of ancient Carmona, the granary of Seville. To date, several hundred tombs have been excavated, mostly dating from the 1st to the 4th century. Some of the funerary chambers were built in the style of patrician residences and were decorated with frescos and sculptures. The most remarkable were the circular mausoleum of Servilia and the so-called "mausoleum of the elephant", named after the statue that it contained. The ritual objects discovered on the site can be seen in its small museum.

Iglesia de San Pedro. The Calle de Seville is extended by the Paseo del Estatuto and the Calle San Pedro. In the latter stands the Iglesia de San Pedro, begun in the 15th century but not completed until the 18th, when a spectacular Baroque tower, the Giraldilla, was built (1783) in the image of its Sevillian counterpart. San Pedro also has a splendid Capilla Sacramental (1760) by Ambrosio de Figueroa, who used similar techniques to those adopted for the Iglesia de San Luis in Seville ▲ *168*. The exterior of the dome is covered in shining *azulejos* ● *56*, *73* depicting archangels, and surmounted by a statue of Faith. Below the church is the Alameda de Alfonso XIII with its medieval fountain, the Fuente de los Leones.

Alcázar de la Puerta de Sevilla. The Calle San Pedro leads to the foot of the old city walls and the Puerta de Seville. The gate was formerly the watchtower of an *alcázar* that, together with the Alcázar de Arriba and what was the Alcázar de la Reina, was one of Carmona's three fortified palaces. The Puerta de Sevilla was originally built by Carthaginian soldiers between 237 and 206 BC. Between the 2nd and 1st centuries BC it became the entrance to the Roman acropolis and consisted of twin gates, which still exist today,

Fortifications
Carmona's first fortifications date from the 9th century BC. Between the 3rd and 1st centuries BC the Carthaginians and then the Romans built an enclosure wall 2½ miles long.

Alcázars
The Alcázar de Arriba (or de la Puerta de Marchena) was built in the 10th century and extended in the 12th by the Almohads. In the 14th century Pedro I transformed it into a palace, and it became one of his favorite residences. The appearance bestowed upon it by the Nazarite architects won it the nickname "little Alhambra". Today it houses the tourist office.

Churches and convents
The tall outlines of the towers and bell towers of churches and convents are silhouetted against the sky above the old city of Carmona. From left to right, the Convento de Santa Clara, founded in 1640, and three examples of Mudéjar architecture: the 14th-century Iglesia de Santiago, the Iglesia de San Felipe (c. 1300) and the tower of San Bartolomé.

Plaza de Arriba
The plaza is the nerve center of the old city and stands on the site of the Roman forum. It has all the scenic qualities of the big Castilian plazas, with

its *casas-mirador*, several stories high, providing an ideal vantage point from which to watch public spectacles. Most of the buildings date from the late 16th and early 17th centuries.

bossed walls from the Roman period, classical central openings and a temple (which no longer exists) on the upper terrace. The walls were restored between 1023 and 1067 during the reign of the Banu Birzal Berbers. In the 12th century the Almohads added the slender Torre del Oro to the bastion, as well as another tower, the Salón de los Presos ("room of captives"). The fortifications were strengthened after the town surrendered to Ferdinand III, in 1247, and saw active service again in the 15th century during the feudal conflicts and wars with the kingdom of Granada.
The old city. Several streets radiate outward from the Puerta de Sevilla: the Calle de la Torre del Oro runs northwest along the ramparts; the Calle Prim, the main thoroughfare, cuts through the center of the old city; and the Calle de San Felipe follows the section of the walls running southeastward. They enclose picturesque districts echoing with the muffled sounds from behind the porches of the white *casas-patio*. The Calle de la Torre del Oro leads into the former Jewish quarter around the Iglesia de San Blas, once a synagogue. Carmona's Jewish community prospered during the reign of Pedro I and then declined until 1391 when it was virtually decimated ● *33*. The Calle de San Felipe leads to the church of the same name, a Gothic edifice rebuilt in 1470

"And the clear, silver sound of a cantilena / from the Arab courtyard, and the serenade / that carries the scent of flowered prayers / to the miradors and mullioned windows… "

Antonio Machado

by the Mudéjar Martín García who added an elegant façade-tower and decorated its three naves with Mudéjar woodwork. The IGLESIA DE SAN BARTOLOMÉ, at the end of the Calle Prim, is a fine example of late 15th-century Mudéjar architecture, in spite of its Baroque decorative elements (1785). The Calle Prim leads onto the Plaza de Arriba dominated by the Convento de la Madre de Dios, whose church dates from 1542, and the TOWN HALL. This former Jesuit school houses valuable historical archives, including a handwritten letter by Cervantes, and a collection of paintings. Nearby is the Baroque Iglesia de San Salvador (1720).

IGLESIA DE SANTA MARÍA. A little further on the Calle Martín Lopez, with the beautiful 17TH- AND 18TH-CENTURY MANSIONS OF THE RUEDA AND AGUILAR FAMILIES, leads to the impressive church of the priory of Santa María, a veritable miniature cathedral. A 6th-century Hispano-Visigoth calendar, engraved on one of the columns of the Patio de los Naranjos, is a reminder of the Visigoth basilica, the first sanctuary to stand on the site. It was succeeded by a mosque, which collapsed, and the Gothic church built between 1424 and 1518. On the Renaissance altar stands the elegant 14th-century figure of the town's patron saint, Nuestra Señora de Gracia. The treasury contains a remarkable custodial by the goldsmith Francisco Alfaro. Opposite stands the CONVENTO DE LAS DESCALZAS, whose church dates from 1748.

DISTRICT OF SANTA MARÍA. The Calle Santa María de Gracia leads to the CONVENTO DE SANTA CLARA, with its double portal and bell tower, and the HOSPITAL DE LA MISERICORDIA Y CARIDAD. The hospital, founded in 1510, has a magnificent Baroque entrance of brick and *azulejos*. The Calle Dolores Quintanilla, to the right, leads to the magnificent QUINTANILLA MANSION and follows the enclosure wall to the Puerta de Córdoba, in the form of a classical triumphal arch set in the city walls.

FROM THE CITY WALLS. At the end of the Calle Calatrava is the 14th-century IGLESIA DE SANTIAGO, flanked by a former minaret, while the *calles* María Auxiliadora and General Freire lead to the top of the rocky outcrop occupied by the ALCÁZAR DE ARRIBA. On the slopes below stand the hermitages of San Mateo and Nuestra Señora de Gracia.

CIVIL ARCHITECTURE
The old city of Carmona has a splendid range of buildings constructed between the 15th and 18th centuries. They tend to be concentrated around Santa María, Santiago and San Felipe. On the Plaza de Arriba stands the Casa de los Azulejos (mid-16th century), Carmona's only Mudéjar residence ● *70*, ▲ *356*, with its polychrome tiled façade and geminate windows. Next door is a Renaissance *casa-mirador* (1588), which used to house the law courts.

PUERTA DE CÓRDOBA
The gate, with its two octagonal towers, is set in the north of the city wall and opens onto the plain of Carmona. It was originally Roman but has had several transformations, the last in 1800 by the architect José Echamorro.

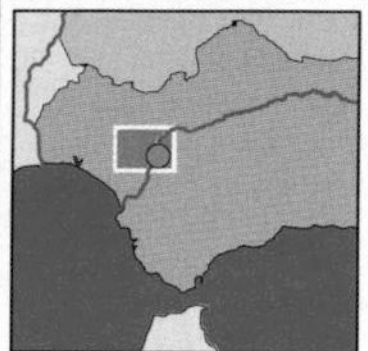

⏱ Half a day
🚗 38 miles

◆ A C3

Idol (right) dating from the 3rd century BC excavated at Valencina de la Concepción.

A fertile region
Studies of such sites as El Carambolo, which has become the symbol of Tartessian culture (11th–6th century BC) ● *30*, have revealed that El Aljarafe was the first inhabited region in the southeast of the Iberian peninsula. Its present name is derived from the Arabic name *al-Saraf* ("the summit"). Its villages, which were once described as "stars in a sky of olive trees", offer visitors a pleasant excursion with an opportunity to sample the local wines in picturesque *tabernas*.

To the west of Seville the hills and slopes of El Aljarafe, which incorporates the plateau situated between the valleys of the Guadalquivir and the Guadiamar, form an insular shelf that descends southward to the Marisma, or delta marshes ▲ *287*. Today the region is part of the urban community of Seville.

Valencina de la Concepción

The village grew up around the Hacienda de Tilly, whose oil mill can still be smelt today, and the parish church. Outside Valencina de la Concepción, near a fortified hacienda, the Capilla de Torrijos contains a remarkable sculpture of Christ and some *ex votos* dating from the 18th and 19th centuries.

Dolmens of La Pastora, Matarrubilla and Ontiveros ★. These megalithic tombs are the most important in western Andalusia. The funerary chamber in which they are found is reached via a long corridor built of huge stone slabs and covered by a mound. The best-preserved tombs are those of La Pastora and Matarrubilla. These examples of prehistoric hypogea attest to the wealth of the inhabitants of Valencina, the bridge-head of the Guadalquivir valley during the Copper Age (3rd millennium BC). The small museum in the Casa de la Cultura de Valencina (idols, pottery, clothes, arrow heads) complements visits to the various sites.

Olivares

The town of Olivares experienced its hour of glory in the 17th and 18th centuries, when it was the capital of one of the three *estados del reino*, "states" with voting rights in the Spanish political assembly, which dated from 1188. Olivares was in the state of the Guzmán family, one of the most powerful families in Andalusia ▲ *173*, *206*, *277*. In the plaza stands the Renaissance-style Ducal Palace of the Conde de Olivares, the chamberlain of Philip IV and chancellor of the Indies. The Collegiate Church is a vast edifice which was begun in 1623 and completed in the 18th century. It was built in the form of a Latin cross, with three portals, three naves and a tower, and houses one of the province's most important treasures: *retablos* and sculptures, choir stalls, paintings (Zurbarán school), a collection of gold items and reliquaries.

The duke and his palace
Don Gaspar de Guzmán (1587–1645), Conde de Olivares and Duque de Sanlúcar la Mayor, was the plenipotentiary of Philip IV, the rival of Cardinal Richelieu of France and master of most of the villages in the El Aljarafe region. The ducal palace in the town of Olivares, nestling among the olive groves, lay at the very heart of his estates. He defended the interests of Spain within Europe from 1621 until 1643 when, as the Spanish empire began to decline, he was disgraced by the failure of his policies.

Olives, wheat and wine
In the 1st millennium BC the region of Olivares was known a the "Garden of Hercules" because the mythical hero was said to have

introduced the olive trees that flourished there. Exports of oil, wine and cereals made the region the granary of Seville ■ *25*, ● *84*.

CHURCHES OF LORETO AND UMBRETE
In the 13th and 14th centuries, the Iglesia de Umbrete (right) belonged to the Church of Seville.

WINE-MAKING IN EL ALJARAFE
The vineyards of El Aljarafe produce the region's characteristic white wines. From September and throughout the fall, the grapes are harvested and pressed. This is also the time of village festivals.

SANLÚCAR LA MAYOR

The town, originally the Roman settlement of Solúcar or *locus solis* ("region of sun"), flourished during the Middle Ages under the Muslims and Christians as the administrative capital of El Aljarafe. Here are found the remains of the 12th- and 13th-century ALMOHAD WALLS, a 17th-century CARMELITE CONVENT and the Mudéjar churches of San Pedro, San Eustaquio and Santa María.

IGLESIA DE SANTA MARÍA. The church's three portals, stained-glass windows, glazed brick oculi, three naves separated by arcades, wooden ceiling and ribbed apse make it one of the most representative examples of the Sevillian Mudéjar-Gothic architectural style ● *70*. Its treasury contains, in particular, the 14th-century Gothic sculpture of the *Cristo de San Pedro* and a collection of crosses, which are fine examples of 15th- and 16th-century gold work.

HACIENDAS OF EL ALJARAFE. In the vicinity of Sanlúcar and Espartinas are such haciendas ● *84* as BENAZUZA (converted into a hotel) and TABLANTE where, in 1599, the poet Juan de Arguijo received the Marquesa de Denia with great ceremony. The HACIENDA DE PATA DE HIERRO (1682) at Villanueva de Ariscal today houses the Bodegas Góngora. This typical and well-preserved farm, which produces oil and wine and tans leather, is open to the public.

CONVENTO DE LORETO. The convent stands in the heart of El Aljarafe and is the venue for a famous pilgrimage in September. It comprises a 13th-century tower, the convent proper, its chapel and a hacienda. The oldest part of the complex, the Claustro del Aljibe, was built in 1525 when the convent was founded by the Franciscans. The rest was built in the 17th and 18th centuries in Baroque style. The convent provided accommodation for the missionaries responsible for preaching the Gospel in America, including the renowned saint, Francisco Solano, and has a collection of Baroque gold work and an original Hispano-Philippine ivory crucifix.

UMBRETE

Toward the end of the 15th century, after the Reconquest, the town was given to the Church of Seville by the Catholic monarchs. It became the retreat of the archbishops who were responsible for its most distinguished edifices, including the 17th- and 18th-century archbishop's palace. The arcades of its main courtyard are linked to the church by a small bridge.

IGLESIA DE LA CONSOLACIÓN. This single-nave Baroque church is remarkable for its impressive size, carved brick façade and twin towers. It was designed by the architect and sculptor Diego Antonio Díaz, who was working in Seville in 1570,

and built during the first half of the 18th century. It contains a magnificent *retablo* by Pedro Duque Cornejo (1677–1757), the Churrigueresque sculptor and goldsmith, and a large collection of sculptures and paintings.

AZNALCÁZAR TO SEVILLE

AZNALCÁZAR. The old town of Castilleja de Talhara lies in a romantic setting between Benacazón and Aznalcázar. All that remains of the town, founded in 1369, are the ruins of a beautiful 14th-century Mudéjar hermitage and a hacienda, reminders of a bygone age when the rural population was as important as it was large. A little further on Aznalcázar, whose original Arabic name means "fountain of the palace", stands on the banks of the Guadiamar. The remains of its fortifications and an ancient, very poorly preserved bridge attest to the town's strategic importance during the Roman and Muslim periods. Its last building of note is the IGLESIA DE SAN PABLO, a triple-naved Mudéjar edifice constructed in the 14th and 15th centuries, whose largest polygonal chapel has a magnificent ribbed vault. Its great tower was crowned in 1764. Its beautiful portals have pointed, brick arches (one in shades of yellow and red), with finely twisted ornamentation.

ERMITA DE CUATROVITAS. The tower of the Ermita de Cuatrovitas stands like a milestone on a bend in the road from Aznalcázar to Bollulos de la Mitación. The elegant 12th-century Mudéjar edifice, originally a mosque for the four local haciendas, was adapted for Christian worship after the Reconquest. Its festival of the Virgin in October, is the occasion of a joyous pilgrimage that resounds with cries of "Long live the Queen of El Aljarafe! Long live the Queen of the Olive!"

BOLLULOS DE LA MITACIÓN. A *retablo* in the IGLESIA DE SAN MARTÍN is set with four canvases by Francisco de Zurbarán ▲ *139*, *158*, *182* in which he combines the influences of the Flemish and Venetian schools, Spanish polychrome sculpture and the naturalism of Caravaggio. They depict saints similar those of the Museo de Bellas Artes ▲ *180* in Seville.

CASTILLEJA DE LA CUESTA. The El Aljarafe itinerary ends at Castilleja, which offers a panoramic view of the valley and Seville, and is renowned for its *galletas*.

CONVENTO-HACIENDA DE ESPARTINAS
(Loreto).

PEASANT FROM EL ALJARAFE
The region has retained its rural character despite its proximity to Seville.

ERMITO DE CUATROVITAS
At the end of May pilgrims bound for El Rocío ● *51* gather at this delightful hermitage on the edge of the marshes.

HERNÁN CORTÉS (1485–1547)
This local squire took part in the conquests of Cuba, which began in 1511, and Mexico (1519–24). He spent the last years of his life in a *palacio* in Castilleja de la

Cuesta (left). In a *palacio* in the Calle Real, now very different from what it once was, the village honors the memory of the *conquistador* who founded its literary academy to make amends to the Court of Madrid. He had left for Mexico in 1518 against orders, and had been declared a rebel.

▲ THE GUADALQUIVIR BELOW SEVILLE

1. SEVILLE
2. GELVES
3. CORIA DEL RÍO
4. LA PUEBLA DEL RÍO
5. VILLAFRANCO DEL GUADALQUIVIR

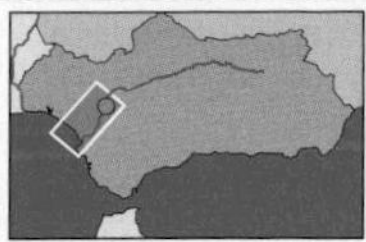

One and a half days
50 miles
◆ A C3-4

RIVER BASIN
During the year Sevillian oarsmen take part in a number of international competitions held in the newly developed river basin.

THE LOWER GUADALQUIVIR

From Seville the drive down the Guadalquivir valley takes you via San Juan de Aznalfarache, Gelves, Coria del Río, La Puebla del Río and Villafranco del Guadalquivir, where a ferry across the Brazor brings you to Isla Mínima and the highway leading to Sanlúcar de Barrameda. Alternatively, there are pleasure boats that go down the river from the quays of the Torre del Oro to its estuary.

RIVER BAETIS. The exact origin of the Roman name for the Guadalquivir ● *31* is not known. The Ancients also referred to it as the "Tartessos" by association with the legendary kingdom on its banks. The Baetis was mentioned for the first time by the historian and geographer Strabo (58 BC–AD 24). The river was an important communications route for the

ROMANTIC VIEW OF SEVILLE
Oil painting (anonymous, mid-19th century) showing the Guadalquivir at Seville. The artist chose to paint the city at dusk with small pleasure and fishing craft in the foreground. The softness and picturesque quality of this charming painting conform to the romantic image expressed in the travel accounts of the great writers of the period.

6. Almonte
7. Sanlúcar de Barrameda
8. Lebrija
9. Trebujena
10. Rota
11. Chipiona

Romans: ships with a deep draft could sail up the river to Hispalis (Seville). The smaller ships could continue as far as Córdoba. During the reign of Augustus it contributed to the economic expansion of Baetica, with the region's agricultural and metallurgical products being shipped downriver to the Atlantic and, from there, to the far reaches of the Mediterranean, the Netherlands and Britain.

Lacus Ligustinus. In ancient times, the sea reached Seville and formed the Lacus Ligustinus. After the Roman period, the river widened its shallow bed and formed a delta with many meanders, river branches and islands surrounded by marshes extending to its present broad estuary. With the fluvial plain thus formed, at almost the same level as the river, it becomes wider as it approaches the sea.

The "great river". It was the Arabs who called the river *wadi el-Azim*, which translates as "the magnificent river", or *wadi el-Kabir* ("the great river"), from which its present name is derived. In 845 the Normans sailed up the river and into the very heart of Seville itself, destroying many buildings as they made their way, including part of the ramparts and the mosque of Seville, which had been constructed six years earlier by Abd el-Rahman II. The Normans were finally driven out by reinforcements from Córdoba, but for two months they remained entrenched in the marshes between Tejada and Isla Menor and continued to harass the western shores of the river.

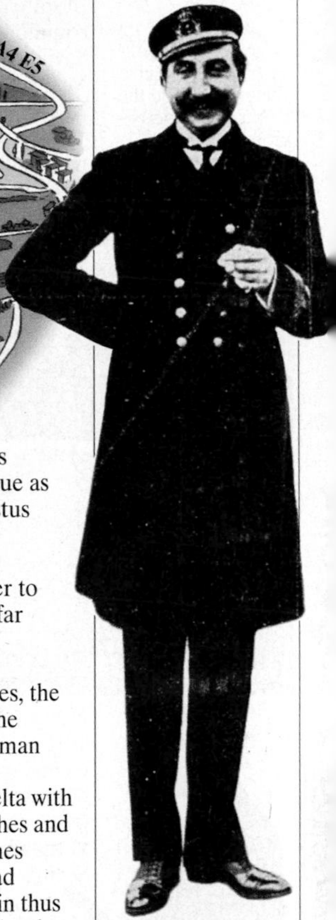

Steamship officer, early 20th century.

The Baetis
Allegorical figure of the River Baetis, illustration by Juan de Mal Lara (1570).

The Guadalquivir in the early 20th century, from San Juan de Aznalfarache.

The Sanlúcar steamship
Mid-19th century watercolor showing a group of travelers on board the Seville–Sanlúcar de Barrameda steamship.

In spite of this episode, the Guadalquivir remained a major commercial route during the Muslim period. The port of Seville was given arsenals, jetties and a landing stage. Mansions were built and, in 1220, the Torre del Oro. Like the Nile, Tigris and Euphrates, the Guadalquivir can also offer elegant pleasure cruises against a setting of beautiful riverside residences and gardens much extolled by poets.

The village of Gelves (below, top) and the Coria del Río ferry crossing the river (below, bottom).

THE ROUTE OF THE GALLEONS ● *34*. From the 15th to the 17th century the Guadalquivir was used by the great fleets sailing between Seville and the Indies. River traffic included powerful great galleons on their way to the Americas, galleons returning with their holds packed full of precious metals, elegant caravels as well as more modest galleys and ships and simple sailing barges. However, the commercial decline of the river began in the mid-17th century as ships became much heavier and were unable to sail up a waterway whose irregular rate of flow and floods caused by high tides made its sandy bed extremely dangerous.

NAVIGATION COMPANY. By the early 18th century the situation had reached catastrophic proportions. The Royal Navigation Company of the Guadalquivir was founded in 1815 to improve navigation and boost the river's declining commercial activity. Its members presented the king with a development project that involved cutting the winding course of the river and creating canals, including the Canal de Fernandino. The first fleet of steamships covered the Seville–Sanlúcar–Cádiz route. In about 1860 the number of companies increased, destinations were extended to include European ports and the docks of Seville became the third largest in Spain.

VILLAGES OF THE GUADALQUIVIR

SAN JUAN DE AZNALFARACHE. On the right bank of the river is the site of the Roman town of Osset where Bacchus was worshiped. The town developed and was fortified during the Muslim period when it became known as Hisn el-Faray ("castle of the visionary"). Its fortress was the residence of Seville's poet-king, El-Mu'tamid ▲ *144*. San Juan was also the camp of the elite troops of Ferdinand, El Católico, the military order of Santiago. There is a magnificent view from the MONUMENTO A LOS SAGRADOS CORAZONES.

HASEKURA
The Japanese ambassador in Seville in the 17th century.

Extracting sand from the river is a traditional occupation.

“The Baetis, a navigable river with a considerable rate of flow which, at high tide, rises some three to four cubits and becomes slightly saline; the waters become fresh again at low tide...”

Jeronimo Munzer, 1494

GELVES. This small hillside town, surrounded by market gardens and orchards, will soon have a marina. Its Arabic name, Ge-Bal, meant “mount pleasant”. It was the birthplace of one of Andalusia's most famous bullfighters, Joselito el Gallo (1895–1920) ● *53*, ▲ *211*.

CORIA DEL RÍO. About 7½ miles below Seville, Coria stands at the crossroads of three regions: El Aljarafe ▲ *218*, the Ribera region and the Marismas (marshes). The town appeared at the end of the prehistoric era, on top of the hill of San Juan, and was extended during the Tartessian and Roman periods. It struck its own coins which bore the head of a warrior and a fish of the shad family. The Muslims and Christians considered it a district of Seville and were careful to ensure its prosperity. It faces the river, and its townsfolk are made up of farmers, fishermen, sailors and ship carpenters. The Guadalquivir can be seen from the Paseo, a tree-lined avenue with kiosks and terraces.

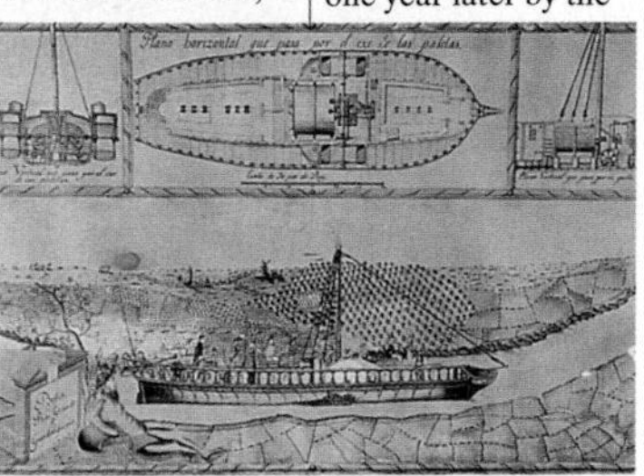

ERMITA DE LA VERA CRUZ. The steps of the Calle San Juan climb the hill to the Ermita de la Vera Cruz or del Cerro (“hill”) from where there is a panoramic view of the surrounding area. According to legend, Saint James the Apostle sailed up the river into Spain. He had with him three statues of Christ to be placed in three different locations. When he reached Coria his ship ran aground, a sign that he had reached his first destination. The hermitage's statue of Christ Crucified is said to be one of the three statues brought by the Apostle.

SAMURAI IN CORIA. In 1617 Luis Sotelo, a Franciscan from Seville, sailed up the river accompanied by a Japanese delegation sent by the *daimyo* Date Masamune of Mutsu Province. The emissaries stopped in Seville on their way to Rome as they bore gifts and letters (now preserved in the town hall) to the city from the *daimyo*. During their stay several Japanese warriors decided to remain in Coria del Río. Today some six hundred townspeople are descended from these 17th-century samurai and have the patronym Japón.

LA PUEBLA DEL RÍO
Unlike its neighbor Coria, La Puebla del Río faces inland. This agricultural community comprises the three islands formed by the branches of the river (Mayor, Menor and Mínima) where the caliph El-Mansur bred his horses. The village marked the starting point of the modern colonization of the marshes.

“REAL FERNANDO”
Plans for the first Guadalquivir steamship, the *Real Fernando*, nicknamed the *Betis*. Launched in 1817, it was replaced one year later by the *Neptuno*, then the *Trajano* and, finally, the *Teodosio*.

THE GUADALQUIVIR BY DELACROIX
In 1832 the French artist Delacroix, who had been crossed in love, set sail from Seville on his way to Cádiz. In his journal he wrote: “Boat, departure. A woman in an officer's uniform. Banks of the Guadalquivir, a dreary night. Alone among several passengers playing cards . . .”

Rice fields and plots that flood.

MAKING THE HULL OF A SHIP
Tools include: an adze; small soft-iron tacks for the planks; nail punches for embedding the nail

RICE GROWERS
The former inhabitants of the marshes were fiercely independent shepherds, hunters and horsemen. They have been replaced by farmers, the descendants of the settlers who came from all over Spain in the 1940's and 1950's to cultivate the newly created plots of rice fields. Rice growers (right) in Villafranco del Guadalquivir.

LAND RECLAMATION
The draining of the marshes and their conversion into agricultural land have transformed the once wild landscape of the lower Guadalquivir valley.

STURGEON
Sturgeon fishermen in the lower Guadalquivir working for the caviar factory in Coria del Río.

TRADITIONAL CRAFTS

Coria has two major types of craftsmen. There are the "land" craftsmen who make tiles, earthenware jars and pottery, and the "river" craftsmen who make fishing boats, nets and rigging. During the golden age of trade with the Indies, there were many carpenters and caulkers plying their trade in Coria.

SHIP CARPENTRY. Today ship carpenters only make small craft, but the techniques they use have remained unchanged for centuries. The "body" is added to the keel, which rests on a high support. The framework is made of wild olive-wood or eucalyptus. The pine ribs are soaked in the river, which makes them flexible enough to be shaped. The hull is then caulked by pressure filling each joint with tow (flax fiber). The craft is finally given a coating of tar to make it watertight.

FISHING. Many types of fish and shellfish are carried into the lower stretch of the river by the tides: red mullet, carp, shad, bleak, eels, crabs and shrimps. The most widely used types of fishing tackle are the eel pot or Dutch net, the trammel net, the bottom line or trawl, and the trolling spoon used by the many shrimp boats found between Coria and the river mouth. The trolling spoon consists of two wooden rods (5½–11 yards long), with a piece of net stretched between them that catches the shrimps as the boat moves against the tide. The funnel-shaped eel pot consists of six rings, about 68 inches apart, which decrease in size and are held together by a net.

CAVIAR. Sturgeon was once plentiful in the waters of the lower Guadalquivir. In 1932 a caviar factory was built at Coria, the only one of its kind in Spain, run by a Russian ichthyologist. However, in the 1960's, the construction of the Alcalá del Río dam above Seville led to the disappearance of the sturgeon and the closure of the caviar factory.

RICE GROWING. About 99,000 acres of marshland on either side of the Guadalquivir are devoted to rice growing. The first rice mill began operating in 1931. The population of the rice

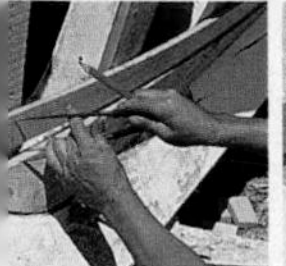

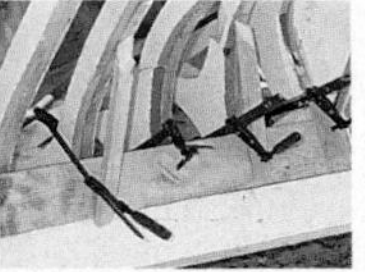
heads in the wood; a hammer and sliding screw jacks to secure the various sections.

fields consists mainly of settlers who came there after the Spanish Civil War (1936–9) and their descendants. The area now constitutes Europe's second largest rice-producing region after Italy. The capital of the marshes is the town of VILLAFRANCO DEL GUADALQUIVIR, which is renowned for its delicious "duck with rice". This dish can be sampled in local restaurants.

BULLS. The low-lying areas of marshland, which are susceptible to flooding and difficult to cultivate, have been used for breeding bulls since ancient times. In one of his poems dedicated to Geryon, Stesichoros (640–555 BC) likened the King of Tartessos to a herdsman because of the many herds in his kingdom. From the river, wild bulls may often be seen grazing on the banks. The breed that is raised in this inhospitable region is a favorite in the bullring because of its great courage. At present the islands of the Guadalquivir have eight establishments that breed bulls for bullfights.

HUNTING. The lower Guadalquivir has always been an exceptionally good region for hunting, which has been a way of life and means of subsistence for its inhabitants, because of its natural conditions. J. A. Valverde describes a typical scene: "With the onset of autumn came the hundreds of thousands of ducks and geese from the north that Juan Ramón pointed out to his donkey, Platero, and with the ducks came the hunters: amazing, solitary men who left the villages with a horse, a gun and some form of cover when the October rains began to bring the birds to the shores of the marshes. They had big guns, big calibers, they called them. They made their own powder according to a time-honored formula, reminiscent of the first arquebusiers: one third saltpeter, one third sulfur and one third coal. They made this powder in large stone mortars, crushing it with a thick piece of olive-wood so that it didn't make sparks. They filled their saddlebag with it and, with their gun on their shoulder, set off to hunt. It could take several days before there were enough ducks for a good shoot, before they killed enough, and could return to the village to sell their game." From 1856, the marshes of the Guadalquivir were frequented by kings, noblemen and naturalists, and became internationally renowned.

TROLLING SPOONS AND EEL POTS
Shrimp boats are easily recognized by the characteristic trolling spoons fixed to the bows. Eel fishermen use eel pots (center).

SHIP CARPENTRY
One of the last ship carpenters on the banks of the river.

Framework of a fishing boat.

▲ The Guadalquivir below Seville

Allegory
Allegory representing the Guadalquivir, the source of prosperity (19th-century engraving).

Fernando Villalón
This stock-farmer and owner of a large estate on the Guadalquivir marshes is better known for his poetry.

Bonanza
A great fish and shellfish market is held in the old warehouses of the port of Sanlúcar de Barrameda.

The Guadalquiver estuary

Aerial photographs clearly show the so-called "plume": the cloudy waters mixed with sand and mud that accumulate in the estuary. The river bed is extremely unsettled as a result of this residue of silt. The thousands of tons of mud carried down by the river and the vast quantities of sand that fall from the cliffs in the province of Huelva have created a mobile coastline whose rapid development has been revealed by modern methods of detection. The coastal dunes that border the Coto de Doñana in the north are among the most beautiful in Europe. In recent centuries the land has advanced into the sea by between half and one mile, a fact borne out by the San Jacinto watchtower. The tower was built on the shore at the end of the 16th century and is today lost among the dunes, between a quarter and half a mile from the water's edge. The coast to the south of the estuary has also been significantly altered. The land today occupied by the *barrio bajo* (meaning "lower town") of Sanlúcar de Barrameda was still being flooded in the 15th century, when the sea used to wash against the cliff occupied by the present *barrio alto* ("upper town"). As the sea gradually receded, the port of Sanlúcar was transferred to the present site of Bonanza in the 18th century.

La Barra. One of the main features of the Guadalquivir estuary in fact lies under the water. La Barra is a line of reefs that stretches out to form an obstruction to the entrance to the estuary, which made this an extremely difficult maneuver for galleon pilots. The sandy bed of the estuary is littered with wrecks of all kinds and from all ages, looking like the exhibits in some strange museum of shipwrecks.

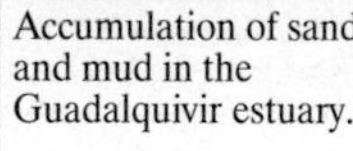

Accumulation of sand and mud in the Guadalquivir estuary.

Steamship
The steamship *Sevilla* was built in 1870 for the Navigation Company of Seville which operated the Seville–Marseille service. It carried passengers and cargo.

Seville to Córdoba

THE GUADALQUIVIR VALLEY

Two days
90 miles
◆ A D2-4

Roman coins from Alcalá del Río (below right).

The itinerary along the Guadalquivir valley passes through the beautiful countryside that is typical of this region. As you leave Seville on the A-431, you soon find yourself driving through plantations of orange trees and fields of maize, wheat and sunflowers. The green expanses stretching into the distance are an ever-present reminder that agriculture is the mainstay of the Andalusian economy. The dense vegetation along the banks of the river includes copses of elm, ash and poplar. Whitewashed farms, with palm trees in their yards, bask in the sun on the hillsides overlooking the cultivated valley.

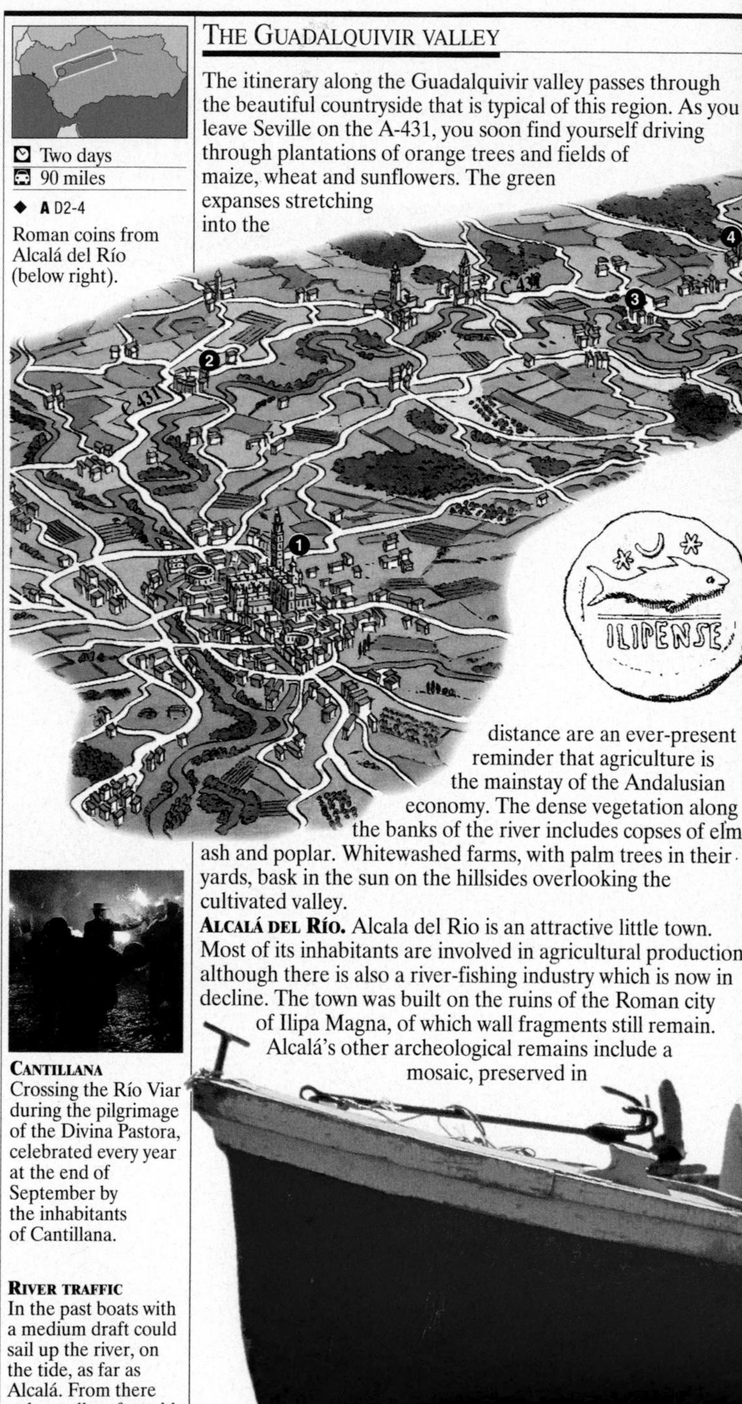

ALCALÁ DEL RÍO. Alcala del Rio is an attractive little town. Most of its inhabitants are involved in agricultural production, although there is also a river-fishing industry which is now in decline. The town was built on the ruins of the Roman city of Ilipa Magna, of which wall fragments still remain. Alcalá's other archeological remains include a mosaic, preserved in

CANTILLANA
Crossing the Río Viar during the pilgrimage of the Divina Pastora, celebrated every year at the end of September by the inhabitants of Cantillana.

RIVER TRAFFIC
In the past boats with a medium draft could sail up the river, on the tide, as far as Alcalá. From there only small craft could continue to Córdoba.

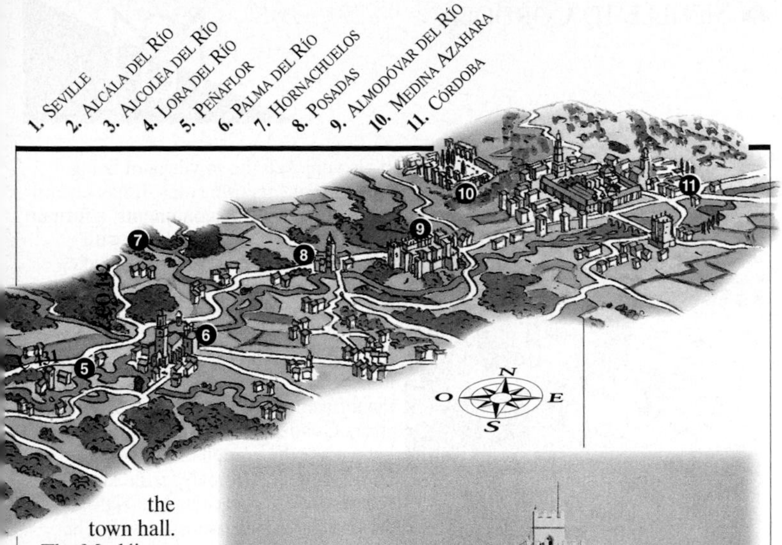

1. Seville
2. Alcála del Río
3. Alcolea del Río
4. Lora del Río
5. Peñaflor
6. Palma del Río
7. Hornachuelos
8. Posadas
9. Almodóvar del Río
10. Medina Azahara
11. Córdoba

the town hall. The Mudéjar Iglesia de la Asunción, built in the 14th century, houses a silver Gothic reliquary and a lovely reredos.

Torre de la Reina
This magnificent, 13th-century fortified bastion near La Algaba has been converted into a hotel.

Alcolea del Río. Alcolea was a strategic river enclave in Roman Baetica. Most of the amphoras used to transport wine and oil to all parts of the Roman Empire came from here. Water mills built by the Muslims (for example, La Aceña) were used to produce flour ● *66*. The river crossing is made from the public landing stage behind the mills, in a boat pulled by a cable. The method has not changed since the days of the bandits. In the center of the village the Iglesia de San Juan Bautista, constructed in the 16th century, is well worth a visit.

Lora del Río. Pliny referred to Lora del Río as "Axati", but its present name is derived from the laurel (*lora*) that grows in abundance in the vicinity. In the town center the Sevillian Baroque buildings of the town hall, the Casa de los Leones (1765), with its beautiful verandah, and the Casa de Quintanilla attest to the importance of the commercial and cultural activities of Lora during the 18th century. The Iglesia de Nuestra Señora de la Asunción was built in the 15th century in Sevillian Mudéjar style ● *70*. It has a brick portal and its tower has several distinct sections. The Capilla Sacramental contains a superb collection of gold and silver work, which includes a 15th-century, solid silver censer.

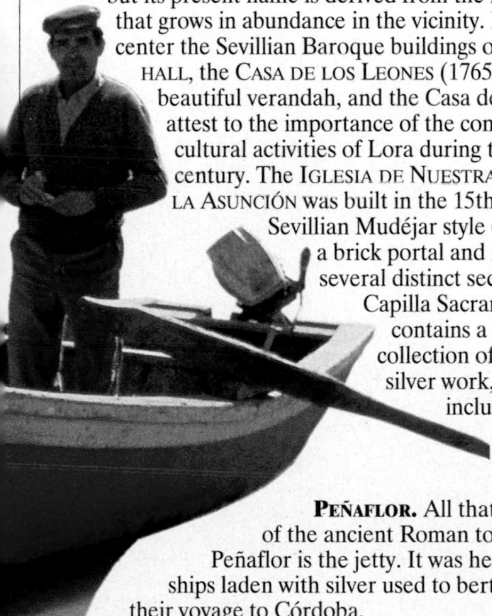

Lora del Río
The tower of the Iglesia de la Asunción dominates the village.

The Baroque hermitage of San Francisco in Lora del Río.

Peñaflor. All that remains of the ancient Roman town of Peñaflor is the jetty. It was here that ships laden with silver used to berth on their voyage to Córdoba.

It also enjoyed the privilege of being able to strike its own coins. It has several interesting historic monuments: a former pottery workshop, a sepulcher with carved niches for cinerary urns and the castle-sanctuary of Villadiego.

Palma del Río. This town, served by the A-453, was founded in AD 1085 by the Roman Aulio Cornelio Palma, after whom it was named. It occupies a magnificent site on the confluence of the rivers Guadalquivir and Genil, and was known as "the garden of Andalusia" because of its extremely fertile land. Palma still has part of its late 12th-century Almohad enclosure wall. The 18th-century Iglesia de la Asunción has a fine Baroque tower after the style of Écija. The former convent of San Francisco, built between the 16th and 18th centuries, provided accommodation for missionaries on their way to America, including Fray Junípero Serra, who preached the gospel in California. The carefully restored convent today houses a hotel, while its church serves as the parish church.

Hornachuelos. A slight detour (take the CO-140 off the A-431 toward the sierra) brings you to Hornachuelos, on the edge of a protected ecological site within a nature reserve. High on the hillside are the early 16th-century Gothic Iglesia de Santa María de las Flores and the nearby Convento de Santa María de los Angeles which overlooks the gorges of the Bembézar river. The Cordovan Romantic writer and duke of Rivas, Angel de Saavedra (1791–1865), used this as the setting for *Don Álvaro o la Fuerza del Sino*, which provided the inspiration for Verdi's opera *La Forza del Destino*.

Posadas. The A-431 carries on past the Moratalla estate, formerly a hunting reserve for royalty and the aristocracy and somewhat reminiscent of Versailles. Soon

Palma del Río
The first Cordovan town built upstream from Seville was the birthplace of the famous bullfighter Manuel Benítez "Cordobés". In the center of the old town are the Plaza de Andalusía and the seigneurial palace of Portocarrero.

Washerwomen on the banks of the Guadalquivir in the early 20th century.

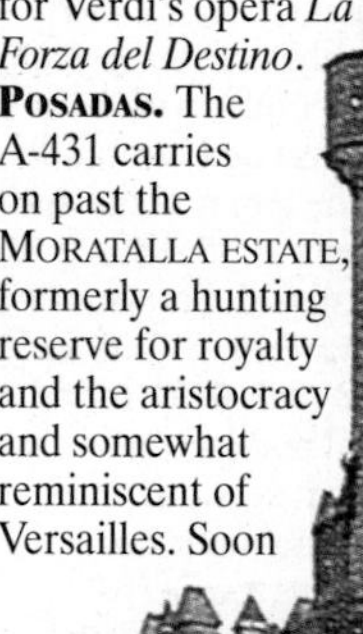

Castillo de Almodóvar
This impressive fortress controlled land and river traffic between Seville and Córdoba.

Brand marks
Fighting bulls from the prestigious cattle farms graze on the pastureland of Palma del Río and Almodóvar.

The Guadalquivir at Almodóvar del Río.

afterward you come to Posadas, which grew up around a group of dwellings built by order of Ferdinand (El Católico) in the late 15th century. According to popular belief, this was one of the main bandit strongholds, a theme that fired the 19th-century Andalusian Romantic imagination. The parish church of Nuestra Señora de las Flores, built in the 16th century in late Gothic style, has a fine Renaissance portal by Hernán Ruiz the Elder (1474–1547) ● *73*, ▲ *240*.

Castillo de Almodóvar del Río ★. The Castillo de Almodóvar del Río, built on a granite outcrop over the river, is one of the most beautiful fortified castles in Spain. All that remains of the original Roman fortress is a section of its walls, which were rebuilt by the Moors in 740 and withstood the attacks of Christian troops for four hundred years! It was extended again in 1226 by King Baza, a vassal of Ferdinand III ● *32*, ▲ *176*, who took it over in 1236. The castle's final structure, based on a Mudéjar-Gothic layout, was the result of renovations carried out in the 14th century by Pedro I and Henry II. According to legend, the castle is supposed to be haunted by the ghosts of those who died while imprisoned within its walls. At night they are said to roam the neighborhood in the form of bats. Juana de Laura, the Lady of Biscaye, was imprisoned there by order of Pedro I, who had oubliettes and a treasure chamber built in the castle. There is a magnificent view from the battlements, above the whitewashed houses of the village clinging to the hillside below.

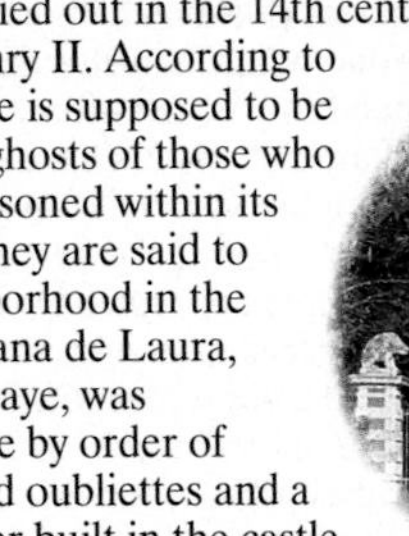

Moratalla estate
The Moratalla estate, at the foot of the Sierra de Hornachuelos, was once a great hunting reserve.

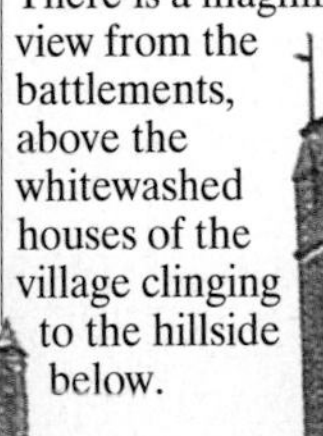

The Castillo de Almodóvar del Río has a series of very fine towers, the Square and Round towers, and the towers of Homage, of the School, and of the Bells.

CALIPH OF CÓRDOBA Abd el-Rahman III el-Nasir (891–965) founded the caliphate of Córdoba in 929. He was described as well built and elegant, with dyed-black hair, a fair complexion and dark blue eyes.

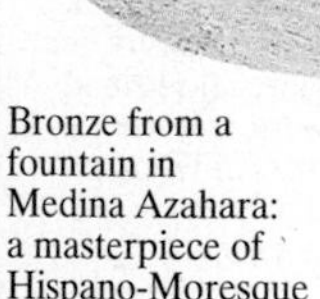

Ruins of the palace complex.

Bronze from a fountain in Medina Azahara: a masterpiece of Hispano-Moresque art.

MEDINA AZAHARA ★

At an intersection a few miles outside Córdoba, take the road to Trassierra, which runs past the ruins of the Medina Azahara.

JEWEL OF THE CALIPHATE. The splendor and refinement of the Medinat el-Zahra ("city of the flower") made it the jewel in the crown of the caliphate of Córdoba. Today the elements that have been restored, even though they only represent a tiny part of the whole, give some idea of the original architectural beauty and harmony.

PALATINE CITY. The city was built by order of Abd el-Rahman III, who wanted to establish his residence and court near Córdoba. The Ommiad dynasty was in the habit of taking up residence on the outskirts of a city, as illustrated by the Syrian palaces near Damascus. According to tradition the caliph chose the site in the foothills of the Sierra Morena and near the so-called "mountain of the betrothed", and dedicated the edifice to one of his favorites, Zahra. Work was begun in 936 and continued for the next forty years, until the reign of El-Hakam II. Many chroniclers have described this vast undertaking, which employed a workforce of over ten thousand men under the direction of the architect Maslama Ibn Abad. The fortified complex occupied an area of 550 x 1,094 yards and included palaces, barracks, servants' quarters, a mint, baths and a great mosque. The complex, with its pool of quicksilver, alabaster screens and silvered tiles, was a dazzling example of oriental splendor that inspired awe and amazement in all who saw it. The caliph is said to have had almond trees planted all the way from the Medina to Córdoba, creating the impression of a carpet of snow when they were in bloom.

THE SHINING TERRACE. The Medina Azahara, which covered an area of almost 300 acres and was enclosed by a thick wall flanked by towers, was built on three descending terraces. On the upper, or "shining", terrace were the *alcázares* of the caliph and his court as well as the administrative and residential quarters, which included some four hundred houses. The royal apartments stood on the edge of the terrace, next to three vast reception halls. These included the so-called "house of the army", whose great portal opened onto a parade ground. To the east was the famous throne room, whose walls were entirely covered with marble and translucent jasper. It was surmounted by a dome covered in gold and silver and decorated with a magnificent hanging pearl, a gift from the emperor of Byzantium.

SOUTH TERRACE. The middle level, occupied by gardens and pavilions, has the finest excavated remains. The pavilion of Abd el-Rahman III, with its richly decorated *salón*, is a fine example of the synthesis of Cordovan art, which combines Greco-Roman and Islamic traditions in the exuberant

> "When kings want to bequeath to posterity the memory of their most elevated thoughts, they do so through the language of beautiful constructions."
>
> Abd al-Rahman III

decoration of the marble plaques and capitals. On the lowest, or "mosque", terrace was the city proper, with its *souk*, stores and the houses where the twelve thousand people who served the court lived.

ANCIENT CÓRDOBA. In 1010 Berber troops led by Suleyman el-Mustain captured the Medina Azahara with the help of King Sancho of Castile. This was the beginning the break-up of the caliphate into numerous small kingdoms, or *taifas*. The city of 4,300 ancient columns, the symbol of the magnificence of the caliphate, was burned, pillaged and destroyed. Its architectural wealth was, to a large extent, dispersed. Some of the fragments were incorporated into Moorish buildings in Córdoba, Seville and Marrakesh. Gradually the remains were buried and the city lay forgotten until the excavations carried out in the 20th century.

REAL MONASTERIO DE SAN JERÓNIMO DE VALPARAISO. Near the Medina Azahara stands the convent of San Jerónimo de Valparaiso, built in the 15th century using materials taken from the ancient Moorish city. The convent, which is now under private ownership, offers a magnificent view of the valley leading to Córdoba. There are numerous religious establishments and sanctuaries in the vicinity, in particular SCALA COELI, SANTO DOMINGO and the famous thirteen hermitages. These hermitages have been continuously inhabited since the 6th century by Cordovan hermits.

RICHLY DECORATED "SALÓN"
The art of the caliphate reached the height of sophistication in the *salones* of the pavilion of Abd el-Rahman III, designed and created between 953 and 957. They were reserved for royal guests as well as government meetings.

REAL MONASTERIO DE SAN JERÓNIMO
One of Córdoba's most impressive Gothic buildings.

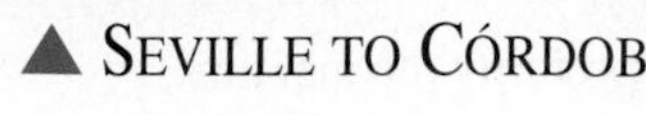

CÓRDOBA IN THE MID-19TH CENTURY
Panoramic view showing the Roman bridge, the mosque and the *alcázar*.

CÓRDOBA

Córdoba provides a dazzling synthesis of the cultures that have left their mark on Andalusia. This ancient city was visited by the Phoenicians, founded by the Carthaginians, became the capital of Roman Baetica and, in the 10th century, the capital of the great caliphate. It then became the greatest spiritual and scientific center in the Western World, with its luxurious palaces, three hundred mosques and great university attracting scholars and artists from all over Europe. Muslims, Jews and Christians lived together in the city until the arrival of Ferdinand III of Castile ● *32*, ▲ *176* in 1236. Thenceforth it underwent a long period of decline marked by religious intolerance and the degeneration of agriculture after the abandonment of the irrigation system built by the Muslims.

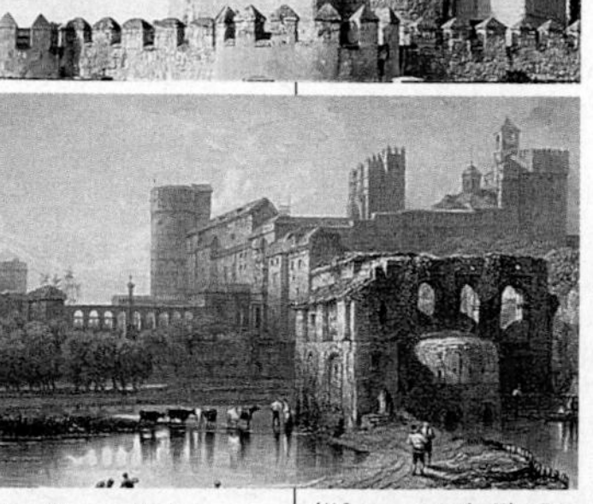

The Torre de la Calahorra (above, top), which now houses the Museo de las Tres Culturas, the water mills and the Alcázar de los Reyes Católicos (above).

TORRE DE LA CALAHORRA. The tower stands in the Campo de la Verdad, on the opposite side of the river to Córdoba. It once guarded the access to the Puente Romano. It was converted into a fortress by the Moors who named it Calahorra ("free castle"). Its two towers were joined in the 15th century.

MUSEO DE LAS TRES CULTURAS. The Torre de la Calahorra houses the Museo Histórico, an interesting museum where an institute for intercultural understanding, directed by Roger Garaudy, presents an exhibition of the city's tri-cultural past, with special focus on the contribution of Islam. There are models of La Mezquita and the Alhambra in Granada.

“O sublime walls! O towers crowned with glory, majesty and valiance! O great river, great king of Andalusia…”

Luis de Góngora

Puente Romano. The 656-foot-long Puente Romano was part of the Via Augusta, the main thoroughfare of Roman Baetica. The bridge has been restored many times, especially during the reign of Hixem I, and of the original Roman structure only part of its foundations remain. A statue (1651) of the city's patron saint, the archangel Raphael, stands here.

Water mills ● *66*. These former Moorish water mills were built in the Guadalquivir. The huge wheel of La Albolafia was used to irrigate the gardens of the Alcázar de los Reyes Católicos, which lay along the banks.

Puerta del Puente. On the far side of the Roman bridge stands the Puerta de Felipe II, a Renaissance-style triumphal arch designed by Juan de Herrera, the favorite architect of Philip II, and built by Hernán Ruiz (1536–1606), son of Hernán Ruiz the Younger ● *73*. The gate opens onto the south façade of La Mezquita. To the left stands the *Triunfo de San Rafael*, another remarkable monument representing the patron saint of Córdoba.

Alcázar de los Reyes Católicos. This *alcázar* lies in the western part of the city, between the Guadalquivir and the Campo Santo de los Mártires. It was built in 1328, at the instigation of Alfonso XI, on the ruins of a former caliphal fortress that was itself built on Roman foundations. It was the residence of the Catholic monarchs, or Reyes Católicos, during military operations against the Kingdom of Granada. Christopher Columbus ▲ *136*, *283*, *304* went there in 1486 to request their support for his planned voyage to the Indies. The *alcázar* became the seat of the Inquisition and then a prison. It was restored in 1951 and now houses a museum whose archeological exhibits include two richly colored Roman mosaics (2nd century). The layout of the gardens, with their fountains, pools and wealth of different plants, are reminiscent of Moorish gardens. There is a magnificent view of the river's banks from the walls.

Persian wheel of La Albolafia
The remains of this 9th-century water mill attest to the exceptional hydraulic skill of the Muslims of El-Andalus.

Roman sarcophagus
The Alcázar de los Reyes Católicos has an extremely valuable archeological collection. This sarcophagus, which came from a Roman workshop and was completed in Córdoba around the middle of the 3rd century, is one of its most remarkable pieces.

Seneca, the philosopher
Lucius Annaeus Seneca (4 BC–AD 65) is known as one of the greatest philosophers of the ancient world. He was born into the Cordovan aristocracy, when Córdoba was the capital of Roman Baetica ● *30*.

Aerial view of La Mezquita.

LA MEZQUITA ★

The cathedral-mosque of Córdoba is one of Spain's grandest monuments. Although the construction of majestic Christian buildings has altered its overall plan, the world's biggest mosque after the one at Mecca has remained a symbol of the era of greatness experienced by the capital of El-Andalus from the 8th century to the beginning of the 11th century.

Puerta el-Hakam II.

THE GREAT MOSQUE. When the Muslim invaders arrived in Córdoba in 711, they initially used the existing places of worship. But the city was rapidly elevated to the status of capital of an independent emirate, and its governor, Abd el-Rahman I, decided to endow it with a mosque to rival Islam's greatest shrines. In 785 he bought back the part of the Basílica de San Vicente dedicated to Christianity from the Mozarabs and had the chapel razed. The mosque was completed in the 10th century, with the addition of several naves, to the south and east. In the words of the geographer and traveler from Ceuta, Mohammed el-Idrisi (1100–72), the resulting structure was "unparalleled for the beauty of its architecture and the vastness of its dimensions as well as the sumptuousness of its decoration". The edifice, about 27,500 square yards in area, was built according to a rectangular plan and faced south, like the Great Mosque of Damascus, rather than southeast, toward Mecca, in accordance with Islamic tradition. It would seem that it was decided to observe the traditions of the Syrian Ommiad dynasty, of whom the El-Andalus princes were descendants.

"PUERTAS" AND "PATIO". The Puerta de San Miguel and Puerta de San Esteban, the extremely ancient entrances of the mosque which open onto the Calle Torrijos, have some beautiful 10th-century Moorish decorations. The Mudéjar Puerta de los Deanes and Puerta del Perdón, in the north wall, give access to the delightful Patio de los Naranjos. This former court of ablutions a 10th-century well, the *aljibe* of Almanzor, and some Mudéjar and Baroque fountains. In the

THE MEZQUITA AND THE JUDERÍA ✪
Behind its austere sandstone ramparts, the Mezquita is home to numerous architectural treasures, the most spectacular of which are the prayer room of the original mosque, the *mihrab* (a recess facing Mecca), the *maqsura* (a space reserved for the caliph) and the chapel of Villaviciosa. The sense of wonderment continues in the winding streets of the Judería, the old Jewish district with its whitewashed walls and charming courtyards.

"As for its great mosque, there is none more important, none so grand, so marvelous or so perfect, in all the Islamic world."

Anonymous, 14th–15th century

centre is the Santa María fountain, dating back to the 17th century and also known as the Caño del Olivo, or "fountain of the olive tree". According to tradition, unmarried people who drink from it will find their partner immediately.

TORRE DEL ALMINAR. The tower on one side of the Patio de los Naranjos was originally a minaret, built in 957 during the reign of Abd el-Rahman III. It was converted into a Renaissance (16th–17th century) bell tower by the architects Hernán Ruiz the Younger and Asensio de Maeda when it was decided to erect a symbol of Christianity within the former mosque (as in the case of La Giralda in Seville) for the Council of Trent. From the top of the tower there is a panoramic view of the entire city.

THE PRAYER ROOM. As you enter the Mezquita via the Puerta de la Palmas, a veritable forest of columns seems to stretch out as far as the eye can see. In the 8th century nave, above these columns, double arcades surmount horseshoe and semicircular arches in alternating shades of brick and ocher. The height and space of this innovative architecture is thought to have been inspired by the Roman aqueducts of ancient Baetica ● *30*.

The columns seem to converge toward the southern wall of the *qibla*, with its *mihrab*, a masterpiece of caliphal Moorish art. This most sacred part of the mosque is extremely ornate: its wall, galleries and are decorated with stuccos, mosaics and multicolored marble. The caliph El-Hakam II, who directed work in 961, had craftsmen brought from Byzantium to create the masterly designs in *pâte de verre* decorated with gold leaf, a technique known as *fusaifisa* in Arabic.

THE COLUMNS
The columns came from all over the Islamic world, from Constantinople and from Roman and Visigoth temples on the Iberian peninsula. They were in every

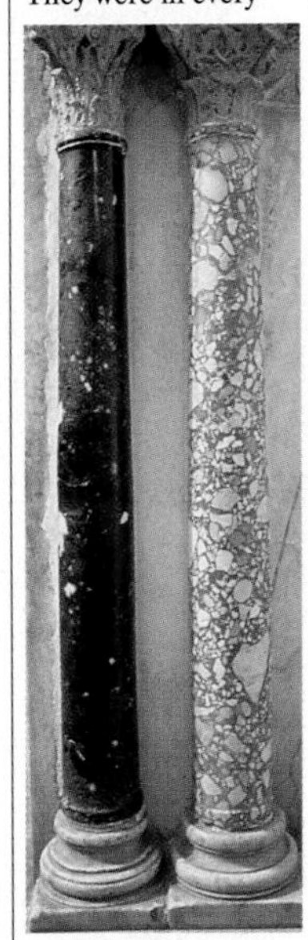

style, color and form imaginable. Since the construction of the cathedral only 856 of the original 1013 columns remain.

THE "MAQSURA"
The Mezquita's most beautiful dome is the the one in the prayer hall reserved for emirs and caliphs, which is marked off by an openwork fence opposite the *mihrab*. The dome is covered with geometric and plant motifs on a gilded mosaic background.

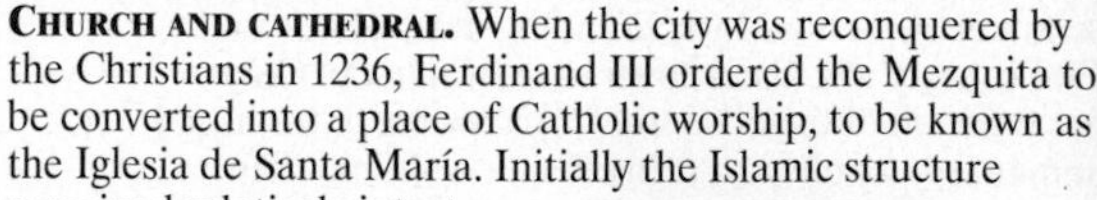

CAPILLA DE VILLAVICIOSA
The chapel's horseshoe arches rest on columns set in a polychrome marble wall-covering of classical inspiration.

CHURCH AND CATHEDRAL. When the city was reconquered by the Christians in 1236, Ferdinand III ordered the Mezquita to be converted into a place of Catholic worship, to be known as the Iglesia de Santa María. Initially the Islamic structure remained relatively intact, although the entrances on the north façade (with the exception of the Puerta de las Palmas) were blocked up and more than thirty chapels were gradually built onto the side of the outer wall. Alfonso X built the CAPILLA DE SAN CLEMENTE in 1254 (one of its portals, to the left of the *mihrab*, can still be seen today) and the CAPILLA REAL (1258), decorated with the Mudéjar stuccowork of the Granadan Nasrid dynasty. Over the years the forest of columns dwindled and, in the early 16th century, the future of the Mezquita gave rise to some bitter controversy. In 1523, in an attempt to prevent its defacement, the mayor of Córdoba, Luis de la Cerda, issued a ban condemning to death anyone who destroyed so much as a single column. Bishop Alonso Manrique, who favored the construction of a cathedral, responded by excommunicating the mayor. The matter was referred to the emperor Charles V, who sided with the Church, a decision he later bitterly regretted. From 1523 to 1617, the massive cathedral structure 60 yards long, designed by Hernán Ruiz the Elder and Younger, Juan de Ochoa and Diego de Praves, was incorporated into the very heart of the mosque. In 1599 the transept was crowned with an original oval, Mannerist-style coffered vault. The choir, created in 1607 by Juan de Oliva, is of Florentine inspiration and has Haitian mahogany choir stalls. Although the Renaissance structure, which incorporates Gothic and Baroque elements, is not without a certain charm, one cannot help recalling the words of Charles V on seeing the work completed: "You have built here what you or anyone might have built anywhere else, but you have destroyed what was unique in the world."

CHOIR STALLS
This masterpiece of Andalusian Baroque sculpture was the work of Pedro Duque Cornejo, between 1747 and 1757. As specified in the contract for the commission, it has 181 alternating reliefs executed "to the best of the master's skill and ability".

JUDERÍA

The entire tri-cultural history of Córdoba is condensed into the immediate vicinity of the Mezquita. To the northwest of the cathedral-mosque lies the city's former Jewish quarter. Initially harshly treated by the Visigoths, Córdoba's Jewish community prospered under the Moorish occupation, especially during the caliphate (929–1031), when they were appreciated for their administrative and scientific ability and enjoyed the protection of the

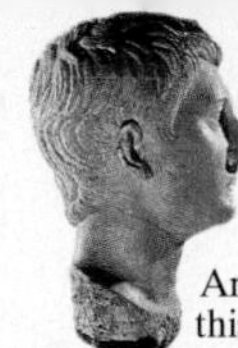
The fine collection of Roman sculptures in the Museo Arqueológico includes this head of Drusus.

sovereigns. As a result large numbers of Jewish scholars flocked from all over Europe to Córdoba, which also had a great Talmudic school. Today the Judería (Jewish quarter), the city's oldest district, still has all the charm of an old medieval town. The best way to enjoy it is to take a leisurely stroll through the maze of narrow, winding streets (El Pañuelo, Las Flores), where the whitewashed façades are covered with geraniums, and discover peaceful courtyards hidden beyond porchways (6, Calle Albucasis) and delightful little plazas. The district extends to the old city walls and the 14th-century Puerta de Almodóvar. Outside are statues of the famous Cordovan-born philosophers Seneca and Averroès (1126–98), the latter was also a theologian, astronomer, mathematician and physician, and disseminated the metaphysics of Aristotle in his works.

"Sinagoga". The synagogue, which stands in the Calle Judíos, was built by Isaac Majeb in 1315, during the reign of Alfonso XI. The interior of the small Mudéjar-style temple is decorated with stucco tracery and Hebrew inscriptions. It is Andalusia's only medieval synagogue and one of only three in the whole of Spain.

May festivals. During the first ten days of May the Judería is a blaze of color as residents take part in the Fiesta de los Patios. The houses around the Mezquita, which are usually covered in flowers throughout the year, vie with each other to produce the best floral display. The festival known as Las Cruces de Mayo ("crosses of May") ● *49* is also held during this period. Elaborately decorated crosses are placed throughout the city, and the event heralds much wine-drinking. The celebrations continue toward the end of the month with the Feria de la Salud, a large cattle-market dedicated to Nuestra Señora de la Salud. Bullfights are organized, stalls selling drinks and *tapas* are erected along the Paseo de la Victoria, and the wine flows freely in an atmosphere of general rejoicing.

Interior of Córdoba's synagogue (left).

Moisés Maimónides (1135–1204)
The Jewish philosopher and Talmudist was born in Córdoba's Judería

during the decline of the caliphate. He was driven from the city by the Almohads and sought refuge at the Ayyubid court in Egypt where he became physician to Saladin and wrote a number of important works in which he attempts to reconcile the Bible with the teachings of Aristotle.

Funerary stele (left) of the Rabbi Amicos (11th century), Museo Arqueológico.

The Calleja de las Flores, and an everyday scene in the old town (below).

11TH-CENTURY CÓRDOBA
The ditch surrounding the town was 13½ miles long and enclosed an area significantly larger than the modern city.

JULIO ROMERO DE TORRES
The work of this modern Cordovan artist is as popular as it is controversial. Some see it as a powerful interpretation of the spirit of Andalusia.

BULLFIGHTING TRADITION ● *52*
Córdoba has two centers dedicated to the bullfighting tradition: the bullring on the outskirts of the city and the Museo Taurino. The museum is dedicated, in particular, to four great bullfighters known as the "four caliphs of Córdoba": Rafael Molina "Lagartijo", Rafael Guerra "Guerrita", Rafael González "Machaquito" and Manuel Rodriguez "Manolete".

TEMPLE OF CLAUDIUS MARCELLUS
The many Roman remains scattered throughout the city attest to its vitality during antiquity. Near the Plaza de las Tendillas, the heart of modern Córdoba, is the colonnade of a 1st-century temple dedicated to Claudius Marcellus.

MUSEUMS OF CÓRDOBA

Córdoba's main museums are situated near the Mezquita.
MUSEO TAURINO. This beautiful 16th-century residence in the Plaza de las Bulas, near the synagogue, houses one of the most important museums of its kind. *Aficionados* will be delighted by its paintings, sculptures, trophies and costumes. A replica of his tomb pays poignant homage to "Manolete", killed in the bullring at the age of thirty.
MUSEO ARQUEOLÓGICO. The museum is housed in a magnificent Renaissance palace in the Plaza Jerónimo Páez to the northeast of the Mezquita. It is renowned for its extremely valuable and well-presented collections. The collection of Roman remains from the province includes statues, some remarkable sarcophagi and some very beautiful mosaics. There are also stone lions from the Iberian period, Moorish caliphal-style capitals and such unique pieces as the bronze fawn from the Medina Azahara and a statue of the god Mithras.
PLAZA DEL POTRO. The name of the Plaza del Potro, which lies near the river, to the east of the Mezquita, is derived from the stone statue of a colt (*potro*) on its 16th-century fountain. The plaza is famous for the inn of the same name which has stood there, unchanged, since 1435 and was mentioned by Cervantes in *Don Quixote*. Cervantes is even said to

have stayed in the inn and written part of his novel there. The MUSEO DE BELLAS ARTES and the MUSEO ROMERO DE TORRES also stand on the plaza.

MUSEO DE BELLAS ARTES. The museum, housed in the former Hospital de la Caridad, has an interesting collection of Andalusian Baroque paintings, in particular works by Goya, Zurbarán, Valdés Leal and Murillo ● *91*.

MUSEO ROMERO DE TORRES ★. The adjoining residence once housed the studio of the Cordovan artist Julio Romero de Torres (1874–1930), which was converted into a museum on his death. This brilliant portraitist painted Andalusian women at their most sensual and provocative. Sometimes harshly criticized for his sinister representations of Spain, he caused the greatest scandal with his "hyperrealistic" nudes, especially *Vividoras del amor*, which was banned from the 1906 National Exhibition of Fine Arts.

DISTRICTS OF THE LOWER CITY

At the height of the Islamic period Córdoba was divided into two areas, each surrounded by walls: the Medina or upper city, around the Mezquita, and the Ajarquía or lower city, to the north and east of a line corresponding to the modern Calle San Fernando.

PLAZA DE LAS TENDILLAS AND PLAZA DE LA CORREDERA. The Plaza de las Tendillas, to the north of La Mezquita, is the city's main plaza. It is linked by the Calle Claudio Marcelo to the Plaza de la Corredera (or Plaza Mayor) which is surrounded by classical-style arcades and is the only one of this type (widely found in Castile) in Andalusia. It took the form of an arena in the 17th century when it was used for official ceremonies and celebrations (*autos-da-fé*, tournaments, balls). Today a large, busy market is held here in the mornings.

IGLESIA DE SAN LORENZO. The districts in the northeast of the

POPULAR DISTRICTS
In the past, travelers and muleteers stayed in the *corral* (courtyard) of the Posada del Potro ("inn of the colt"). On weekday mornings the stalls of a small market, which had replaced an earlier cobblers' market, were set up beneath its porches.

IGLESIA DE SAN LORENZO
When Córdoba was conquered by the Christians in 1236, Ferdinand III established fourteen parishes, whose fortified churches illustrate the transition from the Romanesque to the Gothic style.

Poster for the Fiesta de los Patios, during the Feria de Nuestra Señora de la Salud.

city take their names from the churches built there after the Reconquest: Santa Marina, San Pablo, San Andrés, San Rafael, San Agustín and San Lorenzo. The latter was built to a rectangular layout and the alternate courses of its walls are typical of the bonding used in Moorish caliphal structures. Its bell tower was erected on a minaret. The Ronda ("sentry walk") del Marrubial follows the line of the former Moorish enclosure wall and marks the limit of these districts.

PALACIO DE VIANA ★. This palace in the Santa Marina district is a magnificent example of aristocratic architecture. The 14th-century edifice has undergone several modifications and combines the Renaissance style with sophisticated ornamentation of Islamic inspiration. It was converted into a museum in 1980. Its various collections include paintings, tapestries, firearms, Cordovan leather, porcelain and ceramics. Visitors can relax in its luxuriant garden or in the shade of one of its fourteen arcaded patios with their ornamental pools.

PLAZA DE COLÓN. To the south of this vast plaza, the 18th-century calvary of the CRISTO DE LOS FAROLES ("lanterns") stands in the tiny Plaza de los Dolores. It is decorated with wrought-iron lanterns, which are lit up at night. To the north of the Plaza de Colón is the 15th-century TORRE DE LA MALMUERTA and the nearby Baroque Convento de la Merced, whose façade is embellished with "marble".

IGLESIA DE SAN NICOLÁS DE LA VILLA. The church, northwest of the city center, was founded by Ferdinand III. Its octagonal bell tower was erected in 1496 following a dispute between the bishop and an aristocratic family living opposite the parish. The motto on the tower, "Patience and Obedience", refers to the victory of ecclesiastical over civil power.

CONVENTO DE LA MERCED
The façade of the Baroque convent (1741–57) has trompe l'oeil "marble" décor.

TORRE DE SAN NICOLÁS
The tower is the emblem of the city of Córdoba. The replica built for the 1929 World Fair can still be seen in Seville. Fiesta de la Cruz (right) held in May ● *49*.

La Campiña

▲ La Campiña

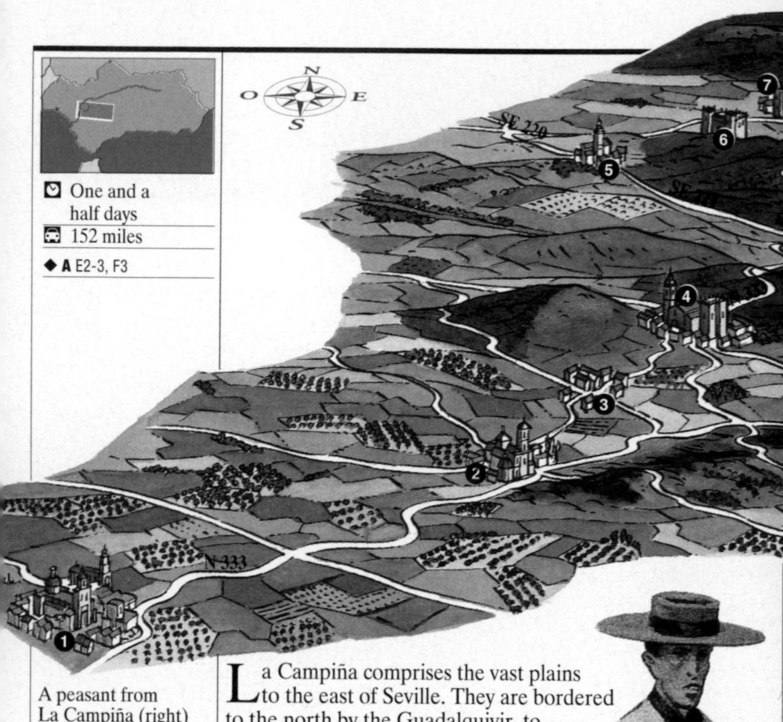

One and a half days
152 miles
◆ **A** E2-3, F3

A peasant from La Campiña (right) in the early 20th century.

La Campiña comprises the vast plains to the east of Seville. They are bordered to the north by the Guadalquivir, to the east by the Genil and to the south by the Guadaira. Although flat, the landscape is far from monotonous, since it is made up of a patchwork of different crops, pastureland, valleys and agricultural towns. La Campiña is defined geographically and historically by its so-called "dry" agriculture. Large and small towns have been established on ancient sites on hills, near fords, at intersections or simply on the most fertile land. Écija, Marchena, El Arahal, Utrera, Morón de la Frontera and Osuna are the largest and most populous towns in the province.

Roman settlement. La Campiña was the theater for the wars between the armies of Pompey and Julius Caesar. The Romans established a series of small *villae*, farms producing mainly cereals and olives. Most survived through the ages, becoming Moorish farms during the Muslim occupation and today's haciendas and market gardens ● *84*. The Christian conquest ● *32* was followed by a division of territory which placed the populations under the jurisdiction of a specially empowered council or a local lord. Behind the fortified enclosure walls of these Andalusian-Moorish towns lies a maze of narrow, winding streets which, in Écija and Marchena, have given rise to such (official or popular) street names as the "Calle de Siete Revueltas" ("street of the

Agricultural tradition
La Campiña has remained an essentially agricultural region (above). Its villages were once the main suppliers of grain and grapes to Seville and, for a long time, the most envied social status was that of landowner in La Campiña.

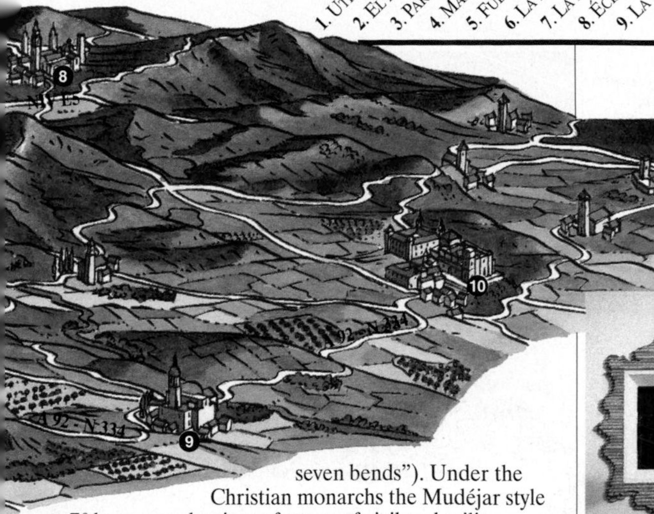

1. Utrera 2. El Arahal 3. Paradas 4. Marchena 5. Fuentes de Andalucía 6. La Monclova 7. La Luisiana 8. Écija 9. La Puebla de Cazalla 10. Osuna 11. Estepa

seven bends"). Under the Christian monarchs the Mudéjar style ● *70* became a dominant feature of civil and military architecture and blended harmoniously with the Gothic style of Castile. The predominance of Mudéjar architecture gives these towns their distinctive character.

Agricultural towns. In the 18th century economic and demographic development led to the towns being extended, as evidenced by the many instances of the name "Calle Nueva" ("new street"). Although the national criteria for civil architecture were largely applied in the region, they did not preclude certain local peculiarities. From the 18th century the most typical type of house had one or two floors, a *zaguán* (large vestibule), a *soberado* (granary), a small courtyard and a work yard. In the 19th century all towns began to whitewash their walls in the style of Morón.

The myth of the "bandoleros". La Campiña was also the haunt of the *bandoleros*, the cut-throats extensively described by 19th-century travelers. The men were known as *guapos* ("tough guys") and the women as *capitanas* ("captains"). They preferred to operate in the area between Écija, Osuna, Estepa, Antequera and Lucena, usually in the vicinity of the Genil river.

Church window in La Campiña, near Écija.

Urban development
The cloistered towns of La Campiña are crossed by narrow streets that open onto public plazas, areas devoted to socializing and festivals (mainly mounted bullfights). Urban communities of this kind are widely found in Andalusia and are known as "convent" or "granary" towns. Plaza de España, Écija (below).

Towers
Écija's brick Baroque towers, decorated with *azulejos* ● *56* and weather vanes, are the work of local craftsmen. The Torre de San Juan (below) and a *casa-mirador* on El Salón (below, right).

Écija

Écija is the provincial capital of La Campiña. It lies in a depression 56 miles east of Seville (via the N-IV/E-5), on the banks of the Genil. Its coat of arms has earned it the name of "the town of sun" and its high summer temperatures (above 115°F) that of "la sartén de Andalucía" ("the frying-pan of Andalusia").

Roman Astigi. The originally Tartessian town later became the Roman town of Astigi, renowned for its mosaics (remains can be seen in the chapterhouse of the town hall) ● *64*. The forum was located near the present-day Plaza de España. According to tradition, Astigi was converted by Saint Paul, who is honored by a Baroque monument near the bridge across the Genil. As well as being the capital of a Roman district, it was also a bishop's see.

From Muslim to Christian town. In the 11th century Écija was the capital of a small Muslim kingdom. In the 12th century it was surrounded by ramparts, some fragments of which can still be seen today. After it was conquered by Ferdinand III in 1240 ● *32*, ▲ *176*, *236*, it became the property of the Crown and was used as a bridgehead for the conquest of the rest of Andalusia. Écija gradually became a major center for agriculture and traditional crafts, and experienced its

As in the time of the great Roman estates, or *latifundia*, La Campiña belongs to a small number of landowners.

golden age in the 18th century, as evidenced by the magnificent monuments erected during this period.

The town of seven towers. The road leading down into Écija offers a splendid view of the Río Genil and the town nestling in its hollow in the rolling countryside. With its many religious establishments, Écija could well be called a "convent town" just as its towers and bell towers, most of which were erected in the 18th century after the earthquake of 1755, would justify the "town of towers". The road leads into the Avenida de Andalucía and the Calle Cervantes, which in turn leads onto the main plaza, El Salón.

Plaza de España: El Salón. El Salón is the popular name for the Plaza de España, the rectangular plaza in the town center. Its ornamental gardens and central fountain are overlooked by the town hall, several religious buildings and a series of *casas-mirador*, several stories high and mostly built in the 18th century. Their galleries once provided a vantage point from which to watch festivals, equestrian events and bullfights.

Iglesia de Santa María. On a small plaza adjoining El Salón is the huge Iglesia de Santa María, founded after the Reconquest, restored in the 16th and totally rebuilt in the 18th century. A Rococo entrance opens onto the church's three naves, separated by pillars and surmounted by vaulted ceilings and a dome supported by a drum. Its paintings on wood (Sevillian school, 16th century) are its main attraction. The church is flanked by parish dependencies and a cloister, which houses a collection of Roman archeological remains, including a bust of the emperor Germanicus.

Iglesia de Santa Cruz. From El Salón the Calle Santa Cruz leads to the parish church of the same name, which was built (1776–1836) by the architect Antonio Matías de Figueroa on the site of a former mosque. The arcades of the unfinished church reach skyward and the adjoining courtyard has some Mudéjar remains. A 5th-century Christian sarcophagus forms the frontal of the altar, which bears a much-restored statue (14th century) of Nuestra Señora de la Valle, the patron saint of Écija. The sacristy contains a silver *monstrance* (1586) made by the goldsmith Francisco de Alfaro ▲ *216*.

Historic district. The Barrio de Santa Cruz is the town's most picturesque district. The *calles* Zayas, Armesto and Marquesa form a veritable maze overlooked by the façades of the many convents. In the Calle Conde is the Convento de San José (or "de las Teresas"), erected on the Mudéjar-Gothic palace of the Conde de la Palma, a complex built in the 14th and 15th centuries complemented by a 17th-century church. The itinerary continues via the Calle Sor Angela de la Cruz to the south of the complex. The *calles* Fernández Pintado and Elvira lead into the new district dominated by the 18th-century Palacio de los Condes de

Palacio de los Condes de Valverde
The early 18th-century palace is a fine example of the grand residence of Écija. It has a splendid brick façade and two watchtowers. The main staircase leads off from the patio, with its double arcaded gallery, which also gives access to the main stable yard.

Decorative door-knocker (above) on a monumental door.

Écija in 1701
Écija used to have a large sheep population and was a major center for the textile industry. The fleeces were washed in the waters of the Río Genil.

Palacio de los Marqueses de Peñaflor
The Palacio de los Marqueses de Peñaflor (1726) is the most remarkable of Écija's palaces, with its escutcheoned entrances.

Valverde and the Palacio de Benameji, part of which is open to the public.

Iglesia de Santiago. The Calle Cánovas leads to the Puerta de Osuna and the Plaza de Santiago, with its 15th-century, Mudéjar-Gothic church of the same name. The elegant tower (18th century) is one of several additions made to the building. The church's wood-paneled naves contain 16th-century, flamboyant Gothic *retablos* decorated with paintings by Alejo Fernández. There is also a *Cristo de la Expiración*, sculpted by Pedro Roldán in 1685 ▲ *189*, and works from the studio of the Flemish artist Pierre de Champaigne (mid-16th century). The *calles* Cava and Cervantes lead into the Calle Castelar and the magnificent façade of the Palacio de Peñaflor, which is decorated with inscriptions and wall paintings, and has a wrought-iron balcony running its length.

Iglesia de San Gil. A small detour along the Calle San Antonio brings you to San Gil, Écija's other parish church. It was built in Mudéjar-Gothic style in the 15th and restored in the 18th century. Its most beautiful sculpture (c. 1500) is the *Cristo de la Salud*. Its paintings include two panels, one of San Gregorio and the other of San Ambrosio, by Villegas Marmolejo (1520). The coffered ceiling of the sacristy is the work of a local artist, Juan Guerrero.

Iglesia de San Juan. Retrace your steps to the Calle Castelar and cross the tiny plaza of San Juan with its 17th- and 18th-century, single-naved church of the same name, which, like other churches in the town, was never completed. It has a charming brick Baroque tower inlaid with *azulejos* and houses a number of Baroque *retablos*. The *retablo* in the sanctuary, which is decorated with a painting of the archangels, is signed by the Sevillian artist Juan Espinal. The sacristy has a sculpture of Christ by Pedro Roldán.

Santa Florentina
This 16th-century Dominican establishment is one of Écija's many convents.

Castillo de la Monclova
Built against the Castillo de la Monclova (opposite) is the tiny Iglesia de la Luisiana.

Luis Vélez de Guevara (1579–1644). The dramatist and novelist Luis Vélez de Guevara is one of Écija's celebrities. He joined the army as a young man and took part in the Italian and Algerian campaigns. He later became a gentleman and frequented the court of the Duke of Lerma. In his latter years he worked on *de repente* (improvized) plays, which were extremely popular with Philip IV. Guevara died in poverty, in spite of being much admired by his contemporaries, including Cervantes, who dedicated poems to him.

"This lofty chain that separates Andalusia from La Mancha was, at the time, the haunt of smugglers, bandits and a few Bohemians…"
Jean Potocki, *The Manuscript Found in Saragossa* (1804)

Écija to Marchena

La Luisiana. La Luisiana lies 8½ miles west of Écija. It was built in the second half of the 18th century during the reign of the enlightened despot, Charles III, and was founded in accord with the program for the repopulation of the Sierra Morena. The idea was to cultivate the deserted lands of the region, which had become a veritable bandits' stronghold. Its individual character is derived from the regular layout of its streets and the simply designed settlers' houses completed by back yards.

Castillo de la Monclova. Near La Luisiana is the "castle-hacienda" of the Castillo de la Monclova. It was built near the site of the Turdetan town of Obúlcula, referred to in Latin texts. Its ramparts and towers are the oldest parts of the edifice and date from the 14th century, when the castle and its village were given to the admiral Micer Egidio Bocanegra for services rendered during the capture of Algeciras (1344). Various Spanish and Italian architectural elements from different periods were incorporated into its restoration in 1910, including a Baroque portal and a patio with a double arcature (1668) from the ruined Convento de la Merced de Lorca (Murcia) and Roman columns excavated in Córdoba.

Fuentes de Andalucía. The village of Fuentes de Andalucía nestles between the *ríos* Genil and Corbones. It belonged to the town of Carmona until it gained independence in the 18th century. Near the Calle General Armero (the main street) are the remains of its originally Moorish castle, modified in the 15th and 16th centuries, the former residence of the local *marqueses*. Nearby, on the plaza of the

Portrait of the writer Luis Vélez de Guevara, a native of Écija.

Iglesia de la Luisiana.

José María el Tempranillo
This famous bandit was born in 1805. He later joined the ranks of the police and was himself assassinated by bandits in 1833.

Brick architecture in Fuentes
The characteristic appearance of Fuentes was created by its master masons. The prosperity of the 18th century gave rise to extensive construction. Local masters Juan and Alonso Ruiz Florindo created buildings with irregular lines, and

façades elaborately decorated with pedestals and finials. During this period the exceptional virtuosity of Fuentes' brick architecture reached its peak. Entrance of the Iglesia de San Francisco and of an aristocratic residence (above).

The walls of Marchena
The enclosure walls of the town are dominated by a Moorish citadel (11th–12th century). The pisé walls and towers were largely reconstructed in freestone after the Christian reconquest of the town in about 1430. A few remaining fragments, incorporated into later buildings, can be seen here and there as you wander through the streets: for example, the Puerta de Morón and the Puerta de Sevilla (right), also known as the Arco de la Rosa.

same name, is the 17th-century Iglesia de Santa María de las Nieves which has an 18th-century tower. Inside there is a 17th-century *San José* by Juan de Mesa (b. Córdoba, d. Seville 1627 ▲ *179*) and, in the crypt, a Gothic sculpture of the Virgen de Noruega. There are some fine examples of Baroque houses opposite the church, in the Calle Carrera and at No. 8 in the neighboring Calle Lora. Their brick entrances, balconies, large grilled windows surrounded by moldings and elegant miradors (whose tiny roofs are supported by fine marble columns) are of particular interest.

Marchena

The ancient Roman town of Martia was surrounded by the agricultural *villae* of the Río Corbones valley.

Capital of the seigneury of Ponce de León. The Castilians captured Marchena from the Muslims in 1240. In 1309 it became the capital of the seigneury of the house of Ponce de León (the dukes of Arcos), one of the most powerful families in Andalusia and the sworn enemies of the Guzmán family, lords of Sanlúcar and counts of Niebla ▲ *173*. Marchena was the birthplace of Diego Lopez de Arenas, an exceptionally talented master carpenter and author of the treatise *Carpinteria de lo Blanco*, published in 1633, one of the rare works devoted to the Mudéjar architectural tradition ● *70*, ▲ *356*.

According to tradition, the *cante flamenco* ● *54* originated among the corporations of itinerant ironsmiths, such as those seen here in the vicinity of Marchena.

The upper town. The visit begins in the upper town with the Castillo de la Mota, the ducal palace and the Iglesia de Santa María de la Mota. The Mudéjar-Gothic church was built in the 14th century on the site of a mosque. Its 16th-century bell tower is in pure Renaissance style. A nearby colonnaded courtyard with Roman capitals is all that remains of the ducal palace. Its 15th-century portal was dismantled and incorporated into the Alcázar of Seville ▲ *142*. The Arco de Alcazaba opens onto the Plaza Ducal, the former parade ground of the fortress, restored in the 18th century. The porticoed plaza is bordered by balconied houses and the former town hall, which today houses archeological remains.

Iglesia de San Juan Bautista. The Calle Pedro Marchena leads to the Mudéjar Iglesia de San Juan Bautista, built in the early 16th century. Its works of art include a huge, 16th-century *retablo* painted by Alejo Fernández and two 17th-century sculptures of *La Inmaculada*, one by Alonso Cano and the other by Pedro de Mena. The dependencies of the church house the Museo Zurbarán, which has nine paintings dating from 1637: six *Apóstoles*, a *San Juan Bautista*, the church's patron saint, a *Crucifixión* and *La Inmaculada*, undoubtedly the most beautiful ▲ *139*, *158*, *182*. The treasury contains precious religious vestments, silver coins and a silver censer (1580) by the goldsmith Francisco de Alfaro.

Los Cuatro Cantillos. The Calle San Juan leads to the Arco de la Rosa, which marks the boundary of Marchena's old enclosure wall. From here the Calle Rojas Marcos leads to the Plaza del Ayuntamiento in the center of the town. Nearby the huge Torre de la Puerta de Morón stands on the intersection of Los Quatro Cantillos. The tower houses a museum devoted to the work of a local sculptor and exponent of late 19th-century realism, Lorenzo Coullaut-Valera (1876–1932). Its two rooms contain photographs, sketches and small-scale sculptures. The most famous of Coullaut-Valera's many works, found throughout Spain and Latin America, is the monument to Gustavo Adolfo Bécquer ▲ *178* in Seville's Parque de María Luisa ▲ *200*.

Convento de San Agustín. The *calles* San Pedro and Sevilla run from the town center to the former Convento de San Agustín (late 18th century). Its austere façade, flanked by towers, is typically Castilian in style and provides a striking contrast with the exuberance of its interior decoration. The plasterwork of the three naves is covered with brightly painted, Aztec-style motifs, which are strongly reminiscent of the Baroque colonial style.

"Marchena is the most important fief of the Duke of Arcos: it brings in 12,000 ducats a year and breeds good saddle horses."
Andrea Navagero, 1526

"Cantaora" La Niña
Although Marchena's summer festival is dedicated to the guitar, the *cante* is also well represented. Local celebrities include La Niña and the famous Pepe Marchena, a native of Seville, who was one of the first *cantaores* to perform on stage ● *54*, ▲ *391*.

"Cierros"
Cierros are projecting windows that rest on a small stone ledge built against the wall. They are a typical feature of the popular architecture of Marchena and part of La Campiña.

Utrera

El Arahal
Entrance to an 18th-century house in the Calle Pozo Dulce.

Herdsman
Utrera lies in what has always been a cattle-rearing region, the so-called "cradle of fighting bulls" that has produced some of Spain's most famous bulls.

Castle and town of Utrera
The modern town lies around the original site, a plateau dominated by the castle and the main churches.

Utrera lies to the southwest of Marchena on the N-333. About 10 miles from Marchena the road passes through the town of El Arahal, which was founded by the Muslims and expanded considerably during the 18th century. Its most interesting monument is the neoclassical Iglesia de Santa María Magdalena (1785–1800) in the town center, the largest church in the diocese of Seville.

A populous town. Utrera is situated 15 miles from El Arahal, on a small plateau in the center of a cultivated plain. Its population of some 43,000 inhabitants is one of the largest in the province. It was the birthplace of the popular dramatists Serafín (1871–1938) and Joaquín (1873–1944) Alvarez Quintero, whose works contain a number of Andalusian stereotypes. Utrera is also famous for its gastronomic speciality, the *mostachón* (macaroon), a thin, round biscuit baked on brown paper.

Frontier castle. The Calle Corredera runs to the foot of the hill and climbs to the Plaza Santa Ana, overlooked by the castle. Utrera was captured by the Christians shortly after Seville, in 1248, and subsequently changed hands several times. The castle was built in the 14th and 15th centuries around a 13th-century tower. It was the main fortified complex of the Banda Morisca, which formed the frontier line with the Moorish kingdom of Granada. Its *pisé* dungeon has been strengthened with freestone and has an interior, octagonal vault.

Iglesia de Santiago. Opposite the castle is the military-looking, Gothic Iglesia de Santiago (15th and 16th centuries). Its magnificent portal in the style of the Reyes Católicos opens onto three beautiful naves with stellar vaults. The old fortified enclosure, the most characteristic part of the town, lies between the *iglesias* of Santiago and Santa María. A walk through the picturesque streets provides an opportunity to admire Utrera's beautiful Baroque residences, such as the one now occupied by the Cultural Center in the Calle Rodrigo Caro which leads to the Plaza Santa María de la Mesa.

Iglesia de Santa María. The several renovations undergone by this 15th-century Gothic church include the addition of a remarkable 16th-century coffered portal, the restoration of the choir and the dome in c. 1600 and the construction of several chapels at the end of the 18th century. Its five naves have ribbed vaults and the sacristy contains a Madonna painted by Bernardino Luini (1485–1532), a rival of Leonardo da Vinci.

" Utrera is the most important town in the Banda Morisca, or the recently founded province of La Campiña."

Juan de Mal Lara, *Recebimiento*, 1570

In front of the church stands a statue of Rodrigo Caro (1573–1674), a native of Utrera renowned in the field of Baroque literature, who wrote a famous poem dedicated to the ruins of Itálica. Behind the Iglesia de Santa María is the PLAZA DEL ALTOZANO. Although recently defaced, it has still retained some of its old houses and its popular atmosphere.

SANTUARIO DE LA CONSOLACIÓN. As you leave the town via the Avenue Juan XXIII, you come to a sanctuary dedicated to Nuestra Señora de la Consolación, the patron saint of travelers who, in recognition of her protection, have covered the sacristy with votive offerings. The sanctuary, which was originally a convent founded in the 16th century, is visited by many pilgrims, especially on the occasion of the *romería* held on the August 8. The interior decoration of its single-naved church, which was built in 1635, is in 19th-century, neo-Mudéjar style. On the *retablo mayor* stands a 15th-century sculpture, the *Virgen de la Consolación*.

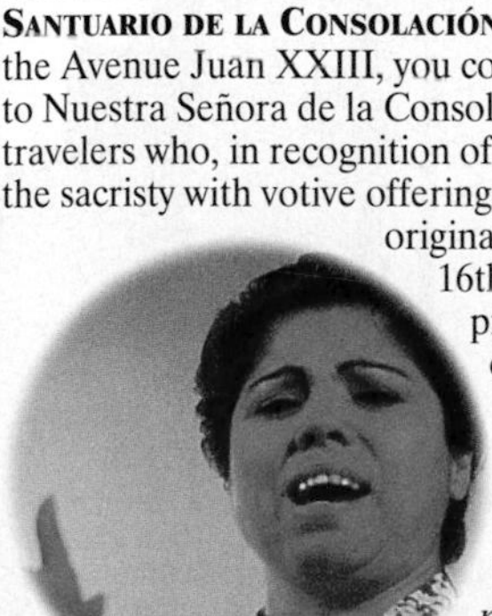

SANTIAGO
This sculpture on the portal of the Iglesia de Santiago represents the saint fighting the Infidels.

SANTA MARÍA DE LA MESA
The church has a beautiful tower-façade and a vaulted, coffered portal in the form of a triumphal arch.

NUESTRA SEÑORA DE LA VIRTUDES
The church is the largest in La Puebla de Cazalla. It was built in the 16th and 17th centuries according to a centralized plan, and is surmounted by a huge dome.

GIPSY TRADITION
Utrera is one of the capitals of the flamenco *cante* ● *54*. The gipsy *cantaora*, Fernanda (left), takes part in the local celebrations. The annual festival, called the "Potaje de Utrera" or "Utrera Broth" (sometimes flamenco festivals are named after dishes), draws large crowds at the end of June.

Osuna, an agricultural town
Osuna is a typical agricultural town in La Campiña. It owes its remarkable state of preservation to the widespread use of stone in its construction.

Universidad de Osuna
In 1548 the aristocracy of Osuna founded a university which functioned until 1820. The Renaissance building is the only one of its kind.

Collegiate church of Osuna
This impressive Renaissance church, built between 1531 and 1535, dominates the town.

Osuna

The itinerary continues eastward, doubling back along the N-333 in the direction of Osuna. At Monteplacio take the A-92 motorway to La Puebla de Cazalla which, like other towns in the duchy of Osuna, experienced its golden age in the 16th century. It was during this period that its church, the Nuestra Señora de las Virtudes, was built. Osuna lies 12 miles further on and is built on a hillside, with the oldest houses near the top. Originally a hilltop village, in the 16th century it began to spread gradually down to the plain. The visit starts in the Plaza Mayor at the foot of the hill.

Museo Arqueológico. At the bottom of the Cuesta de San Antón, not far from the Plaza Mayor, is the 14th-century Torre del Agua, now a museum. Its four rooms present an overview of local history. The town dates from the middle of the 1st millennium BC. Between the 3rd and 1st centuries BC Urso was an

important Roman town whose necropolis was discovered in 1903. The museum has copies of the sandstone sculptures decorating the tombs, the originals being in the Museo Arqueológico in Madrid and the Louvre in Paris. These key pieces of Iberian art include a magnificent bas-relief representing a funeral procession attended by warriors, ladies and musicians. The museum has a copy of another remarkable piece, known as the *Bronzes of Osuna*, a valuable Roman legal document discovered in 1871. It comprises five plates engraved with the laws of the town in 43 BC. In that year Urso, which had previously allied itself with Pompey, had been conquered by Julius Caesar and renamed "Colonia Genitiva Iulia". Other Iberian and Roman (sculptures, ceramics, glass and coins) and Visigoth (5th-century carved bricks) items complete the collection.

DUCAL COURT. Ferdinand III conquered the Moorish town of Ushuna in 1239. In 1445 the domain, which belonged to the Order of the Knights of Calatravas, passed into the hands of its commander, Pedro Girón. In 1562 his successors, the dukes of Osuna, went on to collect titles and offices (in particular the viceroyship of Naples) and amass a legendary fortune. According to a popular saying, they could cross Spain without leaving their lands. They established a court within the city which they endowed with prestigious buildings: a collegiate church, a university and a sepulcher.

COLEGIATA DE LA ASUNCIÓN. The Cuesta de San Antón climbs the hill to the upper town, dominated by the massive bulk of the collegiate church and the university, which attest to Osuna's 16th-century prosperity. The great church was founded in 1531 by Juan Téllez Girón (d. 1558), the fourth Conde d'Ureña and the town's greatest patron of the arts.

MONASTERIO DE LA ENCARNACIÓN
The monastery has some remarkable *azulejo* panels.

PLAZA MAYOR
Typical façade on the Plaza Mayor.

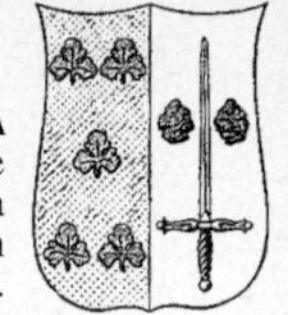

COAT OF ARMS OF ESTEPA Charles V gave the seigneury of Estepa to Genoan-born Adán Centurión.

VIEWS OF OSUNA Osuna's bell towers and white houses (above). Entrance to the Cilla del Cabildo, a tithe warehouse, and the Arco de la Pastora (below).

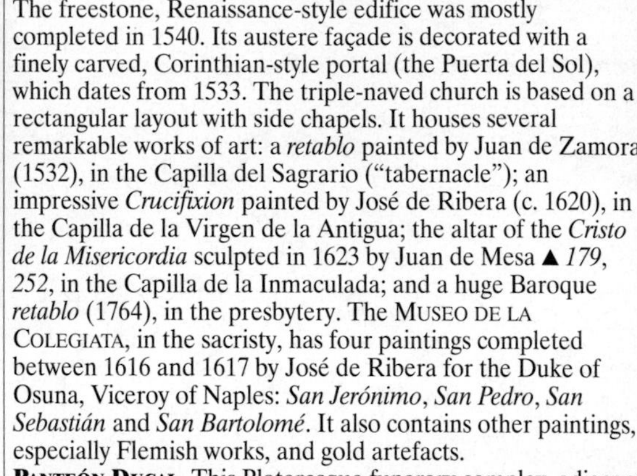

The freestone, Renaissance-style edifice was mostly completed in 1540. Its austere façade is decorated with a finely carved, Corinthian-style portal (the Puerta del Sol), which dates from 1533. The triple-naved church is based on a rectangular layout with side chapels. It houses several remarkable works of art: a *retablo* painted by Juan de Zamora (1532), in the Capilla del Sagrario ("tabernacle"); an impressive *Crucifixion* painted by José de Ribera (c. 1620), in the Capilla de la Virgen de la Antigua; the altar of the *Cristo de la Misericordia* sculpted in 1623 by Juan de Mesa ▲ *179, 252*, in the Capilla de la Inmaculada; and a huge Baroque *retablo* (1764), in the presbytery. The MUSEO DE LA COLEGIATA, in the sacristy, has four paintings completed between 1616 and 1617 by José de Ribera for the Duke of Osuna, Viceroy of Naples: *San Jerónimo*, *San Pedro*, *San Sebastián* and *San Bartolomé*. It also contains other paintings, especially Flemish works, and gold artefacts.

PANTEÓN DUCAL. This Plateresque funerary complex, adjacent to the museum, was built in 1545. The entrance, whose pediment is decorated with death's-heads, opens onto the Patio del Santo Sepulcro which in turn leads to the underground chapel and sepulcher. The omnipresence of the theme of death is impressive. The courtyard is decorated with polychrome plaster panels and the chapels with beautiful sculptures and paintings (mostly 16th century).

UNIVERSIDAD. The former university, founded in 1548, stands behind the collegiate church. It was built in the form of a quadrilateral, punctuated by small towers, around a central, galleried courtyard. Its oratory contains seven paintings (1548) by the Flemish artist Hernando de Esturmio.

CONVENTO DE LA ENCARNACIÓN. This former convent, founded in 1626 and now a museum, stands opposite the collegiate church, next to San Antón. Its Baroque-style buildings were constructed during the 17th and 18th centuries. The central cloister is bordered by a double, colonnaded gallery. The plinths of the columns are decorated with 18th-century *azulejos* ● *56*, ▲ *128* which constitute a unique collection of Sevillian ceramics, both

Olive picker.

in terms of their quality and quantity. They include images of the five senses, the seasons, the Alameda de Hércules in Seville and traditional scenes of hunting and bullfighting. The rooms surrounding the cloister form the museum proper and house collections of paintings, sculpture and *objets d'art*. One of the rooms ("de los Niños") contains a curious collection of statues (16th–19th century) of the infant Jesus, worshiped extensively in nunneries. The convent offers a view of the CANTERAS (quarries), a site formed by the extraction of stone and by a troglodyte necropolis from the Romano-Iberian period.

BAROQUE PALACES. Beyond the IGLESIA DE LA MERCED (1775) and its fine bell tower the *calles* Granada and Cueto, bordered by 16th-century houses, lead down to the Plaza Mayor and the galleried town hall (16th century). Leading off the busy, central plaza, the *calles* de la Huerta, de Sevilla and especially San Pedro offer an opportunity to take a leisurely stroll and discover the local civil architecture. There are a number of 18th-century palaces, whose elaborately carved doorways open onto entrance halls and courtyards: the PALACIO DE LOS CEPEDA, in the Calle de la Huerta, is decorated with mid-18th century sculptures; and in the Calle San Pedro are the impressive façades of the CILLA DEL CABILDO (1773) and the palace of the Marquis of Gomera (1770). With its stone entrance, cornice and mirador-tower, this last palace is possibly the most beautiful.

"SLEEPING BEAUTY"
This Roman sculpture (1st century AD), discovered in Estepa, can be seen in the town hall.

ROMAN BAS-RELIEF FROM ESTEPA
Roman soldiers dressed for battle.

Estepa, a hillside town in a crop-growing region.

ESTEPA

Estepa is built on a high hillside 15 miles east of Osuna on the A-92 freeway. It lies in the geographical center of Andalusia and has always been a strategic crossroads between the west and east of the province.

ASTAPA, A WARRIOR-TOWN. The Iberian town of Astapa is renowned for its fierce resistance to the Romans. It was destroyed in 208 BC and rebuilt by its conquerors, who renamed it Ostippo. Excavations have uncovered oriental objects dating from the 7th century BC and remains from the Romano-Iberian period, in particular bas-reliefs from the 1st century BC representing warriors, today preserved in the Museo Arqueológico in Seville ▲ *204*.

ARCHITECTURE IN ESTEPA
Detail of the Baroque Torre de la Victoria of the (now non-existent) Convent of the Minims.

"El Pernales" Francisco Río (1879–1907), a native of Estepa, was the last *bandolero* in Andalusia. He was known as "Pernales o Pedernales" ("toughest of the tough"). When he was finally shot by the police, all he was carrying was a blanket, a bottle of wine and a bag containing a piece of bread.

Cerro de San Cristóbal. The visit begins at the top of the hill crowned with the remains of the medieval ramparts. This Moorish fortress was conquered by the Christians in 1240 and occupied by the Knights of the Order of Saint James (Santiago). The parts of the walls and the dungeon that can still be seen were rebuilt in the 14th century. The dungeon was transformed into a palace by the house of Centurión, marquises of Estepa from the 16th century. Next to the palace is the fortified Iglesia de Santa María, a masterpiece of Andalusian Gothic architecture. Begun in the 14th century, its stone baptismal fonts were added in the 15th and its three naves in the 16th century. Opposite is the Convento de Santa Clara, founded in 1598, whose church is decorated with wood paneling and wall paintings. The nuns make delicious pastries, which they sell to visitors.

Iglesia del Carmen The magnificent Baroque portal (1768) is decorated with local stone and jasper.

Torre de la Victoria. In the 16th century Estepa began to spread gradually down the hillside. Its streets, which follow the contour lines, are intersected at intervals by *cuestas* (steep streets or hills). From the Iglesia de Santa Maria a stone street leads down to the Calle Ancha. On a plaza to the right stands the Baroque Torre de la Victoria (1760–6). The emblem of the town, it is more than 130 feet high.

El Salón. At the foot of the tower a series of flights of steps leads down to the town's main plaza (El Salón), with its town hall and Iglesia del Carmen (18th century). The church is one of the most representative examples of Andalusian Baroque architecture, in particular its portal and its ornate and colorful nave.

Calle Mesones. The Calle Mesones leads from El Salón to two fine examples of mid-18th century architecture: the Iglesia de la Asunción and Palacio de los Cerverales, whose entrance is decorated with *salomónicas* (barley-sugar columns). The street opens onto the Plaza del los Remedios, where a sanctuary dedicated to the Virgin (1743) provides another example of local Baroque architecture.

The hillside of Estepa offers one of the most spectacular views of La Campiña.

"Mantecados". In summer Estepa is pervaded by the aroma of *mantecados* (right), a sweet, shortcake type of biscuit. The Museo del Mantecado, opened in the Camino de las Piedras by a local factory, shows visitors how this traditionally baked biscuit is made, using butter, flour, caramel, cinnamon, sesame and almonds.

Sierra Morena

STAGECOACH DRAWN BY MULES (1912)
This itinerary follows the routes to the north of Seville and Huelva that have linked western Andalusia with Estremadura and Portugal since Roman times. The N-630 follows the former Roman road commonly known as the Ruta de la Plata, a distortion of the Latin *lata* ("wide") or the Arabic *balate* ("paved").

CAZALLA
The former Carthusian monastery stands in a truly magnificent setting. Accommodation available.

ARACENA
The castle church has an early 16th-century Mudéjar tower. A cross of the Order of the Knights Templar completes the *sebka* ● *68*, the type of geometric decoration used for La Giralda in Seville.

SIERRA MORENA

The Sierra Morena mountain range ■ *26* lies to the north of the provinces of Seville and Huelva, and forms a natural frontier between Andalusia and the rest of Spain. It is bordered in the south by the Guadalquivir valley. Its slopes rise, from east to west, over a distance of some 300 miles, its heightest peaks reaching about 3,280 feet. The principal blocks of the western Sierra Morena are the Sierra Norte de Sevilla and the Sierra de Aracena. The quality of the natural environment and the beauty of the landscapes has led to the establishment of two nature reserves near Aracena and Constantina.

ORIGINS OF THE NAME. The name of the Sierra Morena ("dark-haired mountain") is thought to have come from the slate-rich soil, thick scrub and holm-oak forests covering its slopes. Its other name, the "Cordillera Mariánica", is traditionally associated with Sextus Marius, an Iberian who owned most of the region's mines in Roman times. There is another theory that it derives from "Mons Marmorum" ("mountain of marble"), a reference to the marble quarries of ancient Pagus Marmorarius, the modern town of Almadén de la Plata.

HISTORY. The Sierra Morena has large deposits of copper, iron, coal, manganese and lead. This natural wealth has been exploited since prehistoric times by the early Bronze-Age peoples, the Tartessians and Phoenicians (from the 8th century) and the Romans (from the 3rd century BC) who systematically exploited the copper mines and built a series of roads, including the one linking Hispalis to Emerita via the Sierra Norte de Sevilla. The Sierra Morena, overlooking the Guadalquivir valley and crossed by the main routes linking Castile with the southern coast of Spain, has always been of great strategic importance. It was the frontier of the conflict between Christians

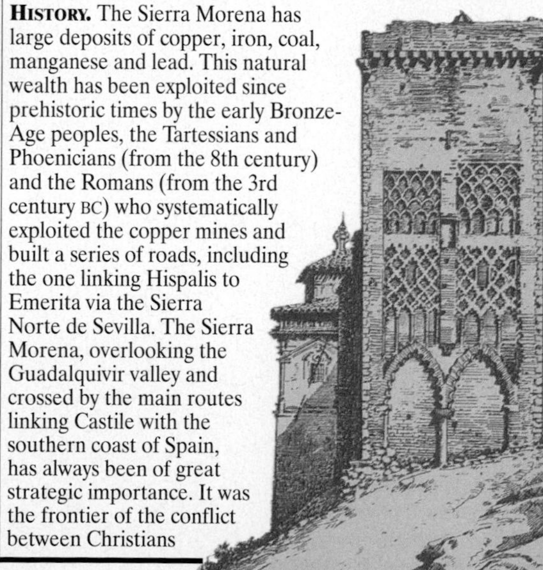

Anis Cazalla
One of the most famous anisettes from the Sierra Morena.

and Muslims during the Reconquest, the natural fortress that halted the Portuguese advance in the 14th century and the stronghold of the partisans of the Duke of Arcos during the feudal wars of the 15th century. In the past both areas of the Sierra Morena were dependencies of Seville. After the Reconquest they became part of the Tierra de Sevilla, a group of estates placed under the city's jurisdiction. They formed the so-called Banda Gallega ("Galician line") and served as a reminder of the origin of the Christian settlers introduced into the region during this period.

Almonaster la Real
Looking down on the town from the ruins of the castle, the (virtually intact) mosque and the 19th-century amphitheater.

Sierra Norte nature reserve. The reserve lies in the province of Seville and is crossed by the *ríos* Viar, Huéznar and Retortillo. It covers an area of some 407,330 acres and is planted with holm- oaks, cork-oaks and common oaks. It contains wildlife which includes deer, wild boar, wildcats, otters and birds of prey.

Sierra de Aracena nature reserve and the Pico del Aroche. The reserve covers an area of 454,675 acres in the province of Huelva. Its pastureland is planted with holm-oaks, cork-oaks, white and black poplars and cistus, and surrounded by chestnut forests. Since the 1960's, this area, which abounds with weasels, martens, badgers, eagles and vultures ■ *26*, has been invaded by non-native eucalyptus.

Alanís
The castle, its hexagonal tower and the Ermita de San Juan Evangelista.

Traditional "industries". The pastureland, planted with holm- and cork-oaks, supports a large population of acorn-fed (predominately Iberian) pigs, which forms the basis of the region's ham industry. The villages of Jabugo, Cortegana and Cumbres Mayores, in the Sierra de Huelva, are renowned for their *jamón de pata negra* ("mountain ham"). The slaughtering of the pigs in December and January is a family event in the local villages and hamlets.
Another traditional industry among the inhabitants of the sierra is the making of brandies and anisettes, the most famous of which are those made in Cazalla, in the Sierra Norte de Sevilla, and Zalamea la Real, which is in the Riotinto mining basin.

"Solanas" and fountain-laundries
Flowered balconies and *solanas* (south-facing galleries used for drying fruit, herbs and spices) are a common sight in the Sierra de Aracena. The streets and plazas still have their fountains and public laundries.

Castles and popular architecture. The rugged relief of the Sierra Morena, together with its characteristic architecture, lend the landscape its distinctive appearance. The many castles of the region (which were mostly built or rebuilt at the end of the 18th century in response to the threat from the kingdom of Portugal) are perched high up in the mountains. On the hillside below are the white houses of the terraced villages, with their narrow windows and red-tiled roofs.

SIERRA NORTE DE SEVILLA

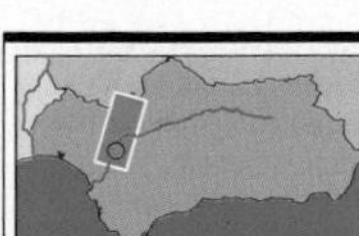

One day
77½ miles
◆ A D1-2, E1-2

VILLANEUVA DE RÍO Y MINAS
Remains of the industrial architecture on the site of the former coalfields of La Reunión.

MULVA OR MUNIGUA
The Romans founded the *municipium* on the site of an Iberian settlement (4th century BC) to exploit the mines. It began to flourish under the Flavians in the 1st century AD. Its terraced sanctuary is the only one of its kind in Spain.

To reach the Sierra Norte from Seville, take the A-431, then the C-433 to Castilblanco de los Arroyos (the setting for Cervantes' novel *Las Dos Doncellas*) and EL PEDROSO. Alternatively, follow the A-431 to Lora del Río (making a detour to the ruins of Multa, linked by a dirt track to the 19th-century mining village of Villanueva del Río y Minas, built over a giant coal tip), then the A-455 to Constantina.

CONSTANTINA. From El Pedroso, the SE-190 leads to Constantina, the largest and oldest town in the sierra, which has retained its medieval character. It is thought to have been founded by the Celts, and its CASTLE (of which only the medieval ruins remain) to have been built by Hannibal. At the time of the civil wars between Julius Caesar and Pompey ● *30* it was known to the Romans as Constancia Iulia. It became Cotinena under the Muslims until it was conquered by Ferdinand III in 1247. Constantina's most interesting edifice, the IGLESIA DE LA ENCARNACIÓN, stands in the center of the town in the Plaza del Llano del Sol. The original structure, formed by the three naves, the porch and the first story of the façade-tower, was built in Mudéjar style, probably in the 14th century. Hernán Ruiz the Younger, the architect of La Giralda ● *68*, *73*, worked on the Renaissance portal and the upper stories of the tower (16th century). The town has a number of other religious buildings, but most are abandoned and in a poor state of repair. At the foot of the ruined castle lies the district of LA MORERÍA with its characteristically medieval steep streets. The whitewashed houses with their irregularly placed windows, porches and red-tiled roofs are typical of the region. The living accommodation is on the first floor, while the upper floor is reserved for the *soberado*, a loft for storing crops. To the northeast of the town lies the ERMITA DE NUESTRA SEÑORA DEL ROBLEDO, in the direction of the observatory. Originally a Mudéjar building and extended in the 18th century, it is dedicated to the patron saint of Constantina and is a place of pilgrimage on the last Sunday of September.

CERRO DEL HIERRO ROUTE. To the right of the SE-163 is the impressive and irregularly shaped building of the POZOS DE LA NIEVE, built by Juan de Moya in 1696, where the snow and ice destined for consumption in Seville were stored in wells.

SAN NICOLÁS DEL PUERTO. The SE-163 comes to an end in San Nicolás del Puerto. A 16th-century stone cross stands at the entrance to the village. Its most noteworthy building, the Mudéjar IGLESIA DE SAN SEBASTIÁN (c. 1400), has a 16th-century freestone portal and a remarkable, three-story façade-tower. San Nicolás was the birthplace of the Franciscan Diego de Alcalá (c. 1400–63) who lived the life of a

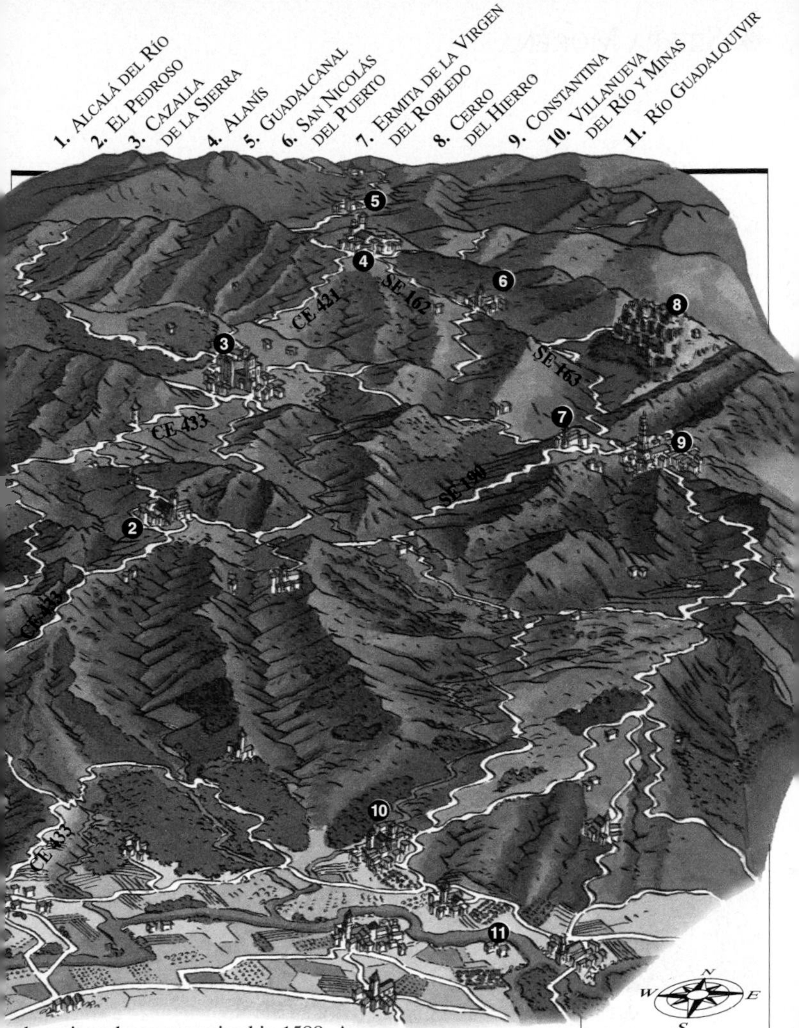

1. Alcalá del Río
2. El Pedroso
3. Cazalla de la Sierra
4. Alanís
5. Guadalcanal
6. San Nicolás del Puerto
7. Ermita de la Virgen del Robledo
8. Cerro del Hierro
9. Constantina
10. Villanueva del Río y Minas
11. Río Guadalquivir
CE 421
SE 162
SE 163
CE 433
SE 190
CE 433
N
W
E
S

hermit and was canonized in 1588. As the town's patron saint, he is also worshiped at the Ermita de San Diego which lies 1½ miles further east. The 15th-century Mudéjar hermitage is one of the most typical and most frequented in the region.

Alanís. The road to Alanís (the SE-162) crosses the Río Galindón by way of a double-arched freestone bridge, which was initially of Roman construction but was rebuilt in the Middle Ages. According to one school of thought, Alanís was originally founded by the Celts, as the town of Iporci, and the Roman colony of Ordo Iporcensium was situated in the vicinity. Howeve, Alanís was almost certainly founded by the Muslims, as the name "Al-Haniz" (which translates as "prosperous land") suggests. The houses of the town are dominated by the Ermita de San Juan Evangelista and by an irregularly shaped, polygonal castle with a hexagonal tower, which is a late 14th-century construction. The castle was rebuilt and equipped with artillery by the French army during the War of Independence ● *39* because of its strategic importance. The oldest church in Alanís is the 14th-century Iglesia de San Sebastián, which has now been partially destroyed.

Cerro del Hierro
To the right of the road running from Constantina to San Nicolás del Puerto lies the rugged Cerro del Hierro ("iron mountain") whose mines have been exploited since ancient times.

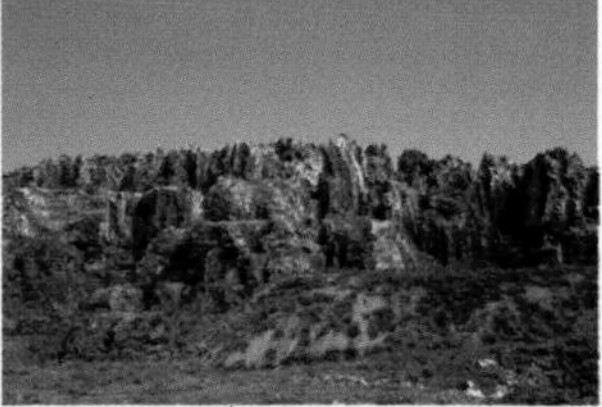

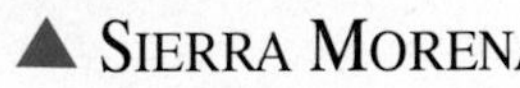

The town's most interesting religious building is undoubtedly the Mudéjar IGLESIA DE NUESTRA SEÑORA DE LAS NIEVES, which is of early 14th-century construction but was renovated during the 18th century. It has a remarkable façade-tower and, inside, a magnificent *retablo* (dating back to about 1500) and 15th-century Mudéjar baptismal fonts in cut stone. Situated next to the church is the Plaza de Santa María. The plaza has a delightful fountain dating from the reign of Charles V. Alanís has several Mudéjar and Renaissance houses.

The bridge across the Río Galindón and the banks of the Huéznar, near San Nicolás del Puerto.

GUADALCANAL. The C-432 runs northwest from Alanís along the Sierra del Agua. Archeological excavations carried out in the caves of Santiago and San Francisco have confirmed that the region was inhabited during the Upper Paleolithic period (35,000–9000 BC). The Iberians and Romans were attracted by its mineral deposits, but the town experienced its golden age under the Muslims who fortified it (only a few scattered remains have survived) and named it Wadi al-Kanal. In 1568 Pedro Ortega, a native of Guadalcanal, discovered the Solomon Islands in the Pacific and named one of the islands after his village. In the 17th century the Függer family, descendants of the famous German bankers from the time of Charles V, tried to re-open the Guadalcanal mines but had to abandon the project after making huge losses. Today only a few seams of barite are still worked. The visit begins in the main plaza with the IGLESIA DE LA ASUNCIÒN. The Mudéjar church was built in the 14th and 15th centuries, on the ruins of an Almohad *alcázar*, and extended in the 16th and 18th centuries. The horseshoe arch in the lower part of the façade was part of the original Moorish walls. The church's three naves are separated by lines of cruciform pillars

NUESTRA SEÑORA DE LAS NIEVES (ALANÍS)
Detail of the *retablo mayor*, a Gothic work of the Sevillian school (c. 1500).

House with a stone porch, Alanís.

Alanís
Official seal of the town council of Alanís.

Cazalla
Official seal of the town council of Cazalla.

supporting pointed arches. Its polygonal choir is surmounted by a vault with intersecting ribs and it has a five-story brick tower. The local market is held in front of the nearby Iglesia de San Sebastián, a Gothic edifice that has retained fragments of its strange, late 15th-century ribbed vaults. The Ermita de Guaditoca, to the north of the village, is decorated with early 18th-century frescos. Founded in 1647, it is dedicated to the patron saint of the village. From Alanís, the C-421 to Cazalla passes through some spectacular countryside dotted with olive groves and haciendas. The Hacienda del Inquisidor is flanked by an unusual mill and oil press.

Cazalla de la Sierra. The town's Arabic name of Kazala means "fortified town". The town itself, which is renowned for its brandies and anisettes, was already producing good-quality wine in Roman times, when it was called "Calletum". During the 16th and 17th centuries, it exported wine and brandy to America. The Iglesia de Nuestra Señora de la Consolación stands on the Plaza de los Mártires. The two horseshoe arches enclosing the courtyard are part of the 13th-century Almohad fortifications. The church was begun during the 14th century and combines several architectural styles. It has a Mudéjar façade-tower, while the section dating from 1538 is recognizably Renaissance; and the features added in the 18th century are Baroque in style. Two panels of the *retablo mayor*, which depict the Annunciation and the Circumcision, are by Juan Oviedo y de la Bandera (1565–1625), who was one of the great masters of the Mannerist school ● *180*. On the same plaza are a Mudéjar house (No. 20) and the Baroque façade of the former town hall, decorated with Tuscan pilasters and columns. The present town hall occupies the former convent of San Agustín of the early 17th century, on the nearby Plaza del Doctor Nosea.

Environs of Cazalla. A minor road leads to the Cartuja de la Inmaculada, almost 2 miles from Cazalla. The Carthusian monastery, which was founded in 1483 and extended in the 18th century, also displays a combination of architectural styles, encompassing the Mudéjar-Gothic, Renaissance and Baroque. The modest Ermita de Nuestra Señora del Monte lies nearly 2 miles southeast of Cazalla on a different road. A *romería* is held at the hermitage in mid-August. After a midnight mass, the patron saint is carried aloft by a colorful procession of pilgrims, some of whom are on foot while others ride in carts and on horseback. From Cazalla the C-433 returns to Seville, just over 45 miles away.

Women from the sierra spinning in a family workshop (19th century).

Iglesia de la Consolación (Cazalla)
One of the most interesting churches in the Sierra Morena.

Brandy "factory"
Cherry brandy is one of Cazalla's most famous spirits.

SIERRA DE ARACENA

Take the N-630 from Seville to Las Nieves and then the N-433 into the province of Huelva. The road is bordered by holm- and cork-oaks, which provide acorns for the region's many pigs. In the heart of the sierra are chestnut and walnut forests. The fields and the farms hereabouts are enclosed by low stone walls.

VIEW OF ARACENA FROM THE CASTLE The castle offers magnificent views of the town and the sierra, and makes an ideal starting point for the visit.

ARACENA. Aracena is the capital of the part of the Sierra Morena belonging to Huelva. Its name is usually associated with the Arabic word *alsenaâ*, meaning "a construction perched high". Aracena, captured from the Moors by the Portuguese in 1251, was handed over shortly afterward to the Castilians and became part of the Tierra de Sevilla ● *32*. It appears to have been in the hands of the Knights Templar until the Order was dissolved by Pope Clement V in 1312. During the reign of Philip IV, it was given to the Duke of Olivares as a seigneury which passed, after his death, to the counts of Altamira. Aracena was a summer resort, as can be seen from the residences along the road to Alájar.

CERRO DEL CASTILLO The hill is crowned by the Iglesia de Nuestra Señora del Mayor Dolor and the remains of the fortress.

It lives up to the motto on Aracena's coat of arms: *Hac itur ad astra* ("From here to the stars"). Deep in the hillside is the Gruta de las Maravillas.

CERRO DEL CASTILLO. The IGLESIA DE NUESTRA SEÑORA DEL MAYOR DOLOR stands among the ruins of the Almohad fortress that was turned into a castle by the Portuguese. The original edifice was built in Sevillian Mudéjar style in the 14th century. The 15th-century Gothic renovations are particularly noticeable on the north entrance, the so-called Puerta de las Mercedes, where there are crosses of the Order of the Knights Templar and a Solomon's seal. The church houses a *Virgen del Mayor Dolor*, sculpted by Juan de Astorga in 1813, and the gisant of the prior Pedro Vázquez by the Italian artist Miguel Florentín, who was working in Seville in the 16th century.

THE OLD TOWN. Below the castle, the paved streets of the oldest part of Aracena offer a pleasant opportunity for a leisurely stroll. In the Plaza Alta, bordered by Renaissance buildings, stand the IGLESIA DE LA ASUNCIÓN (begun in 1528 but never completed) and the former town hall, whose late 16th-century entrance is attributed to Hernán Ruiz the Younger. Near the plaza is a number of houses with Baroque entrances, irregular façades, projecting roofs, and balconies running the length of the building. Behind the Iglesia de la Asunción are a former synagogue, now the IGLESIA SANTA CATALINA, and the new

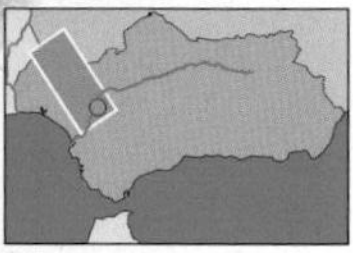

1. Aroche 2. Cortegana 3. Almonaster la Real 4. Jabugo 5. Alájar 6. Fuenteheridos 7. Linares de la Sierra 8. Aracena 9. Zalamea la Real 10. Minas de Riotinto 11. Nerva

One day
121 miles

◆ A B1-2, C1

town hall, built in red brick (1911) by Aníbal González, the master of the Regionalist school ● *86*, which combines Moorish motifs and modern architectural elements.

Gruta de las Maravillas ★. The Gruta de las Maravillas ("cave of marvels") is about half a mile south of Aracena, at the foot of the Cerro del Castillo and on the road to Alájar (H-551). The cave, discovered in 1911, is the biggest underground network of its kind open to the public in Spain, comprising twelve chambers, six lakes and almost 4000 feet of arcades adorned with limestone concretions in a host of shapes and colours. Visitors start with the Room of the Organs, then progress to the Gallery of the Quail, before reaching the Great Lake beneath its 230-foot vault. The choir has two superb stalagmites known as the Twins.

Gruta de las Maravillas
The chamber known as La Choza ("hut").

A land of water
Springs, fountains and public laundries . . . there is no shortage of water in the mountain villages.

Alájar
View of Alájar from La Peña, the retreat of the humanist Benito Arias Montano (1527–98), a former Escorial librarian who studied natural history, philosophy, theology, history, philology and literature. He spoke Hebrew, Greek, Latin, Chaldean, Arabic, Flemish,

German, French, Italian and Portuguese, and directed the publication of the Antwerp polyglot Bible.

Fuenteheridos
Plaza with characteristic elements of popular architecture and a marble cross dating from 1792.

The series of chambers and lakes continues with the magical Room of the Mirror, the Room of Buttocks and the magnificent Great Chamber. There is a small geological museum at the entrance to the cave and, nearby, an open-air museum of contemporary sculpture and a traditional fountain-laundry.

Alájar. The H-521 leads to Alájar, whose originally Arabic name means “the stone”. The hermitage that stands on the peak (La Peña de Arias Montano) to the northwest of the town is dedicated to Nuestra Señora de los Ángeles and is the object of a pilgrimage held on September 7 and 8 ● *50*. The site is believed to have been of sacred and magical importance to ancient civilizations. Arias Montano, counsellor and chaplain to Philip II, withdrew to the

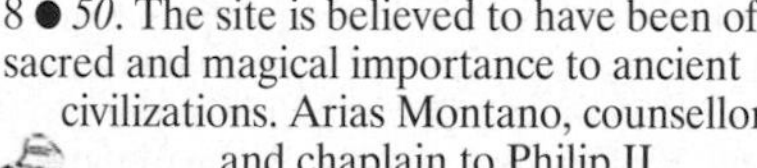

"The archaic beauty of its interior mountain areas possibly [makes it] the most unspoilt sierra in Spain, in spite of such famous towns as Aracena and Jabugo."

Fernando Quiñones

Popular tradition
The curved, red tiles of the roofs, with their projecting eaves (far left), are typical of Sierra Morena architecture.

Herds of brown or black pigs (left), which are the source of the famous *pata negra* ham, forage in semi-liberty in the oak forests.

hermitage. When the King visited him in 1570, he is supposed to have expressed a wish to sit in the cave that became known as the "Sillita de Rey". The nearby monumental stone, the "Naveta", was possibly an ancient altar or funerary megalith.

Jabugo. The most scenic route to Jabugo is via Fuenteheridos and Galaroza. Not far from the central Plaza del Corso in Fuenteheridos is a fountain with twelve water jets. It is also worth stopping in the Plaza Enrique Ponce in Galaroza. Jabugo, surrounded by chestnut forests and orchards, is renowned for its hams (*jamón*), sausages and pâtés. The *Sánchez Romero* curing factory, at the entrance to the village, is open to the public in the mornings.

Almonaster la Real. The town undoubtedly occupies the site of an ancient Roman settlement and its original Arabic name of El-Munastyr suggests the existence of a Christian monastery prior to the Muslim conquest. An early 10th-century mosque still stands among the ruins of the castle. It incorporates Roman and Visigoth capitals, and its *mihrab*, the prayer niche facing Mecca, is the oldest in Spain. The Mudéjar Iglesia de San Martín is a fine example of the rich and complex Manueline style characteristic of late 15th- and early 16th-century Portuguese Gothic architecture. Its early 16th-century Puerta del Perdón bears the coat of arms of Manrique de Lara, Archbishop of Seville, who in fact owned Almonaster until 1578. The houses of the village are in Mudéjar, Gothic, Baroque and regional architectural styles.

Mosque
The 10th-century mosque became the church of the Castillo de Almonaster la Real.

Cortegana. Cortegana, identified with the Turdetan town of Corticata, is reached via the N-433. The medieval castle, which still has Roman and Gothic sections, dates from the end of the 13th century. There is a magnificent view from the top of its towers. The town also has two interesting churches, the *iglesias* de San Sebastián and del Divino Salvador, built in the early 16th century in Mudéjar-Gothic style.

Aroche. The N-433 continues to Aroche, which was the important Roman outpost of Arucci Vetus. Its castle, built by the Almoravids in the 11th and 12th centuries, and rebuilt by Sancho IV

Cortegana
The oldest part of the castle was built between 1284 and 1295. According to legend, the knight Pedro Domingo withdrew to Cortegana where he built the fortress and became one of the paladins in the border conflict with Portugal.

“CORTAS”
The British began open-cast mining by excavating huge quarries, or *cortas*. In 1907 the Corta Atalaya, over 1,100 feet deep, was added to those of the north and the south.

Malachite (natural copper carbonate) stalactites (Museo Minero, Fundación de Riotinto).

toward the end of the 13th century, has an AMPHITHEATER and a modest ARCHEOLOGICAL MUSEUM where finds from local excavations (primarily Roman pieces) are on display. The treasury of the huge IGLESIA DE LA ASUNCIÓN (late 15th century) contains the cross of Cardinal Mendoza and a 17th-century Russian icon. Nearby is the FORMER CONVENTO DE SAN JERÓNIMO, known as “La Cilla” (“cellar”) since it was used as a storehouse by the religious community. Aroche also has several SEIGNEURIAL RESIDENCES, including those of the Count of Alamo (18th century) and the Marquis of los Arcos (17th century). The nearby ERMITA DE SAN MAMÉS (13th century) offers a fine example of the Toledan Mudéjar style.

ROMAN WATERWHEEL
The Romans mined gold, silver and copper in small chambers. Waterwheels, like the one found in the north seam in the late 19th century, were used to evacuate the water from the galleries ● *66*.

MINAS DE RIOTINTO

Return along the N-433 and head south onto the N-435 near Jabugo. Continue southward to the intersection leading to the ERMITA DE SANTA EULALIA (built on the site of a Roman mausoleum and decorated with mid-15th-century wall paintings representing the exploits of Santiago Matamoros). Maintain a southerly direction along the N-435 until you see the slagheaps from the Riotinto mines, then turn onto the C-421 just before you get to Zalamea la Real. The mines mark part of the pyritic seam of southwestern Spain: hundreds of deposits rich in iron, copper and sulfur in the lower

"Beyond the lake lies Mount Argentario, as it was known to the Ancients. As the first rays of the sun begin to warm the land, the ore glistens and sparkles on its slopes."

Avenius

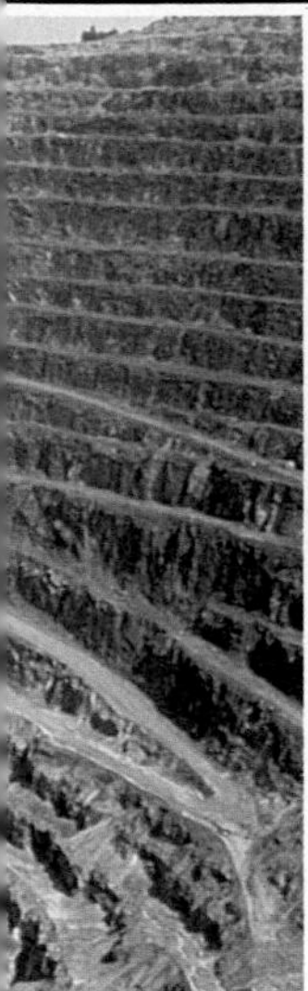

foothills of the sierra and the Andévalo de Huerta. The Minas de Riotinto have been exploited for almost five thousand years and, after the mines of Cyprus, are the oldest in the world. They cover an area of 5 square miles and contain the largest known volume of copper pyrites. However, the mines have become economically unviable and are now under threat of closure.

MINING MUSEUM AND PARK. The Fundación de Riotinto has established a MUSEO MINERO (mining museum) in the former British hospital. It presents information on the history, geology and archeology of the mines. The railway section contains the "Maharajah's carriage", built for Queen Victoria's visit to India. A marked footpath takes visitors via Bellavista, the Corta Atalaya, the Cerro Colorado, the Roman necropolis of La Dehesa and the various sections of the mine. It is also possible to visit the mining village of Nerva and the village of Zalamea.

HISTORY OF THE MINES. Mining began at the end of the 3rd millennium BC and continued until the height of the Tartessian culture. It was taken up by the Romans and then abandoned during the Visigoth and Muslim periods until the mines were rediscovered in 1556. In 1724 Philip V leased them to Liebert Wolters, a Swede, whose nephew Samuel Tiquet built the first houses of the mining village (at a time when the company had only sixteen employees). By the latter part of the 18th century, the mines had 780 employees working under the direction of Francisco Tomás Sanz, a stonecutter from Valencia, who established a village here, with its own Baroque church. In 1828 the mines, which had been virtually abandoned during the War of Independence, were leased to the Marquis of Remisa, who increased production. However, the open-air oxidation process used at the time destroyed the region's forests and polluted the air with sulfurous fumes. In 1841 the mining community established its independence from Zalamea. From 1859 the mines remained under state control until they were bought, in 1873, for 92 million pesetas by a consortium led by the Scottish banker Hugh Matheson.

RIOTINTO COMPANY LIMITED. Between 1873 and 1954, when the mines reverted to a Spanish company, the British-owned Riotinto Company built a railway and the ore-loading quay in the port of Huelva (1875–6), began open-cast mining, improved on-site techniques for the treatment of copper ore, and increased the sale of the copper and sulfur used to obtain

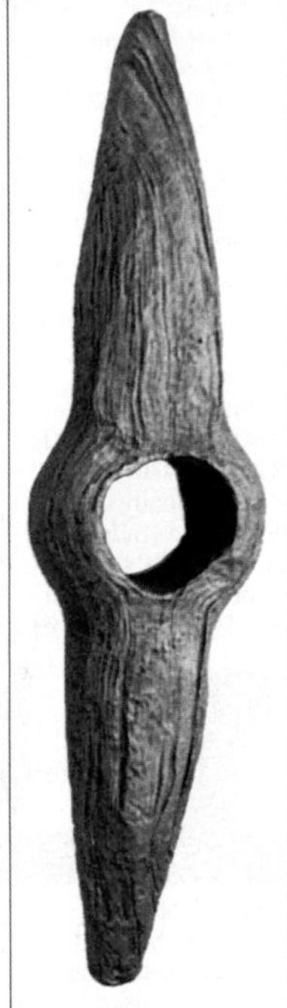

Pick belonging to a Roman miner (Museo Minero, Fundación de Riotinto).

SHAFTS AND GALLERIES
The Riotinto mines use a complex system of underground extraction to reach the deepest seams of ore.

LA MINA
The first Riotinto mining village was abandoned when the *corta sur* (south excavation) began to be worked in 1908. Its church was dynamited in 1928.

THE MINERS
Monument to the miners in the Plaza de Riotinto. The region is traditionally one of libertarian trade unionism, as evidenced by the fact that Nerva used to be called "Villa de la Libertad" and that the local district of Salvochea was named, during the Second Republic, after the great 19th-century anarchist from Cádiz. The crisis in the mining industry and the imminent closure of the mines has led to social unrest in recent years.

sulfuric acid. By 1887 the Riotinto mines were producing 40 percent of the country's copper and the British company was the largest in Spain, its workforce increasing from one thousand in 1873 to some seventeen thousand in 1909. With the land, underground mines, and the buildings and houses of the mining community, the company owned a total of some 24,700 acres. It exerted great political influence in Huelva, and Roger Browning, its managing director from 1908, was known as the "King of Huelva". At the same time harsh working conditions and smoke pollution provoked strikes and demonstrations which were harshly suppressed.

BELLAVISTA AND EL VALLE. The British colony now inhabiting the area was chiefly characterized by its isolationism. The district of Bellavista, which was established in 1879, was populated by an exclusively British community. Its Victorian architecture, semi-detached houses, club, Scottish Presbyterian chapel and Protestant cemetery constituted an exotic enclave where the British played tennis and cricket. They introduced the game of football into Spain, and the first two Spanish football clubs (Riotinto F.C. and Huelva Recreation Club) were founded on their initiative in 1890. The present village of Riotinto, formerly known as "El Valle", became the "capital" of the mines in 1928. Its division into districts and eclectic colonial architecture are the work of the English architect Alan Brace.

THE BRITISH
The images of the British community of Riotinto are, as David Avery wrote, reminiscent of the British Raj.

The province of Huelva

1. MANZANILLA
2. VILLALBA DEL ALCOR
3. LA PALMA DEL CONDADO
4. NIEBLA
5. LUCENA DEL PUERTO
6. SAN JUAN DEL PUERTO

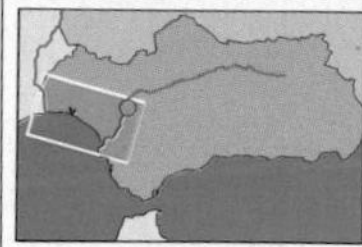

⏲ Two days
🚗 143 miles

◆ **A** B2-3, C2-4

The region of El Condado corresponds to the former Condado ("county") de Niebla. Although not recognized in geopolitical terms, the name is still used to refer to what is essentially a geographical and especially an historical region.

TOWERS OF EL CONDADO
Baroque towers are a constant feature of the landscape of El Condado. The tower of Bollulos (below).

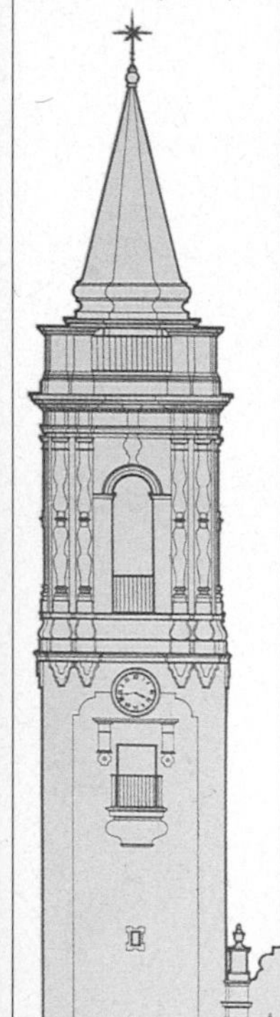

SEVILLE TO HUELVA

Seville is linked with the coast by the A-472 and the A-49, which cross the plain of Huelva, bordered to the north by the foothills of the Sierra Morena. The open landscape of hillsides and Mediterranean crops is punctuated by celebrated vineyards and old villages. For centuries most of this region formed the Condado de Niebla, the domain of the house of Medina Sidonia ▲ *176*, *206*, which was one of the oldest and most important fiefdoms in Andalusia.

TEJADA. After crossing the Guadiamar, the A-472 runs through pastureland grazed by the famous Pabloromero bulls, renowned for their courage ● *52*, and into the countryside of Tejada. The parish church of MANZANILLA is clearly visible on the horizon, as is the nearby CILLA DEL CABILDO ("cellar of the chapter") where the tithes levied by the Church were stored.

VILLALBA DEL ALCOR. The most remarkable building in this picturesque village of Mudéjar and Baroque houses, wine-making plants and mills (El Diezmo, for example), is the IGLESIA DE SAN BARTOLOMÉ. The original structure was a 12th-century Almohad mosque, succeeded in the 14th and 15th centuries by the Mudéjar church.

LA PALMA DEL CONDADO. This wine-producing village, the scene at the end of September of a major vintage festival, also makes a fine brandy. The main street leads to the Plaza de España and the IGLESIA DE SAN JUAN BAUTISTA. Its tower was built in the 18th century by Pedro de Silva.

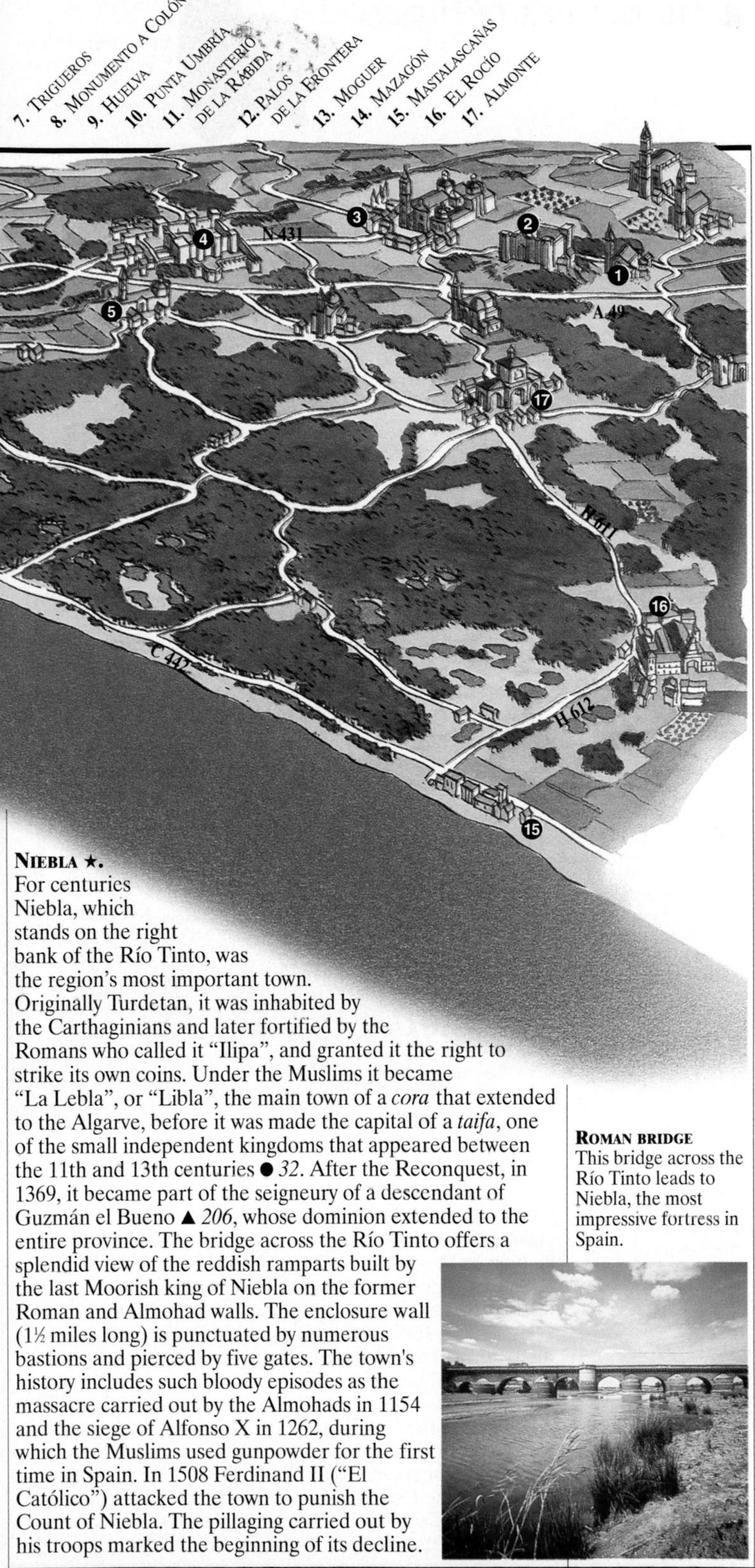

Niebla ★. For centuries Niebla, which stands on the right bank of the Río Tinto, was the region's most important town. Originally Turdetan, it was inhabited by the Carthaginians and later fortified by the Romans who called it "Ilipa", and granted it the right to strike its own coins. Under the Muslims it became "La Lebla", or "Libla", the main town of a *cora* that extended to the Algarve, before it was made the capital of a *taifa*, one of the small independent kingdoms that appeared between the 11th and 13th centuries ● *32*. After the Reconquest, in 1369, it became part of the seigneury of a descendant of Guzmán el Bueno ▲ *206*, whose dominion extended to the entire province. The bridge across the Río Tinto offers a splendid view of the reddish ramparts built by the last Moorish king of Niebla on the former Roman and Almohad walls. The enclosure wall (1½ miles long) is punctuated by numerous bastions and pierced by five gates. The town's history includes such bloody episodes as the massacre carried out by the Almohads in 1154 and the siege of Alfonso X in 1262, during which the Muslims used gunpowder for the first time in Spain. In 1508 Ferdinand II ("El Católico") attacked the town to punish the Count of Niebla. The pillaging carried out by his troops marked the beginning of its decline.

Roman bridge
This bridge across the Río Tinto leads to Niebla, the most impressive fortress in Spain.

Hub ornament from a Tartessian chariot, discovered in the necropolis of La Joya, Huelva.

SAN ANTONIO ABAD This Gothic church, crowned with crenelations, was built on the foundations of a *ribat*, a *marabout* (Muslim ascetic) hermitage from the Almohad period.

HACIENDA DE LA LUZ This former Hieronymite convent, situated between San Juan and Lucena, was founded in 1500 by María de Cardenas and Diego de Oyón. Its composite style includes cloisters and a Gothic church, which are particularly remarkable. Today it has been converted into a farm.

TRADITIONAL COSTUME OF HUELVA The province of Huelva has maintained such original popular traditions and festivals as the *romería* of El Rocío ● *51*.

The ruined castle of the HOUSE OF GUZMÁN was once a truly remarkable building, a magnificent palace whose Torre del Homenaje rivalled La Giralda ● *68*. It was damaged by the 1755 earthquake and demolished on the orders of Field-Marshal Soult during the War of Independence.
The interesting Iglesia de SANTA MARÍA DE LA GRANADA was built on the site of an 11th-century mosque, of which important elements (such as the base of the minaret) can still be seen today.

DOLMEN DEL SOTO. Between Niebla and San Juan del Puerto, a minor road leads off the A-472 to Trigueros. It passes close to the ZANCARRÓN DE SOTO, a megalithic monument from the 3rd millennium BC. The burial mound has, among other things, a wide corridor leading to a funerary chamber with a central pillar.

TRIGUEROS. In the mid-13th century Trigueros was captured from the Muslims by an army of Christian knights, which undoubtedly included the Templars. It became part of the Condado de Niebla and, from the 16th until the 18th century, was the cultural center of the region. The IGLESIA DE SAN ANTONIO ABAD was built during the first half of the 14th century, although its façade and tower were renovated in

the 18th century. Inside are late 15th-century wall paintings and medieval and Renaissance sculptures, including works by Juan de Mesa (1583–1627) ▲ *164*, *179*. Other buildings of note in Trigueros are the CONVENTO DEL CARMEN and the IGLESIA DEL COLEGIO DE SANTA CATALINA, founded by the Compañía de Jesús in the 16th century. At the end of January the Festival of San Antonio Abad, one of Andalusia's most picturesque events, is held here.

SAN JUAN DEL PUERTO AND LUCENA DEL PUERTO. The N-435 runs south to the Río Tinto. The former merchant ports of San Juan and Lucena grew up on opposite sides of the river at a time when Spain was trading with America. San Juan was founded by the Duke of Medina Sidonia in 1468. Its parish church has a *Cristo de la Misericordia* sculpted by Juan de Oviedo in 1591 ▲ *180*.

Huelva's coat of arms.

Huelva

The city of Huelva, the capital of the province of Huelva, lies 8 miles from San Juan along the N-431. Today it has a population of more than 140,000, the result of the chaotic growth that followed the construction of an industrial site in the environs of Huelva in 1964. In spite of the present predominance of a manufacturing sector largely based on the chemical industry, maritime traffic and fishing are still important. In this respect the inhabitants live up to their reputation as *choqueros* (meaning "fighters"), since Huelva is Spain's leading port for seafood and shellfish.

Mineral wealth. Huelva dates back to prehistoric times. The choice of the site for these early settlements can be explained by the rich copper deposits in the nearby sierra and its proximity to the mouth of the *ríos* Tinto and Odiel. Its name appears to have come from a Phoenician temple dedicated to Onus Baal. The arrival of the Phoenicians and Greeks from the 7th century BC gave rise to the enigmatic Tartessian culture ● *30*. The Roman town of Onuba Æstuaria became the Muslim town of Ghelbah. After the Reconquest it was attached to the kingdom of Seville and then the seigneury of the dukes of Medina Sidonia. This small agricultural and fishing town, which became the provincial capital in 1833, was drastically changed by the "mining fever" of the late 19th century, when foreign companies bought and established themselves in the nearby mines ▲ *272*.

Santuario de Nuestra Señora de la Cinta. This chapel in the Mudéjar style (13th century) has been Huelva's best-known religious building since Christopher Columbus came here to pray to the local patron saint. Perched on a hill known as El Conquero, it dominates the vast landscape of the Odiel marshes.

Churches and convents. The Calle Manuel-Siurot leads down from El Conquero and past the Instituto de la Rábida, a regional educational establishment attended by the poet Juan Ramón Jiménez (1881–1958). Nearby San Pedro, the city's oldest parish church, was built on the site of an old mosque. On the adjacent Plaza de la Merced is the former convent of the same name, founded in 1605 by the counts of Niebla.

Portus Maris

"All these people, and especially the mariners, are extremely courageous and intrepid, and perpetuate the memory of the many great deeds of yesteryear." Huelva's finest hour was as a maritime port. The Genoese navigator Christopher Columbus ▲ *136*, *283*, *304* was drawn to Spain by the fact that he had relatives, the Muliart family, living in Huelva. He recruited the crew for his first voyage in the streets of the town and placed himself under the protection of its patron saint, Nuestra Señora de la Cinta, before embarking upon the great voyage that led to the discovery of America.

Iglesia de San Pedro

The church stands at the top of the hill once crowned by the castle. It was built in Mudéjar style in the 14th and 15th centuries and its tower and portal were renovated in the 18th century by Pedro de Silva and Antonio Matías de Figueroa. It houses a silver tabernacle from Mexico.

RIOTINTO QUAY
Late 19th-century photograph showing the port of Huelva with its ore-loading quay. The quay, built in 1874 by the British engineers George Bruce and Thomas Gibson, consists of a broad wooden platform, resting on metal crosspieces. These are supported by foundation pillars set in the river bed.

CALLE CONCEPCION
Like the Calle del Puerto, the Calle

Concepción is characterized by its modern buildings, for example the Colegio de Arquitectos.

Its church (1758) is the finest Baroque edifice in the region. It was built by Pedro de Silva, one of the great architects employed by the archbishop of Seville to rebuild the churches destroyed by the earthquake of 1755. It houses the *Virgen de la Cinta*, a statue by Martínez Montañés, and *San Lorenzo* painted by Francisco de Herrera (the Elder). It has been an episcopal see since 1953. The dependencies of the former convent and hospital today house the university. Near the Plaza de las Monjas is the early 17th-century Convento de SANTA MARÍA DE GRACIA, which has a small Mudéjar cloister and a Renaissance courtyard.

ENGLISH ARCHITECTURE, MODERNISM AND REGIONALISM
The traditional architecture of the streets in the city center is interspersed with examples of late 19th- and early 20th-century Modernist, Regionalist ● *86* and eclectic architectural styles. These include, near the Plaza del Mercado, the PALACIO DE MORAS CLAROS, the SANZ DE FRUTOS CLINIC and the PLAZA DEL GRAN TEATRO. The *Cinema Rábida* and the commercial buildings of the port are characteristic of a more Rationalist form of architecture. But it is the constructions of the Riotinto Company ▲ *272* that give Huelva its architectural originality. The most exceptional of these is the *muelle-embarcadero del mineral* (ORE-LOADING QUAY) in the port.

Calle del Puerto.

Tartessian bronze ● *30* (7th century BC) from the necropolis of La Joya, Huelva (Museo Provincial).

The workers' district
In 1916 the Riotinto Company built the Barrio Reina Victoria for its workers. It was designed by two architects from Huelva, Aguado and Pérez Carasa, and the English architect R. H. Morgan, one of the masters of the British colonial style.

The ¾-mile-long quay was built in 1874 and used to load some 130 million tons of ore before it gave way in 1975. There are currently plans to restore it. The Avenida Sundheim and the surrounding area also have several late 19th-century buildings: the Casa Colón hotel, which was built in 1892 to commemorate the 400th anniversary of the discovery of America, the Hospital Inglés (the "English hospital") and the Barrio Reina Victoria, also known as the Barrio Obrero (the "workers' district").

Museo Provincial. The museum's archeological collection includes objects from the megalithic sites of El Pozuelo and La Zarcita, Tartessian treasure discovered in the necropolis of La Joya, such Greek pieces as a fragment of a painting by Kleitias, a vase by artists of the Komast group, and Roman remains from the mines, including a waterwheel. The medieval Moorish and Christian periods are also represented. The section devoted to the fine arts includes several paintings by the Cubist Nerva Daniel Vázquez Díaz (1882–1969). There is also an ethnology section devoted to the region of Huelva.

Punta Umbría
Holiday bungalow on the Punta Umbría, built by the Riotinto Company in the late 19th century for the British colony.

Costa de la Luz. Huelva is only about 10 miles from the Costa de la Luz. The H-414 runs southwest to the beaches of Punta Umbría and El Rompido. The former was a favorite resort with the British in the last decades of the nineteenth century, and still has bungalows built by the Riotinto Company.

Monumento a Colón. The N-442, in the direction of La Rábida, leads to the Punta del Sebo on the confluence of

MONASTERIO DE LA RÁBIDA
For centuries, the Monasterio de la Rábida stood in isolation on a barren hillside at the confluence of the *ríos* Tinto and Odiel. The photograph (right) shows the monastery before it was restored in 1892. The major restoration work undertaken to commemorate the 400th anniversary of the discovery of America included planting trees and laying out gardens.

the *ríos* Tinto and Odiel. On the *punta* stands the *Monumento a Colón*, dedicated to Columbus in 1929. The monument, by the New York sculptor Gertrude Whitney (1875–1942), was a gift from the United States.

MUDÉJAR CLOISTER
● *70*, ◆ *356*
The 15th-century cloister was based on that of San Isidoro del Campo ▲ *162*. The upper story was added in the 18th century. Its octagonal brick pillars and the wall paintings of its galleries help to make it the most beautiful part of the monastery.

MONASTERIO DE LA RÁBIDA

The Monasterio de Santa María de la Rábida played an important part in the discovery of America: it not only supported Columbus's project, but also received the remains of Martín Alonso Pinzón and was the scene of the meeting between Hernán Cortés and Francisco Pizarro.

AVATARS. The name "Rábida" is derived from the word *ribat*, a fortress defended by *marabouts* (Muslim ascetics) whose hermitages must once have stood on this hill. In 1412 Benedict XIII authorized the Franciscans to found a monastery, which was built in Mudéjar style. When it was damaged in the Lisbon earthquake (1755), the monks decided to abandon it. It was pillaged by French troops during the War of Independence. In 1828 the writer Washington Irving (1783–1859) deplored the state of its "empty, silent" cloisters. There were no buyers when the monastery was put up for auction in 1834, and demolition was even considered. It was finally saved, however, by the Romantic movement: the dukes of Montpensier sponsored its restoration, and the monastery

"While it is still standing, the Convent of La Rábida will always arouse deep emotion and interest."
Washington Irving, *Visit to Palos*, 1828

was classified as an historic monument in 1856.
MONASTERY VISIT. Visitors enter the monastery via the gardens with their monument dedicated in 1892 to the "discoverers" of the New World.
To commemorate the 500th anniversary of the discovery, a new building was constructed near the Franciscan cloister and the CELESTINO MUTIS BOTANICAL GARDEN was created. Beyond the brick and freestone entrance are the forecourt and gatehouse, which lead onto the PATIO DE LA HOSPEDERÍA (or PATIO DE LAS FLORES), restored in the 18th century. A horseshoe arch from the original Moorish building leads into the church where the former sacristy was decorated in 1930 with frescos depicting scenes from the life of Columbus, by Vázquez Díaz. The lecture-room and refectory open onto the small MUDÉJAR CLOISTER. On the upper story, built in the 17th and 18th centuries, is a remarkable SALA CAPITULAR, paintings, models of caravels and a porcelain bas-relief portrait of Christopher Columbus (1505). There is a belvedere offering a fine view of the estuary.
COLUMBUS AT LA RÁBIDA. Columbus visited the convent for the first time in the spring of 1485. He was received by Fray Antonio de Marchena, who supported his project when he presented it to the Catholic monarchs, and recommended it to the dukes of Medina Sidonia and Medinaceli when it was rejected by the Court. Columbus, discouraged, was ready to leave for France, but made another attempt at the end of

IGLESIA DE LA RÁBIDA
The present state of the church is the result of restoration work undertaken in 1891 by R. Velázquez Bosco to commemorate the 400th anniversary of the discovery of

America. The Baroque vaults were replaced by a Mudéjar-style armature and the intersecting ribs of the vault of the main chapel were reconstructed. The representation of Christ Crucified dates from the end of the 15th century.

THE NAVIGATOR'S LESSON
▲ *136, 304*
Most of the paintings of Columbus at La Rábida are the work of the 19th-century Sevillian Romantic school ● *92*. The scene (left) showing the Genoese navigator explaining his project to the Franciscans and García Hernández was painted in Paris by Eduardo Cano (1856). The physician of Palos and Fray Antonio de Marchena, whom the Queen named "El Estrólogo", were versed in cosmography.

PORT OF PALOS
In the 15th century ships and caravels such as the *Santa María* (above) were a common site in the port of Palos. Its activity declined several years after the discovery of the New World and today only a few fishing boats remain (right).

1491 when Fray Juan Pérez, the former confessor of Queen Isabella, managed to obtain another audience. When Columbus returned to the convent for the third time, to prepare his voyage, the Franciscans recommended Pinzón and the mariners of Palos.

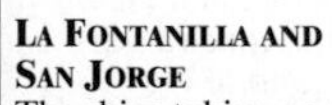

LA FONTANILLA AND SAN JORGE
The ships taking part in the expedition probably took their water supplies from the Mudéjar fountain below the Iglesia de San Jorge.

PALOS DE LA FRONTERA

The H-624 leads to this small town whose name is also linked to Columbus's first voyage to America.

GLORY AND DECLINE. When Columbus arrived here in 1485, the town probably had a fleet of some fifty or so caravels and boats with a shallow draft and lateen sails, built in Palermo. Its sailors traveled as far as the Gulf of Guinea. Chosen by the Reyes Católicos as the port from which Columbus would set sail, in 1492, Palos provided the navigator with half of his crew and two boats. In spite of the expedition's success, the port declined in the 16th century. In 1634, the local poet Rodrigo Caro wrote: "The place known as Palos [. . .] although of no importance and virtually destroyed, since its population totals no more than one hundred or so souls, will always conserve the glory of its name."

IGLESIA DE SAN JORGE. The Mudéjar-Gothic church of San Jorge was constructed during the 14th and 15th centuries, although the PUERTA DEL MEDIODÍA, with its noticeably Romanesque influences, is older. It was through the Puerta de los Novios that on August 3, 1492, Christopher Columbus and his crew left to board their three ships and begin their historic voyage across the "ocean sea".

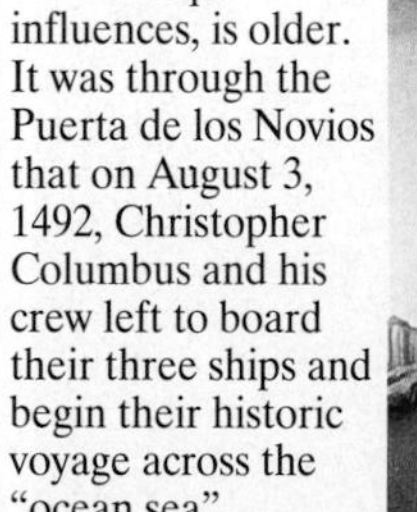

THE PINZÓN BROTHERS OF PALOS
Martín Alonzo Pinzón (right) played a decisive role in Columbus's first voyage. His decision to take part in the expedition, in spite of his initial lack of enthusiasm, gained the support of local mariners. His brother Vicente Yáñez (far right) made several voyages to America, sailed around Cuba and explored the coast of Brazil.

Iglesia de San Jorge (Palos de la Frontera) Columbus called the mariners of Palos together in the church

to ask them to take part in his expedition of 1492.

Casa-museo de Martín Alonso Pinzon. This 16th-century casa, now a museum, is traditionally linked with the Pinzón family. Beyond its beautiful entrance it houses a collection of documents, maps, models and a library.

Moguer

From Palos, the A-494 then the H-640 lead to Moguer. In the late Middle Ages the local lords, the Portocarrero family, made it one of the most important towns of the Tierra Llana de Huelva. Its mariners took part in the discovery of America (including the Niño brothers, who owned *La Niña* ● *34*, one of the three caravels used to make the crossing), explored the Amazonian and the Río de la Plata basins, and participated in the conquest of Mexico. Just outside the town are the remains of a medieval castle. The TOWN HALL and the IGLESIA DE SANTA MARÍA DE LA GRANADA, whose "tower, seen close to, resembles La Giralda seen from afar", date from the 18th century. The town center has Mudéjar and Baroque houses, such as the one where the American writer Washington Irving stayed in 1828 (situated on the intersection of the *calles* Nueva and Molinode la Coba), and the house of Admiral Hernández Pinzón, which is near the parish church.

Convento de Santa Clara
This magnificent Mudéjar-Gothic edifice situated on the Plaza Santa Clara was founded in 1337 and served as a model for the first convents that were established in America. Inside is a small Mudéjar cloister and the larger Claustro de las Madres. Within the Gothic church, which still has several Mudéjar elements, are the alabaster tombs of the Portocarrero family, the founders of the convent.

Claustro de las Madres (Convento de Santa Clara)
The 14th-century cloister was built in the Almohad tradition. The upper section dates from the 16th century. Columbus maintained a correspondence with Inés Enriquez, a relation of Ferdinand el Católico and mother-abbess of the convent. On his return from America, Columbus gave thanks in the convent church for having survived the storm that had threatened *La Niña* in the Azores.

DOÑANA NATURAL PARK, A UNIQUE NATURAL SPACE ✪
Doñana comprises almost 6,000 square miles of lagoons, marshes and dunes, split between the national park, created in 1969, and the nature reserve on its outskirts. Classed a "heritage of humanity" by UNESCO, it is chiefly of interest because of the sheer variety of its ecosystems and for its wildlife, which includes endangered species such as the Spanish lynx and the imperial eagle, as well as numerous types of migrating bird. Explore it on foot, in a four-wheel drive or in a cruiser (departures from Seville or Sanlúcar de Barrameda).

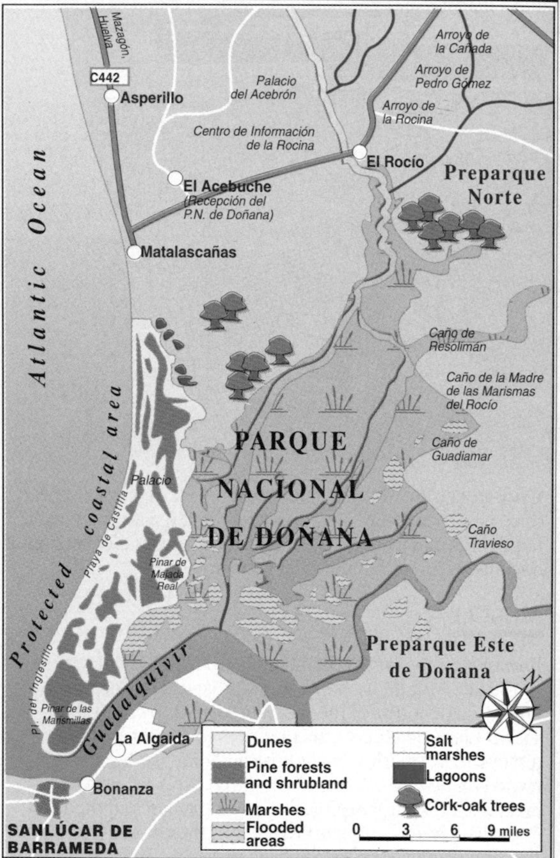

Mazagón, Huelva
C442
Asperillo
Palacio del Acebrón
Centro de Información de la Rocina
El Rocío
Arroyo de la Cañada
Arroyo de Pedro Gómez
Arroyo de la Rocina
Preparque Norte
El Acebuche (Recepción del P.N. de Doñana)
Matalascañas
Atlantic Ocean
Protected coastal area
Playa de Castilla
Palacio
Pinar de Majada Real
PARQUE NACIONAL DE DOÑANA
Caño de Resolimán
Caño de la Madre de las Marismas del Rocío
Caño de Guadiamar
Caño Travieso
Preparque Este de Doñana
Pl. del Inglesillo
Pinar de las Marismillas
Guadalquivir
La Algaida
Bonanza
SANLÚCAR DE BARRAMEDA
Dunes
Salt marshes
Pine forests and shrubland
Lagoons
Marshes
Cork-oak trees
Flooded areas
0 3 6 9 miles

The most valuable items in the convent are the Mudéjar choir stalls (14th century), sculpted from pine and pomegranate and decorated with an *azulejos* plinth. Nearby, the convent of San Francisco has a magnificent Renaissance courtyard.

PALACIO DEL ACEBRÓN
This unusual, classical-style hunting lodge was built in 1961 for the former owner of the estate, Luis Espinosa. Its exhibition, on "Man and La Doñana", is complemented by an interesting walk through the woods bordering the lagoon.

DOÑANA NATIONAL PARK

The A-494 runs through an area of strawberry fields on its way from Palos to the little seaside resort of Mazagón, then follows the coast to Matalascañas, the tourist hub of Playa de Castilla. There are also roads from the national parador and from the Torre del Oro to this beach, which stretches for more than 37 miles and which owes its other name, Arenas Gordas ("gypseous sands"), to the spectacular fossilized dunes of Asperillo, near Matalascañas.

RECEPTION AND INFORMATION CENTERS. El Acebuche, the reception center for Doñana national park, is housed in a former farm approximately 1¾ miles north of Matalascañas on the A-483. The top of the tower offers a panoramic view of the *cotos*, dunes anchored by

Parque Nacional de Doñana
ICONA - MAPA

The birds of Doñana
With birds from central and northern Europe overwintering in the park, Doñana has a population of some 300,000 birds representing some twenty or so common species and several rare species. Until the 18th century, swans were still a common sight. Today wild ducks and geese are the most numerous.

scrub. The El Acebuche center has a permanent exhibition on the Doñana nature reserve, a footpath that winds its way through cistus and heathers, and hides overlooking the Laguna de los Pájaros ("lagoon of birds"). About 6½ miles further on, the information center of Las Rocinas also has a footpath (1½ miles) and hides. It is an ideal place to watch birds of prey in winter and spring. A path leads to the Palacio del Acebrón, which has a permanent exhibition on the history and ethnography of the region. The El Acebrón footpath is likely to be of great interest to botanists and landscape enthusiasts. On the estuary of the Guadalquivir, which borders the National Park to the southeast, is the center of Bajo de Guía de Sanlúcar de Barrameda. It has an exhibition on the wetlands of Andalusia, a river route to the *salinas* (salt pans) of San Isidoro ▲ *308* and a visit to the hut village of La Plancha.

Natural areas. Visits to the natural areas must be reserved in advance and start from the *Centro de Recepción del Acebuche*. The 4-hour circuit in a four-wheel-drive vehicle enables visitors to really appreciate the different types of landscape. The shoreline, from Matalascañas to the Punta de Malandar, is edged by a vast beach which is frequented by seagulls, curlews and terns. It is dotted with fishermen's huts and the remains of three crenelated towers, built in the 16th century by order of Philip (Felipe) II as coastal watchtowers. There are visits to the hut village of La Plancha and the Palacio de Marismillas in the pine forests of El Faro and Marismillas. Countless waterfowl overwinter in the *marismas*, the marshes that cover half the total area of the park, and deer and wild boar are found along the borderline between marshes and dunes. The dunes and the so-called "hill of geese" (Los Ansares), near the enclosed breeding areas, are covered with clumps of pines and scrub. On winter mornings they are invaded by wild geese who forage in the sand with their beaks, to feed on the roots of Andalusian cypress grass.

Hides
The hides at the park entrances offer visitors the opportunity to observe certain birds in their natural surroundings. From the hides at El Acebuche it is sometimes possible to see spoonbills, and one of Doñana's most interesting birds, the purple gallinule.

ROYAL HUNT
In 1624 Philip IV led the most prestigious hunt ever held in Doñana. The ten-day hunting party, which brought together some ten thousand people and included bullfights and theatrical performances, ruined its host, the Duke of Medina Sidonia, the richest nobleman in Spain.

Plan of the Castillo de San Salvador at the mouth of the Guadalquivir (right).

ARISTOCRATIC ESTATE
The dukes of Montpensier hunted on the Doñana estate. At the end of the 19th century the Duke of Tarifa bought it for a group of aristocrats and members of the Anglo-Spanish bourgeoisie living in Jerez ▲ *294*. Alfonso XIII, who liked hunting wild boar, often joined their hunting parties.

Hut (right) in the pine forest of El Faro.

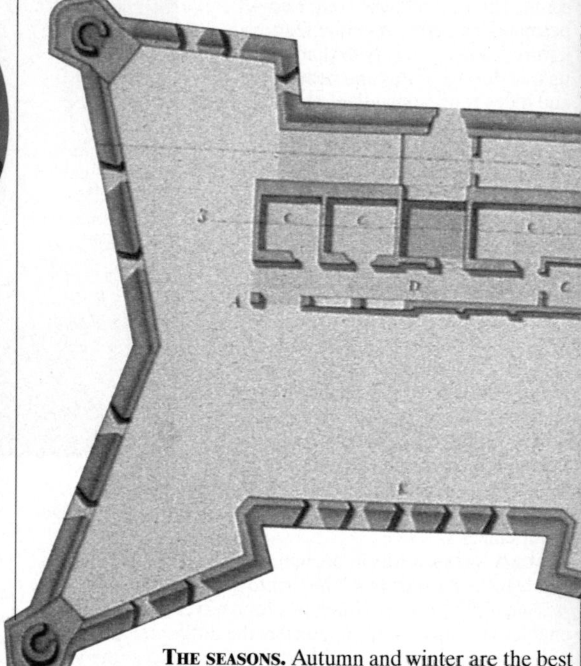

THE SEASONS. Autumn and winter are the best times to visit the Doñana National Park. Flocks of wild geese, herons, flamingos and spoonbills arrive with the first autumn rains. In winter the birds gather to breed and the bottom of the marshes is covered with cypress grass and fescue, creating a mirror-like effect. The water level rises with the spring rains, the marsh plants flower and huge flocks of birds gather in the coastal marshes, preparing their young for migration. In summer the marshes dry up and become a vast expanse of cracked clay where wild horses and cattle search for the last remaining blades of grass.

ORIGINS. The Doñana region was formed some six thousand years ago by alluvial deposits that blocked the mouth of the Guadalquivir on the site of Lake Ligur (the Lacus Ligustinus of the ancient texts). The remains of the Roman towns excavated by the German archeologist, Schulten, on the hills at Trigo, revealed that their inhabitants lived on fish, which

was either salted or macerated to make the sauce known as *garum*.

A HUNTING PRESERVE. Game is one of Doñana's age-old resources. Following the conquest of the kingdom of Niebla in 1262, Alfonso X established the royal hunt at Las Rocinas. In 1309, the land at the heart of the park was ceded to the descendants of Guzmán el Bueno ▲ *206* and for centuries belonged to the seigneury of Medina Sidonia. In the 19th and early 20th centuries, the nobility and prominent figures in the fields of the arts and sciences often hunted there: the naturalists, Buck and Chapman wrote an account of their stay in *Unexplored Spain* (1910). For other, more discreet hunters, known as *venaderos* (deerhunters) or *corsarios* (corsairs), Doñana served as a source of provision in times of shortage.

PALACES AND HUNTING LODGES. Although the PALACIO DEL REY of the former royal estate of Loma del Grullo is the oldest building in the park, the PALACIO DE DOÑANA, now the headquarters of the Estación Biológica, is still the most impressive. The seventh duke of Medina Sidonia had it built in 1585 for his wife, Doña Ana de Silva y Mendoza, after whom the estate is supposed to have been named (although in fact it would seem to have been named after another, less distinguished Ana ...). The PABELLÓN DE LAS NUEVAS is a 20th-century structure, as is the PALACIO DE MARISMILLAS built by the Duke of Tarifa in 1912 in a colonial style of clearly northern influence.

RESOURCES OF DOÑANA. Doñana has always profited the local population and the dukes of Medina Sidonia who controlled its exploitation. As well as hunting and fishing, it offered many resources: coal and wool, cork, honey and wax, bulrushes and reeds for chair-makers and coopers, barley and fescue and, above all, grazing land for cattle. El-Mansur (938–1002) was already breeding horses here in the 10th century and, in 1584, the dukes of Medina Sidonia employed individual herdsman for deer, goats and horses, as well as a grazier and five cowherds. Many shepherds' huts can still be seen today, especially in the marshes.

HUT VILLAGES. These 18th-century villages, reminiscent of the Neolithic age, are found in the PINAR DEL FARO ("pine forest of the lighthouse"). They attest to the agricultural policies of the dukes, who tried to introduce vines to Doñana, sowed parasol pines in the Marismillas region and even had the idea of establishing colonies in the El Rocío region. They consist of two or three huts surrounded by a briar fence. A few families still live in them.

"SALINAS". Salt is one of Doñana's oldest resources. The exploitation of the salt-marshes, like the use of the tunny nets used for tuna fishing, were also part of the agricultural

THE HUTS OF DOÑANA
These rectangular huts have a pinewood frame covered with tightly packed grass stems that form the wall and double-pitched roof.

HUNTERS AND WARDENS
Since ancient times, hunters have come to these dunes and marshes in search of more unusual game. Gamekeepers are responsible for the surveillance of the park.

EL ROCÍO PILGRIMAGE ● *51*
El Rocío is one of the world's most important centers for the worship of the Holy Virgin. Its pilgrimage brings together more than one million people, including the brotherhoods of Seville, Cádiz and the villages of Huelva. The pilgrims follow the *simpecado* (the banner bearing the Virgin's image) on foot, on horseback and in carts.

"AZULEJO" DE LA VIRGEN DEL ROCÍO
When she was restored in the 15th century, the Virgin's face and hands took on a late Gothic quality and she was dressed in rich garments. The current embroidery and garments date from the 18th century. The Virgin is invoked as the Reina de las Marismas ("queen of the marshes"), Blanca Paloma ("white dove") and Divina Pastora ("divine shepherdess").

IGLESIA DE LA ASUNCIÓN
The entrance and tower of this 15th-century church are in later, Baroque style.

policies of the dukes of the *ancien regime*. The abandoned salt pans of San Diego, San Rafael and San Isidoro have not changed since Roman times. A new park information center will soon be opening at San Isidoro.

EL ROCÍO AND ALMONTE

EL ROCIO. The hamlet of El Rocío, to the north of the park, consists mainly of small hermitages and brotherhood houses.

THE HERMITAGE. El Rocío began with the construction of the Ermita de Santa María de las Rocinas by Alfonso X in the 13th century. Toward the end of the century the region, which formed the frontier of the Almohad empire, was repeatedly raided by the Muslim armies. The statue of the patron saint of the hermitage, the Virgen del Rocío, was hidden in a tree, either an ash or an olive, and was not found until the 15th century, when it was discovered by a hunter from Villamanrique. The event was marked by the construction of a new hermitage. Another sanctuary was built in 1964.

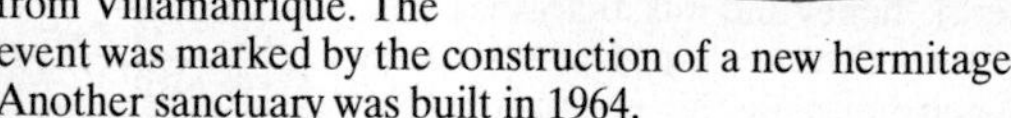

THE PILGRIMAGE. The inhabitants of Villamanrique were the first to make a pilgrimage to El Rocío. In the 17th century Almonte adopted the Virgin as its patron saint (1653) and the local brotherhoods were founded. The pilgrimage, held on Whit Sunday, brings together eighty-five brotherhoods, including the parent brotherhood of Almonte, which is the only one entitled to carry the Virgin in the procession. The small pilgrimage of El Rocío is held on August 19 to give thanks to the Virgin for protecting the village of Almonte during the War of Independence.

ALMONTE. The territory of this town of agricultural and stock farmers extends to the Doñana National Park, and includes El Rocío and Matalascañas. On its main plaza stand two remarkable buildings: the 18th-century TOWN HALL and the IGLESIA DE LA ASUNCIÓN, where a spectacular procession brings the *Virgen del Rocío* every seven years. On July 26, the day of the Saca de Yeguas ("herd of mares"), the marshland horses are taken there to be branded.

Seville to Cádiz

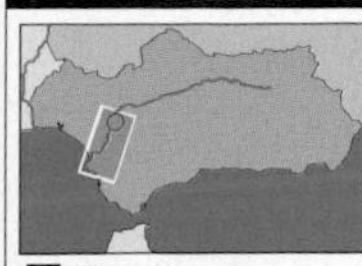

⏲ Two days
🚗 125 miles
◆ A C4-5

THE CÁDIZ COAST

This itinerary covers the coastal area that lies within the triangle formed by Jerez de la Frontera, Cádiz and Sanlúcar de Barrameda, on the Guadalquivir estuary. It has the characteristic low relief of the areas bordering the Atlantic.

ANCIENT HISTORY. The Cádiz coast was explored and colonized by the end of the 2nd millennium BC. In ancient times it was an outpost of the urban Mediterranean civilizations and was visited by the Phoenicians and Greeks, who settled there and assimilated it into their culture. According to Greek mythology, the pillars of Hercules, which marked the borders of the known world, were located at Cádiz, while the philosopher Plato situated the legendary island-kingdom of Atlantis between the southern end of the Cádiz coast and Africa. The disappearance of this extraordinarily sophisticated civilization was thought to have been caused by a major natural catastrophe, possibly the eruption of the Santorin volcanic chain that shook the Mediterranean in about 1500 BC.

THE FLEET OF CÁDIZ Painting depicting the fleet setting sail for Veracruz in the 18th century. From 1680, until the colonies gained independence in 1824, Cádiz was the leading port for trade with America.

SEA AND WINE. Wine-making and fishing are the region's two traditional activities. The proximity of the sea led to the development of commerce and industry in the towns of Cádiz (which currently has a population of 143,000) and San Fernando (84,000). The town of Jerez de la Frontera, on the other hand, owes its success to its wine production, which expanded in the 18th century as a result of the export facilities offered by the neighboring ports. Today it has the largest

Proclamation of the first Spanish Constitution (1812) in the Oratorio de San Felipe Neri, in Cádiz.

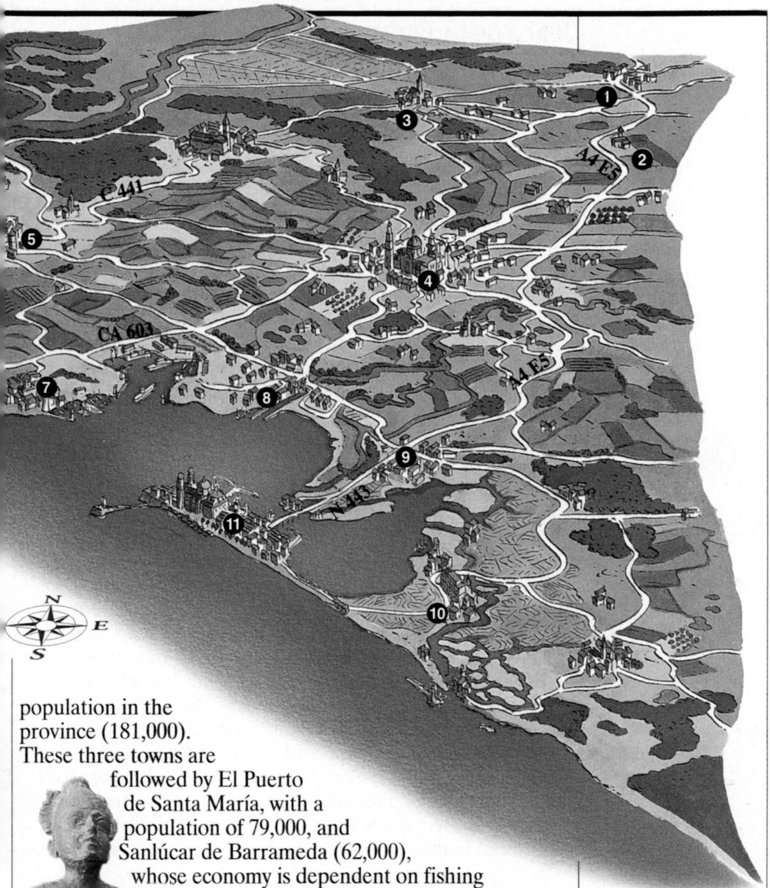

1. Los Palacios y Villafranca
2. Las Cabezas de San Juan
3. Lebrija
4. Jerez de la Frontera
5. Sanlúcar de Barrameda
6. Chipiona
7. Rota
8. El Puerto de Santa María
9. Puerto Real
10. San Fernando
11. Cádiz

population in the province (181,000). These three towns are followed by El Puerto de Santa María, with a population of 79,000, and Sanlúcar de Barrameda (62,000), whose economy is dependent on fishing and viniculture. It will therefore come as no surprise that wine, fish and seafood form the basis of the region's gastronomy and are an important part of every festive occasion.

Seville to Jerez de la Frontera

The A-4 freeway crosses a crop-growing region, bordered on either side by marshland, where there is no marked change between the provinces of Seville and Cádiz. Situated around 6 miles south of Dos Hermanas is Los Palacios, the summer residence of Pedro I (Pedro the Cruel) and, nearly 14 miles further on, is the town of Las Cabezas de San Juan. Dominating Las Cabezas de San Juan is the Baroque church of San Juan Bautista, and next to the church stands the villa that was the seat of the 1820 uprising led by General Riego, who opposed the absolute monarchy of Ferdinand VII. The C-441 leads to the hilltop town of Lebrija. The town's church, the Iglesia de Santa María de la Oliva, was once a mosque. Amongst its notable features are a remarkable series of Mudéjar vaults and a *retablo mayor* by the 17th-century Baroque painter, sculptor and architect Alonso Cano (1601–67).

Melkart/Hercules
Phoenician bronze discovered in Cádiz.

"Bodegas"
Jerez, known as "sherry" in English and *xérès* in French, is the best-known Spanish wine. Jerez, Puerto de Santa María and Sanlúcar are the main centers of production.

Roman coin from Orippo (representing a bull). The originally Turdetan town stood on the site of what is now Dos Hermanas.

PLAZA DE LEBRIJA IN THE 1920'S
Lebrija was the birthplace of the humanist Elio Antonio de Nebrija (1444–1532), the author of the first Spanish grammar, a Latin grammar and a number of other scholarly works.

JEREZ DE LA FRONTERA

MONASTERIO DE LA CARTUJA ★. La Cartuja de Santa María de la Defensión is situated 3½ miles east of the center of Jerez, on the banks of the Guadalete. It was founded in 1463 by Don Alvaro Obertos de Valeto and is one of the masterpieces of Spanish architecture. The Renaissance-style entrance, completed in 1571 by Andrés de Ribera, opens onto a courtyard bordered by the façade of the church. Most of the edifice is in a superb, flamboyant Gothic style. The interior of the church, the refectory, the Claustrillo (small cloister) and the Claustro de los Muertos (great cloister) are truly magnificent. Opening off the latter are the cells, the dormitory, the study room and the oratory, which overlook the garden to the rear. Works by Albrecht Dürer, Francisco de Zurbarán and Alonso Cano once hung in the monastery, but were dispersed at the time of the Napoleonic invasion (1810) and the secularization of Church wealth (1835). The monastery also housed the royal stud, which produced the Cartujano breed (by crossing German and Neapolitan stock), famed for its mettle, speed and aptitude for dressage.

THE TOWN OF JEREZ. Two thousand years ago this town, known to the Greeks as Xera, was already exporting amphorae of a wine famous in Rome. Under the Almoravids and Almohads it was one of the principal towns of El-Andalus. Its Moorish name, "Sherish", has survived in the English word "sherry". Alfonso X conquered the town in 1264 and renamed it. Until the end of the Middle Ages, it was used as a military base for expeditions launched against the kingdom of Granada. In modern times, it became

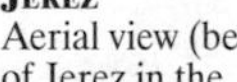

JEREZ
Aerial view (below) of Jerez in the mid-19th century. In the foreground, the *iglesia* and the Barrio de Santiago.

an important center for the production and commercialization of wines exported to the rest of Europe and to America. In the 18th century several British, French and Spanish commercial dynasties (Haurie, Byass, Garvey, Osborne, Domecq, Terry, Duff, Pemartín) renovated the vineyard estates of Jerez and Puerto de Santa María and created huge *bodegas*. The vineyards of Jerez experienced their finest commercial hour in the late 19th century, when other parts of Europe were suffering from phylloxera.

WALLS AND ALCÁZAR. The 11th-century Moorish enclosure wall (of which only a few sections remain) was punctuated by fifty towers and pierced by four gates. The most remarkable monuments in Jerez lie within its (quadrilateral) perimeter. At the southwestern corner stands the 12th-century *alcázar* which includes the Torre del Homenaje ("tower of homage"), an octagonal tower, a cistern, the remains of a *hammam* and a former mosque, converted into the Gothic chapel of Santa María la Real by Alfonso X.

CATHEDRAL. To the northwest of the *alcázar* stands the town's most prestigious architectural work, the collegiate church of San Salvador, which was granted the status of cathedral in 1980. The church has five naves, is surmounted by an octagonal dome and flanked by an isolated bell tower. It was built between 1695 and 1778 on the ruins of a 13th-century church, by a number of architects, including Moreno Meléndez and Torcuado Cayón. It is a hybrid edifice which combines Baroque and neoclassical elements. Its rich interior décor includes some remarkable works: the 14th-century sculpture, the *Cristo de la Viga*, and the *Virgen Niña* by Francisco de Zurbarán ▲ *139*, *158*, *182*.

Hillside vineyard near Jerez.

Muleteer (left) from Jerez, 19th century.

FAÇADE OF THE IGLESIA DE LA CARTUJA
The church, built in 1667 under the direction of Fray Pedro del Piñar, is decorated with sculptures by Francisco de Gálvez.

IGLESIA DE SAN MIGUEL
Along with the cathedral, this is the most remarkable church in Jerez. Its interior (15th and 16th century) is in flamboyant Gothic style. Between 1672 and 1701, Diego Moreno Meléndez sculpted the many Baroque decorations of the portal beneath the façade-tower.

CHURCHES, PALACES AND "BODEGAS"
The architectural character of Jerez is defined by its churches, palaces and *bodegas.* The many religious buildings and palaces within the ramparts of the old town are equaled by the number of *bodegas* that lie beyond its walls. View of the Alcázar (right) in 1835.

IGLESIA DE SAN MIGUEL. From the busy Plaza del Arenal, to the northeast of the Alcázar, the Calle San Miguel leads to the Gothic church of the same name. The intersecting ribs of its three naves are supported by fasciculate pillars. The 17th-century *retablo* of the high altar, by José de Arce ▲ *137* and Juan Martínez Montañés ● *48*, ▲ *139*, *206*, is one of the province's most precious Baroque works.

PLAZA AND IGLESIA DE SAN DIONISIO. Back in the Plaza del Arenal, the itinerary continues via the Calle Pescadería and the Calle Letrados, which leads onto the Plaza de San Dionisio in the center of the old town. On either side of the plaza stand the Renaissance palace of the Cabildo Viejo and the Iglesia de San Dionisio. The church, built in 1664, has an early Gothic façade and portal (13th century) and Mudéjar interior decoration (15th century). It houses a magnificent sculpture of the *Virgen del Mayor Dolor*, attributed to Juan Martínez Montañés. Its Torre de la Atalaya, built in the mid-15th century, is typical of the superimposition of Islamic and Christian Gothic architectural styles. The Calle Francos runs northwest to the Plaza de San Mateo and the Museo Arqueológico.

IGLESIA DE SANTIAGO. The Calle Oliva leads to the Plaza and the Iglesia de Santiago. This flamboyant late Gothic edifice, built outside the Moorish enclosure wall, is distinctively heterogeneous in its decoration. Its three naves, with their beautiful intersecting ribs, contain a *Cristo del Prendimiento*, which is carried in procession during the Semana Santa.

CATHEDRAL
The three huge portals of its façade are decorated with stone reliefs.

CABILDO VIEJO
The former chapterhouse is decorated with sculptures of Hercules and Julius Caesar and has an Italian loggia. It is the work of Andrés de Ribera, Martín de Oliva and Bartolomé Sánchez, and was completed in 1575. It still houses the municipal library.

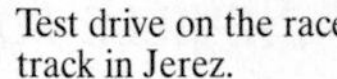

Test drive on the race track in Jerez.

REAL ESCUELA ANDALUZA DEL ARTE ECUESTRE. The Calle Juan Torres joins the Calle Porvera, which marks the eastern boundary of the old town and opens onto a vast esplanade. The Convento de San Domingo, which stands on the esplanade, has a beautiful 15th-century cloister in late Gothic style. The Royal Andalusian School of Equestrian Art lies to the north, on the Avenida del Duque de Abrantes. It stands in the romantic setting of the gardens of the Palacio del Recreo de las Cadenas, designed in 1867 by Charles Garnier, the architect of the Opéra de Paris. The School's presentation, *Como Bailan los Caballos Andaluces* ("How the Andalusian horses dance"), demonstrates the beautiful carriage of this breed and its great aptitude for dressage and schooling. The Feria del Caballo ("horse fair"), held in May, is another popular event with equestrian enthusiasts. To the southwest, the Palacio de la Atalaya in the Calle Leales houses the MUSEO DE LOS RELOJES (clock museum) which has one of the finest collections in Europe.

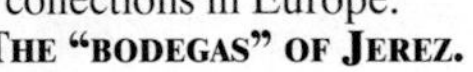

THE "BODEGAS" OF JEREZ. There are many *bodegas* scattered throughout the town. These have vast (aboveground) cellars that combine the optimum conditions of temperature and ventilation in which the wine can mature. *Bodegas* are usually open to the public in the morning, and, as well as being technically and often architecturally interesting, visits also provide an opportunity to sample the wines of Jerez. The Domecq *bodega*, near the cathedral in the Calle de San Ildefonso, has a Moorish interior, while González Byass, in the Calle Manuel María González, has a metallic cellar designed by Gustave Eiffel. There is also a cellar-museum, the CASA DEL VINO, on the Avenida Alvaro Domecq. The vintage festival is held in September.

FLAMENCO. The gipsy districts of San Miguel and Santiago produced the first flamenco *cantaores* ("singers"), including Luis de la Juliana or "El Tío" ("the uncle"), an early 19th century water-seller and the first known flamenco singer. The real magic of Jerez is found here, among the convents and palaces, courtyards and *tabernas*, where *bulería* (local flamenco singing), *tonás*, *martinetes*, *soleares* and *seguidillas* are heard at every kind of gathering. The CENTRO ANDALUZ DE FLAMENCO (flamenco center) in the Plaza de San Juan presents information on all aspects of the art of flamenco.

MANUEL TORRE (1878–1933)
The gipsy *cantaor* from Jerez was one of the first great names in flamenco ● *54*, ▲ *391*.

GREEK BRONZE HELMET
The helmet (7th century BC) was discovered on the bed of the Río Guadalete (Museo Arqueológico, Jerez).

BULLS AND HORSES
Bullfighting ● *52* and horses are, with wine and flamenco, the great passions of Jerez: Rafael de Paula (below), the gipsy matador from Jerez; performance by the Real Escuela Andaluza del Arte Ecuestre (bottom).

View of Sanlúcar in 1567.

GUADALQUIVIR ESTUARY
Sanlúcar stands on the Guadalquivir estuary. Throughout history it has been the sea port of Seville, in spite of one major drawback: a *broa*, a bar of sand and rock, that has been the cause of many shipwrecks. Today a regularly dredged canal has improved the situation for maritime and river traffic. Sanlúcar has a large fishing fleet.

SANLÚCAR DE BARRAMEDA

The A-480 links Jerez to Sanlúcar via the Ruta del Vino (wine route), where farms cling to the vine-covered hillsides. As you approach the sea, the air becomes sharper and the land chalky: these are the *albarizas* that produce the excellent *manzanilla* sherry of Sanlúcar ▲ *306*.

A SEIGNEURIAL TOWN. Classical authors refer to a temple dedicated to Venus (both the evening star and the goddess born of the sea) that stood on the Guadalquivir estuary. The existence of an early settlement is evidenced by the Phoenician, Greek and Roman remains found in the vicinity. The chronicles of the conquests of Alfonso X refer to it for the first time as the "sacred place", San Lucar. The Muslim village that stood on the site was repopulated by Christians and became the fief of Alonzo Pérez de Guzmán ("El Bueno") ▲ *206* as a reward for his heroic courage in the defense of Tarifa. For more than three hundred years Sanlúcar flourished as the seat of the seigneury of Guzmán, counts of Niebla and dukes of Medina Sidonia ▲ *176*. It traded with Mediterranean and Atlantic ports and, with the opening of the route to America and the establishment of Seville's trading monopoly ● *33*, it became one of Europe's busiest ports and an obligatory port of call for transatlantic and other associated fleets.

BARRIO ALTO AND CASTILLO
The town of Sanlúcar is divided into two districts, the *barrio bajo* (lower district) and the *barrio alto* (upper district). The Avenida de la Constitución and then the Calle Sevilla lead to the small castle plaza in the *barrio alto*. This is the town's oldest district, built and fortified on a promontory overlooking the *ría* (estuary). On the edge of the cliff, in one of the angles of the wall, stands the Castillo de Santiago, a fortress built in 1477. It has an impressive hexagonal dungeon, massive towers

JUAN SEBASTIAN ELCANO
In 1519 Magellan's ▲ *194* fleet set sail from Sanlúcar on the first round-the-world voyage. Three years later the only surviving ship, commanded by Juan Sebastián Elcano (1476–1526), returned to port.

The tower of the Iglesia de la O stands at the top of the *barrio alto* (upper district), overlooking the *barrio bajo* (lower district), in the foreground.

and a double enclosure wall. On the river side is a gate with an ogee arch and a statue of a siren.

Bodegas de Manzanilla. The castle is surrounded by *bodegas*, like those found in the *barrio bajo*. Beneath their lofty vaults *manzanilla*, the vintage sherry ▲ *306* exclusive to Sanlúcar, is matured in casks. It has a dry, smooth, subtle flavor and is a beautiful pale yellow color. Its character is derived from the fresh, salty sea air. There are two varieties of *manzanilla*: *fina*, and *pasada* (which has a higher alcohol content).

Iglesia de Nuestra Señora de la O. The Calle Luis Eguilaz, bordered by *bodegas* and vast residences, leads to the center of the *barrio alto*. Here, on the Plaza de la Paz, are the Palacio Ducal and the Iglesia de Nuestra Señora de la O, begun in 1360. Its grandiose Mudéjar portal is in cut stone and bears coats of arms and geometric Moorish and Gothic decorations. The magnificent bell tower, built in 1604, was designed by Alonso de Vandelvira, the great architect of the dukes. The three naves and chapels are surmounted by the most beautiful coffered Mudéjar vault in the Cádiz region. The richness of its furniture and works of art are evidence of the magnificence of the dukes' patronage. Its large collection of 16th-century paintings includes the polyptych by the Flemish artist Hernando de Esturmio (c. 1515–56), the *San Sebastián* by the Portuguese artist Vasco Pereira and a *Descent from the Cross* by Pierre de Champaigne of Brussels.

Palacio Ducal. Next to the church is the austere façade of the Palacio Ducal, with its distinctive *reja de la pendencia* ("grille of the quarrel"), a wrought-iron filigree (16th century). The palace was begun in 1424 and extended several times. It has some magnificent *salones* (particularly the Grand Salon and Room of Columns) containing a profusion of carpets and paintings, galleries and gardens. The archives of the Casa Ducal (which are of great historical value) are also contained in this, the residence of the powerful dukes of Medina Sidonia, who occupied high offices in the government, army and navy. The seventh duke commanded the Invincible Armada, which set sail for England in 1588 and, in 1624, the eighth duke organized a memorable reception in honor of Philip IV ▲ *288*. The decline of the line and its economic power began with the ninth duke, who was involved in the conspiracy (1641) to bring about the secession of Andalusia. The plot was discovered and the duke was imprisoned and stripped of his possessions in Sanlúcar in 1645. A governor appointed by the king then occupied the palace.

Las Covachas and Palacio Ducal
The Gothic reliefs known as *Las Covachas* (top) in the Cuesta de Belén between the *barrio alto* and the *barrio bajo*. Façade of the Palacio Ducal (above).

Signature of Francisco de Goya (1746–1828)
The artist ▲ *139*, *145* spent a season in Sanlúcar with the Duchess of Alba, with whom he had an affair.

Convent of the Barrio Bajo
Sanlúcar is a peaceful town with many convents. Convent (above) in the Calle Regina.

CALLE ANCHA AND PLAZA DEL CABILDO
These are the centers of everyday life in the *barrio bajo*.

STREETS OF THE BARRIO ALTO. To appreciate the district's "rich gift of silence and memories" simply walk from the Plaza de la Paz to the Puerta de Jerez. En route you pass the Convento de las Descalzas (1675) and the beautiful portal and tower of the IGLESIA DE LA CARIDAD, designed by Alonso de Vandelvira and built in Mannerist style in 1612. The church houses the Virgen de la Caridad, the town's patron saint.

CUESTA DE BELÉN. This steep street leads down from the Plaza de la Paz to the *barrio bajo*. It is bordered by the gardens of the PALACIO DE ORLÉANS, now the town hall. The *palacio* dates from 1852 when Antoine d'Orléans, Duke of Montpensier, was living in Seville ● *39* and decided to spend the summer in Sanlúcar. In doing so, he turned this small town into one of the most fashionable resorts of the day. The Mudéjar-style edifice with its bicolored brickwork, courtyards and romantic park, is reminiscent of the Alhambra of Granada. It also attests to the spread of Regionalist architecture ● *86*. Within this setting stands the elegant IGLESIA DE LA MERCED, built at the beginning of the Baroque period and the early part of the 17th century. Beyond the

SANTO DOMINGO
This freestone gateway (1606) in the Calle Ancha leads to the convent church. The church, surmounted by a huge coffered dome, houses the gisants of the dukes of Medina Sidonia.

"A town that gives shelter / To so many nations, / English, Flemings, Bretons, / Distinct in their language, / Their clothes, their stature and features."

Anonymous (17th century)

church the Cuesta de Belén leads to the remarkable COVACHAS: a building decorated with a Gothic cornice frieze (15th century) which may once have belonged to the monumental entrance of the ducal palace above. The erosion of the stone emphasizes the fantastical effect of the dragons and monsters sculpted in relief. A morning market is held nearby, selling fish, shellfish and agricultural produce.

BARRIO BAJO. Beyond the Covachas, the Cuesta de Belén leads into the *barrio bajo*, originally the merchant district of La Ribera. The Bretons formed Sanlúcar's first merchant community in the 14th and 15th centuries, trading in French fabrics and local fruit. They were succeeded by the English and Flemish. A busy market lies between the Calle Bretones and the Plaza de San Roque. It is separated from the Plaza del Cabildo, the modern center of the town, by the TOWN HALL (1730). Off the Plaza de San Roque are picturesque streets and convents (for example, MADRE DE DIOS in the Calle Baños), where the nuns sell confectionery. The *calles* Ancha, San Juan and Bolsa, the town's main streets, converge on the Plaza del Cabildo. The CALLE ANCHA is a major thoroughfare bordered by shops, mansions and the CONVENTS OF SAN DOMINGO AND SAN FRANCISCO.

PROMENADES AND BEACHES. The broad PASEO CALZADA runs from the Plaza del Cabildo to the beach. Apart from some early 20th-century villas (now restored), this is the modern district of Sanlúcar. In May it is the scene of the Feria de la Manzanilla and, in August, the Fiesta de Agosto and the Fiesta de la Exaltación del Guadalquivir. The PASEO MARÍTIMO leads to the beach of Bajo de Guía. At the top end of the promenade is one of the reception centers for the Doñana National Park, which lies on the opposite bank of the Guadalquivir ▲ *286*. A little further on is an arcaded street, lined with bars and restaurants. The itinerary ends at the fishing port of BONANZA ▲ *228*, where an extremely colorful auction is held at around 3pm each day. Local fish and shellfish, including *langostinos* (giant shrimps), plaice and whiting, are sold amid much shouting and animated discussion.

BAJO DE GUÍA
Since 1845, horse races have been held on this beach in August, where fishing boats once unloaded their catches.

BOATMEN OF THE GUADALQUIVIR
They will ferry you across the river, to the edge of the Doñana National Park. Boats leave from the beach of Bajo de Guía, near the Olaso pier, and make the brief crossing to the sand banks on the Punta de Malandar. A short walk takes you to the boarding point for the steamship *Real Fernando,* which stops at Doñana, the salt pans and the port of Bonanza.

CHIPIONA
An aerial view of the village and the coast toward Sanlúcar. In the foreground is Spain's tallest lighthouse (205 feet), completed in 1867.

CHIPIONA AND ROTA

The coastal roads between Sanlúcar and the Bay of Cádiz pass through a number of small villages where you can stop and quench your thirst and sample a few *tapas* ● *60*. The coast near Chipiona is bordered by *corrales*, large rectangles formed by stone walls that act as holding tanks for fish carried in on the tide.

CHIPIONA. This fishing port, which has maintained its traditions in spite of the increase in summer tourism, is renowned for its sweet Muscatel wine. Near the jetty protecting the port are the ruins of the Turris Caepion, a tower built by the Romans in memory of Scipio Africanus to mark out the Guadalquivir estuary. In front of the lighthouse, other ruins, including the Piedra de Salmedina, bear witness to the Roman occupation. The seafront promenade ends at the MONASTERIO DE NUESTRA SEÑORA DE REGLA, thought to have been founded in the 5th century, which has a Baroque cloister and a neo-Gothic church.

EL PUERTO DE SANTA MARÍA IN 1567
In the 16th century Santa María was the home port for the Spanish galleys that protected the coast against pirates. Its extensive salt pans, which still exist today, can be seen in the foreground.

ROTA. The road from Chipiona to Rota runs beside the long, sandy beaches of the Playa de la Ballena and the Punta Candor. The true essence of this small coastal town is found in the old districts, in and around the fishing port. Its CASTILLO DE LUNA, built in the 13th century on the site of a *ribat* of Muslim (warrior) ascetics, was converted into a palace in the 16th century. Built against its walls is the 16th-century IGLESIA DE LA O, whose austere, military-looking appearance contrasts with its richly decorated Gothic interior.

Coat of arms of El Puerto de Santa María, with the Virgin Mary above the sea and a castle.

El Puerto de Santa María

The CA-603 skirts round Rota's US military base on its way to El Puerto de Santa María. The town is mainly known for its wine, and its seaside location makes it an extremely popular place in summer.

La Victoria and Ribera del Marisco. The best way to approach the town is via the main Cádiz road. Near the road to Jerez is the Monasterio de la Victoria, now a prison. It has a single-naved church and chapels opening onto a large cloister. It was founded in the 16th century by the Minim order and received the early preachers of the gospel in America. It has many reminders of the port's close relations with the New World. The *calles* de la Virgen de los Milagros and Ribera del Río lead into the town's busiest district, La Ribera del Marisco, on the banks of the Guadalete: an ideal opportunity to sample the excellent wine and seafood on the terrace of one of its restaurants. Lower down, in the Plaza de las Galeras, is the fountain from which the galleys took their water supply. It is only a few steps from the landing stage where you can board the steamer to Cádiz.

Castillo de San Marcos. The Calle Micaela Aramburu leads into the old town, where you make your way to the Plaza del Polvorista past colonial-style religious buildings, old exporters' houses and the former fish market, with its arcaded Baroque façade, now the *Resbaladero* restaurant. Nearby is the plaza of the Castillo de San Marcos, the first edifice built by the Christians after the conquest of Moorish El-Qanatir, in 1264. They also built the fortified Iglesia de Santa María (which gave its name to the town) on the site of the mosque. The Mudéjar castle is built in an unusual architectural style, in which the stonework and brickwork, polygonal towers and horseshoe arches denote a strong Moorish influence.

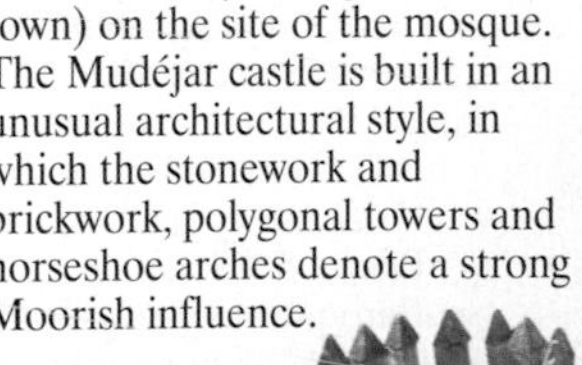

Basketwork
The gipsies of El Puerto and the Bay of Cádiz have traditionally made objects from willow. This community has produced generation upon generation of flamenco singers.

Exporters' houses
El Puerto de Santa María has large numbers of houses with warehouses, built in the 17th and 18th centuries for rich merchants who exported to America. Most are now apartment blocks. The Casa Vizarrón (above) on the Plaza del Polvorista.

Castillo de San Marcos
The castle is the symbol of El Puerto de Santa María. Built at the request of Alfonso X, between 1265 and 1270, under the direction of the master of works, Alí, it is based on the structure of the Muslim *ribats*, fortified mosques, and includes a Christian church.

RAFAEL ALBERTI
The poet Rafael Alberti was born in El Puerto de Santa María in 1902. He was a member of the "Generación del 1927" with García Lorca, Aleixandre, Salinas, Gerardo Diego and other great names in modern Spanish literature. He is the author of an important collection of poetry, a graphic and pictorial work and an autobiography, *La Arboleda Perdida*. A study center and a museum will soon be dedicated to him.

LA VICTORIA
The Convento de la Victoria was built between 1504 and 1517 in late Gothic style. It was the sepulcher of the town's lords, the dukes of Medinaceli. Gallery of the cloister (above).

"LA NIÑA"
This replica of one of Columbus's caravels crossed the Atlantic in 1990. It is anchored in El Puerto de Santa María's marina, Puerto Sherry.

The center of the complex, surrounded by a double rampart wall incorporating eight towers, is occupied by the CHURCH and a garden. The present parvis was once the parade ground. Inside the triple-naved church is a *mihrab*, an early Gothic chapel, and a series of Visigoth, Moorish and Christian pillars and capitals. Christopher Columbus is said to have stayed in the castle between 1483 and 1486 when he came to meet the dukes of Medinaceli. Although he did not sign a contract with the dukes, he did sign one with Juan de la Cosa, the armorer, mariner and cartographer whose bust can be seen in the plaza. Juan de la Cosa procured the *María Galante* (renamed the *Santa María*), and accompanied Columbus on his voyages. He was the first to feature the New World on his Mapa Mundi in 1500. The PALACIO DE ARANÍBAR (1660) stands on the same plaza. It takes its name from one of the powerful Basco-Navarrese clan that controlled most of the trade between the Bay of Cádiz and America in the 17th and 18th centuries.

BULLRINGS AND "BODEGAS". The Calle Santo Domingo leads down into the old town; No. 26 is the HOUSE OF THE POET RAFAEL ALBERTI. The streets to the left lead to the bullring and the *bodegas*. The great PLAZA DE TOROS, built in 1880, is famous throughout Spain and attests to the citizens' passion for bullfighting. The great matador Joselito used to say: "If you haven't seen the bulls of El Puerto, you haven't seen a bull." This is also the district of the vast *bodegas* of Duff, Gordon, Osborne, Terry, Caballero and other English, French and Spanish *bodegas* which, since the 18th century, have perpetuated the town's flourishing wine and brandy trade. Like those of Jerez and Sanlúcar, the *bodegas* of El Puerto are open to the public and have their own small museums ▲ *306*.

IGLESIA MAYOR PRIORAL. The Calle Santa Lucía leads to the Plaza de España, also known as the Plaza de la Iglesia, in the heart of the city. All that remains of the original structure of the Iglesia Mayor Prioral, built in freestone, in Gothic style, in the early 16th century, is the lateral Puerta del Perdón. It was renovated in the 17th century and the Puerta del Sol, a Baroque stone *retablo* in the style of Jerez, was added. The three naves are dominated by the 13th-century statue of the Virgen de los Milagros, which belonged to the castle. The most remarkable chapel is the Capilla del Sagrario, whose altar has a silver *retablo*. Opposite the church is the house of the Marquesa de Candia, now the MUSEO MUNICIPAL, which has archeological remains from the 10th century BC, discovered on the site of the ancient port. On its way to the Guadalete, the Calle Palacios crosses the Calle Larga, the main street, whose houses display coats of arms, stucco and wrought-iron work.

Puerto Real and San Fernando

You can either go direct to Cádiz on the N-443, or follow the bay via Puerto Real and San Fernando.

Puerto Real. This small town, founded in the 15th century around a natural port, was badly damaged during the wars of Succession and Independence. It has, however, retained its original urban grid system and a beautiful collection of houses representing the 17th- and 18th-century architecture of Cádiz, particularly in the Calles Ancha and Amargura. They are decorated with Baroque cornices and pinnacles, large wrought-iron grilles and reliefs carved in the conchitic limestone of the bay.

San Fernando. By 1769 San Fernando, on the island of León, was Andalusia's most important port; its buildings were reconstructed on neoclassical principles. All that remains of the old town is the 13th-century Castillo San Romualdo in the Calle Real. The two main buildings of interest are the Observatorio Astronómico (1793) in the Torre Alta district, with its historical and scientific collections, and the Panteón de los Marinos Ilustres.

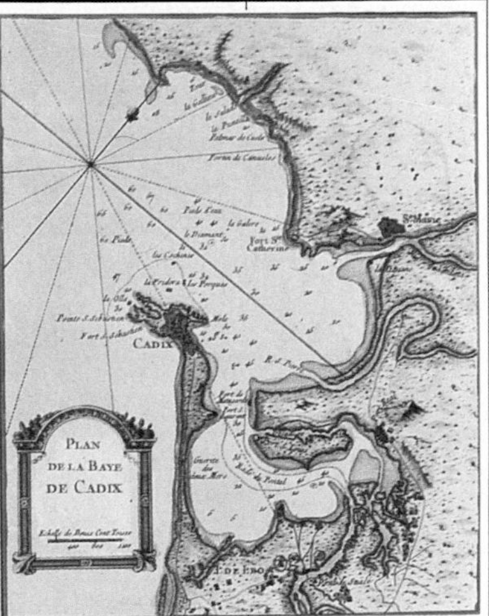

Bay of Cádiz (18th century)
The map shows the island of León and El Trocadero, near Puerto Real.

Matagorda
Near the Puerto Real and the Cádiz bridge is the Matagorda shipyard, opened in 1863. The first propeller-driven ship was built there. In the reception room, an exhibition of photographs traces the yard's history. The launching of the *Magallanes* (left) in 1920.

Town Hall, Puerto Real
This settlers' town was founded in 1483 by the Catholic monarchs.

The wines of Jerez, which date from ancient times, are the product of a successful combination of climate and soil. They were produced throughout the Muslim period, and in the Middle Ages, they were exported in vast quantities to northern Europe. An evolutionary development took place in the 18th century when, instead of the *mostos* (musts) obtained by treading, old wines began to be produced by more elaborate methods. Today Andalusian sherry is distributed throughout the world.

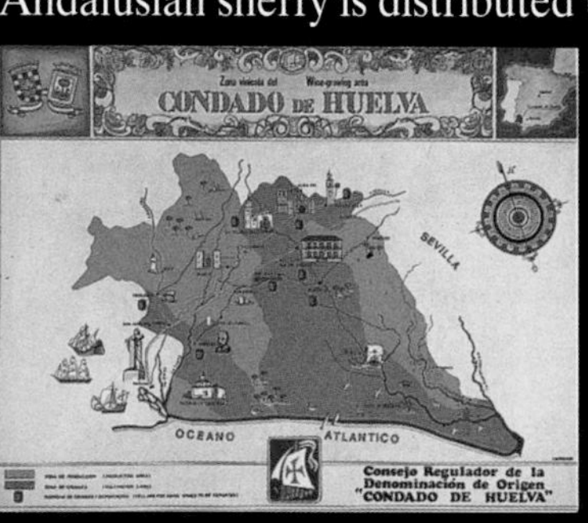

CONDADO DE HUELVA WINES ▲ *276*
As well as the *denominación de origen* "Jerez", western Andalusia also produces "Condado de Huelva" wines of a similar quality.

PRODUCING SHERRY
First of all the grape juice is left to mature in casks that are not quite full. The climate favors the formation of a film of yeast, or bloom, on the surface of the must. This first stage of development produces *finos*, or vintage sherries. If the must is brought into contact with the air, it oxidizes, matures without a bloom and produces *olorosos* or fragrant sherries. As well as this passive method of production, there is also an active method. The pulps are transferred into another cask and mixed to obtain a superior quality and greater consistency. In the rows of casks, known as *escalas* ("ladders"), the young pulps move from the *criaderas* (top rows) to the soleras (bottom rows) from which the desired quality of sherry is produced. This process takes at least five years.

Picking grapes.

Grapes in wicker baskets.

Grapes being carried by donkey, Sanlúcar.

COOPERAGE
The use of handmade American oak casks, known as *botas* and *bocoys*, is one of the secrets of producing good sherry. The *bota bodeguera*, in which it is matured, has a capacity of nearly 145 gallons.

TYPES OF VINE
Palomino and Listán are used for dry sherries, and Pedro Ximénes and Muscatel for sweet varieties.

Luxury sherries
The production of sherry and *manzanilla* requires rigorous selection and very strict controls from vine growing to the maturing process, which precludes low-priced mass production. These luxury sherries are very popular with connoisseurs.

Casks
The cooper assembles 32 or 33 oak staves, which are held in place with metal hoops.

The taster sucks the sherry through a long pipette, or *venencia*, to oxygenate it, and then pours it into the tasting glass, or *catavini*. His opinion is decisive in determining its maturity.

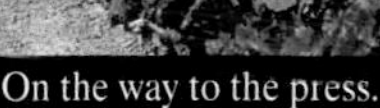
On the way to the press.

The grapes are left in the sun for several hours to ensure they are fully ripe.

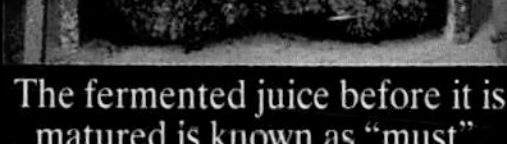
The fermented juice before it is matured is known as "must".

Jerez, xérés, sherry
This *denominación de origen* applies to wines produced in Jerez, El Puerto de Santa María and Sanlúcar (the main triangle), and in Chiclana, Puerto Real, Rota, Chipiona and Trebujena.

The main varieties are: *fino* (15–17 %), the most delicate, dry, light and golden; *manzanilla*, *fino de Sanlúcar*, paler, light and slightly bitter; *amontillado* (17–18 %), a mature *fino*, sweet, amber-colored; *oloroso* (18–20 %) matured for longer, deep golden color, dry, full-bodied; *palo cortado*, superior-quality *oloroso*; *pedro ximénes*, old sherry, very sweet and syrupy, mahogany color; *muscatel*, a rich sweet wine.

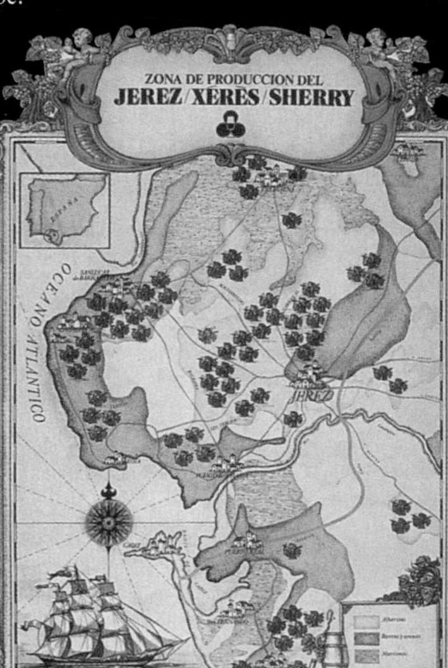

The exploitation of fishing grounds and salt, used as a preservative for the fish, have been the principal activities of the Cádiz coast since time immemorial. The Phoenicians and Romans developed the fishing industry and established numerous salting works where *garum* was produced. This sauce, made from fish that had been macerated in salt, was served with various dishes. It was even exported to Rome.

Sea salt
Constant sunshine, frequent and dry easterly winds and the vast tidal areas, have made the Cádiz coast the ideal place for salt pans. The most important are located around the bay, at El Puerto de Santa María, San Fernando and Sanlúcar de Barrameda. From April to October, salt-pan workers (photo, left) would collect the salt with broad, long-handled rakes and pile it up in "pyramids".

Salt pans of Cádiz
The salt pans were established by the Romans. They flourished from the Middle Ages until the 19th century, when the salt was exported to northern Europe and America. The 20th-century crisis reached its height in the 1970's with the introduction of industrial methods.

Catching tuna
To catch tuna, the boats form a square and then raise the net.

Exploiting the salt pans
In the center of the salt pans are the office, the warehouses, the salt mill and the yard where the salt is stacked.

Traditional salt pans
A system of low walls and sluices channels the sea water, via canals and pools, into the reservoirs where the salt crystalizes.

Fishing in the estuaries
Sea bream, bass, sole and shellfish are bred and fished in the estuaries, the network of canals and lagoons fed by salt water. This particularly saline environment is thought to give them more flavor.

Fishing with tunny nets
A barrier of nets (2½–3 miles long), anchored near the shore, is used to drive the shoals of tuna into a central chamber. Once this is full, a group of boats sets about catching the fish. This age-old method is still used on the coast between Cádiz and the Straits of Gibraltar.

"Levantá"
This is the crucial moment, when the net is thrown and harpoons are used to "catch" the tuna, which can weigh up to 1,100 lbs.

Bluefin tuna
Tunny nets are used on the migration route of the bluefin tuna, which spawns in the Mediterranean.

Export
The meat of the bluefin tuna is reputed to have the most flavor, but is also the most expensive because of the rarity of the species and the cost of fishing. All the tuna caught (approximately three thousand per year) are bought and prepared *in situ* by Japanese teams, before being exported to Japan.

Cutting up tuna (right).

PUERTA DE TIERRA Like most of the city's defenses, this gate was built in the 18th century on an older structure: the tower dates from the 16th century and the Baroque gateway, by José Barnola and Torcuado Cayón, from 1756. In front of the gate are statues of the region's patron saints.

Cádiz and its bay in 1565.

CÁDIZ

ANCIENT GADIR. Cádiz stands on a rocky island opposite the Guadalete estuary. According to the chronicles of Phoenician travelers, it was founded in 1104 BC by the mariners of Tyre. Gadir ("fortified town") was the first colony situated beyond the Pillars of Hercules and is the oldest Atlantic port in the Western World. Between the 8th and 5th century BC, it became the principal market for trade with inland Andalusia, controlling local and imported products (ceramics, luxury items) and exporting metals from the Sierra Morena (gold, silver and copper) and salt fish. Huge temples were built, including the famous temples of Melkart/Hercules and Astarte/Venus, whose lights acted as beacons for mariners out at sea. During the Roman period, Gadir increased in power and spread onto the neighboring island.

AN EVENTFUL HISTORY. Like other coastal towns, Cádiz suffered from a decline in trade under the Visigoths until, by the end of the Middle Ages, it was merely a small town open to plunder. During the Muslim period it was attacked by the Normans in 844 and 858. Alphonso X conquered and repopulated the town in 1262. It flourished once more with the discovery of America and, in 1493, Christopher Columbus set sail from Cádiz on his second voyage. It was soon considered the best Atlantic port for the voyage to the Indies, in spite of Seville's official monopoly ● *33*. Its activity made it a target for the corsair Francis Drake who, in 1587, sacked the town and determined to "singe the king of Spain's beard" by

"Cadiz, rising on the distant coast,
Calls forth a sweeter, though ignoble praise."
Lord Byron, *Childe Harold's Pilgrimage*, Canto I, LXV

Cádiz, likened to a siren of the sea by Lord Byron and the sea's brightness by Manuel Machado, is known to its inhabitants as the "New Penny".

setting fire to the galleons anchored in the bay. In 1596 it was attacked and pillaged by the Anglo-Dutch fleet of the Earl of Essex and the library of the bishop's palace, which was part of the booty, went to enrich the collections of the University of Cambridge. Cádiz recovered and flourished during the 18th century, developing all the necessary facilities for trade with America. It became a commercial and intellectual center. At the end of the century, it took part in the war against England. In 1805 Admiral Nelson defeated the powerful Spanish fleet only a few miles away, at Cape Trafalgar. During the War of Independence, French troops besieged the town from 1810 until 1812, when it was the seat of the Spanish liberal government, the Cortes. Cádiz began to decline when the Spanish colonies gained independence in 1824. The spearhead of liberalism during the Romantic period, it was modernized during the 19th and 20th centuries and became the industrial sector of the isthmus.

SANCTI PETRI
The famous Temple of Hercules stood on this island opposite the isthmus.

CONVENTO DE SANTO DOMINGO. The PUERTA DE TIERRA leads into the historic center of Cádiz, surrounded by a defensive wall that runs between the shoreline and the urban grid system. The steep Calle de las Calesas leads to the Convento de Santo Domingo, whose church was built between 1652 and 1675, and the cloister in c. 1725. The church is dedicated to the Virgen del Rosario, the town's patron saint. The stuccowork of its three naves evokes the American colonial style. The

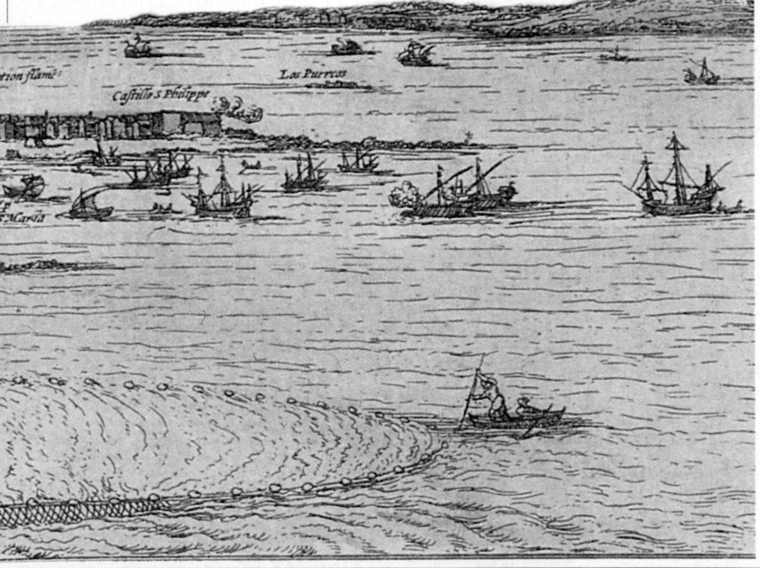

SANTO DOMINGO
The church's 17th- and 18th-century Baroque stuccowork is decorated with geometric and sculptural motifs.

retablo of the high altar and that of the so-called Chapel of the Genoese, on the right, are in Italian polychrome marble. The convent also houses *La Galeona*, another representation of the Virgen del Rosario, who accompanied the fleets of the Indies placed under her protection. The teaching-ship, the *Juan Sebastián Elcano*, continues the tradition by taking the statue on its annual round-the-world voyage. Opposite the port are the Plaza de Sevilla and the Avenida del Puerto. On the left is Cádiz's largest open space, the PLAZA DE SAN JUAN DE DIOS, the nerve center of the city. The Ayuntamiento (city hall) is situated on the south side of this busy plaza, well known for its friendly bars and restaurants.

BARRIO DEL PÓPULO. The ARCO DEL PÓPULO stands at the end of the Calle de la Pelota. It leads into the district of the same name, where the streets are steeped in the atmosphere of old Cádiz and are a turmoil of excitement at carnival time. Fading *palacios* have been converted into apartment blocks.

PLAZA DE SAN JUAN DE DIOS
The neoclassical façade of the Ayuntamiento ("city hall"), surmounted by its clock tower, dominates Cádiz's largest plaza. The first part of the edifice was built (1779–1825) by the architect Torcuado Benjumeda (1757–1836), who was extremely active in Cádiz. Work was completed in 1865. The jewel of the edifice is its luxurious Sala Capitular.

Local figures from the Romantic period: a smuggler, a sailor and a woman worker (c. 1830).

CÁDIZ IN 1782
View of the port and the town at the height of its power, showing the fortifications, its densely built houses (several stories high), the watchtowers and the fleet at anchor in the mouth of the bay.

On the left, the Calle Marqués de Cádiz leads past the CASA DEL ALMIRANTE to the tiny Plaza de San Martín. The *casa*, built in 1687, was the residence of Ignacio de Barrios, commander of the new Spanish fleet. Its Baroque entrance, decorated with marble, was made in the Genoese workshop of Andrea Andreoli, who had a number of clients in Cádiz.

IGLESIA DE SANTA CRUZ. A little further on, the Iglesia de Santa Cruz (the former cathedral) stands on the Plaza de Fray Félix. All that remains of the original edifice, founded in 1263 by Alfonso X, are some of the intersecting ribs of the vault and the baptismal fonts. The church, destroyed in the pillaging of 1596, was rebuilt in 1602 according to plans by Cristóbal de Rojas. The result was an edifice of great soberness to which a large tower was added. The original structure of the three naves, in which the pendentives of the vaults are supported by Tuscan columns, is rarely found in Andalusia. The side chapels on the left contain the votive images of the various brotherhoods, including the extremely popular "El Greñúo" of the Nazarene brotherhood. It is carried in procession during the Semana Santa, which is a particularly beautiful and moving event in Cádiz.

CATHEDRAL. The Callejón de los Piratos leads to the Plaza de la Catedral, where the apse of the huge, white-stone cathedral overlooks the Atlantic. The idea of giving the city a prestigious cathedral dates from the end of the 17th century. Vicente Acero drew an initial, ambitious plan, begun in 1722. As the work dragged on, the plans were simplified and the project directed by a series of architects, including Torcuado Cayón (from 1759) and Juan Daura who,

ARCO DE LA ROSA
The Arco de la Rosa spans the passageway leading to the Plaza de la Catedral. With the Arco del Pópulo and the Arco de los Blancos, it is one of the old gates in the fortified enclosure

wall built by Alfonso X. The medieval town corresponded to the present-day Barrio del Pópulo around the former cathedral. Its ramparts, churches and houses were rebuilt after the Anglo-Dutch attack in 1596.

WATCHTOWERS
The towers were added to a number of houses in the 17th and 18th centuries, to keep watch on maritime traffic.

CAMPO DEL SUR
This seaward-facing promenade follows the walls of El Vendaval. Rising beyond the brightly colored façades are the towers and dome (covered in yellow *azulejos*) of the cathedral.

Interior of the cathedral of Cádiz.

in 1838, completed the dome, which turned out to be smaller than originally planned. The cathedral is therefore a blend of Baroque and neoclassical styles. Its façade has a triple-arched portal and two towers. The sanctuary, in the form of a Latin cross, has three naves, an ambulatory around the apse and vaulted side chapels. The choir and the tabernacle of the high altar are centrally aligned. The crypt, below the altar, has an ambitious freestone vault almost 60 feet high, by Vicente Acero. It houses the tomb of Manuel de Falla (1876–1946), the great composer from Cádiz who introduced Spanish rhythms into classical music. The CATHEDRAL TREASURY on the Plaza del Fray Felix contains marbles, sculptures, embroidery and gold and silver work, such as the engraved silver monstrance (11 feet high), created in 1664 by Antonio Suárez to receive the custodial (1528), which was known as "El Cogollo".

PHOENICIAN SARCOPHAGI
These are the most impressive pieces in the archeological section of the Museo Provincial. The marble tombs, discovered on the isthmus of Cádiz, date from 475 to 400 BC and are unique in Europe. They are similar to the work of the stonecutters of Sidon, and the figures are clearly of Greek influence. The anthropomorphic form suggests funerary rites similar to those of Ancient Egypt.

ORATORIO DE SANTA CUEVA. The 18th-century district, with its regular layout, is reached via the Calle Compañía as far as the busy Plaza de Topete, and then the Calle Columela, which leads to the Plaza del Rosario and the Oratorio de Santa Cueva. This elliptical chapel was built by Torcuado Cayón in 1781. Its oval dome is supported by jasper columns hung with works by Goya, painted in later life (c. 1797): the *Marriage at Cana*, the *Last Supper* and the *Feeding of the Five Thousand*.

CONVENTO DE SAN FRANCISCO. The Calle del Rosario comes to an end, in the northwest, on the Plaza de San Francisco, once the courtyard of the convent of the same name. The convent, founded in 1566, was renovated in the 17th and 18th centuries. Its single-naved church has a *retablo mayor*, a masterpiece of regional Rococo art by Gonzalo Pomar (1763).

MUSEO PROVINCIAL (MUSEO DE CÁDIZ). Continue along the Calle Tinte to the Plaza de Mina, popular among the inhabitants of Cádiz as a place of relaxation and enjoyment,

A piece of Phoenician jewelry found in Cádiz.

and surrounded by a great many bars. The Museo Provincial stands on one side of the plaza. The archeological section contains Phoenician and Roman pieces, mainly found in the old town and its necropolis. The collection of 17th-century paintings in the fine-art section includes works by Ribera, Zurbarán ▲ *138*, *158*, *182*, Van Dyck, a *Holy Family* painted on copper by Rubens, and the last works of Murillo ● *91*, ▲ *138*, *182* painted for the Capuchin convent. The ethnology section traces the development of popular culture via examples of traditional crafts and the *títeres de la tía Norica*, the puppets used in street performances.

ALAMEDA DE APODACA. The Calle Antonio López leads to the Plaza de España, where there is an impressive monument to the Constitution of 1929. The Calle de Argüelles, with its CASA DE LAS QUATRO TORRES, built in 1745 for the Armenian merchant Juan de Fragela, joins the Alameda de Apodaca, the most pleasant and agreeable seafront promenade in Cádiz. To the northwest lie the BASTIÓN DE LA CANDELARIA, restored and converted into a museum, and the IGLESIA DEL CARMEN (1764), built in Caribbean colonial style.

PLAZA DE SAN ANTONIO. The promenade brings you back to the heart of the old town and the Plaza de San Antonio, whose church is surrounded by colored façades. The windows overlooking the plaza are decorated with elaborate iron or wooden grilles, which let in the air while providing protection against the wind.

ORATORIO DE SAN FELIPE NERI AND THE MUSEO MUNICIPAL. Turn right off the picturesque pedestrian precinct of the Calle Ancha into the *calles* San José and Santa Inés, where the Oratorio de San Felipe Neri has various inscriptions commemorating the official declaration of the first Spanish constitution in 1812. The deliberative assembly met in the elliptical church, built between 1688 and 1719. Its dome was damaged by the earthquake of 1755 and rebuilt in 1764. The largest of its seven chapels has a *retablo* whose center is decorated with a magnificent *Inmaculada* (1680) by Murillo.

The major part of the fine-art collection of the Museo Provincial consists of fourteen works painted by Francisco de Zurbarán for the Carthusian monastery of Jerez in 1639. They include the painting of *John Houghton* (above).

Iglesia del Carmen.

Playa de la Caleta.

Poster for the *Festival de Teatro Iberoamericano*, which takes place in Cádiz every summer.

POPULAR DISTRICTS OF CÁDIZ
The districts that have preserved the true essence of Cádiz are the *barrios* de Santa María and del Pópulo, near the cathedral, and de la Palma and de la Viña, near the Playa de la Caleta. Iglesia de la Palma (1763) (below).

Houses are often divided into small apartments. The galleries surrounding the courtyards are either open (above) or enclosed by glass.

"CHIRIGOTA"
The festivals of the carnival are an occasion for celebration and enjoyment. The groups (*coros*, *comparsas*, *chirigotas*) prepare their costumes and try out their new dance steps: *cuplés*, *pasadobles*, *popurrís*. In early February, the entire population of Cádiz is in the streets. The Barrio de la Viña, the Plaza San Antonio and the Calle Ancha (the route of the grand parade on the first Sunday of Lent) are the most crowded.

The Capilla del Sagrario has a composition of marble Italian reliefs. Next to the church, the Museo Municipal has a collection of paintings and objects relating to the region's history, including a model of Cádiz (1777–9) showing the original plans for the cathedral. These plans were never completed.

BARRIO DE LA VIÑA. The Calle Sagasta leads down into the popular district of La Viña. To the right, the TORRE DE TAVIRA, on the corner of the *calles* Solana and Real Tesoro, offers a splendid view of the town and bay. Further down the Calle Sagasta is the former HOSPITAL DE LAS MUJERES, now the bishop's palace, a magnificent Baroque edifice completed in 1749 by Luis de San Martín. Its façade has a freestone foundation and richly decorated stonework with atlantes and pilasters on the upper stories. The main staircase, with six double flights of stairs, separates two courtyards decorated with Tuscan columns, Genoese paving and Delft ceramics. Further on is the Calle de la Rosa, in the heart of the Barrio de la Viña, the birthplace of gipsy traditions. Its inhabitants live in the crowded buildings that line the narrow streets and tiny plazas, like the Plaza del Tío de la Tiza, which takes its name from a carnival character. La Viña is linked to the sea by the Playa de la Caleta, where the BAÑOS DE LA PALMA were constructed in 1926. It is bordered on either side by the fortresses built on the former Phoenician and Roman city: the CASTILLO DE SANTA CATALINA (1598) and the CASTILLO DE SAN SEBASTÍAN, erected in 1706 on an isolated reef that can be reached by way of a narrow footbridge.

CARNIVAL. The origins of this festival date from the 15th century when the town had a Genoese community. The *Erizada*, the popular seafood festival, is held in the Barrio de la Viña one month before the carnival. This is followed by the *Concurso de Coros*, *Comparsas y Chirigotas*, a competition of song and dance, held three weeks later in the TEATRO FALLA. The carnival itself takes place during the week preceding the first Sunday of Lent, known as *Piñata* after the "lucky pot" broken on that Sunday. The high point of the carnival takes place on the first and second days of February, when the streets are invaded by the crowds, masked revelers and dancers.

The White Towns route

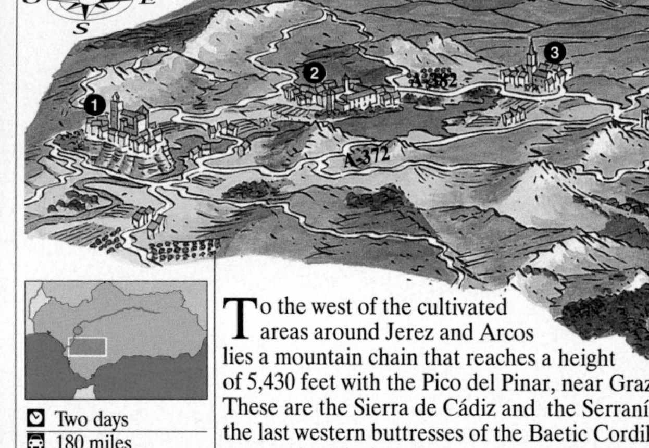

⌚ Two days
🚗 180 miles
◆ A C4-D4-E4

A NATURAL PARADISE
The region has two nature reserves: Grazalema and the Sierra de las Nieves, near Ronda (below).

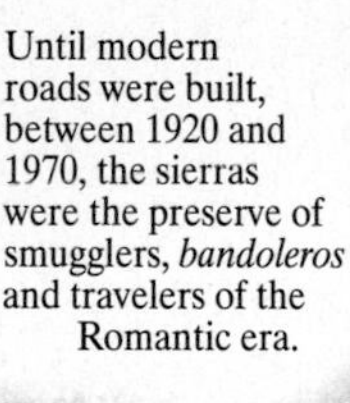

To the west of the cultivated areas around Jerez and Arcos lies a mountain chain that reaches a height of 5,430 feet with the Pico del Pinar, near Grazalema. These are the Sierra de Cádiz and the Serranía de Ronda, the last western buttresses of the Baetic Cordillera which crosses Andalusia from east to west. These mountains cover a total surface area of some 1,160 square miles to the north of the provinces of Cádiz and Málaga. They are bordered, to the north, by the Guadalete and separated, in the southeast, by the Guadiaro. Their limestone slopes, planted with cork-oaks ■ 26 and *pinsapos*, and punctuated with white towns and villages, offer landscapes of unrivalled beauty.

A BORDER REGION. The region's hilly relief has favored its isolation, its role as a border region and the preservation of vast natural areas. It was first inhabited during the Paleolithic period when tribes of hunter-gatherers sought refuge in the caves and recesses of the sierra. During the 1st millennium BC, the establishment of such towns as Arcos de la Frontera and Ronda was linked to the Roman presence. Muslim domination between the 8th and the 15th century gave the villages their characteristic features. The region, which was suited to stock-farming, was settled by Berber shepherds from North Africa, who founded numerous small towns and hamlets. The mountains were deeply affected by the Reconquest and, in 1250, became the frontier between the kingdoms of Castile

Until modern roads were built, between 1920 and 1970, the sierras were the preserve of smugglers, *bandoleros* and travelers of the Romantic era.

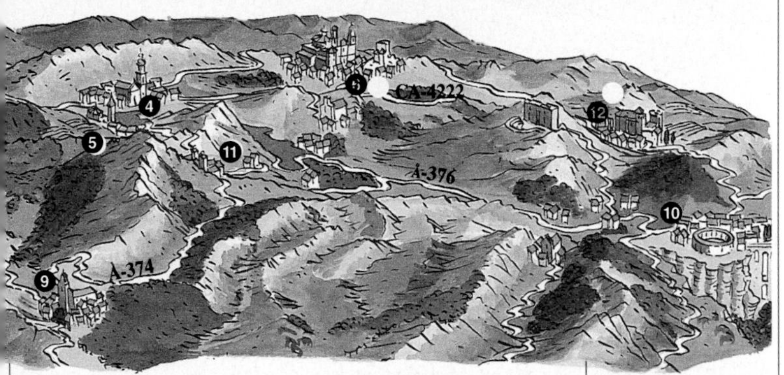

and Granada. The peaks bristled with castles and towers that, as the target of constant raids and attacks by both sides, were continually changing hands. Two eagle's nests faced each other: on one side, Arcos, a Christian military base, and on the other Ronda, which remained the capital of an independent emirate until 1485. After the Reconquest, the knights were rewarded with vast seigneuries, and until their expulsion from Spain many Mudéjars participated in the development of these great domains alongside the Christian settlers. New towns, such as Villamartín, appeared and, in the 18th century, Prado del Rey. The sierra fiercely opposed the armies of Napoleon and became the refuge of smugglers and *bandoleros* when farming declined in the 19th century. It also sheltered members of the Andalusian resistance, who harassed Franco's troops after the clashes of 1936.

Arcos de la Frontera ★

The A-382 runs from Jerez to Arcos, reputedly the most beautiful of Spain's "white towns".

Myth and history. According to legend, the town was founded by one of Noah's sons at the time of the Flood. Numerous remains have been unearthed here, from the Tartessian and also the Phoenician and Roman periods ● *30*. Because of its location, which was easily defensible and had an abundant supply of water and orchards, Arcos thrived during the Muslim period and acquired its urban appearance. In the 11th century it was ruled by a Berber prince from the Jizrun tribe. Arcos surrendered after the conquest of Seville, in 1248. After the Mudéjar rebellion in 1264, the Muslim inhabitants were driven out and the town was repopulated by Christians. It passed into the hands of the house of Ponce de León ▲ *172*, counts and dukes of Arcos, who used it to launch their military campaigns against the western flank of Granada.

The white towns
The mountain itinerary from Cádiz to Ronda has become known as the Ruta de los Pueblos Blancos ("White Towns"), as the towns on the route all have the same whitewashed walls and red-tiled roofs. Their tightly packed houses, linked by narrow, winding streets, cling to the hillsides and are usually dominated by the remains of a castle.

The houses of Grazalema (above).

ARCOS
Arcos is perched on a peak overlooking the Guadalete. The towers of Santa María and San Pedro stand out clearly above the town. One of the most charming features of Arcos is its popular architecture. A courtyard (right).

THE OLD TOWN. La Corredera is the road that winds its way up into Arcos. Beyond the Hospital de San Juan de Dios, the Cuesta de Belén climbs to the Palacio de los Condes del Águila with its magnificent, 15th-century Gothic façade. A narrow ramp, whose bends are protected by columns, leads to the Plaza del Cabildo occupied by the town hall, the Parador, the castle and the IGLESIA DE SANTA MARÍA. The interior of this former mosque has some extremely impressive star-vaulting and several 14th-century murals combining Italian and Mudéjar influences. The castle is a former Moorish *alcázar*, renovated in 1460. According to legend, before setting off on a journey from which he would not return, King Abdun Ibn Jizrun had the woman he loved immured alive in the *alcázar*. The woman's soul took the form of a bird of prey which, on nights when the moon was full, could be seen soaring above the town in search of her loved one. The "balcony" of Arcos overlooks the sheer drop on one side of the plaza, offering the visitor a most spectacular view.

DISTRICTS AND TRADITIONS. The hilly streets lead under small arches and past seigneurial residences toward San Pedro, the town's other great parish church. Its impressive freestone façade-tower was added, in 1765, to the first structure, begun in the 14th century. Steep streets lead down to the PUERTA DE LA MATRERA, part of the 11th-century walls, and

SANTA MARÍA D'ARCOS
The church was built in the 14th century and rebuilt in the 16th, in flamboyant Gothic style. Its uncompleted Gothic tower dates from 1758.

"Arcos de la Frontera is one of these villages: imagine the *meseta*... rising, falling, undulating; and scatter it with small, white houses."

Azorín, *Los Pueblos*

the lower town or *barrio bajo* with its ASILO DE LA CARIDAD, an elegant, colonial-style building (1779). This district has a number of mills and popular dwellings that inspired Manual de Falla's *Sombrero de Tres Picos*. In Arcos the Semana Santa ● *44* celebrations culminate at Easter when the *toro de Aleluya* is released in the streets.

ZAHARA DE LA SIERRA
This fortified town, which guarded the northern access route to the Serranía de Ronda, was bitterly disputed during the frontier wars. After being conquered by the Catelans in 1407, it was repeatedly attacked. The Muslim affront in 1481 gave the Catholic monarchs the excuse to launch their ultimate offensive against the kingdom of Granada.

FRONTERA DEL GUADALETE

The A-382 follows the northern slope of the sierra, linking the small towns perched high above the Guadalete.

BORNOS. This small Iberian and then Muslim town experienced its hour of glory during the Renaissance, when the Riberas, its lords and patrons, built a castle and superb gardens in the 16th century. Its Gothic IGLESIA DE SANTO DOMINGO has a magnificent 17th-century Baroque *retablo*. Bornos's several convents include the 16th-century CONVENT OF CORPUS CHRISTI, with its beautiful, Sevillian-style courtyard.

VILLAMARTÍN. The town was founded in 1520 by the farmers and shepherds who colonized the area, abandoned after the frontier wars. It is dominated by the IGLESIA DE NUESTRA SEÑORA DE LAS VIRTUDES, built in the 16th century and later renovated, which has a painting by Bocanegra. Villamartín is renowned for its saddlery.

OLVERA
Like many hilltop villages, Olvera is dominated by a fortress.

ALGODONALES. This immaculately whitewashed, 16th-century village stands on the Sierra de Líjar. The portals and 130-foot tower of the parish church (1773–84) make it the most impressive monument in the sierra.

ZAHARA DE LA SIERRA. The houses of Zahara de la Sierra cling to the slopes of a rocky peak, facing Algodonales. This hilltop town, which has had an eventful history, is crowned by the dungeon of a 13th-century Nazarite castle. It provides an extremely picturesque setting for an important Corpus Christ celebration. The nearby hermitage of La Garganta Verde ("green gorge"), built in a cave bristling with stalactites and stalagmites, is open to the public.

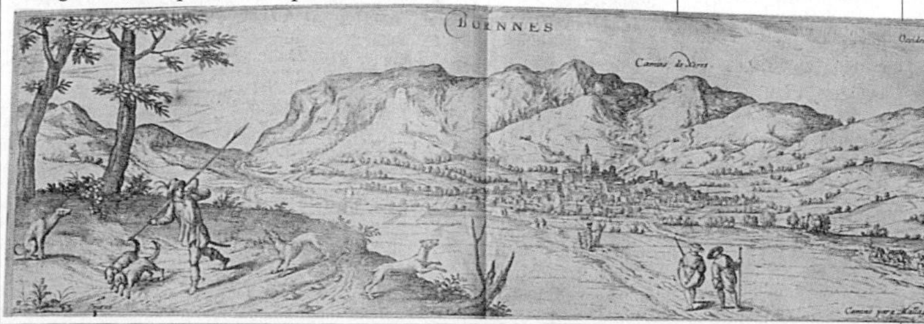

Bornos on a 16th-century engraving.

EL PINAR
This limestone mountain, in the heart of the nature reserve of the Sierra de Grazalema, has the heaviest rainfall on the Iberian peninsula. Its forests of pines are unique in Europe and constitute one of the natural riches of the reserve.

BENAMAHOMA
Place names beginning with *ben*, an Arabic word meaning "son of", attest to the Moorish and Berber origin of certain villages in the sierra: for example, Benaocaz, Benaoján and Benamahoma.

UBRIQUE LEATHER
Ubrique is famous for its leatherwork, a craft that dates back to the Moorish period but flourished in the 18th century with the adoption of modern tanning methods. From the manufacture of shoe soles, production extended to incorporate morocco-leatherwork by Maltese craftsmen. In the 20th century the Catalan Emilio de Santa María laid the foundations of the trade's present success by developing its international commercialization.

OLVERA. Olvera's architecture bears the mark of a lasting Moorish influence. The upper part of the town, surrounded by ramparts, is dominated by a 12th-century Moorish citadel, which was strengthened by the Castilians who conquered it in 1327. This frontier post granted asylum to criminals if they promised to take up arms, which gave rise to the popular refrain: "kill a man and go to Olvera". Its impressive neoclassical Iglesia de la Encarnación was completed in 1843 with the financial help of the Duke of Osuna, Lord of Olvera. The interior is clad in Italian marble.
SETENIL. The CA-4222 leads to Setenil via the town of Torre-Alháquime, dominated by the Castillo del Cementerio. Setenil is also known as Setenil de las Bodegas because, until recently, it was a wine-producing town. With its houses built into the rock, worn down by the Río Trejo, it has a somewhat fantastical appearance. The village still has a Moorish dungeon and a Gothic church, built after the Christian conquest in 1484. A mile or so away EL GASTOR, perched 1,700 feet above a gorge (El Lagarín), is known as the "belvedere of the white towns" because of its panoramic views.

THE HEART OF THE SIERRA

From Arcos the A-372 climbs into the highest and steepest regions of the Sierra de Cádiz.
PRADO DEL REY. A minor road leads to this former settlers' village, founded in 1768 by Charles III with a view to converting former pasture into cultivated land. Its typically 18th-century, regular layout is based around the town hall and the church (1830).
UBRIQUE. This is the most active and productive town in the sierra. At the end of the 15th century the village founded by the Muslims, now Ubrique el Alto, became a refuge for Mudéjars as well as welcoming new settlers.

From the 16th century onward, the town continued to expand as a result of its tanneries. The IGLESIA DE SAN ANTONIO, with its fine bell tower, is the most impressive monument in the old town, which also includes the parish church, the 16th-century Iglesia de la O, and the great Capuchin monastery (1660). Most of the leather shops are found on the intersection of the avenues in the lower part of the town. As well as the traditional *petacas* (cigarette cases) and *carteras de ganadero* (herdsmen's bags), they also sell all kinds of modern articles. The road to Grazalema offers a fine view of the white village of BENAOCAS, clinging to a rocky hillside, before passing through VILLALUENGA DEL ROSARIO, with its magnificent amphitheater carved out of the rock.

NATURE RESERVE OF GRAZALEMA. The reserve covers a total area of 127,740 acres and includes thirteen parishes. The information center and main entrance are situated in EL BOSQUE, a village that grew up around the hunting lodges of the dukes of Arcos. The Sierra de Margarita includes some extremely rare ecosystems. Its pine forest, which covers an area of 988 acres between Grazalema, Zahara and Benamahoma, has been declared part of the World Network of Reserves in the Biosphere by UNESCO. Common oaks and laurels surround the viewpoint on the PUNTO DEL BOYAR. The oak forests are concentrated in the GARGANTA VERDE ("green gorge") on the slopes around Zahara, interrupted by the Punto de las Palomas (4,450 feet). The reserve is an ideal place for walks and has a wide range of fauna: roe-deer, goats, red deer, golden eagles and griffon vultures.

GRAZALEMA. This originally Berber town (Benzalema) nestles in a valley in the Sierra del Endrinal, at a height of 2,715 feet. It is one of the small towns of the sierra where the Muslim influence is most visible. Its textile industry, now in decline, made it very prosperous in the 17th century when its *iglesias* de la Encarnación, de la Aurora and de San José were built.

TEXTILES
The mountain pastures favored the development of a traditional textile industry, which was at its most prosperous in the 19th century. There are still looms at Arcos, Ronda and Grazalema, renowned for its mantillas ● 42.

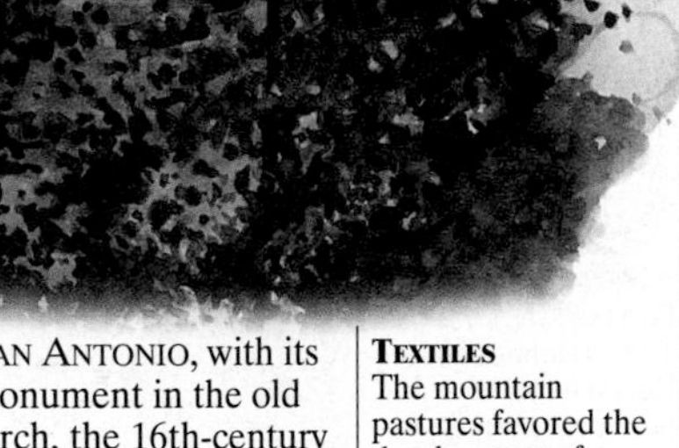

CUEVA DE LA PILETA
The Cueva de la Pileta, near Benaoján, is decorated with cave paintings.

EL TAJO
This narrow gorge, some 330 feet deep and over a quarter of a mile long, was carved out by the waters of the Guadalevín. It is crossed by the Puente Nuevo, built between 1751 and 1793.

OUTLAWS
The mountains of Ronda were the preserve of bandits for centuries. They sheltered Mozarabic opponents to the Córdoba government in the 9th century, Pedro Machuca and his three hundred brigands in the late 16th century, and famous smugglers such as El Tempranillo and Tragabuches in the 19th century. Pasos Largos, the last of these *bandoleros*, was shot down in 1934. A 19th-century inhabitant of Ronda (above) with his *catite* (a kind of crush hat), jacket, cloak, blunderbuss and cigar.

ROMAN THEATER, ACINIPO
The theater still has its tiered seats, carved out of the limestone rock, and stage wall.

SERRANÍA DE RONDA

The A-376 enters the province of Málaga and climbs through the foothills of the mountains of Ronda.

CUEVA DE LA PILETA. The karstic reliefs of Montejaque and Benaoján are honeycombed with caves that were inhabited in the distant past. The CUEVA DEL GATO on the way out of Benaoján is a potholers' paradise with almost 3 miles of galleries bristling with stalactites and stalagmites. About 2½ miles south of Benaoján, the CUEVA DE LA PILETA, discovered in 1905, has some magnificent cave paintings that are about 25,000 years old, and some beautiful rock formations. The chambers are decorated with reindeer, goats, bulls, horses, fish, abstract symbols, and in the so-called El Santuario chamber, simplified human forms.

ACINIPO TO RONDA. The archeological site of Acinipo lies about 8 miles north-west of Ronda. Excavations have revealed that it corresponds to a Phoenician settlement that flourished during Roman times. It is thought to have been razed by the Vandals in 429 and then abandoned. The little-known Celtic village of Arunda stood on the opposite slope (probably in the 6th century BC) and is thought to have become the Roman town of Laurus ("castle of the laurel") which later became Ronda.

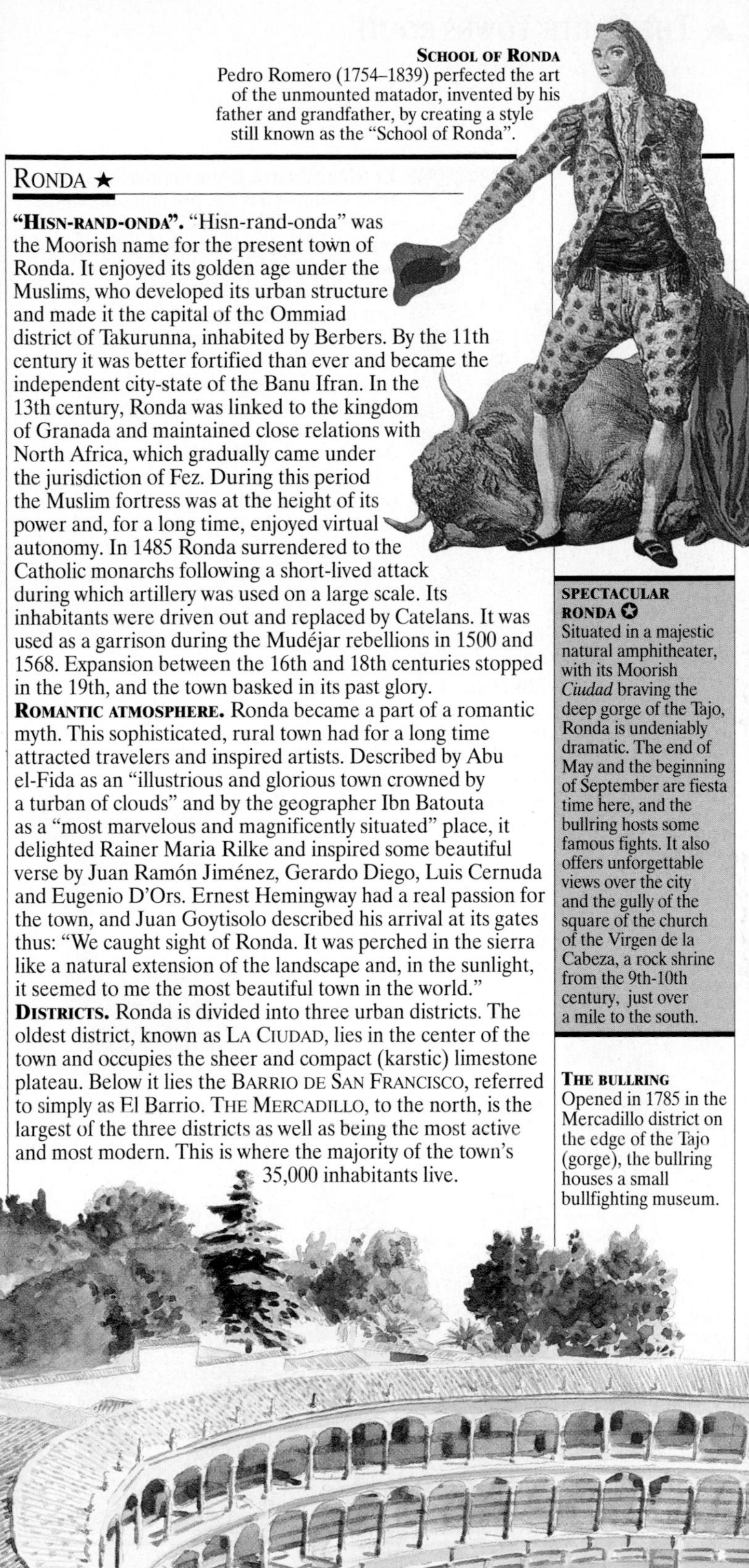

School of Ronda
Pedro Romero (1754–1839) perfected the art of the unmounted matador, invented by his father and grandfather, by creating a style still known as the "School of Ronda".

Ronda ★

"Hisn-rand-onda". "Hisn-rand-onda" was the Moorish name for the present town of Ronda. It enjoyed its golden age under the Muslims, who developed its urban structure and made it the capital of thc Ommiad district of Takurunna, inhabited by Berbers. By the 11th century it was better fortified than ever and became the independent city-state of the Banu Ifran. In the 13th century, Ronda was linked to the kingdom of Granada and maintained close relations with North Africa, which gradually came under the jurisdiction of Fez. During this period the Muslim fortress was at the height of its power and, for a long time, enjoyed virtual autonomy. In 1485 Ronda surrendered to the Catholic monarchs following a short-lived attack during which artillery was used on a large scale. Its inhabitants were driven out and replaced by Catelans. It was used as a garrison during the Mudéjar rebellions in 1500 and 1568. Expansion between the 16th and 18th centuries stopped in the 19th, and the town basked in its past glory.
Romantic atmosphere. Ronda became a part of a romantic myth. This sophisticated, rural town had for a long time attracted travelers and inspired artists. Described by Abu el-Fida as an "illustrious and glorious town crowned by a turban of clouds" and by the geographer Ibn Batouta as a "most marvelous and magnificently situated" place, it delighted Rainer Maria Rilke and inspired some beautiful verse by Juan Ramón Jiménez, Gerardo Diego, Luis Cernuda and Eugenio D'Ors. Ernest Hemingway had a real passion for the town, and Juan Goytisolo described his arrival at its gates thus: "We caught sight of Ronda. It was perched in the sierra like a natural extension of the landscape and, in the sunlight, it seemed to me the most beautiful town in the world."
Districts. Ronda is divided into three urban districts. The oldest district, known as La Ciudad, lies in the center of the town and occupies the sheer and compact (karstic) limestone plateau. Below it lies the Barrio de San Francisco, referred to simply as El Barrio. The Mercadillo, to the north, is the largest of the three districts as well as being thc most active and most modern. This is where the majority of the town's 35,000 inhabitants live.

Spectacular Ronda ✪
Situated in a majestic natural amphitheater, with its Moorish *Ciudad* braving the deep gorge of the Tajo, Ronda is undeniably dramatic. The end of May and the beginning of September are fiesta time here, and the bullring hosts some famous fights. It also offers unforgettable views over the city and the gully of the square of the church of the Virgen de la Cabeza, a rock shrine from the 9th-10th century, just over a mile to the south.

The bullring
Opened in 1785 in the Mercadillo district on the edge of the Tajo (gorge), the bullring houses a small bullfighting museum.

BAÑOS ÁRABES The Arab baths were built at the end of the 13th or beginning of the 14th century. Their horseshoe arches, resting on brick pillars, support vaults with star-shaped vents.

EL MERCADILLO. If you approach Ronda from Cádiz or Seville, you enter the town via El Mercadillo. The district already existed in the Muslim period, but did not begin to expand until the 16th (lower part of the district) and 18th–19th centuries (the part near the Tajo). In this latter part stands the HOTEL DE LA REINA VICTORIA, whose gardens on the edge of the gorge contain a statue of Rainer Maria Rilke. The Austrian poet and author wrote his *Trilogie espagnole* (*Spanish Trilogy*) and other poems here during the winter of 1912. His room (No. 208) has been converted into a small museum. Climbing from north to south toward the Puente Nuevo, via the *calles* de Juan Villegas Redondo and de la Virgen de la Paz, you come to the IGLESIA DE LA MERCED (1585), the ALAMEDA DEL TAJO, an avenue with a viewing platform, and the MAESTRANZA, the oldest *plaza de toros* in Spain. Every year, on September 1, the *corrida goyesca* recreates the atmosphere of an 18th-century *corrida*, in honor of Pedro Romero, the famous matador of Ronda. Beyond the Maestranza lies the Carrera Espinel, the main street of the Mercadillo, with its many bars and shops. It is named after the local writer and musician, Vicente Espinel (1550–1624), who added a fifth string to the guitar, and wrote the picaresque novel *Vida del Escudero Marcos de Obregón* (*Life of Marcos de Obregón*). A little further on is the busy Plaza de España at one end of the Puente Nuevo, the spectacular bridge built by José Martín de Aldehuela (1802) who was also the architect of the Maestranza.

ANIYA LA GITANA (1855–1933) One of Ronda's great popular flamenco singers.

SANTA MARÍA The collegiate church, which dominates the main plaza of La Ciudad, was built on the site of a mosque. Its brick tower (c. 1523) is in Mudéjar style. Its balcony was added in 1570 as a stand for watching street events.

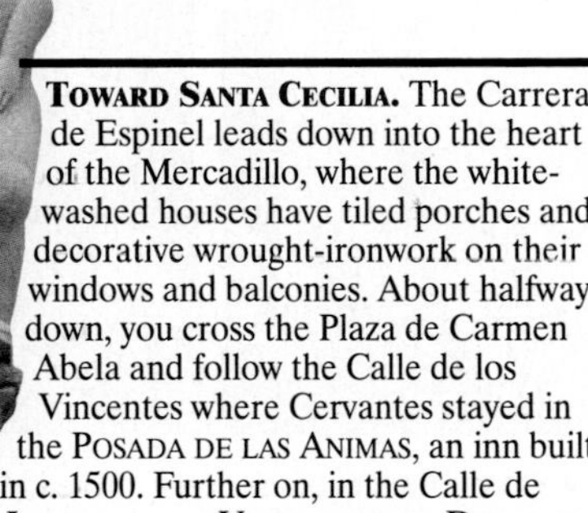

TOWARD SANTA CECILIA. The Carrera de Espinel leads down into the heart of the Mercadillo, where the white-washed houses have tiled porches and decorative wrought-ironwork on their windows and balconies. About halfway down, you cross the Plaza de Carmen Abela and follow the Calle de los Vincentes where Cervantes stayed in the POSADA DE LAS ANIMAS, an inn built in c. 1500. Further on, in the Calle de Santa Cecilia, is the IGLESIA DE LA VIRGEN DE LOS DOLORES (1734), decorated with effigies of condemned souls. On the tiny Plaza de la FUENTE DE LOS OCHO CAÑOS stands the former IGLESIA DE SANTA CECILIA, now the Iglesia del Padre de Jesús. It was built in the 15th and 16th centuries, in Gothic style, and has an impressive freestone façade-tower. Next to the church, the former CONVENTO DE LA MADRE DE DIOS (mid-16th century) is in Mudéjar style, incorporating Gothic and classical elements. The Guadalevín separates El Mercadillo from the district of La Ciudad, over the originally Roman Puente San Miguel (or Viejo), a 14th-century Moorish bridge, restored in 1616.

LA CIUDAD. Churches, convents, palaces and seigneurial residences are centered on the plateau, surrounded by ramparts and gorges. To the right of the Puente San Miguel is the Calle Alejo Linares and the Casa del Rey Moro. According to legend, it stands on the site of the palace of the Merinid prince, Abd el-Malik, the son of the sultan of Fez who proclaimed himself King of Ronda in 1333. A flight of 365 steps leads

PRE-COLUMBIAN SCULPTURES
These decorate the façade of the Palacio del Marqués de Salvatierra (1798). The descendants of Montezuma, himself a descendant of the last Aztec king, settled in Ronda.

PALACIO DE RONDA
There are a number of seigneurial residences in the narrow streets of Ronda. One of the

most remarkable is the Casa del Rey Moro (top), on the edge of the Tajo. This 18th-century palace is surrounded by terraces and gardens designed in the 1920's by J. N. Forestier. The Casa de Mondragón (above) is renovated in Mudéjar style.

"[Ronda] is where you should go if you ever go to Spain on a honeymoon or if you ever bolt with anyone. The entire town and as far as you can see in any direction is romantic background."
Ernest Hemingway, *Death in the Afternoon*

RAMPARTS
The much-restored remains of the Moorish defenses (late 13th century) can still be seen to the west of the town. In the background is the Iglesia del Espíritu Santo, completed in 1505.

ARCO DE FELIPE V
The arch was built in 1742 at the end of the road linking El Mercadillo with La Ciudad, via the Puente Viejo.

SMUGGLERS
The mountains between Gibraltar and Ronda are crossed by numerous smugglers' paths.

HOUSE OVERLOOKING THE TAJO
The house (right) has characteristically irregular windows.

down to the bottom of the gorge and La Mina, the 13th-century structure that harnessed the spring to provide water for La Ciudad. The old curse, "Go and die in Ronda carrying water skins", evokes the sad fate of the prisoners who had to carry the water up to the town. On the far side of the tiny Plaza del Sillón del Moro are the PALACIO DEL MARQUÉS DE SALVATIERRA and the ARCO DE FELIPE V. In the Calle Teniente Gordo to the right you can see one of the few remaining 14th-century Moorish houses, the CASA DEL GIGANTE, and the minaret-tower of SAN SEBASTIÁN, from the same period, with its delicate brick cladding. Further on, the Plaza Mayor is bordered by the arcaded façade of the town hall (1734) and the IGLESIA DE SANTA MARÍA DE LA ENCARNACIÓN. This remarkable collegiate church stands on the site of a 13th-century mosque; the *mihrab* still remains. The narrow streets lead to the Plaza del Campillo, which offers a magnificent view of the Tajo. At the far end, on the right, the Camino de los Molinos winds toward the Puente Nuevo, passing beneath the Moorish Arcos del Viento and del Cristo. To the left it leads to the PALACIO DE MONDRAGÓN (now the municipal museum), a beautiful 15th-century Mudéjar residence with a 16th-century portal. The palaces of Abu Melik and Ahmed al-Zegrí, the last Muslim governor of Ronda, once stood within its enclosure wall. Continue south, via the Plaza de la Duquesa de Parcent and the Calle Acminan, to the IGLESIA DEL ESPIRITU SANTO, in Gothic style.

EL BARRIO. The huge circular towers and metalwork arches of the Moorish PUERTA ALMOCÁBAR (13th century) and the classical PUERTA CARLOS V (16th century) open onto the Barrio de San Francisco. The Alameda (avenue) crosses the network of streets bordered by rustic-style houses, and leads to the CONVENTO DE SAN FRANCISCO. The former Franciscan convent (early 16th century) has a beautiful Isabelline Gothic portal ● *70*.

Eastern Andalusia

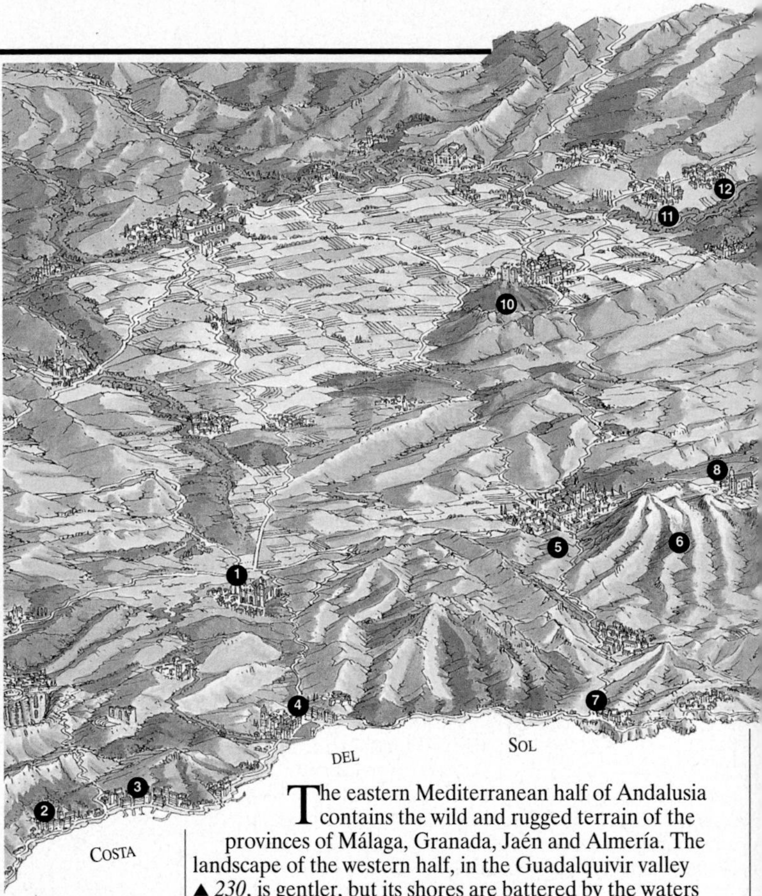

The eastern Mediterranean half of Andalusia contains the wild and rugged terrain of the provinces of Málaga, Granada, Jaén and Almería. The landscape of the western half, in the Guadalquivir valley ▲ *230*, is gentler, but its shores are battered by the waters of the Atlantic. This is a huge region which encompasses densely populated urban centers and tourist attractions, areas of intensive farming and dynamic local economy, as well as enormous stretches of land which are barely populated at all. It is exceptionally rich in natural resources, and ancient traditions struggle to survive. The Baetic Cordillera range cuts across eastern Andalusia from east to west, from Jaén to Cádiz, an undulating chain of limestone rock formations which marks out the southern edge of the Guadalquivir valley. The peaks of the Sierra Nevada rise up to the south, their slopes plunging into the Mediterranean,

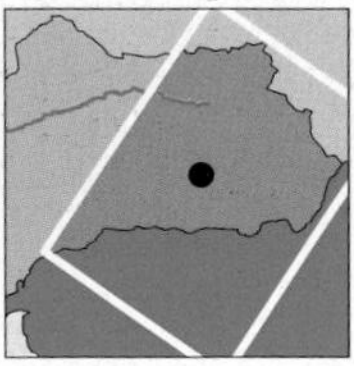

◆ **A** F4-5

◆ **B** A4-5, B2-5, C1-5, D1-5, E2-5

THE ROOF OF THE IBERIAN PENINSULA
The Sierra Nevada boasts the highest peaks in the Iberian peninsula, Mulhacén (11,420 feet) and Veleta (11,129 feet). On the southern slopes of these snow-capped mountains are Las Alpujarras (opposite).

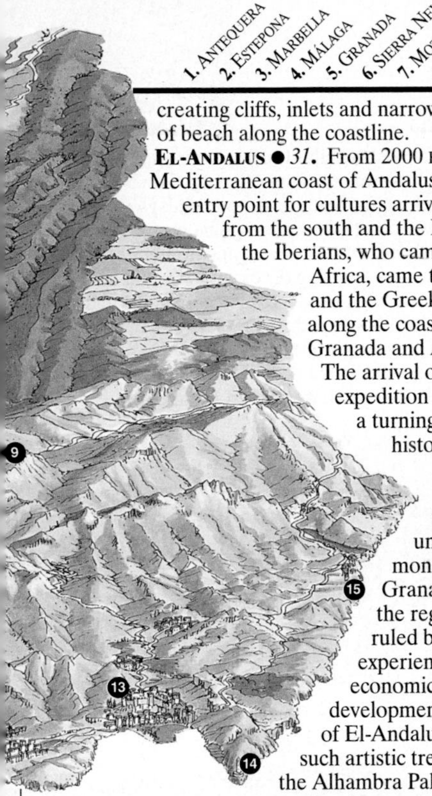

1. Antequera 2. Estepona 3. Marbella 4. Málaga 5. Granada 6. Sierra Nevada 7. Motril 8. Guadix 9. Baza 10. Jaén 11. Baeza 12. Úbeda 13. Almería 14. Cap de Gata 15. Mojácar

creating cliffs, inlets and narrow stretches of beach along the coastline.

El-Andalus ● *31*. From 2000 BC the Mediterranean coast of Andalusia was an entry point for cultures arriving by sea from the south and the Levant. After the Iberians, who came from North Africa, came the Phoenicians and the Greeks, settling along the coasts of Málaga, Granada and Almería.

The arrival of a Muslim expedition in 711 was a turning point in the history of western Andalucia.

For more than 800 years, until the Catholic monarchs seized Granada in 1492, the region was ruled by Islam and experienced huge economic and cultural development. The legacy of El-Andalus includes such artistic treasures as the Alhambra Palace ▲ *338*, as well as innumerable customs to do with food and farming. The former capital of the Nasrid emirate, Granada established itself as the region's main administrative town after the Reconquest, while Málaga remained its economic heart.

Epilogue to Islamic Spain
In 1492 the kingdom of Granada, the last enclave of Muslim Spain, fell. Moriscos were the Muslims who converted to Christianity and remained therc until their final expulsion in the 17th century.

Antequera

This town sits in a vast fertile plain at the foot of the Sierra del Torcal, a limestone mountain transformed into a whimsical maze of fantastically shaped rocks by the wind and rain. At the geographical center of Andalusia, Antequera has been inhabited since the Bronze Age, as can be seen from the imposing megalithic monuments from the 2nd and 3rd centuries BC in the northeast of the town: the Caves of Menga (whose funerary chamber is 82 feet long, 20 feet wide and 13 feet high), Viera and El Romeral. The Alcazaba, an Arab fortress captured by the Christians in 1410, crowns the site of the medieval city, near the Renaissance Colegiata de Santa Maria la Major. The churches and palaces of limestone and brick create one of the most beautiful ensembles of Renaissance and Baroque architecture in Andalusia. The iglesia de San Sebastian on the plaza of the same name is unmissable, as are the capela de la Virgen del Sorrocco, on plaza del Portichuelo, and the Palacio de Najera, which houses the Municipal Museum.

The Mediterranean coast
The coastline of Málaga, Granada and Almería is jagged and rocky, its enchanting inlets and sandy beaches bathed by the Mediterranean. Below, the Torre de Cautor (La Mámola).

COSTA DEL SOL

This is one of the most popular tourist destinations in the world thanks to its warm and sunny climate. The N-340 freeway runs the length of the coast from Málaga for more than 90 miles toward Gibraltar, through beautiful countryside, lined with an ever-increasing number of holiday homes, leisure centers, housing developments, golf courses and marinas, linking what used to be small fishing villages.

ESTEPONA. The livelihood of this peaceful village was once dependent on fishing and farming. It nestles beneath the Sierra Bermeja and the Sierra de las Nieves, and it is this beautiful natural setting and more than 12 miles of beach that have made tourism its main business. Despite the tourists it has still managed to retain its small-town Andalusian charm.

MARBELLA. Founded in 1600 BC by the Phoenicians, Marbella was, according to Pliny, already a holiday destination in Roman times. Sheltered by the Sierra Blanca, its climate is good all year round, and it is the Costa del Sol's most cosmopolitan town. The rich and famous come here to relax and enjoy themselves. Spend an afternoon wandering through the alleyways, squares and gardens of the historic town center, and stop off at the 16th-century town hall, which houses the Municipal Museum. The MUSEUM OF CONTEMPORARY SPANISH ENGRAVING, one of the best of its kind, also deserves a visit. The city center is nevertheless mostly made up of hotels, apartment blocks and large areas of flat parkland, but there is a beautiful marina at nearby PUERTO BANUS which attracts luxurious yachts and sailing boats from all over the world.

BEACH RESORTS
Fuengirola and Torremolinos were once Phoenician and Roman colonies and trading posts, with ancient ruins and fortifications such as the Almoravid Castillo de Sohail. They have now been transformed into tourist complexes with good terrace cafés specializing in fish and shellfish.

Ojén, a mountain village in the hills behind Marbella.

PABLO PICASSO
(1881–1973)
Although he spent only the first ten years of his life in Málaga, it was here that Picasso discovered his vocation. In 1988 the Fundación Casa Natal de Picasso was opened in his childhood home.

MÁLAGA

According to Strabo, the Phoenicians founded the town of Malaka. The Carthagians followed, and then the Romans,

The Alcazaba and the Cathedral

The Archeological Museum, housed in the galleries of the Puerta de Granada in the Alcazaba, has a wonderful collection of Arab gilt ceramics. In the living quarters of the former governors, reached through the Granada Gate, are palaces, courtyards and fine gardens.

who developed the town center. In 711 it was seized by the Moors who made it the capital of a small state/emirate. It was conquered by the Catholic monarchs in 1488. With a population of more than 500,000, it is now the second largest city in Andalusia, a tourist attraction both for its beaches and its historical architecture. The Semana Santa celebrations in Málaga, as amazing as those in Seville ● *44*, have been declared a national tourist attraction. Some thirty brotherhoods process through the streets with a parade of monumental floats. The float of Jesus the Bountiful has retained the power to pardon a prisoner since the reign of Charles III. Málaga is also famous for its fish and seafood restaurants around the Alameda, and on the seafront in the suburbs of Pedregalejo and El Palo.

Alcazaba and the castle of Gibralfaro. These are the most important Muslim sites in Málaga, situated in a sheltered enclave to the southwest of the city. The Alcazaba, an old Roman fortress, was built in the 11th century and modified 200 years later. Now the living quarters belonging to the former governors are restored, the visitor can see the towers, the gates, the plaster sculptures and the gardens. The 14th-century Castle of Gibralfaro, linked to the fortress by a long, double wall, stands on a hill.

Cathedral. The cathedral, on the Plaza del Obispo, is the most important monument in the city. It was constructed on top of an ancient mosque during the 16th, 17th and 18th centuries, and has a Gothic floor plan, a Renaissance high altar, Baroque vaults and a Baroque façade and tower. It was never finished, and its missing tower earned it the nickname "La Manquita" ("the one-armed lady"). The choir stalls, which were sculpted in the middle of the 17th century, are decorated with forty statues of saints by Pedro de Mena. The other remarkable feature is the painting of the *Triumph of the Virgin* by Alonso Cano ▲ *293*, which adorns the third chapel on the right aisle.

Museo de Bellas Artes. Housed in the Palace of the Counts of Buenvista in Plaza San Agustín (a grand Renaissance building with two courtyards), it displays paintings from the 16th- and 17th-century Flemish school and by Alonso Cano, Murillo and Zurbarán, as well as examples of Málagan painting and works from Picasso's childhood.

"Las verdiales"
These songs from Málaga are said to be older than the *cante jondo* ● *54*. They are sung to the accompaniment of guitars, tambourines, flutes, cymbals and sometimes the violin, with a single dancer, but sometimes two or three. Groups known as *pandas* celebrate festivals such as San Juan (June 24), San Andrés (November 30) and the Innocents (December 28).

The Sanctuary of Victory, and Málaga in the distance.

BOABDIL
Nicknamed "El Rey Chico" ("the Boy King"), and known as Boabdil (from his real name Abu 'Abd Allah) he was the last ruler of the Nasrid dynasty and of Islamic Spain. As Muhammad XI, he was King of Granada (1482 –3, and 1486–92), and sought exile in Morocco after his defeat by the Catholic Monarchs. His rather bumpy career has inspired many artists.

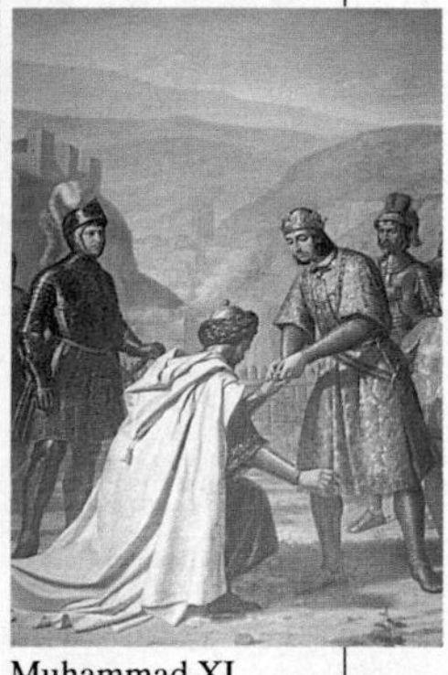

Muhammad XI (Boabdil) surrendering the keys of Granada to Ferdinand III.

GRANADA ★

Granada is the capital of eastern Andalusia, situated at the top of the fertile Genil valley, in the foothills of the Sierra Nevada. First on every traveler's list of places to visit, this fascinating city, with a population of 300,000, has a history brimming with myths. The amazing richness of its history, and the unforgettable countryside which surrounds it, give the city an irresistible appeal.

FROM ELVIRA TO GHARNATA. Granada's charm derives from a combination of eastern and western influences. It all began with the tiny Iberian settlement of Iliberis which prospered at the time of the Romans and the Visigoths under the name of Elvira. The town was the seat of the first Spanish council in the 4th century AD. Some years after the arrival of the Muslims, the inhabitants moved across to the neighboring hill, Gharnata el-Jehud, which had until then mainly been inhabited by Jews. In the 11th century this settlement rapidly developed into one of the many principalities of the fragmented El-Andalus (Muslim Spain ● *31*), under the Zirid dynasty. In 1238 Muhammad Ibn el-Ahmar proclaimed the Nasrid sultanate of Granada in the provinces of Málaga, Granada, Almaría and part of the province of Jaén, at a time when the Christians' advance seemed unstoppable. Nevertheless the Nasrid kingdom stood its ground as the last bastion of Islam in the peninsula for 250 years, a period punctuated by wars and intrigues but also a time of fantastic artistic and cultural achievements which culminated in the completion of the Alhambra Palace. Finally, however, on January 2, 1492, the banner of the Catholic Monarchs was raised over Granada. The Moors and natives of Granada who stayed suffered greater and greater oppression which resulted in the uprisings of 1500 and 1568, and ultimately in their expulsion. The new rulers commissioned an abundance of churches, palaces and other buildings to create a formidable ensemble of Gothic, Renaissance and Baroque architecture to compete with the Nasrid achievements.

"Granada is the Damascus of El-Andalus, nourishing our eyes and uplifting our souls, blessed with an impregnable alcazaba and beautiful buildings."
El-Saqundi
13th century

Granada and the Sierra Nevada.

The main façade of the cathedral.

City center. Most of the city is built along the banks of the rivers Darro and Genil, beneath the Albaicín and Alhambra hills. The Gran Vía Colón, the Calle Reyes Católicos and the Puerta Real are the principal axes in the city center. All around a maze-like network of streets and squares evokes memories of times gone by, its nooks and crannies crammed with interesting monuments. The Plaza Bib-rambla, for example, is a peaceful, well-liked spot with terrace cafés and flower sellers, which was formerly the site of bullfights and *autos-da-fé*. Nearby, the Plaza de las Pasiegas is just opposite the cathedral.

Cathedral. The largest church in Granada was built in the heart of the Muslim *medina*, with a Gothic floor plan designed by Enrique de Egas. In 1528, Diego de Siloé took charge, and built a grandiose Renaissance temple (380 feet by 220 feet), that had five naves, enormous Corinthian columns and a circular Capilla Mayor, with a dome nearly 150 feet high. The main façade is Baroque, designed in 1667 by Alonso Cano (1601–67), an artist from Granada who also produced various paintings and sculptures which are part of the cathedral's rich collection of artefacts. The cathedral's treasures and other valuable objects are displayed in the sacristy.

Capilla Real. The Royal Chapel stands next to the cathedral. The tomb is Gothic in style, and was designed by Enrique de Egas (1505–21) to shelter the marble cenotaph of the Catholic Monarchs, completed by Domenico Fancelli in 1517, and that of their heirs. The Calle de los Oficios, which runs alongside the Capilla Real and the Lonja, cuts through the heart of the Nasrid city.

The Royal chapel
The chapel houses such riches as Queen Isabella's precious collection of paintings and the large Plateresque gate by Master Bartolomé de Jaén (1520).

Federico García Lorca (1899–1936)
Spain's greatest modern poet was born in the small village of Fuente Vaqueros ▲ *342*.
He and his work are still intimately linked to the region of Granada. Much of it is inspired by local oral traditions to which he was introduced by Manuel de Falla. His most popular work is the collection of poems called *Romancero gitan*.

Right, a typical example of Guadix ceramics ▲ *344*. These can be bought in the Albaicín.

EL-BAYYAZIN
According to some, "El-Bayyazin" means "the neighborhood of balconied houses", according to others "the neighborhood of Baeza" (people from Baeza settled in Granada in the 13th century after their town was taken by the Christians).

The Puerta de las Pesas and the Albaicín (above) and a view of the Albaicín.

View of the Convento de Santa Isabel la Real and the Palacio Dar el-Horra in the Albaicín, seen from Mirador de San Cristóbal (right).

The remains of the MADRAZA, a 15th century Islamic school, and its oratory decorated with delicate stuccowork, are concealed behind an 18th-century façade. The ALCAICERIA is at the end of the street: this enclosed shopping precinct made up of extremely narrow alleys is now a tourist market. Further east across the Calle Zacatín and the Calle Reyes Católicos is the CORRAL DEL CARBON, formerly the corn market, and the 14th-century caravanserai used by Nasrid merchants. Its beautiful gateway is decorated with an arch made of horseshoes; nowadays it houses craft stores and the tourist office.

EL TRIUNFO, SAN JERONIMO AND LA CARTUJA. West of the historic district, near the Plaza del Triunfo, are some of the city's most remarkable buildings: the 16th-century HOSPITAL REAL, now the university, and the MONASTERIO DE SAN JERÓNIMO, built at the beginning of the 16th century for the burial of the Gran Capitán, one of the most powerful noblemen of his time. The MONASTERIO DE LA CARTUJA, further away from the city center, was founded in the 16th century but not completed until the 18th. Its exterior is unbelievably austere compared to the vibrant explosion of decoration which covers the tabernacle and the sacristy within. This wonderful interior, by Hurtado Izquierdo, is one of the greatest examples of Spanish Baroque.

ALBAICÍN. More than anywhere else in the city, it is in the Albaicín that the unmistakable heart of Muslim Granada still beats. The cone-shaped network of tightly packed white houses, dotted with belvederes and cypresses, spreads across the hill next to the Alhambra. It traces a delightful maze of slopes, steps and paved alleyways which run alongside the walls of the houses and *carméns* (villas owned by Christianized Muslims) with terraced gardens, of which the inhabitants of Granada were so fond. In the bends of the alleyways there are small clearings and squares, churches where once there were mosques, and the remains of ancient walls, gates and palaces. On street corners there are lively bars and stores, and busy craftsmen's studios producing everything from traditional brass lanterns and ironwork to marquetry (wood decorated with marble inlay) and ceramics. The Triunfo sits at the bottom of the Alhacaba hill alongside the ruins of 11th-century walls and towers which are part of the ancient *alcazaba*, the first fortress to be built in Granada by the Moors. The CONVENTO DE SANTA ISABEL LA REAL is further on, past the Plaza Larga and the Puerta de las Pesas, near to the PALACIO DE DAR EL-HORRA, the queen's house.

Crafts from Granada
Detail of a carpet made from a mixture of cotton and wool.

This elegant Nasrid residence, complete with an ornamental pond and galleries, dates back to the end of the 15th century. It was once the home of Boabdil's mother. Make a small detour to the IGLESIA DE SALVADOR further up the hill, where ritual ablutions used to be performed in the courtyard of the original building, a large mosque. The MIRADOR DE SAN NICOLÁS, a charming square nearby, has fantastic panoramic views over the city, the valley, the Alhambra and the Sierra Nevada. The MIRADOR DE SAN MIGUEL ALTO, above the Albaicín, also has a splendid panoramic view over the Albaicín, the Alhambra and the mountains beyond. From the Chapiz hill, take the SACROMONTE road up to the abbey where the remains of San Cecilio, patron saint of Granada, are preserved. Performances of the flamenco and the *zambra* take place in the caves in the gipsy quarter, a pretty area which is always popular with tourists.

Dancers from the Sacromonte.

Carrera del Darro and Plaza Nueva. The Albaicín district descends all the way down to the romantic Carrera del Darro, which winds its way between the Albaicín and Alhambra hills. Historic buildings line up one after another along the street between the promenade of Los Tristes and the Plaza Nueva. The CASA CASTRIL, with its distinctive Plateresque gateway, houses the ARCHEOLOGICAL MUSEUM which contains objects dating from the Paleolithic age up to the Islamic era. A few yards away, thick walls conceal the CONVENTO DE SANTA CATELINA, and the CASA DE ZAFRA, an amazingly opulent Nasrid residence. The entrance to the Arab Nogal baths, the BAÑUELO, is at 31, Carrera del Darro. Built in the 11th-century Zirid style, this is a magical place which is quiet and rarely visited. The vaulted ceilings of the three rooms are pierced with star shapes and the columns are crowned with horseshoes. The Darro is hidden for a while beneath the Plaza Nueva, the district's main square, which is dominated by the magnificent Mannerist façade of the CHANCILLERÍA and the IGLESIA DE SANTA ANA, a typical 16th-century Granadan Mudéjar church (its design heavily influenced by Moorish architecture); its tower used to be a minaret and there is a beautiful ceiling in the Capilla Mayor. Along the CUESTA DE GOMÉREZ, toward the Alhambra, there are craft and souvenir stores, and excellent guitar stores.

"Granada sits, unmoving, within the surrounding hills. It is different from cities by the sea, or cities with wide rivers flowing through them, which can travel, and then return home enriched by what they have seen. Granada, solitary and pure, turns in upon itself, curbing its extraordinary soul, with nothing to show but its natural lofty position as a star."
Federico García Lorca, *Impressions and Landscapes*, 1918

Festivals in Granada
The anniversary of the capture of the city is celebrated on January 2; the Tarasca, a popular parade made up of giants and enormous heads, on Corpus Christi; and there are always several moving processions during Holy Week.

▲ THE ALHAMBRA

The Alcazaba.

In 1238 Muhammad Ibn el-Ahmar decided to build a formidable fortification on the Sabika hill, opposite the Albaicín. It was known as "Al-hamra" ("The Red"), a reference either to the red earth or the fortress's red walls. The site was developed throughout the 13th and 14th centuries by his successors, in particular Yusuf I and Muhammad V. They added walls, towers, mosques, palaces and gardens to create a gigantic military and residential complex. In the 15th century the Nasrid dynasty fell into decline and only a few minor modifications were made. Restored by the Catholic monarchs, then left to ruin at the beginning of the 18th century, the fortress was only rediscovered by artists and travelers in the 19th century, when it was restored.

THE WORLD'S BEST-PRESERVED MEDIEVAL ARAB PALACE ✪
This treasure of Hispanic-Moorish art and its garden are fascinating – if you manage to ignore the crowds, that is. The best plan of action is to book a ticket for an early-morning or evening visit, though only El Generalife and certain rooms in the Nasrid palace are open at night.

1. Torres Bermejas
2. Puerta de las Granadas
3. Pilar de Carlos V
4. Puerta de la Justicia
5. Torre de las Cabezas
6. Torre de los Siete Suelos
7. Torre del Agua
8. Torre de las Infantas
9. Torre de la Cautiva
10. Torre de los Picos

La Alcazaba
11. Torre de la Vela
12. Torre Quebrada
13. Torre del Homenaje
14. Jardines del Adarve
15. Puerta del Vino
16. Patio de Machuca

Mexuar
17. Sala del Mexuar
18. Patio del Cuarto Dorado
19. Cuarto Dorado

Palacio de Comares
20. Patio de Comares
21. Sala de la Barca
22. Torre de Comares
23. Baños Reales

Palacio de los Leones
24. Patio de los Leones
25. Sala de los Mocárabes
26. Sala de los Reyes
27. Sala de las Dos Hermanas
28. Sala de los Abencerrajes
29. Jardín de la Daraja
30. Peinador de la Reina
31. Jardines del Partal
32. Torre de las Damas
33. Oratorio

El Generalife
34. Jardines nuevos
35. Teatro
36. Patio de la Acequia
37. Pabellón Sur
38. Pabellón Norte
39. Patio de la Sultana
40. Escalera del Agua
41. Palacio de Carlos V
42. Iglesia de Santa María
43. Calle Real
44. Baños públicos Árabes
45. Parador de San Francisco

THE APPROACH TO THE ALHAMBRA
From Plaza Nueva, Cuesta de Gomérez leads up to the Puerta de la Granadas (14th century, reworked by Charles V). The Torres Bermejas, once the state prison, rise up on the south side. The path winds through the cool shade of the woods that surround the fortress as far as the fountain known as the Pilar de Carlos. Past the remarkable Puerta de la Justicia (above), a gate built by Yusuf I in 1348, lies Plaza de los Aljibes next to the Puerta del Vino.

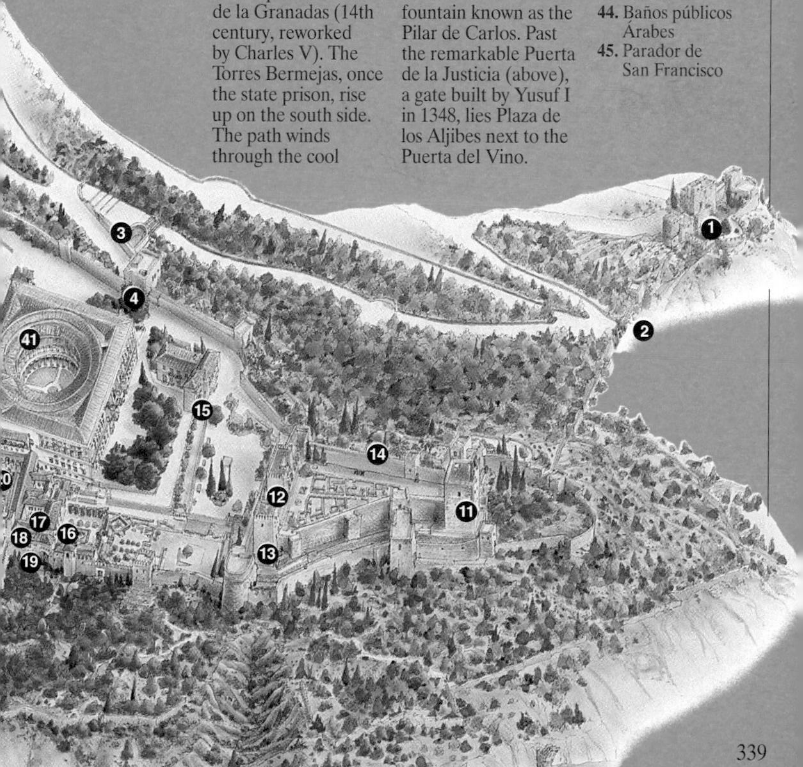

CARLOS V FOUNTAIN
Water is the central feature of the Alhambra. Right, detail of the Pilar de Carlos V, the Renaissance fountain erected in honour of the Emperor Carlos V.

THE STRUCTURE OF THE ALHAMBRA
One part of the Alhambra, the Alcazaba, is military, while the central area surrounding the Torre de Comares is residential. A series of gardens separates the Partal from the Generalife, and the rest of the complex is made up of buildings where servants and courtiers used to live and work.

PALACIO DE CARLOS V AND THE MUSEUMS. The Palacio de Carlos V, built in 1526, towers over one side of the Plaza de los Aljibes. It is the most important Christian structure in the Alhambra, an imposing Renaissance triumphal building which was begun by Pedro Manchuca, an architect from the circle of Raphael Sanzio, and remained unfinished until recently. Its design is unusual: a square palace made of stone, built around a circular central courtyard, which is in stark contrast to the oriental style and materials (adobe, brick, plaster, ceramics) of the surrounding buildings. It also has a sensational classical façade. The galleries now house the Museum of Spanish-Muslim Art, which contains some fantastic pieces of Nasrid art, and the Museo de Bellas Artes, which has an excellent collection of paintings and sculpture.

ALCAZABA. The Alcazaba is the oldest part of the Alhambra, built in the middle of the 13th century by the first sultan. It has sturdy perimeter walls within which the armory and military quarters occupy a court lined with towers: the Torre del Homenaje is the highest of the towers, and was the first royal residence, the Torre de las Armas has a fine doorway, and the huge Torre de la Vela (or Torre de la Campana), where the Catholic monarchs raised their banner over the city, has the best panoramic view over Granada and the valley beyond.

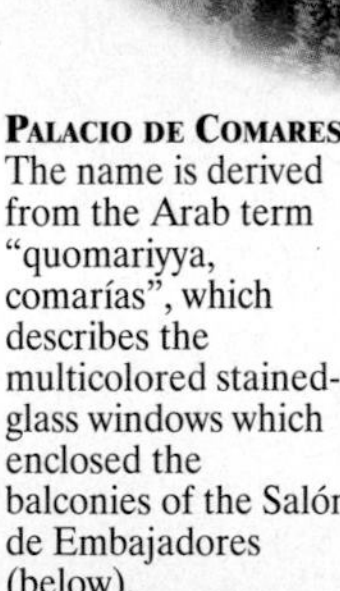

THE CASA REAL, THE MEXUAR, THE PALACIO DE COMARES. Past the Palacio de Carlos V you will reach the Casa Real Vieja, an exquisitely designed and decorated residential complex. Most of it was built in the 14th century by Yusuf I and his son and successor, Muhammad V, in the form of an elaborate labyrinth in which the distinct parts once hosted different functions in court life. Thus, while official business centered around the Mexuar and the Palacio de Comares, the Palacio de los Leones formed the focus of the private quarters which incorporated the Partal, the towers and the gardens. Your visit starts in the Patio de Machuca, before you pass into the Mexuar where viziers and ministers used to gather, and then into a small oratory and the Cuarto Dorado, in which the sultan used to sit in judgement over his subjects. From the adjacent courtyard you might catch a glimpse of the façade of the Palacio de Comares. This is an interior façade, in the tradition of Islamic domestic architecture, a superb example of stuccowork with an outer roof made of wood. It was designed as a triumphal portico in honor of Muhammad V,

PALACIO DE COMARES
The name is derived from the Arab term "quomariyya, comarías", which describes the multicolored stained-glass windows which enclosed the balconies of the Salón de Embajadores (below).

> "To the traveler imbued with a feeling for the historical and poetical... the Alhambra is as much an object of devotion as is the Caaba to all true Muslims."
>
> Washington Irving, *The Alhambra*, 1829

who had it built in 1370 to celebrate his victory over the Christians at Algéciras. A narrow passageway opens out onto the wonderful Patio de los Arrayanes (left), also known as the Patio de la Alberca, where the Torre de Comares is reflected in the ornamental pond. An elegant gallery leads into the main room, the Salón de Embajadores, which is the largest room in the Alhambra, and which used to be the sultan's audience room. This is where Boabdil signed the surrender of Granada and the Catholic monarchs received Christopher Columbus before his departure for the Indies. The interior is finely decorated with Nasrid brickwork, plasterwork and ceramics, beneath a wooden framework symbolizing the seven heavens which await Muslims after their death, before they arrive at God's throne. Every surface is decorated with an amazing variety of Arab inscriptions: phrases from the Koran, and poems in praise of the kings and the glory of their palaces.

Palacio de los Leones. A zigzag path leads into the royal family's private quarters and the harem surrounding the Patio de los Leones, a spectacular cross-shaped courtyard with a gallery supported by 124 marble columns. Miniature canals, representing the rivers of paradise, spring from the fountain in the center and divide the courtyard in four. The twelve lions supporting the fountain are ancient symbols; according to tradition there was a similar fountain in the palace of Yusuf ben Nagrela, the 11th-century Jewish vizier of Granada, which in turn was inspired by the fountain in the temple in Jerusalem that represented the twelve tribes of Israel. The carvings which decorate the courtyard are breathtakingly beautiful, and ghosts seem to lurk in every corner. Beyond is the Sala de los Abencerrajes, where several members of the Abencerraje family are said to have been assassinated on the sultan's orders. It has a wonderful dome pierced with windows that light the niches in the stalactite vaulting, laid out according to mathematical principles and creating a fantastic rhythmical design across the ceiling. The Sala de las Dos Hermanas opens onto the Mirador de Daraxa (from "*al-ain dar Aixa*" or "eyes of the Sultana"), which looks over a little garden, the Patio de Lindaraja, and across to Charles V's apartments, where Washington Irving once lived. Between the Palacio de Comares and the Patio de los Leones, the beautiful Baños Reales are bathed in a mysterious half-light, coming from tiny pierced stars in the vaults. The luxurious Sala de los Reyes, where receptions and banquets were held, accentuates the palace's oriental atmosphere. The ceilings of its three alcoves are covered with scenes of horsemen and Nasrid noblemen, painted on leather. This is unexpected, as the Koran forbids the representation of people, so these pictures may have been painted by a Christian artist at the end of the 15th century.

Washington Irving (1783–1859)
Washington Irving was familiar with the romantic legends associated with the Alhambra. A writer, diplomat and traveler from New York, he stayed there when he journeyed through Spain, and it became the inspiration for his greatest work, the *Tales of the Alhambra*.

Below, the Patio de los Leones and the Sala de los Reyes.

El Partal.

PARTAL AND THE TOWERS. East of the Palacio de los Leones lie the ruins of other palaces and gardens as well as the remains of some of the old court buildings. All that is left of the Palacio del Partal, the oldest palace in the Alhambra, built by Muhammad III at the beginning of the 14th century, is a beautiful pavilion and its reflection in a rectangular pond. Its portico forms the front section of the Torre de las Damas, from where there is a superb view over the Albaicín. Next door, the fine chapel attached to the mosque is also worth seeing. A little further on a path leads toward the Generalife and several more tower-palaces built to to the same plan in the 14th century, including the Torre de la Cautiva and the Torre de las Infantas with their richly decorated rooms.

GENERALIFE. Also known as the "High Garden" (Djinat el-arif) or "Architect's Garden", this was once the summer palace, set in 75 acres of grounds. The palace is built at the heart of the gardens and orchards, on a hill rising to the east of the Alhambra outside the enclosure's perimeter walls. This is where the sultans used to retreat, to escape the intrigues of court life. Water is the most important feature of the gardens, where the canals and fountains never cease their murmuring. Muhammad II began work on them at the end of the 13th century, and Ismail I made further modifications around 1319. Granada's prestigious international festival of music and dance takes place there, in the amphitheater in front of the two little courtyards that lead into the Alcázar near the Jardines Nuevos. The palace is set out around the long Patio de la Acequia, in the middle of which flows the Acequia Real, providing the water supply to the whole complex. The harmonious proportions and beautiful decoration of the Sala Regia, on the north side of the courtyard, make it the most impressive of all the Alhambra's outbuildings. Next door are the Patio de la Sultana (also known as the Patio del Ciprés), where Zoraya, the wife of the emir Abu El-Hassan, used to meet her Abencerraje lover, and the Jardines Altos, which contain the Escalera del Agua, an extraordinary Nasrid hydraulic system that enables water to reach even the highest terraces.

IN MEMORIAM GARCÍA LORCA
Two sites near Granada summon up the memory of the poet ▲ *335*. In the suburbs, toward Calle la Virgen Blanca, is the HUERTA DE SAN VICENTE, a house where Federico García Lorca spent his summers. Converted into a little museum, it retains the flavour of the poet's era and some of its original furniture. At FUENTE VAQUEROS (about 11 miles from Granada), the village where he was born, the MUSEO LORCA has manuscripts, copies of his works and some personal belongings.

The gardens in the Generalife.

SIERRA NEVADA

The Sierra Nevada boasts the highest road in Europe. The A-395 climbs more than 10,000 feet into the Alpine massif, linking the villages of Las Alpujarras.

VELETA AND MULHACÉN. At 11,420 feet Mulhacén is the highest mountain in Spain, named after Boabdil's father, emir Abu El-Hassan. When he died, his Christian wife Soraya ordered his body to be taken to rest there, on safe ground. On a clear day this mountain range can be seen from as far away as Africa. Its

LAS ALPUJARRAS, A DIFFERENT WORLD ✪
This region, with its long tradition of independence, still stands out by virtue of its wild landscape and unique customs. From Pampaneira, it is possible to get to Bubión on foot in 45 minutes. From there you can enjoy a magnificent view over the Granada sierra and listen to the tranquil murmur of the waterfalls as they feed the undergrowth.

second and third highest peaks are Veleta (11,148 feet), which has a ski resort on its slopes, and Alcazaba (11,043 feet). The mountain-top vegetation is the most remarkable in Europe, with many unique species and a wildlife that is so rich that UNESCO has made it a nature reserve. There is an infinite number of roads and paths to choose from, offering anything from a strenuous climb to a gentle stroll.
THE SLOPES OF THE SIERRA NEVADA. Pradollano (or Solynieve), 22 miles from Granada, is the sunniest ski resort in Europe. Reaching an altitude of 6,890 feet, it played host to the World Alpine Skiing Championships in 1996 and has excellent amenities.

Situated on the Poqueira Gorge, Capileira (above) and Pampaneira (below) are typical of the towns high up in the mountains.

LAS ALPUJARRAS

Las Alpujarras is the region, 50 miles wide and 20 miles long, which stretches between the Sierra Nevada and the sea. The Sierra de Lújar, the Sierra de la Contreviesa, the Sierras de Gádor and other smaller ranges run from the Sierra Nevada down to the seashore. This area has a distinctive character, with steep cliffs, gullies and raging torrents, and beautiful valleys dotted with small towns and villages. Little has changed over the centuries: the land is cultivated using traditional methods, the architecture was inherited long ago from the Arabs, and the local dishes and crafts have been passed down from generation to generation. Its name is of Iberian origin, referring to a high place (*alp*) and to the goddess of bright light (Ujar). The gorge has retained the grandeur and beauty that has been appreciated by artists throughout the centuries. The houses still perch on the hillside, surrounded by an abundance of elm trees, willows and poplars despite recent deforestation.
CAPILEIRA, BUBION AND PAMPANEIRA. These three charming villages perched above a deep gorge, the Barranco de Poqueira, make excellent hiking bases. The white houses of

POPULAR HOUSING
In Las Alpujarras the roof terraces of the houses are made from shale sheets set on chestnut, oak or pine beams and covered with a layer of clay, following the Berber model.

«MOROS Y CRISTIANOS»
Nearly 50,000 Moors found refuge in Las Alpujarras after the fall of Granada in 1492. Persecution by the Christians gave rise to revolts in 1500, then the guerrilla war of 1568–70. Survivors were sent away, before being banished from Spain altogether in 1609. The *Moros y Cristianos* village fêtes hark back to these violents incidents of the Reconquest. The most famous is held on September 15 at Válor, the village where the leader of the 1568 uprising was born.

Capileira sit at an altitude of nearly 5,000 feet. To savor the atmosphere at its best, visit the Plaza del Calvario, Calle de la Campana and the Mudéjar church which underwent some modifications in the 17th century. The small town of Bubión, a few miles away, offers the best view of the ravine, and has an interesting craft center. At a lesser altitude, Pampaneira is dotted with fountains, and its church has a lovely Mudéjar coffered ceiling. There are some delicious local gastronomic specialties, notably traditional gipsy stews and farmhouse *migas*, as well as excellent game.

TREVÉLEZ. Trevélez, at an altitude of nearly 5,000 feet, is thought to be the highest village in Spain, and has exceptional views from its terraces, if few buildings of any architectural interest. It holds a festival in honor of strangers on August 15, when its famous *jamón serrano* is eaten (the climate is perfect for preserving this dried meat). The empress Eugenie de Montijo used to arrange for some to be delivered to Paris.

YÉGUEN. This village is worth a detour for its wonderful view of the mountains. British writer Gerald Brenan (1894–1987) settled in Yéguen in the 1920's and devoted several of his works to Las Alpujurras and their inhabitants.

THE TROPICAL COAST

The strip of coast on the edge of the province of Granada is the narrowest in Andalusia because of the mountains which descend steeply to the sea. Its climate is sometimes dry and sometimes subtropical.

SALOBREÑA AND MOTRIL. The nearest town to Salobreña is Motril, which has a lively port, and its church and town hall are both worth a visit. Salobreña itself has been nicknamed "Little Cuba" because of the sugar-cane plantations that have thrived in its exceptional climate since the 10th century.

SALOBREÑA
The N-323 descends from Granada to Salobreña, an old Phoenician enclave near the river Guadalfeo at the foot of the Sierra de Guajar, whose traditional white houses surround the Spanish-Muslim fort. It celebrated its finest hours under Arab rule.

ALMUÑECAR. Founded by the Phoenicians in 800 BC and colonized by the Romans, this town became one of the defensive ports of the emirate of Granada before being conquered by the Catholic monarchs in 1489. This history can be traced by visiting the archeological museum, the Roman aqueduct, the ruins of an *alcázar* and the Renaissance parish church of La Mayor.

GUADIX, BAZA AND THE MARQUESADO

From Granada the N-92 follows the wooded foothills of the Sierra Nevada eastward, then plunges into the vast eroded basins of Guadix and Baza, which saw their first human habitations in Paleolithic times.

GUADIX. Princess Himiloé, the wife of Hannibal, owned a famous silver mine called Bébele in the region. The Iberian town of Acci, established at the main crossroads of eastern Andalucia, became a Roman colony on the Via Augustus. From 1489 the new Christian regime slowly erased most traces of Muslim life; now all that remains are the ruins of the Alcazaba, the Torre Gorda. Most of the monuments are

Almuñecar
This town at the foot of the Sierra de Almijara is now given over to tourism.

Christian, and there are numerous churches, convents, grand houses and an imposing cathedral which took centuries to complete; at first glance it appears to be mainly Baroque in style, but a closer look reveals a mixture of many different styles and periods. Guadix is famous for its cave dwellings, with their distinctive chimneys, which can be seen all around the outskirts of the town. They were originally inhabited by the Moors who had been expelled from mainstream society.

Baza. Following the A-92-N east you will come to the town of Baza, in the northeast corner of the region. It is surrounded by the Sierra Baza, near a large valley. There are more cave dwellings here, as well as settlements from other eras. The town's location at a crossroads has made it a popular conquest through the ages, and there are traces of both medieval and Muslim eras. The archeological museum, the 10th-century baths in the Jewish quarter, the church of Santa María, with its lovely plateresque portal, and the 16th-century palace of Enríquez are all worth seeing.

Marquesado del Cenete. If you take the A-92 in the direction of Almería you will reach a raised plateau. The landscape seems dreary and the climate is harsh, but it is lush and there is a cluster of villages: Huéneja, Dólar, Aldeire, Lacalahorra and Jeres del Marquesado. This region was created at the time of the settlement of land after the Reconquest. The word *zenete* means "slope", but it is also possible that in this instance it comes from the name of the Zanata, an Arab tribe who once lived in the area. You can still see Arab baths in almost every village in this land of Moors and Mudéjars; the best conserved is in Huéneja where you can also see the remains of the fortress.

Lacalahorra. The fortress-palace that crowns the former capital of the Marquesado is a strange but brilliant piece of Spanish architecture dating from the 16th century. Its massive walls surround an exquisite courtyard built in the style of the Italian Renaissance, with very fine galleries and a splendid marble staircase.

Cascamorras
Every September 6 the young people of Baza, doused in petrol from head to toe, pursue through the streets of the town a clown sent from Guadix to reclaim a statue of the Virgin. The fête commemorates a one-time dispute between Guadix and Baza.

Below, Guadix cathedral, the Arab baths at Baza, and a cluster of cave dwellings.

JAÉN

The province of Jaén is one of the gateways to Andalusia. The city's strategic position, at an important crossroads, means that it has been inhabited from Paleolithic times.The Romans knew it as "Auringis" (it was conquered by Scipion in 207 BC), and it passed into Arab hands in 712, thence to the Christians in 1246.

CASTLE. Perched right at the top of the Santa Catalina hill, the castle looks down on the town at its foot. The panoramas from here across the surrounding countryside are superb. The fortified enclosure was built by the Spanish Muslims, with modifications made by Ferdinand III after he captured the town. It now houses a *parador*, part of the state-owned chain of luxury hotels. From the TORRE DEL HOMENAJE there is a magnificent view of the cathedral, which towers over the dense cluster of buildings making up the old town.

CATHEDRAL The best surviving example (below) of Andalusian Renaissance architecture, the cathedral was built in the 16th and 17th centuries after a design by Andrès de Vandelvira. The main façade, flanked by sturdy towers, is beautifully carved.

ARAB BATHS. Climb up the Calle Martínez Molina, one of the main axes of the historic district, to the PALACIO DE VILLARDOMPARDO, a 16th-century nobleman's house. Inside are the best-preserved Arab baths in the region (above), rediscovered in 1913 and are now open to the public; their restoration was awarded the Europa Nostra prize in 1984. They are typical of 11th- and 12th-century El-Andalus culture and it is still possible to follow their original layout: the entrance hall is followed by the cold, warm and hot rooms, with pierced vaulted ceilings. The rest of the building houses the MUSEO DE ARTES Y COSTUMBRES POPULARES and the MUSEUM OF NAIVE ART.

TREASURES OF JAÉN CATHEDRAL
The inside of the cathedral is as splendid as its façade: the choir has elaborately sculpted stalls (16th century), the Capilla Mayor contains a stone tabernacle, and the little museum in the sacristy (below) boasts some magnificent silverware. But the most precious treasure here is the cloth that Saint Veronica is said to have used to wipe

Christ's face on the road to Calvary, and which, it is claimed, has retained the imprint of his features.

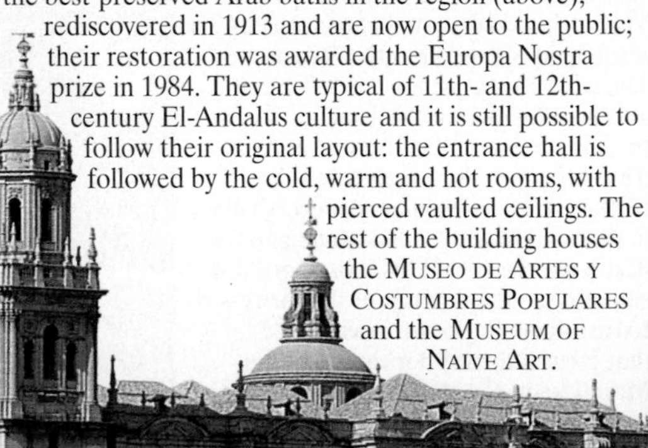

Antonio Machado ● *104*
When his wife Leonor died in 1912, the great Spanish poet asked to be given the first teacher's post to become vacant. He was posted to Baeza, where he stayed until 1919.

Below: the Palacio de Jabalquinto, the Plaza del Pópulo, a window in the Palacio de Jabalquinto, the seminary in Baeza.

Baeza

Baeza is 30 miles from Jaén, along the N-321, near the city of Ubeda at the province's geographical center. Its fields were the subject of a song by Antonio Machado. The name "Baeza" probably comes from the town's Arab name, "Biesa".
Plaza del Populo. All that remains of the ancient fortified square are parts of the battlements, sections of wall and some of the gates. The Jaén Gate in the Plaza del Pópulo supports the arch built in 1521 to commemorate the battle of Villalar, when the *communeros de Castilla* confronted Charles I. The square is surrounded by the Antigua Carnicería, a Renaissance building which now houses the town archives and the Municipal Museum. Situated just behind the arch, the Casa del Pópulo, with its Plateresque façade, is now the tourist office. A statue of an Iberian woman surrounded by four lions stands in the center of the fountain in the middle of the square.
Cathedral. The cathedral is situated on the Plaza Santa María, which is adorned with a beautiful 16th-century fountain. Following the precedent set in other cities, Ferdinand II demanded that the cathedral should be built upon the site of the former mosque, traces of which still remain in the cloister. The cathedral was badly damaged in 1567, with restoration work ensuing until 1593, and displays a mixture of widely different styles: Mudéjar-Gothic (Puerta de la Luna, east), from the reign of Isabella (Puerta del Perdón, south), Renaissance (altars and reredos) and classical (choir stalls).
Palaces and churches. Baeza's historic center is one of the richest architectural ensembles in the country. Next to the cathedral is the Casa Consistoriales Altas with its Gothic façade. In the Plaza de Santa Cruz are the Palacio de Jabalquinto with its beautiful 15th-century Gothic façade, Renaissance courtyard and Baroque staircase, and the ancient university. Continuing toward the Plaza d'España via the Torre de los Aliatares, the last remnant of the old city walls with its beautiful belvedere, you pass the town granary and the arcades of the ancient Alhóndiga (grain stores). This narrow walkway leads to the Ayuntamiento (1599) with its splendid Plateresque façade, and the San Andrés district (*iglesias* de Santa María and del Salvador).

ÚBEDA

Situated on the C-321, 5 miles from Baeza and 35 miles from Jaén, Úbeda looks down over the mountains of the Sierras Mágina, Aznaitín and Cazorla from the top of its hill. Known in Roman times by the name "Bethula", after the nearby river Baetis, it was called "Ubbadat-el-Arab" by the Arabs, who built a wall round it. It grew to be an extremely important city, known for its pottery and ceramics.

THE TRIUMPH OF THE RENAISSANCE. Conquered in 1234 by Ferdinand III, Úbeda recaptured its former glory under Charles I and Philip II. Cees Nooteboom described the city as "cold, distant, peaceful; a classic jewel carved from the fiery soul of Andalusia", at times Arab, at times Baroque. The greatest triumphs of the Renaissance echo through its silent streets. The architects Diego de Siloé and Andrés de Vandelvira stamped the city with Andalusia's distinctive style; the unrivalled quality of Vandelvira's work in particular is clearly recognizable in its most important buildings.

LOCAL CLANS. The history of Úbeda, like that of Baeza, is strewn with the rivalries between the nobles who inherited the land after the Reconquest. The principal families in the local aristocracy, the Aranda and the Trapera, and their descendants, the Cuevas and the Molina, battled to establish their power over the city, feuding throughout the Middle Ages and building magnificent palaces in an effort to outdo one another.

A WALK THROUGH THE PALACES. The PLAZA VÁZQUEZ DE MOLINA is the very essence of the city, with its typical ensemble of palace, churches, towers and spectacular doorways decorated with coats of arms. The most remarkable monuments include the IGLESIA DEL SALVADOR, with its elaborately sculpted monumental portal, the PALACIO DE LAS CADENAS and the collegial church of SANTA MARÍA DE LOS REALES ALCÁZARES, which was begun in 1234 on the site of the great mosque and which combines various different styles. Before leaving the city, you must also take the time to visit the HOSPITAL DE SANTIAGO. Founded in 1562 and designed by Vandelvira, it is one of the masterpieces of the Spanish Renaissance.

BAEZA AND ÚBEDA, TREASURES OF THE ANDALUSIAN RENAISSANCE ✪
The exceptional architecture (15th to 17th century) of these rival towns just 5 miles apart has led to a joint UNESCO world heritage listing. The best time to visit is early evening when the rays of the setting sun bring out the ocher façades of the monuments.

ANDRÉS DE VANDELVIRA
One of the greatest Spanish architects, Vandelvira was born in Alcaraz in 1509, and spent most of his life in Jaén where he died in 1575 while working on the cathedral. There are periods of his life about which we have little information, but he is known for his wonderful architectural designs, which incorporate elements from Italian and Castillian architecture into his typically Andalusian style.

SIERRAS DE CAZORLA, SEGURA AND LAS VILLAS

These mountain ranges adjoining the Sierra de Albacete and the Sierra de Granada in the east of the province of Jaén form a national park that UNESCO has classed as a biosphere reserve and bird sanctuary. The beautiful towns of Cazorla, Segura de la Sierra, La Iruela and Quesada are worth a visit.

Cazorla, overlooked by the Castillo de la Yedra.

CAZORLA AND LA IRUELA. At the entrance to the park, Cazorla retains traces of Arab architecture, such as CASTILLO DE LA YEDRA (11th–13th centuries), also known as Castillo de la Cinco Esquinas. For many years the surrounding towns were frontier towns and they still contain interesting ruins of defensive fortifications. A good example is the village of La Iruela, perched on a hill east of Cazorla. The ruins of its castle, on a rocky outcrop, are particularly spectacular.

SEGURA AND HORNOS. Segura de la Sierra lies to the east of Jaén along the N-322. It was once an Islamic town known as "Saqura", which flourished for many years before it fell into the hands of the Christians in 1242 following several battles. Its origins are lost in the mists of time, but an imposing FORTIFIED CASTLE and some ancient ARAB BATHS give testimony to its glorious past. It was famed for the production of wood for the imperial fleet, which was sent down river and used in the construction of ships for the so-called "invincible" army. It is worth visiting the small village of Hornos, near the Tranco dam, to see its MUSLIM CASTLE and the superb view across an enormous stretch of pine forest.

THE NATURE RESERVE
This covers about 85,000 acres and has endless tracks and paths in all directions. Landmarks include the sources of the Guadalquivir and Segura rivers, the natural lake at Valdeazores, and the pasture land and dam at Tranco de Beas. The reserve contains many different kinds of pine trees, various species of oak, maple, ash and wonderful native flora such as the Cazorla violet. There is an enormous variety of wildlife: stags, wild boar, moufflons (wild short-haired sheep with extravagant horns), wild goats, vultures, otters and more than a hundred species of bird, including the bearded vulture.

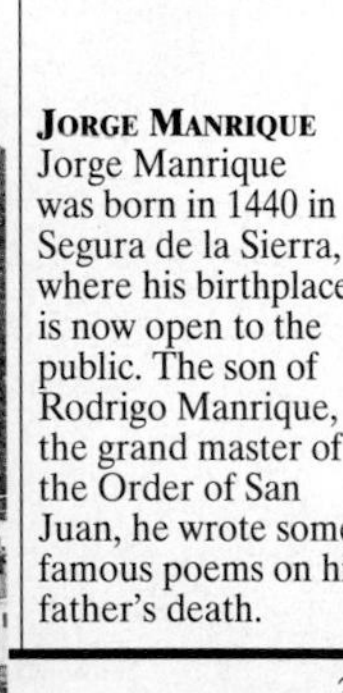

JORGE MANRIQUE
Jorge Manrique was born in 1440 in Segura de la Sierra, where his birthplace is now open to the public. The son of Rodrigo Manrique, the grand master of the Order of San Juan, he wrote some famous poems on his father's death.

THE CASTLE AT VÉLEZ BLANCO
The impressive castle-palace at Vélez Blanco was begun in 1506 on the orders of Don Pedro Fajardo. In 1904 the American millionaire George Blumenthal bought its courtyard, one of the masterpieces of the Spanish Renaissance, and removed it from the castle. It is now exhibited at the Metropolitan Museum of Art in New York.

SIERRA DE MARÍA AND THE VÉLEZ

The landscape on the easternmost border of Andalusia is made up of narrow, fertile valleys with villages clustered between solitary chains of mountains.

SIERRA DE MARÍA NATURE RESERVE. This nature reserve spreads across more than 10,000 acres at the extreme north of the province, east of the high plateaus of Granada, between the villages of María and Vélez Blanco. Unlike the other rather arid and desolate mountain ranges in the region, the Sierra de María is green and lush. Its slopes and crannies, wedged between limestone escarpments, are covered with Mediterranean vegetation, scrub, native black pine and extensive woodland where golden eagles, goshawks, squirrels and wild boars seek refuge.

VÉLEZ BLANCO AND VÉLEZ RUBIO. After Granada was seized, much of the land in the Almería region passed into the hands of the Fajardo, the noblemen who had been leaders in that part of the country during the war. Emboldened by their title, the marquises of Vélez settled in these highly desirable mountain villages. In Vélez Blanco a medieval atmosphere still pervades the winding streets. Churches and other buildings from the 16th, 17th and 18th centuries sit in the shadow of its castle-palace, a worthy rival of the neighboring castle at LACALAHORRA. On the edge of the road leading to Vélez Rubio you will come across the CUEVA DE LOS LETREROS, which is decorated with paintings dating from 5000 BC, including the figure of El Indalo, which has become the symbol of the province of Almería. Vélez Rubio's main attraction is the IGLESIA DEL ENCARNACIÓN, an elegant Baroque building from 1768 with twin towers decorated with the marquises' coat of arms.

View of Almería with the Alcazaba and the port (lithography by Chapuy, 1835).

ALMERÍA

This ancient Phoenician trading post, which the Arabs made into one of the great ports and cultural centers of El-Andalus, called El-Mariyya ("the mirror"), sits in the curve of a Mediterranean bay. Its fortunes, based mainly on textile trading, took a turn for the worse after the Christian conquest of 1489 and the earthquake of 1522, but in the 19th century, cattle breeding and farming, now supplemented by tourism, gave it new life.

ALCAZABA. Almería stretches out across the bottom of a hill which is crowned by some of the best

preserved fortifications in Andalusia. The construction of this complicated system of large towers and walls was begun in the 10th century and later strengthened by minor local kings and Nasrid sultans. After seizing the city in 1489 the Catholic monarchs completed the defensive system by erecting a Gothic bastion at the top of the hill. The Alcazaba is made up of three enclosures: the barracks, the living quarters (the lords of Almería lived here in the 11th century) and a section dating from the time of the Christians which includes the Torre del Homenaje and the ramparts. A long wall links the Alcazaba with the neighboring castle of San Cristóbal.

THE CITY AND THE PORT. Although most of the city is ruined by impersonal contemporary housing developments, the humble CHANCA district, still clinging to the slopes of the Alcazaba, contains remnants of the town's traditional housing. These cave dwellings and brightly painted cube-shaped houses have left a great impression on many writers, including Richard Ford, Gerald Brenan and Aldous Huxley. The PUERTA DE PURCHENA is in the town center; on the outskirts the Plateresque IGLESIA DE SANTIAGO is worth seeing, as are the porticos in the PLAZA VIEJA, where you will also find the town hall, and the CATHEDRAL, a fine Renaissance fortified church dating from the 16th century. A short walk takes you from the cathedral to the NICOLÁS SALMERÓN PARK, which leads you to the port itself.

MODERNISM IN ALMERÍA
Almería (above) is a wealthy city because of its minerals and its export of grapes and other fruit. This has led to a proliferation of modernist architecture in the town center, for example in this detail of the railway station (below).

THE DESERT AND THE COAST OF ALMERÍA

The coastal plains east of Almería, toward El Ejido and Mijar, are covered with serried ranks of polytunnels. Further inland, the Tabernas Desert lies at the foot of the Sierra Alhamilla and the Sierra de los Filabres.

THE TABERNAS DESERT. The village of Tabernas is made up of a huddle of geometric white houses perched under the 11th-century Arab *alcázar*, surrounded by desolate, arid lands: one of the rare areas of desert in Europe. This strange rather godforsaken area of land is characterized by the scarcity of rain, the sparse scrub, the cacti and palm trees, the hills beyond, the "bad lands" and the gullies. Several westerns have been filmed here and the panels of a gigantic solar power station, right at the heart of the steppe, utilize the almost constant source of light. This lunar landscape continues all the way to SORBAS, a nature reserve where reliefs have been carved out of the rocks and caves.

SPAGHETTI WESTERNS
In the 1960's and 1970's the Tabernas desert (not unlike the desert of North Africa) was the setting for several popular westerns. *A Fistful of Dollars* and *The Good, The Bad and The Ugly* were both filmed here. The film sets remain a popular tourist attraction.

Cloth from Almería. The figurine, called El Indalo, is the symbol of the province of Almería.

CABO DE GATA, UNTOUCHED NATURE ✪
A lighthouse stands on the cliffs of this imposing promontory, in an arid and singular area barely 125 miles from the coast of North Africa. Nearby are some of the most beautiful beaches of Andalusia.

NÍJAR. Nijar is one of the many villages made up of white, cubic houses. Its first-class craft center is well known for fine ceramics and textiles, especially multicolored patchwork blankets. From the village there is a good view of the enormous plain dotted with spiky plants, greenhouses and whitewashed farmhouses. This typically Mediterranean landscape continues all the way down to the row of mountains which separates it from the sea.

FROM THE CABO DE GATA TO MOJÁCAR. The 20,000-acre national park of Cabo de Gata begins a few miles east of Almería. This is the only protected area in Andalusia which is part land, part sea. It offers an extraordinarily varied landscape of coastal plains, salt marshes and swamps, with steppes and volcanic reliefs which break up into a succession of cliffs and ridges to create a rocky labyrinth beneath the clear waters, an ideal place for underwater fishing. The vegetation is that of an arid region, with small palm trees, native European dwarf palms, jujube trees and scrub, and there is a remarkable variety of sea life: you might even catch a glimpse of some flamingos. This coast is extremely beautiful all the way along to the tip of the cape which rises toward the north. Its strategic position and its richness in ores made it popular with the Phoenicians, the Romans and the Arabs. Later it would become a refuge for Berber pirates who roamed the Spanish coast. It is a magical land with several places worth visiting, including the PUNTA NEGRA, the inlet at GÉNOIS, the tiny villages of SAN JOSÉ which are shared by fishermen and tourists alike, the ISLETA, the NEGRAS and AGUA AMARGA (a fishing village and development near to a pretty bay), and the PUNTA DE LOS MUERTOS, which is named after the corpses thrown up by shipwrecks. When you leave the park in the direction of Murcia you will pass through the industrial port of CARBONERAS and then MOJÁCAR, which is the most popular tourist outpost in the region, at the source of the river Aguas. This dazzling whitewashed village is perched on a promontory from where there is a magnificent view of the shore. On the BELMONTE hill there are still the remains of a necropolis from Los Millares.

A street in Mojácar and sunset over the beaches at Cabo de Gata, at Andalusia's easternmost point.

Practical information

Key

- Town center
- Animals not allowed
- Air conditioning
- Swimming pool
- Television
- Telephone
- Live music
- Quiet
- Terrace
- View
- Park or garden
- Parking
- Private parking

ADDRESSES

→ **SPANISH CONSULATES**

■ **Canada**
Simcoe Place
200 Front Street,
Suite 2401
Toronto, ON M5V 3K2
Tel. (416) 977 1661
Fax (416) 593 4949
email: cgspain.toronto@mail.mae.es

■ **United Kingdom**
20 Draycott Place
London SW3 2RZ
Tel. (020) 7589 8989
Fax (020) 7581 7888

■ **United States**
– 2375 Pennsylvania Ave., N.W.
Washington, DC 20037
Tel. (202) 728 2330
Fax (202) 728 2302
– 5055 Wilshire Blvd
Suite 960
Los Angeles, LA 90036
Tel. (323) 938 0158
Fax (323) 938 2502
– 2655 Le Jeune Rd
Suite 203
Coral Gables, Miami
FL 33134
Tel. (305) 446 5511
Fax (305) 446 0585
– 150 East 58th St
30th and 31st Floors
New York, NY 10155
Tel. (212) 355 4080
Fax (212) 644 3751
www.spainconsul-ny.org
– For consulates in other US cities:
www.spainemb.org

→ **SPANISH TOURIST OFFICES**

■ **United Kingdom**
22-23 Manchester Square
London W1U 3PX
Tel. (020) 7486 8077
0906 364 0630 (for brochures)
www.tourspain.co.uk
email: info.londres@tourspain.es

■ **United States**
– 8383 Wilshire Blvd
Suite 960
Beverly Hills,
Los Angeles,
CA 90211
Tel. (213) 658 7188
Fax (213) 658 1061
email: losangeles@tourspain.es
–1221 Brickell Ave.
Suite 1850
Miami, FL 33131
Tel. (305) 358 1992
Fax (305) 358 8223
email: miami@tourspain.es
– 666 Fifth Ave.
35th Floor
New York, NY 10103
Tel. (212) 265 8822
Fax (212) 265 8864
email: ontny@tourspain.es

→ **CULTURE AND LANGUAGE**

■ **United Kingdom**
Spanish Education Office (part of the Consulate)
20 Peel Street
London W8 7PD
Tel. (020) 727 2462
Fax (020) 229 4965
www.sgci.mec.es/uk
Instituto Cervantes
102 Eaton Square
London SW1W 9AN
Tel. (020) 235 0353
Fax (020) 235 0329
www.cervantes.es

■ **United States**
Spanish Education Office
358 5th Ave.
Suite 1404
New York, NY 10001
Tel. (212) 629 4435
Fax (212) 629 4438
Instituto Cervantes
122 East 42nd St.
Suite 807
New York, NY 10168
Tel. (212) 661 6011
Fax (212) 545 8837
www.cervantes.org

CUSTOMS

Foreign and national currencies over €7,600 must be declared. Objects for personal use (with the exception of weapons and cultural-heritage items) are admitted freely throughout the European Union, of which Spain is a member.

FORMALITIES AND DOCUMENTS

→ **DRIVING LICENSE**

European or international driving license, a car registration document and a green (international insurance) card.

→ **ID PAPERS**

Members of the European Union can enter Spain with an ID card or passport for stays not exceeding 6 months. If you intend to stay longer, you must apply for a *tarjeta de residencia* (residence permit) or a visa at a Spanish consulate. Non-EU visitors should check entry requirements with a Spanish consulate.

→ **DISCOUNT CARDS**

The International Student Card (ISIC), Euro<26 card and pensioner's card entitle the holders to reductions on the public transport system, in museums and at tourist sites.
***Tip:** Take photocopies of your ID papers with you as well.*

HEALTH

European Union members can obtain an E111 form from their local post-office or health authority, which facilitates medical care and admission to hospital. Visitors from outside the EU should take out medical insurance before leaving (*see also* "Travel insurance" ◆ *355*).

MONEY

1 euro (€)= £0.64/$1 (at time of printing).

→ **CREDIT CARDS**

Are accepted almost everywhere. Autotellers take American Express, Eurocard/Mastercard and Visa (instructions in several languages).

→ **TRAVELER'S CHECKS**

Can be changed in many banks and bureaux de change (you get better exchange rates with checks issued in foreign currencies than with cash).

TELEPHONE

→ **CALLING ANDALUSIA**

From the UK: 00 + 34 + 9-digit number.
From the US: 011 + 34 + 9-digit number.

→ **ENQUIRIES**

■ **Internet**
White pages: *www.paginasblancas.es*
Yellow pages: *www.paginasamarillas.es*

→ **MOBILE PHONES**

Request an international extension from your mobile company.

TIME DIFFERENCE

GMT + 1 hr in winter, GMT + 2 hrs from the final Sun. in March until the final Sun. in Oct. When it is noon in New York, it is 6pm in Seville.

TRAVEL BY AIR

Main airports: Málaga and Seville.

→ **REGULAR FLIGHTS**

■ **From the UK**
British Airways
Direct flights to Barcelona, Seville and Madrid, then change for connecting flights to Granada and Málaga with other carriers.
Reservations/sales:
Tel. 0845 773 3377
Travel Shops:
Tel. 0845 606 0747
www.britishairways.com
Easyjet
Direct flights from London Luton to Málaga.
Tel. 0870 600 0000
www.easyjet.com
Go
There are still direct flights from London Stansted to Málaga at the time of going to press, but with Easyjet's purchase of Go, routes may change in the near future.
Tel. 0870 60 76543
www.go-fly.com
Iberia
Direct flights from London Heathrow to Seville and Málaga;

flights to Granada via Barcelona or Madrid.
Tel. 0845 601 2854
www.iberia.com
email: eurores1@ iberia.es

■ **From the US**
Direct flights to Madrid, then change for connecting flights to Seville, Málaga and Granada with Spanish carriers.
Information:
American Airlines
Tel. 1 800 433 7300
www.aa.com
Continental Airlines
Tel. 1 800 231 0856
www.continental.com
Delta Airlines
Tel. 1 800 241 4141
www.delta.com
Iberia
Direct flights from Chicago, Miami and New York to Madrid, then change for connecting flights to Seville, Málaga and Granada.
Tel. 800 772 4642
www.iberia.com

→ OTHER FLIGHTS
Cheaper flights (charters/promotional offers) are usually available. Consult the Internet and the press for special fares and packages.

TRAVEL BY CAR

The best way to take a car from the UK to Seville is to put it on the train between Paris and Madrid (*see below* "Travel by train").

TRAVEL BY COACH

Eurolines
From London
Tel. 01582 404 511
www.eurolines.com
www.gobycoach.com

TRAVEL BY TRAIN

No direct rail links between London and Andalusia. The fastest and most comfortable form of rail travel is by Eurostar train between London and Paris, arriving at Paris-Gare du Nord, then change stations. From Paris-Austerlitz daily departure at 7.43pm arriving at Madrid-Chamartín 8.58am. Return ticket (adult) from €100. From Madrid-Atocha, AVE trains for Seville (every hour 7am–10pm; duration: about 2½ hours). Fare from €60.70 in *turista* class.

■ **Information (UK)**
Eurostar
Tel. (020) 7928 5163
www.eurostar.com
Rail Europe
178 Piccadilly
London W1
Tel. 08705 848 848
www.raileurope.co.uk
Spanish Railways (RENFE) representative
Prestige International UK Ltd.
Berkeley Sq. House
Berkeley Sq.,
London W1X 5PE
Fax (020) 7409 0379
email: Spanishrail@ prestigein.co.uk

■ **Information (US)**
Rail Europe
Tel. (877) 257 2887
www.raileurope.com
Spanish Railways (RENFE) representative
CIT Tours Corp.
15 W. 44th St. 10th Fl
New York, NY 10036
Tel. (212) 730 2121
Fax (212) 730 4544

■ **SNCF (France)**
Tel. 08 36 35 35 35
www.sncf.fr
■ **RENFE (Spain)**
Tel. (34) 902 24 02 02
www.renfe.es

→ FARES
Vary according to the class of train (*turista*, *preferente*, *club*) and rush hour times (*valle*, *plana*, *punta*).

→ REDUCTIONS
Eurail, Eurodomino, Europass and Interrail cards are accepted on the Spanish railway network (RENFE).

TRAVEL INSURANCE

Before contracting a policy to cover travel cancelation, loss and/or theft of luggage and tickets, third-party liability and repatriation in case of mechanical or health problems, check that these items are not already covered by your multirisk car and home insurance policies or by your credit card company.

WHEN TO GO

The best times to go are between Apr.–June and Sep.–Oct. as the Andalusian climate is Mediterranean, with mild winters and pleasant summer temperatures on the coast, but harsh winters and scorchingly hot summers inland.

AVERAGE TEMPERATURES AND RAINFALL

	°F	MM
January	50	22
February	54	64
March	59	42
April	61	40
May	68	35
June	75	22
July	86	5
August	82	2
September	77	25
October	64	78
November	59	40
December	54	15

■ **Spring**
Pleasant temperatures, spring blossoms, *ferias* and *fiestas*.
■ **Summer**
Torrid (a siesta is an absolute must during the hottest part of the day). Sevillians tend to head for the coast during the summer months.
■ **Fall**
Mild temperatures. Grape harvest months. Rainfalls mostly in October.
■ **Winter**
Cold nights and sunny days. Hunting and olive harvesting season.

WHAT TO TAKE

■ **April to October**
Light clothing, sunglasses, sunhat, sun protection lotion and insect repellent.
■ **November to March**
A few sweaters, a raincoat and mid-season clothing.
■ **Any season**
Walking shoes. Binoculars for nature parks and/or bullfights. Formal clothes (suit and tie for men) are compulsory in the more elegant places.

AIRPORTS

→ ADDRESSES AND INFORMATION

■ Málaga
5½ miles west from the city center
Tel. 95 204 84 84
Flight information
Iberia: 95 213 61 66
Airport transfer
Taxis, trains every 30 mins (Málaga–Fuengirola line), buses

■ Seville
5 miles from the city center on the N-IV
Tel. 954 44 90 00
Flight information
Iberia: 954 22 89 01
Airport transfer
Taxis and buses

■ Granada
10½ miles southeast of the city on the road to Málaga
Tel. 958 24 52 23
Iberia: 958 22 75 92
Airport transfer
Taxis and buses

■ Almería
Road to Nijar, km 9 (5½ miles)
Tel. 950 21 37 15
Iberia: 950 25 11 35
Airport transfer
Taxis and buses

■ Jerez de la Frontera
6¼ miles north of the city on the N-IV Madrid–Cádiz
Tel. 956 15 00 00
Airport transfer
Taxis

BICYCLES

Bicycles can be hired on an hourly or daily basis in major cities, Costa del Sol resorts and mountain holiday resorts.

BOATS (CRUISES ON THE GUADALQUIVIR)

Cruises down the Guadalquivir from April to October. The trip from Seville to Sanlúcar de Barrameda offers some magnificent views of villages, riverside landscapes, marshes and the landscapes and wildlife of the remarkable Doñana National Park. Boats moor in the gourmet paradise of Bajo de Guía.
Departure Sat. at 8.30am. Around €23.
Cruceros Turísticos "Torre del Oro"
Muelle Torre del Oro
Tel. 95 421 13 96

BUSES

→ SEVILLE

Orange buses belonging to the bus company TUSSAM run between 6am and 11.45pm. *Circulares* (C1 to C4) operate around the city center. Night buses (A1 to A6) service certain parts of the city, leaving from Plaza Nueva every hour between midnight and 2am. If you buy your ticket on the bus after 9pm, make sure you have the right change as drivers do not give change at this time of night.

■ Information
Destinations and times are available from all TUSSAM counters and tourist offices.
Tel. 900 71 01 71 (toll-free number)
www.tussam.es

■ Tickets
On sale in tobacconists' stores, at news stands, from the bus company and on board.
– One-way ticket: *billete sencillo* or *univiaje* (€0.90);
– *Bonobus*: 10-journey ticket without transfer (€3.80), or with transfer (€4.50);
– *Tarjeta turística* (tourist ticket): 1 day (€3), 3 days (€7) or 7 days (€10).

→ SEVILLE REGION

Various companies operate in the Seville region. Buses leave from:
– Plaza de Armas for the western region and El Aljarafe;
– Paseo de Colón for San Juan de Aznalfarache and Coria del Río;
– Prado de San Sebastián for Dos Hermanas and the southern region.

→ CÓRDOBA AND GRANADA

Buses operate in these two cities but do not go past the main monuments, which are situated in the pedestrian zone.

CAR AND MOTORCYCLES

→ ROAD NETWORK

Fast expressways and good national roads. There is a toll fee on expressways (*autopistas*) between the towns of Seville, Jerez and Cádiz, and between Málaga, Marbella and Estepona.
The state of minor roads may vary.
Traffic information
Tel. 91 535 22 22

→ GAS

Lead-free (*sin plomo*): octane 95 or *Eurosuper* and octane 98 or *Súper Star*; super and diesel (*gasóleo*).
No LPG. Credit cards are accepted in all gas stations.

→ HIGHWAY CODE

Signs are the same as in the rest of Europe, but they can be inconsistent as obsolete signs are not always removed.
■ Vehicles coming from the right have right of way, as well as those already engaged around a traffic circle or a city square.
■ Seatbelts must be worn by passengers both in the front and the back of the vehicle.
■ Motorcycles over 125cc: crash helmets must be worn and lights must be on at all times.
■ Drink-driving
Maximum level of alcohol in the blood: 50 mg/100 ml.
■ Speed limits
– Freeways: 75 mph (120 km/h)
– Fast roads: 62 mph (100 km/h)
– Roads: 50 mph (80 km/h)
– In the city: 30 mph (50 km/h)
Speeding incurs severe penalties.

→ DRIVING IN SPAIN

Spain is one of the countries leading the European list for traffic accidents. Spanish drivers are not the most patient in the world and tend to make excessive use of the horn. They do not regard flashing one's lights as a friendly gesture to give right of way but as an aggressive way of demanding it!

→ IN BUILT-UP AREAS

Driving in the narrow little streets of Seville, Córdoba and some villages can be difficult. You are advised to leave your car in a parking lot and continue your journey on foot or by public transport.

→ RENTAL

■ Cars
There are many national as well as international car rental companies in Andalusian cities and airports. The smaller, local companies tend to offer more attractive rates and usually collect their clients from the airport. Booking a car before leaving your country is recommended, especially in the high season.
Drivers must be aged over 21 (or 23) and have held a driving license for at least one year.
■ Motorcycles and mopeds
Motorcycle and moped rental is rare and very expensive.

→ **TRAFFIC POLICE**

Seville
Tel. 95 462 11 11
Córdoba
Tel. 957 20 30 33
Granada
Tel. 958 15 36 00
Málaga
Tel. 95 239 19 00/04/08

COACHES

→ **REGIONAL AND LONG-DISTANCE LINES**

Various companies offer fast, regular services in air-conditioned coaches to most cities and villages in Andalusia.

■ **Destinations and timetables**
Available from tourist offices, in the local press or from the bar nearest to the coach station or stop.

■ **Tickets**
From the coach companies, at coach stations or on the bus for minor routes.

→ **COACH STATIONS**

■ **Seville**
Plaza de Armas
Coaches for Seville's northern region, Huelva province and Madrid
Tel. 95 490 80 40 or 95 490 77 37
Prado de San Sebastián
Coaches to Jerez, Cádiz, Arcos de la Frontera, Ronda, Córdoba, and the villages of the interior (Carmona, Osuna, Estepa, Écija), Algeciras, Granada, Costa del Sol, Valencia and Barcelona
Tel. 954 41 71 11

■ **Málaga**
Paseo de los Tilos (¾ mile west of the city center, next to the railway station).
Tel. 95 235 00 61

■ **Granada**
Av. de Jaén (1¾ miles northwest of the city center)
Tel. 958 25 13 58

■ **Córdoba**
C. Federico García Lorca, 3
Tel. 957 40 40 40

■ **Cádiz**
Calle Doctor Fleming
Tel. 902 24 02 02
Cia Comes
Tel. 956 22 42 71
Cia Los Amarillos
Tel. 956 28 58 52

■ **Almería**
Plaza de Barcelona (in the eastern part of the city)
Tel. 950 21 00 29

→ **FARES AND JOURNEY DURATION**

■ **Seville–Cádiz**
Compania Comes
Tel. 95 441 68 58
Duration: 1¾ hrs
One way: around €8.50
Return: around €13

■ **Seville–Granada**
Compania Alsina
Tel. 95 441 88 11
Duration: 3 hrs.
One way: around €15
Return: around €24

■ **Seville–Málaga**
Compania Alsina
Duration: 2½ hrs
One way: around €12
Return: around €21

HORSE-DRAWN CARRIAGES

In Seville: near the cathedral, in the Parque María Luisa, near the Torre del Oro and outside Hotel Alfonso XIII. In Córdoba: around La Mezquita. Tariffs are usually displayed or they can be negotiated (€27–€60 for a horse-drawn excursion, depending on the season).

MAPS

Map section of this guide p. 415. Michelin map no. 446 (South of Spain) can be bought at local gas stations and in bookstores. City maps are available from tourist offices.

PLANES

There are no air links betwen the various cities in Andalusia.

TAXIS

White taxis with an orange strip and a logo on passenger doors, can be found in all cities, day and night. Minimum fare around €3; 25% surcharge at night and on public holidays.

→ **RESERVATIONS**

■ **Seville**
Tel. 95 458 00 00
Tel. 95 462 22 22
Tel. 95 467 55 55

■ **Cádiz**
Tel. 956 21 21 21
Tel. 956 26 26 26

■ **Córdoba**
Tel. 957 47 51 53
Tel. 957 27 23 74

■ **Granada**
Tel. 958 15 14 61
Tel. 958 28 06 54

■ **Málaga**
Tel. 95 232 00 00
Tel. 95 233 33 33

TRAINS

→ **REGIONAL SERVICES**

■ The *Grandes Lineas* from Barcelona and Madrid also serve the major Andalusian cities (see p. 355). From Madrid-Atocha AVE trains go to Seville (2½ hrs) and to Córdoba (1¼ hrs); Talgo 200 trains go to Málaga (4½ hrs), Cádiz (5 hrs) or Huelva (4½ hrs).

■ The cheaper *Regionales, TDR* and *cercanias* are regional and local trains.

→ **REDUCTIONS**

■ Only Spanish residents are entitled to Iberrail reductions.

■ Special conditions for foreign tourists:
– return journey on the same route;
– for vehicles carried on the train;
– Paris–Madrid and Paris–Barcelona Talgo services (for under-26s and over-60s).

■ **RENFE**
Tel. 902 24 02 02
www.renfe.es

→ **"AL-ANDALUS" EXPRESS**

This train consists of period carriages dating from the early 20th century and operates a round-trip from Seville to Córdoba, Granada, Baeza, Úbeda, Ronda and Jerez, including guided tours to the major monuments, and lasts 7 days. Individual trips from March to November, from €2,565. Special prices for honeymooners. Departure Sat. night.

■ **Information**
Tel. 902 333 666
www.alandalus expreso.com

CONTENTS

ACCOMMODATION

→ INFORMATION
Yearly *Hotel and Pension Guide* and *Camping Guide* are published by the Spanish Secretary of State for Tourism. Both are on sale in local bookstores and at tourist offices.
■ **Reservations**
(in Spanish)
www.seneca.web.com

→ HIGH SEASON
The busiest times are between Easter and October (July and August in particular), Christmas and New Year holiday period, Easter week and when major local celebrations or festivals are held. Reservations are essential during the high season, and rates tend to be 30% higher than those offered in the low season. The prices indicated are usually exclusive of tax ("IVA", 7%).

→ HOTELS
■ **"Hoteles"**
Hotels are classified according to a star system (1 to 5) and indicated by a white H on a blue-painted sign. They usually include a restaurant.
■ **"Hoteles residencias"**
("HR"). No food served.
■ **"Hostales" and "pensiones" (boarding houses)**
From 1 to 3 stars ("Hs"). They are as comfortable as hotels in similar categories, but cheaper.
■ **"Hostales residenciales"**
("HsR") for long-term residents. No food served.
■ **Rates**
From €30 for a double room.

→ "PARADORES"
Run by the Ministry of Tourism, these establishments have both elegance and charm. With a few modern exceptions, "paradores" tend to occupy classified historic monuments such as old palaces, monasteries and castles, and enjoy great locations.
■ **Rates**
From €90 for a double room.
■ **Reservations**
Paradores de Turismo
Calle Requena, 3
28013 Madrid
Tel. 91 516 66 66
Fax 91 516 66 57
www.parador.es
General number
Tel. 902 177 177

→ COUNTRY HOMES AND ROOMS IN PRIVATE HOMES
For a room in a private manor house, a small farm or a "troglodyte"-style (rock-cut) house. Brochures available from tourist offices.
■ **Rates**
From €30 for a double room.
■ **Reservations**
Red de Alojamientos rurales
Tel. 902 44 22 33
Fax 950 27 16 78
www.raar.es
SENECA
Tel. 952 92 02 10
Fax 952 92 02 16
www.seneca-web.com
www.andalucia.org
Viajes Rural Andalus
Tel. 952 27 62 29
Fax 952 27 65 56

→ SEASONAL ACCOMMODATION
For appartments, houses and villas to let, contact a tourist office, a specialized real-estate agent, a tour operator or consult the press.

→ YOUTH HOSTELS
("Albergues juveniles") There are some 20 comfortable youth hostels (bed linen provided) in Andalusia, most part of Inturjoven. They are usually open all year and accept bookings for three consecutive nights. No cooking facilities but reasonably priced meals are served. International or National YHA membership card needed.
■ **Information UK**
Youth Hostel Association
Dimple Road
Matlock
Derbyshire DE4 3YH
Tel. 01629 592600
www.yha.org.uk
■ **Information US**
Hosteling International
891 Amsterdam Ave (W. 103rd St)
New York
Tel. (212) 932 2300
www.hostels.com
■ **Prices**
From €8 to €16 per night, depending on the season.
■ **Reservations**
Inturjoven
Miño, 24
41011 Seville
Tel. 902 510 000
www.inturjoven.com

→ CAMPSITES
Over 120 campsites, most of them well equipped, along the coast or near nature reserves. Three categories (1st to 3rd class), according to the facilities provided.
■ **Prices**
About €2.10 to €4 per adult per day.

→ "REFUGIOS"
Mountain and national park refuges are administered by the Andalusian Mountain Sports Federation.
■ **Fed. Andaluza de Montañismo**
Camino de Roda, 101
Edificio Atalaya 1°
Oficina 7 G
18003 Granada
Tel. 958 29 13 40
www.fedamon.com

DRESS CODE

Proper dress (no shorts, deep-cut clothes or bare shoulders) in religious buildings. Bathing suits and daring summer wear are best kept for the beach; in city centers nor in country places, they can even be offensive. The Spaniards like to dress up, especially in the evening.

DRINKS

→ BEER ● *60*
In Andalusia light beers are brewed and served in bottles or on draft (ask for *una caña de cerveza*).

→ COFFEE
Andalusians often take a small glass of equal amounts of coffee and milk (*café con leche*) for breakfast or a mid-morning break. If there is more milk than coffee, people talk of a *sombra*. The equivalent of an espresso is known as *café solo*.

→ WATER AND FRUIT JUICE
Although tap water is drinkable, Andalusians prefer sparkling (*agua mineral con gas*) or still mineral water (*sin gas*). In bars you can get freshly

squeezed orange juice (*zumo de naranja natural*), grape juice (*mosto*) or tiger nut milk (*horchata*).

→ WINE ● 60 ▲ 306
Andalusian wine tends to be served as a pre-dinner drink, to go with *tapas*. Wines from other Spanish regions are served during a meal. Easily spotted in its golden robe, the *fino*, the Andalusian wine par excellence, is a sherry wine (*jerez*) that owes its taste to its *flor* ("bloom", or film of yeast on the surface of the must produced during the fermentation process) and has an alcohol content of 15° to 17°. Order *una copa de vino fino* as a pre-dinner drink: delicate and light, it goes beautifully with cured ham (*jamón serrano*) and spiced olives. *Fino* matured in casks is known as *amontillado* (or *fino viejo*), a full-bodied wine with a deep golden color. If the "bloom" has not developed as much, *jerez* produces *oloroso*, a sweeter, amber-colored wine with a higher alcohol content (18° to 20°).

→ SPIRITS
The three main Spanish spirits are *aguardiente*, *coñac* and *moscatel*. They are taken with desserts or as post-dinner liqueurs. *Aguardiente* tends to be an anis-based spirit. Those from Jerez are known as *coñac*. The more famous *Moscatel* is produced in the Málaga region (*vino Málaga*).

ELECTRICITY
220 V, 50 Hz
Two round-pin plugs.

ENTERTAINMENT

→ BULLFIGHTING ● 52
The bullfighting season begins on Easter Sunday, with appearances by the best *toreros* (bullfighters). After that, *corridas* are held on Saturdays and Sundays until the Wednesday before the Feria de Abril ◆ *364*, when the bullfighting festival begins and *corridas* are held every day. On the second Sunday after Easter, there is a mounted *corrida*. After April, *corridas*, and especially *novilladas* (fights using young bulls), are held on public holidays. Those held in the month of August are particularly well known. The Feria de San Miguel, in September, marks the end of the season. Bullfights start at 5pm or 6.30pm, depending on the season. **Tickets** are on sale at Calle Adriano, 37 or at the bullring, Paseo de Colón. Tickets sold in city-center ticket offices (for example, Calle Sierpes, Calle Tetuán, Avda. de la Constitución) have a 10% surcharge.
Tarifs *Tendio de sol* (seat in the sun): around €21; *tendio de sombra* (in the shade): around €42.

→ FLAMENCO ● 54
Flamenco is an important part of most popular festivals and has its own particular venues.

■ "Peñas" and "Tablaos"
Peñas (circles) are fairly closed associations of flamenco aficionados to which it is virtually impossible to gain admittance without being recommended by a member. *Tablaos*, or *tablaos flamenco*, are bars where flamenco performances are held year round ◆ *380*.

■ Festivals
Flamenco festivals are usually held in summer. For example: La Bulería (Jerez de la Frontera), El Potaje (Utrera), El Gazpacho (Morón), La Caracolá (Lebrija) and the biennial flamenco festival (Seville) in the month of September in even years ◆ *365*.

→ THEATER, DANCE AND CLASSICAL MUSIC

■ Seville
The main theaters in Seville are the **Teatro de la Maestranza** (Paseo de Colón, 22 ◆ *396*), **Teatro Lope de Vega** (Avda. María Luisa ◆ *396*) and **Teatro Central** (on the Isla de la Cartuja ◆ *396*), and in some churches, in particular **Iglesia del Divino Salvador** ◆ *395*, and in the **cathedral** ◆ *394*.

■ Córdoba
Performances and concerts throughout the year in **Gran Teatro** (Av. del Gran Capitán, 3 ◆ *385*). Classical music every weekend in July and Aug., near the Judería (Callejas de las Flores, del Indiano, Plaza de la Concha and Plaza Judá-Levi); concerts and movies at the **Ermita de la Aurora**. Movie shows (at 10pm and midnight) in the courtyards of some of the city's monuments.

■ Granada
Concerts, plays and other performances at the **Auditorio Manuel de Falla** (Paseo de los Mártires ◆ *387*) and at the **Teatro Alhambra** (Calle Molinos, 56 ◆ *388*). Classical music concerts, exhibitions and conferences are also held at the palace of **El Carmen de los Martires**, next to the Alhambra.

FOOD
In Andalusia, lunch is at 2pm or 3pm, and dinner at about 10pm. Various cultures have left their mark on the region (Phoenician, Roman, Jewish,

Arab, and Latin American), resulting in a rich, varied cuisine. *Tapas*, or pre-dinner snacks (*tapeo*), are the best example of the Andalusian culinary tradition.

→ COASTAL CUISINE
Based on fish and seafood – grilled, fried or baked with salt (*a la sal*), it includes mussels (*mejillones*), small fried or grilled fish (*pescaíto frito*), anchovies fried in batter (*rebozados*) or marinated in vinegar (*boquerones*), red mullet, squid, sardines in kebabs or marinated in white wine with garlic, olive oil, parsley and lemon (*moraga*), and prawns (*langostinos*), all served with rice.

→ COUNTRY CUISINE
Bread crumbs (*miga*) are much used; there is even a *miga* festival (*Fiesta de las Migas y de los Vinos*), held in Torrox in December. Specialties of the mountain villages include *salmojero* (a popular dressing of tomato and bread crumbs), *potajes* (pulse dishes), *pucheros* (broth), *tortillas de patatas* (potato omelet served with wild asparagus or beans), *rabo de toro* (oxtail in paprika sauce), El Bosque trout, vegetables such as cabbage and celery, game animals and birds (jugged hare, stews, pigeon with olives) and cooked meats – *salchichón, chorizo, morcilla* (blood sausage) and *jamón ibérico* (ham).

→ TAPAS ● *60*
Served between *Tapas* consist of small dishes (*raciones* or even *media raciones* – half portions) of salt meat and fish, seafood, meat cooked in sauce, vegetables, olives, eggs, etc. This is usually done standing up or sitting on a stool at the counter, with a glass of wine or a beer.

→ GAZPACHOS ● *58*
Another Andalusian specialty, a cold soup made of tomatoes, bread and garlic, and served with diced vegetables and croutons. A white version, *ajo blanco*, is made from almonds and crushed garlic (the Ajoblanco festival in Almachar is held in August).

→ PATISSERIES
Many of Seville's and Granada's convents make and sell confectionery. Jewish and Arab influences are also reflected in some of these *dulces*, such as the typical Córdoban cake flavored with orange-flower blossom and covered in angel's hair, *pestiños* and *buñuelos* (doughnuts), sesame-seed feuilletés, quince paste (*membrillo*), and *turrones* (nougat). The traditional Christmas biscuits (*polvorones*, *roscones and mantecados*) are flavored with almonds, cinnamon or aniseed.

→ FRUIT
Andalusia produces a great variety of fruit, which take pride of place at the end of all meals. Apart from oranges and strawberries, which are widely exported, figs, persimmon fruit, muskmelons, pomegranates and grapes are also grown in the region.

HEALTH

There are no specific health requirements.

→ PHARMACIES
Indicated by an illuminated green or red cross, *farmacias* are open during normal business hours. They sell many medicines over the counter, including antibiotics. A list of emergency pharmacies is posted in all pharmacy windows and published in the local press.

→ EMERGENCIES
In case of an emergency go to the *urgencias* department of the nearest clinic or to the *ambulatorio* (hospital belonging to the Spanish national health service), carrying form E111 if you are an EU citizen. See Health ◆ *354*.

→ HOSPITALS

■ **Seville**
Nuestra Señora de Valme
Crta de Cádiz
Tel. 95 459 60 00
Virgen de la Macarena
C. Doctor Fedriani, 3
Tel. 95 500 80 00
Virgen del Rocio
Av. de Manuel Siurot
Tel. 95 501 20 00

■ **Córdoba**
Hospital de la Cruz
Paseo de la Victoria
Tel. 957 29 34 11
Los Morales
Crta los Morales
Tel. 957 21 70 00
Hospital Provincial
Av. Menéndez Pidal
Tel. 957 21 76 00
Reina Sofia
Av. Menéndez Pidal
Tel. 957 77 15 00

■ **Granada**
San Cecilio
Av. Doctor Oloriz, 16
Tel. 958 27 69 00
Complejo Hospitalario
Av. de las Fuerzas Armadas, 2
Tel. 958 24 11 00

■ **Málaga**
Hospital Costa del Sol
Ctra Nacional 340, km 187, Marbella
Tel. 95 286 27 48
Carlos Haya
Av. Carlos Haya
Tel. 95 239 04 00

MAIL

→ LETTERS
Sending a letter or a postcard to European Union countries costs €0.45, to the rest of the world €0.72. Stamps (*sellos*) can be bought from post offices (*oficinas de correos*) and tobacconists' stores (*estancos*). Delivery time to the EU is about 3 or 4 days, to other countries from one week to 15 days.

→ MAIN POST OFFICES

■ **Seville**
Av. de la Constitución, 32
Tel. 95 421 64 76

■ **Cádiz**
Plaza Topete
Tel. 956 21 21 71

■ **Córdoba**
Calle Cruz Conde, 15
Tel. 957 47 91 96

■ **Granada**
Puerta Real 1
Tel. 958 22 11 38

■ **Málaga**
Av. de Andalucía, 1
Tel. 95 234 84 31
or 902 19 71 97

MEDIA

→ PRESS

■ **General Spanish newspapers**
Andalusian editions of the daily national newspapers *El País*, *El Mundo* and *ABC* are available, as well as regional papers such as *El Diario de Andalucía* and *El Correo de Andalucía*, and the main provincial papers *Huelva Informacíon*, *La Voz de Almería*, *Diario de Cádiz*, *Diario de Jerez*, *Europa Sur* (Cádiz), *Ideal* (Granada), *Córdoba*, *Jaén*, *Sur* (Málaga), *Diario de*

Sevilla and *ABC* (Seville). All give information on cultural events, sports and transport, as well as useful telephone numbers.

■ **Cultural reviews**
La Tribuna, a weekly review distributed free of charge in Córdoba, the monthly *El Giraldillo* in Seville, and the *Guía del Ocio* in Granada and Málaga all contain guides to cultural and leisure activities.

■ **Foreign press**
Usually delivered on the same day of publication, or on the following day, and available in airports, main railway stations and tourist centers.

→ RADIO
RNE 1 (general-interest station), RNE 2 (classical music), RNE 3 (jazz, blues, rock, pop) and RNE 5 (information) as well as four Radio Nacional de España stations broadcast in FM. So does Canal Sur Radio (general-interest station) and Andalucía Información, the two Andalusian public stations. Some private stations, such as Radiolé and Cadena Dial, only play music. Several English-language stations can be received on the coast.

→ TELEVISION
There are five national channels, including two public ones (TV1 and La 2) and three private ones (Antena 3, Tele 5 and Canal+). There are also two regional public channels (Canal Sur 1 and Canal 2 Andalucía), and many local channels (Giralda Televisión, Canal 47, Sevilla Televisión, Málaga TV, Telenova – Huelva).

MONEY

→ CURRENCY
Since Jan.1, 2002, the monetary unit has been the euro (€), in denominations of €5, €10, €20, €50, €100, €200 and €500 (notes) and €1, €2, 1, 2, 5, 10, 20 and 50 eurocents (coins). See also Money ◆ *354*

NIGHTLIFE

■ **Seville**
In summer, bars turn their terraces into open dance floors along the river and stay open until dawn. People go for *tapas* in Calle Betis, in the Triana district. In the fall and in winter, nightlife tends to be centered around the *tapas* bars of Plaza del Salvador, which are always crowded both around lunchtime (from about noon until 4pm) and in the evenings between 8pm and midnight, and in the nightclubs of the Alfalfa, Arenal, Barrio de Santa Cruz and Alameda de Hércules.

■ **Córdoba**
In summer, nightlife is concentrated around the districts of the Brillante and Tablero (terraces), and Arenal (bars, nightclubs). In winter the fine *tapas* bars of the Judería remain busy and lively.

■ **Granada**
Thanks to its university and student population, Granada is always lively in winter. The nightclubs of the Calle Pedro Antonio de Alarcón, of the Camino del Darro and Plaza Nueva are popular with the younger crowds, while the bars and refreshment stalls (*kioskos*) on Plaza Birambla tend to attract a quieter clientele. The Albaicín tearooms are the perfect place for those in search of peace and luxury.

OPENING TIMES

■ **Banks**
Mon.–Sat. (Mon.–Fri. in summer) 8.30am–2pm

■ **Stores**
9am/9.30am–1.30pm and 4.30pm–8pm or 5pm–8.30pm; department stores do not close for lunch. In summer, stores tend to close later, especially in seaside resorts, and are open 7 days a week.

■ **Post offices**
Mon.–Fri. 8.30am– 8.30pm, Sat. 9am–1.30pm.

PUBLIC HOLIDAYS

See Festivals and holidays ◆ *364*

SAFETY

Thieves operate in all tourist places, especially in Seville and Málaga. Beware of pickpockets and "steal-and-run" thieves. Do not leave any valuables in your vehicle, not even in the trunk, unless your car is in a supervised parking lot. Carry photocopies of your ID papers, leaving the originals in a secure place such as your hotel safe.

→ LOSS AND THEFT

■ **Objects**
After reporting the loss or theft of your property at the nearest police station, ask for a copy of the declaration form if you want to make a claim with your insurers. You can also try the Lost and Found Office (*Oficina de objetos perdidos*) at the townhall, or at the police or railway stations.

■ **ID papers**
Contact your embassy or consulate for a temporary ID document.

■ **Credit cards and traveler's cheks**
American Express
Tel. 91 570 77 77
Diners Club
91 547 40 00
Thomas Cook
Tel. 91 431 64 91
Visa
Tel. 900 94 11 18

SHOPPING

→ ANTIQUES
Essentially 19th-century items (Ronda ceramics, genre paintings, furniture and objets d'art).

→ CERAMICS AND POTTERY ● *56*
Seville's patron saints, Santa Justa and Santa Rufina, both made pottery in the Triana district, which still has a number of ceramic workshops. The city and its region (Carmona, Lebrija, Lora del Río, Osuna, Sanlúcar la Mayor) produce a wide range of ceramics, such as glazed and dry-rope, as well as tiles with 16th-, 17th- and 18th-century motifs.

Córdoba and Granada are famous for their Mudéjar-style ceramics in traditional colors (blue, green and black on a white background). So is Úbeda for its distinctive green enameled terracotta and Lucena for its ceramics with their green and yellow geometric motifs.

→ LEATHERWORK ● *62*
With its crowned lion motif, *repoussé* (embossed) leather is Córboba's century-old specialty. Other towns also have specialties: Ubrique (Cádiz region) is famous for its travel goods.

Andalusian artisans also produce jackets, belts, purses and shoes (Almería, Antequera and Montoro), boots (Valverde del Camino), horseriding items (Jerez de la Frontera) and hunting goods.

→ METALWORK
The tradition of metalworking (copper, brass and wrought iron) has been kept alive at Lucena, Seville, Úbeda et Granada. Padlocks, lamps, umbrella-holders and other decorative items are some of the best examples of this work.

→ GOLDWARE, SILVERWARE AND JEWELRY ● *62*
The Spanish capital of goldwork and silverwork, Córdoba is renowned for its filigree work, even if it is now partly done by machine. The Tesoro del Carambolo (6th century BC) provided a starting point for the tradition of gold and silverwork in Seville. The prevalence of religious celebrations has meant that the tradition is still very much alive in Seville and Granada, with artisans specialized in the production of religious objects, such as processional paraphernalia (lanterns, insignia and candleholders).

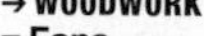

→ WOODWORK
■ **Fans**
The finest fans are made of fabric and of engraved, hand-painted wood.
■ **Musical instruments**
The best Spanish guitars come from Granada, though Seville, Córdoba and Almería are also known for their fine instruments.
■ **Inlaid work**
Granada is famous for its chess sets, boxes, caskets, frames and furniture with mother-of-pearl, ivory, amber and colored-wood inlays in the Mudéjar style.

→ TEXTILES
Delicately embroidered Manila shawls, mantillas and other items of traditional *sevillanas* costumes, woollen blankets from Grazalema, Mudéjar-style carpets and hangings woven in Las Alpujarras are some of the region's most traditional crafts. Hangings, carpets and soft furnishings with reproductions of 17th- and 18th-century motifs are also produced in Málaga.

SPORTS

→ CYCLING
Information and the brochure *120 Itineraries around Andalusia on a Mountain Bike* are available from tourist offices.

→ GOLF
Andalusia is a golfers' paradise, with some 60 golf courses on the Costa del Sol, aptly nicknamed "Costa del Golf".
■ **Information**
Tourist offices and *www.sopde.es*

→ HORSERIDING
Horses are a vital part of rural life in Andalusia. A variety of horseriding facilities are available for all levels (beginners' classes, dressage, short rides or longer rides on the coast or in the sierra).
■ Dressage demonstrations at **Real Escuela Andaluza de Arte Ecuestre** in Jerez de la Frontera ◆ *390*.
■ **Information**
www.tourspain.es
Brochures available from tourist offices.

→ HIKING
The best time for walking and hiking is between mid-July and September in the Sierra Nevada, and from April until June and in September and October in other parts of Andalusia. ***Warning:*** *Walking paths are not always well marked.*

→ MOUNTAIN CLIMBING
The Sierra Nevada offers many climbing locations, such as the Peak of Mulhacén, the highest mountain in Spain (11,413 feet). The gorge of El

Chorro (Málaga region), Sierra de las Nieves, near Ronda, Sierra de Grazalema and Sierra Magina (Jaén region), Sierra Filambres and Sierra María (Almería region) are also excellent climbing spots.

■ **Information**
Tourist offices
Fed. Andaluza de Montañismo
Cam. de Ronda, 101
Edificio Atalaya 1ª
18003 Granada
Tel./fax 958 29 13 40

→ SCUBA DIVING
Foreigners must have a diving permit certified by a Spanish club member of the Underwater Activities Federation.

■ **Best locations**
Cabo de Gata, Las Negras, La Isleta, San José and Morrón de los Genoveses in the Almería region, La Herradura in the Granada region, from Nerja to the coast of Granada in Málaga province.

■ **Information**
Fed. Andaluza de Actividades Subacuáticas
Playa de las Almadrabillas, 10
04007 Almería
Tel. 950 27 06 12
www.fedas.es
www.buceo.com

→ SKIING
Granada is only 18½ miles away from the snow slopes of the Sierra Nevada (peaks range from 6,800 feet to 11,155 feet high). The 1996 World Ski Championships were held at the Pradollanos ski resort (Solynieve), the southernmost skiing location in Europe. Most ski resorts are open Dec.–April only.

■ **Information and reservations**
For information on resorts, snow, hotels:
Tel. 902 70 80 90
www.tele-ski.com

→ WATERSPORTS
There are more than 515 miles of coastline, around 30 marinas in towns and villages, as well as sailing, windsurfing and water skiing clubs in most seaside resorts. Canoeing and kayaking activities are also possible on the lakes and rivers inland.

■ **Information**
www.webnautica.es
Fed. Andaluza de Piragüismo
Apartado de Correos 442 – Cádiz
11080 Cádiz
Tel. 956 25 21 87

Fed. Andaluza de Vela
Avda. de la Libertad
Puerto Sherry
El Puerto de Santa María
11500 Cádiz
Tel. 956 87 48 05

TELEPHONE

→ PHONING WITHIN SPAIN
All numbers to fixed lines have 9 digits. Numbers beginning 900 are freephone numbers; those with 901 are local call rate numbers; those with 902 are national call rate numbers; and with 6, mobile phone numbers.

→ PUBLIC TELEPHONES
Some call boxes take cards (*tarjetas teléfonicas*, €10 and €20), bought at tobacconists' stores. A local call costs around €0.15 and an international call €1.20. Operating instructions are given in several languages. Bars and cafés often have a public phone, but calls are more expensive.

→ MOBILE PHONES
Telephone shops now sell mobile phones without contracts. You purchase the phone and at least €30 worth of calls for about €120. The card can then be recharged in €30 units as required.

→ CALLING FROM SPAIN
To phone the UK: Dial 00 + 44 + the number (omitting the initial 0 of the regional code).
To phone the US and Canada: Dial 00 + 1 + the number you need.

TIPPING

A service charge (*servicio*) is usually included in hotel and restaurant bills. Tipping is not compulsory, but tips (*propinas*) are usually given in restaurants, bars and taxis.

USEFUL NUMBERS

Inquiries:	1003
International inquiries:	025
First aid:	061
Guardia Civil (police):	062
Fire service:	080
National police:	091
Local police:	092
Alarm calls:	096
Ambulances, fire brigade, police, civilian rescue:	112

USEFUL ADDRESSES

→ CONSULATES
Most consulates or consular agencies are open Mon.–Fri. morning and one or two hours in the afternoon.

■ **British consulates**
Granada:
C de S. Cristobal
Ctra de Murcia s/n
Tel. 958 27 47 24
Malaga:
C. Duquesa de Parcent, 8
Tel. 95 221 75 71
Fax 95 222 11 30
Seville:
Plaza Nueva 8
Tel. 95 422 88 74
Fax 95 421 03 23

■ **US consulates**
Malaga:
Av J Gómez "Juanito", 8
Tel. (95 247 48 91
Fax (95) 246 51 89
Seville:
P de las Delicias, 7
Tel. (95) 423 18 85
Fax (95) 423 20 40

■ **Canada consulate**
Seville:
Av. Constitución, 30
Tel. (95) 422 94 13

→ TOURIST OFFICES
Details in "Places to visit" p. 382

→ INTERNET SITES
www.andalucia.org
www.okspain.org
www.tourspain.es
www.turismo.sevilla.org
Language resources:
www.linguanet.org.uk

◆ FESTIVALS AND HOLIDAYS

CARNIVAL
Imported from Venice in the 16th century, the February carnival is celebrated with great exuberance in many Andalusian cities and villages. The most lavish are those of Cádiz and Málaga.

CORPUS CHRISTI ● *49*
Celebrated throughout Andalusia with a procession on the second Thursday following Whit Sunday. The streets and shops are decorated for the occasion. In Seville, young boys in medieval costume, the *seises* ● *49*, dance in the cathedral in front of the altar before the start of the procession. In Granada, a carnival dragon and effigies of Christian and Moorish kings join the procession.

FERIA DE ABRIL ● *50*
Originally a cattle market, the "April fair" takes place 1–2 weeks after Holy Week. It is held in a whitewashed area known as the "Real", where wood and canvas stands (*casetas*) are decorated with lanterns, shawls and bullfighting motifs. These *casetas* are rented by families, companies or associations and people come to them to dance, eat and drink. Every day there is a procession of horseriders and magnificently harnessed horse-drawn carriages, and *corridas* are held in the bullrings.

→ OTHER "FERIAS"
Held on local saint's days, including:
■ **Feria del Caballo** Jerez, in May (horse riders' parades, competitions, *corridas* and flamenco).
■ **Festival de los Patios** in May (competitions and flamenco) and **Feria de Mayo** in Córdoba.
■ **Fiesta de la Virgen del Carmen** In many coastal locations, around July 15 (regattas and other sports events). The Virgin's shrine is carried out to sea on a fishing boat.
■ **Fiesta estivale** In Málaga, in Aug. (parades, concerts, *corridas*, bands)
■ **Feria de Pedro Romero**, with *goyesca corrida*, in Ronda, Sep. 15.

HARVEST FESTIVALS
The main aim of the festivals held after the grape harvest, usually in September, is to find buyers for the wine that has been produced. Cellars are open to the public, who are invited to taste the new wine.
■ The most famous harvest festival is at Jerez de la Frontera and coincides with a literary competition.
■ In the Cádiz region, similar festivals are held at Chipiona, Puerto Real, Rota, Sanlúcar de Barrameda and Trebujena.
■ The harvest festival of Villanueva del Ariscal (Seville region) coincides with a pilgrimage to the monastery of El Loreto, in which the float of Saint Ginés de la Jara is preceded by the festival queen, horsewomen and flamenco dancers. Some of the grapes are pressed and the first must is dedicated as a gift to the saint. It can be tasted in the cellars and taverns of the villages of El Aljarafe, Umbrete, Olivares and Bollullos de la Mitación.

PILGRIMAGES

→ ROMERÍA DE NUESTRA SEÑORA DE LA CABEZA
At Andújar (Jaén region), on the final weekend in April. On the Saturday, some 250,000 pilgrims go to the sanctuary (18½ miles) on foot, on horseback or in carts. The next day the Reina de la Sierra Morena is carried in procession.

→ ROMERÍA DEL ROCÍO
The most famous and most popular pilgrimage in Andalusia. At Whitsun, more than one million pilgrims arrive at the sanctuary on foot, on horseback and in carts. They feast for two days, then at dawn on Whit Monday, the statue of the Virgen del Rocío is taken out of the sanctuary to welcome the pilgrims.

→ GIPSY ROMERÍA
On the 3rd Sunday in June at Cabra (Córdoba region). Thousands of gipsies escort the Virgen de la Sierra to her sanctuary where a *flamenca* mass is then held.

→ ROMERÍA DE VALME
On the 2nd Sunday in October at Dos Hermanas, near Seville. The statue of the Virgin is carried in a procession then, after a traditional rural meal has been held, returned to her chapel.

SEMANA SANTA ● *44*
The week betwen Palm Sunday and Easter, Semana Santa (Holy Week), is Seville's most famous festival. Over one hundred brotherhoods take part in a procession. To appreciate it fully, it is essential to be involved in the whole event (although parts of it are more spectacular than others). If not, it will be little more than a procession of penitents and floats. If you want to see all the brotherhoods, you can reserve a seat on the official route (*carrera oficial*) from the Plaza de la Campana to the cathedral. However, when the processions are over, it is worth exploring the unofficial parts of the city as the brotherhoods return to their local districts.

→ PROGRAM
You can buy the official program (*programa oficial*) from a news stand, or look in the *ABC* newspaper, which publishes the full daily program. In the morning, visit the churches of the brotherhoods taking part in the day's processions to admire the banners, embroidery and flowers, and soak in the atmosphere.

→ THE "VELA" (VIGIL)
Possibly the most interesting moment of Holy Week. The vigil is held during the night of Maundy Thursday, before the procession of the Virgin of Macarena, in which six different brotherhoods take part from about 1am until dawn.

→ THE "SAETA"
A solemn religious song, related to flamenco. It is sung *a cappella* as the brotherhoods enter and leave their church.

FESTIVALS AND EVENTS		
JAN. 1–8	ALMUÑECAR	CERTAMEN INTERNACIONAL DE GUITARRA CLÁSICA ANDRÉS SEGOVIA
JAN. 2	GRANADA	DÍA DE LA TOMA (COMMEMORATION OF THE EXPULSION OF THE MOORS)
2ND OR 3RD WEEK OF FEB.	EVERYWHERE, BUT MOST IMPRESSIVELY IN CÁDIZ	LOS CARNAVALES (CARNIVAL)
FEB./MAR.	SEVILLE	FESTIVAL DE MÚSICA ANTIGUA
MAR. (FRI., 9 DAYS BEFORE PALM SUNDAY	ORGIVA	CRISTO DE LA EXPIRACÍON
PALM SUNDAY/ GOOD FRIDAY	EVERYWHERE, BUT MOST IMPRESSIVELY IN SEVILLE	SEMANA SANTA (EASTER WEEK)
APR. (2ND WEEK AFTER EASTER)	SEVILLE	FERIA DE ABRIL (APRIL FAIR)
APR. 25 OR NEAREST SUNDAY	OHANES	FIESTA DE SAN MARCO
LAST SUNDAY OF APR.	ANDÚJAR	ROMERÍA DE NUESTRA SEÑORA DE LA CABEZA
MAY 3	GRANADA	FIESTA DE LAS CRUCES
1ST WEEK OF MAY	GRANADA AND CÓRDOBA	DÍA DE LA CRUZ
MAY	SEVILLE	FESTIVAL INTERNACIONAL DE TEATRO Y DANZA
1ST & 2ND WEEKS OF MAY	JEREZ DE LA FRONTERA	FERIA DEL CABALLO
2ND WEEK OF MAY	CÓRDOBA	FESTIVAL DE LOS PATIOS AND (EVERY 3 YRS: 2001, 2004, ETC.) CONCURSO NACIONAL DE FLAMENCO
MAY 14–15	JEREZ DE LA FRONTERA	ROMERÍA DE SAN ISIDRO
4TH WEEK OF MAY	CÓRDOBA	FERIA DE MAYO
BEG. MAY OR END JUNE	ALMONTE (HUELVA)	ROMERÍA DEL ROCÍO
	GRANADA AND SEVILLE	FERIA DEL CORPUS CHRISTI
3RD SUNDAY OF JUNE	CABRA	ROMERÍA DE LOS GITANOS
JUNE 23–24	EVERYWHERE	DÍA DE SAN JUAN (SAINT JOHN'S DAY)
MID JUNE/BEG. JUL.	GRANADA	FESTIVAL INTERNACIONAL DE MÚSICA Y DANZA
END JUNE/BEG. JUL.	CÓRDOBA	FESTIVAL DE LA GUITARRA
MID JUL.	ON THE COAST	FIESTA DE LA VIRGEN DEL CARMEN
JUL. 15–17	GRAZALEMA	LUNES DE TORO
END JUL./BEG. AUG.	HUELVA	FIESTAS COLOMBINAS (MUSIC AND DANCE)
AUG. 15	GRANADA AND SEVILLE	FIESTA DE LA VIRGEN DE LOS REYES (PROCESSION OF THE VIRGIN)
2ND & 3RD WEEKS OF AUG.	MÁLAGA	FERIA
3RD WEEK OF AUG.	SANLÚCAR DE BARRAMEDA (CÁDIZ)	FIESTAS DE LA EXALTACIÓN DEL RÍO GUADALQUIVIR
4TH WEEK OF AUG.	ALMERÍA	FERIA
1ST & 2ND WEEKS OF SEP.	RONDA	FERIA DE PEDRO ROMERO (BULLFIGHTING)
SEP. 6–9	BAZA	FIESTAS PATRONALES DE LA VIRGEN DE PIEDAD
2ND OR 3RD WEEK OF SEP.	LA PALMA DEL CONDADO	FIESTA DE LA VENDIMIA (GRAPE HARVEST)
SEP. 14–15	VÁLOR	MOROS Y CRISTIANOS (RECREATION OF THE RECONQUISTA)
SEP. 15–30 (EVEN YEARS)	SEVILLE	BIENAL DE ARTE FLAMENCO
FINAL SUNDAY	GRANADA	FIESTA DE LA VIRGEN DE LAS ANGUSTIAS
OF SEP.	TORREMOLINOS	ROMERÍA DE SAN MIGUEL
SEP./OCT.	SEVILLE	SEVILLA EN OTOÑO
	JEREZ DE LA FRONTERA	FIESTAS DE OTOÑO
OCT. 5–9	CADIAR	FIESTA DEL VINO
3RD & 4TH WEEKS OF OCT.	CÁDIZ	FESTIVAL IBEROAMERICANO DE TEATRO
BEG. NOV.	GRANADA	FESTIVAL INTERNACIONAL DE JAZZ
3RD & 4TH WEEKS OF NOV.	HUELVA	FESTIVAL DE CINE IBEROAMERICANO
DEC. 28	MÁLAGA	FIESTA DE LOS VERDIALES

PUBLIC HOLIDAYS		
JAN. 1	SPAIN	AÑO NUEVO (NEW YEAR'S)
JAN. 6	SPAIN	DÍA DE REYES (EPIPHANY)
FEB. 28	ANDALUSIA	DÍA DE ANDALUCÍA
MAR./APR.	SPAIN	MAUNDY THURSDAY AND GOOD FRIDAY
MAY 1	SPAIN	LABOR DAY
AUG. 15	SPAIN	LA ASUNCIÓN (ASSUMPTION)
OCT. 12	SPAIN	NATIONAL DAY (COLOMBUS' DAY)
NOV. 1	SPAIN	DÍA DE TODOS LOS SANTOS (ALL SAINTS' DAY)
DEC. 6	SPAIN	CONSTITUTION DAY
DEC. 8	SPAIN	LA INMACULADA CONCEPCIÓN
DEC. 25	SPAIN	CHRISTMAS
DEC. 26	ALMERÍA	SAN ESTEBAN (SAINT STEPHEN'S DAY)

◆ HOTELS, RESTAURANTS AND BARS
ALMERÍA

Towns are listed in alphabetical order.
▲ refers to the Itineraries section, while ◆ refers to the Map section.
For a full list of symbols, see page 337.

< €50
€50–€130
€130–€300
> €300

ALMERÍA
▲ 350 ◆ **B** D4

HOTELS
Almería has tended to cater to modest budget tourism, and latterly the main business drive has come from the huge industry based on intensive agriculture under plastic. The hotel offerings remain limited in range.

Costasol***
Paseo de Almería, 58
Tel. 950 23 40 11
Simple and good value but in a busy part of town. Also has a pleasant restaurant.
55 rooms

Gran Hotel Almería****
Av. Reina Regente, 8
Tel. 950 23 80 11
Fax 950 27 06 91
Modern, well-run with a wide range of facilities but lacking in charm.
117 rooms

Sol Almería**
Ctra de Ronda, km 193 (120 miles)
Tel. 950 27 18 11
Fax 950 27 37 09
The best of the small hotels, with a pleasant family atmosphere.

RESTAURANTS

Balzac
Gerona, 29
Tel. 950 26 61 60
Closed Sat. lunch, Sun.
The Balzac is the most interesting and untypical of the restaurants inside the town, which for the most part are uninspired with garish decor. As the name implies there is a French touch which blends especially well with the Mediterranean fish dishes.

Belavista
Urbanización Bellavista (near the airport)
Tel. 950 29 71 56
Closed Sun. evening and Mon.
The Belavista retains its reputation as a highly successful family-run restaurant using great flair with the best of local ingredients. Everyone who has eaten here recommends it highly.

El Bello Rincón
Ctra N-340, km 436 (271 miles), about 3 miles from the town center
Tel. 950 23 84 27
Closed Mon., and July–Aug.
El Bello Rincón provides a consistently wide variety of seafood simply but very well cooked, which ensures a faithful clientele.

TAPAS BARS AND PUBS

Bar Bahía de la Palma
Pl. de la Constitución
Ideal for pre-dinner drinks.

Bar El Ajolí
C. Padre Alfonso
A wide choice of chacinas (grilled meats).

Bar El Alcázar
Paseo de Almería, 4
Popular bar serving seafood and fried squid.

Bar Pavía
Plaza Pavía, 10
Near the fishing port. Excellent fish and seafood.

Bodega El Patio
C. Real, 84
All the charm of an old bodega.

Bodega Las Botas
C. Fructuoso Pérez, 3
Mountain ham, soused hake. Wines: fino *(jerez) and* manzanilla.

Bodega Montenegro
Plaza Granero
Near the cathedral. Good wine and seafood.

Casa Joaquin
C. Real
Popular tapas bar. Fine food.

Casa Puga
C. Lope de Vega, corner of Jovellanos
Popular tapas bar.

Mojito
Paseo de Almería
Caribbean-style bar. Drink specialty: mojito.

Molimalón
Paseo de Almería
Pleasant Irish pub.

Rincón de Juan Pedro
Plaza del Carmen
Local specialties.

CÁDIZ
▲ 310 ◆ **A** C5, **H**, **I**

HOTELS
Cádiz has allowed a magnificent Atlantic beach front to be developed by unappealing modern glass and concrete high rise hotels and apartments. Until recently it had done little to exploit its fine historic center. All this reflects the traditional emphasis on a low income Spanish tourist clientele, rather than the curious traveler. Another new development has been the arrival of big cruise ships.

Francia y Paris***
◆ **I** B2
Pl. San Francisco, 6
Tel. 956 21 23 19
Fax 956 22 24 31
www.hotelfrancia.com
A well-run hotel with a lot of character but some rooms can be gloomy.
57 rooms

Meliá La Caleta****
◆ **H** A1
Av. Amílcar Barca, 47
Tel. 956 27 94 11
Fax 956 25 93 22
Part of the Melia chain, offering standardized comfort. It is right on the main seafront and principal beach but the location is inconvenient for those solely wishing to explore the old town.
143 rooms

Parador Hotel Atlántico****
◆ **I** A3
Av. Duque de Najera
Tel. 956 22 69 05
Fax 956 21 45 82
www.parador.es
email: cadiz@parador.es
The best aspect of this hotel is its position on a spur at the edge of the city, with unrivalled views toward the Atlantic and over the huge Bay of Cádiz with its lively traffic of shipping and sailing boats. It is also by far the most comfortable hotel in the old town. Good restaurant
149 rooms

RESTAURANTS

Achuri
◆ **I** C2
Plocia, 15
Tel. 956 25 36 13
Closed Sun. evening
A great port restaurant close to Plaza de San Juan, offering seafood with

< €20
€20–€30
€30–€50
> €50

a mix of local and Basque dishes at very reasonable prices.

El Aljibe
Plocia, 25
Tel. 956 26 66 56
Closed Sun. evening
A relative newcomer to the portside restaurants, El Aljibe's seafood is considered among the best value for money in town.

El Faro
◆ **I** B3
San Felix, 15
Tel. 956 21 10 68
This remains the most outstanding restaurant within Cádiz and attracts regulars from near and far who marvel at the seafood-based cuisine and its ability to maintain a consistently high standard while being unafraid to experiment. It is advisable to book ahead, especially at weekends.

La Costera
◆ **H** B2
Paseo Marítimo
Tel. 956 27 34 88
La Costera serves reliable seafood at affordable prices, with a location on the main beachfront.

Ventorrillo del Chato
◆ **A** C5
Via Augusta Julia (on the road linking Cádiz to San Fernando)
Tel. 956 25 00 25
Closed Sun.
Though outside the city boundaries, the Bentorillo del Chato is to all intents and purposes a Gaditano *restaurant, run by the same family as El Faro (see above). The menu seeks to be a bit more sophisticated and international without losing its local roots in the presentation of superbly cooked fresh seafood. It also has the attraction of being without the parking worries which bedevil all the city restaurants.*

BARS, TAPAS BARS AND NIGHTLIFE

Bahía
◆ **I** B2
Av. Ramón de Carranza, 69
The Bahía is a pleasant bar serving chops and potatoes prepared in a number of different ways.

Café Levante
◆ **I** B2
C. Rosario
Exhibitions, Cádiz carnival music.

Cambalache
◆ **I** B2
C. José del Toro
Pub with live music (flamenco, jazz). Great atmosphere.

Casa Lucas
◆ **A** C5
Plaza Cruz Verde
Famous for its rice dishes.

Casa Manteca
◆ **I** B3
C. Corralón de los Carros, 66
Sea urchins, Jabugo ham and regional wines.

Cervecería el Puerto
◆ **I** B2
C. Zorrilla, 4
Closed Wed.
One of the best beer bars (cervecerías) in Cádiz – so it's always busy.

El Consuelo
◆ **H** B1
Av. Marconi
Oysters and clams.

El Pito
◆ **I** B3
C. Corralón de los Carros
Fish and smoked meats.

La Bodega
◆ **H** B2
Paseo Marítimo
Good-quality tapas and excellent fish dishes.

La Cava
◆ **I** B2
C. Antonio López
Flamenco shows every night.

Las Pérgolas
◆ **H** B2
Paseo Marítimo
Edificio Europlaya
Bar overlooking the beach, below the Las Pergolas pub.

Poniente
◆ **I** B2
C. Antonio López
Trendy bar.

CÓRDOBA

▲ *236* ◆ **A** F1-2, **F**

HOTELS

For a city with such a major architectural heritage, Córdoba has been slow to cater to overnight visitors and the choice of good hotels remains surprisingly small.

Abetos del Maestre Escuela****
◆ **A** F1–F2
Av. de San José de Calasanz (approx 1.2 miles from the city center).
Tel. 957 28 21 05
Has the advantage of being good value in an attractive location, away from the heat and noise of the center. The only inconvenience lies in the fact that the magnificent mosque complex is a 40 minute walk away.
36 rooms

Alfaros****
◆ **F** D3
Alfaros, 18
Tel. 957 49 19 20
Fax 957 49 22 10
This is a most attractive hotel with well-finished rooms and relaxing patios in the centre.
133 rooms

Al-Mihrab***
◆ **F** D1
Av. del Brillante (approx 1.8 miles from the city center)
Tel. 957 27 21 80
Fax 957 27 21 98
A small hotel with considerable charm, offering good value for money but outside the city center.
29 rooms

El Califa***
◆ **F** B3
Lope de Hoces, 14
Tel. 957 29 94 00
Fax 957 29 57 16
Lots of atmosphere in this small, competitively priced hotel in central Córdoba.
14 rooms

El Conquistador****
◆ **F** B4
Magistral Gonzales Francés, 15
Tel. 957 48 11 02
Fax 957 47 46 77
Built in the 16th century as a private villa, El Conquistador occupies a superb position next to the great mosque complex. Its facilities have been recently upgraded so that it really exploits its potential. If looking at Córdoba's great Moorish past is the main purpose of your visit then this is the best place to be.
102 rooms

Maimonides***
◆ **F** B4
Torrijos, 4
Tel. 957 47 15 00

< €50
€50–€130
€130–€300
> €300

Fax 957 48 38 03
Ideal location next to the Mezquita. Maimonides has benefited from a recent substantial modernization. With its charming plant-filled patio and very comfortable rooms, it has become a pleasure to stay in.
82 rooms

Meliá Córdoba****
◆ F B2
Jardines de la Victoria
Tel. 957 29 80 66
Fax 957 29 81 47
www.solmelia.es
Now part of the Meliá chain, this is one of the city's oldest establishments, with the most comprehensive views of the main monuments from a location in the heart of the old Jewish quarter. It is also one the least homogenized of all the Meliá hotels.
144 rooms

Parador La Arruzafa****
◆ F north of D1
Av. Arruzafa, 3
(1.2 miles north of Plaza de Colon)
Tel. 957 27 59 00
Fax 957 28 04 09
www.parador.es
email: cordoba@parador.es
This is part of the national chain of paradors and the first modern hotel in Córdoba to be clearly aimed at the tourist. It overlooks the city on a hill and is surrounded by a large garden, which helps to offset the sometimes unbearable heat in the town center during the summer months.
94 rooms

RESTAURANTS

Almudaina
◆ F D5
Jardines de los Campos Mártires, 1
Tel. 957 47 43 42
Closed Sun. evening
In a former Moorish palace and onetime prison during the Inquisitino, this restaurant has acquired a reputation for adapting traditional regional dishes to new tastes. It is also famous for its desserts, which when in season make imaginative use of chestnuts.

PARADOR DE LA ARRUZAFA/DR

Astoria Casa Matías
◆ F D1
El Nogal, 16
Tel. 957 27 76 53
Closed Sun. in summer
Family-run with great attention to detail and respect for traditional Andalusian ingredients, the Astoria Casa Matíaas rremains a local favorite for its quality and value.

Casa Pepe de la Judería
◆ F B4
Romero 1
Tel. 957 20 07 44
www.casapepedela juderia.com
The most popular tavern in the old Jewish quarter, with a delightful patio. Regulars say it is better to eat tapas than take the formal meals.

Ciro's
◆ F B3
Paseo de la Victoria, 19
Tel. 957 29 04 64
Ciro's has stayed faithful to a successful formula of well-cooked simple Andalusian dishes. Just because Córdoba is a long way from the sea, do not be afraid to eat their excellent fish.

El Blasón
◆ F B3
C. José Zorrilla, 11
Tel. 957 48 06 25
Closed Sun.
El Blasón occupies a well-restored house, once the venue of literary gatherings attended by the writer Zorilla. The restaurant is a venture by José Manuel García, son of "Pepe" García Marín, Córdoba's best-known restaurateur (see below El Caballo Rojo). The cuisine is imaginative, and clearly benefits from a son trying to prove he can do better than his father.

El Caballo Rojo
◆ F B4
C. Cardenal Herrero, 28
Tel. 957 47 53 75
Pepe García Marín (see above) has made a name for himself by bringing back to life recipes used during the period of the Moorish Caliphate. This culinary art is mixed in with traditional dishes such as rabo de toro *(bull's tail). Competition between father and son keeps each on their toes.*

El Churrasco
◆ F B4
C. Romero, 16
Tel. 957 29 08 19
Closed Aug.
www.elchurrasco.com
This is the most sophisticated of Córdoba's restaurants – both in the décor of the carefully restored historic building with a collection of paintings by prominent local artists, and in the broad range of dishes based on "Cordobese" traditions. Even with the choice of some of the finer wines from the extensive cellar, the bill is nearly always a pleasant surprise.

Pic-Nic
Ronda de los Tejares, 16
Tel. 957 48 22 33
Closed all day Sun., Mon. evening and Aug.
Don't be put off by the confusing name – this charming little family-run restaurant has little do with a picnic as it serves a mix of local and more typical Spanish dishes on a constantly changing menu.

BARS AND TAPAS BARS

Bodega Guzmán
◆ F B4
C. Judíos, 9
Typical bodega with a "bullfighting" atmosphere.

< €20
€20–€30
€30–€50
> €50

Casa Paco Acedo
◆ F D2
C. Adarve, 87
Cod, hake and oxtail.

Casa Rubio
◆ F B4
Puerta de Almodóvar, 5
Traditional taverna near the bullfighting museum. Fine tapas. Very good value.

Casa Salinas
◆ F B4
Puerta de Almodóvar, 2
Opposite the Casa Rubio, as you enter the Jewish quarter. Córdovan specialties.

Gaudí
◆ F C2
C. Gran Capitán, 22
All kinds of beer and first-rate tapas *and* migas *(soups with garlic and bread crumbs) are served at the Gaudi. It is also a good place for breakfast.*

Los Toneles
◆ F C6
C. Fernando de Córdoba, 6
A selection of excellent cheeses and very good wines.

GRANADA

▲ 334 ◆ B B3-B4, G

HOTELS

The bulk of Granada's hotels continue to be geared to one-night stop-overs for tourists "doing" the Alhambra once in their lives. The result is an offering dominated by large, and often rather soulless, functional hotels. This is a pity because the glories of this city need to be soaked up slowly – especially the sunsets – no matter what the time of year. Most people thus remember the gems of Moorish art and architecture, not their hotels.

→ **HOTELS INSIDE THE ALHAMBRA COMPLEX** (◆ G E1–E2)

Alhambra Palace****
◆ G E2
Pena Partida, 2
Tel. 958 22 14 68
Fax 958 22 64 04
www.h-alhambra palace.es
The best things about this hotel are its position with easy access to all the main sites, and the magnificent views looking to the distant Sierra Nevada (snow-capped through spring). It tends to get booked well in advance by groups and conventions because of its superb location. The décor, which once looked a bit kitsch beside the surroundings, has improved with time.
129 rooms

Parador San Francisco****
◆ G E2
Real de la Alhambra
Tel. 958 22 14 68
or 958 22 14 40
Fax 958 22 22 64
www.parador.es
Rooms in this converted Franciscan monastery, once the burial place of Spain's Catholic kings, are the most coveted in the whole national parador chain. Everyone keen to visit Granada should try to stay here for sheer atmosphere and the privilege of being so close to one of mankind's greatest achievements in architecture and landscape gardening. It is pure luck whether space is available. Those trying to book should note that both the Spanish government and the Andalusian regional government tend to reserve a certain number of rooms throughout the year for visiting dignitaries. At short notice space can become available because these rooms are not taken up, so it is worth trying even at the last minute and insisting. But on occasions the need to honor VIPs can undo even the surest of confirmed individual reservations.
36 rooms

→ **HOTELS OUTSIDE THE ALHAMBRA COMPLEX**

Ana Maria***
◆ G A5
Paseo de Ronda, 101
Tel. 958 28 99 11
Fax 958 28 92 15
Well-managed, small hotel, located conveniently close to the Alhambra.
30 rooms

Carmen***
◆ G E4
Acera del Darro, 62
Tel. 958 25 83 00
Fax 958 25 64 62
Big and functional hotel in the heart of the old city.
283 rooms

Corona de Granada***
◆ G D5
Pedro Antonio de Alarcón, 10
Tel. 958 52 12 50
Ideal for a one-night stop-over.
93 rooms

Cortijo Landete***
◆ off map
In the Vega of Granada, less than 4 miles from the city center
Tel. 958 50 66 60
For those with cars, this is an ideal spot to enjoy superb views, have easy access to the monuments and take advantage of a well-converted farmhouse dating back to 1880.. The Cortijo also has a good restaurant. Golf course nearby.
7 rooms

Gran Hotel Luna de Granada****
◆ G C6
Pl. Manuel Cano, 2
Tel. 958 20 10 00
Fax 958 28 40 52
The largest hotel in town offering a good range of facilities but somewhat lacking in charm.
253 rooms

Meliá Granada****
◆ G E3
Ángel Ganivet, 7
Tel. 958 22 74 00
This is the Meliá chain's flagship in Granada, located close to the city center and a five-minute walk from the Alhambra. It tries to please but visitors report that at times staff seem overwhelmed by groups.
197 rooms

Princesa Ana****
◆ G A4
Av. de la Constitución, 37
Tel. 958 28 74 47
Fax 958 27 39 54
This medium-sized hotel on a busy central avenue has been recently redecorated and offers a much more welcome aspect.
61 rooms

Palacio de Santa Inés***
◆ G D2
Cuesta de Santa Inés, 9
Tel. 958 22 23 62
Fax 958 22 24 65
The most charming of the small hotels,

< €50
€50–€130
€130–€300
> €300

in a restored 16th-century palace. It is worth trying to stay here if you plan to spend a few days in the city. Located in the Albaicín quarter, it looks across to the Alhambra.
9 rooms

Rallye****
◆ G C5
Camino de Ronda, 107
Tel. 958 27 28 00
Fax 958 27 28 62
Although on the outskirts of Granada, the Rallye is quieter than more central hotels and seems to have more time to deal with its customers.
79 rooms

Reina Cristina***
◆ G D4
Tablas, 4
Tel. 958 25 32 11
Fax 958 25 57 28
www.hotelreinacristina.com
Fans of 1930's Granadine poet Federico García Lorca should make a point of coming to this converted mansion where he spent his last fateful days before being seized by Francoist police. The tragi-romantic figure of Lorca casts a big spell over the city and this hotel is as good a place as any to make an acquaintance with his poetry.
43 rooms

Triunfo Granada***
◆ G C3
Pl. del Triunfo, 19
Tel. 958 20 74 44
Fax 958 27 90 17
www.h-triunfo-granada.com
Unpretentious small hotel in the city center with staff anxious to please.
40 rooms

RESTAURANTS

Carmen de San Miguel
◆ G E2
Pl. Torres Bermejas, 3
Tel. 958 22 67 23
Closed Sun.
Ambitious menu aimed at a local and international clientele. Though at times pretentious, the quality is reliable.

Chikito
◆ G E4
Pl. del Campillo, 9
Tel. 958 22 33 64
Closed Wed.
Like several other eateries, this lives off the folklore of García Lorca. However, this restaurant has the cachet of being where he and his 1930's artistic friends held their tertulias (literary gatherings). Such a past adds to the mystique of the plaza setting and the food, though usually very good, often takes second place.

El Rincón de Lorca
◆ G D4
Tablas, 4
Tel. 958 25 32 11
Less authentic Lorciana but this restaurant serves excellent meats.

Horno de Santiago
◆ G E3
Pl. de los Campos
Tel. 958 22 34 76
Closed Sun. evening and Aug.
The size of this restaurant with dining rooms on different levels can be off-putting, but it is well run and the varied menu is of a high standard and good value.

Jardines Alberto
◆ G F1
Av. de los Alixares
Tel. 958 22 48 18
Closed Sun. evening
This has the great virtue of being in the Alhambra complex. More welcome still, it does not exploit its superb location: instead the staff seem happy to treat clients to some very imaginative dishes at reasonable prices – trapping the tourist in the best way. And some of the vegetables served are home grown.

Las Tinajas
◆ G E5
Martínez Campos, 17
Tel. 958 25 43 93
Closed July
www.suinsa.es/las tinajas
Las Tinajas made its reputation on well-cooked, simple local dishes but it also offers gastronomic menus featuring every aspect of the Spanish cuisine. Excellent whichever way you choose. Friendly and popular.

Mirador de Morayma
◆ G D1
Pianista García Carillo, 2
Tel. 958 22 82 90
Closed Sun. evening
www.alqueria morayma.com
In the Albaicín quarter overlooking the Alhambra. The view, which is most evocative in the evening, has made this an obligatory rite of passage for the great and good visiting Granada. Happily for such a setting, neither the menu nor the cuisine are a let-down.

Sevilla
◆ G D3
Oficios, 12
Tel. 958 22 12 23
Closed Sun. evening and Mon.
Very central and right by the cathedral, this restaurant offers high-quality local ingredients cooked to a uniformly high standard.

BARS AND NIGHTLIFE

Casa Enrique
◆ G E4
Acera del Darro, 8
Small tavern. Fine wines and cooked meats.

Distrito-10
◆ G C4
C. Gran Capitán, 5-7
Tel. 958 28 21
Nightclub open from midnight until 6am.

El Corral del Príncipe
◆ G E2
Campo del Príncipe
Shows and live music.

El Ruido Rosa
◆ G C5
C. Pedro Antonio de Alarcón
Pub.

El Secadero
◆ B B3-4
Alhendin
Ctra Bailén–Motril, km 53 (33 miles)
Tel. 958 55 80 39
Live music on Fri. and Sat. at midnight.

El Tragaluz
◆ B B3-B4
C. Nebot, 26
Bar-restaurant. Plays and exhibitions.

Los Molinos
◆ G E3
Cuesta de los Molinos
Mussels and fried fish.

Medinaceli
◆ G D5
C. Cristo de Medinaceli, 6
Ahumados *(smoked meats)* and ham.

- < €20
- €20–€30
- €30–€50
- > €50

Novecento
◆ G C5
C. Martínez de la Rosa
Trendy snack-bar.

Peña Partida
◆ G E2
Patio de los Aljibes, 13
Flamenco circle (peña) in the Albaicín district.

Poetas Andaluces
◆ G C5
C. P. Velázquez, 5
Tel. 958 20 09 06
Pub.

Snooker
◆ G C4
C. Gran Capitán, 25
Tel. 958 27 05 78
Trendy snack-bar. Sandwiches and drinks until 3.30am.

HUELVA

▲ *279* ◆ A B3

HOTELS

Hotels principally cater to holidaymakers from Seville who come during the summer months for the fine beaches. There are few foreign visitors, save for the annual Rocio festival in nearby Doñana. As a result the hotels are modern and well-equipped but tend to be large and functional.

Costa de la Luz**
C. José María Arno, 8
Tel./Fax 959 25 64 22
One of the small hotels with friendly service and few frills.
35 rooms

Luz Huelva****
Alameda Sundheim, 28
Tel. 959 25 00 11
Fax 959 25 81 10
Recently renovated, this hotel offers the best range of facilities.
110 rooms

REINA CRISTINA/DR

Monte Conquero***
Pablo Rada 10
Tel. 959 28 55 00
Fax 959 28 39 12
Big and comfortable but lacking in character.
166 rooms

RESTAURANTS

El Estero
Av. Martín Alonso Pinzón, 13
Tel. 959 28 27 11
Set in the Hotel Tartessos, this has an extremely good selection of Huelva's famous seafood.

El Paraíso
Av. Guatemala, 44
On the Huelva–El Portil road, km.11 (6.8 miles)
Tel. 959 27 19 58
Excellent value seafood as well as pata negra *(locally cured ham).*

Las Candelas
At Aljaraque: Under 6 miles from Huelva going to Punta Umbria
Tel. 959 31 83 01
Closed Sun.
One of the best-known fish restaurants in the Huelva area, but it also has a good repertoire of meat dishes.

Las Meigas
Av. Guatemala, 44
Tel. 959 27 19 58
Closed Sun. in summer
A touch of Galician cuisine to add variety to the local fish dishes.

BARS, TAPAS BARS AND NIGHTLIFE

Agmanir
C. Concepción
Closed Sun.
Bar-cafeteria. Wide choice of tapas.

Bajamar
C. Miguel Redondo, 4
Closed Wed.
An ideal place to sample regional specialties.

Cervecería La Ria
C. Fariñas
Good beer and top-quality seafood.

Ibiza
C. Ginés Martín
Cozy wine bar. Pleasant service.

José
Plaza de la Merced
Fresh seafood and fish dishes.

Lagares
C. Bonares
Typical Huelva taverna.

Las Tinajas
C. Alfonso XIII, 5
The shellfish are a must. Excellent salpicón *(dressing).*

Ocho
Plaza de la Merced
Very popular pub.

Ottawa
C. Berdigón, 1
English pub. Always crowded.

Piranchelo
C. Legión Española, 2
Closed Mon.
Nightclub.

JAÉN

▲ *346* ◆ B B2

HOTELS

Jaén is a useful stop-over town for travelers going either north/south or east/west across Andalusia.

Castillo de Santa Catalina****
Tel. 953 23 00 00
email: jaen@parador.es
What remains of this mighty castle, built on the orders of the Moorish King Alhamar responsible for Granada's Alhambra, has been turned into a hotel in the national chain of paradors. The view perched atop a steep hill is sensational and enough to tempt any traveler to stay. The hotel itself is as good as can be and has a perfectly acceptable restaurant but whatever is on offer pales beside the

▪ < €50
▪ €50–€130
▪ €130–€300
▪ > €300

location.
45 rooms

Condestable Iranzo***
Paseo de la Estación, 32
Tel. 953 22 28 00
Fax 953 26 38 07
Large and functional, hotel-restaurant with few pretentions other than offering a comfortable night.
159 rooms

Xauen**
Pl. de Dean Mazas, 3
Tel. 953 24 07 89
This hotel located in the heart of the historic city center has a pleasant atmosphere and maintains its reputation for being good value.
35 rooms

RESTAURANTS

Casa Antonio
Fermín Palma, 3.
Tel. 953 27 02 62
Closed Sun. and Aug.
Sometimes a bit pricey, but the restaurant also serves top-quality products, especially game in season.

Casa Vicente
C. Francisco Martín Mora, 1
Tel. 953 23 22 22
Closed Sun. evening and Aug.
An attractive setting in a restored house near the cathedral with its own courtyard. Interesting menu that makes good use of the abundant local partridges. The lamb dishes are among the best in the area.

Pilar del Arrabalejo
Milán de Priego, 49
Tel. 953 24 07 81
The Pilar del Arrabalejo has the best atmosphere in town, and regulars swear that, with its strong meat and game base, it remains the most authentic purveyor of Jaén cuisine. It is also extraordinarily good value.

BARS AND NIGHTLIFE

Abaco
C. Muñoz Grande
Café-pub.

Auringis
C. Consuelo
Quiet pub.

Bar Nuevo
C. Nueva
Fish and seafood.

California
C. Millán de Priego
Snack-bar serving good-quality tapas.

El Gorrión
Arco del Consuelo, 7
Century-old bar with a wide choice of tapas.

Moet
Av. Andalucía
Pub.

MÁLAGA

▲ *332* ◆ **A** F5, **B** A5

HOTELS

Most foreign visitors see only Málaga Airport before heading for the beach resorts and golf courses of the Costa del Sol. However, this big, bustling ancient Mediterranean port city has a long tradition of welcoming foreigners. In anticipation of the opening of a museum dedicated to Pablo Picasso – the city's most famous son – hotel owners are looking for a new type of visitor and enhanced interest in Málaga's often neglected monuments.

California**
Paseo de Sancha, 17
Tel. 95 221 51 65
Very pleasant small hotel in the least spoiled residential part of town, with easy access to the seafront.
25 rooms

Don Curro***
C. Sancha de Lara, 7
Tel. 95 222 72 00
Fax 95 221 59 46
118 rooms
The décor and location are not memorable but the hotel is practical and well run.
118 rooms

Don Paco**
C. Salitre, 53
Tel. 95 231 90 08
Fax 95 231 90 62
A friendly small hotel often preferred by businessmen.

Guadalmar****
Urbanización Guadalmar on the coastal road to Cádiz (km 234)
Tel. 95 223 17 03
Fax 95 224 03 85
This big modern hotel is aimed at people who want to be by the sea yet enjoy easy access to the city – although the clogged central Málaga traffic makes this less and less practical.
195 rooms

Larios****
Marqués de Larios, 2
Tel. 95 222 22 00
Fax 95 222 24 07
www.hotellarios.com
Named after one of the best-known Málaga families, who also have given their name to a brand of gin, this well-run hotel boasts a fine terrace and a bar with superb vistas.
39 rooms

Los Naranjos***
Paseo de Sancha, 35
Tel. 95 222 43 19
Fax 95 222 59 75
Like its neighbor, the California, Los Naranjos is in a very pleasant part of town. The hotel is both comfortable and reasonably priced – except during Holy Week.
35 rooms

Parador Málaga-Gibralfaro****
Castillo de Gibralfaro
Tel. 95 222 19 02
Fax 95 222 19 04
www.parador.es
email: malaga@parador.es
Again, a hotel part of the national parador chain which magnificently exploits a site among the ruins of an ancient fortress dating back to Phoenician times. Staying here, perched above the city, gives a wonderful sense of superiority. The rooms are spacious and luxurious. The hotel is especially enjoyable during the winter months where one can find many a sun trap to warm in. It is so agreeable, that you may sometimes find it hard to summon the energy to descend into the hurly-burly below.
38 rooms

RESTAURANTS

Adolfo
Paseo Marítimo Pablo Ruiz Picasso, 12
Tel. 95 260 19 14
Closed Sun.

< €20
€20–€30
€30–€50
> €50

One of the best seafront seafood restaurants – and always full.

Antonio Martín
Plaza de la Malagueta
Tel. 95 222 73 82
The city's most famous fish restaurant, which still manages to stay head and shoulders above the rest. The prices are accordingly higher.

Café de París
C. Vélez Málaga, 8
Tel. 95 222 50 43
Closed Sun. and last two weeks in July
This restaurant contains a happy mix of Spanish and more international cuisine, accompanied by attentive service. For those who come by car, there is the added convenience of a parking attendant. Some Malagueños say it has become a bit too expensive.

Casa Pedro
C. Quitapenas, 121
Paseo Marítimo
El Palo
Tel. 95 229 00 13
Closed Mon. evening
Of the seafood restaurants by the sea and reasonably central, this is considered to be among the most fairly priced. But as it is popular and packed, it is often noisy.

El Cabra
Paseo de Pedregal
Tel. 95 229 25 95
A fish restaurant much frequented by locals, who usually like to order one of the many types of fried fish. Simple and no frills: eating is the essence.

Figón de Juan
Pasaje Esperanto, 1
Tel. 95 228 75 47
Closed Sun. and Aug.
Here you will find high-quality fried fish as well as salt-baked recipes, at affordable prices.

Monte Sancha
Montes de Sancha 6
Tel. 95 260 31 76
Closed Sun. and the first half of Aug.
This is a restaurant based round a catering school. The apprentice chefs are forever anxious to demonstrate their culinary prowess and visitors with big appetites should not hesitate to try one of the gastronomic menus.

BARS AND NIGHTLIFE

Antigua Casa Guardia
Alameda, 18
The oldest taberna in town, dating back to 1840, serves good-quality fish and seafood.

Antonio
C. Fernando Lesseps, 7
Tapas bar serving excellent ham.

Arribabá
C. Mundo Nuevo
Bar-cum-art gallery.

Bourbon Street
Cerrado de Calderón
Edif. Multicentro 2–15
Wine bar.

El Pimpi
C. Granada, 62
Tavern.

La Cosecha
C. Echegaray, 4
Tel. 95 222 74 93
Good selection of wines.

La Manchega
C. Marín García, 4
Ham, cheese from the Mancha and tapas.

La Tasca
C. Marín García, 12
Fine wines from Jerez and Montilla.

Latino Bar
Av. Cánovas del Castillo, 12
Tel. 95 222 86 23
Live Latin American and West Indian music.

Lo Güeno
C. Marín García, 11
One of Málaga's most picturesque taverns.

7 de Julio
Av. Cánovas del Castillo, 12
Cuisine from Navarra and tapas.

Terraza Bar Britannia
C. Bolsa, 10
Tel. 95 222 21 60
Open noon–dawn
Shows and live music.

SEVILLE

▲ 128 ◆ A D3, C, D, E

HOTELS

The most popular times to visit Seville are during Holy Week (Semana Santa) and the annual week-long Fair (Feria) two weeks later. Demand for hotel space is heavy and even though some hotels do not specifically say so, they all raise their prices during this period.

Since Spain still treats Holy Week as one long holiday – and the Feria is still seen as a major social occasion for many non-Sevillianos – the demand continues to grow for hotel space from within Spain. The crowds in Holy Week are such that the processions are now guided by satellite navigation. So unless you specifically wish to visit for these events it is better to avoid the city or book well in advance. If you are set on visiting for these occasions and find hotels booked, it is worth considering staying in Carmona which is less than 25 minutes away by car past the airport.

With temperatures rising above 30°C from May to October, those who want to stay cool may well be more comfortable in the big but rather featureless hotels that have been built over the past ten years at strategic points on the outskirts. Because the latter also cater to a growing business clientele who need accommodation during weekdays, they often have attractive weekend package. But as Seville is essentially a place to walk around and savor, it is best to visit from late October until May, and to look for somewhere central.

The volume of visitors passing through the hotels is such that some staff can be blasé and off-hand. Nevertheless, few complaints are aired because people forget the incidents quickly in the general magic of the city. Most visitors still spend only one night here, and too many hotels still cater on this basis with what they offer. However, in the past few years there has been a determined attempt to improve standards and exploit the city's wealth of

< €50
€50–€130
€130–€300
> €300

old buildings, to provide a more sophisticated, design-orientated, type of hotel appealing to those keen to use Seville as a base for short breaks.

Most hotels now have their own websites or are in the process of acquiring them; these usually give a better idea of what is on offer than the traditional travel agents' brochures.

ALFONSO XIII/DR

Al Andalus Palace****
◆ **A** D3
Av. La Palmera
Tel. 954 23 06 00
Fax 95 423 19 12
The most luxurious and high-tech of the new hotels that have sprung up in sites located away from the historic center. It is geared to offer every sort of convenience for the busy traveler whether on business trips or pure tourism. For short stays its location on the way out to Cádiz could be inconvenient.
328 rooms

Alfonso XIII*****
◆ **E** D5
San Fernando, 2
Tel. 95 491 70 00
Fax 95 491 70 99
www.hotelalfonsoxiii.com
One of the great traditional luxury hotels in Spain. Built for the 1929 Seville international exhibition in grandiose neo-Mudejar style, it has remained the doyen of Seville's hotels and is the first choice for visiting VIPs. Purists occasionally complain that modernization has removed some of the charm but most visitors appreciate the improved air conditioning and luxury additions to keep pace with the demands of top-class comfort. Even if you can't afford to stay, its elaborate decoration with extensive use of tiles which reflect the Andalusian revival of the Moorish architectural tradition, make it worth a look. But you will need to look smart to get past the doorman. Its location also makes the Alfonso XIII an ideal meeting point for a drink (if you're trying to impress your date or simply want to feel self-important). And if a little comfort, peace and quiet is needed after a morning on the city's streets, the hotel's San Fernando restaurant justifies the cost.
146 rooms

América***
◆ **D** B5
Jesús del Gran Poder, 2
Tel. 95 422 09 51
Fax 95 421 06 26
The location could not be more central, in the commercial heart of the old city, but it can be noisy. Lacks charm but good value.
100 rooms

Bécquer****
◆ **E** A2
C. Reyes Católicos, 4
Tel. 95 422 89 00
Fax 95 421 44 00
Ideal for being close to the Cathedral and the historic area of the Barrio de Santa Cruz. Has a steady business clientele which mixes well with the tourists.
120 rooms

Don Paco***
◆ **D** E6
Pl. Padre Jerónimo de Córdoba, 4
Tel. 95 422 49 31
Fax 95 422 28 24
Of the bigger hotels in the city center, Don Paco is among the most comfortable and sensibly priced. But the location is very noisy and the building lacks charm.
220 rooms

Doña María****
◆ **E** D3
C. Don Remondo, 19
Tel. 95 422 49 90
Fax 95 421 95 46
www.hdmaria.com
For years the discerning traveler has been staying at the Doña Maria for its intimacy and fine Spanish antique furnishings. Its rooftop terrace complete with small swimming pool also offers one of the most privileged panoramas looking onto the Giralda. Yet with all these things going for it, the hotel sometimes gives the impression of sitting on its laurels while too obviously exploiting its assets.
68 rooms

Fernando III****
◆ **E** E3
C. de San José, 21
Tel. 95 421 73 07
Fax 95 422 02 46
Within easy walking distance of all main monuments, and good value for a central location.
157 rooms

Giralda***
◆ **C** D3
Sierra Nevada, 3
Tel. 95 441 66 61
Fax 95 441 93 52
The kind of place where you will remember the town more than the hotel: well-run and unremarkable in a central location.
98 rooms

Hotel Amadeus**
◆ **E** E3
Farnesio, 6
(linking San Jose with Fabiola)
Tel. 95 450 14 43
Fax 95 450 00 19
www.hotelamadeussevilla.com
The most unusual addition to the city's hotels. As its name implies, music is the theme and this small 16th-century restored house is aimed at musicians and music lovers. It's an original idea and on a small enough scale to work. There is a lovely roof terrace with fine views over the city's rooftops and La Giralda. The hotel sometimes stages small classical concerts (hence the grand piano in the lobby).
14 prettily decorated rooms

Hotel Corregidor***
◆ **D** C4
Morgado 17
(next to Iglesia de San Martin)
Tel. 95 438 51 11
Unpretentious and

< €20
€20–€30
€30–€50
> €50

with a pleasant patio, the Corregidor retains its reputation for being well-run with staff showing a good feel for the varying needs of the visitor. Surprisingly quiet, too.
77 rooms

Inglaterra****
◆ **E** C2
Pl. Nueva, 7
Tel. 95 422 49 70
Fax 95 456 13 36
The name is for nostalgics of the Grand Tour but more often this hotel is booked by tour groups who find it caters easily to site-sore visitors.
116 rooms

La Rábida**
◆ **E** B3
Castelar 24
Tel. 95 422 09 60
Fax 95 422 43 75
For those seeking the essentials of a modestly priced place to stay while being close to the main monuments.
100 rooms

Las Casas de la Judería***
◆ **E** F3
Callejón Dos Hermanos, 7
Tel. 95 441 51 50
Fax 95 442 21 70
www.casasypalacios.com
The hotel, promoted by a prominent local aristocrat as part of a move to restore old buildings in the historic center, has become one of the "in" places to stay for its charm and fine sense of simple decoration respecting traditional styles. It brings together a group of buildings in the old Jewish quarter which once housed the dependents of the Duke of Béjar's household.
70 rooms

Las Casas de los Mercaderes***
◆ **E** D2
Álvarez Quintero, 9–13
Tel. 95 422 58 58
www.casasypalacios.com
Based on the same principle as its like-named sister hotel above, this is housed in a fine 18th-century building in the city center and based round a covered multi-columned patio. Staying here gives a good sense of absorbing the great traditions of Andalusian domestic architecture, while being good value.
47 rooms

Las Casas del Rey de Baeza****
◆ **E** F1
C. Santiago (Pl. Jesús de la Redención)
Tel. 95 456 14 96
www.casasypalacios.com
This the third and most recent addition to the highly successful "Casas" with the difference that it aims at a richer, more exclusive clientele, and is priced accordingly. Set back off a small and very quiet pedestrian square, it matches the best of refined modern interior design with the charm of its ancient structure. This is based round three tiers of balcony-corridors that give onto internal patios. There is a great view from the rooftop pool. It also has a restaurant offering nouvelle Andalusian cuisine.
44 rooms

Los Seises****
◆ **E** D3
Segovias, 6
Tel. 95 422 94 95
Fax 95 422 43 34
www.hotellosseises.com
Sited in the 16th-century archbishop's palace next to the Giralda, in terms of history, location and building it is one of the more spectacular places to stay, though the hotel itself does not always match expectations. Small rooftop swimming pool with terrace and spectacular views of La Giralda. If you stay here, remember to look in on the restaurant which has some Roman remains (stones not food!).
43 rooms

Meliá Colón****
◆ **E** A2–B2
Canalejas, 1
Tel. 95 422 29 00
Traditionally the home of famous bullfighters (the Maestranza's bullring is five minutes away), Colón is large and comfortable, and central. Even if some people feel that it has become a bit pricey and failed to move with the times, it remains a good place to stay and a great place to meet as it boasts two well-used restaurants: El Burladero and La Tasca.
218 rooms

Meliá Lebreros****
◆ **C** E3
Avda Luis de Morales
Tel. 95 457 94 00
or 900 14 44 44 (freephone reservations)
Fax 95 458 23 09
One of the Meliá chain hotels in the city, offering functional high-standard comfort with good in-house restaurants for the busy traveler in high-rise Seville. Not as central as the Colón, the Lebreros is however very well located, close to the Santa Justa main high speed Madrid–Seville train (AVE) terminal, and just off the main avenue leading to the airport 5 miles away. It is also near the Sanchez Pizjuan sports stadium. If you are the type who doesn't like being mixed up in conferences or conventions, then be wary of these large places.
437 rooms
The sister
Meliá Sevilla****
◆ **C** D6
closed July-Aug.
is especially geared to conferences
364 rooms
while the
Meliá Confort Macarena****
◆ **D** E1
caters in part to those going to the nearby Isla Magica adventure park on the remains of the 1992 Quincentenary exhibition grounds.
331 rooms

Monte Triana***
◆ **A** D3
C. Clara de Jesús Montero, 24
Tel. 95 434 18 32
or 95 434 31 11
Fax 95 434 33 28
Good value modern hotel in the Triana district. Although it is set across the river from the main monuments, the area is exceptionally lively at night and home to Seville's community of industrial and artisan ceramicists. In summer it can be a bit cooler and is

< €50
€50–€130
€130–€300
> €300

within easy reach of good riverside restaurants.
117 rooms

Murillo**
◆ E E4
López de Rueda, 7
Tel. 95 421 60 95
Fax 95 421 96 16
Simple, characterful hotelr, named after the eponymous favorite-son painter. It is located among some of the most typical of the old narrow streets in the Santa Cruz district. Though the rooms are well priced, some of them can get uncomfortably hot in summer.
57 rooms

San Gil***
◆ D D2
Parras, 28
Tel. 95 490 68 11
Fax 95 490 69 39
email: hasangil@arrakis.es
Converted former palacio in the town center which offers a good feel of old Seville in simple taste and modest prices.
39 rooms

Simón*
◆ E C3
C. García de Vinuesa, 19
Tel. 95 422 66 60
Fax 95 456 22 41
www.hotelsimonsevilla.com
email: hotel-simon@jet.es
Excellent-value small hotel, located in a typical 19th-century house in one of the quieter streets close to the cathedral. Book well ahead.
29 rooms

Taberna del Alabardero****
◆ E B2–B3
Zaragoza, 20
Tel. 95 456 06 37
tabernadelalabardero.com
Late 19th-century palacio on three floors, converted into very elegant suites with lots of authentic atmosphere (and each has a jacuzzi). As it also boasts one of the best restaurants in town, it's a favorite with visitors. It's not easy to get bookings here so try well ahead. The hotel is closed in August.
7 rooms

Zenit Sevilla****
◆ E A5–A6
Pages del Corro, 90
Tel. 95 434 74 34
Fax 95 434 2707
One of the best places to stay in the Triana district, with functional, well-sized rooms and friendly bar service. It is also quiet, being off the road in a large back courtyard.
128 rooms

RESTAURANTS

Seville offers a vast selection of restaurants of every category in every part of the city. This means it is rarely necessary to look beyond easy walking distance of one's hotel to eat well at a reasonable price. Menus tend to vary little between summer and winter, and are often remarkably similar save where there is a specialization in fish or meat – the local clientele have conservative tastes and visitors are offered the same.

Menus that have too international a range of dishes can be disappointing. Also the price can be deceptive of quality. You should be aware that your bill will be more a function of décor, comfort, size of chair and scale of service rather than quality of food. The décor in some of the more expensive restaurants can be overwhelmingly pretentious and geared to unquestioning business expense accounts.

Because the city is at the heart of a major agricultural region, the basic products – fruit, vegetables, meat and fish – are almost all local and of good quality. The meat is well flavored, reflecting the free-range style of cattle farming. All types of fish and seafood are abundant, delivered daily from the nearby Atlantic fishing ports. Admittedly, there is a lot of frying but even the cheaper establishments use good oil. A useful test is to check the color of the olive oil/vinegar containers placed on tables – the yellower the better.

Eating – seated – in a restaurant is seen as a very different social activity to standing at a bar and picking at tapas, or even taking tapas casually at a table. Sitting down in a restaurant is considered a serious and lengthy affair – and portions will be generous as restaurateurs assume you will want a solid, relaxed meal. Most first-time visitors to Seville will be better off sticking to the ubiquitous tapas bars – it is a great way to get to know the Sevillian lifestyle. The décor of these places is unpretentious and usually the tables are bursting onto the street. One orders at the bar (where it is easy to point at unfamiliar or unpronounceable food) and then carries the order to a table. It is worth remembering that a single tapa is a large portion, meant to be shared or treated as a main item. Thus many people order half portions (tapitas or media raciones) and ask for several different items.

Non-smokers should remember that the cigarette and the cigar are important elements in the eating-out habits of Andalusians – and most Spaniards, from whatever city. The better restaurants tend to be indoors and air conditioned but the wafting smoke of the post-prandial cigar in a room can sour a great lunch or dinner for non-smokers. However this can be avoided by ensuring you leave the luncheon table by 4.30pm and the dinner table before midnight, when smokers tend to get into their stride!

The following list of restaurants is a highly selective and is intended merely as a point of reference – especially to those wandering around the city who feel overwhelmed by the amount of choice in every street. When eating out, the most important rule is never be put off by unfamiliar names for dishes: these might be the best items on the menu. Try to have them explained to you or carry or small phrasebook, as disappointments

< €20
€20–€30
€30–€50
> €50

are usually caused by not fully knowing what you have ordered!

Becerrita
◆ E F2
Recadero, 9
Tel. 95 441 20 57
Closed Sun. evening
Recently enlarged to build on its reputation of presenting the best of local cuisine along with excellent tapas. The chef is not afraid to make imaginative use of local vino oloroso *in dishes and produces a fine* tocino de ceilo *desert which is difficult to make so light.*

Casa Robles
◆ E D3
Álvarez Quintero, 58
Tel. 95 421 31 50
www.robles restaurantes.com
Reliable and centrally located, offering both restaurant and tapas service. Best for fish and a good place to try some of the regional cheeses. Its deserts are also home-made, a rare thing these days.

Casa Román
◆ E E4, next to P Andreu
Pl. de los Venerables, 1
Tel. 95 422 84 83
Hotels often direct clients here for its location in the heart of the Santa Cruz quarter and its standard offerings such as freshly cut cured ham from the nearby Sierra (jamon Jaburgo or pata negra) washed down with a sherry 'fino'.

Casablanca
◆ E B3
C. Zaragoza, 50
Tel. 95 422 46 98
Closed Sun.
This restaurant is still basking in the memory of an unexpected stop-over by King Juan Carlos during the 1992 Quincentenary celebrations. It excels in its guisos *(stews which are either fish, seafood, meat-based or purely vegetarian); the most tasty is often chickpea based (garbanzos).*

Don José
◆ C D6
Doctor Pedro de Castro
Tel. 95 441 44 02
Closed Sat.–Sun. in August
Good value, with a fixed menu. Visitors should make a point of asking about the guiso of the day. If one has enough Spanish it is also worth asking how it is made.

Dona Clara
Off map, west of ◆ E A6
Virgen del Valle, 10
Tel. 95 428 30 33
Closed Sun.
Reliable standard Andalusian fare. A good bet for anyone who is in this area of the city.

Egaña Oriza
◆ E D5
San Fernando, 41
Tel. 95 422 72 11
Closed Sat. lunch, Sun. and Aug.
www.restauranteoriza.com
An exceptionally good restaurant with superb ambience giving onto part of the walls of the Murillo Gardens. José María Egana brings all the flair of Basque nouvelle cuisine to the south in a happy symbiosis of flavors. This is for serious gourmets who are unlikely to be disappointed. Reservations are advisable.

El Bacalao
◆ E F1
Pl. Ponce de León, 15
Tel. 95 421 66 70
Closed Sun.
As its name implies, the specialty is a variety of cod and hake-based dishes. But it also offers top-quality meat, especially steaks. The formula is repeated at two sister restaurants: Victoria Eugenia (Pl. Villasis) and Columnas de Bacco (Tarifa 4).

El Espigón
◆ A D3
C. Bogotá, 1
Tel. 95 423 92 56
Closed Sun.–Mon.
Specializes in seafood of all types and produces a fine salt-baked fish.

Enrique Becerra
◆ E C3
C. Gamazo, 2
Tel. 95 421 30 49
Closed Sun.
Innovative recipes for traditional local products and much appreciated by Sevillianos. Regulars swear the tapas at the bar are better than the restaurant proper but if you have time it's worth trying both.

La Albahaca
◆ E E4
Pl. de Santa Cruz, 12
Tel. 95 422 07 14
Closed Sun. and Aug.
Well-located, in elegant surroundings with a terrace on the plaza, this restaurant offers an imaginative range of dishes. On most days diners enthuse, but occasionally the chef gets carried away using too many varied ingredients.

La Dorada
◆ C E6
Av. Ramón y Cajal (in the Viapol building)
Tel. 95 492 10 66
Closed Sun. evening
This is traditionally known as the best big fish restaurant in Seville. Big, noisy and informal, it continues with its emphasis on excellent raw materials simply cooked and served. Salt-baked sea bass brought to the table and then broken open with the knock of a hammer is an attraction in its own right.

La Parra
Off map, south of ◆ C D6.
Gustavo Gallardo, 14
Tel. 95 461 29 59
Closed Sat. lunch, Sun, and Aug.
Eclectic menu successfully mixing Andalusian and Arab (Moroccan) dishes as well as being unafraid to venture into curries.

Mesón Don Raimundo
◆ E D3
Argote de Molina, 26
Tel. 95 422 33 55
Suggestive setting in an old convent coupled with its concentration on dishes inspired by Moorish recipes make this special restaurant well worth a visit.

Modesto
◆ E F4
Cano y Cueto, 5
Tel. 95 441 68 11
www.grupomodesto.com
About as "typical" a Sevillian tavern/tapas bar as can be

⊡ < €50
⊡ €50–€130
⊡ €130–€300
⊡ > €300

found in the city, with the advantage of being very close to the main monuments in the Santa Cruz quarter. Good on anything fried. A few doors away is the tapas bar La Juderia, from the same owners.

Ox's
◆ E B6
Betis, 61
Tel. 95 427 95 85
Closed Sun. evening
Offers some of the best grilled meat in the city, with generous portions in a menu strongly influenced by Basque cuisine.

Poncio
Victoria, 8
Tel. 95 434 00 10
Closed Sun. and Aug.
This is by far the best recent addition to the choice of restaurants in the Triana district. Though the menu is small, it is constantly changing depending on what produce is available. It is well worth a special trip to Triana to savor this imaginative modern Andalusian/ Mediterranean cuisine.

Porta Rossa
◆ E B3
Pastor y Landero, 20
Tel. 95 421 61 39
Closed Sun. evening and Mon.
For those anxious for a break from local food and decor, this offers a welcome breath of reasonably authentic Italian cuisine in a lively atmosphere.

Salvador Rojo
◆ E D5–E5
San Fernando, 23
Tel. 95 422 97 25
Closed Sun. and first two weeks in Aug.
This highly praised restaurant takes its name from the chef who set up on his own after working at La Alqueria, which boasts the best cuisine in southern Spain (see Hacienda Benazuza p. 380). Unpretentious décor, with the emphasis squarely on top-quality food served to those who appreciate a flourish of new ideas. Be sure to save room for the sumptuous desserts.

MESON DON RAIMUNDO/DR

EGAÑA ORIZA/DR

Taberna del Alabardero
◆ E B2
Zaragoza, 20
Tel. 95 456 06 37
Closed mid July–mid Aug.
www.tabernadel alabardero.com
Located in a well restored 19th-century palacio, this expensive but much admired restaurant attracts those who want to eat well on a night out in elegant surroundings. The chef takes care to change the menu regularly and the sauces are always a surprise. For foodies a cooking school is run in the same building, and a hotel *(see p. 376).*

BARS AND NIGHTLIFE

Aduana
◆ A D3
Av. de Bonanza
Nightclub situated near Alfonso XIII bridge. Always lively.

Antigüedades
◆ E D3
C. Argote de Molina, 48
Lively bar with frequently changing decor.

Área
◆ C A3
Corner of Albuera and Marqués de Parada
Open until dawn.
Lively bar with four video screens.

Bar La Estrella
◆ E F3
C. Estrella, 3
Tel. 95 456 14 26
Closed Mon.
Popular, relaxed place offering a vast choice of tapas.

Bar Las Teresas
◆ E E4
C. de Santa Teresa, 2
Tel. 95 421 30 69
In the Santa Cruz district. Chacinas *and* tapas.

Bar Laredo
◆ E C1
C. Sierpes, 90
Tel. 95 421 30 16
Closed Sun.
Near the town hall.

Blue Moon
◆ C E3
C. Juan Antonio Cavestany, 10
Tel. 95 454 08 11
Open 10pm–dawn
Jazz concerts.

Bodega Belmonte
◆ E D3
C. Mateos Gago, 24
Tel. 95 421 40 14
Next to the cathedral. Good choice of wines and fine tapas.

Bodega Morales
◆ E C3
C. García de Vinuesa, 11
Former wine cellar (founded 1850) where you can enjoy a glass of wine with the fried fish bought from a nearby stand. Simple, good tapas.

Bodega Salazar
◆ E C3
C. García de Vinuesa, 20
Tel. 95 421 31 81
Closed Sun.
Typical bodega. Specialty: berenjenas *(aubergines).*

Bodeguita Alfalfa
◆ E E2
C. Aguilas
This bar's excellent tapas go very well with a glass of manzanilla.

Bourbon
◆ E D2
C. Álvarez Quintero, 7
Closed summer
Overlooking a parking lot in the

■ < €20
■ €20–€30
■ €30–€50
■ > €50

alleyway of the Calle Francos.
♫

Café del Casino
◆ E E6
Av. María Luisa
Tel. 95 423 66 59
The Casino's terrace offers a magnificent view of Parque María Luisa.

Café Europa
◆ E D1
C. Siete Revueltas, 35
One of the city center's best bars, ideally located and perfect for a quiet drink. The fod is really good too.

Café Maestranza
◆ E B4
C. Dos de Mayo, 28
Tel. 95 456 22 00
Quiet café next to the theater.

Café Universal
◆ E D2
C. Blanca de los Ríos
Tel. 95 422 47 70
Near Plaza Salvador. Great choice of tapas and raciones*.*
♫

Casa Cuesta
◆ C A4
C. Castilla, 3-5
Tel. 95 433 33 37
Closed Tue.
A bar-restaurant serving traditional Andalusian home cooking. Specialty: oxtail.

Catedral
◆ E C2
Cuesta del Rosario, 12
Late-night bar, pub and nightclub.
♫

Centro
◆ E D2
C. Alvarez Quintero, 3
Tel. 95 421 87 84
Closed Sun.
In the heart of Seville, as the name indicates. Breakfast and tapas.

Cervecería Giralda
◆ E D3
C. Mateos Gago, 1
Tel. 95 422 74 35
A popular tapas bar located closed to the cathedral. Excellent tapas.

Cervecería Internacional
◆ E C3
C. Gamazo, 3
Tel. 95 421 17 17
Closed Sun.
Good selection of draft beers and tapas. The place is famous for its frankfurters.

Chile
◆ E C6
Paseo de las Delicias
Tel. 95 423 52 58
Overlooking the Guadalquivir, near the Palacio de San Telmo.
♫

Discoteca Nodo
◆ E C3
C. Federico Sánchez Bedoya, 20
Tel. 95 421 60 39
Open until dawn
Closed summer
Nightclub located in the heart of the Arenal.
♫

El Aljibe
◆ A D3
C. Monzón (Behind Avenida Reina Mercedes)
Trendy bar, renowned for its beer.
♫

El Jota
◆ C D4
Av. Luis Montoto, 52
Small, friendly bar. Excellent draft beer and cod dishes.

El Kiosko
◆ D D1
Av. Ramón de Carranza
Beer and tapas in the Parque de Los Príncipes.

El Kiosko de las Flores
◆ C A4
Plaza del Altozano
Tel. 95 433 38 98
Beer and fried fish.

El Rinconcillo
◆ D D5
C. Gerona, 40
Tel. 95 422 31 83
Seville's oldest bar, dating back to the 17th century. Delicious tapas.

El Tremendo
◆ D D6
C. San Felipe, 15
Closed Wed.
Next to Santa Catalina. Excellent beers and tapas (especially cod and smoked tuna dishes).

Fun Club
◆ D B4
Alameda de Hércules, 86
Shows, exhibitions, live music.
♫

Kiosko Bar El Líbano
◆ C B6
Av. de la Palmera
A pleasant venue set in the gardens of Las Delicias. Tapas served during the day, bar at night.

La Bodeguita
◆ E D2
Plaza del Salvador
Closed Mon.
Specialties: "gambas" *and* "chacinas"*. A lively bar at all times of day and night.*

La Carbonería
◆ E E3
C. Levíes, 18
Tel. 95 421 44 60
Open 7pm–3am
Art exhibitions, flamenco and live music in this former coal merchant's store.
♫

La Esquina del Puente
◆ E A4
C. Betis, 1-3
Closed Tue.
Bar-restaurant. Specialties: fish and seafood.

La Mina
◆ E D2
Pl. de la Pescadería
Typical bodega*. Beer and* altramuces *(lupin-seed) tapas.*

La Raza
◆ C C6
Av. Isabel la Católica, 2
Tel. 95 423 38 30
A conveniently located, pleasant bar. Terrace in summer. Parking facilities.

Pub Abades
◆ E D3
C. Abades, 13
Tel. 95 422 56 22
Open 9pm–3am
In a 19th-century building.
♫

O' Flaherty Irish Bar
◆ E C3
C. Alemanes, 7
Tel. 95 421 04 51
Near the cathedral. For nachos, caesar salad, jacket potatoes... and Guinness
♫

Raynela Bar
◆ E D4
C. Miguel de Mañara, 9
Bar situated near the cathedral. Breakfast, tapas and drinks. Pleasant setting.

Sol
◆ D E5
Corner of Calle Sol and Calle Matahacas
Open 9pm (10pm weekends)–dawn
Live music.
♫

Sol y Sombra
◆ C A4
C. Castilla, 151
Tel. 95 433 39 35
In the Triana district. Delicious fish, meat and chacinas*. Unusual décor.*

Sopa de Ganso
◆ D C6, E D1
C. Pérez Galdós, 8
Tel. 95 421 25 26
A late-night bar near the Alfalfa. Tapas.
♫

⚀ < €50
⚁ €50–€130
⚂ €130–€300
⚃ > €300

→ **FLAMENCO: PEÑAS AND TABLAOS**

Arenal
◆ **E** B4
C. Rodo, 7
Tel. 95 421 64 92
Show at 9pm.

El Patio Sevillano
◆ **E** B4
Paseo de Colón, 11
Tel. 95 421 41 20
Spanish cabaret and flamenco. Shows: Mar.–Oct. at 7.30pm, 10pm and 12.30am.

Los Gallos
◆ **E** E4
Pl. de Santa Cruz, 11
Tel. 95 421 69 81
One of the best tablaos *in Seville. Shows take place at 9pm and 11.30pm.*

Torres Macarena
◆ **D** D1
Calle Torrigiano, 29
Peña *for both onlookers and specialists.*

AROUND SEVILLE

HOTELS

The following are about 30 minutes from Seville by car/bus.

Cortijo Aguila Real****
◆ **A** C2
On the Guillena–Burgillos road
Tel. 955 78 50 06
www.sol.com/cortijo/aguila/real/
This well restored former cortijo *shows the simple elegance that is typical of this combination of Andalusian country house and farm. Located just north of Seville, it is ideal for a restful weekend. But for keen horse riders there are extensive stable facilities in addition to a plaza de toros for bullfight enthusiasts.*
12 rooms
⚂

Casa Palacio Casa de Carmona*****
Plazuela de Lasso, 1
41410 Carmona
Tel. 954 414 41 51
Fax 954 19 01 89
www.casadecarmona.com
Set in the heart of one of the most ancient towns in Andalusia, this is a superbly restored 16th-century palace with each room decorated with distinctive antiques, a magnificent ocher-tiled loggia giving onto a small swimming pool. Less than 20 minutes from Seville airport, the hotel is an interesting luxury alternative to staying in Seville proper: However it is best to avoid coming in August as Carmona is dubbed the frying pan of Andalusia.
33 rooms
⚂

Cortijo El Esparragal***
Near Gerena off the main road to Merida, less than 15 miles from central Seville.
Tel. 955 78 2 702
www.sol.com/cortijo/esparragal/
On a big cattle- and bull-breeding ranch, a classic cortijo *converted into a comfortable hotel. Rich antique furnishings add to the atmosphere.*
18 rooms
⚂

Hacienda Benazuza*****
◆ **A** C2
Sanlucar La Mayor (approx 15 miles west of Seville)
Tel. 955 70 33 44
www.hbenazuza.com
An evocative conversion of a country house whose origins date to the Moorish domination of Andalusia in the 10th century. Complete with heliport and 15th-century private chapel, it offers the ultimate in luxury, down to individual jacuzzis. This is topped off by the La Alqueria restaurant which boasts one of the best – if not the best – cuisine and wine list in southern Spain. Those who can afford all this are unamimous in their praises.
44 rooms

Hacienda San Ignacio****
◆ **A** C3
Castilleja de la Cuesta, 4.5 miles from central Seville in the direction of Huelva
Tel. 954 16 04 30
This magnificent 17th-century converted hacienda has been running successfully as a hotel for ten years, relying on good service and pleasant surroundings with an especially fine patio. It also attracts a discerning clientele to its Almazara ("olive press") restaurant.
13 rooms

Parador Alcazar Rey Don Pedro
◆ **A** D2
Carmona
(20 minutes from Seville airport off the Seville–Córdoba freeway)
Tel. 954 14 10 10
www.parador.es
email: carmona@parador.es
Part of the state-run parador chain of hotels, the Alcazar Rey Don Pedro is set in a spectacular position by the old city walls of Carmona and on a bluff overlooking a huge open landscape towards the Sierra of Ronda. Although the paradors have been slow to adapt to changing tourist tastes and their décor is a bit severe, this hotel is very reliable and has a superbly sited swimming pool.
63 rooms

◆ PLACES TO VISIT

Opening times of tourist services, sites and monuments often change in Andalusia, and many churches are open only for services. You are advised to telephone beforehand to confirm that the information given here is still valid.

ACINIPO	◆ A E4	
ROMAN RUINS Tel. 952 21 36 40 *7¾ miles northwest of Ronda*	*Open Wed.–Sun. 9am–3.30pm.*	▲ *324*

ALCALÁ DE GUADAIRA	◆ A D3	
CASTILLO Esplanada del Castillo Tel. 955 69 91 16	*Restoration works. Visit by appointment.*	▲ *212*

ALCALÁ DEL RÍO	◆ A D2	
IGLESIA NUESTRA SEÑORA DE LA ASUNCIÓN Calle Padre Ruíz Paez Tel. 955 65 07 69	*Services Mon.–Sat. 7.30pm, Sun. 11am and 7.30pm.*	▲ *230*

ALCOLEA DEL RÍO	◆ A D2	
IGLESIA DE SAN JUAN BAUTISTA Plaza de España Tel. 955 64 40 24	*Services Tue.–Thur. 8pm, Sun. noon.*	▲ *231*

ALMERÍA	◆ B D5	
ALCAZABA Calle Almanzor Tel. 950 27 16 17	*Open Tue.–Sun. 9am–6.30pm.*	▲ *350*
ANCIENT HISTORY ROOM (CITY MUSEUM) Archivo Histórico Provincial Calle Infanta, 12 Tel. 950 22 50 58	*Open Tue.–Sat. 9am–2pm.*	
CATHEDRAL Plaza Catedral Tel. 609 57 58 02	*Open Mon.–Fri. 10am–4.30pm, Sat. 10am–1pm.*	▲ *351*
PREHISTORY ROOM (CITY MUSEUM) Biblioteca Pública Calle Hermanos Machado Tel. 950 23 03 75	*Open Tue.–Fri. 9am–2pm, Sat. 9.30am–1.30pm.*	
REGIONAL TOURIST OFFICE Parque de Nicolás Salmerón Tel. 950 27 43 55	*Open Mon.–Fri. 9am–7pm, Sat.–Sun. 10am–2pm. Closed public hols.*	

ALMODÓVAR DEL RÍO	◆ A F2	
CASTILLO Tel. 957 63 51 16 *At the top of the village*	*Visit by appointment.*	▲ *233*

ALMONASTER LA REAL	◆ A B1	
IGLESIA DE SAN MARTÍN Av. de San Martín Tel. 959 14 30 03	*Services daily 5.30pm.*	▲ *271*
MEZQUITA (MOSQUE) Tel. 957 14 30 03 *In the upper part of town*	*Open daily 9.30am–6.30pm (if it is closed, the key is available from the town hall on the main square).*	▲ *271*

ALMUÑECAR	◆ B B5	
ARCHEOLOGY MUSEUM Cuevas de Siete Tel. 958 63 11 25	*Open Tue.–Sat. 10.30am–1.30pm and 4–6.30pm (5.30–9.30pm in Jul.–Aug.); Sun. and public hols. 10.30am–1.30pm.*	▲ *344*
TOURIST OFFICE Palacete la Najarra Av. de Europa Tel. 958 63 11 25	*Open daily May–June, Sep.–Oct.: 10am–2pm and 5–8pm; July–Aug.10am–2pm and 5–9pm; Nov.–Apr.: 10am–2pm and 4–7pm.*	▲ *344*

ANTEQUERA	◆ A F4	
ALCAZABA, COLEGIATA DE SANTA MARÍA LA MAYOR *In the upper part of town*	*Open Tue.–Fri. 10.30am–2pm and 4.30–6.30pm, Sat.–Sun. 10.30am (Alcazaba Sun. 11.30am)–2pm*	▲ *331*
CUEVAS DE MENGA Y VIERA *¾ mile northeast of Antequera, on the Málaga-Granada road*	*Open July–Aug.: Wed.–Sun. 9.30am–3.30pm; Sep.–June: Tue.–Sat. 9am–6pm, Sun. 9am–3.30pm.*	▲ *331*

Places to visit are listed by city in alphabetical order.
The ▲ symbol refers to the Itineraries section and the ◆ symbol to the Map section.

CUEVA DEL ROMERAL *From La Azucena traffic circle, 2 miles northeast of Antequera*	*Open July–Aug.: Wed.–Sun. 9.30am–3.30pm; Sep.–June: Tue.–Sat. 9am–6pm, Sun. 9am–3.30pm.*	▲ 331
PALACIO DE NAJERA (TOWN MUSEUM) Plaza del Coso Viejo Tel. 952 70 40 21	*Open Oct.–Mar.: Tue.–Fri. 10am–1.30pm and 4–6pm, Sat. 10am–1.30pm, Sun. 11am–1.30pm; Apr.–Sep.: Mon.–Fri. 10am–2pm, Sat.–Sun. 11am–2pm.*	▲ 331
TOURIST OFFICE Plaza de San Sebastián, 7 Tel. 952 70 25 05	*Open Mon.–Sat. 9.30am–1.30pm and 4–7pm; Sun. and public hols. 10am–2pm.*	
ARACENA		◆ A C1
GRUTA DE LAS MARAVILLAS Calle Pozo de la Nieve Tel. 959 12 83 55	*Open daily 10.30am–1.30pm and 3–6pm.*	▲ 269 ▲ 268
IGLESIA DE LA ASUNCIÓN Plaza Alta	*Open for services: Mon.–Sat. 7pm, Sun. noon.*	
IGLESIA DE NUESTRA SEÑORA DEL MAYOR DOLOR, CASTILLO *Upper part of town*	*Open daily 10am–6.30pm.*	▲ 268
TOURIST OFFICE Plaza de San Pedro Tel. 959 12 82 06	*Open daily 10am–2.30pm and 4–6.30pm.*	
ARCOS DE LA FRONTERA		◆ A D4
IGLESIA DE SANTA MARÍA Plaza del Cabildo	*Open Mon.–Fri. 10am–1pm and 3.30–6.30pm, Sat. 10am–2pm.*	▲ 320
TOURIST OFFICE Plaza del Cabildo Tel. 956 70 22 64	*Open Mon.–Fri. 10am–2pm and 5.30–7.30pm, Sat. 10am–2pm and 5–6.30pm, Sun. and public hols. 10.30am– 12.30pm.*	
AROCHE		◆ A B1
CASTILLO *Top of the village*	*Visit by appointment. Contact Sr. Manuel Amigo, tel. 959 14 02 61. Reserve two days before.*	▲ 271
IGLESIA DE LA ASUNCÍON Plaza de Juan Carlos I	*Visit by appointment organized by Manuel Amigo, tel. 959 14 02 61. Reserve two days before.*	▲ 272
AZNALCÁZAR		◆ A C3
IGLESIA DE SAN PABLO Av. Juan Carlos I, 5 Tel. 955 75 03 25	*Open for services.*	▲ 221
BAEZA		◆ B C1
ANTIGUA CARNICERÍA Plaza de los Leones Tel. 953 74 04 44	*Currently undergoing restoration works.*	▲ 347
CATHEDRAL Plaza Santa María Tel. 953 74 41 57	*Open June–Sep.: daily 10.30am–1pm and 5–7pm; Oct.–May: daily 10.30am–1pm and 4–6pm.*	▲ 347
PALACIO DE JABALQUINTO Plaza de Santa Cruz	*Open Tue., Thur.–Sun. 10am–2pm and 4–6pm.*	▲ 347
TOURIST OFFICE Casa del Pópulo Plaza del Pópulo Tel. 953 74 04 44	*Open Mon.–Fri. 9am–2pm, Sat. 10am–1pm.*	
BENAOJÁN		◆ A E4-E5
CUEVA DE LA PILETA Tel. 952 16 73 43 *2½ miles south of Benaoján, on the road to Cortes de la Frontera*	*Open June–Sep.: daily 10am–1pm and 4–6pm; Oct.–May: daily 10am–1pm and 4–5pm.*	▲ 324
CABO DE GATA-NÍJAR (NATURE RESERVE)		◆ B E5
CENTRO DE INTERPRETACIÓN LAS ALMOLADERAS Tel. 950 16 04 35 *1½ miles northwest of Ruescas*	*Open Holy Week and July–Sep.: Tue.–Sun. 10am–2pm and 5–9pm; the rest of the year: Tue.–Sun. 9.30am–3.30pm.*	▲ 352
CÁDIZ		◆ A C5
CITY TOURIST OFFICE Plaza de San Juan de Dios, 11 Tel. 956 24 10 01	*Open Mon.–Fri. 9am–2pm and 5–8pm, Sat.–Sun. and public hols. 10am–1pm and 4–6.30pm.*	

BASTIÓN DE LA CANDELARIA Alameda Marques de Comillas Tel. 956 22 24 74	*Open June–Sep.: Mon.–Fri. 11am–2pm and 6–9pm; Oct.–May: 11am–2pm and 5–8pm.*	◆ I A1-A2 ▲ 315
CASA MUSEO PALACIO DE LOS MORA Calle Ancha, 26 Tel. 956 211 409	*Open Sat. 10am–1pm.*	◆ I B2
CASTILLO DE SANTA CATALINA Campo de las Balas Tel. 956 22 63 33	*Open Mon.–Fri. 10am–6.30pm, Sat.-Sun. and public hols. 10am–1pm.*	◆ I A3 ▲ 316
CATHEDRAL Plaza de Pío XII Tel. 956 28 61 54	*Open Tue.–Fri. 10am–1pm and 4.30–6.15pm, Sat.–Sun. 10am–1pm. Services Wed., Fri. 7pm, Sun. 11am.*	◆ I C2 ▲ 313
CONVENTO DE SAN FRANCISCO Plaza de San Francisco, 5 Tel. 956 21 37 10	*Open daily 11am–12.45pm and 7–9pm. Services daily 7.30pm (July–Aug. noon and 8.30pm).*	◆ I B2 ▲ 314
CONVENTO DE SANTO DOMINGO Plaza de Santo Domingo Tel. 956 26 37 09	*Open Mon.–Sat. 8.45am–noon and 7–8.45pm. Sun. services 8am, noon and 8pm.*	◆ I C2 ▲ 311
HOSPITAL DE LAS MUJERES Palacio Arzobispal Calle Hospital de Mujeres, 2 Tel. 956 22 36 47	*Open Mon.–Fri. 10am–1pm.*	◆ I B2-B3 ▲ 316
IGLESIA DE SANTA CRUZ Plaza del Fray Félix Tel. 956 28 77 04	*Services Mon.–Sat. 7pm, Sun. 11.30am and 7pm.*	◆ I C2 ▲ 313
IGLESIA DE SANTA CUEVA Calle Rosario Tel. 956 22 22 62	*Open 10am–1pm. Closed Sun. and public hols. morning. Oratorio de Santa Cueva: Mon.–Fri. 10am–1pm and 4.30–7.30pm, Sat.-Sun. 10am–1pm.*	◆ I B2 ▲ 314
IGLESIA DEL CARMEN Calle Bendición de Dios Tel. 956 21 42 06	*Services daily 9am and 7.30pm.*	◆ I A2 ▲ 315
MUSEO CATEDRALICIO Plaza del Fray Félix Tel. 956 25 98 12	*Open Tue.–Fri. 10am–1pm and 4–7pm, Sat.–Sun. 10am–1pm.*	◆ I C2 ▲ 314
MUSEO DE CÁDIZ Plaza de Mina, 5 Tel. 956 21 22 81	*Open Tue. 2.30–8pm, Wed–Sat. 9am–8pm, Sun. 9am–2pm.*	◆ I B2 ▲ 314
MUSEO DEL MAR Calle Paseo del Parque Genovés Tel. 956 22 24 74	*Open Mon.–Fri. 11am–2pm and 6–9pm, Sat.–Sun. and public hols. 11am–2pm.*	◆ I A2
MUSEO HISTÓRICO MUNICIPAL Calle Santa Inés, 9-11 Tel. 956 22 17 88	*Open Tue.–Fri. 9am–1pm and 4–7pm (June–Sep. 9am–1pm and 5–8pm), Sat.–Sun. 9am–1pm.*	◆ I B2 ▲ 315
ORATORIO DE SAN FELIPE NERI Calle Santa Inés Tel. 956 21 16 12	*Open Mon.–Sat. 10am–1.30pm.*	◆ I B2 ▲ 315
REGIONAL TOURIST OFFICE Calle Calderón de la Barca, 1 Tel. 956 21 13 13	*Open Mon. and Sat. 9am–2pm, Tue.–Fri. 9am–7pm.*	
TEATRO ROMANO Calle San Juan de Dios Tel. 956 21 22 81	*Open Tue.–Sun. 11am–1.30pm.*	◆ I C2
TORRE DE TAVIRA-CÁMARA OSCURA Calle Marqués del Real Tesoro, 10 Tel. 956 21 29 10	*Open June 15–Sep. 15: Mon.–Fri. 10am–8pm; Sep. 16–June 14: 10am–6pm.*	◆ I B2 ▲ 316
CARMONA		◆ A D2
AYUNTAMIENTO Calle El Salvador, 2 Tel. 954 14 00 11	*Open Mon.–Fri. 8am–3pm.*	
IGLESIA DE SAN BARTOLOMÉ Calle San Bartolomé Tel. 954 14 11 75	*Open for services.*	▲ 217
IGLESIA DE SAN PEDRO Arco de la Carne, Calle San Pedro Tel. 954 14 12 70	*Open Mon., Thur.–Fri. 11am–2pm and 5–7pm, Sat.–Sun. 11am–2pm.*	▲ 215
IGLESIA DE SANTA MARÍA DE GRACIA Plaza de Cristo Rey, 2 Tel. 954 19 14 82	*Open Mon.–Fri. 10am–2pm and 5.30–7pm, Sat. 10am–2pm.*	▲ 214

IGLESIA DE SANTIAGO Calle Calatrava	*Open Mon.–Fri. 10.30am–2.30pm.*	▲ 217
IGLESIA DE SAN SALVADOR Calle El Salvador	*Open Mon.–Fri. 4–6pm, Sat.–Sun. 10.30am–2.30pm. Closed July–Aug.*	▲ 217
MUSEO DE HISTORIA Casa Palacio del Marqués de las Torres Calle San Ildefonso, 1 Tel. 954 14 01 28	*Open Wed.-Mon. 11am–7pm, Tue. 11am–2pm.*	
NECRÓPOLIS ROMANA Av. Jorge Bonsor, 9 Tel. 954 14 08 11	*Open (except public hols.) Sep. 16–June 14: Tue.–Fri. 9am–5pm, Sat.–Sun. 10am–2pm; June 15– Sep. 15: Tue.–Fri. 8.30am–2pm, Sat. 10am–2pm.*	▲ 215
TOURIST OFFICE, ALCÁZAR DE LA PUERTA DE SEVILLA Arco de la Puerta de Sevilla Tel. 954 19 09 55	*Open Mon.–Sat. 10am–6pm, Sun. and public hols. 10am–3pm.*	▲ 215
CAZALLA DE LA SIERRA	◆ A D1	
AYUNTAMIENTO Plaza de Manuel Nosea, 2 Tel. 954 88 40 00	*Open Mon.–Fri. 8am–3pm.*	
CARTUJA DE LA INMACULADA *1¾ miles southeast of Cazalla*	*Open daily 9am–8pm.*	▲ 267
IGLESIA DE NUESTRA SEÑORA DE LA CONSOLACIÓN Plaza Mayor Tel. 954 88 40 43	*Services daily 8pm.*	▲ 267
CAZORLA	◆ B D2	
MUSEO DEL ALTO GUADALQUIVIR Castillo de la Yedra Tel. 953 71 00 39	*Open Tue. 3–8pm, Wed.–Sat. 9am–8pm, Sun. and public hols. 9am–1pm.*	▲ 349
TOURIST OFFICE Plaza de la Constitución, 1 Tel. 953 71 02 81	*Gives information on the town and the nature reserve of Cazorla, Segura y las Villas.*	
CHIPIONA	◆ A C4	
TOURIST OFFICE Plaza de Andalucía Tel. 956 37 28 28	*Open Apr.–Sep.: Mon.–Fri. 10am–1.30pm and 6–8pm, Sat. 11am–1pm; Oct.–Mar.: Mon.–Fri. 10am–1.30pm and 5–7pm, Sat. 11am–1pm.*	
CONSTANTINA	◆ A D1	
ERMITA DE NUESTRA SEÑORA DEL ROBLEDO Tel. 954 88 45 16 *About 1 mile from Constantina*	*Open all day.*	▲ 264
IGLESIA DE LA ENCARNACIÓN Plaza del Llano del Sol Tel. 955 88 13 06	*Services Apr.–Sep.: Mon.–Sat. 8.30pm, Sun. noon and 8.30pm; Oct.–Mar.: Mon.–Sat. 7pm, Sun. 8pm.*	▲ 264
TOURIST OFFICE Paseo de la Alameda, 7 Tel. 955 88 12 97	*Open daily 10.30am–2pm and 5–8pm.*	
CÓRDOBA	◆ A F1-F2	
CITY TOURIST OFFICE Plaza de Judá Levi Tel. 957 20 05 22	*Open Mon.–Sat. 8.30am–2.30pm, Sun. 9am–2pm.*	
ALCÁZAR DE LOS REYES CATÓLICOS Calle Caballerizas Reales Tel. 957 42 01 51	*Open Tue.–Sat. 10am–2pm and 4.30–6.30pm (Aug. 8.30am–12.30pm), Sun. and public hols. 9.30am–2.30pm.*	◆ F A5-B5 ▲ 237
CATHEDRAL, LA MEZQUITA, TESORO CATEDRALICIO Calle Torrijos, 10 Tel. 957 47 05 12	*Open Mar., July–Oct.: Mon.–Sat. 10am–6.30pm, Sun. and public hols. 2–6.30pm; Apr.–June: Mon.–Sat. 10am–7pm, Sun. and public hols. 2–7pm; Feb. and Nov.: Mon.–Sat. 10am–5.30pm, Sun. and public hols. 2–5.30pm; Dec.–Jan.: Mon.–Sat. 10am–5pm, Sun. and public hols. 2–5pm.*	◆ F B4-B5 ▲ 238
GRAN TEATRO Av. del Gran Capitán, 3 Tel. 954 48 02 37/954 48 06 44	*Plays, music and dance. Box office open Mon.–Sat. 11am–2pm and 6–9pm; Sun. 11am–2pm.*	◆ F C2 ◆ 360

IGLESIA DE SAN LORENZO Plaza de San Lorenzo Tel. 957 48 34 79	*Services daily 11am, noon, 8pm and 9pm.*	◆ F F3 ▲ 244
IGLESIA DE SAN NICOLÁS DE LA VILLA Plaza de San Nicolás Tel. 957 47 68 32	*Services daily 9am, 10am, 11.30am, 6pm, 7pm and 8pm.*	◆ F B3 ▲ 244
MUSEO ARQUEOLÓGICO Plaza Jerónimo Páez, 7 Tel. 957 47 40 11	*Open Tue. 3–8pm, Wed.–Sat. 9am–8pm, Sun 9am–3pm.*	◆ F C4 ▲ 242
MUSEO DE BELLAS ARTES Plaza del Potro, 1 Tel. 957 47 33 45	*Open Tue. 3–8pm, Wed.–Sat. 9am–8pm, Sun and public hols. 9am–3pm.*	◆ F D5 ▲ 243
MUSEO DIOCESANO DE BELLAS ARTES PALACIO EPISCOPAL Calle Torrijos, 12 Tel. 957 49 60 85	*Open June, July and Sep.: Mon.–Fri. 10.30am–2pm and 4–6.30pm, Sat. 9.30am–1.30pm; Oct.–May: Mon.–Fri. 9.30am–1.30pm and 4–6pm, Sat. 9.30am–1.30pm. Closed in Aug.*	◆ F B5
MUSEO ROMERO DE TORRES Plaza del Potro, 2 Tel. 957 49 19 09	*Open Tue.–Sat. 10am–2pm and 4.30–6.30pm, Sun. and public hols. 9.30am–2.30pm.*	◆ F C5-D5 ▲ 243
MUSEO TAURINO Plaza Maimónides, 5 Tel. 957 20 10 56	*Open May–Oct. 15: Tue.–Sat. 10am–2pm and 5.30–7.30pm, Sun. and public hols. 9.30am–2.30pm; Oct. 16–Apr.: Tue.–Sat. 10am–2pm and 4.30–6.30pm, Sun. and public hols. 9.30am–2.30pm.*	◆ F A4-B4 ▲ 242
PALACIO DE VIANA Plaza de Don Gome, 2 Tel. 957 49 67 41	*Open June 16–Sep.: Mon.–Sat. 9am–2pm; Oct.–May: Mon.–Fri. 10am–1pm and 4–6pm, Sat. 10am–1pm. Closed June 1–15.*	◆ F D3 ▲ 244
REGIONAL TOURIST OFFICE Calle de Torrijos, 10 Tel. 957 47 12 35	*Open June–Aug.: Mon.–Fri. 9 .30am–8pm, Sat. 10am–8pm; Sep.–Oct.: Mon.–Fri. 9.30am–7pm, Sat. 10am–7pm; Nov.–May: Mon.–Fri. 9.30am–6pm, Sat. 10am–6pm; all year: Sun. and public hols. 10am–2pm.*	
SYNAGOGUE Calle Judíos, 20 Tel. 957 20 29 28	*Open Tue.–Sat. 10am–1.30pm and 3.30–5.30pm, Sun. and public hols. 10am–1.30pm.*	◆ F B4 ▲ 241
TORRE DE LA CALAHORRA Puente Romano Tel. 957 29 39 29	*Open May–Sep.: daily 10am–2pm and 4.30–8.30pm; Oct.–Apr.: daily 10am–6pm.*	◆ F B6 ▲ 236
DOÑANA NATIONAL PARK	◆ A B3-C3-C4	
INFORMATION CENTERS – El Acebuche Tel. 959 44 87 11 (national park) Tel. 959 45 01 59 (nature reserve) *8 miles southwest of El Rocío (A-483)*	*(see also Sanlúcar de Barrameda ◆ 393)* *Open daily 8am–7pm or 8pm.*	▲ 286
– Las Rocinas Tel. 959 44 23 40 *¾ mile south of El Rocío*	*Open daily 10am–7pm or 8pm.*	▲ 287
– El Acebrón Tel. 959 43 04 32 *2½ miles west of El Rocío*	*Open daily 9am–3pm and 4–7pm.*	▲ 287
MADRE DEL ROCÍO OBSERVATORY Paseo Marismeños Tel. 959 50 60 93	*Open June–Sep.: Tue.–Sun. 9am–2pm and 6–10pm.*	
PARK (GUIDED TOURS) Reservations 959 43 04 32	*Departures: June–Sep.: Mon.–Sat. 8.30am and 5pm; Oct.–May: Tue.–Sun. 8.30am and 3pm.*	
ÉCIJA	◆ A E2	
IGLESIA DE SAN GIL Calle San Antonio Tel. 954 83 07 37	*Open daily 10am–1pm and 5–7pm.*	▲ 250
IGLESIA DE SAN JUAN Plaza de San Juan Tel. 954 83 35 32	*Open daily 10am–1pm and 5–7pm.*	▲ 250
IGLESIA DE SANTA CRUZ Plaza de la Virgen del Valle Tel. 954 83 06 13	*Open daily 10am–1pm and 5–7pm.*	▲ 249
IGLESIA DE SANTA MARÍA Plaza de Santa María Tel. 954 83 04 30	*Open daily 10am–1pm and 5–7pm.*	▲ 249
IGLESIA DE SANTIAGO Plaza de Santiago Tel. 646 11 87 12	*Open daily 10am–1pm and 5–7pm.*	▲ 250

PALACIO DE PEÑAFLOR Calle Emilio Castellar Tel. 954 83 02 73	*Houses the city library, which organizes temporary exhibitions: Mon.–Fri. 11am–1pm and 6–9pm; Sat., Sun. and public hols. 11am–2pm.*	▲ 250
PALACIO DE BENAMEJI AND PALACIO DE LOS CONDES DE VALVERDE MUSEO HISTORICO MUNICIPAL Calle Cánovas del Castillo, 4 Tel. 955 90 29 19	*Open June–Sep.: Tue.–Sun. 9am–2pm; Oct.–May: Tue.–Sun. 9.30am–1.30pm and 4.30–7.30pm.*	▲ 249
TOURIST OFFICE Calle Cánovas del Castillo, 4 Tel. 955 90 29 33	*Open Apr.–Sep.: Tue.–Sun. 9am–2pm; Oct.–Mar.: Tue.–Sun. 9.30am–1.30pm and 4.30–6.30pm.*	
ESPARTINAS	◆ A C3	
CONVENTO DE LORETO Tel. 954 11 39 12 *Km 563 (350 miles) on the A-472 (Seville–Huelva)*	*Open daily 9am–1pm and 4–8.30pm.*	▲ 220
ESTEPA	◆ A F3	
CONVENTO DE SANTA CLARA Cerro de San Cristóbal Tel. 955 91 32 20	*Church open for services: Mon. 5pm, Sat. and Sun. 8–9pm.*	▲ 260
IGLESIA DEL CARMEN Plaza del Carmen	*Services Sun. 1pm.*	▲ 260
PALACIO DE LOS CERVERALES Calle Castillejos, 8	*Tours by appointment. Contact Emilio (Tel. 954 82 00 79 or 677 41 17 75).*	▲ 260
TOURIST OFFICE Calle Saladillo, 12 Tel. 955 91 27 71	*Open Mon.–Fri. 9am–8pm.*	
GRANADA	◆ B B3-B4	
ABADIA DEL SACROMONTE Camino del Sacromonte Tel. 958 22 14 45	*Open Tue.–Sun. 11am–1pm and 4–6pm.*	▲ 337
ALHAMBRA AND EL GENERALIFE Cuesta de Gomérez Tel. 902 44 12 21 Reservations 902 22 44 60	*Open Apr.–Oct.: daily 8.30am–8pm, Tue.–Sat. also 10–11.30pm; Nov.–Mar: daily 8.30am–6pm, Fri.–Sat. also 8–9.30pm. Reservations recommended.*	◆ G E1-E2-F1-F2 ▲ 338, 342
AUDITORIO MANUEL DE FALLA Paseo de los Mártires Tel. 958 22 94 21	*Open Mon.–Sat. 10am–3pm.*	◆ G F2 ◆ 360
BAÑUELO Carrera del Darro, 31 Tel. 958 02 78 00	*Open (except public hols.) Tue.–Sat. 10am–2pm.*	◆ G D2 ▲ 337
CAPILLA REAL (MUSEO DE LOS REYES CATÓLICOS) Calle de los Oficios, 3 Tel. 958 22 92 39	*Open Apr.–Oct.: daily 10.30am (Sun. 11am)–1pm and 4–7pm; Nov.–Mar.: daily 10.30am (Sun.11am)–1pm and 3.30–6.30pm.*	◆ G D3 ▲ 335
CASA DE LOS PISAS Calle Convalenscia, 1 Tel. 958 22 21 44	*Open Mon.–Sat. 10am–1pm and 5–7.30pm. Guided tours 10.30am and 11.30am.*	◆ G D2
CASA-MUSEO F. GARCÍA LORCA Huerta de San Vicente Calle Virgen Blanca Fuente Vaqueros Tel. 958 25 84 66	*Open Tue.–Sun. 45-min. tours: Apr.–June: 10am, 11am, noon, 1pm, 5pm, 6pm and 7pm ; Jul.–Sep.: 10am, 11am, noon, 1pm, 6pm, 7pm and 8pm; Oct.–Mar.: 10am, 11am, noon, 1pm, 4pm, 5pm and 6pm.*	◆ B B3 ▲ 342
CASA-MUSEO MANUEL DE FALLA Calle Antequeruela Alta, 11 Tel. 958 22 94 21	*Currently closed to the public.*	◆ G F2
CATHEDRAL Calle Gran Vía de Colón Tel. 958 22 29 59	*Open Mon.–Sat. 10am–1.30pm and 4–7pm, Sun. and public hols. 4–7pm. Exhibitions Apr.–Oct. 15: Mon.–Sat. 10am–7pm, Sun. and public. hols. 10am–8pm; Oct. 15–Mar.: daily 3.30–6.30pm.*	◆ G D3 ▲ 335
COLEGIATA DEL SALVADOR Plaza del Salvador	*Open Mon.–Sat. 10am–1pm and 4.30–6.30pm.*	◆ G D1
CONVENTO DE SANTA CATALINA AND CASA DE ZAFRA Carrera del Darro Tel. 958 22 61 89	*Services Sun. 1am and 1pm.*	G D2 ▲ 337

Place	Details	Map / Page
CONVENTO DE SANTA ISABEL LA REAL Calle Santa Isabel la Real	*Church open daily 10am–6pm.*	◆ G D3 ▲ 336
CORRAL DEL CARBÓN Calle Mariana Pineda Tel. 958 22 59 90	*Open Mon.–Sat. 9am–7pm, Sun. 10am–2pm.*	◆ G D3 ▲ 336
FUNDACIÓN RODRÍGUEZ ACOSTA Carmen Rodríguez Acosta Callejón Niño del Rollo, 8 Tel. 958 22 74 97	*By appointment., Tue.–Sat. 10am–1.30pm (contact Carolina).*	◆ G E2
HOSPITAL DE SAN JUAN DE DIOS Calle San Juan de Dios Tel. 958 29 52 21	*Open Apr.–Oct.: daily 7.30–11.30am and 6–9pm; Nov.–Mar: daily 10am–noon and 5–7pm.*	◆ G C3-C4
HOSPITAL REAL Av. del Hospicio Tel. 958 24 30 27	*Open Mon.–Fri. 9am–2pm.*	◆ G B3 ▲ 336
IGLESIA DE SANTA ANA Calle Santa Ana, 1 Tel. 958 22 50 04	*Services Mon.–Fri. 6.30pm, Sun. and public hols. 11am, noon and 6pm.*	◆ G D2 ▲ 337
MONASTERIO DE LA CARTUJA Tel. 958 16 19 32 *On the road to Alfacar*	*Open Mon.–Sat. 10am–1pm, Sun. 10am–noon. Also Apr.–Oct.: daily 4–8pm; Nov.–Mar.: daily 4–7pm.*	◆ G A2 ▲ 336
MONASTERIO DE SAN JERÓNIMO Calle Rector López Argüeta, 9 Tel. 958 27 93 37	*Open Mon.–Sat. 10am–1.30pm, Sun. 11am–1.30pm. Also Apr.–Oct.: daily 4–7.30pm; Oct.–Mar: daily 3–6.30pm.*	◆ G C4 ▲ 336
MUSEO ARQUEOLÓGICO **CASA DE CASTRIL** Calle del Darro, 43 Tel. 958 22 56 40	*Open (except public hols.) Tue. 3–8pm, Wed.–Sat. 9am–8pm, Sun. 9am–2.30pm.*	◆ G D2 ▲ 337
MUSEO DE BELLAS ARTES Palacio de Carlos V Alhambra Tel. 958 22 48 43	*Open (except public hols.) June–Sep.: Tue. 2.30–8pm, Wed.–Sat. 9am–8pm, Sun. 9am–2.30pm; Oct.–May: Tue. 2.30–6pm, Wed.–Sat. 9am–6pm, Sun. 9am–2.30pm.*	◆ G E2 ▲ 340 ❀
MUSEO NACIONAL DE ARTE **HISPANO-MUSULMÁN** Palacio de Carlos V Alhambra Tel. 958 22 75 27	*Open Tue.–Sat. 9am–2pm.*	◆ G E2 ▲ 340
PARQUE DE LAS CIENCIAS Carretera Armilla Tel. 958 13 19 00	*Open Tue.–Sat. 10am–7pm, Sun. and public hols. 10am–3pm. Closed last two weeks Sep.*	
TEATRO ALHAMBRA Calle Molinos, 56 Tel. 958 22 04 47	*Plays, jazz, contemporary dance... Box office opens 1 hour before the performance. Tickets can also be bought at the Corte Inglés and Hypercor.*	◆ G F2 ◆ 360
TOURIST OFFICES – Calle Mariana Pineda, 10 Tel. 958 22 59 90 – Av. del Generalife Tel. 958 22 95 75	*Open Mon.–Fri. 9.30am–7pm, Sat. 10am–2pm.*	
GRAZALEMA		◆ A E4
TOURIST OFFICE Plaza de España Tel. 956 13 22 25	*Open Apr.–Sep.: Tue.–Sun. 10am–2pm and 4–6pm; Oct.–Mar.: Tue.–Sun. 10am–2pm and 5–7pm.*	
GUADIX		◆ B C3
ALCAZABA Tel. 958 66 01 60	*Open Wed.–Sat. 10am–2pm and 4–6pm, Sun. 10am–2pm.*	▲ 345
CATHEDRAL, MUSEUM Plaza de la Catedral Tel. 958 66 08 00/10 97	*Open Mon.–Sat. 11am–1pm and 4–6pm.*	▲ 345
MUSEO DE LAS CUEVAS Plaza del Beato Poveda Tel. 958 66 08 08	*Open June–Sep.: Mon.–Sat. 10am–2pm and 4–8pm, Sun. 10am–2pm; Oct.–May: Mon.–Sat. 10am–2pm and 4–6pm, Sun. 10am–2pm.*	▲ 345
REGIONAL TOURIST OFFICE Av. Mariana Pineda Tel. 958 66 26 65	*Open Mon.–Fri. 8am–3pm.*	
HUELVA		◆ A A3
MUSEO PROVINCIAL Alameda Sundheim, 13 Tel. 959 25 93 00	*Open Tue.–Sat. 9am–8pm, Sun. and public hols. 9am–3pm.*	▲ 281

Place	Opening hours	Page
TOURIST OFFICE Av. de Alemania, 12 Tel. 959 25 74 03	*Open Mon.–Fri. 9am–7pm, Sat. 10am–noon.*	
TOURIST REGIONAL COMMITTEE Calle Fernando el Católico, 18 Tel. 959 25 74 67	*Open Mon.–Fri. 8am–3pm.*	
JAÉN		◆ B B2
BAÑOS ARABES, MUSEO DE ARTES Y COSTUMBRES POPULARES, MUSEO DEL ARTE NAÏF Palacio de Villardompardo Plaza Santa Luisa de Marillac Tel. 953 23 62 92	*Open (except public hols.) Tue.–Fri. 9am–8pm, Sat.–Sun. 9.30am–2.30pm.*	▲ 346
CASTILLO Cerro de Santa Catalina	*Open Thur.–Tue. 10am–2pm and 3.30-6pm.*	▲ 346
IGLESIA DE LA MAGDALENA Plaza de la Magdalena	*Open daily 6–8pm.*	
IGLESIA DE SAN ILDEFONSO Plaza de San Ildefonso	*Open daily 8.30am–noon and 6–9pm.*	
MUSEO CATEDRALICIO Plaza Santa María, Tel. 953 22 46 75	*Open May–Sep.: daily 10am–1pm and 4–8pm; Oct.–Apr.: Mon.–Sat. 10am–1pm and 5–7pm, Sun. 10am–1.30pm and 6–7pm.*	▲ 346
MUSEO PROVINCIAL Paseo de la Estación, 27 Tel. 953 25 06 00	*Open (except public hols.) Tue. 3–8pm, Wed.–Sat. 9am–8pm, Sun. 9am–3pm.*	
REGIONAL TOURIST OFFICE Calle del Arquitecto Berges 3 953 24 26 24	*Open Mon.–Fri. 9am–7pm, Sat. 10am–2pm and 5–7pm, Sun. 10am–2pm and 4–7pm.*	
TOWN TOURIST OFFICE Palacio Municipal de Cultura Calle de la Maestra, 16 Tel. 953 21 91 16	*Open May–Aug.: daily 10am–8pm; Sep.–Apr: daily 10am–6pm. Closed Dec. 25., Jan. 1 and 6.*	
JEREZ DE LA FRONTERA		◆ A C4
ALCÁZAR Alameda Vieja Tel. 956 31 97 98	*Open Mon.–Fri. 9am–2.30pm and 4.30–8.30pm.*	▲ 295
BODEGA DOMECQ Calle San Ildefonso, 3 Tel. 956 15 15 00	*Tours Mon.–Fri. 9am–2pm, Sat., Sun. and public hols. afternoon by appointment.*	▲ 297
BODEGA GONZÁLEZ BYASS Calle Manuel María Gonzalez Tel. 956 35 70 00	*Tours (Spanish): Mon.–Fri. 11am, noon, 1pm, 2pm, 5pm, 6pm, 7pm, Sat.–Sun. 5pm, 6pm, 7pm; (English): daily 11.30am, 12.30pm, 1.30pm, 4.30pm, 5.30pm, 6.30pm.*	▲ 297
CATEDRAL DEL SALVADOR Plaza de Arroyo Tel. 956 34 84 82	*Open daily 6.30–7.30pm and for services.*	▲ 296
CENTRO ANDALUZ DE FLAMENCO Palacio Permartín Plaza de San Juan, 1 Tel. 956 34 92 65	*Open (except public hols.) Mon.–Fri. 9am–2pm.*	▲ 297
IGLESIA DE SAN DIONISIO Plaza de Asunción Tel. 956 34 29 40	*Open daily 7am–7pm.*	▲ 296
IGLESIA DE SAN MIGUEL Calle San Miguel Tel. 956 34 33 47	*Services daily at 7pm.*	▲ 296
IGLESIA DE SANTIAGO Plaza de Santiago Tel. 956 18 08 39	*Services Mon.–Sat. 8am, Sun. and public hols. 11am and 8pm.*	▲ 296
MONASTERIO DE LA CARTUJA Tel. 956 15 64 65 *3½ miles from Jerez on the Medina–Sidonia road*	*Currently closed to the public. (Gardens open to the public daily 8am–6pm; only men are allowed to visit the monastery, by appointment Wed. and Sat. 5–6pm)*	▲ 294
MUSEO ARQUEOLÓGICO Plaza del Mercado Tel. 956 33 33 16	*Open Tue.–Sun. 10am–2.30pm; Also Sep.–June 14: Tue.–Fri. 4–7pm.*	▲ 296
MUSEO DE LOS RELOJES Calle Cervantes, 3 Tel. 956 18 21 00	*Open summer: Tue-Sun 9am-2pm and 6-8pm; winter Tue-Sun 10am-7pm.*	▲ 297

REAL ESCUELA ANDALUZA DEL ARTE ECUESTRE Av. del Duque de Abrantes Reservations 956 31 80 08	*Schooling and dressage: Mon.–Wed. 11am–1pm. Show "Como Bailan los Caballos Andaluces": Tue. and Thur. noon–1.30pm. Reservations compulsory.*	▲ 297
TOURIST OFFICE Calle Larga, 39 Tel. 956 33 11 50	*Open Mon.–Fri. 9am–7pm, Sat. 9am–2pm.*	
LACALAHORRA	◆ **B** C3	
CASTILLO *Top of the village.*	*Open Wed. 10am–1pm and 4–6pm. Information from Sr Antonio Trivalo: 958 67 70 98.*	▲ 345
LEBRIJA	◆ **A** C4	
IGLESIA DE SANTA MARÍA DE LA OLIVA Calle Rector Merina, 2	*Open daily but times may vary (enter through the small door to the sacristy).*	▲ 293
TOURIST INFORMATION Casa de Cultura Calle Tetuán, 15 Tel. 955 97 40 68	*Open Mon.–Fri. 9am–2pm and 4–10pm.*	
LORA DEL RÍO	◆ **A** E2	
IGLESIA DE NUESTRA SEÑORA DE LA ASUNCIÓN Calle Martínez Montanés, 14	*Open Mon.–Fri. (except public hols.) 11am–2pm and 5–8pm.*	▲ 231
MÁLAGA	◆ **A** F5, **B** A5	
ALCAZABA - MUSEO ARQUEOLÓGICO Calle Alcazabilla Tel. 95 221 60 05	*Open Apr.–Sep.: Wed.–Mon. 9.30am–8pm; Oct.–Mar.: Tue.–Sun. 8.30am–7pm.*	▲ 333
CATHEDRAL Calle Molina Lario Tel. 95 221 59 17	*Open Apr.–Sep.: Mon.–Fri. 9am–6.45pm, Sat. 9am–5.45pm; Oct.–Mar.: Mon.–Sat. 10am–6.45pm.*	▲ 333
CITY TOURIST OFFICE Av. de Cervantes, 1 Tel. 95 260 44 10	*Open June 15–Sep. 15.: Mon.–Sat. 11am–2pm and 6–9pm, Sun. 11am–2pm; Sep. 16–June 14: Mon.–Sat. 11am–2pm and 5–8pm, Sun. 11am–2pm.*	
FUNDACIÓN CASA NATAL DE PICASSO Plaza de la Merced, 15 Tel. 95 206 02 15	*Open Mon.–Fri. 8am–2pm and 4.30–7pm, Sat. 9.30am–1.30pm.*	▲ 332
GIBRALFARO Alto del Monte Gibralfaro Tel. 95 222 19 02	*Open daily: Apr.–Sep. 9.30am–8pm, Oct.–Mar. 9am–6pm.*	▲ 333
MUSEO DE ARTES Y COSTUMBRES POPULARES Pasillo de Santa Isabel, 10 Tel. 95 221 71 37	*Open June 15–July and Sep.: Mon.–Fri. 10am–1.30pm and 5–8pm, Sat. 10am–1.30pm; Aug.: Mon.–Sat. 10am–1.30pm; Oct.–June 14: Mon.–Fri. 10am–1.30pm and 4–7pm, Sat. 10am–1.30pm.*	▲ 333
MUSEO DE BELLAS ARTES Palacio Buenavista Calle San Augustín, 8 Tel. 95 221 83 82	*Closed. The building is currently being restored. It will house a large museum dedicated to Picasso (possibly from early 2003). The Fine Arts museum will be transfered to a different location.*	
MUSEO DE LA ABADIA DE SANTA ANA DEL CISTER Calle Cister	*Open Mon.–Fri. 10.30am–2pm, Sat. 11.30am–2pm.*	
MUSEO DE LA COFRADÍA DE LA EXPIRACIÓN Av. de la Aurora Tel. 95 236 02 71	*Open Mon.–Fri. 10am–1pm and 7–9pm.*	
MUSEO DE MÁLAGA Paseo de Reding, 1 Tel. 95 222 04 43	*Open daily 10am–8pm.*	
PLAZA DE TOROS DE LA MALAGUETA Paseo de Reding Tel. 95 222 62 92	*Open Mon.–Fri. 10am–1pm and 5–8pm.*	
REGIONAL TOURIST OFFICE Pasaje de Chinitas, 4 Tel. 95 221 34 45	*Open Mon.–Fri. 9am–7pm, Sat. 10am–7pm, Sun. 10am–2pm.*	
MARBELLA	◆ **A** F5	
MUSEO DEL GRABADO ESPAÑOL CONTEMPORÁNEO Calle Hospital Bazán Tel. 952 82 50 35	*Open June–Sep.: Mon.–Fri. 10am–2pm and 6–9pm ; Oct.–May: Tue.–Sat. 10am–2pm and 5.30–8.30pm.*	▲ 332

TOURIST OFFICE Glorietta Fontanilla Tel. 952 77 14 42	*Open Mon.–Fri. 9.30am–9pm, Sat. 10am–2pm.*	
MARCHENA	◆ B C3	
IGLESIA DE SAN JUAN BAUTISTA (Museo Zurbarán) Calle Cristóbal de Morales Tel. 954 84 32 57	*Open Mon.–Fri. 11.30am–8pm (exhibitions) or by request, Sat.–Sun. 10am–1pm.*	▲ 253
IGLESIA DE SANTA MARÍA DE LA MOTA Calle Palacio Ducal, 9 Tel. 954 84 39 83	*Convent: open daily 10am–2.30pm and 4.30–6.30pm. Church: service Sun. 9am.*	▲ 253
TOURIST OFFICE Calle San Francisco, 43 Tel. 955 84 61 67	*Open daily 10am–2pm.*	
MATALASCAÑAS	◆ A B3	
TOURIST OFFICE Av. de las Adelfas Tel. 959 43 00 86	*Open June–Oct.: Mon.–Fri. 9.30am–3pm, Sat. 9.30am–2pm; Nov.–May: Tue.–Fri. 9am–2.30pm, Sat. 9.30am–1.30pm and 2.30–7pm, Sun. 9.30am–1.30pm.*	▲ 286
MEDINA AZAHARA	◆ A F1	
Medinat el-Zahra site Tel. 957 32 91 30 *On the Palma del Río road, 4¾ miles from Córdoba*	*Open Tue.–Sat.: May–June 10 am–2pm and 6–8.30pm; July–Sep. 10am–1.30pm and 6–8.30pm; Oct.–Apr. 10am–1.30pm and 4–6.30pm. Sun. and public hols. 10am–2pm.*	▲ 234
MOGUER	◆ A B3	
CASA MUSEO JUAN RAMÓN JIMÉNEZ Calle Juan Ramón Jiménez, 10 Tel. 959 37 21 48	*Open (except public hols.) Tue.–Sat. 10am–2pm and 3–8pm, Sun. 10am–2pm.*	
CONVENTO DE SANTA CLARA Plaza de las Monjas Tel. 959 37 01 07	*Open Tue.–Sat. 11am–1pm and 5–7pm, Sun. and public hols. 11am–1pm.*	▲ 285
MOJÁCAR	◆ B F4	
TOURIST OFFICE Calle Glorieta Tel. 950 47 51 62	*Open Apr.–Oct.: Mon.–Fri. 10am–2pm and 5–8pm, Sat. 10am–1pm; Nov.–Mar.: Mon.–Fri. 10am–3pm, Sat. 10am–1pm.*	
MONCLOVA (LA)	◆ A E2	
CASTILLO Tel. 955 90 73 94 *On the N IV-E5.*	*Visit by appointment.*	▲ 251
OLIVARES	◆ A C2	
IGLESIA DE NOSTRA SEÑORA DE LAS NIEBLES Plaza de España Tel. 954 11 03 09	*Services Sun. 8.30am, 11am and 2.30pm.*	▲ 219
OSUNA	◆ A E3	
COLEGIATA DE SANTA MARÍA DE LA ASUNCIÓN Y PANTEÓN DUCAL Colegiata Extramuro Tel. 954 81 04 44	*Open May–Sep.: Tue.–Sun. 10am–1.30pm and 4–7pm; Oct.–Apr.: Tue.–Sun. 10am–1.30pm and 3.30–6.30pm.*	▲ 257 ▲ 258
CONVENTO DE LA ENCARNACIÓN Plaza de la Encarnación Tel. 954 81 11 21	*Open. May–Sep.: Tue.–Sun. 10am–1pm and 4–7pm; Oct.–Apr.: Tue.–Sun. 10am–1pm and 4–5pm.*	▲ 258
MUSEO ARQUEOLÓGICO Plaza de la Duquesa Tel. 954 81 22 11	*Open. May–Sep.: Tue.–Sun. 11.30am–1.30pm and 5–7pm; Oct.–Apr: Tue.–Sun. 11.30am–1.30pm and 4–6pm.*	▲ 256
TOURIST OFFICE Plaza Mayor Tel. 955 82 14 00 or 954 81 16 17	*Open Mon.–Sat. 10am–2pm and 5–7pm, Sun. 10am–1pm.*	

PALMA DEL RÍO		◆ A E2
IGLESIA DE LA ASUNCIÓN Calle Cardenal Portocarrero Tel. 957 64 31 91	*Open Mon.–Sat. for the 9pm service, Sun. noon–9pm.*	▲ 232
PALOS DE LA FRONTERA		◆ A B3
IGLESIA DE SAN JORGE Calle Fray Juan Pérez, 19 Tel. 959 35 07 58	*Open Mon.–Fri. 10.30am–1pm and 7–8pm.*	▲ 284
CASA MUSEO DE MARTÍN ALONSO PINZON Calle Cólon, 24 Tel. 959 35 01 99	*Open Mon.–Fri. 10.30am–1.30pm and 5–7.30pm.*	▲ 285
PUERTO DE SANTA MARÍA (EL)		◆ A C5
BODEGAS OSBORNE Calle de los Moros Tel. 956 85 52 11	*Open Mon.–Fri. (by reservation). Closed Aug. and public hols.*	▲ 304
BODEGAS TERRY Calle Santisima Trinidad Tel. 956 48 30 00	*Open Mon.–Fri. (by reservation). Closed Aug. and public hols*	▲ 304
CASTILLO DE SAN MARCOS Plaza de Alfonso X, El Sabio Tel. 956 54 14 66	*Open Tue.–Sun. 10am–2pm.*	▲ 303
IGLESIA MAYOR PRIORAL Plaza de España Tel. 956 85 17 16	*Open Mon.–Fri. 8.30am–1pm and 6.30–8.30pm, Sat. 8am–12.30pm and 6.30–8.30pm.*	▲ 304
FUNDACIÓN RAFAEL ALBERTI Calle Santo Domingo, 26 Tel. 956 85 09 60	*Open June–Sep.: Mon.–Fri. 10.30am–2.30pm; Oct.–May: Tue.–Sun. 10.30am–2.30pm.*	▲ 304
MUSEO MUNICIPAL Calle Parador, 1 Tel. 956 54 27 05	*Open Mon.–Sat. 10am–2pm.*	▲ 304
TOURIST OFFICE Calle Guadalete, 1 Tel. 956 54 24 13	*Open June–Sep.: daily 10am–2pm and 6–8pm; Oct.–May: daily 10am–2pm and 5.30–7.30pm. Closed during the "feria".*	
RÁBIDA (LA)		◆ A B3
MONASTERIO DE SANTA MARÍA DE LA RÁBIDA Muelle de los Caravelas Tel. 959 53 05 97	*Open Apr.–Sep. 20: Tue.–Fri. 10am–2pm and 5.45–9pm, Sat.–Sun. 11am–8pm; Sep. 21–Mar.: Tue.–Sun. 10am–7pm.*	▲ 282
RIO TINTO		◆ A B2
MUSEO MINERO DE RIOTINTO Plaza del Museo Tel. 959 59 10 15 Reservations 959 59 00 25	*Open daily: July–Sep. 10am–7pm; Oct.–June 10am–3pm and 4–7pm.*	▲ 273
ROCÍO (EL)		◆ A B3-C3
ERMITA DE NUESTRA SEÑORA DEL ROCÍO *In the center of the village*	*Open daily 8.30am–7.30pm.*	▲ 290
TOURIST OFFICE Centro Ecoturistico Av. de la Canaliega Tel. 959 44 26 84	*Open Mon.–Fri. 10am–2pm.*	
RONDA		◆ A E4
BAÑOS ÁRABES Calle San Miguel Tel. 952 87 38 89	*Open Tue. 9am–1.30pm and 4–6pm, Wed.–Sat. 9.30am–3.30pm.*	▲ 326
CASA DEL REY MORO Cuesta de Santo Domingo, 17 Tel. 952 18 72 00	*Gardens only: open daily 10am–7pm.*	▲ 327
IGLESIA DEL ESPÍRITU SANTO Calle Espíritu Santo Tel. 952 87 49 28	*Open Mon.–Sat. 10am–6.30pm.*	▲ 328
IGLESIA DE SANTA CECILIA Plaza de los Descalzos Tel. 952 87 21 80	*Services Sat. 8pm, Sun. 10am and 8pm.*	▲ 327

IGLESIA DE SANTA MARÍA DE LA ENCARNACÍON Plaza Duquesa de Parcent Tel. 952 87 22 46	*Open daily 10am–6pm.*	▲ 328
IGLESIA DE SANTA MARÍA LA MAYOR Plaza Duquesa de Parcent Tel. 952 87 22 46	*Open June–Sep.: daily 10am–9pm; Oct.–May: daily 10am–6pm. Service Sun. 1pm.*	▲ 326
IGLESIA DE LA VIRGEN DE LA CABEZA Barrio de San Francisco Tel. 649 36 57 72 *Drive about ¼ mile on the road to Algeciras, then turn right and drive 1¼ miles*	*Open Tue.–Fri. 10am–2pm and 4–6pm (Oct.–Mar.), 10am–7pm (Apr.–Sep.); Sat., Sun. and public hols. 10am–3pm.*	
MUSEO DEL BANDOLERO Calle Armiñán, 65 Tel. 952 87 77 85	*Open daily: Mar. 10am–7pm; Apr.–Nov. 10am–8pm; Dec.–Feb. 10.30am–6pm.*	
MUSEO RILKE Hotel de la Reina Victoria Calle Doctor Fleming, 25 Tel. 952 87 72 40	*By appointment.*	▲ 326
PALACIO DEL MARQUÉS DE SALVATIERRA Calle Marqués de Salvatierra Tel. 952 87 12 72	*Open Mon.–Wed., Fri., Sat.; guided tours every 30 mins. 11am–2pm and 4–7pm.*	▲ 328
PALACIO DE MONDRAGÓN Plaza de Mondragón Tel. 952 87 84 50	*Open Mon.–Fri. 10am–7pm (Oct.–Apr.: 10am–6pm); Sat., Sun. and public hols. 10am–3pm.*	▲ 328
PLAZA DE TOROS Y MUSEO TAURINO Calle Virgen de la Paz Tel. 952 87 41 32/15 39	*Open Apr.–Sep.: daily 10am–8pm; Oct.–Mar.: daily 10am–6pm. Bullfighting school: open to the public Mon., Wed. and Fri. 8–10pm.*	▲ 325
REGIONAL TOURIST OFFICE Plaza de España, 1 Tel. 952 87 12 72	*Open Mon.–Fri. 10am–2pm and 4–6.30pm, Sat. 10.30am–2.30pm.*	
SALOBREÑA	◆ B B5	
CASTILLO ÁRABE Fortaleza Tel. 958 61 27 33	*Open July–Sep.: Tue.–Sun. 9.45am–2pm and 3.30–10pm; Oct.–June: Tue.–Sun. 11am–1.50pm and 4–7pm.*	▲ 344
MUSEO ARQUEOLÓGICO Town Library Calle Ángel Ganivet Tel. 958 61 27 33	*Open May–Aug.: Tue.–Sun. 10am–2pm and 4–10pm; Sep.–Apr.: Tue.–Sun. 11am–1.50pm and 4–7pm.*	
TOURIST OFFICE Plaza de Goya Tel. 958 61 03 14	*Open Mon.–Fri. 9.30am–1.30pm and 4.30–7pm, Sat. 9.30am–1.30pm.*	
SANLÚCAR DE BARRAMEDA	◆ A C4	
BODEGAS BARBADILLO Calle Luis de Eguilaz, 11 Tel. 956 36 05 16	*By appointment.*	▲ 299
FÁBRICA DE HIELO DE BAJO DE GUÍA (VISITORS CENTER) Av. de Bajo de Guía Tel. 956 38 16 35 (national park) Tel. 956 36 07 15 (nature reserve)	*Information about tours in the Doñana park. National park office open daily 9am–7pm. Nature reserve office open Tue.–Fri. 10am–2pm and 4–6pm, Sat.–Sun. 10am–2.30pm.*	▲ 287
IGLESIA DE NUESTRA SEÑORA DE LA O Plaza del Conde de Niebla Barrio Alto Tel. 956 36 05 55	*Services July–Sep.: daily 8pm; Oct.–June: Mon.–Fri. 7.30pm, Sun. noon.*	▲ 299
PALACIO DE ORLÉANS Y BORBÓN (Ayuntamiento) Calle Cuesta de Belén Tel. 956 38 80 00	*Open July–Sep. 15: daily 10am–2pm; Sep. 16–June: Mon.–Fri. 10am–2pm.*	▲ 300
PALACIO DUCAL Plaza del Conde de Niebla Barrio Alto Tel. 956 36 01 61	*Open Sun. 10.30am–1.30pm.*	▲ 299
TOURIST OFFICE Calzada del Ejército Tel. 956 36 61 10	*Open Mon.–Fri. 10am–2pm and 6–8pm, Sat., Sun. 10am–2pm and 6–8.30pm.*	

SANLÚCAR LA MAYOR		◆ A C3
IGLESIA DE SANTA MARÍA Calle Calvo Sotelo, 3 Tel. 955 70 25 35	*Open daily 6–8pm.*	▲ 220
SANTIPONCE		◆ A C2
ITÁLICA ARCHEOLOGICAL SITE Av. de Extremadura, 2 Tel. 955 99 73 76	*Open Apr.–Sep.: Tue.–Sat. 8.30am–8.30pm, Sun. and public hols. 9am–3pm; Oct.–Mar.: Tue.–Sat. 9am–5.30pm, Sun. and public hols. 10am–4pm.*	▲ 208
MONASTERIO DE SAN ISIDORO DEL CAMPO Av. de San Isidoro	*Undergoing restoration works. Closed to the public.*	▲ 206
SEVILLE		◆ A D3
AYUNTAMIENTO Plaza Nueva, 1 Tel. 95 459 01 01	*Currently closed to the public.*	◆ E C2 ▲ 132
BASÍLICA DE JESÚS DEL GRAN PODER Plaza de San Lorenzo, 13 Tel. 95 438 54 54	*Open daily 8am–1.45pm and 6–9pm.*	◆ D B4 ▲ 179
BASÍLICA DE LA MACARENA Calle Bécquer, 1 Tel. 95 437 01 95	*Basilica: daily 9am–1pm and 5–9pm; Museum: daily 9.30am–1pm and 5–8pm.*	◆ D D2 ▲ 167
BIBLIOTECA CAPITULAR Y COLOMBINA Calle Alemanes Tel. 95 456 27 21	*Open Mon.–Thur. 9am–2pm and 4.30–7.30pm, Fri. 9am–2pm.*	◆ E D4 ▲ 134
CAPILLA DEL CRISTO DE LA EXPIRACIÓN Calle Castilla	*Open for services.*	◆ C A4 ▲ 197
CAPILLA DE LOS MARINEROS Calle Pureza, Triana	*Services Sat. 9pm, Sun. 11am.*	◆ E A4 ▲ 195
CAPILLA DE SAN JOSÉ Calle Sierpès	*Services daily at 8pm and Mon.–Sat. 9am, 10am, 11am and noon.*	◆ E A4 ▲ 131
CASA DE LA MEMORIA DE AL-ANDALUS Calle Ximénez de Enciso ,28 Tel. 95 456 06 70	*Open daily 10am–2pm and 5–9pm.*	◆ E E3-E4
CASA LONJA – ARCHIVO DE INDIAS Av. de la Constitución Tel. 95 421 12 34	*Currently closed to the public.*	◆ E D4 ▲ 150
CASA MUSEO DE MURILLO Calle Santa Teresa, 8 Tel. 95 422 94 15	*Houses temporary exhibitions: Mon.–Fri. 8am–3pm and 5–8pm.*	◆ E E4 ▲ 155
CASA DE PILATOS Plaza de Pilatos, 1 Tel. 95 422 52 98	*Open June–Sep.: daily 9am–7pm; Oct–May: daily 9am–6pm. Free admission Tue. 1–5pm.*	◆ E F2 ▲ 158
CATHEDRAL, LA GIRALDA Puerta de Aljama Tel. 95 421 49 71	*Open July–Aug.: Mon.–Sat. 10.30am–4pm, Sun. 2–6pm; Sep.–June: Mon.–Sat. 11am–5pm, Sun. 2.30–6pm. Guided tours at 11am, noon, 5pm and 6pm.*	◆ E D3-D4 ▲ 133
CENTRO ANDALUZ DE ARTE CONTEMPORÁNEO Av. Américo Vespucio, 2 Isla de la Cartuja Tel. 95 503 70 70	*Open Apr.–Sep.: Tue.–Sat. 10am–9pm, Sun. 10am–3pm; Oct.–Mar.: Tue.–Fri. 10am–8pm, Sat. 11am–8pm, Sun. 10am–3pm.*	◆ C A1-A2 ▲ 199
CONVENTO DE LA ENCARNACÍON Calle Virgen de los Reyes Tel. 95 422 70 01	*Church open Tue. 7.30am–2pm and 4–8pm.*	◆ E D4 ▲ 141
CONVENTO DEL ESPÍRITU SANTO Calle del Espíritu Santo Tel. 95 422 12 73	*Church open Mon.–Fri. 11am–1pm and 6–8pm. Service Sun. 8.30am.*	◆ D D5 ▲ 171
CONVENTO DE LOS REMEDIOS (MUSEO DE CARRUAJÉS) Plaza de Cuba	*Open daily 10am–2pm; visits afternoon by appointment.*	◆ E B6 ▲ 194
CONVENTO DE SAN CLEMENTE Calle Reposo, 9 Tel. 95 437 80 40	*Services: Mon.–Sat. 8.30am, Sun. and public hols. 9.30am.*	◆ D B2 ▲ 176
CONVENTO DE SAN LEANDRO Plaza de San Ildefonso, 1 Tel. 95 422 41 95	*Open for services: Mon.–Fri. 7.30am, Sat. 8am, Sun. 9am; all day on the 22nd of every month.*	◆ E E2-E3 ▲ 162
CONVENTO DE SANTA ANA Calle Santa Ana, 34 Tel. 95 438 06 03	*Church open daily 4.30–7pm. Services Mon.–Sat. 8am, Sun. 10am.*	◆ D B3 ▲ 178

CONVENTO DE SANTA INÉS Calle Doña María Coronel, 5 Tel. 95 422 31 45	*Visits by appointment. Services, summer: daily 8.30am; winter: daily 7.30pm.*	◆ D D5 ▲ 170
CONVENTO DE SANTA ISABEL Plaza de Santa Isabel Tel. 95 421 89 17/95 442 16 13	*Service Sun. 10am.*	◆ D E4 ▲ 168
CONVENTO DE S. MARÍA DE LOS REYES Calle Santiago, 33 Tel. 95 456 04 44	*Houses temporary exhibitions.*	◆ D E6 ▲ 170
CONVENTO DE SANTA PAULA Calle Santa Paula, 11 Tel. 95 453 63 30	*Open Tue.–Sun. 10.30am–12.30pm and 4.30–6.30pm.*	◆ D E4 ▲ 168
ESPACIO CULTURAL PUERTA TRIANA Isla de La Cartuja Tel. 95 503 70 83	*Open Tue.–Fri. 10.30am–1pm and 4.30–7pm, Sat., Sun. and public hols. 11am–2.30pm and 4.30–8pm.*	◆ C A1-A2 ▲ 198
HOSPITAL DE LA SANTA CARIDAD Calle Temprado, 3 Tel. 95 422 32 32	*Open Mon.–Sat. 9am–1.30pm and 3.30–6.30pm, Sun. and public hols. 9am–1pm.*	◆ E C4 ▲ 188
HOSPITAL DE LAS CINCO LLAGAS (HOSPITAL DE LA SANGRE) Calle Parlamento de Andalucía Tel. 95 459 21 00	*Open Mon. 5–7pm (individuals); Mon.–Fri. 8.30am–2.30pm (groups). Closed Aug.*	◆ D D1 ▲ 167
HOSPITAL DE LOS VENERABLES Plaza de los Venerables, 8 Tel. 95 456 26 96	*Open daily 10am–2pm and 4–8pm.*	◆ E E4 ▲ 155
IGLESIA DE LA ANUNCIACIÓN Plaza de la Encarnación Tel. 95 463 74 96	*Services Sat. noon and 8.30pm, Sun. 12.30pm.*	◆ D C6 ◆ E D1 ▲ 165
IGLESIA DE LA MADRE DE DIOS Calle San José	*Service Sun. 10.30am.*	◆ E E3 ▲ 157
IGLESIA DE LA MAGDALENA Calle San Pablo Tel. 95 422 96 03	*Open Mon.–Sat. 7.30–11am and 6.30–9pm; Sun. 7.30am–1pm.*	◆ E B2 ▲ 179
IGLESIA DEL DIVINO SALVADOR Plaza del Salvador Tel. 95 421 16 79	*Open Mon.–Sat. 6.30-9pm, Sun. 10.30am–2pm and 7–9pm.*	◆ E D2 ▲ 164
IGLESIA NUESTRA SEÑORA DE LA O Calle Castilla Tel. 95 433 75 39	*Open daily 9–11am and 7–9pm. Services Sat. 8pm, Sun. noon.*	◆ C A4 ▲ 197
IGLESIA DE OMNIUM SANCTORUM Plaza C. de la Barca	*Services Sat. 7.30pm, Sun. 10.30am and noon.*	◆ D C3 ▲ 173
IGLESIA DE SAN ANDRÉS Plaza de San Andrés Tel. 95 438 10 17	*Currently being restored. Closed to the public.*	◆ D B2-C2 ▲ 171
IGLESIA DE SAN ESTEBAN Calle Medinacelli, 2 Tel. 95 442 20 54	*Services Sat. 8pm, Sun. 11am.*	◆ E F2 ▲ 158
IGLESIA DE SAN GIL Plaza de San Gil Tel. 95 437 13 68	*Services Sat. 7pm, Sun. 9am and 11am.*	◆ D D2 ▲ 167
IGLESIA DE SAN ILDEFONSO Plaza de San Ildefonso	*Services Sat. 8pm, Sun. 10am and noon.*	◆ E E2 ▲ 162
IGLESIA DE SAN ISIDORO Calle San Isidoro Tel. 95 422 53 13	*Services Sat. 8pm, Sun. 11.30am and 1pm.*	◆ E D2 ▲ 162
IGLESIA DE SAN JUAN DE LA PALMA Calle San Juan de la Palma Tel. 95 422 94 37	*Services Sat. 8pm, Sun. 11am and 12.30pm.*	◆ D C5 ▲ 172
IGLESIA DE SAN LORENZO Plaza de San Lorenzo Tel. 95 438 45 58	*Open Sat.–Thur. 8am–1.45pm and 6–9pm, Fri. 7.30am–10pm.*	◆ D B4 ▲ 178
IGLESIA DE SAN LUIS Calle San Luis Tel. 95 455 02 07	*Currently closed to the public.*	◆ D D4 ▲ 168
IGLESIA DE SAN MARCOS Plaza de San Marcos, 10 Tel. 95 421 14 25	*Services Sat. 9pm, Sun. noon and 9pm.*	◆ D E4 ▲ 168
IGLESIA DE SAN MARTÍN Plaza de San Martín Tel. 95 438 20 05	*Open Mon.–Wed., Fri., Sat. 8–9pm, Sun. 10am–1pm.*	◆ D C4 ▲ 171

Place	Information	Map / Page
IGLESIA DE SAN NICOLÁS Calle Federico Rubio, 4 Tel. 95 422 68 69	*Services Sat. 8pm, Sun. noon.*	◆ E E2 ▲ 157
IGLESIA DE SAN PEDRO Plaza de San Pedro Tel. 95 421 68 58	*Services Sat. 8pm, Sun. 10am, 11am, noon and 8pm.*	◆ D D6 ◆ E E1 ▲ 170
IGLESIA DE SANTA ANA Plaza de Santa Ana Tel. 95 427 13 82	*Services Sat. 8.30pm, Sun. 10am, noon and 8.30pm.*	◆ E A5 ▲ 195
IGLESIA DE SANTA CATALINA Plaza de los Terceros Tel. 95 421 74 41	*Open Mon.–Fri. 7–8pm.*	◆ D D6 ◆ E E1 ▲ 170
IGLESIA DE SANTA CRUZ Calle Mateos Gago Tel. 95 422 73 39	*Services Sat. 8.30pm, Sun. 10am, 1pm and 8.30pm.*	◆ E E3 ▲ 156
IGLESIA DE SANTA MARÍA LA BLANCA Calle de San José	*Open Tue.–Fri. 10am–9pm, Sat. 11am–9pm, Sun. and public hols. 10am–3pm.*	◆ E E3-F3 ▲ 157
ISLA MÁGICA Isla de la Cartuja Tel. 902 16 17 16	*Open Mar. 17–Apr.: Fri.–Sun. 11am–10pm; May–June 21: Tue.–Thur. 11am–7pm, Fri.–Sun. 11am–10pm; June 22–Sep. 8 daily 11am–2am.*	◆ C A1 ▲ 198
MONASTERIO CARTUJO DE SANTA MARÍA DE LAS CUEVAS Calle Americo Vespucio Isla de la Cartuja Tel. 95 503 70 83	*Open Apr.–Sep.: Tue.–Sat. 10am–9pm, Sun. 10am–3pm; Oct.–Mar.: Tue.–Sat. 10am–8pm, Sun. 10am–3pm.*	◆ C A1 ▲ 198
MUSEO ARQUEOLÓGICO Plaza de América Parque María Luisa Tel. 95 423 24 01	*Open Tue. 3–8pm, Wed.–Sat. 9am–8pm, Sun. and public hols. 9am–2pm.*	◆ C C6 ▲ 204
MUSEO DE ARTES Y COSTUMBRES POPULARES Plaza de América, 3 Parque María Luisa Tel. 95 423 25 76	*Open Tue. 3–8pm, Wed.–Sat. 9am–8pm, Sun. and public hols. 9am–2pm.*	◆ C C6 ▲ 203
MUSEO DE BELLAS ARTES Plaza del Museo, 9 Tel. 95 422 07 90	*Open Tue. 3–8pm, Wed.–Sat. 9am–8pm, Sun. and public hols. 9am–2pm.*	◆ D A6 ◆ E A1 ▲ 180
MUSEO MILITAR Plaza de España Puerta de Aragón Tel. 95 423 99 09	*Open Sep.–July: Tue.–Sat. 10am–2pm.*	◆ C C6
PALACIO DE LAS DUEÑAS Calle de las Dueñas Tel. 915 47 66 06	*Visit by permission (Mon.–Sat. 9.30am–2pm and 4–7pm).*	◆ D D5 ▲ 171
PALACIO DE LEBRIJA Calle Cuna, 8 Tel. 95 421 81 83	*Open Mon.–Fri. 11am–1pm and 5–7pm, Sat. 10am–1pm.*	◆ E C1 ▲ 164
PALACIO DE SAN TELMO Avenida de Roma Tel. 95 503 55 00	*Visits by appointment.*	◆ E D6 ▲ 187
PLAZA DE TOROS DE LA MAESTRANZA MUSEO TAURINO Paseo de Cristóbal Colón Tel. 95 422 45 77	*Open daily 9.30am–2pm and 3–7pm (9.30am–3pm on days when bullfighting is held).*	◆ E B3-B4 ▲ 190
REAL MONASTERIO DE SAN CLEMENTE Calle Reposo, 9 Tel. 95 437 80 40	*Church open for services only.*	◆ D B2 ▲ 176
REALES ALCÁZARES Plaza de Triunfo Tel. 95 450 23 23	*Open Apr.–Sep.: Tue.–Sat. 9.30am–7pm, Sun. and public hols. 9.30am–5pm; Oct.–Mar.: Tue.–Sat. 9.30am–5pm, Sun. and public hols. 9.30am–1.30pm.*	◆ E D4-D5 ▲ 142
TEATRO CENTRAL Isla de la Cartuja Tel. 95 503 72 00	*Telephone sales (tel. 902 40 02 22), advance booking at the Corte Inglés and Hypercor.*	◆ C A1
TEATRO DE LA MAESTRANZA Paseo de Colón, 22 Tel. 95 422 33 44	*Open 10am–2pm and 5–8pm.*	◆ E B4-C4 ▲ 189
TEATRO LOPE DE VEGA Av. María Luisa Tel. 95 422 33 44	*Classical music, opera. Box office open daily 10am–2pm and 6–9pm.*	◆ C C5

TORRE DE DON FADRIQUE Real Monasterio de Santa Clara Calle de Santa Clara, 40 Tel. 95 437 99 05	*Undergoing restoration works. Shows some evenings (information from Seville town hall, tel. 954 59 01 01)*	◆ D B2-B3 ▲ 177
TORRE DEL ORO **MUSEO MARÍTIMO** Paseo de C. Colón Tel. 95 422 24 19	*Open Tue.–Fri. 10am–2pm, Sat., Sun. and public hols. 11am–2pm; closed Aug.*	◆ E C5 ▲ 184
TOURIST OFFICES AND INFORMATION – Av. de la Constitución, 21 Tel. 95 422 14 04 Fax 95 422 97 53	*Open (except public hols.) Mon.–Sat. 9am–7pm, Sun. 10am–2pm.*	
– Santa Justa station Av. Kansas City Tel. 95 453 76 26	*Open Mon.–Fri. 9am–8pm, Sat.–Sun. 10am–2pm.*	
– Airport: Autopista de San Pablo Tel. 95 444 91 28	*Open Mon.–Fri. 9am–9pm.*	
– CIS (Centro Información Sevilla) C. Arjona, Naves del Barranco Tel. 95 450 56 00	*Open Mon.–Fri. 8.30am–8.30pm.*	
– Information by telephone: Tel. 95 459 08 85		
SIERRA DE ANDÚJAR (NATURE RESERVE)	◆ B A1-B1	
INFORMATION CENTER Torre del Reloj Plaza de Santa María Andújar Tel. 953 50 49 59	*Open Tue.-Sat.: June–Sep. 8am–2.30pm; Oct.–May 10am–2pm and 5–8pm.*	
SIERRA DE ARACENA Y PICOS DE AROCHE (NATURE RESERVE)	◆ A B1-C1	
INFORMATION CENTER Cabildo Viejo, Plaza Alta Aracena Tel. 959 12 84 75	*Open Mon.–Fri. 9am–2pm.*	▲ 268
SIERRA NORTE DE SEVILLA (NATURE RESERVE)	◆ A D1-2	
INFORMATION CENTER Constantina Tourist Office	*See Constantina ◆ **385***	
ÚBEDA	◆ B C1	
CAPILLA DEL SALVADOR Plaza Vázquez de Molina	*Open July–Sep.: daily 10am–2pm and 5–7.30pm; Oct.–June: daily 10.30am–2pm and 4.30–6pm.*	▲ 348
COLEGIATA DE SANTA MARÍA DE LOS REALES ÁLCAZARES Plaza Vázquez de Molina	*Currently undergoing restoration works.*	▲ 348
HOSPITAL DE SANTIAGO Av. del Cristo Rey Tel. 953 75 08 42	*Open Mon.–Fri. 8am–3pm and 3.30–10pm; Sat., Sun. and public hols. 11am–3pm and 6–10pm.*	▲ 348
MUSEO ARQUEOLÓGICO Calle Cervantes, 6 Tel. 953 75 37 02	*Open Tue. 9am–3pm (groups) and 3–8pm, Wed.–Sat. 9am–8pm, Sun. 9am–3pm.*	
PALACIO DE LAS CADENAS (AYUNTAMIENTO) Plaza Vázquez de Molina Tel. 953 75 04 40	*Open daily 10am–2pm and 5–9pm.*	▲ 348
TOURIST OFFICE Hospital de Santiago Calle Baja del Marqués, 4 Tel. 953 75 08 97	*Open Mon.–Fri. 8.30am–2.45pm, Sat. and public hols 10am–1.30pm.*	
UMBRETE	◆ A C3	
IGLESIA DE LA CONSOLACIÓN Plaza de la Iglesia, 5 Tel. 955 71 63 05	*Open for services.*	▲ 220
UTRERA	◆ A D3	
CASTILLO Calle Ponce de León	*Currently undergoing restoration works.*	▲ 254

IGLESIA DE SANTA MARÍA Calle Antonio Maura Tel. 954 86 03 30	*Open daily 7–9.30pm.*	▲ 254
IGLESIA DE SANTIAGO Calle Ponce de León, 12 Tel. 954 86 02 30	*Open daily 6.30–9pm.*	▲ 254
SANTUARIO DE LA CONSOLACIÓN Paseo de la Consolación	*Open, summer: daily 10am–2pm and 5–9pm; winter: daily 9.30am–2pm and 4–7pm.*	▲ 255
TOURIST INFORMATION Casa de Cultura Calle Rodrigo Caro, 3 Tel. 955 86 09 31	*Open July–Sep.: Mon.–Fri. 10am–2pm and 6–9pm; Oct.–June: Mon.–Fri. 10am–2pm and 4–8.30pm.*	
VALENCINA DE LA CONCEPCIÓN	◆ A C2	
DOLMENS OF LA PASTORA, MATARRUBILLA AND ONTIVEROS	*Visits to the Casa de Cultura by appointment.*	▲ 219
TOURIST INFORMATION Casa de Cultura Plaza de España, 9 Tel. 955 72 02 11	*Open, summer: Mon.–Fri. 8am–3pm and 5–8pm; winter: Mon.–Fri. 9.30am–1pm and 5–8pm.*	
VÉLEZ BLANCO	◆ B E2	
CASTILLO Monte del Castillo 950 41 56 51	*Visits by appointment.*	▲ 350
CUEVA DE LOS LETREROS Monte Maimón 950 41 56 51	*Visits by appointment.*	▲ 350
IGLESIA DEL ENCARNACIÓN Plaza del Encarnación	*Open for services.*	▲ 350
TOURIST INFORMATION Dir. Almacén del Trigo Av. de los Vélez Tel. 950 41 53 54	*Open June 15–Sep. 15: Thur.–Sun. and public hols. 9am–2pm and 5–8pm; Sep. 16–June 14: Thur.–Sun. and public hols. 10am–2pm and 4–6pm.*	
VÉLEZ RUBIO	◆ B D2	
TOURIST OFFICE Calle San Pedro, 1 Tel. 950 41 01 48	*Open Mon.–Fri. 10.30am–2pm and 4.30–8.30pm.*	
VILLANUEVA DEL ARISCAL	◆ A C3	
HACIENDA DE PATA DE HIERRO Bodegas Góngora Calle Cristo de la Veracruz, 59 Tel. 954 11 37 00	*Open June 15–Sep. 15: Mon.–Fri. 7am–3pm; Sep. 16–June 14: Mon.–Fri. 8am–2pm and 4–6.30pm.*	▲ 220
ZAHARA DE LA SIERRA	◆ A D4-D5	
TURISMO RURAL BOCALEONES Calle San Juan Tel. 956 12 31 14	*Open Mon.–Fri. 9am–2pm, Sat.–Sun. 9am–2pm and 4–7pm.*	▲ 321

ESSENTIAL READING

◆ Boyd (A.): *The Sierras of the South: Travels in the Mountains of Andalucia* (HarperCollins, UK)
◆ Burns (J.): *Spain: A Literary Companion* (John Murray, UK)
◆ Capek (K.): *Letters from Spain* (Geoffrey Bles, London)
◆ Hooper (J.): *The Spaniards* (Penguin)
◆ Lowe (A.): *Companion Guide to the South of Spain* (Companion Guides, London)
◆ Pritchett (V.S.): *The Spanish Temper* (Chatto & Windus, London)
◆ Zabalbeascoa (A.): *The New Spanish Architecture* (Rizzoli)

GENERAL READING

◆ Cohen (J.M.): *The Penguin Book of Spanish Verse*(Penguin, UK/US)
◆ Ford (R.): *Gatherings from Spain* (J.M.Dent)
◆ Ford (R.): *Handbook for Travellers in Spain* (Open Gate Press 1966)
◆ Gibson (I.): *Fire in the Blood* (Faber)
◆ Hopkins (A.): *Spanish Journeys: A Portrait of Spain* (Penguin, UK)
◆ McCauley (L.): (ed) *Spain: Travelers' Tales* (O'Reilley, US)
◆ Mitchell (D.): *Travellers in Spain: An Illustrated Anthology* (Cassell, UK)
◆ Woodall (J.): *In Search of the Firedance. Spain Through Flamenco* (Sinclair – Stevenson, UK)

HISTORY

◆ Brenan (G.): *Spanish Labyrinth; Origins of the Civil War; The Literature of the Spanish People* (Cambridge University Press)
◆ Brenan (G.): *South from Granada* (Penguin)
◆ Carr (R.): *Modern Spain 1875–1980* (OUP US/UK)
◆ Carr (R.): *The Spanish Tragedy: The Civil War in Perspective* (Weidenfeld, UK)
◆ Castro (A.): *The Structure of Spanish History* (E.L. King)
◆ Elliot (J.H.): *Imperial Spain 1469–1716* (Penguin, US/UK)
◆ Fletcher (R.): *Moorish Spain* (Orion – Phoenix/California UP)
◆ Fraser (R.): *Blood of Spain* (Pantheon, US)
◆ Gilmour (D.): *Cities of Spain* (Pimlico/Ivan R Dee)
◆ Harrison (R.): *Spain at the Dawn of History* (Thames & Hudson)
◆ Harvey (L.P.): *Islamic Spain, 1250–1500* (Chicago University Press)
◆ Howarth (D.): *The Voyage of the Armada* (Penguin, US)
◆ Keay (S.J.): *Roman Spain* British Museum/ University of California
◆ Kedourie (E.): *Spain and the Jews: The Sephardi Experience, 1492 and After* (Thames & Hudson, UK/US)
◆ Lalaguna (J.): *A Traveller's History of Spain* (Windrush/Interlink)
◆ Lynch (J.): *Spain 1598–1700; Bourbon Spain: 1700–1808* (Blackwells, UK)
◆ Mitchell (D.): *The Spanish Civil War* (Granada)
◆ Preston (P.): *Franco* (HarperCollins, UK/US)
◆ Reilly (B.F.): *The Medieval Spains* (Cambridge University Press)
◆ Richardson (J.): *Roman Spain* (Blackwells, UK)
◆ Shubert (A.): *A Social History of Spain* (Routledge, UK)
◆ Thomas (H.): *The Spanish Civil War* (Penguin/Touchstone)
◆ Watt (W.H.) & Cachia (P.): *A History of Islamic Spain* (Edinburgh University Press)

ART, ARCHITECTURE AND PHOTOGRAPHY

◆ Lojendio (L.): *Navarre Romaine* (French Zodiaque series on Medieval Art)
◆ García Rodero (C.): *Festivals and Rituals of Spain* (Abrams, US)
◆ García Rodero (C.): *España Oculta* (Little, Brown, US)

LITERATURE

◆ Byron (G.G.): *In My Hot Youth – Byron's Letters and Journals, Vol. 1* (John Murray, London)
◆ Carrington (D.): *Carrington – Letters and Extracts from Her Diaries* (Jonathan Cape, London)
◆ Ellis (H.H.): *The Soul of Spain* (Constable & Co., London)
◆ Epton (N.): *Andalusia* (Weidenfeld & Nicolson, London)
◆ Gautier (T.): *A Romantic in Spain* (Alfred A. Knopf, New York and London)
◆ Hare (A.): *Wandering* in Spain (Smith, Elder & Co., London)
◆ Hemingway (E.): *Death in the Afternoon* (Penguin Books/Jonathan Cape, New York, London)
◆ Irving (W.): *The Alhambra* (Macmillan & Co., London)
◆ Koestler (A.): *Dialogue with Death* (Hutchinson, London)
◆ Lomas (J.): *Sketches in Spain from Nature, Art and Life* (Longmans Green & Co., London)
◆ Mérimée (P.): *Carmen – a Romance* (The Folio Society, London)
◆ Morton (H.V.): *A Stranger in Spain* (Methuen & Co Ltd)
◆ Newby (E.): *On the Shores of the Mediterranean* (HarperCollins, London)
◆ Orwell (G.): *Homage to Catalonia* (Penguin)
◆ Rilke (R.M.): *Selected Letters of Rainer Maria Rilke* (Macmillan & Co., London)
◆ Sitwell (S.): *Spain* (B.T. Batsford Ltd, London)
◆ Waugh (E.): *Labels: A Mediterranean Journey* (Penguin, London)
◆ Williams (H.): *Freelancing* (Faber and Faber, London and Boston)
◆ Woolf (V.): *A Passionate Apprentice – The Early Journals 1897–1909* (The Hogarth Press, London)

SPANISH LITERATURE

◆ Alarcón (P. de): *The Three-Cornered Hat* (Everyman Paperbacks, UK)
◆ Atxaga (B.): *Obabakoak* (Vintage/Pantheon)
◆ Calderón de la Barca (P.): *Life is a Dream and other Spanish Classics* (Nick Hern Books/ Players Press)
◆ Calderón de la Barca (P.): *The Mayor of Zalamea* (Absolute Press/Dramatic Publications)
◆ Catalá (V.): *Solitude* (Readers International, UK/US)
◆ Cervantes (M. de): *Don Quixote* (Everyman's Library, UK, Alfred A. Knopf, New York, 1995)
◆ Cervantes (M. de): *Exemplary Stories* (Penguin/UK)
◆ García Lorca (F.): *Three Tragedies and Five Plays* (Penguin)
◆ García Lorca (F.): *Three Plays: Blood Wedding, Yerma, The House of Bernarda Alba* (Farrar Straus Giroux, US or Oxford Paperbacks, UK)
◆ García Marquez (G.): *One Hundred Years of Solitude* (Everyman's Library/Alfred A Knopf, New York)
◆ Goytisolo (J.): *Marks of Identity* (Serpent's Tail/ Consort)
◆ José Cela (C.): *The Family of Pascual Duarte* (Little, Brown, US/UK)
◆ Leopoldo (A.): *La Regenta* (Penguin US/UK)
◆ Marias (J.): *Tomorrow in the Battle Think on Me* (Harvill, UK)
◆ Pardo Bazán (E.): *The House of Ulloa* (Penguin, US/UK)
◆ Pérez de Ayala (R.): *Belarmino and Apolonio; Honeymoon, Bittermoon* (Quartet/California UP)
◆ Pérez Galdós (B.): *Fortunata and Jacinta* (Penguin, UK/US)
◆ Pérez Galdós (B.): *Misericordia* (Dedalus, UK)
◆ Pérez-Reverte (A.): *The Seville Communion* (Vintage)
◆ Pérez-Reverte (A.): *The Fencing Master* (Vintage)
◆ Ríos (J.): *Larva* (Quartet/Dalkey Archive)

MOVIES

◆ Almodóvar (P.): *Pepi, Luci, Bom* (1981); *Labyrinth of Passions* (1982); *Women on the Verge of a Nervous Breakdown* (1988); *What Have I Done to Deserve This?* (1984); *Matador* (1986); *The Law of Desire* (1987);
Kika (1993); *The Flower of My Secret* (1995); *All About My Mother* (1999)
◆ Antonio Bardem (J.): *Main Street* (1956)
◆ Berlanga (L.): *Welcome Mr Marshall* (1953)
◆ Buñuel (L.): *Viridiana* (1961); *Tristana* (1970); *That Obscure Object of Desire* (1977)
◆ Erice (V.): *The South* (1983); *The Quince Tree Sun* (1991)
◆ Saura (C.): *The Hunt* (1965); *The Garden of Delights* (1970); *Cousin Angelica* (1973); *Raise Ravens* (1975); *Blood Wedding* (1981); *Carmen* (1985); *Tango* (1998)
◆ Trueba (F.): *Belle Epoque* (1994)

FOOD AND WINE

◆ Andrews (C.): *Catalan Cuisine* (Headline, UK)
◆ Butcher (N.): *The Spanish Kitchen* (Macmillan, UK)
◆ Casas (P.): *The Foods and Wines of Spain* (Penguin/Knopf)
◆ Millon (M. & K.): *Wine Roads of Spain* (HarperCollins, UK/US)

◆ LIST OF ILLUSTRATIONS

◆ LIST OF ILLUSTRATIONS

LIST OF ILLUSTRATIONS

◆ LIST OF ILLUSTRATIONS

◆ LIST OF ILLUSTRATIONS

We have not been able to trace the heirs or publishers of certain documents. An account is being held open for them at our offices.

A

B

C

D

E

F

G

◆ INDEX

Map section

Key

Freeway
Primary road
Secondary road
Other roads
Marine link
Railroad
Urban area
Principal town
Secondary town
Place of interest
Hospital
▲ Main peak

◆ STREET INDEX

SEVILLE

◆ STREET INDEX

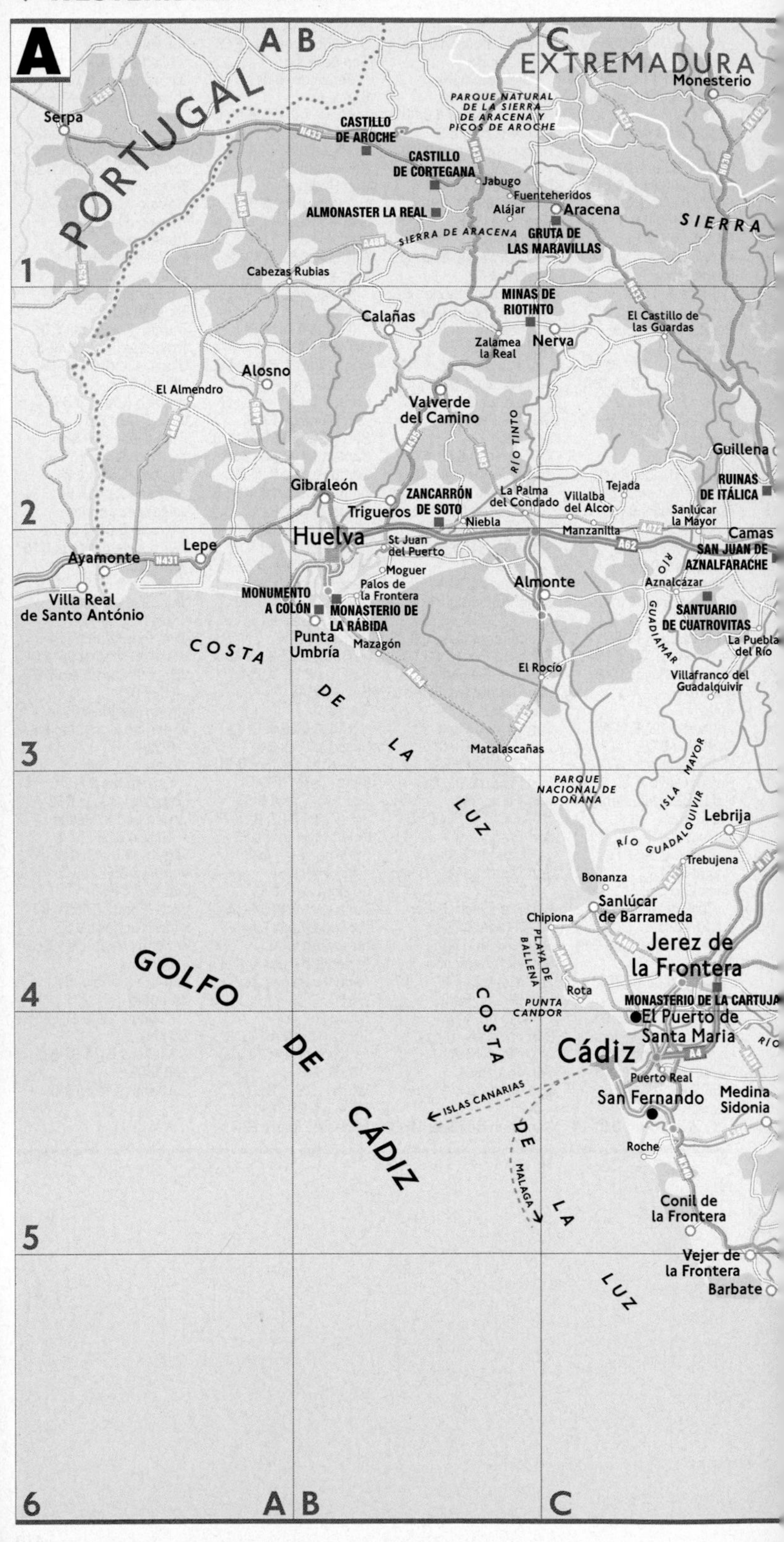
A
EXTREMADURA
PORTUGAL
Serpa
Monesterio
PARQUE NATURAL DE LA SIERRA DE ARACENA Y PICOS DE AROCHE
CASTILLO DE AROCHE
CASTILLO DE CORTEGANA
Jabugo
Fuenteheridos
Alájar
Aracena
ALMONASTER LA REAL
SIERRA DE ARACENA
GRUTA DE LAS MARAVILLAS
SIERRA
Cabezas Rubias
MINAS DE RIOTINTO
Calañas
Nerva
Zalamea la Real
El Castillo de las Guardas
Alosno
El Almendro
Valverde del Camino
RÍO TINTO
Guillena
RUINAS DE ITÁLICA
Gibraleón
Trigueros
ZANCARRÓN DE SOTO
La Palma del Condado
Villalba del Alcor
Tejada
Sanlúcar la Mayor
Niebla
Manzanilla
Camas
Huelva
St Juan del Puerto
SAN JUAN DE AZNALFARACHE
Lepe
Ayamonte
Moguer
Palos de la Frontera
Almonte
Aznalcázar
Villa Real de Santo António
MONUMENTO A COLÓN
MONASTERIO DE LA RÁBIDA
SANTUARIO DE CUATROVITAS
RÍO GUADIAMAR
Punta Umbría
Mazagón
La Puebla del Río
El Rocío
Villafranco del Guadalquivir
COSTA DE LA LUZ
Matalascañas
PARQUE NACIONAL DE DOÑANA
ISLA MAYOR
Lebrija
RÍO GUADALQUIVIR
Trebujena
Bonanza
Sanlúcar de Barrameda
Chipiona
PLAYA DE BALLENA
Jerez de la Frontera
GOLFO DE CÁDIZ
Rota
MONASTERIO DE LA CARTUJA
PUNTA CANDOR
COSTA DE LA LUZ
El Puerto de Santa Maria
Cádiz
Puerto Real
ISLAS CANARIAS
San Fernando
Medina Sidonia
MALAGA
Roche
Conil de la Frontera
Vejer de la Frontera
Barbate
A B C
1 2 3 4 5 6

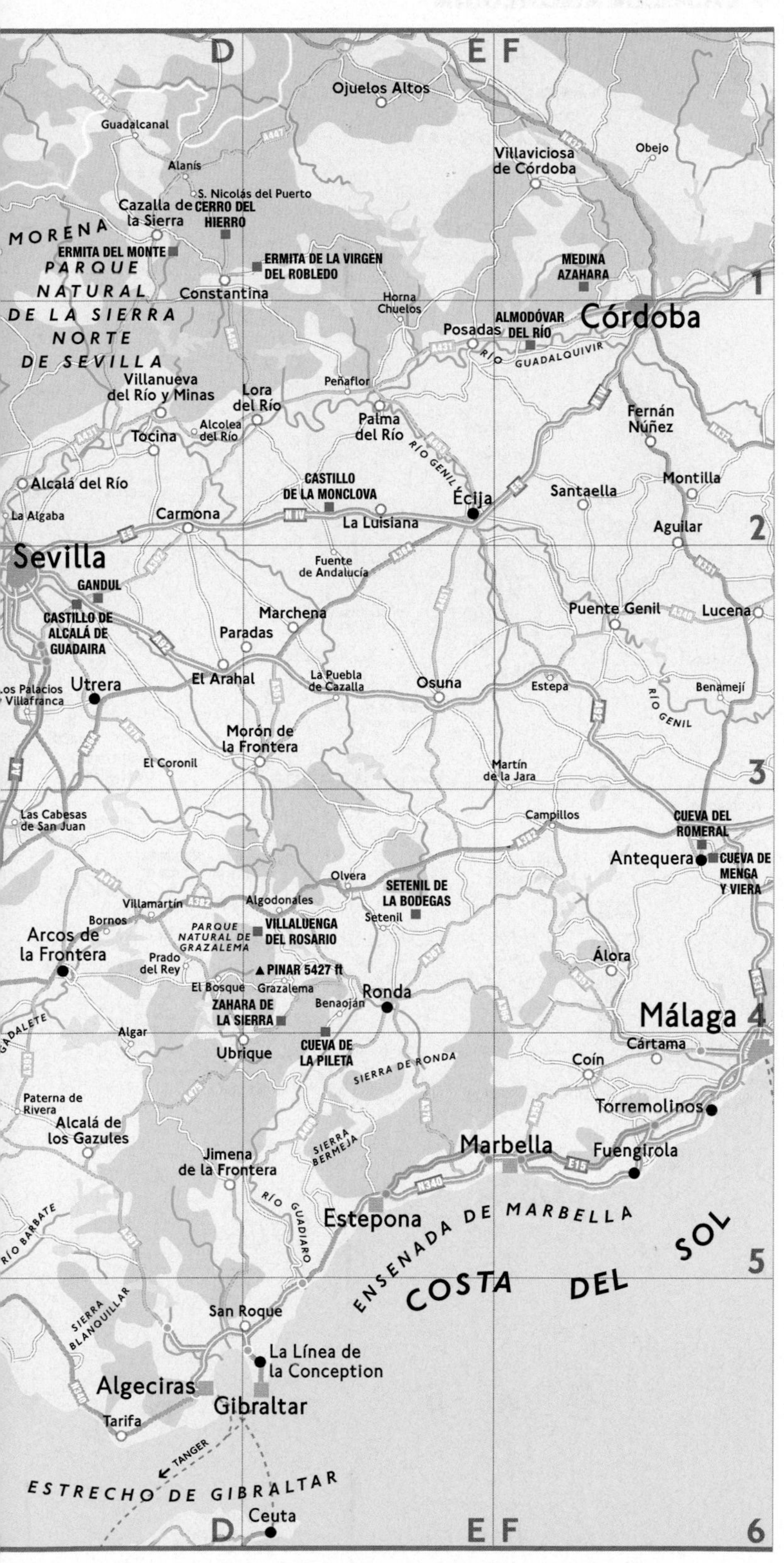

D
E
F
1
2
3
4
5
6
Ojuelos Altos
Guadalcanal
Alanís
Villaviciosa de Córdoba
Obejo
S. Nicolás del Puerto
Cazalla de la Sierra
CERRO DEL HIERRO
MORENA
ERMITA DEL MONTE
PARQUE NATURAL DE LA SIERRA NORTE DE SEVILLA
ERMITA DE LA VIRGEN DEL ROBLEDO
MEDINA AZAHARA
Constantina
Horna Chuelos
ALMODÓVAR DEL RÍO
Córdoba
Posadas
RÍO GUADALQUIVIR
Peñaflor
Villanueva del Río y Minas
Lora del Río
Palma del Río
Fernán Núñez
Tocina
Alcolea del Río
RÍO GENIL
Alcalá del Río
CASTILLO DE LA MONCLOVA
Montilla
Santaella
Écija
La Algaba
Carmona
La Luisiana
Aguilar
Sevilla
Fuente de Andalucía
GANDUL
Puente Genil
Lucena
CASTILLO DE ALCALÁ DE GUADAIRA
Marchena
Paradas
El Arahal
La Puebla de Cazalla
Osuna
Estepa
Benamejí
Los Palacios Villafranca
Utrera
RÍO GENIL
Morón de la Frontera
El Coronil
Martín de la Jara
Las Cabesas de San Juan
Campillos
CUEVA DEL ROMERAL
Antequera
CUEVA DE MENGA Y VIERA
Olvera
SETENIL DE LA BODEGAS
Villamartín
Algodonales
Bornos
Setenil
PARQUE NATURAL DE GRAZALEMA
VILLALUENGA DEL ROSARIO
Arcos de la Frontera
Prado del Rey
Álora
▲PINAR 5427 ft
El Bosque
Grazalema
Ronda
ZAHARA DE LA SIERRA
Benaoján
Málaga
RÍO GUADALETE
Algar
Cártama
CUEVA DE LA PILETA
Ubrique
Coín
SIERRA DE RONDA
Paterna de Rivera
Torremolinos
Alcalá de los Gazules
SIERRA BERMEJA
Marbella
Fuengirola
Jimena de la Frontera
RÍO GUADIARO
Estepona
RÍO BARBATE
ENSENADA DE MARBELLA
COSTA DEL SOL
SIERRA BLANQUILLAR
San Roque
La Línea de la Conception
Algeciras
Gibraltar
Tarifa
TANGER
ESTRECHO DE GIBRALTAR
Ceuta

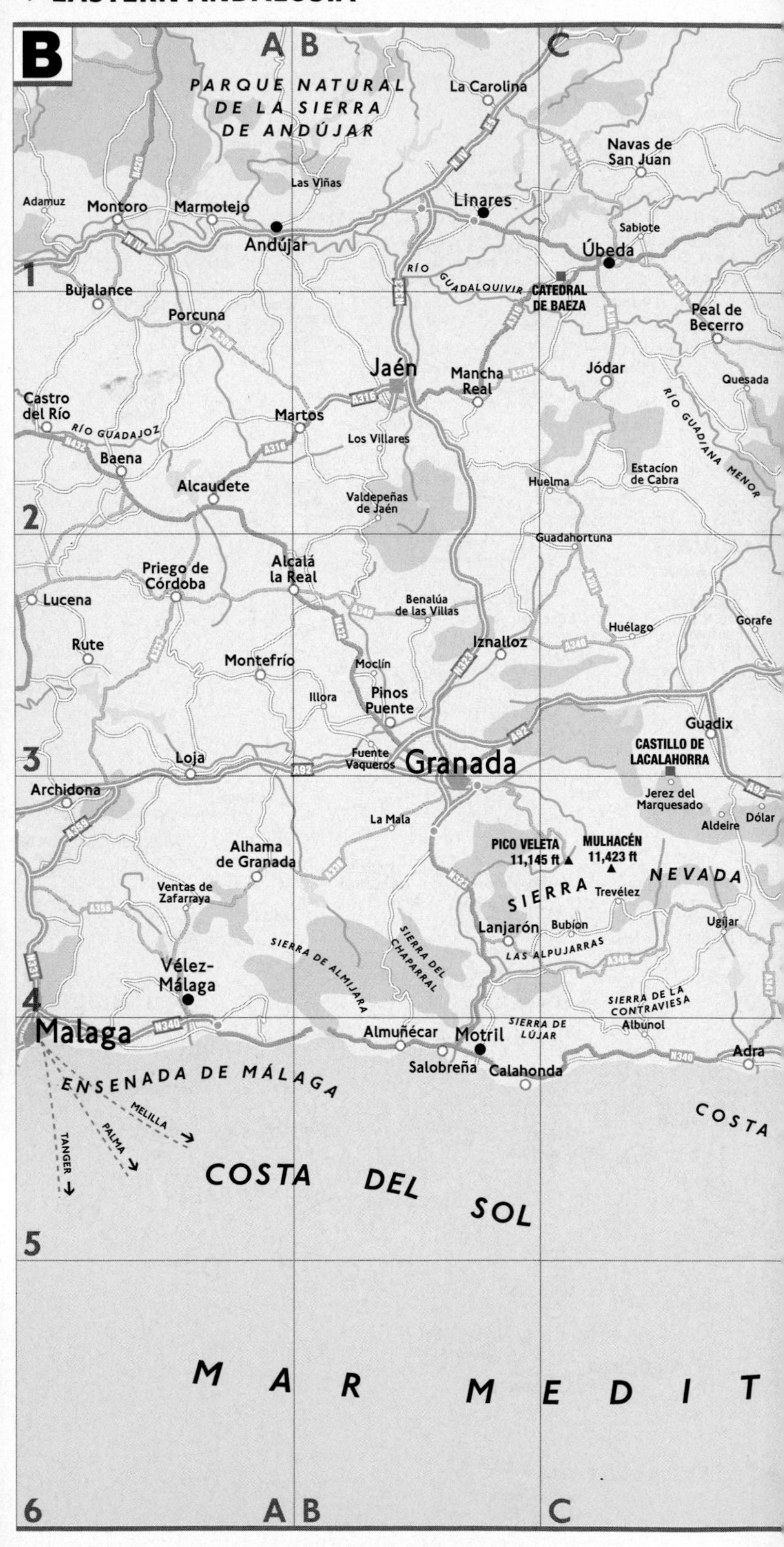
B
A B C
PARQUE NATURAL DE LA SIERRA DE ANDÚJAR
La Carolina
Navas de San Juan
Las Viñas
Adamuz
Montoro
Marmolejo
Andújar
Linares
Sabiote
Úbeda
Río Guadalquivir
Catedral de Baeza
Bujalance
Porcuna
Peal de Becerro
Jaén
Mancha Real
Jódar
Quesada
Castro del Río
Río Guadajoz
Martos
Río Guadiana Menor
Los Villares
Baena
Estacíon de Cabra
Huelma
Alcaudete
Valdepeñas de Jaén
Guadahortuna
Priego de Córdoba
Alcalá la Real
Lucena
Benalúa de las Villas
Huélago
Gorafe
Rute
Iznalloz
Montefrío
Moclín
Illora
Pinos Puente
Guadix
Castillo de Lacalahorra
Loja
Fuente Vaqueros
Granada
Archidona
Jerez del Marquesado
La Mala
Dólar
Aldeire
Pico Veleta 11,145 ft
Mulhacén 11,423 ft
Alhama de Granada
Sierra Nevada
Ventas de Zafarraya
Trevélez
Lanjarón
Bubíon
Ugíjar
Las Alpujarras
Sierra de Almijara
Sierra del Chaparral
Vélez-Málaga
Sierra de la Contraviesa
Malaga
Sierra de Lújar
Albunol
Almuñécar
Motril
Salobreña
Calahonda
Adra
Ensenada de Málaga
Melilla
Palma
Tanger
Costa del Sol
Mar Medit
1 2 3 4 5 6

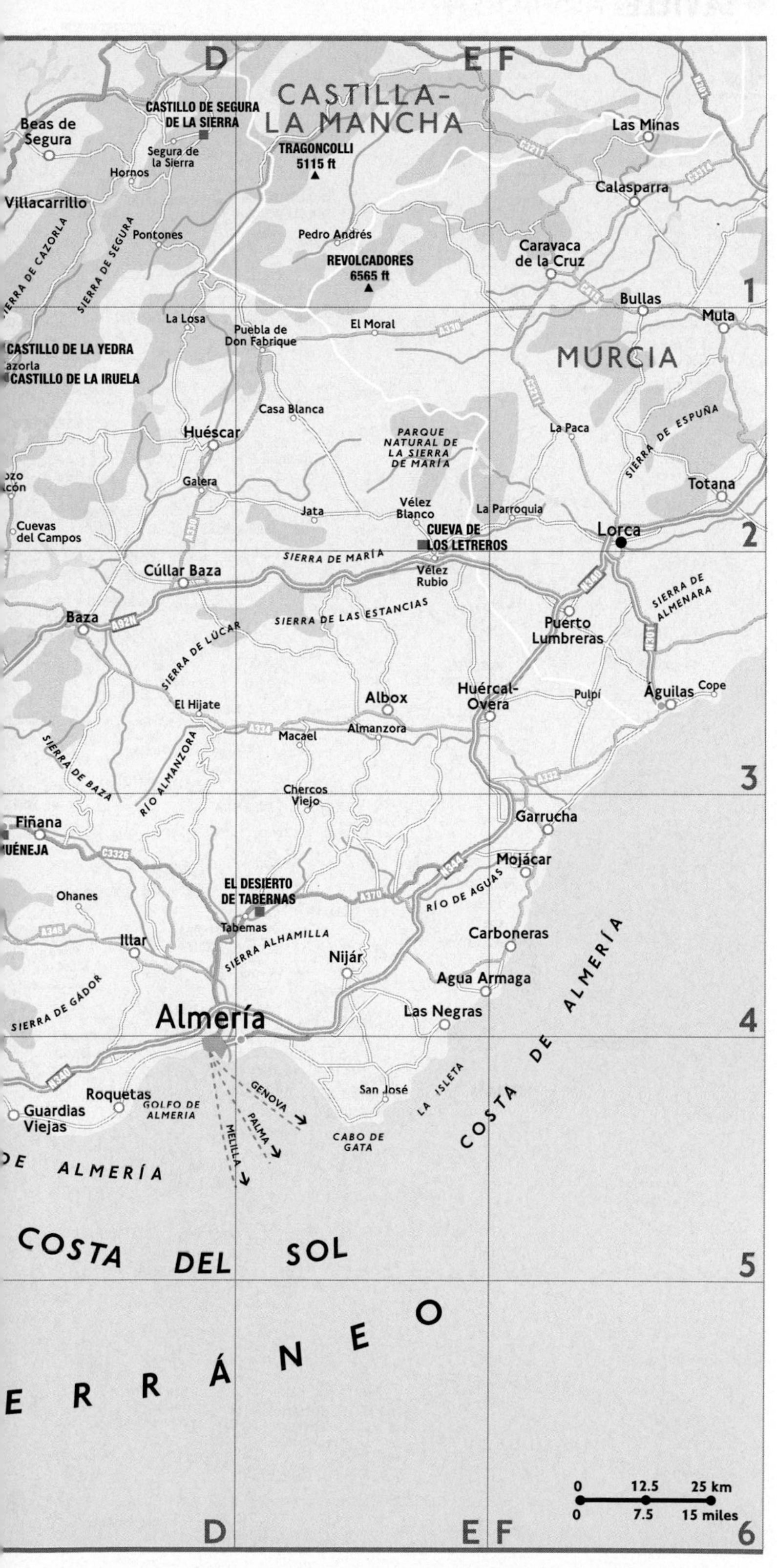

D
E F
CASTILLA-
LA MANCHA
CASTILLO DE SEGURA
DE LA SIERRA
Beas de
Segura
Segura de
la Sierra
Hornos
TRAGONCOLLI
5115 ft
Las Minas
Calasparra
Villacarrillo
SIERRA DE CAZORLA
SIERRA DE SEGURA
Pontones
Pedro Andrés
REVOLCADORES
6565 ft
Caravaca
de la Cruz
Bullas
Mula
1
La Losa
Puebla de
Don Fabrique
El Moral
CASTILLO DE LA YEDRA
CASTILLO DE LA IRUELA
MURCIA
Casa Blanca
Huéscar
PARQUE
NATURAL DE
LA SIERRA
DE MARÍA
La Paca
SIERRA DE ESPUÑA
Galera
Totana
Cuevas
del Campos
Jata
Vélez
Blanco
La Parroquia
CUEVA DE
LOS LETREROS
Lorca
2
SIERRA DE MARÍA
Cúllar Baza
Vélez
Rubio
SIERRA DE
ALMENARA
Baza
SIERRA DE LAS ESTANCIAS
Puerto
Lumbreras
SIERRA DE LÚCAR
El Hijate
Albox
Huércal-
Overa
Pulpí
Águilas
Cope
Macael
Almanzora
SIERRA DE BAZA
RÍO ALMANZORA
3
Chercos
Viejo
Fiñana
Garrucha
Mojácar
EL DESIERTO
DE TABERNAS
Ohanes
RÍO DE AGUAS
Tabernas
Illar
SIERRA ALHAMILLA
Carboneras
Níjar
Agua Armaga
SIERRA DE GÁDOR
Almería
Las Negras
COSTA DE ALMERÍA
4
Roquetas
GOLFO DE
ALMERÍA
Guardias
Viejas
GENOVA
PALMA
MELILLA
San José
LA ISLETA
CABO DE
GATA
DE ALMERÍA
COSTA DEL SOL
5
ERRÁNEO
0 12.5 25 km
0 7.5 15 miles
D
E F
6

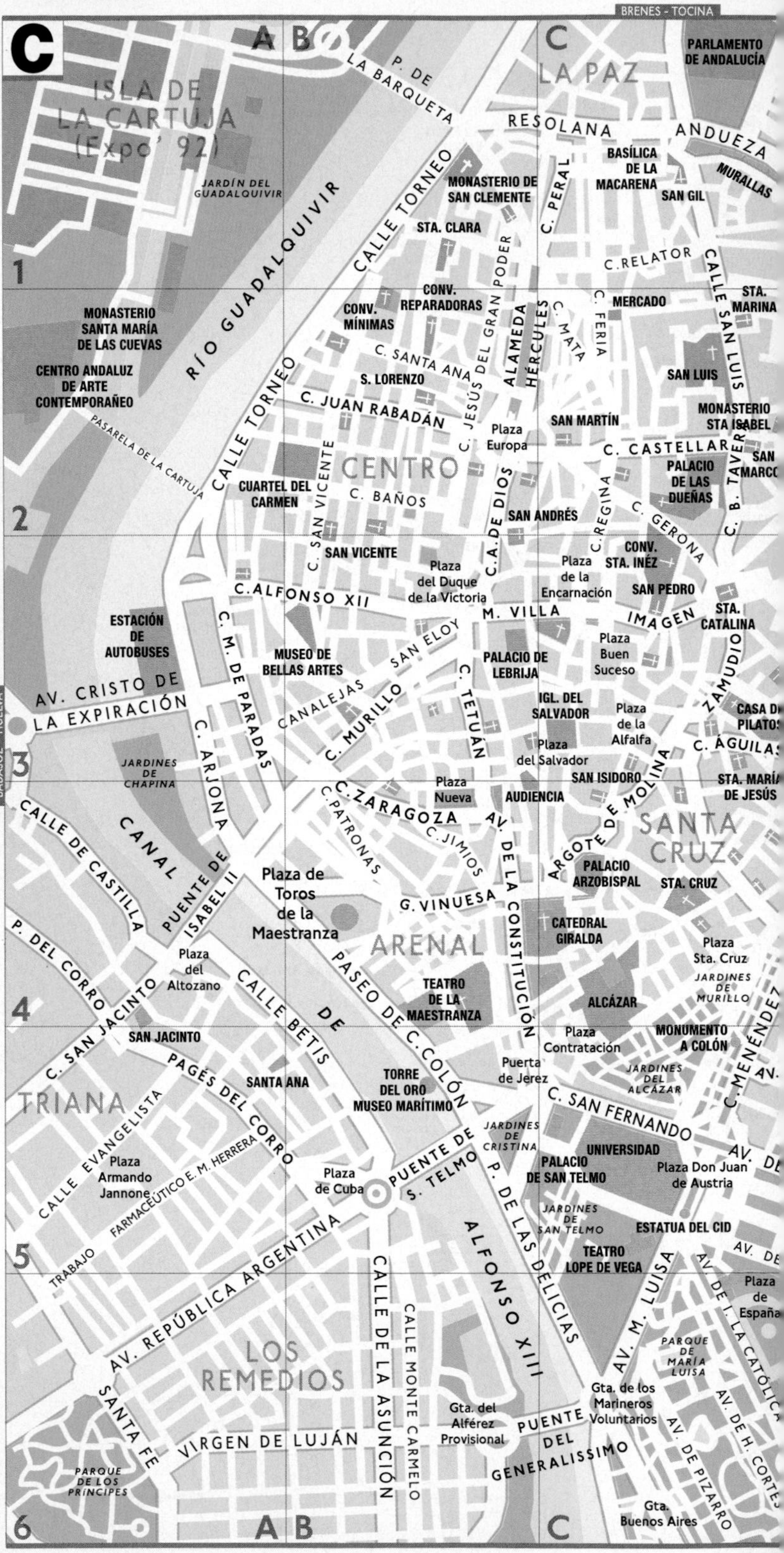

C
BRENES - TOCINA
ISLA DE LA CARTUJA (Expo' 92)
JARDÍN DEL GUADALQUIVIR
P. DE LA BARQUETA
LA PAZ
PARLAMENTO DE ANDALUCÍA
RESOLANA
ANDUEZA
MURALLAS
BASÍLICA DE LA MACARENA
SAN GIL
MONASTERIO DE SAN CLEMENTE
CALLE TORNEO
C. PERAL
STA. CLARA
RÍO GUADALQUIVIR
C. RELATOR
CALLE SAN LUIS
STA. MARINA
MONASTERIO SANTA MARÍA DE LAS CUEVAS
CONV. MÍNIMAS
CONV. REPARADORAS
C. JESÚS DEL GRAN PODER
ALAMEDA HÉRCULES
C. MATA
C. FERIA
MERCADO
CENTRO ANDALUZ DE ARTE CONTEMPORAÑEO
C. SANTA ANA
S. LORENZO
SAN LUIS
C. JUAN RABADÁN
PASARELA DE LA CARTUJA
Plaza Europa
SAN MARTÍN
MONASTERIO STA ISABEL
C. CASTELLAR
C. B. TAVERA
SAN MARCO
CENTRO
CUARTEL DEL CARMEN
C. SAN VICENTE
C. BAÑOS
C. A. DE DIOS
PALACIO DE LAS DUEÑAS
C. REGINA
C. GERONA
SAN ANDRÉS
SAN VICENTE
Plaza del Duque de la Victoria
CONV. STA. INÉZ
Plaza de la Encarnación
SAN PEDRO
C. ALFONSO XII
M. VILLA
IMAGEN
STA. CATALINA
ESTACIÓN DE AUTOBUSES
C. M. DE PARADAS
MUSEO DE BELLAS ARTES
SAN ELOY
PALACIO DE LEBRIJA
Plaza Buen Suceso
ZAMUDIO
AV. CRISTO DE LA EXPIRACIÓN
CANALEJAS
C. MURILLO
C. TETUÁN
IGL. DEL SALVADOR
Plaza de la Alfalfa
CASA DE PILATOS
C. ÁGUILAS
JARDINES DE CHAPINA
C. ARJONA
Plaza del Salvador
SAN ISIDORO
STA. MARÍA DE JESÚS
BADAJOZ - HUELVA
CALLE DE CASTILLA
CANAL
C. ZARAGOZA
C. PATRONAS
Plaza Nueva
AUDIENCIA
ARGOTE DE MOLINA
SANTA CRUZ
C. JIMIOS
AV. DE LA CONSTITUCIÓN
PUENTE DE ISABEL II
Plaza de Toros de la Maestranza
PALACIO ARZOBISPAL
STA. CRUZ
G. VINUESA
P. DEL CORRO
ARENAL
CATEDRAL GIRALDA
Plaza Sta. Cruz
Plaza del Altozano
CALLE BETIS
PASEO DE C. COLÓN
TEATRO DE LA MAESTRANZA
JARDINES DE MURILLO
ALCÁZAR
C. SAN JACINTO
SAN JACINTO
Plaza Contratación
MONUMENTO A COLÓN
C. MENÉNDEZ
PAGÉS DEL CORRO
SANTA ANA
TORRE DEL ORO MUSEO MARÍTIMO
Puerta de Jerez
JARDINES DEL ALCÁZAR
AV.
TRIANA
C. SAN FERNANDO
CALLE EVANGELISTA
JARDINES DE CRISTINA
UNIVERSIDAD
AV. DE
Plaza Armando Jannone
FARMACÉUTICO E. M. HERRERA
Plaza de Cuba
PUENTE DE S. TELMO
PALACIO DE SAN TELMO
Plaza Don Juan de Austria
P. DE LAS DELICIAS
JARDINES DE SAN TELMO
ESTATUA DEL CID
TRABAJO
AV. REPÚBLICA ARGENTINA
ALFONSO XIII
TEATRO LOPE DE VEGA
AV. DE
CALLE DE LA ASUNCIÓN
CALLE MONTE CARMELO
AV. M. LUISA
AV. DE I. LA CATÓLICA
Plaza de España
PARQUE DE MARÍA LUISA
LOS REMEDIOS
Gta. de los Marineros Voluntarios
AV. DE H. CORTES
SANTA FE
VIRGEN DE LUJÁN
Gta. del Alférez Provisional
PUENTE DEL GENERALISSIMO
AV. DE PIZARRO
PARQUE DE LOS PRINCIPES
Gta. Buenos Aires
A B C
1 2 3 4 5 6

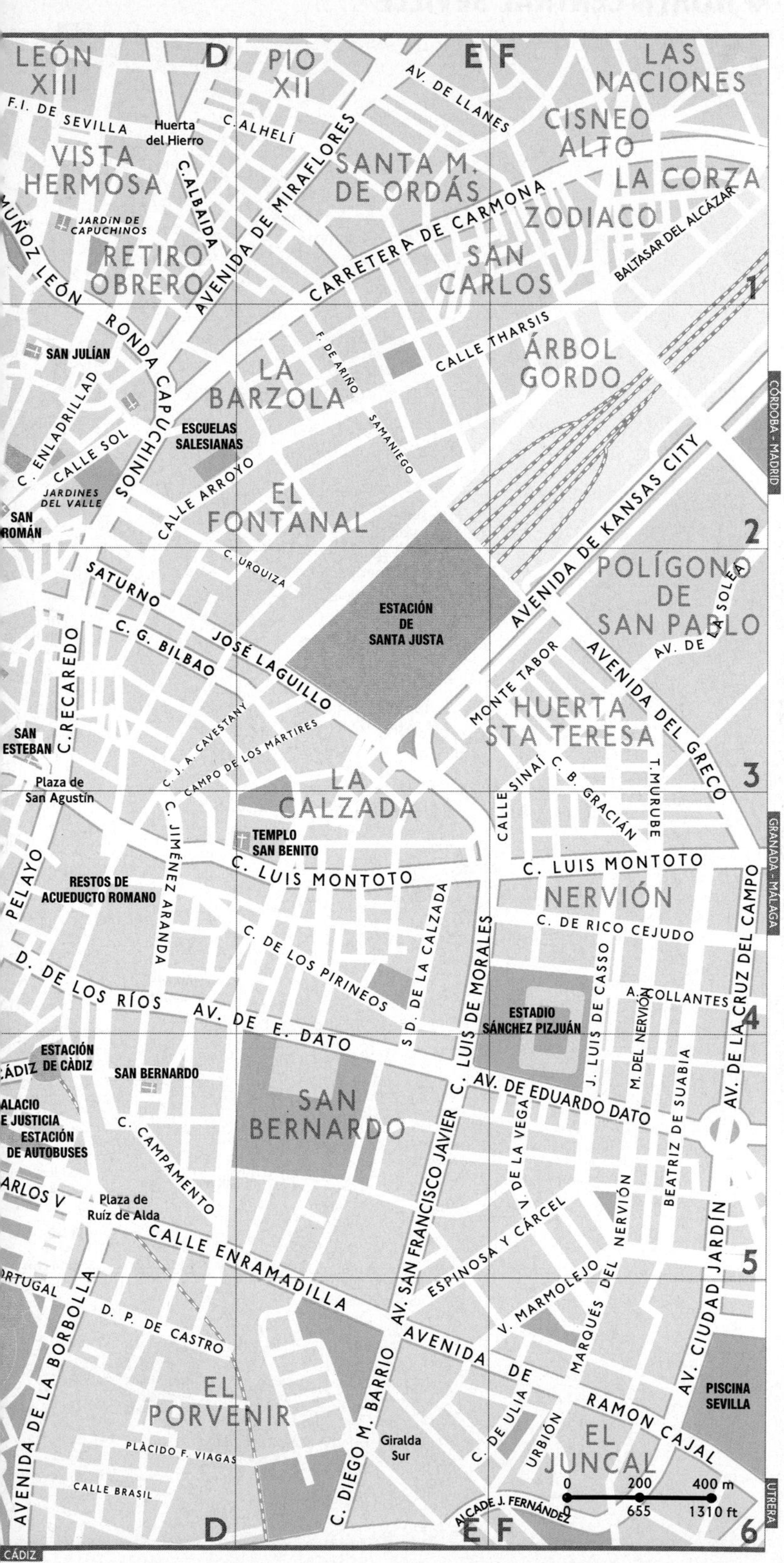

LEÓN XIII
PIO XII
LAS NACIONES
AV. DE LLANES
CISNEO ALTO
F.I. DE SEVILLA
Huerta del Hierro
C. ALHELÍ
VISTA HERMOSA
C. ALBAIDA
AVENIDA DE MIRAFLORES
SANTA M. DE ORDÁS
LA CORZA
ZODIACO
BALTASAR DEL ALCÁZAR
MUÑOZ LEÓN
JARDÍN DE CAPUCHINOS
RETIRO OBRERO
CARRETERA DE CARMONA
SAN CARLOS
RONDA CAPUCHINOS
SAN JULÍAN
CALLE THARSIS
ÁRBOL GORDO
F. DE ARIÑO
LA BARZOLA
C. ENLADRILLADA
CALLE SOL
ESCUELAS SALESIANAS
SAMANIEGO
CÓRDOBA - MADRID
JARDINES DEL VALLE
CALLE ARROYO
EL FONTANAL
AVENIDA DE KANSAS CITY
SAN ROMÁN
C. URQUIZA
SATURNO
POLÍGONO DE SAN PABLO
ESTACIÓN DE SANTA JUSTA
C. G. BILBAO
JOSÉ LAGUILLO
AV. DE LA SOLEÁ
C. RECAREDO
MONTE TABOR
AVENIDA DEL GRECO
HUERTA STA TERESA
SAN ESTEBAN
C. J. A. CAVESTANY
CAMPO DE LOS MÁRTIRES
Plaza de San Agustín
LA CALZADA
CALLE SINAÍ
C. B. GRACIÁN
T. MURUBE
C. JIMÉNEZ ARANDA
TEMPLO SAN BENITO
GRANADA - MÁLAGA
PELAYO
RESTOS DE ACUEDUCTO ROMANO
C. LUIS MONTOTO
NERVIÓN
C. DE RICO CEJUDO
AV. DE LA CRUZ DEL CAMPO
C. DE LOS PIRINEOS
S. D. DE LA CALZADA
C. LUIS DE MORALES
J. LUIS DE CASSO
A. COLLANTES
D. DE LOS RÍOS
AV. DE E. DATO
ESTADIO SÁNCHEZ PIZJUÁN
M. DEL NERVIÓN
ESTACIÓN DE CÁDIZ
SAN BERNARDO
AV. DE EDUARDO DATO
BEATRIZ DE SUABIA
SAN BERNARDO
C. CAMPAMENTO
AV. SAN FRANCISCO JAVIER
V. DE LA VEGA
ESTACIÓN DE AUTOBUSES
Plaza de Ruíz de Alda
ESPINOSA Y CÁRCEL
MARQUÉS DEL NERVIÓN
CALLE ENRAMADILLA
AV. CIUDAD JARDÍN
D. P. DE CASTRO
V. MARMOLEJO
AVENIDA DE LA BORBOLLA
AVENIDA DE RAMON CAJAL
C. DIEGO M. BARRIO
EL PORVENIR
PISCINA SEVILLA
C. DE ULIA
URBIÓN
EL JUNCAL
Giralda Sur
PLÀCIDO F. VIAGAS
CALLE BRASIL
ALCADE J. FERNÁNDEZ
0 200 400 m
0 655 1310 ft
UTRERA
CÁDIZ
D E F
1 2 3 4 5 6

◆ NORTH CENTRAL SEVILLE

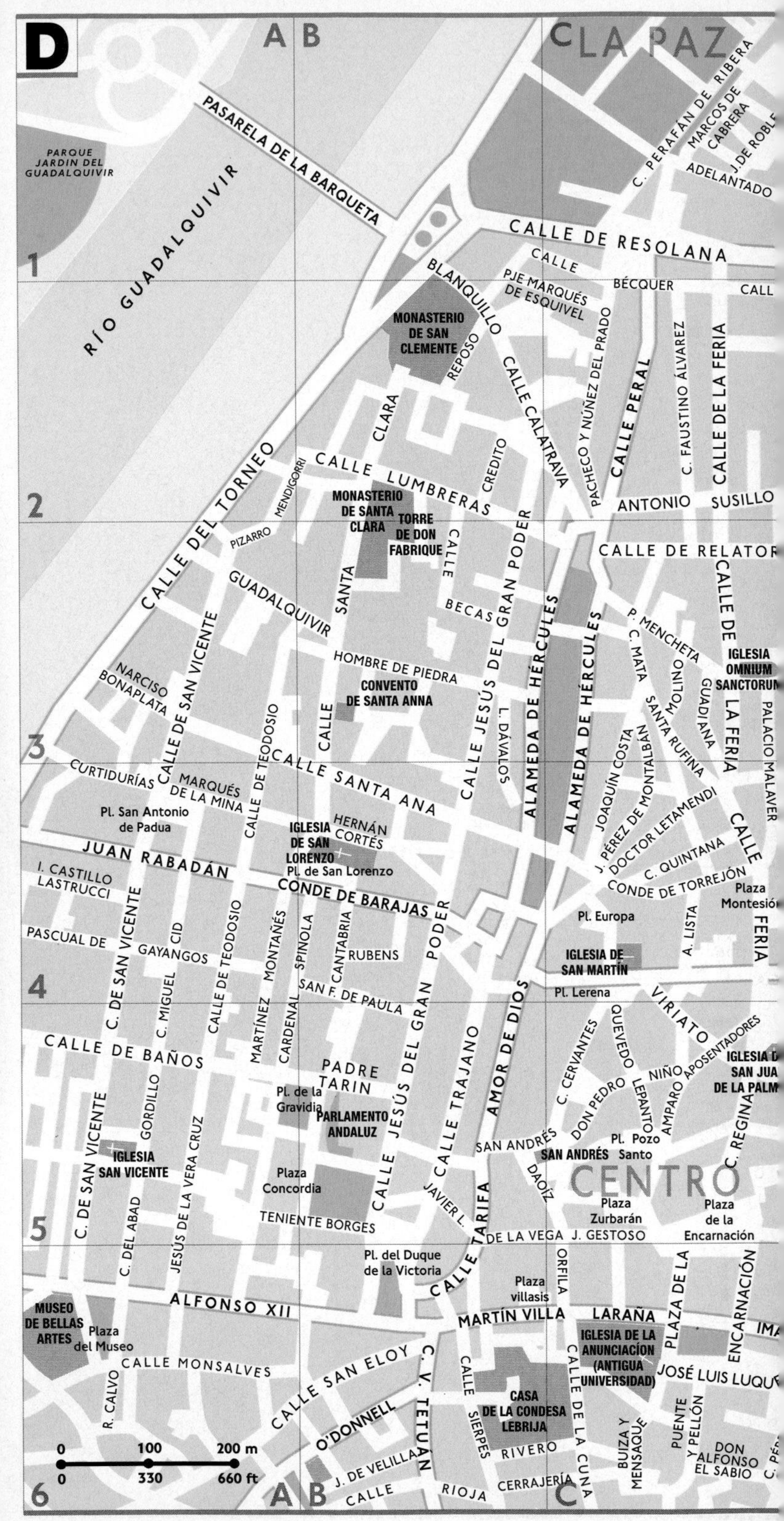

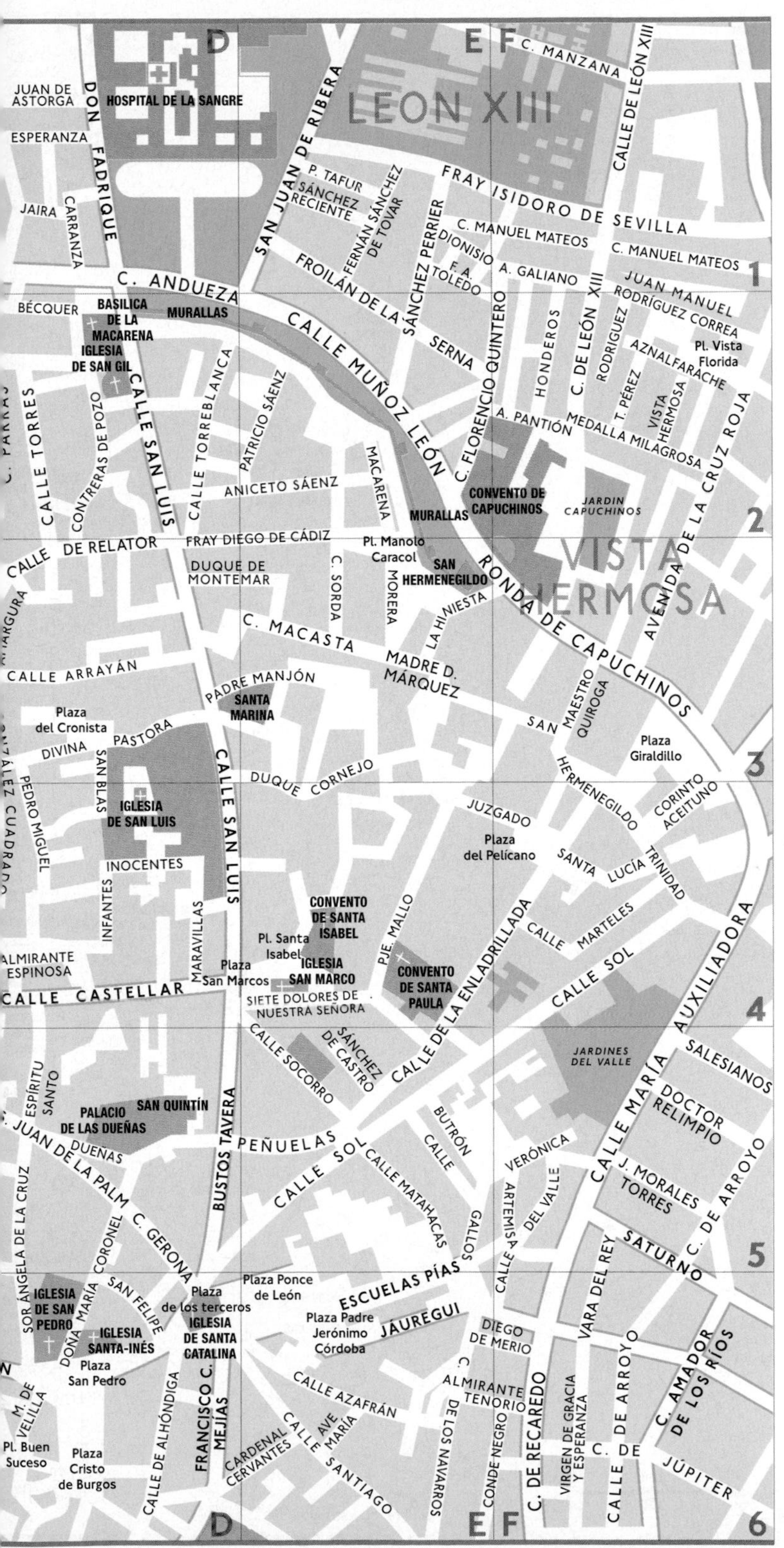
D
E
F
1
2
3
4
5
6
LEON XIII
VISTA HERMOSA
HOSPITAL DE LA SANGRE
JUAN DE ASTORGA
DON FADRIQUE
ESPERANZA
JAIRA
CARRANZA
SAN JUAN DE RIBERA
C. MANZANA
CALLE DE LEÓN XIII
P. TAFUR
SÁNCHEZ RECIENTE
FERNÁN SÁNCHEZ DE TOVAR
SÁNCHEZ PERRIER
FRAY ISIDORO DE SEVILLA
C. MANUEL MATEOS
DIONISIO A. GALIANO
F. A. TOLEDO
FROILÁN DE LA SERNA
JUAN MANUEL RODRÍGUEZ CORREA
C. ANDUEZA
BÉCQUER
BASILICA DE LA MACARENA
IGLESIA DE SAN GIL
MURALLAS
CALLE MUÑOZ LEÓN
C. FLORENCIO QUINTERO
HONDEROS
C. DE LEÓN XIII
RODRÍGUEZ
AZNALFARACHE
Pl. Vista Florida
T. PÉREZ
VISTA HERMOSA
A. PANTIÓN
MEDALLA MILAGROSA
AVENIDA DE LA CRUZ ROJA
C. PARRAS
CALLE TORRES
CONTRERAS DE POZO
CALLE SAN LUIS
CALLE TORREBLANCA
PATRICIO SÁENZ
ANICETO SÁENZ
MACARENA
CONVENTO DE CAPUCHINOS
JARDIN CAPUCHINOS
CALLE DE RELATOR
FRAY DIEGO DE CÁDIZ
Pl. Manolo Caracol
SAN HERMENEGILDO
RONDA DE CAPUCHINOS
DUQUE DE MONTEMAR
C. SORDA
MORERA
LA HINIESTA
C. MACASTA
MADRE D. MÁRQUEZ
CALLE ARRAYÁN
PADRE MANJÓN
SANTA MARINA
SAN HERMENEGILDO
MAESTRO QUIROGA
Plaza Giraldillo
Plaza del Cronista
PASTORA
DIVINA
SAN BLAS
DUQUE CORNEJO
GONZÁLEZ CUADRADO
PEDRO MIGUEL
IGLESIA DE SAN LUIS
CALLE SAN LUIS
JUZGADO
CORINTO
ACEITUNO
Plaza del Pelícano
SANTA LUCÍA
TRINIDAD
INOCENTES
INFANTES
MARAVILLAS
CONVENTO DE SANTA ISABEL
PJE. MALLO
CALLE DE LA ENLADRILLADA
CALLE MARTELES
AUXILIADORA
Pl. Santa Isabel
IGLESIA SAN MARCO
CONVENTO DE SANTA PAULA
CALLE SOL
ALMIRANTE ESPINOSA
Plaza San Marcos
CALLE CASTELLAR
SIETE DOLORES DE NUESTRA SEÑORA
CALLE SOCORRO
SÁNCHEZ DE CASTRO
JARDINES DEL VALLE
SALESIANOS
ESPÍRITU SANTO
PALACIO DE LAS DUEÑAS
SAN QUINTÍN
BUSTOS TAVERA
CALLE MARÍA
DOCTOR RELIMPIO
JUAN DE LA PALMA
DUEÑAS
PEÑUELAS
CALLE SOL
BUTRÓN
CALLE
CALLE MATAHACAS
VERÓNICA
J. MORALES TORRES
C. DE ARROYO
SOR ÁNGELA DE LA CRUZ
CORONEL
C. GERONA
GALLOS
CALLE ARTEMISA
DEL VALLE
SATURNO
IGLESIA DE SAN PEDRO
DOÑA MARÍA
SAN FELIPE
Plaza de los terceros
Plaza Ponce de León
ESCUELAS PÍAS
VARA DEL REY
IGLESIA SANTA-INÉS
IGLESIA DE SANTA CATALINA
Plaza Padre Jerónimo Córdoba
JÁUREGUI
DIEGO DE MERIO
Plaza San Pedro
M. DE VELILLA
CALLE DE ALHÓNDIGA
FRANCISCO C. MEJÍAS
CALLE AZAFRÁN
C. DE LOS NAVARROS
ALMIRANTE TENORIO
C. DE RECAREDO
VIRGEN DE GRACIA Y ESPERANZA
CALLE DE ARROYO
C. AMADOR DE LOS RÍOS
Pl. Buen Suceso
Plaza Cristo de Burgos
CARDENAL CERVANTES
CALLE SANTIAGO
AVE MARÍA
CONDE NEGRO
C. DE JÚPITER

◆ SOUTH CENTRAL SEVILLE

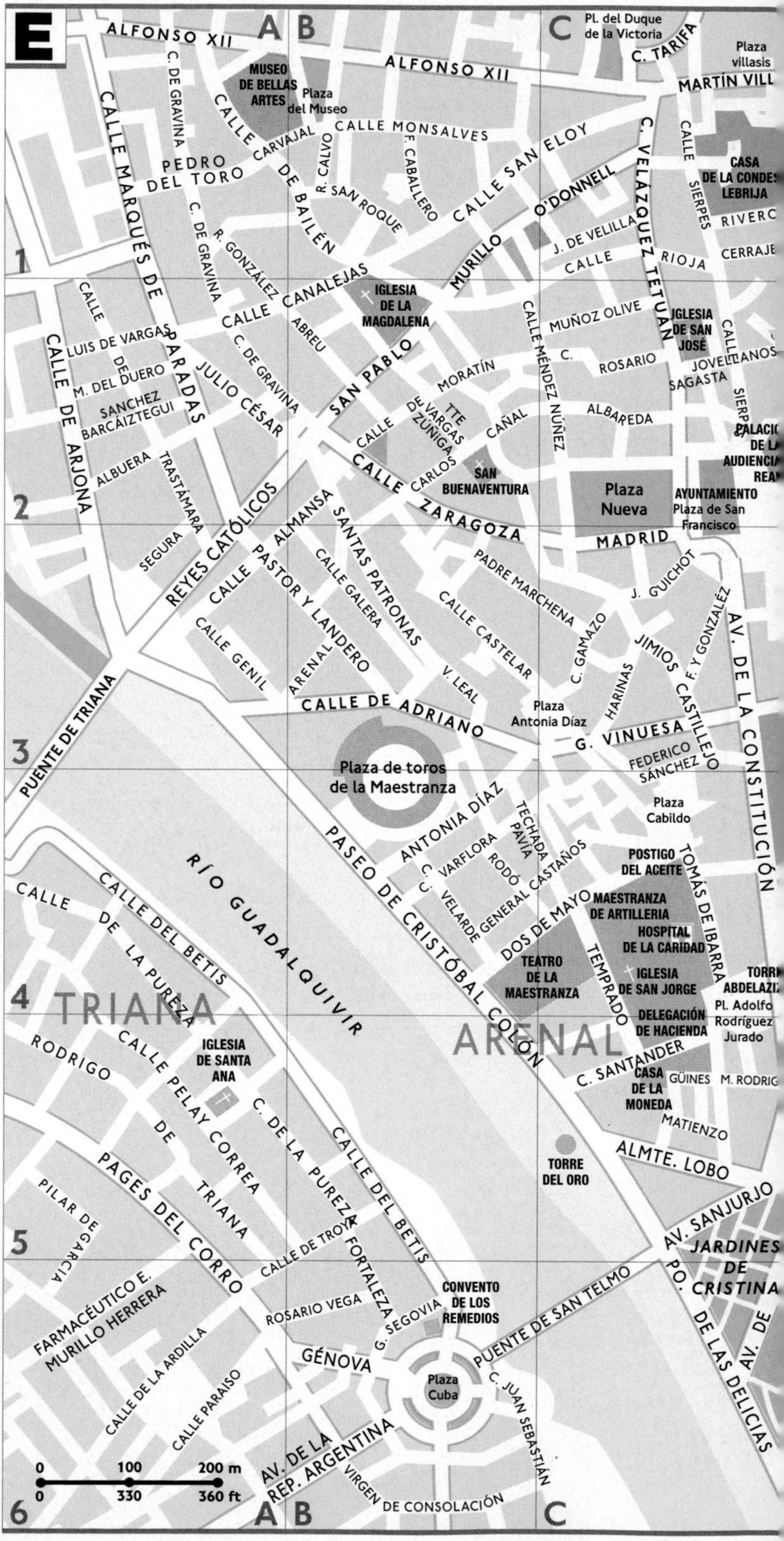

E

Museo de Bellas Artes
Plaza del Museo
Pl. del Duque de la Victoria
Plaza villasis
Casa de la Condesa Lebrija
Iglesia de la Magdalena
Iglesia de San José
San Buenaventura
Plaza Nueva
Ayuntamiento
Plaza de San Francisco
Palacio de la Audiencia Real
Plaza Antonia Díaz
Plaza de toros de la Maestranza
Plaza Cabildo
Postigo del Aceite
Maestranza de Artilleria
Hospital de la Caridad
Iglesia de San Jorge
Teatro de la Maestranza
Delegación de Hacienda
Torre Abdelaziz
Pl. Adolfo Rodríguez Jurado
Casa de la Moneda
Torre del Oro
Iglesia de Santa Ana
Convento de los Remedios
Plaza Cuba
Jardines de Cristina
Río Guadalquivir
Triana
Arenal

0 100 200 m
0 330 360 ft

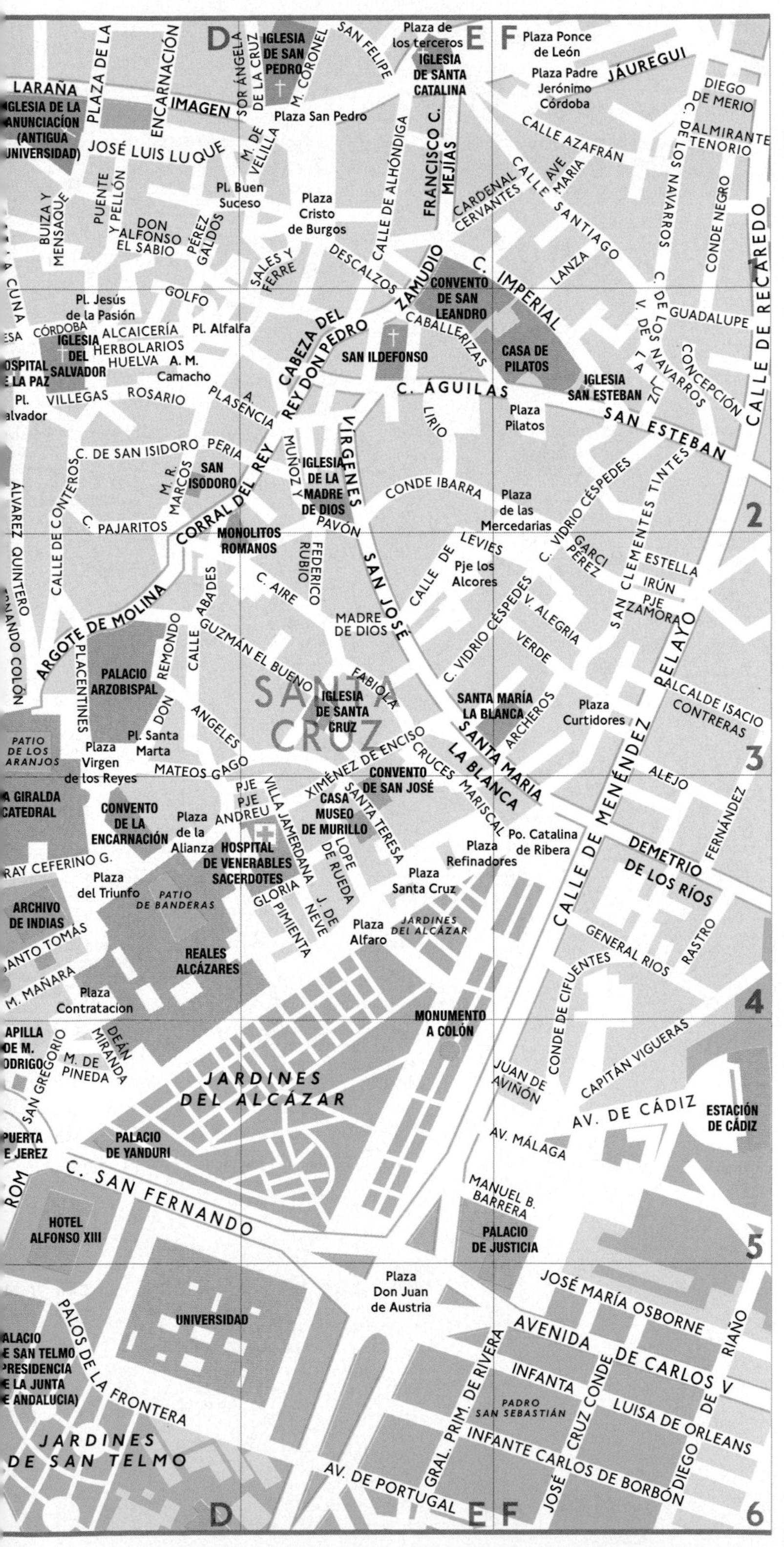

SANTA CRUZ
JARDINES DEL ALCÁZAR
JARDINES DE SAN TELMO
IGLESIA DE SAN PEDRO
IGLESIA DE SANTA CATALINA
CONVENTO DE SAN LEANDRO
CASA DE PILATOS
IGLESIA SAN ESTEBAN
SAN ILDEFONSO
IGLESIA DEL SALVADOR
SAN ISODORO
IGLESIA DE LA MADRE DE DIOS
MONOLITOS ROMANOS
PALACIO ARZOBISPAL
IGLESIA DE SANTA CRUZ
SANTA MARÍA LA BLANCA
CONVENTO DE SAN JOSÉ
CASA MUSEO DE MURILLO
CONVENTO DE LA ENCARNACIÓN
HOSPITAL DE VENERABLES SACERDOTES
ARCHIVO DE INDIAS
REALES ALCÁZARES
MONUMENTO A COLÓN
ESTACIÓN DE CÁDIZ
PALACIO DE YANDURI
HOTEL ALFONSO XIII
PALACIO DE JUSTICIA
UNIVERSIDAD
Plaza San Pedro
Plaza Cristo de Burgos
Pl. Buen Suceso
Plaza Ponce de León
Plaza Padre Jerónimo Córdoba
Plaza de los terceros
Pl. Jesús de la Pasión
Pl. Alfalfa
Plaza Pilatos
Plaza de las Mercedarias
Pje los Alcores
Plaza Curtidores
Pl. Santa Marta
Plaza Virgen de los Reyes
Plaza de la Alianza
Plaza del Triunfo
Plaza Contratacion
Plaza Refinadores
Plaza Santa Cruz
Plaza Alfaro
Po. Catalina de Ribera
Plaza Don Juan de Austria
PATIO DE LOS NARANJOS
PATIO DE BANDERAS
JARDINES DEL ALCÁZAR
PADRO SAN SEBASTIÁN
C. IMPERIAL
C. ÁGUILAS
SAN ESTEBAN
CALLE DE RECAREDO
CALLE DE MENÉNDEZ PELAYO
SAN JOSÉ
SANTA MARÍA LA BLANCA
CORRAL DEL REY
CABEZA DEL REY DON PEDRO
ARGOTE DE MOLINA
C. SAN FERNANDO
AV. DE CÁDIZ
AV. MÁLAGA
AVENIDA DE CARLOS V
JOSÉ MARÍA OSBORNE
INFANTE CARLOS DE BORBÓN
AV. DE PORTUGAL
PALOS DE LA FRONTERA
D E F
1 2 3 4 5 6

◆ CÓRDOBA

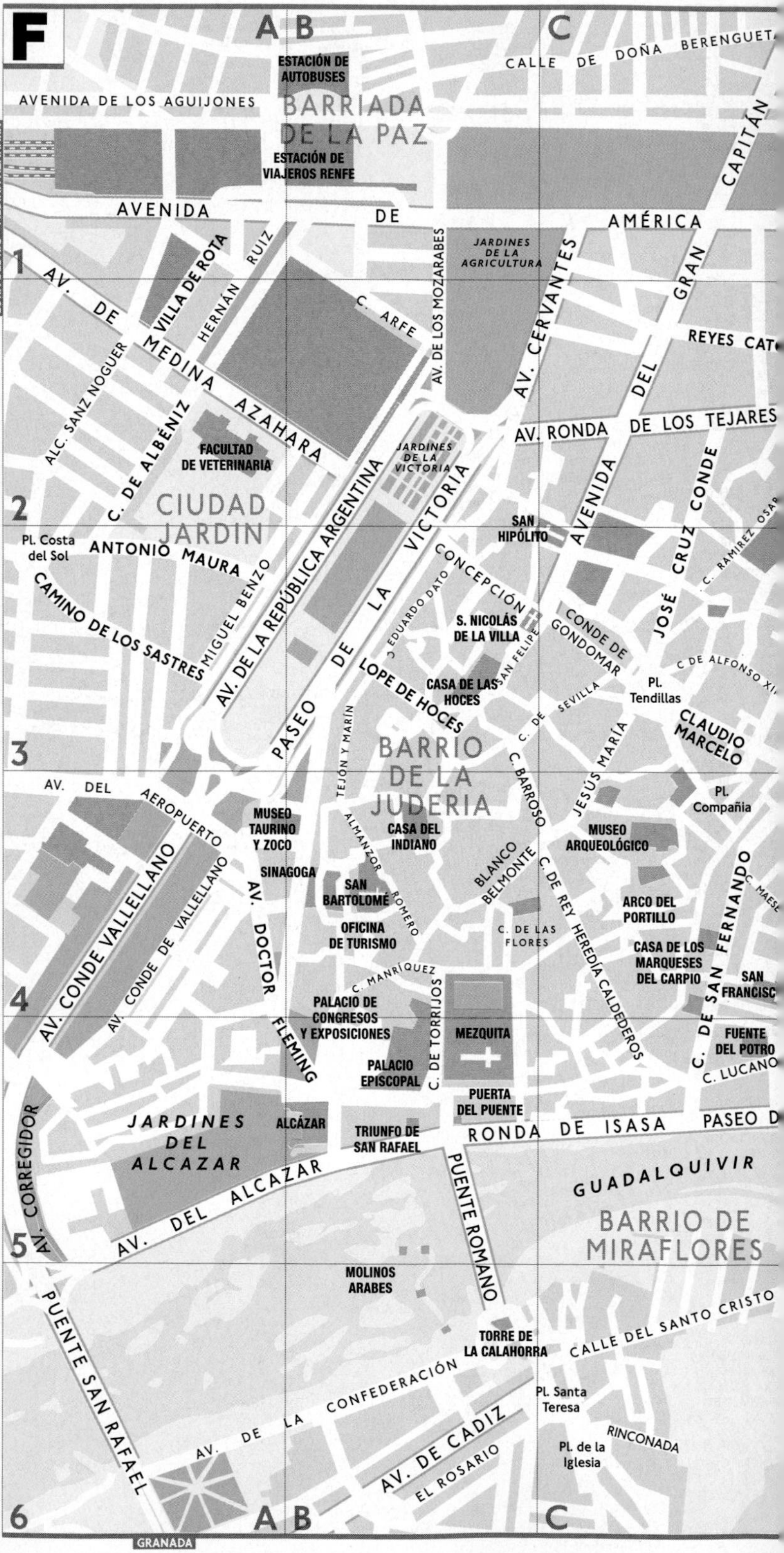

F

A B C

ESTACIÓN DE AUTOBUSES
CALLE DE DOÑA BERENGUELA
AVENIDA DE LOS AGUIJONES
BARRIADA DE LA PAZ
LORA DEL RIO - MEDINA AZAHARA
ESTACIÓN DE VIAJEROS RENFE
CAPITÁN
AVENIDA DE AMÉRICA
JARDINES DE LA AGRICULTURA
AV. DE LOS MOZARABES
VILLA DE ROTA
RUIZ
HERNÁN
AV. DE MEDINA AZAHARA
C. ARFE
AV. CERVANTES
GRAN
REYES CAT
AVENIDA DEL GRAN CAPITÁN
ALC. SANZ NOGUER
C. DE ALBÉNIZ
FACULTAD DE VETERINARIA
JARDINES DE LA VICTORIA
AV. RONDA DE LOS TEJARES
CIUDAD JARDIN
AV. DE LA REPÚBLICA ARGENTINA
PASEO DE LA VICTORIA
SAN HIPÓLITO
AVENIDA
CRUZ CONDE
JOSÉ
Pl. Costa del Sol
ANTONIO MAURA
CAMINO DE LOS SASTRES
MIGUEL BENZO
CONCEPCIÓN
C. EDUARDO DATO
C. RAMIREZ OSAR
S. NICOLÁS DE LA VILLA
CONDE DE GONDOMAR
SAN FELIPE
LOPE DE HOCES
CASA DE LAS HOCES
C. DE ALFONSO XII
Pl. Tendillas
C. DE SEVILLA
CLAUDIO MARCELO
TEJÓN Y MARÍN
BARRIO DE LA JUDERIA
JESÚS MARÍA
C. BARROSO
AV. DEL AEROPUERTO
MUSEO TAURINO Y ZOCO
CASA DEL INDIANO
ALMANZOR
Pl. Compañia
MUSEO ARQUEOLÓGICO
SINAGOGA
AV. CONDE VALLELLANO
AV. CONDE DE VALLELLANO
AV. DOCTOR FLEMING
SAN BARTOLOMÉ
ROMERO
BLANCO BELMONTE
C. DE REY HEREDÍA CALDEDEROS
ARCO DEL PORTILLO
C. DE SAN FERNANDO
C. MAESE
OFICINA DE TURISMO
C. DE LAS FLORES
CASA DE LOS MARQUESES DEL CARPIO
SAN FRANCISC
C. MANRÍQUEZ
PALACIO DE CONGRESOS Y EXPOSICIONES
C. DE TORRIJOS
MEZQUITA
FUENTE DEL POTRO
PALACIO EPISCOPAL
C. LUCANO
PUERTA DEL PUENTE
AV. CORREGIDOR
JARDINES DEL ALCAZAR
ALCÁZAR
TRIUNFO DE SAN RAFAEL
RONDA DE ISASA
PASEO D
AV. DEL ALCAZAR
PUENTE ROMANO
GUADALQUIVIR
BARRIO DE MIRAFLORES
MOLINOS ARABES
PUENTE SAN RAFAEL
TORRE DE LA CALAHORRA
CALLE DEL SANTO CRISTO
AV. DE LA CONFEDERACIÓN
Pl. Santa Teresa
RINCONADA
AV. DE CADIZ
EL ROSARIO
Pl. de la Iglesia

1 2 3 4 5 6

A B C

GRANADA

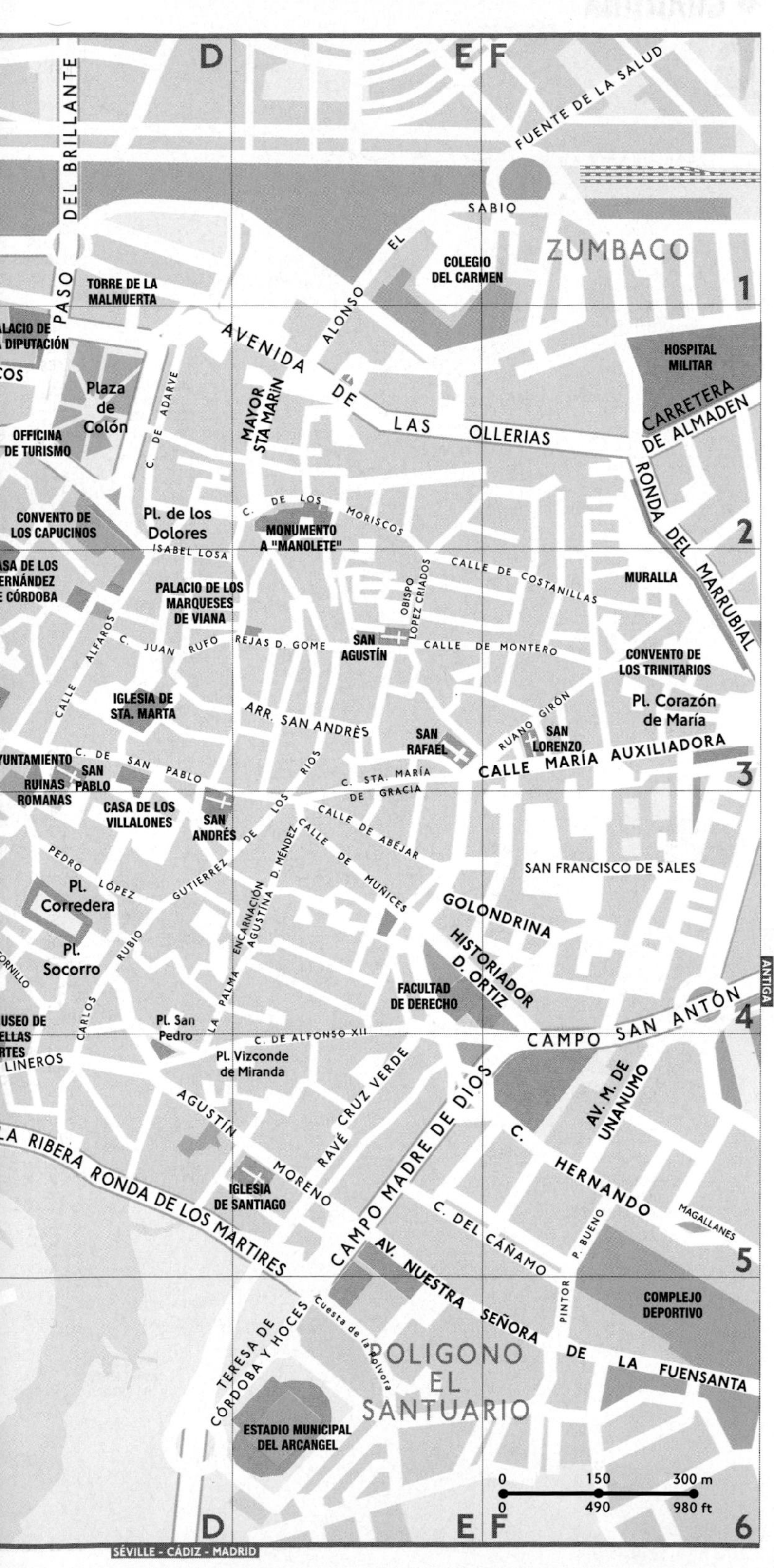

D
E F
FUENTE DE LA SALUD
PASO DEL BRILLANTE
SABIO
ZUMBACO
ALONSO EL
COLEGIO DEL CARMEN
TORRE DE LA MALMUERTA
1
PALACIO DE LA DIPUTACIÓN
AVENIDA DE LAS OLLERIAS
HOSPITAL MILITAR
Plaza de Colón
C. DE ADARVE
MAYOR STA MARIN
CARRETERA DE ALMADEN
OFFICINA DE TURISMO
RONDA DEL MARRUBIAL
C. DE LOS MORISCOS
CONVENTO DE LOS CAPUCINOS
Pl. de los Dolores
MONUMENTO A "MANOLETE"
2
ISABEL LOSA
CALLE DE COSTANILLAS
CASA DE LOS FERNÁNDEZ DE CÓRDOBA
PALACIO DE LOS MARQUESES DE VIANA
OBISPO LÓPEZ CRIADOS
MURALLA
CALLE ALFAROS
C. JUAN RUFO
REJAS D. GOME
SAN AGUSTÍN
CALLE DE MONTERO
CONVENTO DE LOS TRINITARIOS
IGLESIA DE STA. MARTA
ARR. SAN ANDRÈS
Pl. Corazón de María
RUANO GIRÓN
SAN RAFAEL
SAN LORENZO
CALLE MARÍA AUXILIADORA
AYUNTAMIENTO
C. DE SAN PABLO
SAN PABLO
RUINAS ROMANAS
C. STA. MARÍA DE GRACIA
3
CASA DE LOS VILLALONES
SAN ANDRÉS
DE LOS RIOS
CALLE DE ABÉJAR
CALLE DE MUÑICES
PEDRO LÓPEZ
GUTIERREZ
D. MÉNDEZ
SAN FRANCISCO DE SALES
Pl. Corredera
ENCARNACIÓN AGUSTINA
GOLONDRINA
RUBIO
HISTORIADOR D. ORTIZ
Pl. Socorro
TORNILLO
LA PALMA
FACULTAD DE DERECHO
CARLOS
MUSEO DE BELLAS ARTES
Pl. San Pedro
CAMPO SAN ANTÓN
4
C. DE ALFONSO XII
LINEROS
Pl. Vizconde de Miranda
AV. M. DE UNANUMO
AGUSTÍN MORENO
RAVÉ CRUZ VERDE
CAMPO MADRE DE DIOS
C. HERNANDO MAGALLANES
LA RIBERA RONDA DE LOS MARTIRES
IGLESIA DE SANTIAGO
C. DEL CÁÑAMO
P. BUENO
5
AV. NUESTRA SEÑORA DE LA FUENSANTA
PINTOR
COMPLEJO DEPORTIVO
TERESA DE CÓRDOBA Y HOCES
Cuesta de la Polvora
POLIGONO EL SANTUARIO
ESTADIO MUNICIPAL DEL ARCANGEL
ANTIGA
0 150 300 m
0 490 980 ft
6
SÉVILLE - CÁDIZ - MADRID

◆ GRANADA

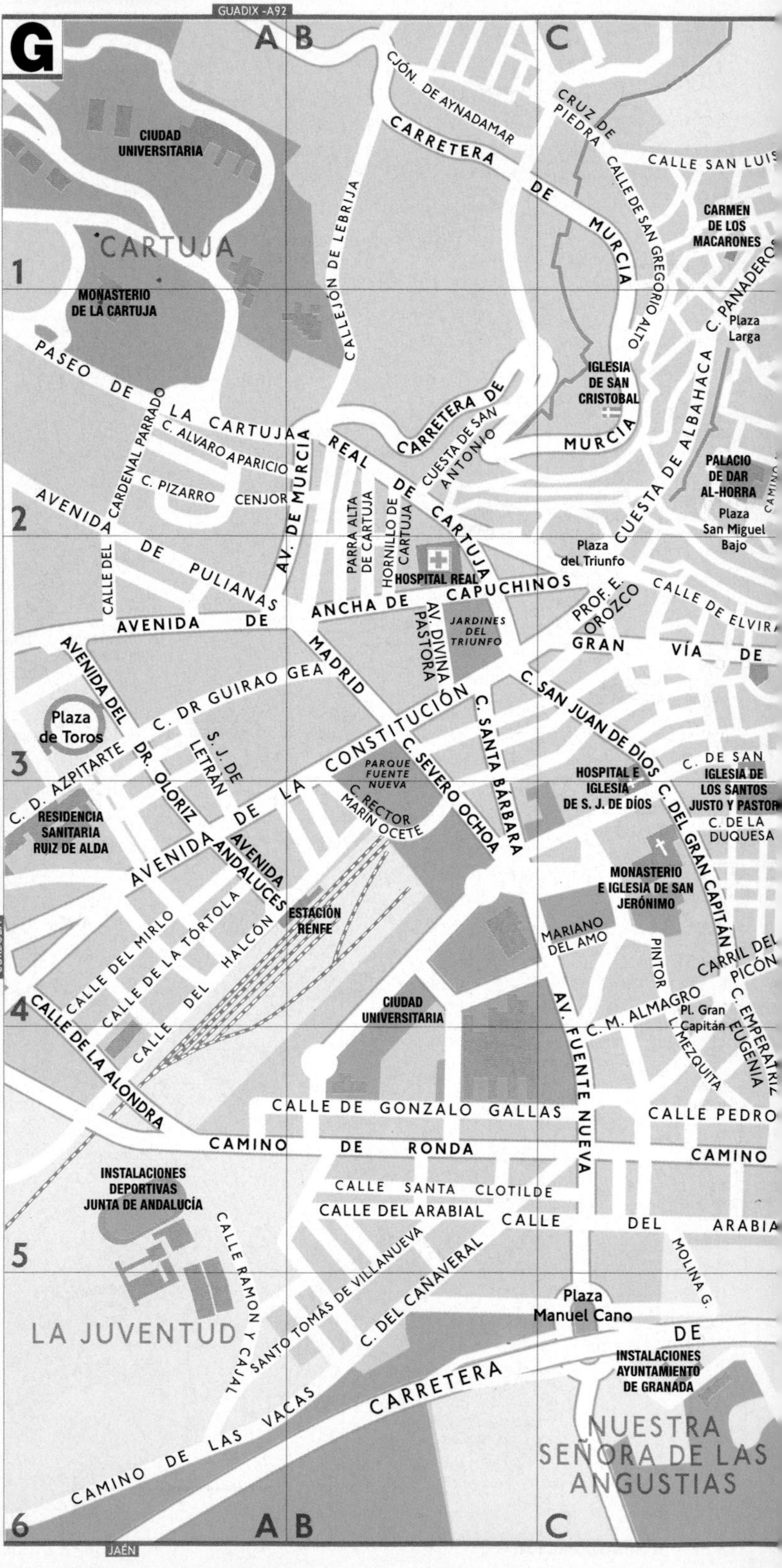
GUADIX -A92
G
A B C
1 2 3 4 5 6
CIUDAD UNIVERSITARIA
CARTUJA
MONASTERIO DE LA CARTUJA
CJÓN. DE AYNADAMAR
CARRETERA DE MURCIA
CRUZ DE PIEDRA
CALLE SAN LUIS
CALLE DE SAN GREGORIO ALTO
CARMEN DE LOS MACARONES
C. PANADEROS
Plaza Larga
CALLEJÓN DE LEBRIJA
IGLESIA DE SAN CRISTOBAL
PASEO DE LA CARTUJA
CALLE DEL CARDENAL PARRADO
C. ALVARO APARICIO
C. PIZARRO
CENJOR
AV. DE MURCIA
REAL DE CARTUJA
CARRETERA DE MURCIA
CUESTA DE SAN ANTONIO
CUESTA DE ALBAHACA
PALACIO DE DAR AL-HORRA
CAMINO
Plaza San Miguel Bajo
Plaza del Triunfo
AVENIDA DE PULIANAS
PARRA ALTA DE CARTUJA
HORNILLO DE CARTUJA
HOSPITAL REAL
ANCHA DE CAPUCHINOS
AVENIDA DE
PROF. E. OROZCO
CALLE DE ELVIRA
AV. DIVINA PASTORA
JARDINES DEL TRIUNFO
GRAN VÍA DE
AVENIDA DEL DR. OLORIZ
C. DR GUIRAO GEA
MADRID
Plaza de Toros
C. SAN JUAN DE DIOS
C. SANTA BÁRBARA
C. SEVERO OCHOA
AVENIDA DE LA CONSTITUCIÓN
C. D. AZPITARTE
S. J. DE LETRÁN
PARQUE FUENTE NUEVA
C. RECTOR MARÍN OCETE
HOSPITAL E IGLESIA DE S. J. DE DÍOS
C. DE SAN
IGLESIA DE LOS SANTOS JUSTO Y PASTOR
C. DE LA DUQUESA
C. DEL GRAN CAPITÁN
RESIDENCIA SANITARIA RUIZ DE ALDA
AVENIDA ANDALUCES
MONASTERIO E IGLESIA DE SAN JERÓNIMO
ESTACIÓN RENFE
CALLE DEL MIRLO
CALLE DE LA TÓRTOLA
CALLE DEL HALCÓN
MARIANO DEL AMO
PINTOR
CARRIL DEL PICÓN
CÓRDOBA
CALLE DE LA ALONDRA
CIUDAD UNIVERSITARIA
C. M. ALMAGRO
Pl. Gran Capitán
L. MEZQUITA
C. EMPERATRIZ EUGENIA
AV. FUENTE NUEVA
CALLE DE GONZALO GALLAS
CALLE PEDRO
CAMINO DE RONDA
CAMINO
INSTALACIONES DEPORTIVAS JUNTA DE ANDALUCÍA
CALLE SANTA CLOTILDE
CALLE DEL ARABIAL
CALLE DEL ARABIA
CALLE RAMON Y CAJAL
SANTO TOMÁS DE VILLANUEVA
C. DEL CAÑAVERAL
MOLINA G.
Plaza Manuel Cano
LA JUVENTUD
DE
INSTALACIONES AYUNTAMIENTO DE GRANADA
CARRETERA
CAMINO DE LAS VACAS
NUESTRA SEÑORA DE LAS ANGUSTIAS
JAÉN

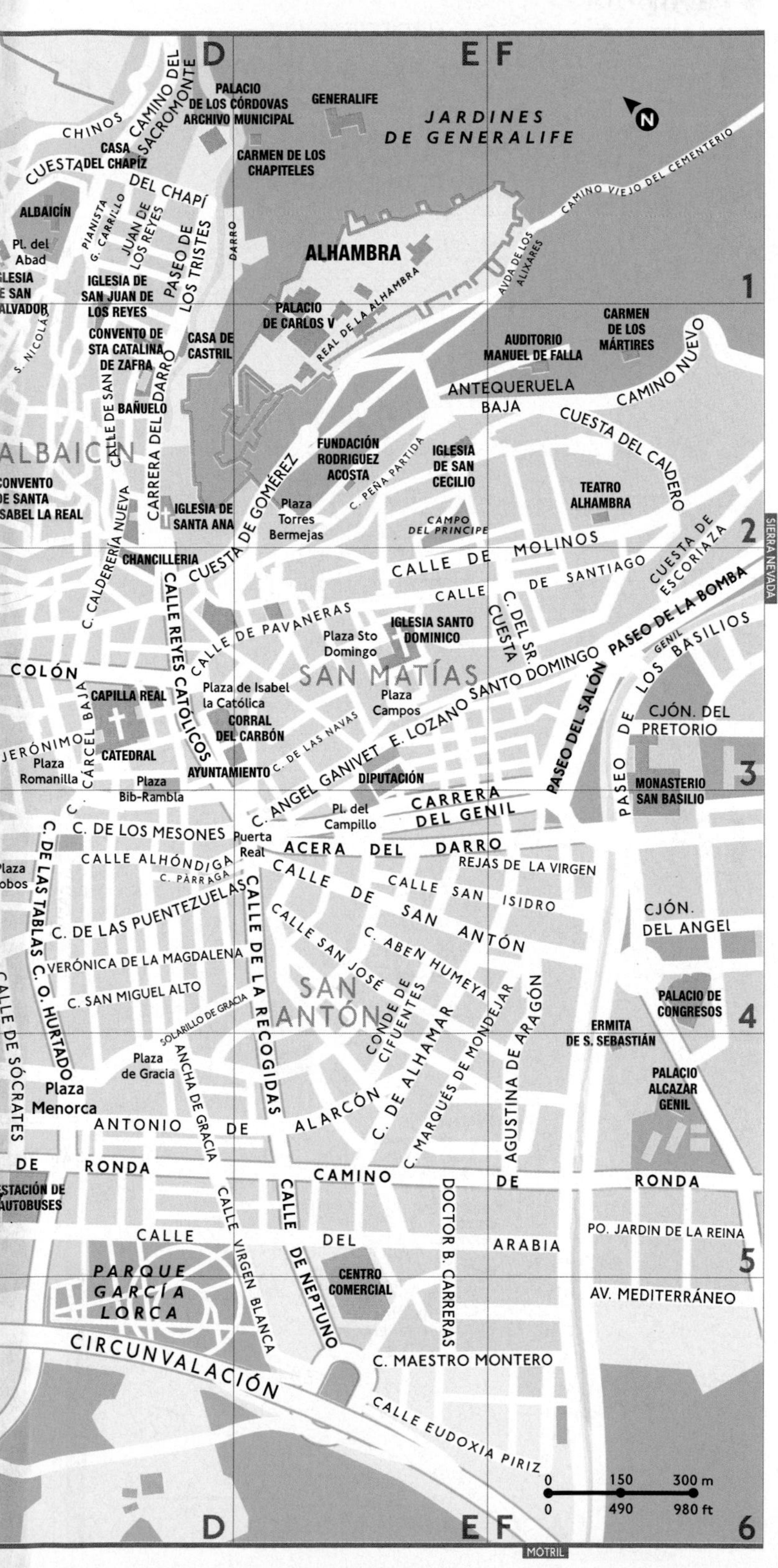
D
E
F
JARDINES DE GENERALIFE
GENERALIFE
PALACIO DE LOS CÓRDOVAS
ARCHIVO MUNICIPAL
CARMEN DE LOS CHAPITELES
CAMINO DEL SACROMONTE
CHINOS
CUESTA DEL CHAPÍ
CASA DEL CHAPÍZ
ALBAICÍN
Pl. del Abad
IGLESIA DE SAN SALVADOR
PIANISTA G. CARRILLO
JUAN DE LOS REYES
PASEO DE LOS TRISTES
DARRO
ALHAMBRA
CAMINO VIEJO DEL CEMENTERIO
AVDA DE LOS ALIXARES
REAL DE LA ALHAMBRA
IGLESIA DE SAN JUAN DE LOS REYES
PALACIO DE CARLOS V
CARMEN DE LOS MÁRTIRES
AUDITORIO MANUEL DE FALLA
CAMINO NUEVO
S. NICOLÁS
CONVENTO DE STA CATALINA DE ZAFRA
CASA DE CASTRIL
CALLE DE SAN
BAÑUELO
CARRERA DEL DARRO
ANTEQUERUELA BAJA
CUESTA DEL CALDERO
ALBAICÍN
CONVENTO DE SANTA ISABEL LA REAL
FUNDACIÓN RODRIGUEZ ACOSTA
C. PEÑA PARTIDA
IGLESIA DE SAN CECILIO
TEATRO ALHAMBRA
CALDERERÍA NUEVA
IGLESIA DE SANTA ANA
CUESTA DE GOMÉREZ
Plaza Torres Bermejas
CAMPO DEL PRINCIPE
SIERRA NEVADA
CHANCILLERIA
CALLE DE MOLINOS
CUESTA DE ESCORIAZA
C. CALDERERÍA
CALLE REYES CATÓLICOS
CALLE DE SANTIAGO
C. DEL SR. CUESTA
PASEO DE LA BOMBA
CALLE DE PAVANERAS
IGLESIA SANTO DOMINICO
Plaza Sto Domingo
GENIL
LOS BASILIOS
COLÓN
SAN MATÍAS
SANTO DOMINGO
CAPILLA REAL
Plaza de Isabel la Católica
Plaza Campos
E. LOZANO
PASEO DEL SALÓN
CJÓN. DEL PRETORIO
PASEO DE
CÁRCEL BAJA
CORRAL DEL CARBÓN
C. DE LAS NAVAS
JERÓNIMO
CATEDRAL
C. ANGEL GANIVET
Plaza Romanilla
AYUNTAMIENTO
DIPUTACIÓN
MONASTERIO SAN BASILIO
Plaza Bib-Rambla
CARRERA DEL GENIL
Pl. del Campillo
C. DE LOS MESONES
Puerta Real
ACERA DEL DARRO
REJAS DE LA VIRGEN
CALLE ALHÓNDIGA
C. PÁRRAGA
CALLE DE SAN ANTÓN
CALLE SAN ISIDRO
CJÓN. DEL ANGEL
Plaza Lobos
C. DE LAS TABLAS
C. DE LAS PUENTEZUELAS
CALLE SAN JOSÉ
C. ABEN HUMEYA
VERÓNICA DE LA MAGDALENA
CALLE DE LA RECOGIDAS
SAN ANTÓN
CONDE DE CIFUENTES
PALACIO DE CONGRESOS
C. SAN MIGUEL ALTO
SOLARILLO DE GRACIA
ERMITA DE S. SEBASTIÁN
C. O. HURTADO
Plaza de Gracia
ANCHA DE GRACIA
C. DE ALHAMAR
C. MARQUÉS DE MONDEJAR
AGUSTINA DE ARAGÓN
CALLE DE SÓCRATES
Plaza Menorca
PALACIO ALCAZAR GENIL
ANTONIO DE ALARCÓN
DE RONDA
CAMINO DE RONDA
ESTACIÓN DE AUTOBUSES
CALLE VIRGEN BLANCA
CALLE DE NEPTUNO
DOCTOR B. CARRERAS
CALLE DEL ARABIA
PO. JARDIN DE LA REINA
PARQUE GARCÍA LORCA
CENTRO COMERCIAL
AV. MEDITERRÁNEO
CIRCUNVALACIÓN
C. MAESTRO MONTERO
CALLE EUDOXIA PIRIZ
0 150 300 m
0 490 980 ft
MOTRIL
1
2
3
4
5
6

◆ CÁDIZ

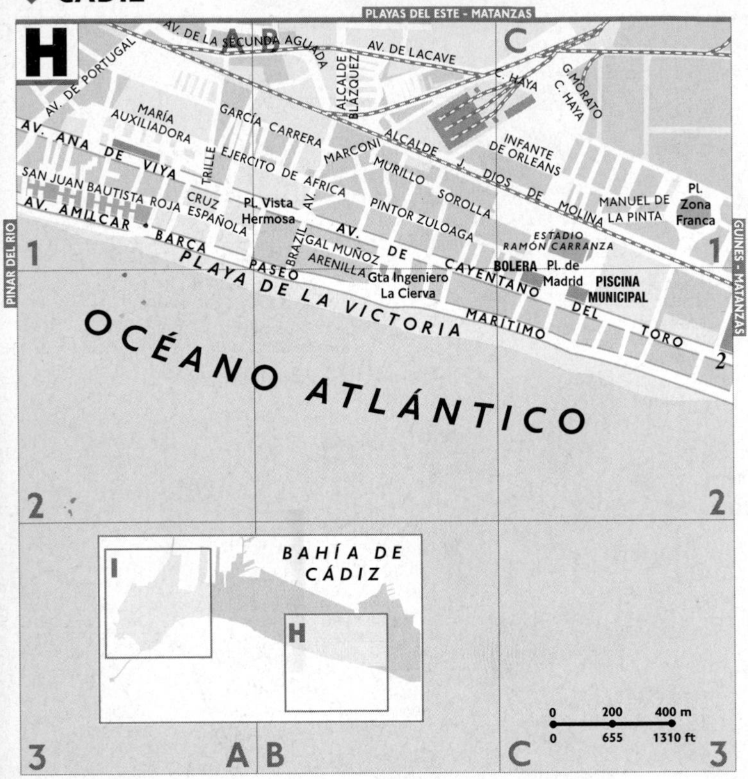

PLAYAS DEL ESTE - MATANZAS
H
AV. DE LA SECUNDA AGUADA
AV. DE LACAVE
AV. DE PORTUGAL
ALCALDE BLÁZQUEZ
C. HAYA
G. MORATO
C. HAYA
MARÍA AUXILIADORA
GARCÍA CARRERA
AV. ANA DE VIYA
TRILLE
EJERCITO DE AFRICA
MARCONI
ALCALDE J. DIOS DE MOLINA
INFANTE DE ORLEANS
SAN JUAN BAUTISTA ROJA
CRUZ ESPAÑOLA
Pl. Vista Hermosa
AV. BRAZIL
MURILLO
SOROLLA
PINTOR ZULOAGA
MANUEL DE LA PINTA
Pl. Zona Franca
AV. AMILCAR BARCA
PASEO
GAL MUÑOZ ARENILLA
AV. DE CAYENTANO DEL TORO
ESTADIO RAMÓN CARRANZA
BOLERA
Pl. de Madrid
PISCINA MUNICIPAL
Gta Ingeniero La Cierva
PLAYA DE LA VICTORIA
MARÍTIMO
PINAR DEL RIO
GUINES - MATANZAS
OCÉANO ATLÁNTICO
BAHÍA DE CÁDIZ
I
H
0 200 400 m
0 655 1310 ft
A B C
1 2 3
I
ESTACIÓN MARITIMA
PUERTO
ESTACIÓN RENFE
HONDURAS
Pl. Pozos de las Nieves
Pl. España
AVENIDA
BATERÍA CANDELARÍA
ALAMEDA APODACA
ALAMEDA MARQUES DE COMILLAS
ANTONIO LÓPEZ
OF. DE TURISMO
Pl. de Mina
RAMON DE CARRANZA
AV. DEL PUERTO
Pl. de Sevilla
CUESTAS DE LAS CALESAS
A. DE CASTRO
PASEO CARLOS III
ENRIQUE DE LAS MARINAS
MUSEO DE BELLAS ARTES ARQUEOLOGICO
ROSARIO
VEEDOR
Pl. de San Antonio
TABLAS
CERVANTES
ANCHA
NOVENA
Pl. Candelaria
Pl. de San Juan
COLUMELA
MUSEO HISTORICO MUNICIPAL
Pl. Las Viudas
COBOS
PELOTA
LA BONERIA
ALV. CABRERA
PASEO DE STA. BARBARA
AV. DR. GOMEZ ULLA
GRAN TEATRO FALLA
SACRAMENTO
LONDRES
LIBERTAD
OF. DE TURISMO
Pl. Catedral
CATEDRAL
CONCEPCIÓN ARENAL
ANTIGUA PRISIÓN
B. PÉREZ GALDOS
HOSPITAL DE MUJERES
HOSPITAL DE MUJERES
DR. MARAÑON
ENCARNACIÓN
CRUZ
MORENO DE MORA
PASQUIN
SAGASTA
AV. DUQUE DE NAJERA
PORLIER
OCÉANO ATLÁNTICO
CASTILLO DE STA. CATALINA
CAMPO DEL SUR
0 200 400 m
0 655 1310 ft
CASTILLO DE SAN SEBASTIAN

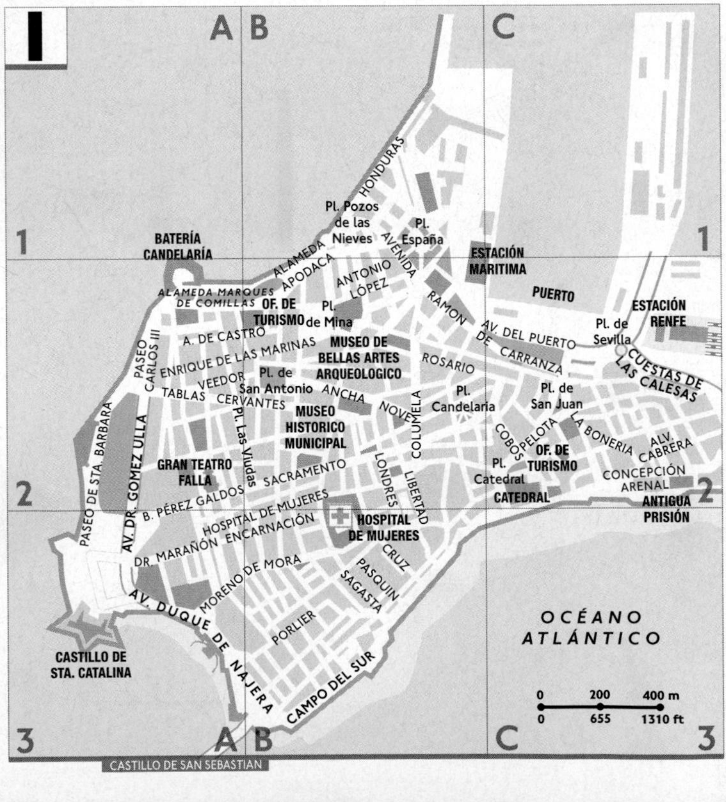

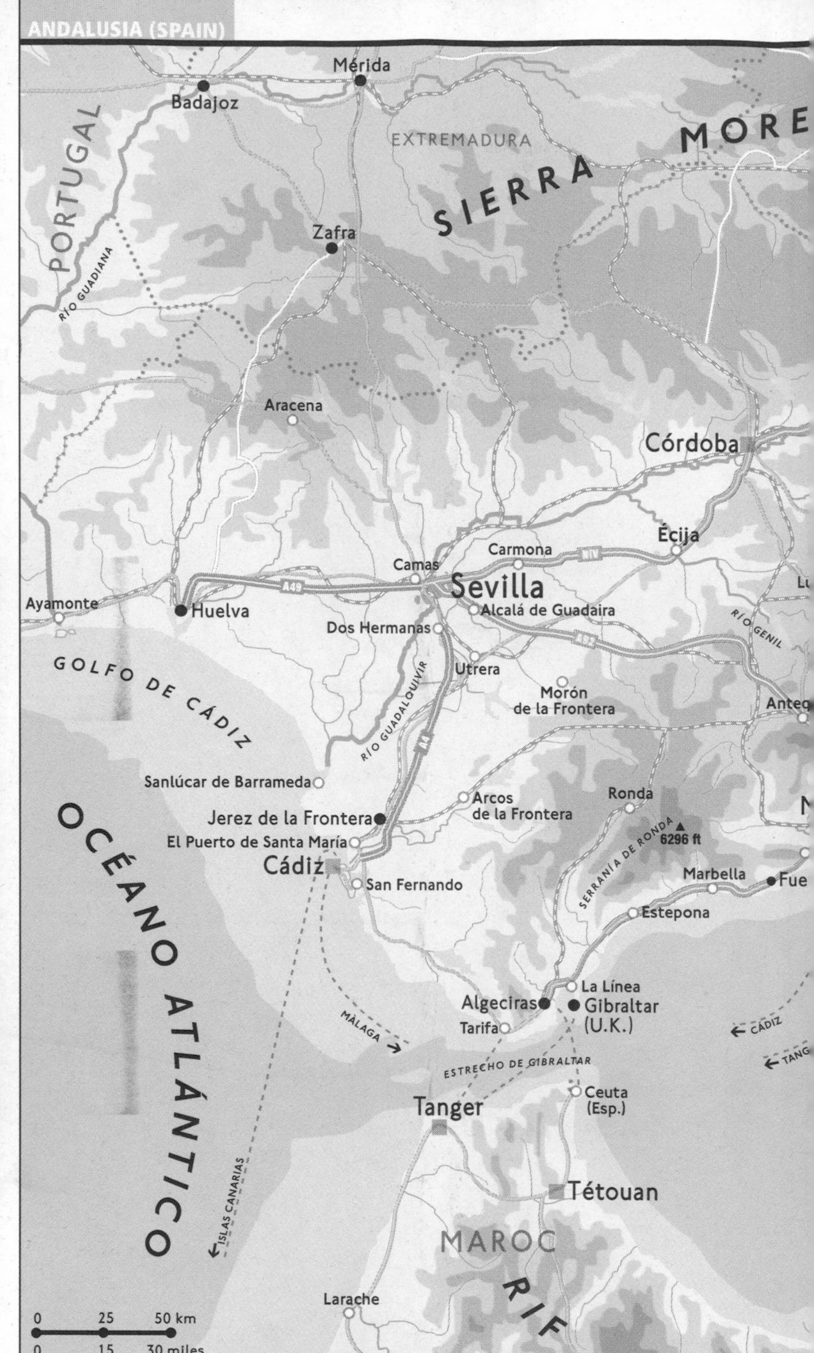

ANDALUSIA FACTS AND FIGURES

Andalusia is one of 17 autonomous regions that make up Spain, with its own president, government, Parliament, administration and Supreme Court.

■ EIGHT PROVINCES
Huelva, Seville, Córdoba, Jaén, Cádiz, Málaga, Granada and Almería.

■ SURFACE AREA
227,000 sq. miles, or 17.35 % of the Spanish territory (1,308,000 squ. miles).

■ REGIONAL CAPITAL
Seville.

■ HIGHEST POINT
Mulhacén (11,420 feet), the highest mountain in Spain.

■ CLIMATE
Mediterranean.

■ POPULATION
7,237,000, or 18,15 % of the entire Spanish population (39,853,000).

POPULATION DENSITY:
33 people/sq. mile, which compares with 31.5 people/ sq. mile for Spain as a whole.